THE ROUTLEDGE HANDBOOK OF COMPARATIVE RURAL POLICY

This volume represents the result of almost two decades of trans-Atlantic collaborative development of a policy research paradigm, the *International Comparative Rural Policy Studies* program. Over this period dozens of scientists from different disciplines but with a common interest in rural issues and policy have collaboratively studied the policies in North America, Europe, and other parts of the world.

A core element of the book is the idea and practice of comparative research and analysis – what can be learned from comparisons, how and why policies vary in different contexts, and what lessons might or might not be "transferable" across borders. It provides skills for the use of comparative methods as important tools to analyze the functioning of strategies and specific policy interventions in different contexts and a holistic approach for the management of resources in rural regions. It promotes innovation as a tool to valorize endogenous resources and empower local communities and offers case studies of rural policy in specific contexts. The book largely adopts *a territorial approach* to rural policy. This means the book is more interested in *rural regions*, their people and economies, and in the policies that affect them, than in *rural sectors*, and sectoral policies per se.

The audience of the book is by definition international and includes students attending courses in agricultural and rural policy, rural and regional studies, and natural resource management; lecturers seeking course material and case studies to present to their students in any of the courses listed above; professionals working in the field of rural policy; policy-makers and civil servants at different levels seeking tools to better understand rural policy both at the local and global scale and to better recognize and comprehend how to transfer best practices.

Matteo Vittuari, PhD, is Associate Professor in Agricultural, Food and Rural Policy and Agricultural Policy Evaluation at the Department of Agricultural and Food Sciences, University of Bologna, Italy.

John Devlin, PhD, is Associate Professor in the Rural Planning and Development Program, School of Environmental Design and Rural Development at the University of Guelph, Canada.

Marco Pagani, PhD, is a Research Fellow in the Rural Policy Learning Commons Project.

Thomas G. Johnson, PhD, is Professor Emeritus at the University of Missouri, USA.

ROUTLEDGE INTERNATIONAL HANDBOOKS

For more information about this series, please visit: www.routledge.com/series/RIHAND

THE ROUTLEDGE HANDBOOK OF COMPARATIVE RURAL POLICY

*Edited by Matteo Vittuari, John Devlin,
Marco Pagani, and Thomas G. Johnson*

Routledge
Taylor & Francis Group

LONDON AND NEW YORK

First published 2020
by Routledge
2 Park Square, Milton Park, Abingdon, Oxon OX14 4RN

and by Routledge
605 Third Avenue, New York, NY 10017

First issued in paperback 2021

Routledge is an imprint of the Taylor & Francis Group, an informa business

Publisher's Note
The publisher has gone to great lengths to ensure the quality of this reprint but points out that some imperfections in the original copies may be apparent.

British Library Cataloguing-in-Publication Data
A catalogue record for this book is available from the British Library

Library of Congress Cataloging-in-Publication Data
Names: Vittuari, Matteo, editor. | Devlin, John F., editor. | Pagani, Marco, editor. | Johnson, Thomas G., editor.
Title: The Routledge handbook of comparative rural policy / edited by Matteo Vittuari, John Devlin, Marco Pagani, and Thomas G. Johnson.
Description: Milton Park, Abingdon, Oxon ; New York, NY : Routledge, 2020. | Series: Routledge international handbooks | Includes bibliographical references and index.
Identifiers: LCCN 2019028108
Subjects: LCSH: Rural development–Government policy. | Land use, Rural–Government policy.
Classification: LCC HN49.C6 .R686 2020 | DDC 307.1/412–dc23
LC record available at https://lccn.loc.gov/2019028108

ISBN 13: 978-1-03-208722-1 (pbk)
ISBN 13: 978-1-138-59411-1 (hbk)

Typeset in Bembo
by Wearset Ltd, Boldon, Tyne and Wear

CONTENTS

Contents

FIGURES

TABLES

CONTRIBUTORS

Mikaël Akimowicz is a Research Fellow at Brandon University, Canada – Rural Development Institute with interests in urban-influenced farming and food system sustainability, which he investigates through the lens of institutional economics.

Reidar Almås is Emeritus Professor of Rural Sociology at NTNU, Trondheim, Norway. He is currently Senior Researcher at Ruralis – Institute for Rural and Regional Research and his publications span the areas of agri-food restructuring, agricultural policy, agricultural history, rural and regional development.

Robert Annis, retired, is the former Director of the Rural Development Institute at Brandon University, Canada, and has served as an Associate Professor of both Indigenous Studies and Psychology.

William Ashton (MCIP) is the Director of Rural Development Institute at Brandon University, Canada, and a professor of public policy in the Department of Rural Development with interests in regional and rural economic development and policy implementation.

Víctor Ávila Akerberg is a full-time Lecturer and Researcher at the Autonomous University of the State of Mexico, with interests in forest ecology and conservation, biodiversity, ecosystem services, and rural tourism.

Keith Baker is an Associate Professor of Public Administration at the College of Brockport, NY, USA. His research and teaching interests focus on state/society relationships and modes of governance within these.

Hilde Bjørkhaug is a Research Professor at Ruralis, Institute for Rural and Regional Research, Norway. His research interests include agricultural restructuring and family farming, ethics, power relations, and financialization in the agri-food value chain.

Natalija Bogdanov is a full Professor at the Faculty of Agriculture in the University of Belgrade, Serbia, with research interests in rural development, agricultural policy, institutional and structural changes in agriculture.

Ray D. Bollman worked for Statistics Canada (1971–2011) where he was the founding editor of their *Rural and Small-Town Canada Analysis Bulletin*. He is now affiliated with Brandon University and Memorial University.

Laura Brenes-Peralta is a Researcher at Tecnológico de Costa Rica with research interests in food and food waste technology.

John M. Bryden is Emeritus Professor of Human Geography at the University of Aberdeen, Scotland. He has conducted many transnational comparative research projects, as well as being a rural policy advisor in several countries.

Lidia Carvajal is an Associate Professor in the Department of Economics at the Autonomous University of the State of Mexico with interests in international migration, remittances, and development in Mexico and North America.

Harry Cummings is a retired Professor in the School of Environmental Design and Rural Development, University of Guelph, Canada, and teaches program evaluation at the university and directs Harry Cummings and Associates Inc.

Allison Davis-White Eyes is affiliate faculty within the School of Public Policy at Oregon State University, USA, with research interests in decolonization, postcolonial theory, and nation-building strategies.

Philomena de Lima is the Director of the Centre for Remote and Rural Studies, University of the Highlands and Islands – Inverness College, Scotland with interests in migration and social justice issues.

Fabio De Menna is an Assistant Professor at the Department of Agriculture and Food Science at the University of Bologna, Italy. He conducts research on the sustainability of food systems, with a specific focus on food loss and waste.

John Devlin is an Associate Professor in the School of Environmental Design and Rural Development at the University of Guelph, Canada, and conducts research on rural environmental and agricultural policy.

Luca Falasconi is an Assistant Professor in the Department of Agriculture and Food Science at the University of Bologna, Italy, with interests in food policy and food waste.

David Fazzino is an Assistant Professor of Anthropology at Bloomsburg University of Pennsylvania, USA. He is a cultural anthropologist trained in law and agro-ecology studying food systems policy and structural violence.

Mary Ferguson is a Senior Partner with Eko Nomos, Canada, a consultancy that specializes in social enterprise development and evaluation.

Patricia T. Fernandez-Guajardo is a PhD student in Public Policy at Oregon State University, USA, with interests in sustainable management of the water–energy–food nexus, especially in agricultural communities.

Sergio Franco-Maass is a Researcher at the Autonomous University of the State of Mexico with interests in the management and conservation of timber and non-timber forest resources.

Maya Fromstein holds an MA from the University of Guelph, Canada, with interests in feminism, soil health, and food and agriculture as tools for social and environmental justice.

Glenna Gannon is a social scientist and artist from Alaska, USA. She holds an MS in Environment and Sustainability from the University of Saskatchewan.

Laura García Herrero is a PhD candidate at the University of Bologna, Italy, with interests in holistic assessment approaches to sustainability in food systems and the energy sector.

Ryan Gibson is the Libro Professor of Regional Economic Development at the University of Guelph, Canada. His research interests include rural development, governance, and philanthropy.

Tanya González Martínez is a PhD student at Autonomous University of the State of Mexico with research interests in environmental education and environmental awareness for biodiversity conservation.

Greg Halseth is a Professor in Geography at the University of Northern British Columbia, Canada, and the Canada Research Chair in Rural and Small-Town Studies and Co-Director of UNBC's Community Development Institute.

Barbara Harrison is Co-Founder and President of Kitab World Education, Canada, a non-governmental organization focused on community-engaged learning and has a deep interest in work related to rural areas.

Thomas G. Johnson is Professor Emeritus at the University of Missouri, USA. He is a co-founder of the International Comparative Rural Policy Studies.

Wayne Kelly is a PhD at University of Galway, Ireland, researching digital youth in rural communities. He also helps lead the Rural Policy Learning Commons at Brandon University, Canada.

Charilaos Képhaliacos is Emeritus Professor of Economics at the Ecole Nationale Supérieure de Formation de l'Enseignement Agricole, France. He researches environmental public goods management in the agricultural sector.

Kathleen Kevany is an Associate Professor and Director of the Rural Research Centre at the Faculty of Agriculture of Dalhousie University, Canada, specializing in sustainable diets, food systems, and plant-rich living.

Philipp Kneis teaches Political Science at Oregon State University, USA. His research and teaching centers on cultural and political theory.

Dezsö Kovács is a retired researcher of the Hungarian Academy of Sciences with interests in rural issues, policy, tourism, heritage, wine-roads, honey, bees and beekeepers, and experience economy.

Denise Lach is a Professor of Sociology at Oregon State University, USA, with interests in community adaptation to climate and other changes, and the use of scientific and local knowledge in decision-making.

Karen Landman is a Professor in the School of Environmental Design and Rural Development at the University of Guelph, Canada, and researches food systems, landscape stewardship, and green infrastructure.

Michelle Landry is an Assistant Professor at the Université de Moncton, Canada, with interests in local governments, social movements, and minority group governance.

Catherine Lang is a consultant/researcher from Canada, with a core interest in rural social enterprise capacity building, policy, and ecosystems development, particularly in the cooperative and non-profit sectors.

Al Lauzon is a Professor in the School of Environmental Design and Rural Development at the University of Guelph, Canada. His research interests focus on community sustainability and well-being and on rural change and development.

Marius Lazdinis is a Deputy Head of Unit, dealing with pre-accession assistance in agriculture and rural development, in the Directorate General for Agriculture and Rural Development of the European Commission.

Luis Angel López Mathamba is a PhD student at the Autonomous University of the State of Mexico, with interests in ecosystem services, biodiversity, rural development, and food science.

Philip Loring is an Associate Professor at the University of Guelph where he holds the Arrell Chair in Food, Policy, and Society. His interests are in food security, community sustainability, and social justice.

Grichawat Lowatcharin is a Lecturer at the College of Local Administration, Khon Kaen University, Thailand, with interests in structure of government and intergovernmental relations.

Brennan Chapman Lowery is a PhD student at Memorial University, Canada, with interests in rural sustainability, asset-based approaches, sustainability indicators, and heritage.

Annie McKee is a social researcher at The James Hutton Institute, Aberdeen, Scotland, focusing on rural governance and institutions. In 2016, she completed an OECD Comparative Research Fellowship in Norway.

Sean Markey is a Professor with the School of Resource and Environmental Management at Simon Fraser University, Canada. His research concerns issues of rural development and community and regional sustainability.

William H. Meyers is Professor Emeritus of Agricultural and Applied Economics, University of Missouri, USA. Areas of teaching and research are trade, agricultural and rural policy, and transition economics.

Sarah Minnes is a Postdoctoral Fellow and registered professional planner, with the School of Environment and Sustainability, University of Saskatchewan, Canada.

Gabino Nava Bernal is a Researcher at Autonomous University of the State of Mexico with research interests in sustainable livelihoods and community-based conservation of crop diversity.

Marco Pagani is a Research Fellow in the Rural Policy Learning Commons Project with interests in the energy–food–climate nexus and in food waste.

Giuseppe Palladino is an Assistant Professor, Department of Agricultural and Food Sciences, University of Bologna.

Suman Pant is the Academic Director of Nepal's Development and Social Change Program and has research interests in rural and international development policy.

Andrew Peach holds an MSc in Rural Planning and Development from the University of Guelph and is currently a Planning Consultant at Shared Value Solutions based in Guelph, Ontario.

Matthew Pezold is a Workforce Specialist for University of Missouri Extension, USA. A social scientist and ethicist, his research and teaching focus on the intersections of poverty, race, justice, and socio-economic mobility.

Simone Piras is an agricultural and rural economist working in the Social, Economic and Geographical Sciences group at the James Hutton Institute. He has an interdisciplinary background in development studies, primarily in Eastern Europe.

Krishna Lal Poudel is an economist at the Missouri Department of Natural Resources, USA. His research involves strategies for improved management of natural resources to promote a healthy environment and economy.

Karen Refsgaard is the Research and Deputy Director at Nordregio, Sweden, being an institutional economist with expertise in rural development and policy, circular economy, and innovation.

Francesca Regoli is Research Officer at the Department of Management – University of Bologna, Italy, with more than 15 years of experience in international projects and in rural development related fields with a particular focus on rural tourism.

Bill Reimer is Professor Emeritus at Concordia University, Canada with interests in capacity building, social support, social capital, immigration, and the informal economy (http://billreimer.ca).

Pedro Fiz Rocha Correa is International Manager at the Campus Terra of the University of Santiago de Compostela, Spain, with interests in rural development policy analysis, especially in mountain areas, and rural strategic planning.

Jordi Rosell Foxà, Associate Professor at the Department of Applied Economics of the Autonomous University of Barcelona, Spain, is a researcher specialized in agricultural and rural economics.

Laura Ryser is the Research Manager of the Rural and Small-Town Studies Program at the University of Northern British Columbia, Canada. Her research interests include small-town community restructuring and resilience.

Andrea Segrè is a Professor of International and Comparative Agricultural Policy, with research interests in food economics and policy. He is the creator of Last-Minute Market, an academic spin off, and he is also president of the Edmund Mach Foundation in San Michele all'Adige (Trento), and of the FICO Foundation.

Victòria Soldevila-Lafon is a Lecturer of Applied Economics at Universitat Rovira i Virgili in Spain. Her research interests include agri-food value chains, rural development, and food security.

Judith I. Stallmann, is Professor at the University of Missouri, USA, with interests in rural development, public finance, and decentralization of government.

Brent S. Steel is Professor of Political Science in the School of Public Policy at Oregon State University, USA. His research interests include rural, environmental, and renewable energy policy.

Glenn Sterner is an Assistant Professor of Criminal Justice at Pennsylvania State University, USA, whose interests include criminal and hidden networks and the scholarship of engagement.

Houston Sudekum is a doctoral student at the University of Missouri, with research interest in the water–energy–food nexus.

Casey Taylor is Assistant Professor at the University of Delaware with interests in environmental, renewable energy and endangered species policy.

Diana E. Valero is a Research Associate and Project Coordinator at the University of the Highlands and Islands, Scotland, with interests in local development, governance, social innovation, and social justice issues.

Lourdes Viladomiu is an Associate Professor at the Department of Applied Economics of the Autonomous University of Barcelona, Spain, specialized in local and rural development.

Heidi Vinge is a PhD candidate in Sociology at the Norwegian University of Science and Technology and Researcher at Ruralis, Institute for Rural and Regional Research, Norway with interests in sustainable land use, political decision-making, and the relationship between power and knowledge.

Matteo Vittuari is an Associate Professor in the Department of Agricultural and Food Science at the University of Bologna, Italy, with interests in food systems sustainability, food losses and waste, the food and energy nexus, and agricultural, food, and rural policy.

Erika Allen Wolters is Assistant Professor and Director of the Oregon Policy Analysis Laboratory at Oregon State University, USA. Her research interests include the food–water–energy nexus and sustainability policy.

ACKNOWLEDGMENTS

We thank Tony Fuller, Bruno Jean, Doug Ramsey, Thierno Thiam, Robert Zabawa, Timo Aarrevaara, Riikka Kangas, Eeva Aarrevaara, Silvia Gaiani, and all the colleagues who provided a contribution or an inspiration for the book.

RURAL POLICY LEARNING COMMONS

The Rural Policy Learning Commons (RPLC) is a $2.5 million partnership grant funded by the Social Sciences and Humanities Research Council of Canada (SSHRC) and hosted at the Rural Development Institute (RDI) at Brandon University (http://rplc-capr.ca). The major objectives of the RPLC are to develop networks, build rural capacity, and mobilize knowledge to inform rural research and policy.

The RPLC formally began in 2014 and it is a growing network of 31 founding institutions with more than 200 faculty, students, and practitioners participating. While many of the RPLC's formal partners are located in the host country of Canada, this international partnership includes institutions from the United States, Mexico, Italy, the United Kingdom, Ireland, and Spain. The diversity of the members is mirrored by the diversity of their scope, some focusing on local and regional research while others concentrate on international comparative analysis through working relationships among institutions and individual partners. Rural Themed Networks and Services help develop policy deliverables useful to rural policy practitioners and community stakeholders through exchange, expertise, and experiences that cross disciplinary, organizational, and sectoral lines.

Since 2014 the RPLC developed a unique relation with International Comparative Rural Policy Studies (ICRPS). ICRPS and the RPLC are both working to study and increase understanding of rural policy in a comparative and international context. Both networks are also committed to building the capacity of researchers and students regarding rural policy and issues and as a result, many faculty and students belong to both networks. ICRPS's summer institute provides critical learning and networking opportunities for graduate students within the RPLC.

INTRODUCTION

In 2015 the United Nations General Assembly identified 17 universally applied global goals, the *Sustainable Development Goals* (SDGs), to be reached by 2030. These SDGs are designed to achieve a better and more sustainable future for all. They address the compendium of global challenges ranging from poverty to inequality, from climate change to environmental degradation, from prosperity to affordable and clean energy. Most of these challenges are crucial to the development of rural areas. For instance, SDG 2 is to "end hunger, achieve food security and improved nutrition and promote sustainable agriculture". Specifically, goal 2.a calls for increasing "investment, including through enhanced international cooperation, in rural infrastructure, agricultural research and extension services, technology development and plant and livestock gene banks in order to enhance agricultural productive capacity in developing countries, in particular least developed countries".

The *Sustainable Development Goals* suggest that rural development should represent a priority in the agenda of national governments and international organizations since rural areas are where the potential synergies between major development factors such as migration, human capital, energy, health, education, water, food, gender, and economic growth can be realized and exploited.

In approaching this nexus of the factors, this book largely adopts a territorial approach to rural policy. This means the book is focused on rural regions, their people and economies, and in the policies that affect them, rather than on rural sectors and sectoral policies. The key problematic is the role that rural people and places have – or could have – in the largely urbancentric culture and politics of the "northern" world of richer, industrialized countries.

Looking to recent experience the book asks which policies and institutions have been supportive of rural development, and which policies and institutions have not. Looking forward the book asks, what policies and institutions might assure the success and development of such regions? What alliances might be formed between rural and urban interests to the benefit of both?

Equally, the book is concerned with the sustainable development of rural regions, and policies that might support it, rather than with economic growth, or the environment viewed in isolation.

A core element of the book is the idea and practice of comparative research and analysis – what can be learned from comparisons, how and why policies vary in different contexts, and

1

what lessons might or might not be "transferable" across borders. Since the volume of comparative analysis of rural policy is still rather limited, this book describes various comparative methods that researchers can use to assess alternative strategies and specific policy interventions in different contexts.

The book is organized into six parts (see Figure A). Part I introduces the concept of rurality and rural policy with a strong emphasis on comparative theory and methods to carry out comparative rural policy studies. Chapter 1 describes how rurality is a spatial concept, since it involves large areas with low populations and distance from urban centers, together with the concepts of rural development and policy. Historical and geographical factors have profoundly influenced the spatial distribution of human population in rural areas of the world. These factors and their implications are analyzed in Chapters 2, 3, and 4 with a focus on Europe and North America, and OECD countries in general. The other chapters in the section are concerned with conceptual and methodological issues; Chapters 5 and 6 describe how current comparative and process policy theories can be applied to specifically rural issues. Chapters 7, 8, and 9 discuss the roles of territory and decentralization in rural policy evolution and outcomes.

Part II addresses people and society in rural areas, exploring a range of socio-economic issues. Chapters 10 and 11 describe the causes and consequences of rural migration, and depopulation, and issues related to population diversity. Chapter 12 explores the role and potential role of women in agriculture, food security, and rural development. In Chapter 13 the unique causes and consequences of rural poverty and income inequality are examined. Chapters 14 and 15 explore the challenges faced by those providing age-related and health-care services. Finally, Chapter 16 considers the implications of the rural–urban divide.

Part III is focused on natural resources and the relationships between rural policy, resources exploitation, and environment protection. Chapters 17 and 18 discuss the options for environmental and resources policies. Chapters 19, 20, and 21 explore the nexus of water, energy, and climate. Chapters 22, 23, 24, and 25 consider policies influencing food systems, food waste, and food sovereignty. Chapter 26 concludes this section by considering forestry policy.

Part IV analyzes innovation, its typologies, and its implications for rural development processes. Common themes in this section are resilience, adaptation, and evolving governance. Chapter 27 describes how rural social enterprises have evolved to respond to the decline in the public sector's involvement in service delivery. Chapters 28 and 29 describe innovations involved in the emergence of the bioeconomy, primarily in Europe, and the unique opportunity offered by digital technologies, mainly broadband internet access, to rural regions in Canada. Chapter 30 analyzes how rural areas are struggling and innovating to adapt to climate change at the local level in Nepal.

The focus of Part V is rural policy at the macro level. The chapters in this section provide examples of in-depth analysis of policies in specific rural regions. Chapters 31, 32, and 33 describe and assess current rural policies and policy environments in the three main regions studied by the International Comparative Rural Policy Studies Consortium, that is the United States, Canada, and Europe, in the period between the end of World War II and the first decades of the twenty-first century. Chapter 34 describes special policy issues and innovations in Southeastern Europe. The chapters describe how rural policy has evolved in an environment of competing sectoral objectives, macro-economic volatility, and rising globalization. The authors describe the results of policy experimentation and course correction, successes and failures. Together they provide a basis for rich comparative policy assessment.

Part VI is a collection of case studies on selected rural issues. The studies provide in-depth analyses of specific challenges, in most cases, with a comparative perspective to understand the implications of policies in alternative policy contexts. The case studies presented in this final

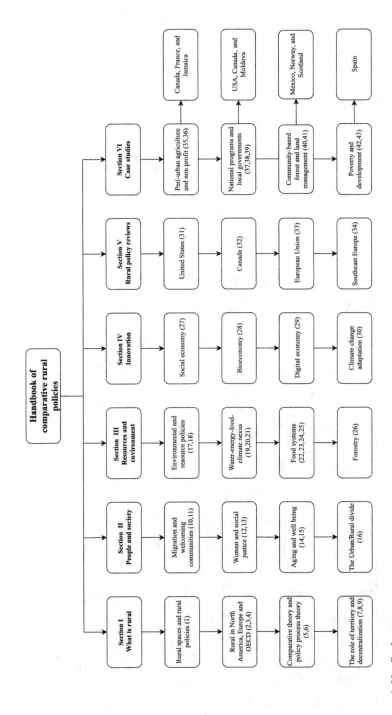

Figure A Handbook structure

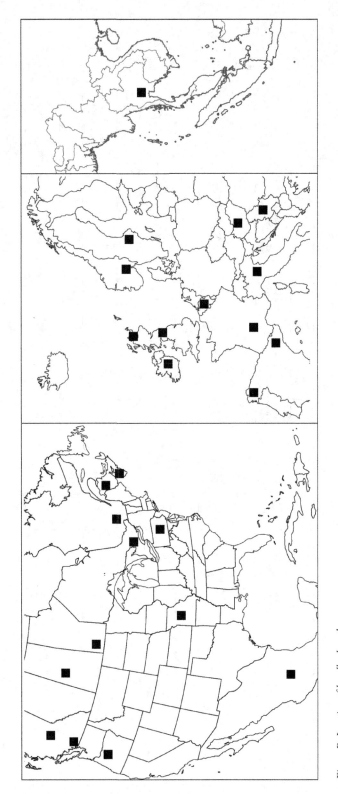

Figure B Location of handbook authors

section address policy questions in rural areas of Europe, North America, and the Caribbean and cover a diverse array of policies including economic development, social inclusion, rural resource management, and governance innovations.

This volume is the result of almost two decades of trans-Atlantic collaborative development of a policy research paradigm, the *International Comparative Rural Policy Studies* program (ICRPS). Over this period dozens of scientists from different disciplines but with a common interest in rural issues and policy have collaboratively studied the policies in North America, Europe, and other parts of the world (see Figure B) through comparative cultural, economic, geographic, historical, institutional, and social lenses. The result is a rich and growing literature on conceptual, methodological, and empirical dimensions of comparative rural policy. The ICRPS program enables students to examine and compare the role of rural policy in different cultural, political, and administrative contexts in Europe and North America, as well as in the Global South.

The International Comparative Rural Policy Studies Consortium continues to explore emerging policy issues in ever more regions and policy contexts. The research generated by researchers and students associated with ICRPS evolves with emerging issues, changing institutions, and new methodological developments. The volume is a record of current knowledge, but equally important, it is also a foundation for future comparative rural policy research.

Box 0.1 Location of ICRPS summer institutes 2004–2020

2004	University of Guelph, Guelph, Canada
2005	Katholeike Universiteit, Leuven, Belgium
2006	Brandon University, Brandon, Canada
2007	Universitat Autònoma de Barcelona, Catalonia, Spain
2008	University of Missouri, Columbia, United States
2009	University of Highlands and Islands, Inverness, Scotland
2010	Oregon State University, Corvallis, United States
2011	Norwegian Agricultural Economics Research Institute (NILF), Ås, Norway
2012	Concordia University, Montreal, Quebec, Canada
2013	University of Bologna, Bertinoro, Italy
2014	Universidad Autónoma del Estado de Mexico, Toluca, Mexico
2015	National University of Ireland, Galway and University College Dublin, Galway, Ireland
2016	University of Alaska, Fairbanks, United States
2017	Universitat Autònoma de Barcelona, Catalonia, Spain
2018	Tuskegee University, Tuskegee, United States
2019	University of Lapland, Rovaniemi, Finland
2020	Brandon University, Brandon, Canada

PART I

Introduction to comparative rural policy studies

1

WHAT IS RURAL? WHAT IS RURAL POLICY? WHAT IS RURAL DEVELOPMENT POLICY?

Ray D. Bollman and Bill Reimer

Introduction

There has been a long-running conversation on the meaning of rural and rurality. Often, observers develop a profile or typology for rural residents, rural enterprises, or rural institutions and then use these characteristics to define rural or rurality. Alternatively, the focus may be on geographical localities (either spaces or places), with the typology developed from the distribution of residents, enterprises, or institutions within and across those localities.

The objective of this chapter is to review this discussion in order to clarify the spatial dimensions that define rurality versus the characteristics of individuals (or enterprises or institutions) along the rural–urban continuum.

Rurality is a spatial concept. The two key dimensions of rurality are the density and distance-to-density of the localities of actors (individuals, enterprises, or institutions). In other words, the dimensions of density and distance-to-density define the rurality of the geographical localities of actors. Many characteristics of rural actors are correlated with rurality. However, these characteristics do not define rurality.

The meaning of rural policy follows directly from the two dimensions of rurality for localities. Specifically, considering the implications of the two rurality dimensions for any given policy would constitute "rural" policy. For example, considering density and distance-to-density implications of development policy would constitute the "rural" in rural development policy. This attention to rurality has been instituted as "rural proofing" or a "rural lens" in a number of jurisdictions.

There are various ways to delineate the grid or the spatial boundaries of geographical localities and to measure their density and distance-to-density. This chapter reviews the considerations required to implement these measures. The exact choice of measures will depend upon the analytic objective being pursued.

The preparation of statistical tabulations and the desire to target public policy requires the determination of the spatial grid (i.e. the boundaries of each locality) and the thresholds for density and for distance-to-density in order to classify localities or regions. These thresholds do not define "rurality". The choice of the threshold simply classifies actors associated with the localities at given points along the continuum of density and distance-to-density

9

For many purposes, analysts should consider the broader regional milieu within which each community is located. Similarly, for an analysis of regions, analysts should consider the mix of rural versus urban communities that comprise each given region.

These perspectives are discussed in the context of historical and current debates on the interpretations of rurality. Discussion questions are offered regarding the nature of the operational trade-offs needed to implement a measure of rurality for any given investigation.

Since the empirical implementation of a measure of each dimension of rurality ultimately depends on the issue(s) being considered, it is critical that analysts are skilled at understanding and evaluating the appropriate way to measure each of the conceptual dimensions when addressing a given issue.

What is rural?

Theory vs operational variables

Before discussing the theoretical idea of rurality versus the empirical measures of rurality, it is important to distinguish between a theoretical construct and an empirical variable that attempts to measure the theoretical construct. One should start with the theoretical concept and then search for ways to measure (or operationalize) that concept.

A theoretical construct (Box 1.1) may be considered to be an abstract feature of a phenomenon or process. Typically, these constructs are not directly measurable.

Box 1.1

A theoretical construct is a relatively abstract construct (or concept) that describes the essential features of a phenomenon. These constructs are (typically) not directly observable.

Operational definitions identify measurable variables that attempt to capture the essence (often partially) of the theoretical concept. This involves two steps:

1   identifying which empirical measure(s) most closely capture(s) the theoretical construct; and
2   identifying which procedure or data collection methodology will be used to generate the empirical measure.

Correlates are variables (usually empirical) which vary together. There may or may not be causal processes driving the correlations.

Once the theoretical constructs are identified, analysts need to search for empirical measures (or variables) that can best represent the concepts. This process involves two decisions: first, one must assess the appropriateness of alternative empirical variables and chose the one(s) that most closely capture(s) the essence of the theoretical construct; and second, one must consider the procedure or the methodology that represents the best way to obtain the empirical measure

Two or more variables may be correlated. In other words, they are interconnected at an empirical level. However, correlation does not mean causality. Specifically, a correlation between two variables may not indicate a causal relationship (i.e. if one sees more of "x", *then one will* see more of "y").

More importantly, these correlated variables should not (or more assertively, must not) be used to define the theoretical concept.

The theoretical concept of rurality

Rural is a spatial concept (Reimer and Bollman, 2009; World Bank, 2009). Whether it is used for statistical, analytical, personal, or polemical objectives, "rural" implies something about the geographical location of its object. Even where "rural" is used in a metaphorical sense, it implies actors in localities with low density and/or a long(er) distance to higher-density localities.

Theoretically speaking, rurality refers to geographical localities with respect to two theoretical dimensions:

- their density; and
- their distance-to-density.

Frequently, density may be indicated by the population size of a locality and distance-to-density may be indicated as the physical distance or the money and/or time expended to travel to a locality of high(er) density. A detailed discussion of measurement issues is provided below.

Thus, localities that are more "rural" are those with a relatively low(er) population or institutional density and/or with a relatively long(er) distance to high(er)-density localities. Urban localities are those with a relatively high(er) density. Variations on these generalizations create a large number of possible propositions regarding the impacts of density and distance-to-density on opportunities and behavior as suggested below.

The relationship between density and distance to high(er)-density localities is most usefully represented as a continuum – as illustrated in Table 1.1. Individuals residing in a locality in the upper-right-hand part of this diagram are residing in a smaller town (i.e. higher rurality in the

Table 1.1 The two dimensions of the rurality of localities on a scale from 1 to 10

		Index of rurality in the density dimension from lower rurality, 0 (higher density) to higher rurality, 10 (lower density)										
		0	1	2	3	4	5	6	7	8	9	10
	0											
	1											
	3											
Index of rurality in the distance dimension from lower rurality, 0 (shorter distance) to higher rurality, 10 (longer distance)	4											
	5											
	6											
	7											
	8											
	9											
	10											

density dimension) that is adjacent to an urban or metro center (i.e. lower rurality in the distance-to-density dimension). Metro-adjacent individuals have easier access to urban or metro jobs and services (e.g. hospitals[1]) and a market to sell their goods and services. At the same time, they are living in a small-town locality (i.e. higher rurality in the density dimension). These individuals likely experience a small-town "way-of-living" (perhaps less air pollution, less crime, fewer traffic jams, etc.) but are able to access a metro market and metro services. Individuals residing in a locality in the lower-left-hand part of this diagram cannot (easily) access the market or services of an urban or metro center (i.e. high rurality in the distance dimension) but are residing in a larger town (i.e. lower rurality in the density dimension). These individuals are constrained to "small-town" or "small-city" opportunities (e.g. employment or services) but are living in a locality with a higher population density that would support the availability of many services, such as found in a regional service center.

Operational definitions

The specification or choice of empirical measures of density and distance-to-density requires one to answer three questions.

1   What are the options for delineating the geographic boundaries or selecting the geographical units (i.e. a geographical grid such as community, county, region, etc.) that are most suitable to study the issue at hand?
2   What are the options for empirical measures of density and distance-to-density?
3   What are the options for establishing thresholds of the empirical measures for:
    a   the tabulation and publishing of statistical tables; and/or
    b   the designation of "rural" localities for targeting policies and programs.

The choice of geographical units for the empirical measures

The first operational choice required is the selection of the geographical unit (e.g. neighborhood, town, county, regional district) that best represents the "places" or "localities" appropriate for the issue being studied (du Plessis et al., 2001).[2] For example, the choice of the spatial unit will depend upon whether one is studying an issue with a neighborhood focus (e.g. daycare), an issue administered at the county level, or an economic development issue to be considered for a functional economic area. This choice will, in turn, represent the "locality" in the grid in Table 1.1.

For many community-level issues requiring community-level data, there will also be a need to know the characteristics of the region within which the community is embedded. Similarly, for many regional-level issues, it may be important to know the characteristics or the mix of communities within the region. For example, what are the differences in family income among the communities in the region? Are all the communities in the region approximately the same size or is there a dominant community in the region? Also, how is the population distributed within the region?

If no data are available for the theoretically appropriate geographic grid, there will be a loss of information. For example, if community is the appropriate spatial grid but data are only available at the county level, then one is missing the variation among the communities in the county as the county-level data will only show the (population-weighted) average for all communities in the county. Using county-level data rather than community-level data will generate (perhaps very) different empirical relationships between rurality measures (density and distance-to-density) and the behavior or outcome that is the object of the analysis. In fact, one would expect (very) different estimates of the size of the empirical relationship between each of the independent factors and the behavior or outcome being analyzed when using county-level data compared to using community-level data.

Measuring density (as a continuous variable)

The choice of this measure will also be determined by the analytic question being considered. Typically, the population size of the locality would be an appropriate choice. In some cases, the population per square kilometer might be more appropriate. However, there may be specific investigations that would call for a density measure such as the density (number) of social networks (perhaps on a per capita basis) or the density (number) of individuals diagnosed with diabetes (again, perhaps on a per capita basis), as two examples. For analytical questions, generally, the chosen measure of density would be entered as a continuous variable in the empirical analysis. Data availability may also constrain the choice of the appropriate geographic grid for the empirical estimate of density.

Measuring distance-to-density[3] (as a continuous variable)

The choice of the measure of distance-to-density would also be determined by the analytic question being measured. For example, the transportation of goods would likely require a different set of measures compared to the transfer of services (such as the transfer of accounting services or travel agent services by the internet).

The road distance might be suitable for many analytic questions. More likely, the time cost and/or the money cost of making the trip would be a more suitable measure. The question of distance to "where" will depend upon the question(s) being investigated. For example, the measure of the distance to daycare versus the distance to a brain surgeon versus the distance to sell your crop of organic peaches would each need to be implemented in different ways. In addition to the money or time cost of distance, for some cases, such as the distance to attend university, the issue of distance may also involve psychological, emotional, cultural, and familial costs (or perhaps benefits) that need to be considered as part of the measure of distance-to-density.

For analytical questions, generally, the chosen measure of distance would be entered as a continuous variable in the empirical analysis. In some cases, a continuous variable would not be appropriate such as the case where residents of a small(er) island must use a ferry or for residents who must cross a mountain pass.

Data availability is always an issue. For example, if the analyst is searching for a measure of distance to a university, perhaps the ideal data would be the longitude and latitude for the exact location of the university. However, the analyst might be constrained to use the distance to the centroid of the municipality (or the boundary of the municipality) where the university is located. The comparison of multiple potential and logical measures of distance-to-density would permit the analyst to test hypotheses about the significance of these various measures of distance-to-density in explaining the behavior or outcome being studied.

A number of countries have generated remoteness or accessibility measures of the distance to urban centers. For Canada, see Alasia *et al.* (2017).

Establishing thresholds for classification into groups

In order to generate a statistical tabulation of the characteristics of individuals, enterprises, or organizations along the rural–urban continuum, one needs to select a threshold of density and a threshold of distance-to-density. In addition, some government agencies need rurality thresholds[4] for targeting government programs.

Thresholds for density

Statistical agencies (almost) always classify their population into rural and urban groups by assigning a threshold for the population size of a settlement (built-up area). One participant at the National Academies (2016) workshop had tried to determine the original justification for the threshold of 2500 inhabitants for the US classification of rural versus urban but the available files in the government department did not provide any rationale for the choice. Statistics Canada has used a threshold of 1000 inhabitants for the rural–urban classification for at least 100 years and it is equally unlikely that the rationale for the original choice of this threshold could be uncovered.

For analysts who are able to assign their own thresholds, the choice of a threshold should be influenced by the research question. In some cases, one will wish to understand the regional context within which each smaller locality is embedded, or, in other cases, one will want to understand the mix of communities that constitute a given region (Isserman, 2005; Partridge and Rickman, 2006).

Thresholds for distance-to-density

Statistical agencies in a number of countries assign a distance threshold. For example, in the US, counties are classified as non-metro based on a density criterion. Then, a distance criterion is applied, to classify non-metro counties into two groups: metro-adjacent and non-adjacent to metro. The rural and small-town definition that is used in Canada (du Plessis *et al.*, 2001) is based on a density criterion of 10,000 inhabitants (in a given census sub-division (CSD), i.e. incorporated towns and incorporated municipalities) plus a distance criterion based on observed commuting flows (specifically, less than 50 percent of resident workforce commutes to a CSD of 10,000 or more). These density and distance-to-density thresholds are illustrated schematically in Table 1.2. The regions delineated as predominantly rural regions by the OECD are classified into two groups – predominantly rural regions close to a city and predominantly rural remote regions (see Brezzi *et al.*, 2011).

For analysts who are delineating their own thresholds, the choice of the threshold should be driven by the issues being analyzed.

Implications

From an analytical point of view, the most important purpose for defining the dimensions of "rurality" is to understand and measure how one's position of density and distance-to-density in geographic space might affect behavior or outcomes. This means that these behaviors or outcomes should not be included as elements of the definition of rurality, but as potential correlates of rurality or urbanity. Indicators such as the percentage of the labor force in agriculture, levels of education, income, attitudes to hunting, or even the feeling or perception of rural identity should remain independent from the theoretical and operational definitions of rurality so that theories and hypotheses regarding the impacts of each dimension of rurality can be empirically tested (Cloke *et al.*, 2006; Halseth *et al.*, 2010; Alasia, 2010; Partridge *et al.*, 2007a, 2007b, 2008; Partridge and Olfert, 2011).

This separation of rurality dimensions and potential correlates includes the interpretation of "rural" as a social representation or construct (Halfacree, 1993; and his comments in the report

Table 1.2 The two dimensions of the rurality with density and distance thresholds

		Index of rurality in the density dimension from lower rurality, 0 (higher density) to higher rurality, 10 (lower density)										
		0	1	2	3	4	5	6	7	8	9	10
	0											
	1											
	3											
	4											
Index of rurality in the distance dimension from lower rurality, 0 (shorter distance) to higher rurality, 10 (longer distance)	5							Rural and small-town outside Census Metropolitan Areas (CMAs) and outside Census Agglomerations (CAs)				
	6											
	7											
	8											
	9											
	10											

Note: These thresholds illustrate in a notional sense the operational definition of "rural and small town" areas where the vertical line represents a population density of 10,000 or more in the population center and the horizontal line represents a "distance" threshold measured by whether 50 percent or more of the employed residents commute to the population center (du Plessis *et al.*, 2001)

by the National Academies, 2016, p. 38). This approach suggests that how people perceive or imagine "rural" geographic space will influence behavior. "Rural" as a social representation should be considered as a potential hypothesis independent of the spatial aspects of density and distance-to-density, rather than a defining characteristic. By separating the definition of rurality using the dimensions of density and distance-to-density from its social construct characteristics, it becomes possible to explore potential empirical relationships between these two elements rather than confound them within the same definition.

The same approach should be used when rurality dimensions are treated as a proxy for indicating the "needs" for targeting a policy or program. If the target is unemployment, health services, or capacity to initiate development programs, then a direct assessment of the "need" would seem to be a more efficient approach than using the dimensions of rurality to target a policy or program. Need and capacity will likely differ across the two rurality dimensions of density and distance-to-density *but* the correlation or linkage of rurality and need or capacity should not be expected to be a one-to-one relationship. In other words, considerable variability of need and capacity would be expected within each cell of Table 1.1. A program targeted at need and capacity should use an independent index of need and capacity rather than an index of rurality in order to implement its initiatives.

This approach means that the characteristics of people in any locality do not define their rurality. The effort to define "rurality" is *not* an effort to generate a socio-economic classification but to ascertain whether or not their location in geographic space has an independent influence on their behavior or outcomes. Thus, the effort to define "rurality" is not to generate a grouping which minimizes within-group variability relative to "urban". Rather, the effort to define "rurality" is to situate individuals in a spatial locality in order to examine how the locality dimensions of density and distance-to-density might affect their behavior, modify their perceptions, constrain or enhance their options, or require special programs for the management of resources or services.

The close association of "place" and "distance" with human intervention reinforces another challenge associated with the dimensions of rurality: its ideological implications. This is especially important for analysts with an interest in social or political change. The thresholds adopted for "place" and "distance" inadvertently (and unfortunately) give preference to certain objectives, infrastructure, and institutions over others. The choice of any given threshold will tend to provide the impression that every locality in the group is the same. They are certainly the "same" with respect to the classification variable, but they would be expected to be (and empirically are) very different in many other respects. This will (or will appear to) diminish important diversity of social, institutional, and political factors within the delineated spatial grouping.

Perhaps obviously, the schematic in Table 1.1 represents the situation at a given point of time. Over time, there are changes in both the advantages and the disadvantages associated with both density and distance-to-density. Notably, the price[5] of distance has been declining over time (Bollman and Prud'homme, 2006). In addition, Lichter and Brown (2011) speak of "changing spatial boundaries" and Lichter and Ziliak (2017) speak of "new patterns of spatial interdependence".

In summary, the conceptual definition for the rurality of localities is density and distance-to-density. Operational decisions regarding the way to measure density and distance-to-density should be specified on the basis of the objectives of the specific issue being considered.

Finally, the analyst should take care to ensure that the behavior or outcomes of individuals, enterprises, or institutions are clearly defined (theoretically and operationally) in a way which keeps them separate from the theoretical and operational definitions of rurality. Only in this way can analysts learn from the empirical analysis instead of suffering the tautological error of finding that the relationships are true by how they are defined.

Discussion

Early analysis of rural qualities and places occurred as a contrast to urban ones. Analysts used the distinction to describe a wide range of contrasting characteristics: economic, productive, social, and political (Marx and Engels, 1848; Simmel, 1964; Weber, 1966). These analyses rarely included empirical studies of specific places, so the challenges of operationalization seldom emerged. Rural regions were often identified with agricultural production, particularly in the European context. The contrast of conditions in urban and rural places was sufficiently strong (at least in its conceptualization) to inspire its use as an explanation for differences such as economic growth, social integration, health, political action, values, and attitudes. This type of analysis was also reflected in the institutional organization of governments, often in the form of agriculture or regional-focused departments.

It was only in the latter part of the twentieth century that a simple contrast of rural and urban regions and the strong identification of agricultural production with rural places faced challenges on empirical and analytical grounds. The reframing of agricultural organization and community characteristics (e.g. Goldschmidt, 1947) and the proliferation of detailed case studies in the North American context (e.g. Hughes, 1963) raised concerns, both conceptual and operational, about the simple contrast between urban and rural places. One of the strongest challenges emerged as international comparisons were made in the search for common indicators of rural and urban places. Driven by the desire for international comparisons, analysts were faced with many different meanings and indicators of "rural" in places as diverse as Greece, Norway, Germany, the US, or Canada (Eurostat, 2015; OECD, 1994). This was reinforced by debates among researchers regarding the explanatory significance of spatial conditions themselves in the face of diverse social, cultural, and power dynamics within rural regions (Alasia, 2010; Cloke *et al.*, 2006; Halfacree, 1993; Halseth *et al.*, 2010; Partridge *et al.*, 2007a, 2008; Partridge, 2017).

As a result of these debates and analyses researchers are now in a much better position to address both the theoretical and operational challenges of understanding rural issues. Analysts now pay more attention to the way in which they define "rural" and "rurality" – often with a distinction between their definition and the characteristics associated with it. At the same time, a plethora of empirical studies which examine those characteristics – using a variety of rural classifications – are still present.

For example, from 1998 to 2012, Statistics Canada published a series of "Rural and Small-Town Canada Analysis Bulletins"[6] that provided a profile of the rural and urban population in Canada. As in other countries, rural residents tended to be older on average, have fewer years of formal education, and have higher unemployment rates due to the intensity of seasonal industries. The OECD rural policy reviews between 2007 and 2014 provide additional examples of both theoretical discussions and empirical analysis of predominantly rural regions. Most recently, Del Real and Clement (2017) reported on a rural survey (The Washington Post and the Kaiser Family Foundation, 2017) that showed the usual socio-economic differences between individuals classified as "rural" versus those classified as "urban" based on a set of thresholds of density and distance-to-density.

The interpretation of these studies still requires careful attention to the dimensions of rurality that have been used. For example, is the unit of analysis appropriate for the issues of concern? Are the measures of density and distance-to-density independent from the characteristics considered? Fortunately, authors of both theoretical and empirical studies are now more likely to make their concepts and procedures more explicit.

What is policy?

Policies are principles or guidelines used to specify or frame decisions within social groups as priorities are considered and choices are made to achieve desired outcomes. Even the decision not to decide would be included as a policy. Policies are often abstract in nature, with a focus on long-term objectives, but the term "policy" is sometimes used to refer to short-term expectations or requirements related to an organization (e.g. policy on dress code or maternity leave).

For some, the meaning of policy is limited to the role of public institutions with their more formal regulations, principles of decision-making or action, and the patterns of decisions they represent. Other actors include non-public organizations such as corporations and more informal groups that research and generate policy proposals. Since policies require mechanisms for their formulation, communication, and enforcement, policy discussions often include the activities, constraints, and incentives which structure their application.

Policies are often codified in constitutions, bylaws, regulations, and contracts with powers to monitor, adjudicate, and impose sanctions or benefits accordingly. In more informal contexts, equivalent functions may be served by mission statements, codes of practice, and traditions of engagement. Because of their relatively general and abstract formulation, there are often multiple options for their implementation. A policy advocating improved health services for remote localities, for example, may be addressed by programs supporting more doctors in those localities, improved medical facilities, more home care, extended telemedicine, improvements in emergency transport, or various combinations of these or similar initiatives. Policy discussions and analysis, therefore, often involve debates and decisions about both the policy and its implementation.

Under the best conditions, policies are based on clearly articulated objectives and rationales for specific implementations, but this is not always the case. Therefore, the identification of policies often requires the analyst to infer the principles of an implicit policy from the cases to which it is applied. Implicit policies are typically driven by political, social, environmental, or ideological objectives. Policy domains are also made complex by the fact that multiple organizations and objectives may be involved. For example, within the public sector, departmental and jurisdictional differences often generate such policy "inconsistencies". Each organization is operating within a given context or set of parameters. Perhaps not surprisingly, the policy objectives and programs of one department may not be consistent with the policy objectives and programs of another department.

Policy analysts provide several taxonomies of policies, usually based on their sphere of concern (e.g. health, agriculture, environmental), the processes by which policies are formulated and applied, and the analysis of the broader context in which policies are developed (Bührs and Bartlett, 1997). There is also considerable discussion regarding various methodologies for the analysis of policy – including both descriptive and evaluation objectives (Salamon, 2002; Simon, 1997; Conteh, 2013). Some of the most useful approaches focus on the evaluation of policies, including Salamon's (2002) analysis of the long-term durability of policies using the following six questions:

- What effects does the policy have on the targeted problem?
- What are the unintended effects of this policy?
- What are the effects of the policy on different population groups?
- What is the financial cost of this policy (including tax credits)?
- Is the policy technically feasible?
- Do the relevant policy stakeholders view the policy as acceptable? ("Policy analysis – Wikipedia", 2017)

What is rural policy?

Although there may be policies which are directed specifically at or to rural places or actors, few, if any, of them have outcomes which are exclusive to those places or actors. As a result, analysts have typically focused on the *analysis* of policy rather than its division into rural vs. non-rural types. At most, they differentiate "narrow" rural policies (those which are targeted specifically to rural localities, actors, or issues) from "broad" policies (those which might have an impact on such localities, actors, or issues, but are not specifically targeted to them) (OECD, 2008). In keeping with this approach, this section will focus on rural policy analysis.

Rural policy analysis is the application of a rural lens (also known as rural proofing) to policy proposals. Rural policy analysis is a consideration of the density and distance-to-density implications of (almost) every policy proposal. Since the assessment of policies for more intensive rural analysis will vary over time as knowledge, institutional priorities, and ideological perspectives change, it behooves analysts to consider all policy as potential candidates for further exploration. Typically, this involves a triage type of process in which all policies are considered, with some of them selected for further, more detailed analysis. Each policy of a government, enterprise, or institution would be considered for their potential outcomes, benefits, and/or costs along the continuums of the rurality dimensions. Policies selected for more intensive analysis would then undergo more thorough analysis of their implications for individuals, enterprises, and institutions.

Typically, a rural policy analyst would ask if the objectives of the policy proposal could be enhanced or made more effective by adjusting the policy or its implementation for citizens, businesses, or institutions in various combinations of low(er) density and high(er) distance-to-density locations. These considerations have been constituted as rural proofing or as a rural lens in a number of jurisdictions. For a number of years, this was one task of the former federal Rural Secretariat in Canada (Clemenson, 1994; Agriculture Canada, 2001; OECD, 2002, 2006a, p. 112, 2010; Hall and Gibson, 2016). Other examples include the initiatives of the UK Department of the Environment, Food and Rural Affairs (DEFRA, 2017), the Rural Ontario Municipal Association (2015a, 2015b), and in Huron County (Procter *et al.*, 2014) in Ontario, Canada.

Although (virtually) all public policies are "rural-related" (i.e. have density and distance-to-density implications), many policies are only indirectly related to the geographical characteristics of rurality (Halseth *et al.*, 2010; Young, 2006). Even agricultural policy, for example, is not solely a rural policy issue (Bollman, 2007) due to urban-based and metro-adjacent farming. Similarly, policies explicitly formulated as "rural policy" – like "Québec's Politique nationale de la ruralité" (see Chapter 33) – create important issues of an urban nature such as the allocation of financial resources for urban concerns. Broad policies such as those of finance, economic development, labor, health, education, transportation, and social welfare require specific consideration of their implications for different density and distance-to-density conditions.

Even where "rural lens" considerations for rural people, enterprises, or organizations are taken into account, there is often little reference to evidence provided by the analytic studies of the differential impacts (or different elasticities of response) along each rurality dimension and/ or little input from rural people. Thus, decisions may be driven by the perceptions of urban-based decision-makers.

What is development policy?

There are various foci of "development policy". Examples include community development policy, social development policy, economic development policy, and regional development policy.

As with all policy, development policy focuses, generally, on improving the well-being of individuals, communities, or groups. "Development" has been considered as both an outcome of well-being and a process to improve well-being.

What is rural development policy?

Rural development policy is an explicit consideration of density and distance-to-density implications in the design and implementation of (community, social, or economic) development policy. In other words, the application of a rural lens or rural proofing would constitute the "rural" in any development policy.

There has been a long history of development policies and programs targeted to rural areas. The discussion of rural development emerged from a focus on regional or sub-national economic development which started in the mid-1900s in Canada and in other OECD countries. This approach has undergone important changes (Harriss, 1982). The OECD has represented these changes in three major paradigms: the Old Rural Paradigm, the New Rural Paradigm (OECD, 2006a, 2006b), and now as Rural Policy 3.0 (OECD, 2017a, 2017b) (Table 1.3).

Table 1.3 Changing paradigms of rural development policy since the mid-1900s

	Old paradigm	*New paradigm – 2006*	*Rural policy 3.0 – implementing the new rural paradigm*
Objectives	Equalization	Competitiveness	Well-being considering multiple dimensions of (i) economy, (ii) society, and (iii) environment
Policy focus	Support for a single dominant resource sector	Support for multiple sectors based on their competitiveness	Low-density economies differentiated by type of rural area
Key actors and stakeholders	Farm organizations and national governments	All levels of government and all relevant departments plus local stakeholders	(i) Public sector (multi-level governance) (ii) private sector (for-profit firms and social enterprises), and (iii) third sector (nongovernmental organizations and civil society)
Policy approach	Uniform applied top-down policy	Bottom-up policy, local strategies	Integrated approach with multiple policy domains
Rural definition	Not urban	Rural as a variety of distinct types of place	Three types of rural: (i) within functional urban area, (ii) close to a functional urban area, and (iii) far from a functional urban area

Source: OECD (2017a, 2017b).

The old paradigm focused on one or two sectors (e.g. agriculture, forestry, mining, energy) as strategic for rural development. Policies were developed by central governments to increase the efficiency of primary production, including the building of a transportation infrastructure for trade. Rural communities competed for large firms in their search for solutions to community decline – without realizing that success often meant ongoing decline since increasing efficiency meant that fewer workers were required to produce more.[7] The subsidies provided by communities to firms meant that the communities had fewer remaining funds for other community development initiatives and the centers of control became more distant from community-level influence.

The old paradigm approach began to face criticism as a result of the research stimulated by the Goldschmidt thesis that linked the style of agricultural production with community characteristics (Goldschmidt, 1947), and the critiques of the first "Green Revolution" export-oriented policies of the World Bank for their inadequate impacts on persistent poverty, gender, and the environment (Pingali, 2012). In 2006, the OECD published *The New Rural Paradigm* that challenged this old view and proposed an approach which was more bottom-up, multi-sectoral, and focused on investments rather than a strategy of subsidies (OECD, 2006a, 2006b). Through a series of extensive national and comparative studies, this new approach was illustrated and documented in a valuable array of both qualitative and quantitative analyses of rural development and the policies that contribute or inhibit it (see the OECD Rural Policy Reviews for Mexico

(2007), Finland (2008), Scotland (2008), Netherlands (2008), Italy (2009), Germany (2009), China (2009), Spain (2009), Quebec (2010), England (2011), and Chile (2014), (OECD, 2019)).

The work of the OECD has continued over the last ten years and contributed to several critiques and refinements of the *New Rural Paradigm* which provide more details regarding the economic and social mechanisms supporting effective policies. These proposals are identified as "*Rural Policy 3.0*" in Table 1.1. Key elements include the reaffirmation of multi-sector collaboration among the public, private, and third sectors for strong rural policy, the explicit identification of the economy, society, and the environment as multiple objectives for the policy, and the role of distance-to-density by recognizing "functional urban areas" as a point of reference for rural localities.

As with any policy discussion, the focus of attention will depend on the issues being considered. For example, if economic development is the focus, Partridge and Olfert (2011) argue that one should not talk about rural development – rather the focus should be on regional development (i.e. the development options for a functional economic area). In this case, the options and the expected outcomes will differ based on the degree of rurality (i.e. density and distance-to-density) of the functional economic area (Stabler and Rounds 1997; Olfert and Stabler, 2002; Munro *et al.*, 2011; Ashton *et al.*, 2013).

Statistics for rural residents/enterprises/institutions

Statistical tables often present a profile of data for observations classified as "rural" using given thresholds for density and for distance-to-density. It is important to identify the theoretical and empirical validity of these thresholds in order to appropriately interpret the data.

First, to emphasize, these thresholds do not define rural – rather, density and distance-to-density define rurality.

However, any given set of thresholds will generate a portrait of the average statistics for observations in the group – and the characteristics revealed in the tabulated data would be different for each alternative set of thresholds for density and distance-to-density.

Given a set of statistics for a group of observations classified as "rural", the next (and arguably most important) step would be to apply a "rural lens" to the tabulated data in order to query:

•   What is the role played by low(er) density in the observed data?
•   What is the role played by long(er) distance-to-density in the data?

and then to query whether there is an opportunity for policy to improve the well-being of "rural" actors.

For example, statistical tabulations typically show that the population in a rural area has a lower level of educational attainment. What is the role of the selected grid (selected boundaries) and the density and distance-to-density in this finding? Are the designated geographical units so large that they are insensitive to pockets of higher education within the region – or so small that they overlook the role of broader regional collaboration? Did low(er) density or long(er) distance-to-density mean that people with higher levels of educational attainment moved away to find jobs (or those who left for education were not able to return due to the lack of jobs)? Did low(er) density or long(er) distance-to-density mean that the availability and quality of the schools or colleges in the locality caused a lower level of educational attainment? Was the lower level of educational attainment observed because many retired people (with lower than average levels of education) have chosen to move to the locality after their retirement? These questions will help to determine the role of rurality in understanding the reasons for the observed data of lower levels of educational attainment in rural areas.

Summary

Rurality is a spatial concept. As noted by Shucksmith and Brown (2016) "people still solve the challenges of everyday life in geographically bounded communities" (p. 664).

Density and distance-to-density are the spatial dimensions of localities that define their rurality. All other factors that may be associated with rurality are characteristics that are found within specific locations. They are characteristics of rural people, enterprises, or institutions. However, it is the density and distance-to-density dimensions that define rurality.

These concepts are not changing. However, the prices, costs, advantages, and disadvantages of each of the two rurality dimensions are changing. For example, in earlier times, a town of a given size could support a hospital. However, these days, most patients want a hospital with the best technology and such a hospital can only be supported by a regional center. In this case, there is a change in the disadvantage of smaller community (i.e. lower density) vis-à-vis hospital services.

The measure of distance-to-density may be physical distance (e.g. kilometers) or the price of distance (e.g. dollars to move a person, goods, or service over a given number of kilometers). A change in these prices constitutes a change in the rurality dimension of distance-to-density.

For the discussion of some issues, such as rural youth who move to the city to pursue further education, there are social, psychological, cultural, or familial advantages *and* disadvantages of making this move. Distance remains "a powerful shaper of human interaction, influence, and exchange" (Young, 2006, p. 262) but the dynamics of this influence are complex since the meaning (or "price") of distance itself is different for different issues being discussed and for the changes over time for any given issue being discussed.

Rural policy analysis means considering the implications of density and distance-to-density for (almost) every policy proposal. In the specific case of development policy, the "rural" aspect of a development policy is the explicit consideration of density and distance-to-density in the design and the implementation of the policy. This approach requires that a rural lens or rural proofing procedure should be applied to each development policy proposal.

The categorization of people, enterprises, or organizations into spatial geographic groups labeled "rural" does not define rurality. Density and distance-to-density define rurality. The classification of observations into spatial groups should consider two factors. First, the nature of the issue (e.g. daycare versus regional economic development) will determine the geographic grid (e.g. neighborhood versus functional economic area) that is chosen to make the classification. Second, the nature of the issue will also drive the consideration of the appropriate level of the thresholds of density and distance-to-density when implementing the classification.

Policy preferences and priorities are complex and changing. Thus, there is seldom a common agreement on interpretations and indicators among analysts and researchers, let alone policy-makers and citizens. It behooves us, therefore, to critically analyze the objectives and analytic approaches to an issue and the choice of measures or indicators that are adopted to quantify the rurality dimensions of density and distance-to-density.

Considerations for moving forward

Readers are invited to consider the following questions when discussing "rural", "rural policy", and the rurality aspects of "regional economic development policy".

1   What are the policy objectives and issues being considered?
  •   What are the implications, advantages, and disadvantages for people, enterprises, and organizations located in lower-density localities *and* in places with a long(er) distance-to-density?
2   What processes are being used to formulate, discuss, and adjust any policy proposal?
  •   How might the processes be modified to improve the consideration of density and distance-to-density?
3   What is the appropriate geographic unit of analysis (e.g. neighborhood, community, county, tourism region, etc.) to use for categorizing and presenting descriptive characteristics of the people, enterprises, or organizations that will be impacted by the policy proposal?
  •   What data are available for the appropriate geographic grid?
  •   What compromises must be made? Are the data published for the geographic grid appropriate for your analysis? If not, can you afford the price of a special tabulation to generate the appropriate data?
4   What are the social and political contexts within which proposed policies are formulated and chosen?
  •   Where should such decisions be made for the given objectives or issues being considered?
5   Who controls or influences the discourse surrounding the issue, related selection of thresholds, and measures associated with the issues you have selected? What are their interests and how do they conflict with others?
6   What are the appropriate indicators for the policy issues selected?
  •   Are the dimensions of distance and distance-to-density being considered?
7   How do they relate to conflicting policies and indicators?

Consider these questions as you proceed through the following chapters. The variety of approaches represented will not only demonstrate the possibilities, but hopefully inspire you to reflect on the implications for your own research and analysis.

Notes

1 Careful readers will recall the earlier statement that the characteristics of a locality do not define the rurality of a locality. Here, examples are used to illustrate the point. Although larger hospitals may be associated with larger localities, one would not expect a one-to-one relationship between a larger hospital and a larger locality. To repeat, the examples in this chapter are simply illustrative.
2 Note that du Plessis *et al.* (2001) provide operational definitions of "rural", not theoretical ones.
3 The 2009 World Development Report of the World Bank acknowledged a third "D", namely "division" (World Bank, 2009, Chapter 3) which includes:

  • the thickness of borders (e.g. tariffs, non-tariff barriers) for the transfer of goods, services, and people from one jurisdiction to another; and
  • ethnic/cultural/language differences ("divisions") that sometimes constrain the transfer of goods, services, and people from one jurisdiction to another. For example, one might imagine a person standing outside a health center in any cell of Table 1.1 and being unable to access the health center due to issues of skin color or ethnicity.

  Thus, access to services (or access to a market for one's goods or services) is often determined by more than density and distance-to-density. However, the dimensions of density and distance-to-density remain as the key rurality dimensions.
4 Some government programs adjust the size of the subsidy based on the degree of rurality of the locality. For example, one participant at the National Academies (2016, p. 83) workshop noted that the US

Rural Development water program used priority points to allow a region to get extra points if it is far below the population threshold.

5 One might think of the "price" of distance as the component of the price of a loaf of bread or an automobile, etc. that is attributable to the component of the retail price that is typically called the expenditure for "freight". For transporting services (such as an accountant providing accountancy services to a business in another locality), technology has changed the "delivery price" from the money and time expenditure to transport a paper copy of the documents to the internet expenditure to transport an electronic copy of the business accounts.

6 Available at www5.statcan.gc.ca/olc-cel/olc.action?objId=21-006-X&objType=2&lang=en&limit=0.

7 Schultz (1972) has noted the pervasiveness of the "increasing value of human time". This has driven the substitution of machines for workers meaning more output can be produced with fewer workers.

References

Agriculture Canada, 2001. *Guide to using the rural lens.* Agriculture Canada, Ottawa, Ont.

Alasia, A., Bedard, F., Belanger, J., Guimond, E., Penney, C., 2017. *Measuring remoteness and accessibility: A set of indices for Canadian communities.* Statistics Canada, Ottawa, Ont.

Alasia, A., 2010. *Population change across Canadian communities, 1981 to 2006: The Role of Sector Restructuring, Agglomeration, Diversification and Human Capital.* Agriculture Division, Statistics Canada, Ottawa, Ont.

Ashton, W., Bollman, R., Kelly, W., 2013. *Identifying and explaining self-contained labour areas in rural Manitoba.* Rural Development Institute, Brandon, MB. www.brandonu.ca/rdi/files/2015/08/Identifying_Explaining_SLAs_in_Rural_Manitoba_Report.pdf.

Bollman, R., 2007. *Factors driving Canada's rural economy, 1914 to 2006.* Research Paper, Catalogue No. 21-601-MIE – No. 083. Agriculture Division, Statistics Canada, Ottawa, Ont.

Bollman, R., Prud'homme, M., 2006. *Trends in the prices of rurality.* Agriculture Division, Statistics Canada, Ottawa, Ont.

Brezzi, M., Dijkstra, L., Ruiz, V., 2011. *OECD extended regional typology: The economic performance of remote rural regions.* OECD Regional Development Working Papers, 2011/06. https://doi.org/10.1787/5kg6z83tw7f4-en.

Bührs, T., Bartlett, R.V., 1997. *Strategic thinking and the environment: Planning the future in New Zealand?* Environmental Politics 6(2), 72–100.

Clemenson, H., 1994. *Mandate for small communities and rural areas,* in: Reimer, B., Young, G. (Eds.), *Development strategies for rural Canada: Evaluating partnerships, jobs and communities.* ARRG Working Papers Series No. 6. The Canadian Agricultural and Rural Restructuring Group, Wolfville, NS, pp. 3–6.

Cloke, P., Marsden, T., Mooney, P., 2006. *The handbook of rural studies.* Sage, London.

Conteh, C., 2013. *Policy governance in multi-level systems: Economic development and policy implementation in Canada.* McGill-Queen's University Press, Montreal, QC.

Del Real, J., Clement, S., 2017. *Rural divide.* Washington Post. www.washingtonpost.com/graphics/2017/national/rural-america/ (accessed 2.22.19).

Department for Environment Food and Rural Affairs (DEFRA), 2017. *Rural proofing: Practical guidance to assess impacts of policies on rural areas.* UK Government.

du Plessis, V., Beshiri, R., Bollman, R., Clemenson, H., 2001. *Mapping the socio-economic diversity of rural Canada.* Agriculture Division, Statistics Canada, Ottawa, Ont.

Eurostat, 2015. *Archive: Urban–rural typology: Statistics explained.* Eurostat. Statistics explained. https://ec.europa.eu/eurostat/statistics-explained/index.php/Archive:Urban-rural_typology (accessed 2.22.19).

Goldschmidt, W.R., 1947. *As you sow.* Harcourt, Brace & Co, New York.

Halfacree, K.H., 1993. *Locality and social representation: Space, discourse and alternative definitions of the rural.* Journal of Rural Studies 9, 23–37. https://doi.org/10.1016/0743-0167(93)90003-3.

Hall, H.M., Gibson, R., 2016. *Rural proofing in Canada: An examination of the rural secretariat and the rural lens.* University of Waterloo; University of Guelph.

Halseth, G., Markey, S., Bruce, D. (Eds.), 2010. *The next rural economies: Constructing rural place in a global economy.* University of Northern British Columbia. CABI, Oxfordshire.

Harriss, J., 1982. *Rural development: Theories of peasant economy and agrarian change.* Hutchinson University Library, London.

Hughes, E., 1963. *French Canada in transition.* Oxford University Press, Don Mills, Ont.; New York.

Isserman, A.M., 2005. *In the national interest: Defining rural and urban correctly in research and public policy*. International Regional Science Review 28, 465–499. https://doi.org/10.1177/0160017605279000.

Lichter, D., Brown, D., 2011. *Rural America in an urban society: Changing spatial and social boundaries*. Annual Review of Sociology 37, 565–592. http://dx.doi.org/10.1146/annurev-soc-081309-150208.

Lichter, D.T., Ziliak, J.P., 2017. *The rural–urban interface: New patterns of spatial interdependence and inequality in America*. The Annals of the American Academy of Political and Social Science 672, 6–25. https://doi.org/10.1177/0002716217714180.

Marx, K., Engels, F., 1848. *Manifest der Kommunistischen Partei (The Communist Manifesto)*. J.E. Burghard, London.

Munro, A., Alasia, A., Bollman, R.D., 2011. *Self-contained labour areas: A proposed delineation and classification by degree of rurality*. Rural and Small Town Canada Analysis Bulletin Catalogue 8(8). Agriculture Division, Statistics Canada, Ottawa, Ont. www150.statcan.gc.ca/n1/en/pub/21-006-x/21-006-x2008008-eng.pdf?st=4bLqZn8H.

National Academies of Sciences, Engineering, and Medicine, 2016. *Rationalizing rural area classifications for the economic research service: A workshop summary*. The National Academies Press, Washington, DC. https://doi.org/ 10.17226/21843.

OECD, 1994. *Creating rural indicators for shaping territorial policy*. OECD, Paris; Washington, DC.

OECD, 2002. *OECD territorial reviews: Canada 2002*. OECD, Paris.

OECD, 2006a. *Reinventing rural policy*. OECD Observer. OECD, Paris.

OECD, 2006b. *The new rural paradigm: Policies and governance*. OECD, Paris.

OECD, 2008. *OECD rural policy reviews: Finland*. OECD, Paris.

OECD, 2010. *OECD rural policy reviews: Québec, Canada*. OECD. Paris.

OECD, 2017a. *New rural policy: Linking up for growth*. Background document prepared for the National Prosperity Through Modern Rural Policy Conference. OECD, Paris.

OECD, 2017b. *Rural policy 3.0*. OECD, Paris.

OECD, 2019. *OECD rural policy reviews*. www.oecd-ilibrary.org/urban-rural-and-regional-development/oecd-rural-policy-reviews_19909284.

Olfert, R.M., Stabler, J.C., 2002. *Saskatchewan in the 21st century: Population projections to 2005*. University of Regina Press, Regina, SK.

Partridge, M., 2017. *The geography of rural American poverty*. Testimony before the House Ways and Means Committee, Subcommittee on Human Resources, The Ohio State University.

Partridge, M., Olfert, M.R., 2011. *The winners' choice: Sustainable economic strategies for successful 21st-century regions*. Applied Economic Perspectives and Policy 33, 143–178.

Partridge, M., Rickman, D., 2006. *The geography of American poverty: Is there a need for place-based policies?* Upjohn Press, Kalamazoo, MI. https://doi.org/10.17848/9781429454872.

Partridge, M., Bollman, R., Olfert, M.R., Alasia, A., 2007a. *Riding the wave of urban growth in the countryside: Spread, backwash, or stagnation?* Land Economics 83, 128–152. https://doi.org/10.3368/le.83.2.128.

Partridge, M., Olfert, M.R., Alasia, A., 2007b. *Canadian cities as regional engines of growth: Agglomeration and amenities*. Canadian Journal of Economics 40, 39–68.

Partridge, M., Rickman, D.S., Ali, K., Olfert, M.R., 2008. *Lost in space: Population growth in the American hinterlands and small cities*. Journal of Economic Geography 8, 272–757. https://doi.org/10.1093/jeg/lbn038.

Pingali, P.L., 2012. *Green revolution: Impacts, limits, and the path ahead*. Proceedings of the National Academy of Sciences of the United States of America 109(31), 12302–12308. https://doi.org/10.1073/pnas.0912953109.

Procter, K., Marr, E., Smith, M., 2014. *Huron County rural lens: A tool to promote rural equity and inclusion*. Huron County Health Unit, Huron County, Ont. www.gatewayruralhealth.ca/uploads/2/4/7/9/24790890/huron_-_full_doc_rural_lens_07apr2014.pdf.

Reimer, B., Bollman, R., 2009. *Understanding rural Canada: Implications for rural development policy and rural planning policy*, in: Douglas, D. (Ed.), *Rural planning and development in Canada*. Nelson College Indigenous, Toronto, Ont., pp. 10–52.

Rural Ontario Municipal Association, 2015a. *A rural and northern lens panel card*.

Rural Ontario Municipal Association, 2015b. *The rural and northern lens and a voice for rural and northern Ontario*.

Salamon, L.M., 2002. *The tools of government: A guide to new governance*. Oxford University Press, Oxford.

Schultz, T.W., 1972. *The increasing economic value of human time*. American Journal of Agricultural Economics 54, 843–850. https://doi.org/10.2307/1239227.

Shucksmith, M., Brown, D., 2016. *Framing rural studies in the Global North*, in: Shucksmith, M. and Brown, D.L. (Eds.), *Routledge international handbook of rural studies*, 1st edition. Routledge, New York, pp. 1–26.

Simmel, G., 1964. *The sociology of Georg Simmel*. The Free Press, New York.

Simon, H., 1997. *Administrative behavior*. Simon and Schuster, New York.

Stabler, J., Rounds, R., 1997. *Commuting and rural employment on the Canadian prairies*, in: Bollman, R.D. and Bryden, J. (Eds.), *Commuting and Rural Employment on the Canadian Prairies*. CABI, London, pp. 193–204.

The Washington Post and the Kaiser Family Foundation, 2017. *The Washington Post-Kaiser Family Foundation rural and small-town America poll*. Washington Post. www.washingtonpost.com/apps/g/page/national/washington-post-kaiser-family-foundation-rural-and-small-town-america-poll/2217/ (accessed 2.24.19).

Weber, M., 1966. *The city*, 2nd edition. ed. D. Martindale. Free Press, New York.

World Bank, 2009. *Reshaping economic geography*. World Development Record.

Young, N., 2006. *Distance as a hybrid actor in rural economies*. Journal of Rural Studies 22, 253–266. https://doi.org/10.1016/j.jrurstud.2005.11.007.

2

COMPARING RURALITIES

The case of Canada and the United States

Bill Reimer and Thomas G. Johnson

Introduction

Framework and scope of this chapter

Chapter 1 describes rurality as characteristics of place: density of population, and distance to the nearest high-density settlement. As such, it is about the geographical distribution of populations, with a focus on those which have relatively low density and/or long distance to high-density places. This approach not only provides a clear focus for analysis, but it promotes the separation of causes and consequences from the definition of rurality itself.

But density and distance-to-density are not static. Populations settle, grow, diminish, and move – and with those changes, the density and distance-to-density shift. Geography, natural resources, political choices, social relations, and cultural practices can all play a part in these dynamics, producing shifts in the distribution of rural and urban places as well as the consequences of those shifts. Comparing and understanding different nations or regions, therefore, requires both diachronic and synchronic approaches to analysis.

In this chapter, a comparison between Canada and the US is used to illustrate the ways in which historical and institutional differences have affected settlement patterns and created different approaches to understanding and responding to rural issues. Both the similarities and differences between these countries offer important insights into the factors that create the foundations for rural policy. The purpose of this chapter is not to compare such policy but rather the contexts within which broad rural policy is made, and to point out how sometimes subtle differences can lead to quite different policy outcomes.

The comparison begins by identifying some of the key geographical and institutional differences between Canada and the US which have conditioned their settlement and policy contexts. Although not rural-focused in a narrow sense, these differences have important implications for rural conditions and options in the two countries. Next, a brief description of current differences between the two countries – focusing on settlement, income, and education as examples – is offered. This section includes a discussion of the units of analysis used to distinguish rural from urban places in the two countries. The third section focuses on density and the ways in which differences in geography, colonization, government structures, and urbanization have led to diverse settlement outcomes in Canada and the US. This is followed by a similar analysis examining changes in the distance-to-density. Finally, the chapter points to some important cultural, identity, and perceptual differences that distinguish the two countries and condition their options before identifying some of the key lessons for international comparison that emerge from this analysis.

The importance of geography

The first major difference between the territories of Canada and the US lies in their geography. About 55 percent of the Canadian land mass is composed of the boreal forest (taiga): a region dominated by trees, lakes, and wetlands (Roi, 2018). North of this zone lies the tundra – a further 26 percent of the Canadian landmass – dominated by permafrost conditions and few, if any trees. The remaining southern part (19 percent) is composed of a variety of temperate, coastal, and deciduous forest regions, savannah and grasslands, wetlands, and heaths, most of them within close proximity to the southern border with the US. It is in the latter region where most of the Canadian population is located.

These topological and ecological conditions have created distinctions in the Canadian public discourse that separate "rural" from "remote" and "northern". Historically, "rural" has been primarily reserved for agricultural regions, "remote" for isolated regions – often with a forestry, mining, or energy focus, and "northern" for places and regions eligible for public tax and stipend support (Canada Revenue Agency, 2004). This financial policy, along with the regional focus of the Canadian constitution, creates conditions where institutional, policy, and research attention is more often on regions and the north than on rural (see Chapter 33) – unlike in the US.

In the US, most of the territory lies south of the 49th parallel, with Alaska being the only exception. The US also includes the state of Hawaii and several island territories. Alaska is similar to the taiga and tundra regions of Canada, and the northern regions of the contiguous 48 United States are similar in many respects to the southern areas of Canada – deciduous forest regions, savannah and grasslands, wetlands, and the eastern maritime region. Other areas of the US are quite different – the Mediterranean-like region of California, the vast intermountain deserts, and the subtropical gulf and Florida eco-region. Since climate, ecology, and topography are so important to settlement, natural resources, economy, and culture, it is little wonder that these geographical differences emerge as important factors driving rural opportunities and challenges within the two countries.

The role of institutions

Canadian and US institutions have evolved in a complex way over the last two centuries. In some cases, they are very different – set by the initial constitutional conditions of the two nations or emerging as a result of different geographical, economic, social, and cultural pressures. In other cases, they are similar, especially where common markets are shared, or multinational organizations operate.

The 1783 Peace of Paris ended the American Revolution, ceded the 13 southern British colonies to the new United States of America, and left the remaining colonies, including those which eventually became Canada, under British control. It roughly set the boundary between Canada and the US (later resolved after several challenges, military actions, and negotiations) and created conditions for continued competition between the merchants and traders of the St. Lawrence River system (primarily via Montreal) and those controlling the Hudson River (primarily via New York). Some argue that a primary motivation for establishing a Canadian dominion from the Atlantic to the Pacific was to secure the western territories as a resource hinterland for those operating through the St. Lawrence River system (Berton, 2001).

The Dominion of Canada was created in 1867 when the British parliament passed the British North America Act (BNA) – just two years after the end of the American Civil War. Contrary to the constitution of the US, where the federal government powers were limited and specific, with all residual (stronger) powers given to the states, the provincial governments' powers in Canada were limited and specified, with residual powers going to the federal government. Since then, these relative powers have shifted, with more power going to the Canadian provinces and less power to the US states (Field, 1992).

These differences place rural issues in different political contexts within the two countries. For example, since natural resources and labor relations are provincial responsibilities in Canada, most of the regulations and negotiations take place with provinces – except were interprovincial or international trade is concerned. In the US, the federal government has interpreted its responsibilities for commerce and international trade much more broadly – requiring greater attention to federal politics and negotiations when considering rural issues. The Canadian constitutional requirements for equalization payments among the provinces have had important impacts on rural places as well, not only with respect to fiscal support for more rural provinces, but via additional federal regional development programs (see Chapter 33 for their impacts on rural and regional poverty).

Canada has taken a second, diverse institutional direction as a result of addressing the language, cultural, and social characteristics of Quebec. The legacy of the French occupation of Lower Canada, special arrangements to deal with their religious and language concerns, (the Royal Commission on Bilingualism and Biculturalism in 1963, and the Official Languages Act of 1969), and the extension of these concerns to an official policy on multiculturalism (1971 and 1988) have created policy and institutional conditions in Canada that contrast considerably with those in the US (more often referred to as a "melting pot" policy with respect to ethnic and cultural integration). The 1969 Official Languages Act, for example, established English and French language rights for education along with bilingual services in all federal institutions across the country. In rural and remote areas this has created special programs where language-based groups are sufficiently large. It has also supported place-based ethnic and language settlements through programs and financial supports for language and cultural practices. Much of this support has gone to rural communities to support schools, language training, and community development initiatives.

The history of land and governance issues relating to Indigenous Peoples in Canada creates a third way in which it is institutionally different from the US. The current plethora of land claims, treaties, and legal challenges has created a context in which institutions are undergoing rapid change as new national groups, rights, and policies emerge – particularly in rural and northern regions. The current government's focus on truth and reconciliation with Indigenous Peoples is also likely to produce significant institutional change in the near future (http://trc.ca).

A fourth important difference between Canada and the US is the former's commitment to regional development and related institutions. These institutions have had particularly important impacts on rural and remote regions. The US on the other hand has numerous tools available for redistribution among the states and regions, but few policies and programs have been devoted to this goal. The few regional development programs that have been funded – the Appalachian Regional Commission, the Tennessee Valley Authority, the Delta Regional Authority – are primarily focused on rural regions and have had impacts on infrastructure and services in the regions but are not systemic in the same way that the five federal Regional Economic Development Agencies are in Canada. These five agencies each have a broad portfolio of responsibilities for their respective regions. Whereas the US agencies were created in response to chronic underdevelopment in the regions, the Canadian agencies are focused on building on the region's strengths.

A fifth difference can be seen in the considerable institutional focus on northern issues as a separate domain in Canada. As discussed above, this attention is reflected in both federal and provincial governments, depending on the extent to which they are geographically connected to northern territories. Within the federal Canadian government, for example, this includes the Department of Indigenous and Northern Affairs Canada (currently undergoing a transformation in design), the Canadian Northern Economic Development Agency, and the Territorial government. These organizations address issues of economic, social, and community development in a multidimensional fashion.

A sixth Canada–US institutional difference can be seen in the countries' approaches to public services. In Canada, for example, there is a tradition of social-democrat sentiment and support for labor mobility that encourages public sector preference for health, education, and welfare (Reimer, 2007). Similar public support is much weaker in the US. Since provincial and federal governments are involved in these sectors, it also means that they have a stronger incentive to address issues of prevention than in the US since prevention initiatives directly affect government costs in the long term. It also means that the provinces are faced with the challenge of providing services in rural and remote areas as a result of their legal mandate.

The US provides a much different social safety net for its citizens. The biggest difference in health and social services is the largely employer-based system of health insurance and retirement benefits. This strategy has its origins during World War II when employers, constrained by price and wage controls, offered health and retirement benefits rather than higher wages to attract employees (Blumenthal, 2006). Since employees of small companies and self-employed workers seldom have access to these benefits, the disparities in health and retirement benefits are large. The social security system and Supplemental Nutrition Assistance Program (SNAP) partially offset these disparities, especially for the aged, but for others, including children, the US social support system is limited.

Finally, because of more open immigration policies, immigration rates in Canada have been higher than in the US for many decades. Over the last century, immigrants have made up between 15 and 22 percent of the population of Canada (Statistics Canada, 2017). Over the same period the immigrants to the US have never exceeded 14 percent and have been as low as 4.7 percent of the population (Migration Policy Institute, 2013). Recent immigration has had much lower direct effects on rural areas than on urban areas (Reimer, 2007). There are indications, however, that a growing number of recent immigrants are settling in small cities and rural communities. In the decade between the 1990 and 2000 censuses in the US, the growth in immigrants in non-metro counties exceeded the rates in metro counties (McGaha and Kudlowitz, 2007). The increase was driven by rising employment in agriculture, food processing, and unskilled manufacturing. This trend seems to be continuing or accelerating (Pew Charitable Trusts, 2014). A remarkable example in Canada can be found in rural southern Manitoba where concerted action by the provincial and federal governments has produced immigration rates that rival urban Toronto (Silvius and Annis, 2007).

Current conditions: density, income, and education in rural Canada and the US

Overall population densities are very different in the US at 34.05 persons per km^2, and Canada at 3.7 persons per km^2. These levels compare to the world average of about 56 persons per km^2. However, because of the vast, largely unpopulated Canadian territories, these national statistics tell us little about the density, and distance-to-density experience of most residents, especially those in rural places.

The OECD has developed a standardized regional typology that allows comparison among its 38 member states based on county-equivalent units of geography (OECD, 2017). This typology distinguishes predominantly urban, predominantly rural, and intermediate regions. Intermediate regions and predominantly rural regions are further divided into those close to cities and those which are remote (see Figure 2.1). Using this unit of analysis, the two countries are more similar. In 2006, 43 percent of the US population and 48 percent of Canadians lived in primarily urban regions. In the US, 38 percent of the population lived in primarily rural regions, compared to 33 percent of Canadians. Of these residents of rural regions, significantly more Canadians, 13 percent, live in remote rural areas than the 4 percent of Americans (Brezzi *et al.*, 2011, p. 7).

The population of most primarily rural regions in Canada and the United States is declining due to internal rural to urban migration. This is especially true of remote rural regions and for younger residents. However, this is not always the case. In Canada, some resource-dependent

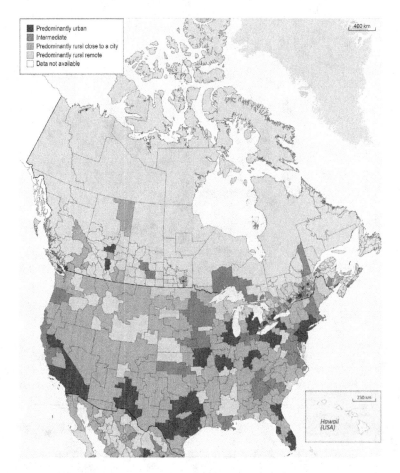

Figure 2.1 OECD regional typology – North America, 2010
Source: OECD (2011).

regions in northern Canada, and some high-amenity rural regions in the US are gaining population (see Figure 2.2).

Rural and urban Americans enjoy comparable income levels. In 2015, median household income in urban US was about $54,000 USD compared to $52,000 USD in the rural US. That same year, the median household income in Canada was higher than in the US at over $56,000 USD. While a comparison of rural and urban median household income is not available for 2015, the Canadian Income Survey of 2014 (Statistics Canada, 2014) indicates urban (population 30,000+) individuals have slightly higher levels of median income than individuals in rural areas (about $31,000 USD and $28,000 USD respectively). Meanwhile, rural poverty rates in the US were lower than urban rates (13.3 versus 16.0 percent). In Canada, the percentages of households below the low-income cut-offs (LICO) are 6.6 percent versus 13.6 percent respectively for rural and urban before taxes and 4.1 percent and 9.6 percent after taxes (see Chapter 12 for details regarding the interpretation of poverty indicators in the US and Canada).

Figure 2.2 Net inter-regional population flows – North America, 2008

Source: Brezzi and Piacentini (2010, Figure 4, p. 7).

Rural Americans lag urban residents in educational achievement levels but are closing the gap. In 2015, 85 percent of US rural residents had at least a high school diploma or equivalent compared to 87 percent of urban residents. In Canada, for 2014, the comparable figures were 76 percent and 86 percent (Statistics Canada, 2014). In the US, 50 percent of rural residents had at least some post-secondary education compared to 62 percent of urban residents (United States Department of Agriculture, 2017a). In Canada, for 2014, the figures were 47 percent and 58 percent respectively (Statistics Canada, 2014).

Educational achievement differs significantly across US regions. Rural and urban residents of northern states have significantly higher levels of educational achievement than residents of southern, especially southeastern states (see Figure 2.3). In Canada, regional differences are also found, with the highest levels of education in 2014 found in British Columbia, Ontario, Alberta, and the Yukon, and the lowest in the north and Newfoundland and Labrador (Statistics Canada, 2019).

The role of territorial units: shaping the visibility of rural and urban places in Canada and the US

There are several operational definitions of rural used in Canada and the US. Choosing an appropriate one is challenging – not only for the identification of rural places within each country, but especially when international comparisons are desired.

The statistical agencies of both Canada and the US identify geographical units that retain quite detailed spatial resolution. However, most data are aggregated up and reported at the county-equivalent level – especially for international comparisons. In Canada for 2016, there are

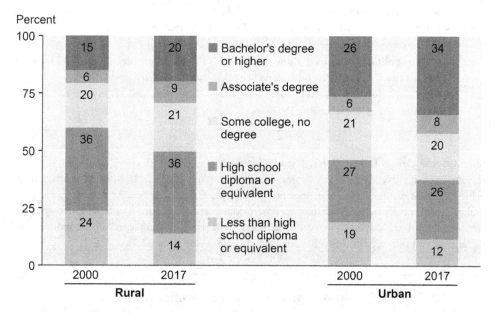

Figure 2.3 Educational attainment in US rural and urban areas, 2000 and 2015

Source: USDA, Economic Research Service using data from the US Census Bureau, Census 2000 and 2017 American Community Survey.

Note: Educational attainment for adults 25 and older. Urban and rural status is determined by Office of Management and Budget metropolitan and nonmetropolitan area definitions.

293 such units. They range considerably in size: from $192\,km^2$ to over $989,000\,km^2$ (Statistics Canada, 2016). The population sizes range from 740 to over 2,730,000. In the US, the evolution of local governments has led to a wide range of county (or county-equivalent) sizes as well. Counties vary in area from $5.2\,km^2$ to $376,860\,km^2$. In terms of population, US counties vary from 113 to over 10,000,000.

Since "rural" has few program implications in Canada, the distinctions have been primarily driven by research interests and a variety of provincial programs like health and welfare. Du Plessis *et al.* (2001) identified six different definitions used by various researchers and agencies in Canada – from which, they suggest, a choice should be made depending on the particular question being asked. Most detailed analyses of rural geography use the Rural and Small Town distinctions (see Box 2.1) (Statistics Canada, 2015).

Box 2.1

Canadian rural and small town (RST) areas refer to individuals in towns or municipalities outside the commuting zone of Census Metropolitan Areas (CMD) or Census Agglomerations (CA) (with 10,000 or more population). RST areas are further classified into Metropolitan Influenced Zones (MIZ), as follows:

- **Strong Metropolitan Influenced Zone**: Census Subdivisions (CSDs) in a RST area where 30 percent or more of the resident workforce commutes to any CMA or CA;
- **Moderate Metropolitan Influenced Zone**: CSDs in a RST area where 5–29 percent of the resident workforce commutes to any CMA or CA;
- **Weak Metropolitan Influenced Zone**: CSDs in a RST area where more than zero but less than 5 percent of the resident workforce commutes to any CMA or CA;
- **No Metropolitan Influenced Zone**: CSDs in a RST area where none of the workforce commutes to a CMA or CA (or the workforce is less than 40 workers); and
- **RST Territories**: CSDs in the Yukon, Northwest Territories, and Nunavut which are outside the CAs of Whitehorse and Yellowknife.

In the US, the Census Bureau (United States Census Bureau, 2016) identifies rural areas as counties remaining after two types of urban areas are identified (see Box 2.2). Both of these urban areas include adjacent counties that are economically linked to the central core. As a result, many very rural places, especially in the western states where counties are large, are classified as metropolitan and therefore urban. Much of the Grand Canyon in Arizona, for example, is in metropolitan statistical areas and thus reported as urban for many purposes (see Figure 2.4).

Box 2.2 The US Census Bureau rural–urban classification

- Urbanized areas (UAs): of 50,000 or more people.
- Urban clusters (UCs): of at least 2500 and less than 50,000 people.
- Rural encompasses all population, housing, and territory not included within an urban area.

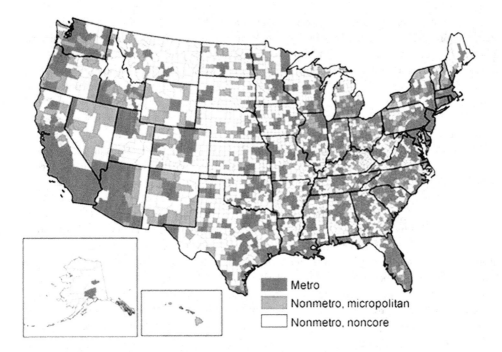

Figure 2.4 County typologies in the US, 2015

Source: USDA, Economic Research Service using data from the US Census Bureau.

Alternatives to the US metro–non-metro system have been developed, although almost all are aggregations of counties. Several of these alternatives attempt to capture the interaction of density and distance-to-density (see OECD, 2011 and United States Department of Agriculture, 2017b). In Canada, the smallest OECD unit (TL3) is the Census Subdivision. In the US, the smallest unit is the Economic Area as defined by the Bureau of Economic Analysis (OECD, 2017).

Given the convenience of the census division geography in Canada and the metro–non-metro system in the US, they are used for making many policy decisions. As a result, the real conditions of some rural residents are often masked because they are defined as urban.

The role of density: settlement patterns in Canada and the US

Unlike much of Europe and parts of Asia, where settlement patterns grew out of feudalism, North American settlement grew out of Indigenous land use; various land grants either purchased or simply claimed by fiat or force; waves of immigration from Europe, Asia, and Africa; the predominance of resource extraction industries during the early waves of immigration; the evolution of institutions over the following decades; and subsequent changes in technology and markets. The details of land ownership evolved as immigrants expanded westward. All of these are conditioned by the wide variety of geographic features of the land: geology, geomorphology, ecology, and climate.

In the early colonization of eastern North America (excluding Quebec), large land grants were made to individuals and companies. These were then subdivided, being sold to individuals in return for passage from Europe. In the southern colonies a system of plantations evolved, based on slave labor.

Outside of current Quebec, British approaches to land tenure applied, with an important modification: they recognized that Indigenous Peoples who lived on the land had a claim to those territories. As a result, all land in Canada, except for a part of southern Quebec, was subject to Aboriginal title. During the expansion of the western provinces from 1871 to 1921, much of this land was negotiated in the form of treaties where the national government (the Crown) took over the land in exchange for annuities along with some legal exemptions and privileges. Many of these treaties are currently being re-negotiated and challenged for non-compliance. In addition, there are many formal land claims and negotiations underway for those lands not ceded. As a result, Canada has a relatively high level of Indigenous and local community land designation or ownership (44%) compared to both the US (2%) and the world (18%) (Rights and Resources Initiative, 2015). This legacy creates substantial complexities in economic development, health, education, and welfare initiatives in rural places.

The provincial governments hold about 48 percent of the land in Canada as Crown lands. The federal government holds about 41 percent and the remaining 11 percent is privately owned (Neimanis, 2013). Federal holdings are primarily in the north where provincial and territorial governments do not have jurisdiction – although they also include national parks, First Nations reserves, and national defense installations. Crown lands have been used in the past to finance major corporate initiatives (e.g. the transcontinental railroad), immigration (e.g. the settlement of the prairie provinces during the latter nineteenth and early twentieth centuries), and direct economic development through leasing arrangements – primarily with forestry, mining, and energy initiatives.

As immigrants moved west in the US, the combination of changing technology, maturing governance institutions, and relationships with Indigenous populations led to new and different types of land grants. Following the revolutionary war (and later, the war of 1812, the Mexican war, and the Indian wars), many US soldiers received land grants in the newly acquired Eastern Louisiana Territory, west of the Appalachian Mountains and east of the Mississippi River. The Louisiana Purchase of 1803 and the Mexican cession of 1848 expanded the land holding of the US government by more than 3.5 million km^2 from the Mississippi River west to the Rocky Mountains, and from the Gulf of Mexico to what is now the Canadian prairies.

The US Homestead Act of 1862 extended land grants to farmers west of the Mississippi River. In most cases these land grants encouraged or required grantees to reside on their farms rather than in villages. As a result, the villages that emerged were small and focused on servicing the dispersed small farmsteads. Many schools were not located in these villages but distributed across the countryside in order to limit the distance between schools and farms to that which could be walked or ridden by horse.

As settlement moved westward, improved transportation and communication allowed larger county governments to replace the system of town and township governments in the east. In the intermountain west the arid climate and low agricultural productivity meant that small farms were impractical. Here population density is very low outside urban centers, and counties are very large. In many cases the economic base of the western region was and still is resource extraction. Resource extraction is subject to boom and bust cycles which have become an endemic part of life in many rural regions in the western US and Canada.

One consequence of these legacies is that significant change has occurred in the density of both urban and rural regions of North America. In the US, the rural population, no matter how it is measured, has grown only slightly over the last century while the urban population has more than quadrupled. In Canada, the pattern is more extreme with urbanization increasing about six times that of rural. But even this is a misleading indicator of rural population density because the rural population has increasingly been concentrated in rural centers. The US farm population peaked in 1916. Since 1916, the US farm population, and thus density, has declined by more than five-sixths.

Furthermore, in much of the US, small villages have largely become obsolete, especially for commodity production. Some small towns have grown to become regional service sectors, while others have disappeared. Agriculture no longer generates sufficient employment or net income to support public and private rural services. Lack of high-quality services has further driven residents from rural areas and declining populations have reduced the political influence of rural residents and businesses. Unstable resource extraction sectors create uncertainty and high levels of in-, and then out-, migration.

Several of these patterns are replicated in Canada, but they are modified in significant ways by the characteristics of more remote regions. As shown in Figure 2.5, rural population decline is felt most strongly in those rural places where the metropolitan influence (MIZ) is moderate or weak. On the other hand, rural regions close to metropolitan regions, those outside the sphere of such influence, and those in the northern regions of the Territories and Nunavut show important population growth. In the case of Strong MIZ regions, this is most likely due to the opportunities and services offered by larger centers, whereas in the No MIZ and Northern regions it is most likely due to the availability of attractive amenities, natural resource exploitation, and the relatively high fertility rates of Indigenous populations.

The role of distance-to-density: rural complexity and interdependence in Canada and the US

The role of population density described above is only part of the story. Remoteness is another feature of rurality that can affect the opportunities and options available. Improvements in transportation and communication technologies have done much to increase rural residents' access to markets and services, but distance continues to be associated with population and employment levels (Partridge *et al.*, 2007).

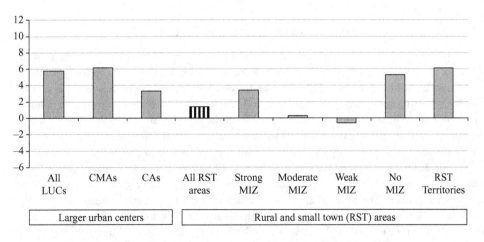

Figure 2.5 Percentage change by urban and rural categories, 2011 to 2016, Canada.

Source: Statistics Canada, Census of Population, 1991 to 2016. (Adapted from: Charts population in rural and small-town areas by MIZ [Metropolitan Influenced Zone] by province 1986 to 2016.pptx – slide 14).

Note: For acronyms, see Box 2.1. Data are tabulated within boundaries applicable at the time of the given census.

Bollman and Prud'homme's (2006) analysis of Canadian data suggests that the price of trade in goods and services has been falling over the last 30 years but that the cost of transporting people has increased over that time. Partridge *et al.*'s (2008a) analysis of hinterland regions in the US, on the other hand, suggests that the cost of distance is increasing and that any advantages of remoteness due to reduced competition are minimal. This raises questions about potential differences between Canada and the US due to special distance and density characteristics of northern communities. It may be, for example, that remote centers have less competition from other service centers and therefore tend to provide a broader range of services than those in the shadow of larger centers.

Partridge *et al.*'s (2008b) analysis of geographic diversity in the US cautions us to consider the continued importance of local effects on employment growth. As access to markets, jobs, institutions of higher education, and other services become more important to the quality of life in rural areas, the cost of distance to the source of services increases. This cost of distance is complicated by declining local density. As rural centers lose population, the range of services provided locally declines and the dependence on larger centers increases. Declining rural density means that schools, hospitals, and other essential services consolidate in larger centers, at a greater distance for those remaining in the rural areas.

Weber and Freshwater (2016) point to the importance of information and communication technologies (ICT) on the significance and perception of distance. Following Murdoch (2000) they point to physical, social, and value or supply chains as important types of networks to consider for economic development. They conclude that good broadband connections are now necessary for economic development but remain equivocal regarding the overall benefits to rural and remote places.

ICT is also affecting the opportunities and nature of social relationships in rural places. The delivery of health, education, and communication services, for example, has already transformed the ways in which people relate both within and across communities. The details of these impacts, however, remain unclear because of the rapid changes in the technologies, the significant digital divide in access and adoption between rural and urban places, and the research challenges in assessing those impacts (Roberts *et al.*, 2017).

Culture, identities, and perceptions

As products of frontier expansion, most Canadians and Americans share the view of the pristine rural as an ideal. Humans are considered invasive species which must be tolerated but contained. National parks, wilderness areas, and conservation reserves are products of this view. This contrasts with the concept of rural in many European countries (and among Indigenous Peoples in Canada and the US), where humans are seen as part of the natural system, and that while balance and conservation are valued, this balance includes human needs and activities.

Rural is perceived differently by Canadians and Americans in other respects. One of Canada's leading authors, Margaret Atwood, argues that Canadian literature is mostly about "survival" when it comes to rural engagement: often pitching people against the challenges of the natural environment (Atwood, 1972). This contrasts with the representation of western settlements in the US where rural culture involves making places safe from threatening people or institutions. Current tourism and recreation marketing continues similar differences which are likely to affect general perceptions of "rural" in the two countries – or across the continents (e.g. rural equals well organized beaches and small-town sites vs. untamed backcountry). This difference in perspectives may partially explain differences in opinion regarding handguns, capital punishment, immigration, and other policies.

Another dimension of rural identity is a perceived distinction between rural and urban values. A recent poll of Americans found that rural residents tended to believe that urban "values" conflict with their own – at least with respect to perceived biases in government assistance, support for immigration, and treatment of non-whites (Kaiser Family Foundation/Washington Post Partnership, cited in The Washington Post, 2017). On the other hand, there are indications that when it comes to the economy, the perceptions of rural and urban residents are more in line. The same survey suggests that both types of residents face economic hardships but that these "show little relation to the feeling that urban residents have different values". Comparable information for Canada is not available.

These perceptions may be subject to important qualifications, however, with the urgency and discourse regarding climate change and the environment (Huddart-Kennedy *et al.*, 2009). Rural places, spaces, and natural resources have become key foci in the perception and initiatives emerging from this crisis. Urban-based people have been prominent in these shifting perceptions as they recognize the importance of rural places for the quality of water and food, carbon capture, and mitigation of rising ocean levels. The significant social action focusing on forest preservation, protection of water from pipeline failure, and enhancing biodiversity all suggest that rural–urban alliances may change the political landscape of both countries (Reimer, 2013).

Conclusions

International comparisons are fraught with challenges. The complexities of different histories, institutional organization, cultures, and economic, social, and political structures mean that even the same words can have different meanings. Using the same indicators does not avoid the challenges since the significance of geographical units, density, distance, and rural/urban thresholds across countries can imply different "actors", policy domains, and implications. In addition, the sensitivities of these indicators will change depending on the issues and outcomes considered (e.g. economic development, poverty, environmental sustainability) since those issues are often perceived and treated differently in various countries. This means that clear rationales, multidisciplinary approaches, and collaboration in comparative analysis are even more important – whether the objective is description, explanation, policy development, or advocacy.

In spite of these challenges, comparisons between Canada and the US are still possible and insightful so long as the limitations are recognized. In addition, there are important lessons to be learned for international comparisons in general. They can be summarized in the following way.

First, is the different political significance of "rural" in the two countries. In Canada, the constitutional and institutional legacies have given priority to "regional" perspectives over "rural" ones. In turn, this has directed the focus of programs and finances for non-urban locations in ways that are different to those in the US. This example suggests that multinational researchers would be well-advised to carefully compare both theoretical and operational foundations for spatial-related programs in different countries as an essential part of their analysis.

The second lesson emerges from the unique characteristics of the Canadian northern geography. Although it is part of rural Canada, its relatively low density and long distances create special challenges for transportation, the delivery of services, economic development, and community support that make it significantly different from both US rural regions and from more southern locations in Canada. This reinforces the importance of considering how sub-regions in rural areas should be part of the analysis of international comparisons.

The high level of land and governance negotiations currently underway with Indigenous Peoples in Canada creates a third lesson for general comparative analysis. It creates local and general conditions of uncertainty for economic, political, social, health, education, and welfare policies to name a few. It also means that the relative power of governments is in flux even as the legal structures and decisions are under development. For international comparisons, these conditions remind us of the temporal nature of rural development: even as contemporary comparisons are made, they are a snapshot of ongoing processes that are rooted in change.

Finally, the different legacies of political responses to rural issues create a variety of opportunities and options for future policy development. In Canada, for example, the creation of a transcontinental railway and its associated conditions established east–west transportation and interdependencies that resisted the "natural" north–south connections encouraged by geography. The establishment of Canadian policies and institutions encouraging labor mobility and regional transfer payments made the national coordination of education, health, and welfare programs easier to implement. In turn, the responses to single-payer health care creates the conditions for government commitment to rural and remote services that counter to some extent the challenges of population density and market failure.

In general, Canadian and US conditions in rural areas are very similar, especially when compared to other nations. These similarities, however, mask important differences that make life in those areas quite different for inhabitants, the impacts of global changes on those regions to vary, and the policy choices available at various levels to be significantly different. It also makes research and analysis of rural places to be more demanding and complex, especially where explanations are desired. More complex analysis is required, along with the collection of more detailed data to match the complexity, but the promise of new insights and improved analysis is sufficiently strong to warrant the effort.

Key research questions and opportunities

This analysis suggests a number of important questions to be asked when conducting comparative analysis among any national entities. Some of the most important are identified below.

- How is "rural" defined and operationalized within the countries considered? How do they relate to similar concepts highlighting spatial entities – like regions, remote, northern, and isolated?
- In what ways are the rural-related concepts associated with specific policies, programs, and initiatives within the countries? Which of them are institutionally mandated for the allocation of infrastructure and/or funds and where do the decisions regarding such allocation take place?
- What are the historical and institutional legacies of current policies and programs within the countries? Which ones are particularly susceptible to change and what is the likely nature of the changes?

References

Atwood, M., 1972. *Survival: A thematic guide to Canadian literature.* House of Anansi, Torronto, Ont.

Berton, P., 2001. *The last spike: The great railway, 1881–1885.* Anchor Canada, Toronto.

Blumenthal, D. 2006. *Employer-sponsored health insurance in the United States: Origins and implications*, New England Journal of Medicine 355(1), 82–88.

Bollman, R., Prud'homme, M., 2006. *Trends in the prices of rurality.* Agriculture Division, Statistics Canada, Ottawa, Ont.

Brezzi, M., Piacentini, M., 2010. *Labour mobility and development dynamics in OECD regions.* Presented at the OECD workshop "Migration and Regional Development".

Brezzi, M., Dijkstra, L., Ruiz, V., 2011. *OECD extended regional typology: The economic performance of remote rural regions*. OECD Regional Development Working Papers, 2011/06. https://doi.org/10.1787/5kg6z83tw7f4-en.

Canada Revenue Agency, 2004. *Northern residents tax reductions: Do you qualify for the northern residents deductions?* aem. www.canada.ca/en/revenue-agency/services/tax/individuals/topics/about-your-tax-return/tax-return/completing-a-tax-return/deductions-credits-expenses/line-255-northern-residents-deductions/line-255-you-qualify-northern-residents-deductions.html (accessed 2.24.19).

du Plessis, V., Beshiri, R., Bollman, R., Clemenson, H., 2001. *Definitions of rural*. Rural and Small Town Canada Analysis Bulletin No. 3(3). Statistics Canada, Ottawa, Ont.

Field, M., 1992. *The differing federalisms of Canada and the United States*. Law and Contemporary Problems 55, 107–120.

Huddart-Kennedy, E., Beckley, T.M., McFarlane, B.L., Nadeau, S., 2009. *Rural–urban differences in environmental concern in Canada*. Canadian Forest Service Publications. Natural Resources Canada, Ottawa, Ont. https://cfs.nrcan.gc.ca/publications?id=30103.

Kaiser Family Foundation/Washington Post Partnership. *Survey probes experiences and views of rural Americans*. The Henry J. Kaiser Family Foundation. www.kff.org/health-reform/press-release/kaiser-family-foundationwashington-post-partnership-survey-probes-experiences-and-views-of-rural-Americans/ (accessed 2.24.19).

McGaha, E., Kudlowitz, 2007. *Immigration and housing in rural America*. Housing Assistance Council, Washington, DC.

Migration Policy Institute, 2013. *U.S. immigrant population and share over time, 1850–Present*. migrationpolicy.org. www.migrationpolicy.org/programs/data-hub/charts/immigrant-population-over-time (accessed 2.24.19).

Murdoch, J., 2000. *Networks: A new paradigm of rural development?* Journal of Rural Studies 16, 407–419. https://doi.org/10.1016/S0743-0167(00)00022-X.

Neimanis, V.P., 2013. *Crown land*. The Canadian Encyclopedia. www.thecanadianencyclopedia.ca/en/article/crown-land (accessed 2.24.19).

OECD, 2011. *OECD regional typology*. OECD, Paris.

OECD, 2017. *Territorial grids of OECD member countries*. OECD, Paris.

Partridge, M., Olfert, M.R., Alasia, A., 2007. *Canadian cities as regional engines of growth: Agglomeration and amenities*. Canadian Journal of Economics/Revue canadienne d'économique 40, 39–68. https://doi.org/10.1111/j.1365-2966.2007.00399.x.

Partridge, M., Rickman, D.S., Ali, K., Olfert, M.R., 2008a. *Lost in space: Population growth in the American hinterlands and small cities*. Journal of Economic Geography 8, 272–757. https://doi.org/10.1093/jeg/lbn038.

Partridge, M.D., Rickman, D.S., Ali, K., Olfert, M.R., 2008b. *The geographic diversity of U.S. nonmetropolitan growth dynamics: A geographically weighted regression approach*. Land Economics 84, 241–266. https://doi.org/10.3368/le.84.2.241.

Pew Charitable Trusts, 2014. *Changing patterns in U.S. immigration and population*. www.pewtrusts.org/en/research-and-analysis/issue-briefs/2014/12/changing-patterns-in-us-immigration-and-population (accessed 2.24.19).

Reimer, B., 2007. *Immigration in the new rural economy*. Our Diverse Cities 3, 3–8.

Reimer, B., 2013. *Rural–urban interdependence: Understanding our common interests*, in: Parkins, J.R., Reed, M.G. (Eds.), *Social transformation in rural Canada: Community, cultures, and collective action*, UBC Press, Vancouver, BC, pp. 91–109.

Rights and Resources Initiative, 2015. *Who owns the world's land? A global baseline of formally recognized indigenous and community land rights*. September 29. https://rightsandresources.org/en/publication/whoownstheland/#.XSvkaugzaUk.

Roberts, E., Beel, D., Philip, L., Townsend, L., 2017. *Rural resilience in a digital society: Editorial*. Journal of Rural Studies 54, 355–359. https://doi.org/10.1016/j.jrurstud.2017.06.010.

Roi, G.H.L., 2018. *Boreal zone*. The Canadian Encyclopedia. www.thecanadianencyclopedia.ca/en/article/boreal-forest (accessed 2.24.19).

Silvius, R., Annis, R.C., 2007. *Reflections on the rural immigration experience in Manitoba's diverse rural communities*, in: Reimer, B. (Ed.), *Migration, economic growth and social cohesion*. Metropolis, Melbourne, pp. 126–133.

Statistics Canada, 2014. *Canadian income survey*. www23.statcan.gc.ca/imdb/p2SV.pl?Function=getSurvey&Id=299499&dis=1.

Statistics Canada, 2015. *Data and definitions.* www150.statcan.gc.ca/n1/pub/21-006-x/2008008/section/s2-eng.htm (accessed 2.24.19).

Statistics Canada, 2016. *2016 census program.* www12.statcan.gc.ca/census-recensement/2016/ref/dict/tab/t1_1-eng.cfm (accessed 2.24.19).

Statistics Canada, 2017. *150 years of immigration in Canada.* www150.statcan.gc.ca/n1/pub/11-630-x/11-630-x2016006-eng.htm (accessed 2.24.19).

Statistics Canada, 2019. *Labour force characteristics by Aboriginal group and educational attainment*, Table: 14–10–0359–01 (formerly CANSIM 282–0228). www150.statcan.gc.ca/t1/tbl1/en/tv.action?pid=1410035901.

The Washington Post, 2017. *New poll of rural Americans shows deep cultural divide with urban centers.* June 17. www.washingtonpost.com/classic-apps/new-poll-of-rural-Americans-shows-deep-cultural-divide-with-urban-centers/2017/06/16/d166c31e-4189-11e7-9869-bac8b446820a_story.html?noredirect=on&utm_term=.426d9d5c00a7 (accessed 2.24.19).

United States Census Bureau, 2016. *A comparison of rural and urban America: Household income and poverty.* The United States Census Bureau. www.census.gov/newsroom/blogs/random-samplings/2016/12/a_comparison_of_rura.html (accessed 2.24.19).

United States Department of Agriculture, 2017a. *Rural education at a glance*, 2017 edition. www.ers.usda.gov/publications/pub-details/?pubid=83077 (accessed 2.24.19).

United States Department of Agriculture, 2017b. *What is rural?* www.ers.usda.gov/topics/rural-economy-population/rural-classifications/what-is-rural/ (accessed 2.24.19).

Weber, B., Freshwater, D., 2016. *The death of distance? Networks, the costs of distance and urban–rural interdependence*, in: Shucksmith, M., Brown, D.L. (Eds.), *Routledge international handbook of rural studies*, 1st edition. Routledge, New York, pp. 154–164.

3

WHAT IS RURAL?

The historical evolution of rural typologies in Europe

John M. Bryden, Jordi Rosell Foxà, and Lourdes Viladomiu

Introduction

In this chapter contemporary and previous concepts of rurality in Europe are outlined, showing how diverse Europe is in terms of its rural history, property ownership, class formation, demography, and politics. This diverse history is reflected in different definitions and concepts of rurality, as well as in the evolution of national and latterly EU and OECD policy frameworks (see also Chapter 33). Using published comparative research, the various theoretical approaches used to analyze the transitions for rural to urban society, and the relationships between them are discussed as well as how rurality (and urbanity) is measured today, drawing on the OECD rural indicators approach as well as the Eurostat definitions. The transition from an "agrarian" understanding of rurality, to the multi-sectoral territorial approach will be outlined. Finally, some recent data on evolving inequalities within and between rural territories in Europe are presented. The point here is that in considering policies that affect rural people and places or territories, it is necessary to consider many policies that are not often considered "rural policies". A narrow concept of rural policy (and related data) is not useful for understanding contemporary developments of rural–rural or rural–urban social and economic inequalities.

The historical origins of rurality in Europe

Until the era of rapid industrialization based on fossil energy from around the mid-nineteenth century in Britain and the US, and up to the middle of the twentieth century, for example in Italy, Spain, and Norway, most people lived outside the densely populated areas called "cities", "towns", "urban areas", or "metropolitan areas". These were often given special powers and status as "burghs". Ideas of "rural" and "city" came from the ancient Latin word "rusticus" on the one hand, and "civitas" and "civic" on the other. The cities were mainly seen as centers of civilization; the rural areas "beyond the pale" – crude, rude, and simple, where the "peasants" lived hard lives under the watchful eye of the Church and the landed aristocracy.[1] Such stereotypes have persisted even into the present day, for example in the work on "the creative class", a concept based almost entirely on city-based professions. The division of space according to powers given to burghs also persisted into the second half of the twentieth century – there were widely varying definitions of "cities" or "urban areas" which largely related to the density of population and nature of settlements. Thus, in sparsely populated countries of northern Europe, an urban area may be only a few hundred people, while in more densely populated southern countries like Italy, an urban area could be several thousand people.

In twentieth-century Europe, the idea of rural became associated with its main functions, notably as a space of primary production – agriculture, forestry, hunting, fishing, and perhaps mining – and as the "lung" for urban people destined to suffer the pollution associated with the Industrial Revolution, to be experienced through recreation, tourism, and special areas such as National Parks. The association of productive functions with space was never entirely accurate, nor did it stay constant over time. Thus most "proto-industrialization" used water, wind, or forests as the key source of energy, and thus industrialization was mainly a rural phenomenon before the revolution in engines and associated use of fossil fuels in the nineteenth and twentieth centuries.

It is thus clear that the idea of rural varied across time and space, sometimes associated with sparsity of population and settlement patterns, distance from cities, political power or the lack of it, economic and social functions, environmental or landscape features including "wilderness", or alleged cultural characteristics. That is why sociologists and human geographers invented the idea of the "social construction of rurality" (Halfacree, 1993; Mormont, 1990; Newby, 1980; Shucksmith, 1994). Scholars such as Mormont, based in highly urban Belgium, argued that the term "rural" should be abolished because it is no different from "urban" in most important respects, while others argued that the modern ideas of rural had been constructed to suit the dominant political interests, in particular of large farmers who were defending large national and then European subsidies.

However, the attacks on the economic, social, and especially environmental outcome of agricultural policy and related public expenditure in the 1970s and 1980s had their impact, as did the enlargement of the European Communities to include Spain, Portugal, and Greece in the 1980s, and the subsequent creation of the European single market in 1986. For reasons explained in Chapter 33, these changes, together with the related international pressures on European agricultural policy, led to the notion of Territorial Rural Policy, where "rural" became a kind of "region". This in turn led to a proliferation of types of rural and indeed urban "region", which will be discussed in greater detail below.

Why is the definition of rurality important?

It is important to understand how different economic, social, and political interests align themselves around different notions of rurality, because only then is it possible to understand the forces acting on policy-makers when opportunities for change emerge. Thus farmers, especially large commercial farmers, support agrarian constructions of rurality that emphasize the importance of farm families and agricultural production and its upstream and downstream industries. On the other hand, environmental interests support notions of rural as "wilderness" and "biodiversity" or producers of "ecosystem services". Urban interests, however, stress the importance of rural areas for open space, recreation, and tourism – the "urban lung". Both urban and environmental interests tend to support urban consumption uses of rural regions through national parks and nature reserves, and the reintroduction of predators such as wolves. They tend to be little focused on the economic and social situation and needs of those working and living in rural areas. The relative political strength of such interests changes the balance of policy effort in different countries and regions.

The "territorial approach" seeks to take a holistic view of the activities and potentials in rural areas, but with a focus on the economic and social welfare of people living in the rural regions. It seeks to escape from the confines of the sectoral and environmental constructions.

Regional typologies in Europe after the 1980s

Southern enlargement of the EU to include Greece in 1981, and Spain and Portugal in 1986 more than doubled the rural population of the EU and increased the number of farms from about 6.6 million in 1970, to some 10 million (Bor *et al.*, 1997, p. 47). In addition, these countries were relatively poor, and their rural regions even more so.

The enlargement occurred during a period when the Commission, encouraged by the UK Conservative government under Margaret Thatcher, was anxious to complete the Single European Market by harmonizing nearly 300 pieces of legislation to remove all remaining technical, physical, and fiscal barriers to the movement of goods, services, and people within the Community (Tracy, 1990). However, the Commission realized[2] that the enlargement would mean that a single market required for trade and people would need to be accompanied by a radical reform of the European structural funds and a significant increase in the resources devoted to socio-economic cohesion. At this time, the structural funds comprised:

- The ERDF – European Regional Development Fund
- The ESF – The European Social Fund
- The EAGGF Guidance Section – the structural component of the European Agricultural Guidance and Guarantee Fund.

The reform involved a doubling of the structural fund spending in real terms over the period 1987–1992.

Five priority objectives were set for this spending, notably:

- Objective 1: Promoting the development and adjustment of the regions whose development is lagging behind (GDP per head less than 75 percent of EC average)
- Objective 2: Converting regions seriously affected by industrial decline
- Objective 3: Combating long-term unemployment
- Objective 4: Facilitating occupational integration of young people
- Objective 5: With two sections defined in coherence with the Common Agricultural Policy reform:
  - 5a. adapting agricultural structures;
  - 5b. promoting the development of rural areas, selected on a range of criteria including high share of agricultural employment, low level of agricultural income and low population density and/or significant depopulation trend.

Objectives 1, 2 and 5b thus required territorial delimitation and mapping according to the specified criteria, and also the development of territorial development plans which departed to a significant extent from the former sectoral approaches to agricultural and regional policy. Thus, the Single European Act of 1987 had explicitly added a new aim to the EEC Treaty "reducing the disparities between various regions and the backwardness of the least-favoured regions" (Art. 130 A–E).

Box 3.1 Schematic evolution of "rural" definitions in the EU after 1970

Pre-1975   Varying national definitions of "rural" and "urban", mainly based on thresh-old settlement size or agrarian characteristics.

1975–1980   After the Less Favoured Areas Directive of 1975 (Council Directive 75/268/EEC of April 28, 1975), EU definition of Mountain and Less Favoured Areas (LFA) used in agricultural policies. Mainly based in agricultural production conditions, but in some member states, LFA include "areas in danger of depopulation".

1981–1990   In the early 1980s, following the experimental Integrated Development Programmes (IDPs) and Integrated Mediterranean Programmes (IMPs), EU definitions begin to take a territorial character. This is consolidated in the late 1980s by the structural funds reform of 1988 which adopts a territorial definition based on the main type of economic and social problem.

1991–2006   In the early 1990s, a new non-sectoral territorial classification is adopted by the OECD, leading to three main categories of regions: remote rural, intermediate areas, and urbanized areas. In the early 2000s this scheme is partially adopted with some variation by Eurostat.

2007–2009   In 2007, the European Commission asks member states to provide the definition used to delimit rural regions in each Rural Development Programme (RDP). A review of the criteria used reveals a lack of coherence, as well as non-compliance with either the OECD or the EU schemes for delimitation of rural regions.

Since 2010   Finally, since 2010, EU proposes a revised urban–rural typology based on a variation of the OECD methodology, in order to avoid distortions.

In 1988 the Commission produced an important document titled "The Future of Rural Society" that signaled a radical departure in rural policy, emphasizing:

1   the context of enlargement, the single market, and political concerns about the environment;
2   that the problems of rural society went far beyond agriculture and farmers;
3   the need for closer integration of the Commissions policy instruments if these problems were to be tackled;
4   the important role of local interests and democratic bodies in defining rural development actions together with the EC and national governments;
5   the diversity of rural Europe – one size would not fit all. In particular it developed the first real EU territorial typology for rural regions, notably specifying the following three types of "standard problem" regions:
  a   regions suffering the pressure of modern development in rural areas accessible from large towns or cities;
  b   regions of rural decline in many, particularly outlying Mediterranean, areas;

c regions of depopulation and the abandonment of the land in areas that are particularly marginal, such as certain hill and mountain areas and islands (Tracy, 1990, p. 16; European Commission, 1988).

As a result, territorial development plans were prepared for Objective 1 (most of them were rural) and 5b regions, and the new Community Initiative "LEADER" (*Liaison Entre Actions de Développement de l'Economie Rurale*, links between actions for the development of the rural economy) was introduced for priority rural regions to engage rural interests and bodies in a more "bottom-up" process of creating new innovative developments. These were the foundation of Europe's territorial rural development policies for the 1990s and, to a considerable extent, thereafter. These plans were to be funded partly by the structural funds at EU level, and partly by member state contributions. This multi-fund approach lasted until the period after 2000 and was partly re-instated after 2013 for the period to 2020.

It must be remembered that the 1980s was also a period of growing pressures on the Common Agricultural Policy – both its stress on increasing production, and the related budgetary expenditures and impacts on the food exporting countries, especially Canada, US, Australia, and New Zealand. This added to the interest in alternative policy approaches to rural problems. Moreover, a growing body of research was providing evidence on the close dependence of farm family economy on local rural economies, especially for those on smaller farms (for example, the research program on farm structures and household pluriactivity between 1986 and 1991: see Bryden *et al.*, 1992; Bryden, 1994).

The European Community was not alone in this quest for alternative policy approaches – Canada had already introduced its Community Futures Programme in 1988, and interest was also strong in the US. Indeed, the US played a major role in establishing the OECD's rural policy committee and subsequent Rural Development Programme in 1991. This Programme was deliberately located outside the Agricultural Division of the OECD, and later became integrated within the Territorial Policies and Governance Division.

The OECD's territorial scheme (1994)

The OECD's territorial scheme was one of the first outcomes of the Programme, published in 1994, and became the global standard (OECD, 1994).

The building block was the definition of rural areas as "communities with a population density below 150 inhabitants/km^2". Having identified these communities, at the regional level, the OECD scheme groups territorial units according to their degree of rurality. This is measured by the share of the rural population in the regional total. The next step involves grouping the 2000 OECD regions (in 1994) into three types of region according to the share of the population living in rural communities. In Predominately Rural Regions over 50 percent of the population lies in rural communities; in Significantly Rural Regions, the share of the population living in rural communities is between 15 and 50 percent, while in Predominately Urbanized Regions the share living in rural communities is below 15 percent. In 1997, however, the term "Significantly Rural Regions" was changed to "Intermediate Regions".

This typology was modified in 2011 to take the size of urban centers into account as follows (OECD, 2011):

• A region classified as predominantly rural by steps 1 and 2 becomes intermediate if it contains an urban center of more than 200,000 inhabitants (500,000 for Japan and Korea) representing at least 25 percent of the regional population.

- A region classified as intermediate by steps 1 and 2 becomes predominantly urban if it contains an urban center of more than 500,000 inhabitants (1,000,000 for Japan and Korea) representing at least 25 percent of the regional population.

The OECD's scheme reflects ideas about rurality as a non-sectoral, or perhaps more clearly as a *cross-sectoral*, issue. It also reflects to some degree the idea that urban–rural interactions – such as those concerning trade, energy, transport infrastructure, governance, commuting, and migration – are important for development. Finally, it covers entire territories, rather than simply dealing with the "rural" space. Perhaps its greatest weaknesses are that it fails to deal with the issue of distance from centers of economic activity (OECD, 2011) or other significant determinants such as energy sources, or international transport hubs. However, it is based on a simple and intuitive classification that has so far stood the test of time.

The OECD's scheme is also useful analytically. It immediately allowed the identification of "leading" and "lagging" regions, for example, and so led to questions about why some rural regions were performing "better" than others over time.[3] In this and other ways, it stimulated

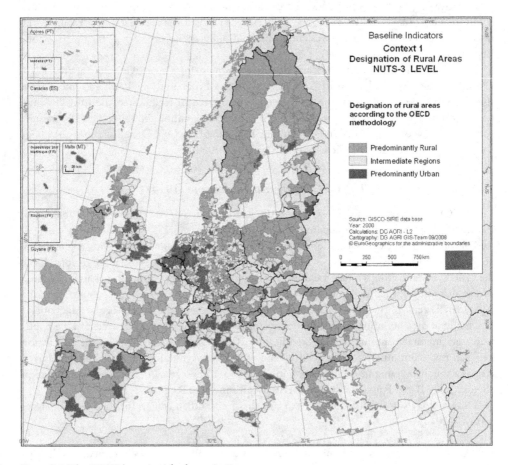

Figure 3.1 The OECD's territorial scheme in Europe
Source: GISCO-SIRE data base.

the creation of knowledge as evidence for the development of territorial development policies in OECD and other countries (Von Meyer, 1997).

The EU's territorial scheme after 2000

The OECD criteria were applied in the EU on NUTS 3 (Nomenclature des Unités Territoriales Statistiques, nomenclature of territorial units for statistics) regions for reasons of data availability; this was a gradual process started in the late 1990s and intensified in the early 2000s when Eurostat became engaged with revisions of its own schemes for territorial classification. As illustrated below, the scheme later created some problems for the delimitation of eligible areas for rural policy in some member states. Indeed, two types of distortions undermine its comparability within the EU. The first distortion is due to the large variation in the "community or municipality area" of Local Administrative Units level 2 (LAU2). The second distortion is due to the large variation in the surface area of NUTS 3 regions and the practice in some countries to

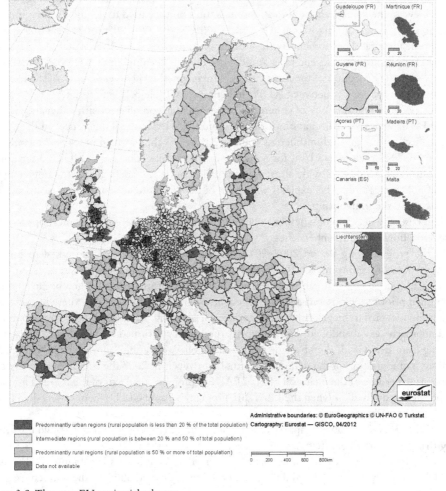

Figure 3.2 The new EU territorial scheme

separate a (small) city center from the surrounding region. The EU scheme seeks to tackle these problems through an approach based on the $1\,km^2$ population grid in order to circumvent the distortion of the variable size of the LAU2s (Eurostat, 2017).

The result of these adjustments is that, although the population share in intermediate regions at the EU level does not change, the share of population in predominantly rural regions increases by 4 percentage points (a relative increase of 20 percent) and the share of population in pre-dominantly urban regions drops by 4 percentage points. At the country level, changes follow the changes at the local level, with the Netherlands and Belgium becoming less urban and Sweden and Finland becoming more intermediate and less rural. In the Baltic member states, Slovenia, the Czech Republic, Slovakia, between 15 and 25 percent of the population shifts between categories. Also in Italy, Greece, and Portugal, 17 percent of the population shifts between categories.

Criteria adopted in different EU member states for the purposes of Rural Development Programmes (2007–2013)

The European Commission asked member states to provide a chapter at the beginning of each Rural Development Programme (RDP) on the definition they used to delimit rural regions for the purpose of programming (Council Regulation (EC) No. 1698/2005 of 20 September 2005 on support for rural development by the European Agricultural Fund for Rural Development (EAFRD)). Nevertheless, several programs did not do this, deciding instead to consider all their regions with the exception of the large cities as "rural zones". The overall result of the exercise was significant differences between RDP rural criteria, as Table 3.1 demonstrates.

This evidence reveals a lack of coherence, as well as non-compliance with either the OECD or the EU schemes for delimitation of rural regions. This reflects real differences in the reality of "rurality" on the ground in different countries as well as the problem of using the large and diverse NUTS 3 regions as a basis for defining rural territories. The use of NUTS 3 territories to delimit rural areas can provide a first approximation but is not adequate for the implementation of policy measures. This explains why most of the programs are committed to a delimitation based on the municipalities.

This raises the question of whether a common definition is needed or if it is more appropriate to leave options to the member states.

In the programming period 2007–2013 the European Commission also asked to build a typology of rural regions in each RDP in order to establish priority areas for intervention.

In fact, in 1988 when it can be said that the EU's Territorial Rural Policy began, the EU established priority regions and delimited these according to certain criteria, thereby excluding regions not deemed to be priorities for EU structural spending. After 2000, however, the multi-fund approach was abandoned, and territorial rural policy returned to DG Agriculture, with funding from EAGGF. It then became a horizontal policy, covering "all rural areas" in the EU, without harmonization of the definition of rural. However, in 2007 the need for a priority criterion arose because of the inclusion of the LEADER program as an axis of the RDP. This need disappeared again in 2014 when the LEADER program became CLLD, Community-Led Local Development (Chapter 33).

In Table 3.2 it is possible to appreciate, the different criteria used in order to build the typology that permitted differentiation between rural zones in some RDPs.

Such differences partly reflect the relative power of different interests lobbying for eligibility in RDPs, but they also reflect real differences in the reality of "rurality" in the different regions of Europe.

Table 3.1 Criteria used by member states to delimit rural areas for EU Rural Development Programmes, 2007–2013. Only the regions and countries with information on rural criteria used in the Rural Development Programmes are included in the table

Criteria	Member states or regions
Total population at municipality level (number of inhabitants)	Austria, Bulgaria, Czech Republic, Brandenburg-Berlin (DE), Rhineland-Palatinate (DE), Saarland (DE), Saxony (DE), Saxony-Anhalt (DE), Schleswig-Holstein (DE), Northern Ireland (UK), Scotland (UK), Latvia, Lithuania, Netherlands, and Balearic Islands (ES)
Population density	Belgium, Asturias (ES), Canary Islands (ES), Castile and Leon (ES), Catalonia (ES), Galicia (ES), Navarre (ES), and Ireland
Employment	France
Population and population density	Estonia, Hungary, and Azores (PT)
Population of the municipalities and accessibility	Sweden
Population, population density, and less favored areas	Continental Portugal
Population, population density, and agricultural employment	Madeira (PT)
Population, population density, and built-up area	Finland
Population density, agricultural employment, and built-up area	Malta
Population, city-planning qualification, and productive specialization	Basque country (ES)
Population, population density, built-up area, and commuting	Baden-Württemberg (DE), Bavaria (DE), North Rhine-Westphalia (DE), Hesse (DE), and Thuringia (DE)
Population density, agrarian surface, altitude, and geographic location	Italy (all the regional programs)
Degree of rurality through 14 indicators	Denmark

Source: Viladomiu and Rosell (2008).

The problem of territorial inequalities in rural regions of the EU

The creation of the European Economic Community in 1957, with the Rome Treaty's goals of a common market, led to fears of emerging and deepening territorial economic inequalities, because the economically strong countries and regions would be able to take most advantage of the widened markets. Seers,[4] in one of the first real efforts to apply "development theory" to the European case, argued that a "core and periphery" were developing in Europe, and that this development would intensify with "southern enlargement" and subsequent enlargements

Table 3.2 Typology of the rural zones in the EU for RDPs. Only the regions and countries with information on rural criteria used in the Rural Development Programmes are included in the table

Criteria	Criteria details	Member states or regions
Accessibility	Time to reach a city	Scotland, Sweden, Bulgaria
Accessibility	Peri-urban degree	France (labor commuting time). Finland (labor commuting time and other indicators)
Accessibility plus socio-economic dynamism	Remoteness, depopulation, farming decline, etc.	Ireland, Denmark, Castilla-La Mancha
Population settlement	Cities, villages, parishes, and isolated houses	England, Wales, Bavaria
Economic specialization	Sectoral participation	Austria, Italy

Source: Viladomiu and Rosell (2008).

(Seers *et al.*, 1979, pp. 3–31). Seers pointed out that "Expenditure by all Community institutions in 1977 was 0.7 per cent of the aggregate gross produce of EEC members, or less than 2 per cent of their total public expenditures". The point was that the resources available at EU level to cope not only with existing disparities, but with potentially increasing disparities over time, were minimal. Seers argued at the time that "The effect was only about 1 per cent of what would be needed to eliminate regional and state disparities" (1979, pp. 27–28).

In the early 1990s a study by Dunford and Kafkalas (1992) concluded that both national and regional divergence in economic performance and inequalities had increased in Europe and, further, that weaker regions would struggle to cope with such divergences. Regional disparities in productivity, unemployment, and GDP were also noted by Amin *et al.* (1992) and Amin and Tomaney (1995), to name but a few.

The 5th Report on Economic and Social Cohesion in the EU illustrates the disparities between member states in 2008 as shown in Figure 3.3.

This shows that, at least in terms of GDP per head, the richest country is more than three times as rich as the two poorest countries. Disparities between the EU regions are naturally even greater than this. Much is written, inside and outside the European institutions, on whether or

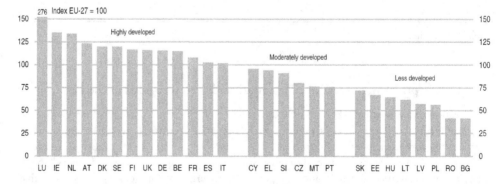

Figure 3.3 Disparities in GDP per head (PPS) in EU member states, 2008

not disparities are increasing or decreasing, but there is no consensus on the question. Nevertheless, it is the case that the EU structural funds as a whole account for only about 0.5 percent of EU GDP and that in some of the countries most severely hit by the economic and financial crisis since 2008, the local impacts of fiscal austerity have been much larger than spending on the structural funds. In this context, it is most probable that disparities have widened (Bryden, 2016).

That question will no doubt be answered in the future. For present purposes what it is important to stress is the role of a range of local and non-local factors in determining local economic performance, rural or urban.

Table 3.3 shows clearly that some rural regions performed better on employment than urban or intermediate regions in the 1980s, although others fared worse.

The OECD work on territorial rural data in the 1990s opened up a whole new field of enquiry, because as Table 3.3 illustrates, it showed that some predominately rural regions outperform other types of region in terms of employment growth. Several research projects tried to explain why some rural areas perform "better" than others: DORA (Bryden and Hart, 2004), RUREMPLO (Terluin and Post, 2000), and the OECD-REMI work using shift-share analysis to examine the role of local (as opposed to national or sectoral) factors in territorial employment dynamics. This clearly demonstrated that in all 15 OECD countries studied, positive local dynamics were what made the difference between "leading" and "lagging" rural regions. One major conclusion, which was to influence subsequent OECD work on rural policies, especially *The New Rural Paradigm* (2006), was that "development analyses and policies should focus much

Table 3.3 Employment change by type of region, 1980–1990

Countries	National 1980 = 100	Predom. rural regions 1980 = 100	Differences in employment change. Regional change minus national change in % points				
			Predominantly rural			Significantly rural	Predominantly urbanized
			Total	Lagging regions	Dynamic regions		
Sweden	112.0	110.8	−1.1	−2.5	2.9	0.2	2.5
Finland	105.0	98.3	−6.7	−10.1	9.9	−1.1	15.8
Denmark	107.2	–	–	–	–	–	–
Austria	104.5	101.7	−2.8	−5.6	3.4	2.9	−0.8
Ireland	101.3	100.1	−1.2	−3.6	1.6	−0.3	1.4
Greece	107.2	97.7	−9.5	−13.0	4.8	2.0	11.1
Portugal	118.2	–	–	–	–	–	–
Czech Republic	101.1	100.2	−0.9	−2.8	2.8	−0.7	1.9
France	103.7	100.6	−3.1	−5.9	4.3	2.1	0.3
Spain	106.7	106.9	0.2	−20.9	7.5	−9.7	11.7
Italy	104.4	–	–	–	–	–	–
Germany	106.7	114.4	7.7	−1.7	9.1	0.7	−0.7
United Kingdom	103.5	108.6	5.1	–	5.1	7.3	−4.5
Luxembourg	119.6	–	–	–	–	0.0	–
Belgium	101.7	104.2	2.4	–	2.4	−4.7	0.8
Netherlands	126.1	–	–	–	–	3.9	−0.7

Source: OECD (1996): Territorial Indicators of Rural Employment Focusing on Rural Development. Rural Employment Indicators Project (REMI). Paris.

more on the territorial, local and regional, conditions and initiatives rather than the sectoral components and structures" (OECD, 1996, p. 56).

Conclusions

The ideas of rurality and the delineation of rural regions have developed in the period since the 1970s due to the changing roles of agriculture, concerns about the non-farming elements and populations in the rural economy, and fears around the environmental and international impacts of agricultural policies, as well as changes in the power of related lobbies. In particular, the need for territorial policies that became more evident after "southern enlargement" in the 1980s led to a rapid development of schemes of territorial classification by the OECD and then the EU. These schemes went hand in hand with the development of territorial rural (and regional) policies even if they have not always been used for the delineation of eligible regions by the member states.

The criteria to identify rural regions and to prioritize rural regions for intervention are very different around Europe and today there is no single generally accepted criterion. Nevertheless, for the RDPs most member states are adopting the density criteria rather than one based on the total number of inhabitants of a municipality and the agrarian specialization. Other member states propose several indicators in their RDP systems of delimitation that are in fact more difficult to manage.

In the establishment of a typology of rural regions the criteria of accessibility is also gaining importance ahead of agrarian performance. Nevertheless, the abandonment of the priority region approach and multi-fund programs since 2000 has reduced the policy relevance of defining and classifying types of rural regions. According to the authors' opinion, the abandonment of the priority criteria and the multi-fund approach was a mistake since it both "watered down" the efforts for territorial cohesion started in the 1988 reform of the structural funds and gave too much power to sectoral lobbies. In fact, the lack of priority criteria also led to some inequity in the system, since richer member states were in a position to include municipalities that in other countries would be ineligible.

Finally, it remains an open question whether territorial development policies have in fact reduced territorial disparities, especially in the light of the impacts of the economic and financial crisis and the Eurozone crisis on "broad" policies that have significant negative impacts on rural (as well as urban) regions.

Notes

1 The English word rustic derived from the Latin *rusticus* "of the country, rural; country-like, plain, simple, rough, coarse, awkward", from *rus* (genitive *ruris*) "open land, country" (see *rural*). Noun meaning "a country person, peasant" is from 1550s (also in classical Latin) (online Etymology Dictionary, s.v. "rustic", www.etymonline.com/word/rustic). It was usually, but not always, used in a pejorative sense; for example, in the positive sense it could also mean "honest", "husbandry", "simplicity" (Leverett, 1842).

2 Jacques Delors, Commission president at the time, agreed to the implementation of the single market on condition that the structural funds were reformed and increased, to which Margaret Thatcher finally agreed.

3 It stimulated several national and transnational research projects to investigate this issue including RUREMPLO and DORA in the EU, New Rural Economy in Canada, and RIMISP in Latin America (Berdegué *et al.*, 2015).

4 Dudley Seers was a British development economist and a critic of neoclassical economics and the "growth fetish". He drew much on his experiences in Latin America, and especially dependency and core–periphery theories, but also structuralism. He became the first director of the new Institute of Development Studies at Sussex University in 1967.

References

Amin, A., Tomaney, J., 1995. *The challenge of cohesion*, in: Amin, A., Tomaney, J. (Eds.), *Behind the myth of European Union: Prospects for cohesion.* Taylor & Francis, London, pp. 9–41.

Amin, A., Charles, D.R., Howells, J., 1992. *Corporate restructuring and cohesion in the new Europe.* Regional Studies 26, 319–331. https://doi.org/10.1080/00343409212331347021.

Berdegué, J.A., Escobal, J., Bebbington, A., 2015. *Explaining spatial diversity in Latin American rural development: Structures, institutions, and coalitions.* World Development 73, 129–137. https://doi.org/10.1016/j.worlddev.2014.10.018.

Bor, W. van den, Bryden, J., Fuller, A.M., 1997. *Rethinking rural human management: The impact of globalisation and rural restructuring on rural education and training in Western Europe.* Mansholt Institute, Kerkwerve, Netherlands.

Bryden, J., 1994. *Interactions between farm households and the rural community*, in: Dent, J.B., McGregor, M.J. (Eds.), *Rural and farming systems analysis: European perspectives.* CABI, Oxfordshire, pp. 243–254.

Bryden, J., 2016. *Causes and consequences of medium and long-term territorial inequalities in a European context, with a focus on rural regions.* Working Paper Series Document No. 182. Territorial Cohesion for Development Working Group, Santiago, Chile.

Bryden, J., Hart, K., 2004. *A new approach to rural development in Europe: Germany, Greece, Scotland, and Sweden.* Edwin Mellen Press, Lewiston, NY.

Bryden, J., Fuller, A., MacKinnon, N., 1992. *Part-time farming: A note on definitions. A further comment.* Journal of Agricultural Economics 43(1), 109–110.

Dunford, M., Kafkalas, G., 1992. *The global–local interplay: corporate geographies and spatial development strategies in Europe.* Belhaven Press, London.

European Commission, 1988. *The future of rural society.* Com (88)501.

Eurostat, 2017. *Urban–rural typology: Statistics explained.* http://ec.europa.eu/eurostat/statistics-explained/pdfscache/7109.pdf.

Halfacree, K.H., 1993. *Locality and social representation: Space, discourse and alternative definitions of the rural.* Journal of Rural Studies 9, 23–37. https://doi.org/10.1016/0743-0167(93)90003-3.

Leverett, P. (Ed.), 1842. *New and copious lexicon of the Latin Language.* Wilkins and Carter, Boston, MA.

Mormont, M., 1990. *Who is rural?*, in: Marsden, T., Lowe, P., Whatmore, S. (Eds.), *Rural restructuring: Global processes and their responses.* David Fulton, London, pp. 21–44.

Newby, H., 1980. *Green and pleasant land? Social change in rural England.* Penguin Books, London.

OECD, 1994. *Creating rural indicators for shaping territorial policy.* OECD Publications and Information Centre, Paris; Washington, DC.

OECD, 1996. *Territorial indicators of employment: Focusing on rural development. Version details.*

OECD, 2011. *OECD regional typology.* Directorate for Public Governance and Territorial Development, Paris.

Seers, D., Schaffer, B., Kiljunen, M.-L., 1979. *Underdeveloped Europe: Studies in core–periphery relations.* University of Sussex, Institute of Development Studies Harvester Press, Hassocks, Sussex.

Shucksmith, M., 1994. *What is rural?*, in: Towards sustainable rural communities. Presented at the Winegard seminar series, Guelph, Ont.

Terluin, I., Post, J. (Eds.), 2000. *Employment dynamics in rural Europe.* CABI, Wallingford.

Tracy, M., 1990. *Rural policy issues.* The Arkleton Trust, Oxford.

Viladomiu, L., Rosell, J., 2008. *Anàlisi comparatiu dels Programes de Desenvolupament Rural 2007–2013 a nivell espanyol i europeu.* Working Paper, DRUAB.

Von Meyer, H., 1997. *Rural employment in OECD countries: Structure and dynamics of regional labour markets*, in: Bollman, R.D., Bryden, J.M. (Eds.), *Rural employment: An international perspective.* CABI, Wallingford, pp. 3–21.

4

A COMPARATIVE RURAL PROFILE ACROSS OECD MEMBER COUNTRIES

Ray D. Bollman

Introduction

International discussions of rural policy options often fail to appreciate the diversity of the rural situation both within and across OECD member countries. International comparative rural policy analysis requires comparing like-to-like, in terms of baseline factors, in order to determine if policy, or a policy change, generates a desirable outcome, or a change in a desirable outcome. Specifically, some basic rural versus urban structural features illustrate the constraints experienced by some countries and the advantages experienced by other countries in promoting an active rural policy agenda. For example, countries with a smaller share of their population residing in predominantly rural regions would have a greater degree of freedom to consider targeted rural policy.

The objective of this chapter is to highlight two key demographic features of OECD member countries that merit consideration in order to improve the international comparative rural policy discourse. This discussion will also help researchers in choosing "similar" countries for comparative rural policy analysis *and* help in the choice of "similar" regions for comparative rural policy analysis.

The overall approach to territorial policies (e.g. metro policies, small city policies and rural policies) will necessarily be advantaged, or constrained, by the population settlement patterns within each country. The discussion in this chapter is an update and extension of Bollman (2004, 2005, 2006).

A note on the value of statistics

Statistics inform decisions – both decisions in the private sector and decisions in the public sector. The value of a statistic may be estimated by the increase in the value of a decision when the statistical evidence is introduced into the decision process. To be clear, it is the increase in the value of a decision that provides value to a data item, a statistic, or an item of information.

Bonnen (1975, 1997, 2000) and Bonnen and Harsh (1995) have noted the value of raw data and the value of statistics in a system that generates knowledge for (public and private) decision-makers. Specifically, raw data are used to generate statistics, or, saying the same thing, statistics provide an interpretation and summary of data.

Numerous authors (Blandford, 2007; Gardner *et al.*, 2006; Just *et al.*, 2002; United Nations, 2007) have documented the value of agricultural statistics to both private and public decision-makers.

Importantly, any statistic would be expected to increase both the value of a decision made in the private sector and the value of a decision made in the public sector.

More generally, from a public policy point of view, statistics benchmark the policy discussion. In other words, the conversation does not dwell on the size of the problem. The conversation can directly start with alternative solutions to deal with the problem.

National indicators do not (necessarily) indicate the regional experience. A specific definition of region is not proposed – generally, a region would constitute a collection of people in a group of communities that is smaller than a province (in Canada) or smaller than a state (in the United States.) Regional statistics address two sets of questions:

- What is the situation among the regional units that are targeted/should be targeted by region-specific policies?
- What are the different impacts across different sub-national regional units that would arise from a given (national) policy proposal?

The OECD regional classification

The OECD has developed a protocol to classify three types of sub-national regions within each member country:

- predominantly urban regions;
- intermediate regions; and
- predominantly rural regions.

The classification of regions is based on the settlement structure within each region.

First, the population density (population per square kilometer) for sub-regional geographic units is determined. Sub-regional geographic units, in most countries, are small(er) administrative units. If the population density is less than 150 inhabitants per square kilometer, the population in the given sub-regional geographic unit is classified as "rural". The population in geographical units with 150 or more inhabitants per square kilometer is classified as "urban".

A region is classified as "predominantly rural" if the settlement pattern within the region has 50 percent or more of the residents living in a "rural" sub-regional geographic unit. A region is classified as an intermediate region if 15–49 percent of the population resides in a "rural" sub-regional geographical unit. A region is classified as "predominantly urban" if less than 15 percent of the residents in the region are living in a "rural" sub-regional geographical unit. These are the general criteria. Additional criteria are applied, such as the presence of a city of a given size, and different levels of population density for countries such as Japan (see OECD, 1994; and Box 3.1 "The OECD Regional Typology and Its Extension" in OECD, 2016, pp. 150–151). The role of distance (see Chapter 1 in this volume) has been recently incorporated into the OECD classification (Brezzi *et al.*, 2011) but is not discussed in this chapter.

The most recent OECD regional database has incorporated changes to the regional classification of each EU county by applying the EU protocol for the classification of regions (Eurostat, 2015). Consequently, the population distribution patterns reported here for 2015 differ from previously published OECD data for a number of EU countries (OECD, 2005–2016).

Population settlement patterns

The population structure of a country frames the opportunities/constraints for targeted rural development initiatives. For example, a country with a large(r) share of their population residing in predominantly rural regions:

a   has a smaller base of taxpayers in predominantly urban or intermediate regions to fund rural development initiatives;

b   but if the policy initiatives are widespread *and* successful, this would have a large(r) impact on national economic development.

In 2015, across 38 OECD member countries, there were three countries with more than 50 percent of their residents residing in predominantly rural regions (Ireland, 60%; Slovenia, 59%; and Romania, 54%) (Figure 4.1 and Table 4.1). These countries have a relatively smaller population in non-rural regions from which to derive additional funds for rural development initiatives. There are an additional nine countries with 33–49 percent of their population residing in predominantly rural regions.

Note that Figure 4.1 also shows the population shares in each of the intermediate and predominantly urban regions. Note that countries with a similar share of their population in predominantly rural regions will often have a very different share of their population in intermediate and predominantly urban regions. For example, each of Australia, Hungary, and Korea has essentially the same share of their population in predominantly rural regions but Hungary has a much lower share of its population in predominantly urban regions. These observations are the basis of a typology proposed below.

Across OECD member countries, there is again an equally wide variation in the share of the population residing in intermediate regions (Figure 4.22 and Table 4.21). In 2015, there were seven countries with over 50 percent of their population in intermediate regions (Luxembourg, 100%; Bulgaria, 69%; Iceland, 65%; Lithuania, 64%; Hungary, 63%; the Czech Republic, 54%; and the Slovak Republic, 51%). These countries:

a   lack the presence of a large population in metropolitan centers that can benefit from agglomeration economies;

b   but these countries do benefit from the presence of small(er) cities which provide the basis for development initiatives designed for intermediate regions.

There are an additional 13 countries with 33–49 percent of their population residing in intermediate regions.

Note that fully 20 OECD member countries (over one-half of OECD countries) have one-third of more of their population residing in intermediate regions. Notably, the OECD has a Working Party on urban (or "metro") policy and a Working Party on rural policy but the analysis of the opportunities/challenges of small city regions is conspicuous by its absence in the OECD program of policy research and analysis.

Figure 4.2 shows that countries with a similar share of their population in intermediate rural regions will often have a very different share of their population in predominantly rural and in predominantly urban regions. For example, each of Norway and Slovenia have equal shares of their population in intermediate regions but Norway has (about) equal shares of their population in each type of region whereas Slovenia has no predominantly urban regions and the predominantly rural population is considerably larger than the population in intermediate regions. These observations also play a role in the construction of the typology proposed below.

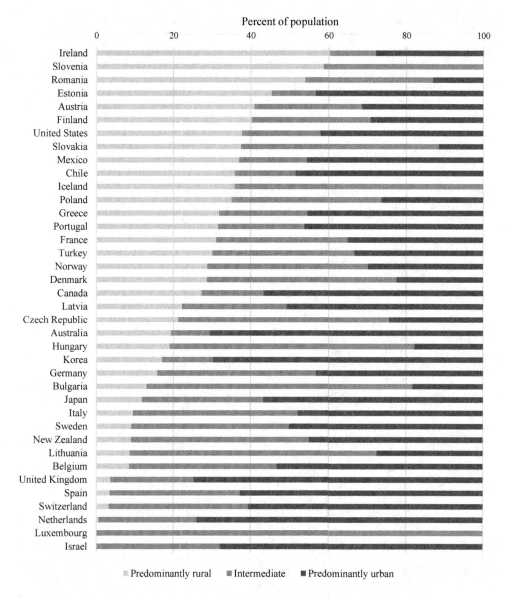

Figure 4.1 Population per type of region, ranked by percent in predominantly rural regions, 2015

Source: OECD regional database.

Finally, in 2015, there were 11 OECD countries with 50 percent or more of their population residing in predominantly urban regions (United Kingdom, 76%; Netherlands, 74%; Australia, 70%; Korea, 70%; Israel, 68%; Spain, 63%; Switzerland, 61%; Japan, 57%; Canada, 57%; Belgium, 53%; and Latvia, 51%) (Figure 4.3 and Table 4.1). In addition, there are another 11 OECD countries with 33–49 percent of their population residing in predominantly urban regions. Countries with a larger share of their population residing in predominantly urban regions are more likely to benefit from the agglomeration economies of their metropolitan centers and thus these countries:

Table 4.1 Distribution of population by type of region, OECD member countries, 2015

Country	Population (thousands) per type of region				Population (percent) per type of region		
	Predominantly urban	Intermediate	Predominantly rural	All regions	Predominantly urban	Intermediate	Predominantly rural
Australia	16,774	2396	4620	23,790	71	10	19
Austria	2703	2371	3511	8585	31	28	41
Belgium	5988	4290	957	11,237	53	38	9
Bulgaria	1317	4938	948	7202	18	69	13
Canada	20,344	5714	9794	35,849	57	16	27
Chile	8720	2823	6464	18,006	48	16	36
Czech Republic	2575	5725	2238	10,538	24	54	21
Denmark	1275	2757	1627	5660	23	49	29
Estonia	570	149	596	1315	43	11	45
Finland	1603	1665	2203	5472	29	30	40
France	23,320	22,456	20,681	66,456	35	34	31
Germany	35,110	33,234	12,854	81,198	43	41	16
Greece	4940	2462	3457	10,858	46	23	32
Hungary	1757	6223	1875	9856	18	63	19
Iceland	–	211	118	329	–	64	36
Ireland	1308	552	2817	4678	28	12	60
Israel	5627	2670	–	8297	68	32	–
Italy	29,085	25,881	5830	60,796	48	43	10
Japan	72,241	39,730	15,137	127,095	57	31	12
Korea	35,568	6754	8693	51,015	70	13	17
Latvia	1009	536	441	1986	51	27	22
Lithuania	807	1859	255	2921	28	64	9
Luxembourg	–	563	–	563	–	100	–
Mexico	55,167	21,043	44,784	121,006	46	17	37
Netherlands	12,488	4306	106	16,901	74	25	1
New Zealand	2067	2113	416	4596	45	46	9
Norway	1543	2135	1488	5166	30	41	29
Poland	10,056	14,621	13,329	38,006	26	38	35
Portugal	4799	2305	3270	10,375	46	22	32
Romania	2593	6565	10,712	19,871	13	33	54
Slovakia	625	2762	2034	5421	12	51	38
Slovenia	–	851	1212	2063	–	41	59
Spain	29,115	15,705	1635	46,450	63	34	4
Sweden	4882	3977	888	9747	50	41	9
Switzerland	4992	2978	269	8238	61	36	3
Turkey	25,958	28,297	23,433	77,696	33	36	30
United Kingdom	48,397	14,104	2374	64,875	75	22	4
United States	135,001	64,725	121,171	320,897	42	20	38
OECD total	610,325	362,446	332,238	1,305,008	47	28	25

Source: OECD regional database.

a   have a large(r) metropolitan taxpayer base available to generate additional funds for rural development initiatives; and

b   at the same time, these agglomeration economies would be expected to contribute to overall national economic development.

Note again the wide differences in population shares within predominantly rural and intermediate regions for countries with a similar share of their population residing in predominantly urban regions. For example, Sweden, Chile, and Italy have a very similar share of their population

Figure 4.2 Population per type of region, ranked by percent in intermediate regions, 2015

Source: OECD regional database.

Percent of population

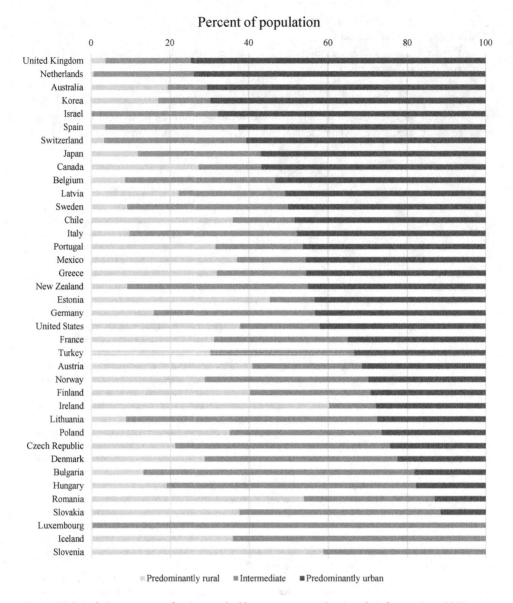

Figure 4.3 Population per type of region, ranked by percent in predominantly urban regions, 2015
Source: OECD regional database.

in predominantly urban regions but Chile has a much larger share of residents residing in predominantly rural regions.

Another way to portray the varying population structures across OECD member countries is to observe:

a there are 21 OECD member countries where the population of predominantly urban regions represent the largest share among the three types of regions within the country (Table 4.1);

b   there are 12 OECD member countries where the population of intermediate regions represent the largest share among the three types of regions within the country; and

c   there are six OECD member countries where the population of predominantly rural regions represents the largest share among the three types of regions within the country.

Most specifically, a minority of countries have their predominantly rural regions contributing the largest share of their population.

This pattern of population distribution across OECD countries generates the pattern of:

- 47 percent of the OECD population residing in predominantly urban regions;
- 28 percent of the OECD population residing in intermediate regions; and
- 25 percent of the OECD population residing in predominantly rural regions (Figure 4.4 and Table 4.2, Row 48).

However, as is demonstrated by the results above (Figures 4.1 to 4.3 and Table 4.1), there is considerable variation in the population settlement patterns across OECD member countries. The OECD-wide population pattern of Figure 4.4a does not truly represent the pattern within any given OECD member country.

Countries with different settlement patterns may be expected to adopt different strategies/options for rural development initiatives.

In order to understand the implications of these varying settlement patterns for international comparative policy analysis, some peer groups of countries are proposed which would suggest that, at least at a macro scale, a common approach to rural policy analysis may be appropriate within each peer group.

For example, there are *six* OECD countries with approximately one-third of their population in each predominantly urban, intermediate, and predominantly rural regions (Figure 4.4b and Table 4.2, Row 7).

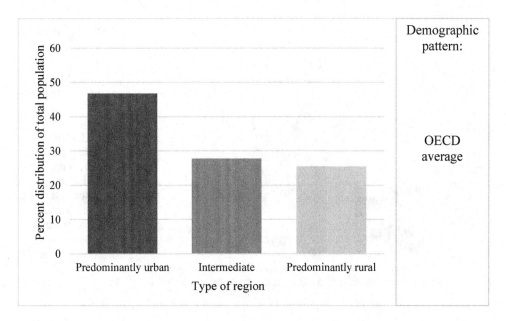

Figure 4.4a Demographic pattern: OECD average

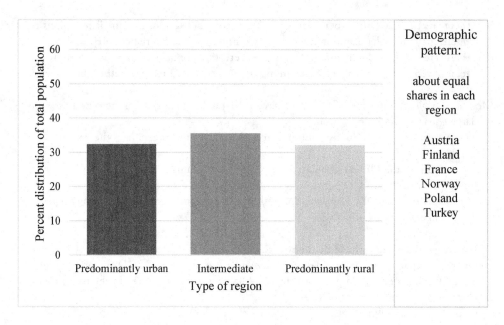

Figure 4.4b Demographic pattern 1: about equal shares in each region

There are *eight* OECD member countries with about two-thirds of their population residing in intermediate regions (Figure 4.4c and Table 4.2, Row 16). For these countries, it would seem that the priority should be a focus on small city or mixed urban–rural policy. Any national focus on "urban" (or "metro") policy and any national focus on "rural" policy should consider the national context of a large population core residing in a settlement pattern defined as intermediate regions.

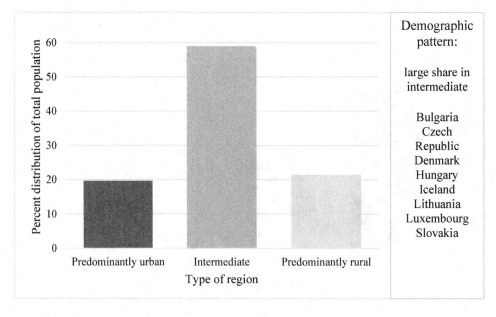

Figure 4.4c Demographic pattern 2: large share in intermediate

Table 4.2 Typology groups for population distribution in OECD countries, 2015

Country	Population (thousands) per type of region				Population (percent) per type of region		
	Predominantly urban	Intermediate	Predominantly rural	All regions	Predominantly urban	Intermediate	Predominantly rural
Austria	2703	2371	3511	8585	31	28	41
Finland	1603	1665	2203	5472	29	30	40
France	23,320	22,456	20,681	66,456	35	34	31
Norway	1543	2135	1488	5166	30	41	29
Poland	10,056	14,621	13,329	38,006	26	38	35
Turkey	25,958	28,297	23,433	77,696	33	36	30
Equal shares PU, IN, and PR					32	36	36
Bulgaria	1317	4938	948	7202	18	69	13
Czech Republic	2575	5725	2238	10,538	24	54	21
Denmark	1275	2757	1627	5660	23	49	29
Hungary	1757	6223	1875	9856	18	63	19
Iceland	–	211	118	329	–	64	36
Lithuania	807	1859	255	2921	28	64	9
Luxembourg	–	563	–	563	–	100	–
Slovakia	625	2762	2034	5421	12	51	38
Large share IN					20	59	21
Belgium	5988	4290	957	11,237	53	38	9
Israel	5627	2670	–	8297	68	32	–
Japan	72,241	39,730	15,137	127,095	57	31	12
Netherlands	12,488	4306	106	16,901	74	25	1
Spain	29,115	15,705	1635	46,450	63	34	4
Switzerland	4992	2978	269	8238	61	36	3
United Kingdom	48,397	14,104	2374	64,875	75	22	4
Large share PU, small share PR					63	30	7
Canada	20,344	5714	9794	35,849	57	16	27
Chile	8720	2823	6464	18,006	48	16	36
Estonia	570	149	596	1315	43	11	45
Greece	4940	2462	3457	10,858	46	23	32
Mexico	55,167	21,043	44,784	121,006	46	17	37
Portugal	4799	2305	3270	10,375	46	22	32
United States	135,001	64,725	121,171	320,897	42	20	38
Equal share PU and PR, small share IN					44	19	37
Germany	35,110	33,234	12,854	81,198	43	41	16
Italy	29,085	25,881	5830	60,796	48	43	10
New Zealand	2067	2113	416	4596	45	46	9
Sweden	4882	3977	888	9747	50	41	9
Equal share PU and IN, small share PR					46	42	13
Australia	16,774	2396	4620	23,790	71	10	19
Korea	35,568	6754	8693	51,015	70	13	17
Latvia	1009	536	441	1986	51	27	22
Large share PU, small share IN and PR					69	13	18
Romania	2593	6565	10,712	19,871	13	33	54
Large share PR, smaller share IN, small share PU					13	33	54
Slovenia	–	851	1212	2063	–	41	59
Larger share PR and large share IN					–	41	59
Ireland	1308	552	2817	4678	28	12	60
Large share PR, smaller share PU, small share IN					28	12	60
OECD total	610,325	362,446	332,238	1,305,008	47	28	25

Source: OECD regional database.

There are *seven* OECD countries with virtually no population residing in predominantly rural regions and where over two-thirds of the population is residing in predominantly urban regions (Figure 4.4d and Table 4.2, Row 24). Nearly two-thirds of the population in these countries resides within predominantly urban regions and approximately another one-third resides in intermediate regions.

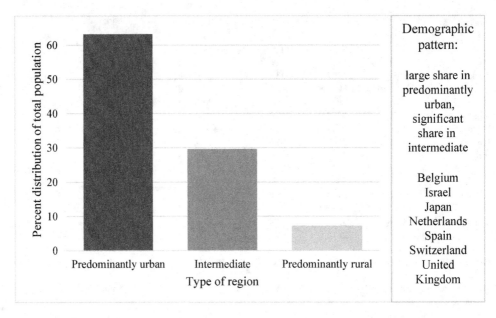

Figure 4.4d Demographic pattern 3: large share in predominantly urban, significant share in intermediate

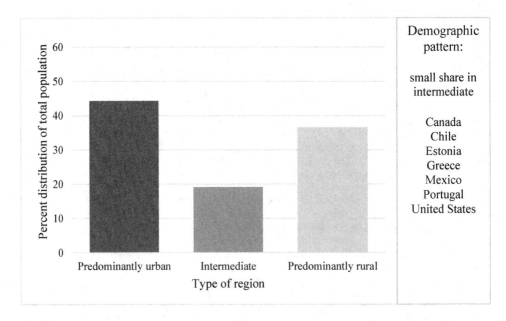

Figure 4.4e Demographic pattern 4: small share in intermediate

There are *seven* OECD countries with a relatively small share of their population residing in intermediate regions (Figure 4.4e and Table 4.2, Row 32). Compared to the typology groups proposed above, these countries represent the case (presently pursued by the OECD) with a focus on urban (or metro) policy analysis and with a focus on rural policy analysis but with no focus on development options for intermediate regions.

There are *four* OECD member countries with approximately an equal share of their population in each of predominantly urban and intermediate regions – and with a small share in predominantly rural regions. (Figure 4.4f and Table 4.2, Row 37).

There are *three* OECD countries with a large share (over two-thirds) of their population in predominantly urban regions with an equal, but small (about one-sixth of) their population in each of intermediate and predominantly rural regions (Figure 4.4g and Table 4.2, Row 41).

Only *one* OECD country has a large share (about one-half) of their population residing in predominantly rural regions but with a strong share (about one-third) in intermediate regions and only about one-seventh in a predominantly urban region (Figure 4.4h and Table 4.2, row 43).

There is *one* OECD country with a large share (over one-half) of its population in predominantly rural regions and a substantial share in intermediate regions but there are no predominantly urban regions (Figure 4.4i and Table 4.2, Row 45).

Finally, there is *one* OECD country, again, with a large share (nearly two-thirds) of their population in predominantly rural regions but with a small share in intermediate regions and with over one-quarter of the population residing in predominantly urban regions (Figure 4.4j and Table 4.2, Row 47).

The settlement pattern of the population within each OECD member country is expected to influence the opportunities and constraints for spatial development policy – and rural development initiatives in particular.

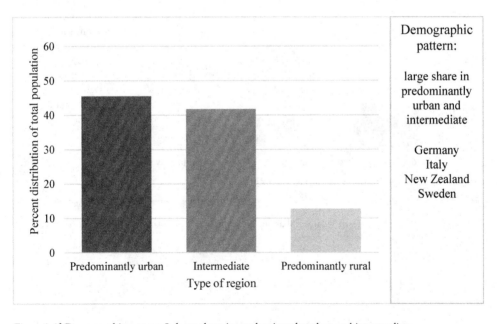

Figure 4.4f Demographic pattern 5: large share in predominantly urban and intermediate

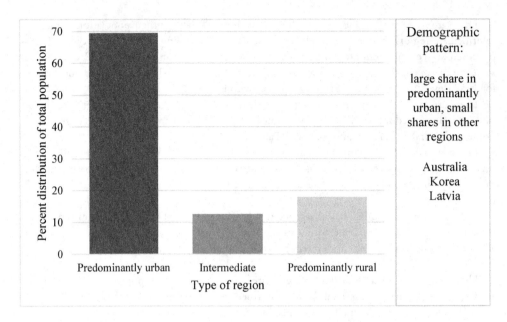

Figure 4.4g Demographic pattern 6: large share in predominantly urban, small shares in other regions

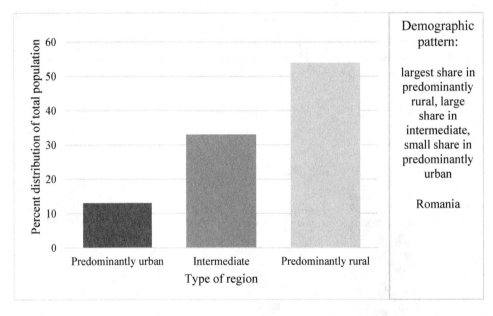

Figure 4.4h Demographic pattern 7: largest share in predominantly rural, large share in intermediate, small share in predominantly urban

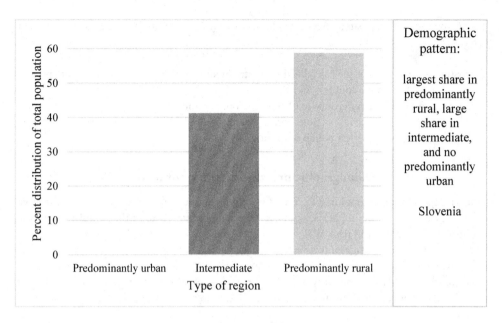

Figure 4.4i Demographic pattern 8: largest share in predominantly rural, large share in intermediate, and no predominantly urban

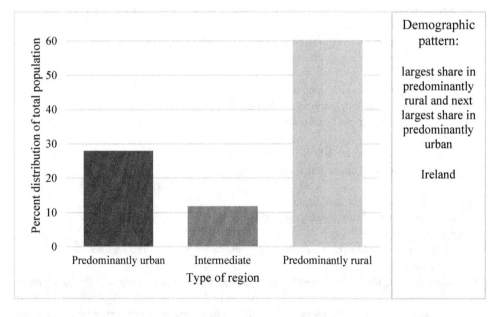

Figure 4.4j Demographic pattern 9: largest share in predominantly rural and next largest share in predominantly urban

The point of proposing these typologies of within-country population settlement patterns is:

- first, to emphasize that the overall OECD settlement pattern (Figure 4.4) does not apply to each OECD member country; and
- second, to propose peer groups of OECD member countries where international comparative analysis of rural policy options and strategies would be expected to improve the international comparative rural policy discussion.

Demographic pressure on the labor force

Another important demographic pattern that would seem essential in international comparative rural policy analysis is the implications of the demographic structure of the population on the potential labor force within regions.

To measure the demographic pressure on the potential labor force, an index is constructed by calculating the number of potential labor market entrants within the next ten years (i.e. the population presently 10 to 19 years of age) as a percentage of the number of potential labor retirees within the next ten years (i.e. the population presently 55 to 65 years of age).

Perhaps obviously, not all individuals 10 to 19 will enter the labor force within ten years – post-secondary schooling and/or travel may delay the entry to the labor market. Also, equally obvious, is that not all individuals will leave the labor force at 65 years of age. Hence, this index of demographic pressure is an indicator of the "potential" impact of the demographic structure on the labor force over the next ten years.

Regions with an index over 100 have more potential labor market entrants than potential labor market retirees. The implications are:

- a potential labor *surplus*; but with an
- opportunity to grow employment levels; but
- otherwise, one may expect out-migration.

Regions with an index under 100 have fewer potential labor market entrants than potential labor market retirees. The implications are:

- a potential labor *shortage*; and thus
- the region can only grow employment if there is:
- net in-migration; as
- otherwise, one would expect a decline in employment levels in the region.

When one calculates this index for each type of region when combining all OECD member countries, one sees that each type of region has shifted from an expected situation of labor surplus (i.e. an index over 100) before the mid-2000s to a situation of expected labor shortages (i.e. an index under 100) by the mid-2010s (Figure 4.5). Specifically, in aggregate across all OECD member countries, this change occurred:

- in 2011 within intermediate regions;
- in 2012 within predominantly urban regions; and
- in 2015 within predominantly rural regions.

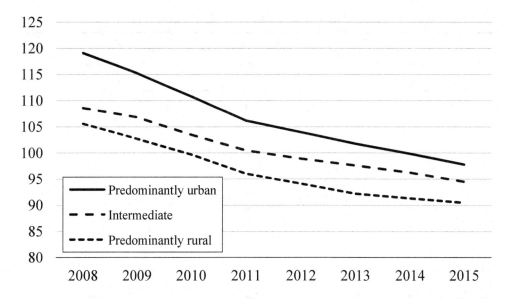

Figure 4.5 Index of the demographic pressure on the labor market: OECD average. The demographic pressure is the number of labor market entrants in the next 10 years (population 10 to 19 years of age) as a percentage of the number of potential labor market retirees in the next 10 years (population 55 to 64 years of age)

Source: OECD territorial database.

As noted in the chart on the cover of Bollman (2014), the rural development challenge has now shifted from "create jobs" to "create workers".

However, as has been emphasized above, not all OECD member countries are in the same situation. In 2015, there were nine OECD member countries with an expected labor market surplus at the national level (an index over 100) (Table 4.3, Column 4). This national context would be expected to be an important factor in the development policy options within each type of region within this group of countries.

In 2015, there were five OECD member countries with their demographic pressure in pre-dominantly rural regions being above 100 (i.e. an expected labor market surplus) (Table 4.4, Column 3). Over the next ten years, one would expect more labor market entrants than retirees and thus job creation/job growth would be (one) rural development strategy for this group of countries.

In order to consider both the demographic pressure on the national labor force and the demographic pressure on the predominantly rural labor force, a relative measure of intensity (also called a "location quotient") is calculated which shows the demographic pressure index within predominantly rural regions as a percentage of the demographic pressure index for the country as a whole. This calculation shows 11 OECD member countries with a location quo-tient above 100 – i.e. relatively larger labor "surplus" (but not necessarily an absolute labor surplus) within predominantly rural regions (Table 4.5, Column 5). There are 21 countries with a location quotient below 100, which indicates a relative larger labor "shortage" (but again, not necessarily an absolute labor shortage).

By reviewing the rankings in the Tables 4.3–4.5, one can generate a typology of countries in terms of their expected approach to economic development policy.

For example, there are eight OECD countries expecting a labor market surplus (more poten-tial labor market entrants compared to the potential number of retirees) (Table 4.3 and the first

Table 4.3 Demographic pressure[a] on the labor market at the country level, 2015

Country	Predominantly urban regions	Intermediate regions	Predominantly rural regions	All regions	Predominantly rural regions location quotient[b]
Turkey	177	190	224	196	115
Israel	162	210	–	177	–
Chile	128	138	143	135	106
Ireland	115	147	121	122	99
Iceland	–	111	118	114	103
New Zealand	123	108	100	114	88
Australia	110	103	96	106	91
Norway	107	108	99	105	94
United States	103	100	102	102	100
Denmark	100	103	92	99	93
Luxembourg	–	99	–	99	–
United Kingdom	104	89	78	99	79
France	110	98	86	98	88
OECD average	**95**	**90**	**98**	**94**	**104**
Sweden	97	90	82	92	89
Netherlands	92	90	73	91	80
Belgium	91	82	95	88	108
Korea	86	87	81	86	95
Austria	87	81	82	83	99
Switzerland	84	83	78	83	93
Canada	87	77	76	82	93
Latvia	78	80	95	81	117
Portugal	82	93	74	81	90
Spain	85	78	62	81	76
Finland	89	77	77	80	96
Greece	76	86	79	79	100
Romania	57	74	87	79	110
Slovakia	–	76	82	78	104
Italy	78	72	72	75	96
Estonia	72	53	78	72	108
Japan	76	69	65	72	90
Germany	74	70	65	71	92
Hungary	60	74	72	71	101
Poland	54	70	80	69	116
Lithuania	64	71	75	68	110
Czech Republic	64	67	66	66	100
Bulgaria	63	63	60	62	96
Slovenia	53	68	61	61	99

Source: OECD regional database.

Notes

(a) Number of potential labor market entrants in the next ten years (population 10 to 19 years of age) as a percentage of the number of potential labor market retires in the next ten years (population 55 to 64 years of age).

(b) Quotient of demographic pressure in predominantly rural regions to demographic pressure in the country as a whole.

Table 4.4 Demographic pressure[a] on the labor market within predominantly rural regions, 2015

Country	Predominantly urban regions	Intermediate regions	Predominantly rural regions	All regions	Predominantly rural regions location quotient[b]
Turkey	177	190	224	196	115
Chile	128	138	143	135	106
Ireland	115	147	121	122	99
Iceland	–	111	118	114	103
United States	103	100	102	102	100
New Zealand	123	108	100	114	88
Norway	107	108	99	105	94
OECD average	**95**	**90**	**98**	**94**	**104**
Australia	110	103	96	106	91
Belgium	91	82	95	88	108
Latvia	78	80	95	81	117
Denmark	100	103	92	99	93
Romania	57	74	87	79	110
France	110	98	86	98	88
Sweden	97	90	82	92	89
Austria	87	81	82	83	99
Slovakia	–	76	82	78	104
Korea	86	87	81	86	95
Poland	54	70	80	69	116
Greece	76	86	79	79	100
United Kingdom	104	89	78	99	79
Switzerland	84	83	78	83	93
Estonia	72	53	78	72	108
Finland	89	77	77	80	96
Canada	87	77	76	82	93
Lithuania	64	71	75	68	110
Portugal	82	93	74	81	90
Netherlands	92	90	73	91	80
Italy	78	72	72	75	96
Hungary	60	74	72	71	101
Czech Republic	64	67	66	66	100
Japan	76	69	65	72	90
Germany	74	70	65	71	92
Spain	85	78	62	81	76
Slovenia	53	68	61	61	99
Bulgaria	63	63	60	62	96
Israel	162	210	–	177	–
Luxembourg	–	99	–	99	–

Source: OECD regional database.

Notes

(a) Number of potential labor market entrants in the next ten years (population 10 to 19 years of age) as a percentage of the number of potential labor market retires in the next ten years (population 55 to 64 years of age).

(b) Quotient of demographic pressure in predominantly rural regions to demographic pressure in the country as a whole.

Table 4.5 Index of demographic pressure[a] on the labor market by the predominantly rural location quotient, 2015

Country	Predominantly urban regions	Intermediate regions	Predominantly rural regions	All regions	Predominantly rural regions location quotient[b]
Latvia	78	80	95	81	117
Poland	54	70	80	69	116
Turkey	177	190	224	196	115
Romania	57	74	87	79	110
Lithuania	64	71	75	68	110
Belgium	91	82	95	88	108
Estonia	72	53	78	72	108
Chile	128	138	143	135	106
OECD average	**95**	**90**	**98**	**94**	**104**
Slovakia	–	76	82	78	104
Iceland	–	111	118	114	103
Hungary	60	74	72	71	101
United States	103	100	102	102	100
Greece	76	86	79	79	100
Czech Republic	64	67	66	66	100
Ireland	115	147	121	122	99
Austria	87	81	82	83	99
Slovenia	53	68	61	61	99
Finland	89	77	77	80	96
Italy	78	72	72	75	96
Bulgaria	63	63	60	62	96
Korea	86	87	81	86	95
Norway	107	108	99	105	94
Denmark	100	103	92	99	93
Switzerland	84	83	78	83	93
Canada	87	77	76	82	93
Germany	74	70	65	71	92
Australia	110	103	96	106	91
Portugal	82	93	74	81	90
Japan	76	69	65	72	90
Sweden	97	90	82	92	89
New Zealand	123	108	100	114	88
France	110	98	86	98	88
Netherlands	92	90	73	91	80
United Kingdom	104	89	78	99	79
Spain	85	78	62	81	76
Israel	162	210	–	177	–
Luxembourg	–	99	–	99	–

Source: OECD regional database.

Notes
(a) Number of potential labor market entrants in the next ten years (population 10 by 19 years of age) as a percentage of the number of potential labor market retires in the next ten years (population 55 to 64 years of age).
(b) Quotient of demographic pressure in predominantly rural regions to demographic pressure in the country as a whole.

column of Table 4.6). However, when one looks at the demographic pressure within pre-dominantly rural regions among these eight countries, one finds:

- Four countries (Turkey, Chile, Iceland, and the United States) with a greater labor market surplus in their predominantly rural regions, compared to the country as a whole. This implies a relatively greater demand for job creation strategies in rural areas.
- Two countries (Ireland and New Zealand) with an expected rural labor market surplus that is less than the expected labor market surplus for the country as a whole. One might expect these countries to focus on job creation strategies in non-rural areas.
- Two countries (Norway and Australia) with an expected labor market surplus at the national level but an expected labor market shortage within predominantly rural regions. Would employers in predominantly rural regions be able to attract potential workers to their community from the non-rural areas of their country?

Table 4.6 Classification of OECD member countries according to the expected demographic pressure on the labor market towards 2025

			Index of demographic pressure at country level		
			Country index ≥ 100 Country surplus	80 ≤ Country index < 100 Country shortage	Country index < 80 Country shortage
Index of demographic pressure within predominantly rural regions	Rural index ≥ 100 *Rural Surplus*	Relatively larger surplus: rural index ≥ country index	Turkey, Chile, Iceland, United States	–	–
		Relatively smaller surplus: rural index < country index	Ireland, New Zealand	–	–
	Rural index < 100 *Rural Shortage*	Relatively less shortage: rural index ≥ country index	–	OECD average, Latvia, Poland, Belgium, Romania	Greece, Romania, Estonia, Slovakia, Hungary, Czech Republic, Lithuania
		Relatively greater shortage: rural index < country index	Norway, Australia	Denmark, France, United Kingdom, Sweden, Netherlands, Korea, Switzerland, Austria, Canada, Portugal, Spain	Finland, Italy, Japan, Germany, Bulgaria, Slovenia

These eight countries are expected to experience a labor market surplus over the next ten years. However, the different situation within the predominantly rural regions would imply possible different approaches to job creation strategies within predominantly rural regions for each group of countries. In other words, each of these three groups of countries in the first column of Table 4.6 would be proposed as a peer group for an international comparative analysis of labor market policy alternatives.

All remaining OECD countries would expect a labor market shortage over the next ten years. As noted above, the index of demographic pressure on the labor force is a simple calculation. Not all individuals who turn 20 years of age would be expected to enter the labor force – schooling and the search for other life experiences would be important considerations. Not all individuals who turn 65 years of age would be expected to retire. Nevertheless, this index does indicate ongoing increasing demographic pressure on the labor market. One implication is that if/when the labor force stops growing, GDP can only grow via increases in productivity (i.e. GDP per worker) as there will not be an increase in the number of workers.

There are 15 OECD countries with a country-level pressure index of 80 to 99 which means there is an expected labor market shortage in the next ten-year period as there are 80 to 99 potential labor market entrants for every 100 potential labor market retirees (Table 4.4 and the second column of Table 6). Within this group of 15, there are four countries where the rural labor market shortage is expected to be less than the national level (Latvia, Poland, Belgium, and Romania) and there are 11 countries where the rural labor market shortage is expected to be greater than at the national level (Denmark, France, United Kingdom, Sweden, Netherlands, Korea, Switzerland, Austria, Canada, Portugal, and Spain). These two groups are proposed as peer groups.

There are another 14 countries with a country-level pressure index that is less than 80 (Table 4.5 and fourth column of Table 4.6). This means that for every 100 potential retirees, there will be fewer than 80 potential entrants to the labor market. There are eight countries where the labor market shortage within predominantly rural regions is expected to be less severe (Greece, Romania, Slovak Republic, Estonia, Hungary, Poland, Czech Republic, and Lithuania). There are six countries where the predominantly rural labor shortage may be expected to be even more intense than at the national level (Finland, Italy, Japan, Germany, Bulgaria, and Slovenia). These two groups are proposed as peer groups.

Overall, Table 4.6 suggests seven possible peer groups that combine the situation of the demographic pressure on the national labor force and the demographic pressure on the labor force within predominantly rural regions.

Pursuing international comparative rural policy analysis

To paraphrase the situation faced by retirees, the international comparative analysis of rural policy is not for the faint of heart. Ongoing exertion and a healthy diet (of statistics?) are two possible routes to success.

In this chapter, two simple but fundamental demographic features are offered as examples of ways to generate peer groups for international comparative rural policy analysis.

Specifically, the varying patterns of population settlement across OECD member countries portray the varying advantages and constraints for the design and the implementation of rural policy. Nine peer groups are proposed where countries within each peer group would, arguably, have similar advantages and constraints for the design and the implementation of rural policy.

Also, the demographic pressure on the labor market would be expected to frame the approach to labor market policies in OECD member countries. Among the countries with an expected labor market surplus in the next ten years, three peer groups of countries are proposed based on the relationship of the expected labor market trajectory within their predominantly rural regions, relative to the national trend in demographic pressure on the labor market.

Among countries with an expected labor market shortage of workers over the next ten years both at the national level *and* within their predominantly rural regions, four peer groups of countries are suggested for the international comparative policy analysis of rural development options.

International comparative rural policy analysis should be pursued among countries (and among regions within countries) with similar demographic advantages and constraints.

References

Blandford, D., 2007. *Information deficiencies in agricultural policy design, implementation and monitoring*. OECD Food, Agriculture and Fisheries Papers No. 6. OECD Publishing.

Bollman, R., 2004. *Information for policy-makers: The use of territorial indicators*. Presented at the International Comparative Rural Policy Studies (ICRPS), University of Guelph, Guelph, Ont.

Bollman, R., 2005. *Information for policy-makers: The use of territorial indicators*. Presented at the International Comparative Rural Policy Studies (ICRPS), Leuven, Belgium.

Bollman, R., 2006. *Information for policy-makers: The use of territorial indicators*. Presented at the International Comparative Rural Policy Studies (ICRPS), Brandon, MB.

Bollman, R., 2014. *Rural Canada 2013: An update. A statement of the current structure and trends in rural Canada*. Federation of Canadian Municipalities, Ottawa, Ont.

Bonnen, J.T., 1975. *Improving information on agriculture and rural life*. American Journal of Agricultural Economics 57, 753–763. https://doi.org/10.2307/1239073.

Bonnen, J.T., 1997. *The changing relationship of statistical data and analysis*. Staff Paper No. 97–17, April. Michigan State University, Department of Agricultural Economics, East Lansing, MI.

Bonnen, J.T., 2000. *Providing economic information in an increasingly difficult policy environment*. Review of Agricultural Economics 22, 500–518.

Bonnen, J.T., Harsh, S.B., 1995. *Establishing a framework for an information system*. Canadian Journal of Agricultural Economics 43, 605–614. https://doi.org/10.1111/j.1744-7976.1995.tb00069.x.

Brezzi, M., Dijkstra, L., Ruiz, V., 2011. *OECD extended regional typology: The economic performance of remote rural regions*. OECD Regional Development Working Papers, 2011/06. https://doi.org/10.1787/5kg6z83tw7f4-en.

Eurostat, 2015. *Archive: Urban–rural typology – Statistics explained*. https://ec.europa.eu/eurostat/statistics-explained/index.php/Archive:Urban-rural_typology (accessed 2.27.19).

Gardner, B., Goodwin, B., Ahearn, M., 2006. *Economic statistics and U.S. agricultural policy*. Presented at the International Association of Agricultural Economists Conference, Gold Coast, Australia.

Just, D.R., Wolf, S.A., Wu, S., Zilberman, D., 2002. *Consumption of economic information in agriculture*. American Journal of Agricultural Economics 84, 39–52. https://doi.org/10.1111/1467-8276.00241.

OECD, 1994. *Creating rural indicators for shaping territorial policy*. OECD Publications and Information Centre, Paris; Washington, DC.

OECD, 2005–2016. *OECD regions at a glance*. www.oecd-ilibrary.org/urban-rural-and-regional-development/oecd-regions-at-a-glance-2005_reg_glance-2005-en (accessed 2.27.19).

OECD, 2016. *OECD regional outlook 2016: Productive regions for inclusive societies*. OECD, Paris.

United Nations, 2007. *Rural households' livelihood and well-being: Statistics on rural development and agriculture household income*. United Nations, New York.

5

WHY COMPARATIVE RURAL POLICY STUDIES?

Comparative theory and methods

Erika Allen Wolters and Brent S. Steel

Introduction

Rural areas are perceived as contextually different from urban counterparts and can be distinctly different from one another. Characteristically, rural areas have a low population density with natural resource use as the primary economic base. In the United States, it has been assumed that rural areas tend to adhere to more traditional land use management practices, are more conservative ideologically, and have political power due to key economic inputs (Sheridan, 2007) from such practices as ranching, forestry, and energy production. Through comparative rural policy (i.e. comparing policy decisions among rural areas) both traditionally held views of rurality can be explored, as well as variations in policy choices among rural areas. Therefore, comparative rural public policy can provide context to the understanding of the drivers behind rural policy.

At its core, "comparative public policy illuminates the various and subtle ways in which politics works to produce choices of a collective or social nature" (Heidenheimer *et al.*, 1990, p. 2). Through a comparative lens "analysis moves beyond the particularities of each case and identifying patterns and regularity across cases, settings and time periods" (Engeli and Allison, 2014, p. 2), which ultimately serves as a baseline against which to test a broader selection of cases. This type of research explores both why policies were enacted, but also why not. Through comparative policy research, the process of policy-making is a key element, but also "of problem emergence and definition, of policy formation, of policy implementation and also evaluation" (Engeli and Allison, 2014, p. 2).

Comparative public policy explores broadly how, why, and to what end policies differ among countries, states, and institutions (Gupta, 2012; Jreisat, 2002). The basis of comparison seeks to clarify these questions:

> First, the "how" of this definition calls for a focus on what goes on inside governmental structures, how these structures operate, and how they arrive at policy decisions ... Second "why" a government pursues a certain course of action is difficult to discover. The inquiry may take the researcher into unfamiliar terrain of the historical, cultural, and motivational factors that may have been instrumental in shaping the

adopted policy ... Third, the "to what effect" question focuses on the impact, the outcome or the payoff of the policy.

(Jreisat, 2002, pp. 82–83)

The difficulty in answering these questions rests in the numerous methodological applications used to study public policy as well as the different disciplines seeking to study public policy. As such, researchers from several disciplines, including economics, political science, and sociology, conduct public policy research through the lens of their discipline. Since many economic factors influence public policy, such as economic growth, productivity, employment, etc. the tools of economics are often used to promote policies or to explain why policies succeed or fail. Political scientists study the political process since this is the process through which policies are made, implemented, and enacted. Sociologists explore community and group activities that are an important part of policy-making, because groups/classes/etc. of people often make political demands that can influence policy outcomes. Thus, comparative public policy draws from economics, political science, and sociology while simultaneously utilizing theories from public policy and other disciplines (Dodds, 2013).

However, with public policy being inherently interdisciplinary, it is subject to criticisms for lacking discipline, particularly lacking theory (Stone, 2012; Robertson and Judd, 1989; Dresang, 1983). Early attempts at policy studies were discretionary leading Dresang to state:

> Policy studies are regarded by many political scientists, economists, and sociologists as second-best research ... the field of inquiry is too broad and varied to fit within a single theoretical framework or set of methodologies. Policy inquiry is not considered a science.
>
> *(1983, p. 1)*

Theoretical frameworks are important for researchers as they allow them to study in a systematic and methodologically sound way. A theory is "a set of principles or assumptions used to explain and ultimately predict some type of phenomena" (Steel *et al.*, 2003, p. 36). A theory is useful at analyzing phenomena if it is valid, economical (simpler than the phenomena being studied), testable (can be tested with quantitative or qualitative methods to determine validity), organized (brings order out of chaos by explaining what is otherwise unexplainable), and heuristic (acts as a catalyst to induce and guide further research) (Frederickson *et al.*, 2011). Thus, theoretical frameworks can lend insight into causal explanations, instill a greater understanding of the world, and bring clarity to significant issues at multiple levels.

Theoretical frameworks and methodological approaches though are particularly useful when studies can be replicated (and therefore more broadly tested) for validity and broad application, especially in comparative public policy research. Gupta's (2012) review of comparative policy research finds that prior studies explored a range of variables from historical experience, key players, interest groups, institutions, values, and the media to explain policy outcomes. Gupta (2012) suggests that while policy research is important, those conducting research often utilized a mix of theoretical frameworks from other fields such as risk analysis and economic theory and ultimately, "this approach widens the gap between comparative policy scholars and those who focus on theories of the policy process to understand policy dynamics" (p. 15). Thus, a more systematic and methodologically similar study of comparative public policy may garner the most helpful and revealing information on policy phenomena.

Conducting comparative public policy research

Of primary importance in comparative policy research is what to study, how that study should be conducted, and a discussion of why the comparative study is significant. First, less critical is the number of cases included in a study (although for comparative policy research a minimum of two is assumed) as is the carefully chosen types of cases that can help with external validity and with broader generalizability (Heijden, 2014). The smaller study (small-N) allows the researcher to delve deeper into variables affecting the how, why, and to what end, but potentially limits the broader application of these findings to other cases. Studies with more cases (medium to large-N) have the opposite problem of being too inclusive of multiple variables potentially making them more generalizable, but less likely to get into specifics or have the ability to control for external variance. Heijden (2014) thus proposes that "instead of aiming to strengthen a research by a sheer increase in the number of cases, the researcher may better aim to strengthen her research by increasing the number of potential explanatory variables" (p. 46).[1]

Large-N studies began in earnest in the 1960s in an attempt to use aggregate data to draw inferences into the public policy process about how policies are derived and modified (Blomquist, 2007). The work by researchers Dye, Sharkansky, and Hofferbert (DSH) has created a template for large-N comparative policy research. The DSH model examines "a set of independent variables that are hypothesized to differentiate cases from one another with respect to some policy" (Blomquist, 2007, p. 267). The independent variables are usually socio-economic in scope or some combination of variables related to political behavior or institutions with the dependent variable being some form of policy output.

However, these large-N studies are criticized for the inability of research to shift levels of analysis due to the data primarily acquired from one level (Coppedge, 1999). Blomquist (2007) offers a more robust critique of large-N studies finding that the DSH model "leave[s] little or no opportunity for policy scholars to explore or pursue the usefulness of the concept of 'levels of action'. In the DSH approach, the political system is not only static, it is a given" (Blomquist, 2007, p. 275). Further, Blomquist finds that due to the inherent nature of large-N studies there are two fundamental flaws to their design and use, first that "the complexity of the policy-process theories will make the information gathering and analytic tasks of even individual case studies daunting", and second that "the large-N comparative study is methodologically inconsistent with a narrative account of policy change over time" (Blomquist, 2007, p. 282).

Another method used to examine comparative policy is through case studies. The case study is useful when examining either a descriptive or an explanatory question (e.g. what is happening, or why did something happen?) (Yin, 2012). In this way, case studies are not limited to single variables, but rather are noted for the comprehensive approach to comparative studies. As Yin (2012) describes it, "the in-depth focus on the case(s), as well as the desire to cover a broader range of contextual and other complex conditions, produce a wide range of topics to be covered by any case study" (p. 4) thus allowing for a very detailed examination of real world situations. Case studies employ both quantitative and qualitative data that further enhances understanding about a particular policy question by allowing the researcher to seek several sources of information that lend discovery. While case studies can broadly seek answers to the "what" and "why" questions, they also can employ theoretical frameworks to further elicit both focus of the research and generalizability of findings (Yin, 2012). Through comprehensive case studies, outcomes of the research can be very useful in providing a detailed description and/or explanation of a policy issue (Jreisat, 2002).

Evolving comparative public policy

Comparative public policy theory is the evolution of years of interdisciplinary attempts to explain comparative policy from the perspective of discipline-specific fields. Broadly, there are four general schools of comparative public policy theory: cultural, economic, political, and institutional. The *cultural* school assumes that culture affects what policies/approaches are acceptable and not acceptable (e.g. some societies are more skeptical about government than others). Within this school, there are two divisions of research: families of nations and public opinion. The families of nations research focuses on groups of countries with similar cultural attributes and histories that (should) lead to similar policies. The public opinion approach explores how public opinion impacts policies in advanced industrial societies (where public opinion influences policy preferences, primarily in Europe and North America). Public preferences and values are shaped by the socio-economic and political environment of developmental years (predominantly post World War II), which leads to generational conflict. Younger cohorts, with greater societal, socio-economic, and political stability are more likely to address preferences pertaining to quality-of-life issues like marriage equality, the environment, etc. whereas older cohorts are more focused on economic and political security.

The *economic* school of thought focuses on the economic forces that are available to a country that shape expectations of citizens and policy-makers. Economic expectations can be based on short-term trends in the economy (e.g. GDP growth rate). For example, short-term growth can lead to policy reform to solve societal problems by generating optimism for problem solving; and more money available to expand current efforts or begin new ones (Adolino and Blake, 2001).

Long-term trends in the economy can also impact policy. Wilensky (1975) and Lindert (2004) found that the affluence of countries was related to greater welfare expenditures – the wealthier the country the more generous the benefits. Finally, this school of thought is also concerned about long-term demographic patterns and the impact on economic capacity (i.e. "graying factor", how declining population rates affect tax revenues and retirement expenditures).

In the 1980s, political scientists started criticizing cultural and economic approaches to comparative public policy as being devoid of politics including political parties and interest groups. As such, the *political* school focuses much more on the role of partisanship and interest groups. For example, labor-oriented political parties can affect policy when in majority or in coalition governments (e.g. expand social welfare policies), with the opposite being true when conservative business-oriented parties are in majority. The type of party control is also examined – such as policy change is easier in parliamentary systems where the executive and legislative branches are integrated and most difficult in presidential systems with separation of powers / checks and balances (e.g. the United States).

Interest groups also play a major role in policy formation in both pluralism and corporatism. Under pluralism (e.g. Dahl, 1961), groups compete openly, and government does not take sides. Group compromise leads to policy (the USA is considered an example by some). Under corporatism (e.g. Wiarda and Skelley, 2005), fewer and larger groups (e.g. major unions, industry, agriculture, etc.) work with government behind the scenes to negotiate policy (Sweden and Japan are good examples).

Finally, the *institutional* school focuses on how institutions (e.g. formal government rules and informal norms in government and nongovernmental institutions) impact policy processes, design, implementation, and effectiveness. Pertaining to formal institutions, Tsebelis (2002) found that multi-tiered federal systems make them prone to slower change because more people/organizations in and outside of government have a chance to challenge policy proposals (hence more access points). In contrast, informal institutions are subject to cultural constraints of prevailing norms. For example, Peters (2002, 1988) and Bouckaert and Peters (2002) found that "bureaucratic politics" and norms have a huge impact on how policies are given priority and implemented.

More recently, New Institutionalism has come from the institutional school wherein there is a strong emphasis on how informal rules (norms and patterns) influence the policy process (Ostrom, 2015; Congleton and Swedenborg, 2006). One illustration of this is the "Seniority Rule" in the US Congress for committee chair selection. Second, while formal government rules remain important, new considerations on how the participation of nongovernmental organizations influences policy framing, formation, implementation, and evaluation are gaining traction in policy research (Scharpf, 1997).

Historically, much of comparative policy research sought to compare the USA, Canada, and European countries that offered the benefit of comparing Western democracies broadly but with different forms of democratic rule. This distinction allowed researchers to examine "policy variation with institutional variables held constant" (Wilder, 2017, p. 548) such as large-N studies and case studies, yet arguably limited the scope to explanations of policy of similar institutional settings (Wilder, 2017). This essentially allowed researchers to examine the ways a policy played out in another country. With governmental structures held as a constant, "one country may serve as a 'laboratory' for another's policy choices" (Marmor *et al.*, 1978, p. 64).

Recently, use of policy theories such as Institutional Analysis and Development (IAD), the Advocacy Coalition Framework (ACF), Punctuated Equilibrium Theory (PET), and the Multiple Streams Approach (MSA) that are inherently comparative have been modified to function across institutional variants, with the exception of the IAD that is already multi-level and cross-institutional in scope (Wilder, 2017). Gupta (2012) suggests that comparative policy studies reside at the intersection of policy theory and comparative case studies. As such, she suggests that comparative policy studies would benefit from "using policy theories to compare issues across contexts (can the ACF explain the evolution of nuclear energy policy in both France and India), and comparing theories to each other (which theory … can better explain healthcare policy in Germany)" (Gupta, 2012, p. 20). It is the intersection of these theories that is beneficial for the study of comparative policy because:

> First, it encourages theoretical refinement by forcing policy scholars to think about how well the different theories can explain policy dynamics in different institutional settings. Second, it helps us better to define the boundaries and synergies associated with the theories by explicitly comparing them to one another and analyzing their ability to answer particular questions.
>
> *(Gupta, 2012, p. 12)*

Further refinement of the policy theories could address policy issues not only at the meso level by examining issues pertaining to cities, states, or communities (policy subsystems), but also at the macro level (national and supranational).

Use of frameworks in comparative public policy research

This next section will briefly review the use of policy frameworks in comparative public policy analysis. For a more in-depth understanding of the theories and frameworks, please see Chapter 6.

Institutional Analysis and Development (IAD)

The IAD is primarily focused on the role of institutions and institutional rules as the boundary to public policy-making. The IAD is useful in exploring multi-levels of engagement in the policy process, allowing researchers to focus on a particular point of entry in order to understand the larger policy picture (the IAD has been especially useful in understanding common-pool resource issues). Specifically, "the IAD framework is thus a general language about how rules, physical and material conditions, and attributes of community affect the structure of action arenas, the incentives that individuals face, and the resulting outcomes" (Ostrom, 2007, p. 46).

Use of the IAD for comparative public policy research is intuitive as the "IAD has been both explicitly comparative and explicitly institutionalist from the outset" (Wilder, 2017, p. S51).

The IAD framework has thus been utilized many times for comparative policy research, particularly in comparative institutional analysis (the focus of the framework). Ostrom's book *Governing the Commons: The Evolution of Institutions for Collective Action* (2015) explores common-pool resource problems and provides eight "design principles" for successful resource management. It is these principles that have helped to set clear boundaries and variables to explore and that have applicability across governing structures and institutions. Therefore, the advantage of the IAD in comparative policy is that it explicitly outlines key "concepts, variables, and evaluative criteria to engage in systematic comparisons" (Schlager and Cox, 2018, p. 234) providing methodological rigor and structure to policy research that can be replicated in different institutional configurations.

Advocacy Coalition Framework (ACF)

The ACF assumes that core beliefs are what drive actors in the policy process. When core beliefs are challenged, or threatened, advocacy coalitions mobilize to influence policies and policy-makers. There are three key elements to ACF. First, that policy-making is shaped by specialists who themselves are impacted by political and socio-economic systems; second, that individuals and their core beliefs affect the policy process; and third, when individuals hold shared beliefs they form around "advocacy coalitions" using collective resources and strategies to shape policy (Jenkins-Smith *et al.*, 2018).

One of the first broad applications of the ACF in comparative policy is the recent work by Weible *et al.* (2016). In this edited volume, the ACF is applied to countries in North America and Europe on the policy issue of hydraulic fracturing. Specifically, Weible *et al.* examine the formation of coalitions under varying governmental structures and the subsequent impact of those coalitions on hydraulic fracturing policies. While the ACF is still limited in the application of comparative policy, the basis of ACF "offers concepts and assumptions that should stimulate and facilitate comparative analysis" (Jenkins-Smith, *et al.*, 2018, p. 157).

Multiple Streams Approach (MSA)

The MSA framework proposes that when three separate, but intricately woven streams of problems, policies, and politics coalesce during a policy window it can facilitate adoption of new policies (Zahariadis, 2007). When a policy window opens, policy entrepreneurs engage in pairing burgeoning policy problems with desired policy solutions that mobilize around a policy goal. This framework, "gives a prominent role to policy-makers' perceptions of issues and to the efforts to shape and change those perceptions through the cultivation and use of information, as well as … to the prospects for rapid change following long periods of stability" (Blomquist, 2007, p. 281).

The MSF has been used for a variety of studies internationally. However, "depending on how much the political system analyzed differs from the US presidential one, it is necessary to adapt the framework to different degrees" (Herweg *et al.*, 2018, p. 35). Currently the MSF is in need of a "systematic adaptation" (Herweg *et al.*, 2018) so the framework can be applied to varying forms of government including parliamentary systems and autocracies for greater application in comparative rural policy research.

For example, parliamentary and presidential governments – the former exemplified by many European countries and Canada, and the latter by the United States – are the two principal forms of democratic governance in Europe and North America. In the USA the president is directly elected, as well as representatives and senators in Congress. The president, with the advice and consent of the Senate, appoints cabinet officers. The president can veto Acts of Congress, but Congress can override the veto by a two-thirds vote in both chambers. The president and one or both of the legislative chambers can be of different political parties, and they typically disagree over policy issues, especially those related to the use of rural policy (e.g. natural resources). This political structure is called a "separation of powers" and often leads to policy "gridlock", where it is very difficult if not impossible to pass legislation. In a sense, there are "many cooks in the kitchen and they all have their own recipe". Passing legislation in the USA can be a very unpredictable and difficult process. A member of the majority party can vote against the wishes of her or his own party and not fear having to run for reelection because the government has fallen, like what could happen in a parliamentary system.

In many parliamentary systems, such as Great Britain, citizens only vote for their own member of the House of Commons. The political party that obtains a majority in the House of Commons then forms the government and is responsible for rural policy without the undue influence of opposition parties, unless the government is part of a ruling coalition of political parties. The leader of the majority party, or head of the coalition, becomes prime minister (head of the government). Unlike in a presidential system like the United States, the prime minister selects other leading party members to become government ministers (defense, foreign affairs, etc.). The prime minister and the other ministers must be members of parliament. The line between the executive and legislative branches of government is therefore blurred in a parliamentary system – a political system typically called "integration of powers" – a clear difference from the USA. The legislative process is much more predictable in this type of system since it is based on the "majority rule" principle. There is also a system of "collective responsibility" whereby members of parliament almost always vote along party lines. The MSA, and other policy theories discussed in Chapter 6 and here, can be useful to identify institutions and processes that influence rural policy processes.

Social Construction of the Target Population framework

The Social Construction of the Target Population framework posits that social perceptions of groups are constructed in ways that can inform policy formation when "target" groups are seen as deserving or undeserving of policy benefits or having a strong or weak political voice. Specifically, "there are strong pressures for public officials to provide beneficial policy to powerful, positively constructed target populations and to devise punitive, punishment-oriented policy for negatively constructed groups" (Schneider and Ingram, 1993, p. 334). These subsequent policy decisions reinforce and communicate group status and codify social perceptions about groups within the general public (Schneider and Ingram, 1993).

The use of social construction of targeted populations has gained momentum in recent years in part because, "the variety of policy domains to which the theory … is being applied demonstrates the theory's portability across contexts and also alludes to a practical dimension as findings contribute to understanding a range of social problems" (Pierce *et al.*, 2014, p. 10). Social construction has also been used in comparative policy studies such as Montpetit, Rothmayr, and Varone's (2005) study of six European democracies and assisted reproductive technology. However, use of the framework to "scale up and down" has been limited, as Pierce *et al.* (2014) find in their meta-study of the application of social construction in policy research. Pierce *et al.* (2014) found that previous use of the social construction framework was primarily focused on federal government and had limited application to state and local policy and even less examining policy at multiple levels (e.g. state and federal, state and local, etc.). And, as the other frameworks discussed here, application of the Social Construction of the Target Population framework would need some modification to be useful in a non-democratic context.

Narrative Policy Framework (NPF)

The Narrative Policy Framework's primary premise is that "narrative plays a fundamental role in how human beings make sense of the world" (Jones *et al.*, 2014). Stories fundamentally help shape policy choices by appealing to selective perceptions and world-views. In order to be considered a policy narrative, a story must contain both a policy stance and, at minimum, one character who plays the role of hero, villain, or victim (Shanahan *et al.*, 2013). Thus by appealing to emotions and reinforcing world-views, narratives become powerful constructs of policy preferences.

The NPF has broad application in micro-, meso-, and macro-level comparative research by exploring the elements of narrative at different scales. In micro- and meso-level analysis the narrative is "constructed by individuals and organizations", while at the macro level the narrative examines the narratives of institutions and cultures (Shanahan *et al.*, 2013, p. 457). However, through examining both established elements of policy formation in addition to narrative, the NPF addresses the gap in comparative policy research:

> Whether scholarly pursuits focus on a country comparison of policies with policy narratives as the data for analysis or a comparison of the use of narrative elements and strategies in different policy contexts (such as comparing narratives across sectors in a single country or across levels of governance), NPF is a viable framework for comparative analysis.
>
> *(Shanahan* et al., *2018, p. 198)*

The NPF has gained momentum as a constructivist framework since its inception. Further refinement of the NPF will allow for greater application in all contexts of comparative policy theory.

The evolution of comparative public policy

In the ever-evolving subfield of comparative public policy, theoretical attempts to answer the how, why, and to what effect questions requires multi-level analysis, an understanding of institutions beyond the USA and Europe, and a keen eye towards rapidly changing policy conditions. The frameworks mentioned above are not exclusive for use in comparative public policy research. The subfield continues to advance with relatively new approaches and iterations of existing frameworks like the Narrative Policy Framework (NPF) and the Ecology of Games Framework (Lubell *et al.*, 2010) that offer to elicit a more comprehensive approach to comparative public policy that functions on a macro, meso, and micro scale.

Finally, there has been a call for a mixed method – qualitative and quantitative – approach to further develop and refine comparative policy theory and frameworks (Denscombe, 2008). While there have been calls for mixed-methods approaches for decades, policy scholars have not systematically pursued such an approach (Biesenbender and Héritier, 2014). The use of mixed-methods approaches will depend on the policies investigated, the time frame of the research, and of course resources, but allow for "triangulation of results" and the ability to generate in-depth insights with qualitative methods, and then the ability to generalize with quantitative approaches. As Biesenbender and Héritier argue:

> the mixed methods strategy offers ways to mitigate the weaknesses of the two broad research approaches within the social sciences … While quantitative analyses are apt to ensure the generalizability of the results, additional qualitative case studies of the processes might help to identify the causal mechanism at work for a subset of the unit of analysis … The value addition of mixed-methods over single-method approaches lies in the ability to draw more robust conclusions from empirical research.
>
> *(2014, p. 238)*

Conclusions

Much of this chapter focused on the various approaches to researching comparative policy. To date, there have been few studies specifically examining comparative rural policy. Therefore, comparative rural policy research is well positioned to provide robust opportunities to further develop policy process theory. Both cross-national and within-country case study approaches provide opportunities to compare policies using one or more of the policy process frameworks provided in this chapter. But, as Tosun and Workman (2018) have argued: "Comparative research both widens and deepens our understanding of political processes. However, when we decide to compare we need to develop ideas about how to collect the appropriate evidence to test the empirical implications of the theoretical models" (2018, p. 354). All of these theories and frameworks have incorporated quantitative and qualitative approaches, but rarely both.

Note

1 Generally, a small-N study is considered less than 12, a medium-N between 12 and 20, and a large-N 20 or more cases.

References

Adolino, J.R., Blake, C.H., 2001. *Comparing public policies: Issues and choices in industrialized countries*, 2nd edition. CQ Press, Washington, DC.

Biesenbender, S., Héritier, A., 2014. *Mixed-methods designs in comparative public policy research: The dismantling of pension policies*, in: Engeli, I., Allison, C.R. (Eds.), *Comparative policy studies: Conceptual and methodological challenges*. Research Methods Series. Palgrave Macmillan, London, pp. 237–264. https://doi.org/10.1057/9781137314154_11.

Blomquist, W., 2007. *The policy process and large-N comparative studies*, in: Sabatier, P.A. (Ed.), *Theories of the policy process*, 2nd edition. Westview Press, Boulder, CO, pp. 261–289.

Bouckaert, G., Peters, B.G., 2002. *Performance measurement and management: The Achilles' heel in administrative modernization*. Public Performance and Management Review 25, 359–362.

Congleton, R.D., Swedenborg, B., 2006. *Democratic constitutional design and public policy*. The MIT Press, Boston, MA.

Coppedge, M., 1999. *Thickening thin concepts and theories: Combining large N and small N in comparative politics.* Comparative Politics 31, 465–476.

Dahl, R., 1961. *Who Governs?* Yale University Press.

Denscombe, M., 2008. *Communities of practice: A research paradigm for the mixed methods approach.* Journal of Mixed Methods Research 2, 270–283. https://dx.doi.org/10.1177/1558689808316807.

Dodds, A., 2013. *Comparative public policy.* Macmillan, New York.

Dresang, D., 1983. *Forward*, in: Paris, D.C., Reynolds, J.F. (Eds.), *The logic of policy inquiry.* Longman, New York, pp. 1–2.

Engeli, I., Allison, C.R., 2014. *Conceptual and methodological challenges in comparative public policy*, in: Engeli, I., Allison, C.R. (Eds.), *Comparative policy studies: Conceptual and methodological challenges.* Palgrave Macmillan, New York, pp. 1–13.

Frederickson, H.G., Smith, K.B., Larimer, C.W., Licari, M.J., 2011. *The public administration theory primer*, 2nd edition. Westview Press, Boulder, CO.

Gupta, K., 2012. *Comparative public policy: Using the comparative method to advance our understanding of the policy process.* Policy Studies Journal 40, 11–26. https://doi.org/10.1111/j.1541-0072.2012.00443.x.

Heidenheimer, A.J., Adams, C.T., Heclo, H., 1990. *Comparative public policy: The politics of social choice in America, Europe, and Japan*, 3rd edition. St. Martin's Press, New York; Macmillan Education, Houndmills.

Heijden, J. van der, 2014. *Selecting cases and inferential types in comparative public policy research*, in: Engeli, I., Allison, C.R. (Eds.), *Comparative policy studies: Conceptual and methodological challenges.* Palgrave Macmillan, New York, pp. 35–56.

Herweg, N., Zahariadis, N., Zohlnhöfer, R., 2018. *The multiple streams framework: Foundations, refinements, and empirical applications*, in: Weible, C.M., Sabatier, P.A. (Eds.), *Theories of the policy process*, 4th edition. Westview Press, Boulder, CO, pp. 17–54.

Jenkins-Smith, H.C., Nohrstedt, D., Weible, C.M., Ingold, K., 2018. *The advocacy coalition framework: An overview of the research program*, in: Weible, C.M., Sabatier, P.A. (Eds.), *Theories of the policy process*, 4th edition. Westview Press, Boulder, CO, pp. 135–172.

Jones, M.D., Shanahan, E., McBeth, M.K., 2014. *The science of stories: Applications of the narrative policy framework in public policy analysis.* Palgrave Macmillan, New York.

Jreisat, J.E., 2002. *Comparative public administration.* Westview Press, Boulder, CO.

Lindert, P.H., 2004. *Growing public.* Cambridge University Press, Cambridge. https://doi.org/10.1017/CBO9780511510717.

Lubell, M., Henry, A.D., McCoy, M., 2010. *Collaborative institutions in an ecology of games.* American Journal of Political Science 54, 287–300. https://doi.org/10.1111/j.1540-5907.2010.00431.x.

Marmor, T.R., Bridges, A., Hoffman, W., 1978. *Comparative politics and health policies: Notes on benefits, costs, limits*, in: Ashford, D.E. (Ed.), *Comparing public policies: New concepts and methods.* Sage, Beverly Hills, CA, pp. 59–80.

Montpetit, E., Rothmayr, C., Varone, F., 2005. *Institutional vulnerability to social constructions: Federalism, target populations, and policy designs for assisted reproductive technology in six democracies.* Comparative Political Studies 38, 119–142.

Ostrom, E., 2007. *Institutional rational choice: An assessment of the institutional analysis and development framework*, in: Sabatier, P.A. (Ed.), *Theories of the policy process*, 2nd edition. Westview Press, Boulder, CO, pp. 21–64.

Ostrom, E., 2015. *Governing the commons: The evolution of institutions for collective action.* Cambridge University Press, Cambridge.

Peters, B.G., 1988. *Comparing public bureaucracies: Problems of theory and method.* University of Alabama Press, Tuscaloosa, AL.

Peters, B.G., 2002. *The politics of tool choice*, in: Salamon, L.M. (Ed.), *The tools of government: A guide to new governance.* Oxford University Press, Oxford; New York, pp. 552–564.

Pierce, J.J., Siddiki, S., Jones, M.D., Schumacher, K., Pattison, A., Peterson, H., 2014. *Social construction and policy design: A review of past applications.* Policy Studies Journal 42, 1–29. https://doi.org/10.1111/psj.12040.

Robertson, D.B., Judd, D.R., 1989. *The development of American public policy: The structure of policy restraint.* Scott Foresman & Co., Glenview, IL.

Scharpf, F.W., 1997. *Games real actors play: Actor-centered institutionalism in policy research.* Westview Press, Boulder, CO.

Schlager, E., Cox, M., 2018. *The IAD framework and the SES framework: An introduction and assessment of the Ostrom workshop frameworks*, in: Weible, C.M., Sabatier, P.A. (Eds.), *Theories of the policy process*, 4th edition. Westview Press, Boulder, CO, pp. 214–252.

Schneider, A., Ingram, H., 1993. *Social construction of target populations: Implications for politics and policy.* American Political Science Review 87, 334–347. https://doi.org/10.2307/2939044.

Shanahan, E., Jones, M.D., McBeth, M.K., Lane, R.R., 2013. *An angel on the wind: How heroic policy narratives shape policy realities.* Policy Studies Journal 41, 453–483.

Shanahan, E.A., Jones, M.D., McBeth, M.K., Radaelli, C.M., 2018. *The narrative policy framework*, in: Weible, C.M., Sabatier, P.A. (Eds.), *The theories of the policy process*, 4th edition. Westview Press, Boulder, CO, pp. 173–213.

Sheridan, T.E., 2007. *Embattled ranchers, endangered species, and urban sprawl: The political ecology of the new American west.* Annual Review of Anthropology 36, 121–138. https://doi.org/10.1146/annurev.anthro.36.081406.094413.

Steel, B., Clinton, R., Lovrich, N., 2003. *Environmental politics and policy.* McGraw-Hill Humanities/Social Sciences/Languages, Boston, MA.

Stone, D., 2012. *Policy paradox: The art of political decision making*, 3rd edition. W.W. Norton & Company, New York.

Tosun, J., Workman, S., 2018. *Struggle and triumph in fusing policy process in comparative research*, in: Weible, C.M., Sabatier, P.A. (Eds.), *Theories of the policy process*, 4th edition. Westview Press, Boulder, CO, pp. 329–362.

Tsebelis, G., 2002. *Veto players.* Princeton University Press, Princeton, NJ.

Weible, C.M., Heikkila, T., Ingold, K., Fischer, M. (Eds.), 2016. *Policy debates on hydraulic fracturing: Comparing coalition politics in North America and Europe.* Palgrave Macmillan, New York.

Wiarda, H.J., Skelley, E.M., 2005. *Dilemmas of democracy in Latin America: Crises and opportunity.* Rowman & Littlefield, Lanham, MD.

Wilder, M., 2017. *Comparative public policy: Origins, themes, new directions.* Policy Studies Journal 45, S47–S66. https://doi.org/10.1111/psj.12200.

Wilensky, H.L., 1975. *The welfare state and equity.* University of California Press, Berkeley, CA.

Yin, R., 2012. *Applications of case study research*, 3rd edition. Sage, Thousand Oaks, CA.

Zahariadis, N., 2007. *The multiple streams framework: Structure, limitations, prospects*, in: Sabatier, P.A. (Ed.), *Theories of the policy process*, 2nd edition. Westview Press, Boulder, CO, pp. 65–92.

6

POLICY PROCESS THEORY FOR RURAL POLICY

Suman Pant, Casey Taylor, and Brent S. Steel

Introduction

Public policy has been defined by Anderson as "a purposive course of action followed by government in dealing with some problem or matter of concern" (1997, p. 330). Similarly, Dye defines it as "anything a government chooses to do or not to do" (1992, p. 2). While there are a variety of other definitions used by scholars, they all concern government activities in a wide range of areas including rural policy.

Academics have identified six stages of public policy process, which include (see Figure 6.1): (1) setting the policy agenda, which is basically getting government to consider taking action on some identified problem or issue; (2) formulating policy, which is the development of a course of action to deal with the identified problem; (3) policy adoption, the process of selecting and then authorizing a course of action; (4) policy implementation, applying the policy to solve the problem; (5) policy evaluation, an effort to evaluate if the policy is actually working or not; and (6) policy feedback to redesign, change, or continue the policy in question.

While it allows an organized way of thinking about policy process, there are two main flaws with this approach; first, it creates an image of "scientific rational" process where policy-makers set the agenda, explore all the possible options, weigh in the costs and benefits of each option, and make a rational decision based on their analysis. This assumption upholds the idea of a technocratic scientific method and does not incorporate the politics and interests that come into play. Second, it shifts the blame of failure away from the policy-makers and is often attributed to the inefficiency of implementation or lack of political will (Scoones *et al.*, 2006).

Policy theory research has shown that policy process is not linear, but complex and iterative (see Figure 6.2). Discourses and narratives often direct the agenda and its presentation, and also influence the analysis and decision-making. Discourse and narratives also affect the implementation stage since it involves a certain interpretation of the policy. The actors and networks are essential components of policy process, since they are a part of the policy-making process as well as the recipients of those policies. Their interests and politics will influence the agenda, the discourse, and decision-making process. Politics and interests are deeply intertwined with the policy-making process, and these interests will affect the process from setting of the agenda to its implementation (Keeley and Scoones, 2003).

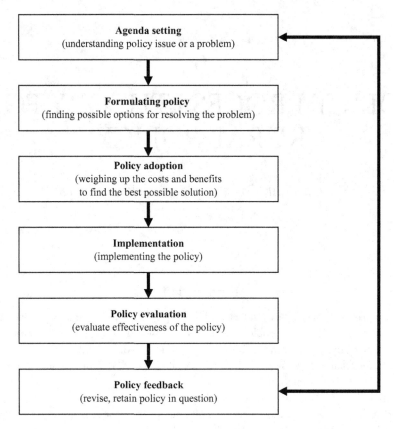

Figure 6.1 Linear model of policy process
Source: Author's illustration.

This chapter will provide a brief overview of the five most prevalent policy process theories used in the literature that could be incorporated into comparative rural policy research (Sabatier and Weible, 2014). The theories include the Institutional Analysis and Development framework, the Social Construction of the Target Population framework, the Advocacy Coalition Framework, the Multiple Streams Approach, and the Narrative Policy Framework.

Institutional Analysis and Development framework

In general terms, the Institutional Analysis and Development (IAD) framework is based on rational thinking and is consistent with game theory, which allows researchers to examine a wide range of empirical studies (Ostrom, 2011). Besides game theory, the IAD framework also provides compatibility with economic theory, theory of public goods, social choice theory, and common-pool resources theory. One of the distinct aspects of the IAD framework is that it helps policy-makers examine and analyze different governance systems that allow individuals to solve problems democratically. In short, its helps researchers and scholars determine how individuals come together and interact with each other and their resources, to produce a certain outcome in an institutional setup.

The IAD, pioneered by Elinor Ostrom and her colleagues, has been extensively used in understanding institutions for rural resource governance and management, collective action for

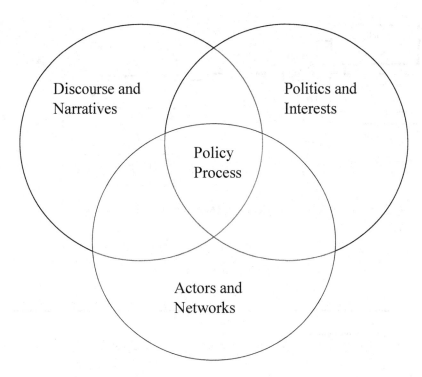

Figure 6.2 The three aspects of policy process
Source: Author's illustration.

common-pool resources, and others pertaining to rural policy issues (see Figure 6.3). Research-ers have applied the framework to examine irrigation governance and management (Shivakoti and Ostrom, 2002), understanding local collaboration in land use and forestation policies, and sustainable governance for natural resource management (Rudd, 2004; Fischer *et al.*, 2007), among others.

Action situations lie at the heart of the IAD framework, and in the realm of rural policy process, actors and interests would be the aspect that IAD focuses on most (see Figure 6.4). Action situations are spaces where actors interact, share (or fight over) resources, and cooperate (or compete) with each other. Although rational choice by itself assumes that these actors will try to maximize their utility, the IAD framework does allow analysts to take additional steps and understand the structure of action situations, which are based on the "bounded rationality" of the actors.

This is very significant for rural policy processes because a rural context provides a certain level of stability in the networks and relationships among actors, where the structure of the action situation is more prominent (as compared to more transient relationships among actors). Since it is assumed that there is cohesiveness and robust networks among actors, with similar values and social attributes, the IAD framework's position on action situations becomes highly relevant. If more people have similar ideas about potential outcomes (their cost–benefit analyses are similar), and there are not significant external variables, regardless of the position they are assigned to, or the power they have, the action situations have a higher potential to produce desired outcomes.

According to the IAD framework, the actors and their allowable actions are associated with the position they hold within the action space. This collectively is linked to potential outcomes,

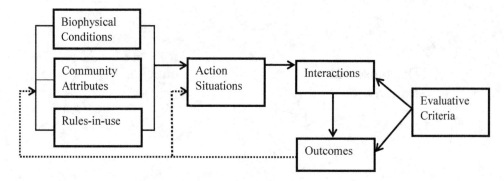

Figure 6.3 Institutional Analysis and Development (IAD) framework

Source: Ostrom (2005).

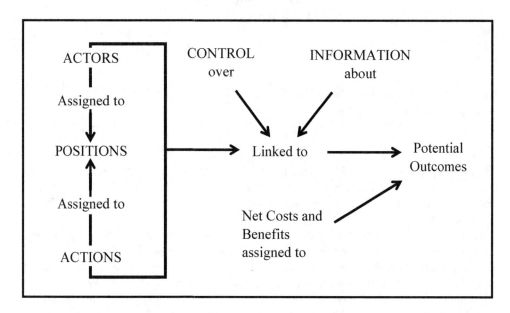

Figure 6.4 Internal components of action situation in IAD framework

Source: Ostrom (2005).

based on their control and information about probable outcomes. The costs or benefits that are assigned to actions and outcomes act as possible incentives or disincentives for the actors. One would assume that in a situation where strong networks, cohesiveness, and transparency are dominant, and where actors have information on potential outcomes, they would work together to increase their "benefits" in a collective manner. To perform certain actions, there has to be a set of formal and informal rules that the actors will use to make decisions.

The IAD framework's focus on the action situation especially in collective action relates significantly to the rural policy process, especially when the external variables are reduced or less significant. Also, due to the stable structure within a rural context, the IAD framework can provide more accurate analysis by understanding the contextual structure (biophysical properties, community attributes, and rules in use) that the action situation is dependent on. Additionally, the cohesiveness in social and behavioral attributes in the rural context allows researchers to understand institutional outcomes using the IAD framework. One of the biggest strengths of the IAD framework is its generalizability, and its ability to examine and evaluate different institutions. This generalizability also allows researchers to select and compare different institutions to understand policy outcomes.

The IAD framework has shown its robustness by proving its applicability on examining collective action (Gautam and Shivakoti, 2005). However, the IAD framework has its criticisms too. For example, Steins and Edwards (1999) highlight the shortcomings of the IAD's design principles, mainly arguing that the framework ignores the larger ecological context and wider political economy, while focusing on internal dynamics. The framework assumes that the outcome of collective action will feed back to the context (biophysical properties, rules in use, and community attributes), so that the learning from the outcome will help actors negotiate and collaborate to improve their institutional arrangement. In an isolated system, this would be true. However, in the real world, with various influencing forces (which are often larger than the institution of collective action), the feedback by itself can have lower significance. An understanding of discourse, politics, interests, and their influence in the local institutions is necessary, and without this knowledge, the IAD framework can be limited to assumptions provided by rational choice.

Social Construction of the Target Population framework

The Social Construction of Target Population framework (SCF) was designed to provide a better understanding of why policies fail to solve public problems or pave the way for equality in citizenship (Ingram *et al.*, 2007). To do so, the framework delves deeper into the social structure to differentiate inequality in power and resources among different groups and how these differences coupled with societal perceptions and stereotypes influence policy decisions. Instead of grouping all actors and their network as homogenous, it allows contestations in the policy process to reveal the winners and losers of policy change. In short, this theory attempts to answer a longstanding puzzle: "who gets what, when, and how?" (Lasswell and Kaplan, 1950).

According to Schneider and Ingram (1993) the target population is differentiated along two main characteristics: (1) their power in the society; and (2) the way society views them. Based on these two characteristics, the social construction framework differentiates the target population in four distinct groups: the advantaged, the contenders, the dependents, and the deviants. The foundation of this framework is built on Edelman's (1988) work on social constructions of knowledge and Arnold's (1990) idea that because public officials care about public reaction to policies and will develop strategies that include public spirit, the construction of target population becomes an important variable in policy-making.

The SCF argues that policy-makers will choose certain policies over others to benefit or burden the target groups, and to do so they will calculate the logical links between the target groups and the objective of the policy (see Figure 6.5). For example, increasing rural employment rates is a widely held public opinion, but it is up to the policy-makers about how to pursue it, and the options are wide and different. They could focus on providing subsidies and tax waivers to large corporations with the rationale that it would increase economic growth, or they could increase employment in the public sector by increasing public services with taxes imposed on the big corporations. Although the logical goal is the same, i.e. increasing rural employment rates, the beneficiaries are different because of different rationale.

Constructions

	Positive	Negative
Strong	**Advantaged:** The elderly Business Veterans Scientists	**Contenders:** Big unions The rich Minorities Cultural elites Moral majority
Weak	**Dependents:** Children Women Mothers Disabled	**Deviants:** Criminals Flag burners Gangs Drug addicts

Power (vertical axis label, Strong / Weak)

Figure 6.5 Social constructions and political power: types of target populations

Source: Schneider and Ingram (1993).

According to the SCF, the advantaged groups are generally the recipients of beneficial policies even in cases where choosing other groups would be more efficient. This is because the advantaged groups, who are powerful and have a positive construction, have considerable control over resources and capacity to get their issues in the forefront of policy agendas. While the benefits are oversubscribed to such groups, the burdens like force and sanctions are usually not imposed on them. The rationale for such oversubscribed benefits and undersubscribed burdens is often attributed to the groups' contribution to public purposes like economic competitiveness and national defense.

The contenders are the groups that have power and resources, but are often viewed negatively by the society. Due to their social construction combined with power, public officials prefer policies that provide these groups with benefits but at the same time hiding those benefits from the scrutiny of the public and the media. In cases where burdens are imposed on them, they usually have the ability to blunt the impact because of their power and resources. Since they are viewed negatively by society, the magnitude of the burden will be overstated, portrayed as a corrective measure for their excessive power.

Groups that do not have power but are viewed positively by the society are categorized as the dependents. Since they are viewed positively by the society, officials and policy-makers want to appear to be sympathetic to their interests but because these groups lack resources and power, it relieves the officials from directing resources towards the benefit of these groups. These groups do not have any control over the policy design, and the benefits they receive often involve some kind of labeling, or in some cases, stigmatization. Beneficial policies are under-subscribed to these groups and they will have to rely on agencies, since they are not considered self-reliant and are not given the support to devise their own solutions. Justice and equality are often emphasized as the rationale behind beneficial policies for these groups.

Deviants do not have legitimate power or resources, and are also viewed negatively by the society. Policies are often geared to inflict punishment and/or coercion on these groups since these groups have little to no power to create electoral retaliation by themselves, and the public approves of these punishments as they are constructed negatively. Even in cases where it is inefficient or illogical to do so, beneficial policies will always be undersubscribed and burdens will be oversubscribed to these groups. Little to no resources geared to rehabilitation programs for criminals and drug abusers are an example of how policies are designed in a specific way for this group. Even when programs are geared to support these groups (like rehabilitation programs), they are intended to change the individual behavior via authoritative means rather than fixing the structural problems. The rationale behind such policies is based on the idea that these groups deserve to be punished.

Although these groups are categorized in a specific quadrant, research has shown that these groups can also move from one quadrant to another. For example, homosexual men with AIDS, who were categorized as deviants in the 1980s, saw a shift to the contenders quadrant by the late 1990s (Donovan, 1997). Building on their previous work, Schneider and Ingram posited that a shift in categorization of the target groups is possible due to: (1) policies that can influence change in public perceptions of the target population; (2) external events that can provide opportunities; and (3) opportunities and skillful manipulation by the entrepreneurs (Schneider and Ingram, 2005). Although these propositions provide some answers, understanding the mechanisms that allow transition from one group to another still remains a key challenge for the framework (Sabatier, 2007a).

The social cohesiveness and stability of rural communities make SCF uniquely relevant for rural policy-making since the rural economy is highly localized and the resources it receives are limited. The powerful groups will often dictate appropriation and utilization of these resources and the discourse and narratives legitimize these decisions and influence the policy process. A broader understanding of the social construction framework in a rural context can help policy-makers and analysts determine "who gets what and when".

Advocacy Coalition Framework

The Advocacy Coalition Framework (ACF) is a framework for understanding "wicked" problems characterized by major goal and value conflicts. Fundamentally, the ACF focuses on the role of personal beliefs and the influence of those beliefs on political behavior. The key ACF concept is the idea of an "advocacy coalition", which is a group of like-minded political actors that share core beliefs and policy preferences. Within a given policy issue, there may be a small handful of competing advocacy coalitions working to achieve policy goals. In addition to a focused role for belief systems, ACF incorporates a variety of ideas from the social psychology literature to provide a more realistic model of individual behavior – one where individuals operate under limits of time and resources, and therefore must make use of heuristics and mental short-cuts in order to function in society. Early applications of the ACF skewed largely towards resource management and energy policies, the areas of expertise for the framework's developers, Paul Sabatier and Hank Jenkins-Smith.

At its core, the ACF has three "foundation stones" (Sabatier, 2007b): first, it assumes that most policy debates occur among specialists within a policy subsystem; second, it bases its hypotheses and conceptual models on developments in social psychology; third, it assumes that the best way to manage the variety of actors involved in a policy subsystem is for them to self-organize into a smaller number of "advocacy coalitions" connected by shared core beliefs and policy preferences.

The ACF focuses specifically on what Sabatier (2007b) refers to as mature policy subsystems, which involve a set of specialized policy participants who share expert knowledge and are involved in affecting the policy domain over an extended period of time (see Figure 6.6). Scientific and technical information are presumed to have an important role in these subsystems, and so researchers and experts are given a central role in the policy process in addition to advocacy organizations and politicians. Moving beyond the rational models offered in economics-based theories, ACF borrows heavily from the social psychology literature to understand individual behavior (Sabatier, 2007b). While an economically rational model assumes individuals make choices based on the pursuit of personal benefit, the ACF allows for choices based in an assessment of values and desired outcomes. The ACF assumes that the more central beliefs are to a person's identity, the more difficult they are to change. Normative, deep core beliefs are expected to be highly resistant to change, while more superficial policy preferences are likely to be more prone to persuasion.

Within a given policy subsystem, there may be dozens of actors and organizations vying to influence policy outcomes, each with their own resources, and strategies. The ACF suggests that the most effective means to achieve policy goals is to form advocacy coalitions with those who share similar values and preferences, and then share resources and strategies (Sabatier, 2007b). Since secondary beliefs are more flexible than core beliefs, they can be traded among coalition

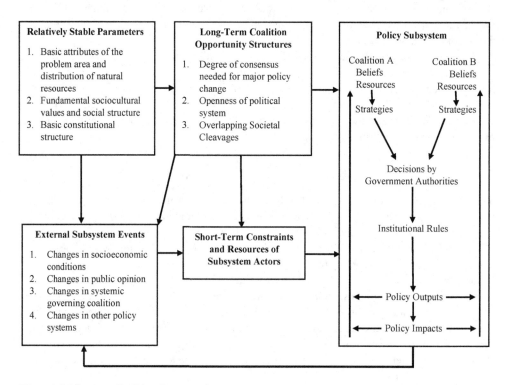

Figure 6.6 Advocacy Coalition Framework

Source: Sabatier and Jenkins-Smith (1993).

members to make progress on deeper shared preferences. Over time, these coalitions may shift in power and resources as the result of internal or external shocks, which provide opportunities for policy change.

Sabatier (2007b) argues that the three ACF foundation stones provide two paths for changing coalition beliefs and subsystem policies – external shocks and policy learning. External shocks can disrupt the subsystem enough to modify beliefs and policies include changes in socio-economic conditions, changes in government leadership, or some sort of social or natural disaster. Policy learning is a slower process where information and experience accumulate that may lead coalition members to reevaluate policy preferences and strategies.

The ACF, with its historical basis in natural resource policy and management, shares a common heritage with important issues in rural policy. Natural resource management continues to be the most frequently applied research area for ACF (see Sotirov and Memmler, 2012), but as the framework gained traction and went through several revisions, its application has expanded to other important policy areas, including public health, finance, social policy, and education (Jenkins-Smith *et al.*, 2018). Because of this, the ACF's proposed principles, typologies, and hypotheses are likely to be particularly useful in understanding the relationships between political actors and their behavior over time. Further, the locally bounded scope of many rural policy questions makes these ripe for analysis at the subsystem level, particularly when examined at the case level.

Reimer *et al.* (2016) utilize the ACF as a strategy for understanding the discourse of rural advocacy organizations in the United States, and how that discourse is used to achieve influence and desired policy outcomes at the federal level. The authors analyzed media reports, congressional testimony, and interviews with representatives of 118 rural advocacy organizations to create discourse networks organized around key words serving as network nodes. These networks allowed the authors to identify clusters of word communities that reflected discourse patterns. The authors found that communications centered on specific federal programs that dominated the rural advocacy discourse, highlighting the role that the federal government plays in rural communities. Similarly, agriculture took a disproportionately dominant place within these networks, operating as a connecting frame covering a wider pool of rural issues.

Reflecting on these results, Reimer *et al.* note that the results did not conform to their expected discourse networks centered on agriculture, rural development, environment, and food. Instead, their analysis shows the power of agricultural interests in dominating rural advocacy discussions, blending agricultural values into discussion of other concerns, including health care, economic development, and environmental management. The authors note that farming interests are better organized and demonstrate higher political capacity than more narrowly focused interests, reflecting successful efforts by the agricultural sector to equate rural issues with agriculture.

The ACF can be usefully applied to rural policy analysis because of several key overlapping features of the framework with the rural policy domain. First, the dominant focus of ACF is on the role of values in connecting individual actors and organizations involved in a policy debate. Second, the ACF was designed to operate within the context of stable policy subsystems over extended periods, usually at least ten years. Rural policy issues abound with examples of historically tightly woven policy subsystems, or "iron triangles", that highlight the interactions of key policy actors over time but which are now facing greater scrutiny and involvement from actors traditionally outside that triangle, such as environmental advocacy organizations.

Multiple Streams Approach

The Multiple Streams Approach (MSA), presented by Kingdon (1995), is a framework that provides a theoretical lens to explain how governments make policies under conditions of ambiguity (Blankenau, 2001; Smith and Larimer, 2009; Zahariadis, 2014). Kingdon (1995) argues that governments and organizations are in fact organized anarchies because of the ambiguity that is inherent in their structure. This ambiguity can be measured by three indicators: fluid participation due to high turnover, unclear and problematic preferences, and unclear technology.

The framework is inspired by organizational theory and can be applied to the entire policy formulation process, including agenda setting, decision-making, and implementation (Zahariadis, 1995, p. 66). The MSA is based on the idea of Cohen et al.'s (1972) "garbage can" model of organizational choice, which argues: "Collective choice is not merely the derivative of individual efforts aggregated in some fashion but rather the combined result of structural forces and cognitive and affective processes that are highly context dependent" (Zahariadis, 2014, p. 68). This is why the unit of analysis in the MSA is essentially the entire policy subsystem or a separate policy decision. The MSA framework assumes that governments are organized anarchies and three streams flow through the policy system:

a   *Problems Stream*: Several problems exist that need to be addressed. The significance and nature of these problems is determined by way of indicators, focusing events, and policy feedback.
b   *Policies/Solutions Stream*: A large number of ideas are floated around by policy specialists, but only the best ones are considered for implementation. The criteria for selection of ideas include technical feasibility, value acceptability, and resource adequacy.
c   *Politics Stream*: The third stream consists of political variables including interest group activity, national mood, and turnover in the government.

According to Kingdon (1995), a window of opportunity is opened whenever these streams join together. He defined this as a "policy window" as "opportunit[ies] for advocates of proposals to push their pet solutions, or to push attention to their special problems" (1995, p. 165). The individuals or corporate actors who make efforts to make possible the confluence of these streams are called "Policy entrepreneurs". While this framework seems to have some similarities with the rational choice model, Zahariadis (2014, p. 68) outlines the distinction between the two; the MSA complements the rationality by assuming that the "Individuals sometimes behave rationally, but the process of making systemic decisions often does not exhibit rational properties". He further explains that the MSA lens categorizes people in two groups: those who manipulate – i.e. the policy entrepreneurs – and those who get manipulated. Figure 6.7 provides an overview of how the MSA conceptualizes the policy process with examples of variables to potentially examine in all three policy streams.

While there have not been any applications of MSA to comparative rural policy, it has been used to compare more general policies that do indeed affect rural populations. For example, Blankenau (2001) has used the MSA to explain why Canada was able to successfully adopt national health insurance in 1960s while the United States' attempt to introduce the universal coverage in the form of Clinton's Health Security Act (HSA) failed.

In this research, Blankenau examined the three streams of MSA in context of the organizational structures in each country. The application of MSA to the case of adoption of national health insurance in Canada and the US highlights striking differences. For the sake of comparison, the

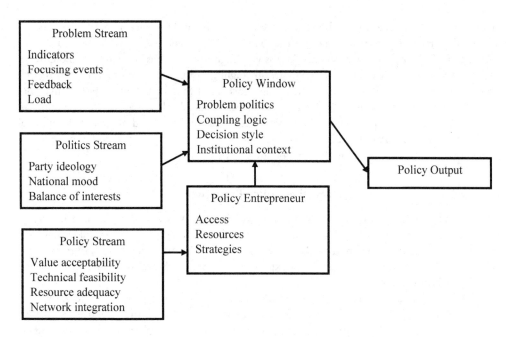

Figure 6.7 Multiple Stream Approach
Source: Zahariadis (2014).

author has used a simple scale for the variables in each of the three MSA streams. The scale categorizes the status of variable as strong: i.e. clear and strong evidence that this variable supports the opening of a window of opportunity; medium, i.e. some evidence that this variable supports, or at least does not inhibit, the opening of a window of opportunity; and weak, i.e. little to no evidence that this variable supports the opening of a window of opportunity.

In the problem stream, Blankenau finds the indicators in both countries to be medium, i.e. they support, or at least do not inhibit, the opening of a window of opportunity. Furthermore, the physicians' strike in Saskatchewan, Canada, and the Wofford Senate election victory in the United States were strong focusing events in the problem stream. The policy feedback in both countries was medium as there were both positive and negative opinions about the incumbent policies.

In the policy stream, Blankenau considered three variables that are of utmost importance in selection of a particular idea: technical feasibility, affordability, and value acceptability. In Canada, a how-to model already existed in the form of a national hospital insurance program and hence technical feasibility was already established. However, in the United States, the feasibility of President Clinton's health-care plan was not established and was being attacked from several ideological and economic perspectives. Similarly, the affordability as well as the value acceptance of the Canadian health-care system appeared to be supporting, or at least not inhibiting, the opening of a window of opportunity while in the United States increasing budget concerns and resistance to increased government intervention subjected the plan to attacks.

In the political stream, Blankenau considers variables like national mood, interest group activity, and turn over. In both countries, the national mood was supportive of the health insurance reforms. The interest group activity in Canada was medium as some interest groups were supporting the reforms while the others were opposing it. However, in the United States, there was strong opposition to the reforms with over 1000 interest groups involved in the matter. Similarly, policy entrepreneurship was very high in Canada as compared to the United States. While the analysis of three MSA streams highlight some major factors that led to the failure of the national health-care initiative in the United States, the author argues that the spillover in moving towards an acceptance of a stronger federal role as well as the separation of powers between legislative and executive branches also contributed to this failure. The application of the MSA in this case provides useful insights into the complex and unpredictable forces that are critical in shaping the rural policy process.

Narrative Policy Framework

The Narrative Policy Framework (NPF) emerged from the study of issue framing in policy studies, when its authors realized that the study of narratives could provide a useful framework for understanding the policy process (McBeth et al., 2014). The NPF recognizes that stories and narratives are fundamental to the human experience and thus a critical tool for understanding political behavior.

Although an objective reality may exist, individuals will perceive that reality differently, and apply different meanings and significance to its elements. Individuals then build narratives in order to make sense of it – narratives that then serve as a filter through which policy problems are understood and communicated. Thus, the way policy problems are understood is socially constructed (e.g. Ingram et al., 2007). The world is too large and too complex to take in completely, so individuals must use tools, such as narratives, to simplify it.

McBeth et al. (2014) identify four core components of a narrative: setting (policy system), characters (policy actors), plot (policy action, relationships between characters, and setting), and moral (policy preference). At the individual level, NPF research has largely focused on the impacts narratives have on policy preferences, especially when narratives are congruent or incongruent with a person's social and cultural identity (McBeth et al., 2014).

The NPF borrows the concept of advocacy coalitions from the Advocacy Coalition Framework, which may include allied interest groups, politicians, media outlets, and individual citizens that share a mutual policy preference (McBeth et al., 2014). Competing coalitions may tell similar stories but strategically assign character roles differently. For instance, in describing the plot of increased government regulation, one coalition might cast the government as the hero, acting to serve the public good by restricting the activities of villainous industry executives, while another coalition frames it oppositely – victimized industries suffering from villainous government interference.

The NPF proposes that competing coalitions will seek to change the scope or causal story described in the narrative in order to meet policy goals (McBeth et al., 2014). A winning coalition is likely to restrict the scope of a conflict in order to maintain the beneficial status quo, while the losing coalition is expected to seek an expansion of scope in order to build membership in their cause. Coalitions are also expected to choose causal stories strategically in their narratives. NPF analysis has found that narratives indicating intentional harm have short-term success in policy action and public influence, although such success is short-lived and is often replaced by narratives of inadvertent action (Shanahan et al., 2013a; 2013b).

There are few formal applications of NPF to comparative rural policy, although there are substantial opportunities to integrate the framework. Many of the existing applications focus on topics relevant to rural communities, particularly resource use and management. Crow and Berggren (2014) used case studies to assess stakeholder strategy selection in issues of energy regulation and water allocation policy in Colorado, and found that policy winners were more likely to assign blame and utilize more narrative components than policy losers. Heikkila *et al.* (2014), also using Colorado as a case study, sought to assess which policy factors and strategies were important in a policy change regarding fracking, and found that characterizations of heroes, villains, and victims varied across coalitions, although noted that some of these characterizations changed over time.

In an analysis reflecting the influx of new populations into rural western communities, Shanahan *et al.* (2011) compare the influence of competing media narratives on different audiences on the issue of snowmobile use in Yellowstone National Park. The authors identify a "New West" narrative that is anchored to environmentalist ideas and preferences for tightly regulated snowmobile use in the park and attributed to liberal urban residents and/or "newcomers" to rural western communities. This is compared to an "Old West" narrative anchored to motorized recreation group ideas and preferences for minimal regulation of snowmobile use and attributed to conservative longtime residents of rural western communities (Shanahan *et al.*, 2011). News articles with similar content but competing New West–Old West narratives were presented to groups of students in regional universities close to Yellowstone National Park, and students were given pre- and post-tests to assess the relative influence of those narratives among different groups. The authors found that after reading one of the assigned news pieces, student opinions were either strengthened or converted by the pieces, depending on how they aligned with their existing beliefs and perspectives, and argue that these "about face" changes in opinion reflect the power of narratives to influence public opinion, at least in the short term. These results are in contradiction of assumptions in the models of the ACF regarding the stability of policy beliefs over time and suggest that more research may be needed to understand the conditions of belief changes (Shanahan *et al.*, 2011).

The NPF promotes the study of the role of narratives and an understanding of their importance in the policy process, which certainly are likely to play a role in rural policy issues. In an assessment of the NPF, Weible and Schlager (2014) noted that prior to the NPF, studies of narrative in policy studies lacked a systematic structure. By introducing key variables to describe narrative characteristics, the NPF makes studies of narrative more easily comparable, which should allow for increased rigor in narrative research. The developers specifically designed the NPF so that the framework's components could be integrated with the Advocacy Coalition Framework, broadening the theoretical scope, while also expanding on some of ACF's concepts, such as devil shift. The NPF also provides a mechanism for understanding the strategies and behaviors of policy coalitions.

Conclusions

The given five policy frameworks have been extensively applied in both theoretical and empirical analysis for various policy domains. It is important to note that these frameworks have their strengths and weaknesses in understanding policies, societies, and the interaction between both (see Table 6.1). For example, while the Advocacy Coalition Framework focuses on how actors and networks influence the policy domain, the Social Construction of Target Population framework focuses on discourse and narratives about certain groups and how power and resources associated with them can influence policy processes. Depending on the research focus and their objective, scholars can utilize one or more of the above policy frameworks to understand policy process in the rural context.

Table 6.1 Strengths and weaknesses of policy theories

Framework	Relevance	Strengths	Weaknesses
Institutional Analysis and Development (IAD) framework	Helps understand and determine how individuals come together and interact with each other and their resources to produce a certain outcome in an institutional setup.	Generalizability. Ability to evaluate and compare institutions on a local level. Ability to determine outcomes if external forces are negligible.	Does not accommodate for larger forces (political, historical, market).
Social Construction of the Target Populations	Focuses on discourse and narratives. Allows policy analysts to determine "who gets what, when and how" by understanding their power and perception in society.	Reveals resource appropriation and legitimization of certain policies. Helps policy-makers frame narratives to appropriate resources for target groups.	Cannot accommodate for actors and their networks. Assumptions regarding political interests are based on the established discourse and narratives.
Advocacy Coalition Framework (ACF)	Helps understand role of personal values and beliefs and their influence on political behavior.	Offers detailed typologies and clear, testable hypotheses for policy subsystem components and attributes.	Subsystem and coalition focus limits capacity to predict individual action. Some areas of framework less developed than others.
Multiple Stream Approach (MSA)	Provides a historical and holistic understanding of policy subsystems through identification of policy windows and entrepreneurs.	Helps understand policy subsystem development ex post facto.	Not predictive and prone to selective causal factors.
Narrative Policy Framework (NPF)	Focuses on the role of policy discourse and narratives. Provides structure for analysis and comparison between studies.	Provides a systematic structure for analyzing and comparing policy narratives. Offers clear integration with Advocacy Coalition Framework to address wider policy questions.	Ambiguity in key concepts, leading to inconsistently applied terminology. Focus is narrow and limited to a single component of policy theory (narratives), but this can be addressed through Advocacy Coalition Framework integration.

References

Anderson, D., 1997. *A common wealth: Museums and learning in the United Kingdom. A report to the Department of National Heritage.* Department of National Heritage, London.

Arnold, R.D., 1990. *The logic of congressional action.* Yale University Press, New Haven, CT.

Blankenau, J., 2001. *The fate of national health insurance in Canada and the United States: A multiple streams explanation.* Policy Studies Journal 29, 38–55. https://doi.org/10.1111/j.1541-0072.2001.tb02073.x.

Cohen, M.D., March, J.G., Olsen, J.P., 1972. *A garbage can model of organizational choice.* Administrative Science Quarterly 17, 1–25. https://doi.org/10.2307/2392088.

Crow, D.A., Berggren, J., 2014. *Using the narrative policy framework to understand stakeholder strategy and effectiveness: A multi-case analysis,* in: Jones, M., Shanahan, E., McBeth, M.K. (Eds.), *The science of stories: Applications of the narrative policy framework in public policy analysis.* Palgrave Macmillan, New York, pp. 131–156.

Donovan, M.C., 1997. *The problem with making AIDS comfortable: Federal policy making and the rhetoric of innocence.* Journal of Homosexuality 32, 115–144. https://doi.org/10.1300/J082v32n03_05.

Dye, T.R., 1992. *Understanding public policy,* 7th edition. Prentice Hall, Englewood Cliffs, NJ.

Edelman, M., 1988. *Constructing the political spectacle.* University of Chicago Press, Chicago, IL.

Fischer, A., Petersen, L., Feldkoetter, C., Huppert, W., 2007. *Sustainable governance of natural resources and institutional change: An analytical framework.* Public Administration and Development 27, 123–137. http://dx.doi.org/10.1002/pad.442.

Gautam, A., Shivakoti, G., 2005. *Conditions for successful local collective action in forestry: Some evidence from the hills of Nepal.* Society and Natural Resources 18, 153–171. https://doi.org/10.1080/08941920590894534.

Heikkila, T., Pierce, J.J., Gallaher, S., Kagan, J., Crow, D.A., Weible, C.M., 2014. *Understanding a period of policy change: The case of hydraulic fracturing disclosure policy in Colorado.* Review of Policy Research 31, 65–87.

Ingram, H., Schneider, A.L., deLeon, P., 2007. *Social construction and policy design,* in: Sabatier, P.A. (Ed.), *Theories of the policy process,* 2nd edition. Westview Press, Boulder, CO, pp. 93–128.

Jenkins-Smith, H., Sabatier, P., 1993. *The study of public policy processes,* in: Sabatier, P., Jenkins-Smith, H. (Eds.), *Policy change and learning: An advocacy coalition approach.* Westview Press, Boulder, CO, 1–9.

Jenkins-Smith, H.C., Nohrstedt, D., Weible, C.M., Ingold, K., 2018. *The advocacy coalition framework: An overview of the research program,* in: Weible, C.M., Sabatier, P.A. (Eds.), *Theories of the policy process,* 4th edition. Westview Press, Boulder, CO, pp. 135–172.

Keeley, J., Scoones, I., 2003. *Understanding environmental policy processes: Cases from Africa.* Routledge, London; Sterling, VA.

Kingdon, J.W., 1995. *Agendas, alternatives, and public policies.* Longman, New York.

Lasswell, H.D., Kaplan, A., 1950. *Power and society: A framework for political inquiry.* Yale University Press, New Haven, CT.

McBeth, M.K., Jones, M.D., Shanahan, E., 2014. *The narrative policy framework and the practitioner: Communicating recycling policy,* in: Jones, M., Shanahan, E., Pierce, J.J. (Eds.), *The science of stories: Applications of the narrative policy framework in public policy analysis.* Palgrave Macmillan, New York, pp. 45–68.

Ostrom, E., 2005. *Understanding institutional diversity.* Princeton University Press, Princeton, NJ.

Ostrom, E., 2011. *Background on the institutional analysis and development framework.* Policy Studies Journal 39, 7–27. https://doi.org/10.1111/j.1541-0072.2010.00394.x.

Reimer, A., Han, Y., Goetz, S., Loveridge, S., Albrecht, D., 2016. *Word networks in US rural policy discourse.* Applied Economic Perspectives and Policy 38, 215–238. https://doi.org/10.1093/aepp/ppv051.

Rudd, M.A., 2004. *An institutional framework for designing and monitoring ecosystem-based fisheries management policy experiments.* Ecological Economics 48, 109–124. https://doi.org/10.1016/j.ecolecon.2003.10.002.

Sabatier, P.A., 2007a. *The need for better theories,* in: Sabatier, P.A. (Ed.), *Theories of the policy process,* 2nd edition. Westview Press, Boulder, CO, pp. 3–20.

Sabatier, P.A., 2007b. *Theories of the policy process,* 2nd edition. Westview Press, Boulder, CO.

Sabatier, P.A., Weible, C.M. (Eds.), 2014. *Theories of the policy process,* 3rd edition. Westview Press, Boulder, CO.

Schneider, A., Ingram, H., 1993. *Social construction of target populations: Implications for politics and policy.* American Political Science Review 87, 334–347.

Schneider, A.L., Ingram, H.M., 2005. *A response to Peter deLeon.* Public Administration Review 65, 638–640. https://doi.org/10.1111/j.1540-6210.2005.00492.x.

Scoones, I., Mehta, L., Leach, M., Waldman, L., 2006. *Understanding policy processes: A review of IDS research on the environment*. Brighton: Institute of Development Studies.

Shanahan, E.A., McBeth, M.K., Hathaway, P.L., 2011. *Narrative policy framework: The influence of media policy narratives on public opinion*. Politics and Policy 39, 373–400. https://doi.org/10.1111/j.1747-1346.2011.00295.x.

Shanahan, E., Adams, S.M., McBeth, M.K., 2013a. *Spin or strategy?: How story construction matters in the formation of public opinion*. Presented at the International Public Policy Conference, Grenoble, France.

Shanahan, E.A., Jones, M.K., McBeth, M.K., Lane, R.R., 2013b. *An angel on the wind: How heroic policy narratives shape policy realities*. Policy Studies Journal 41(3), 453–483.

Shivakoti, G., Ostrom, E., 2002. *Improving irrigation governance and management in Nepal*. ICS Press, Oakland, CA.

Smith, K.B., Larimer, C.W., 2009. *The public policy theory primer*. Westview Press, Boulder, CO.

Sotirov, M., Memmler, M., 2012. *The advocacy coalition framework in natural resource policy studies: Recent experiences and further prospects*. Forest Policy and Economics 16, 51–64.

Steins, N.A., Edwards, V.M., 1999. *Platforms for collective action in multiple-use common-pool resources*. Agriculture and Human Values 16, 241–255. https://doi.org/10.1023/A:1007591401621.

Weible, C.M., Schlager, E., 2014. *Narrative policy framework: Contributions, limitations, and recommendations*, in: Jones, M., Shanahan, E., Pierce, J.J. (Eds.), *The science of stories: Applications of the narrative policy framework in public policy analysis*. Palgrave Macmillan, New York, pp. 235–246.

Zahariadis, N., 1995. *Markets, states, and public policy*. University of Michigan Press, Ann Arbor, MI.

Zahariadis, N., 2014. *Ambiguity and multiple streams*, in: Sabatier, P.A., Weible, C.M. (Eds.), *Theories of the policy process*, 3rd edition. Westview Press, Boulder, CO, pp. 25–58.

7

POLICY OUTCOMES OF DECENTRALIZED PUBLIC PROGRAMS

Implications for rural policy

Judith I. Stallmann and Grichawat Lowatcharin

The structure of government varies among countries from a unitary government to various degrees of decentralized government and elected local officials. In a decentralized structure responsibility for rural policy may be concentrated at one level or dispersed among various levels, or policy may come from one level with implementation at other levels. A basic question that often arises in policy discussions is why countries or nations (used synonymously) choose to structure their governments differently. The obvious second question is how the structure of government affects outcomes of public policies and programs. This article uses a cross-national comparison to address the second question. Zimring (2006) argues that cross-national research allows insights not afforded by single-nation research by revealing both general patterns and exceptions.

The World Bank (2001) is a proponent of decentralizing government. It cites the work of Rondinelli, Nellis, and Cheema (1983) to argue that decentralization increases oversight at the local level, which will result in less corruption and, therefore, more effective delivery of government services. In addition, it is argued that centralized governments often have one-size-fits-all policies that do not fit the diversity of areas, both between and within urban and rural, leading to lower effectiveness. Further, it may be difficult for rural/remote people to access and have voice in a centralized government simply due to remoteness. Yet the research literature on the performance of centralized and decentralized systems of government is limited.

The conceptual framework draws on new institutionalism, decentralization, and fiscal federalism. This is followed by a descriptive comparison of three rural development programs with various degrees of decentralization: the EU LEADER program, the Canadian Community Futures Program, and US local economic development. The comparison suggests that some amount of oversight from a higher level may lead to better results. But this description suffers from the lack of comparisons with more centralized rural programs. The comparative findings are summarized. The final section provides further reflections on governance issues that can arise in a decentralized system. A text box summarizes recent comparative research on the outcomes of centralized and decentralized police systems. Even for a given policy, such as the structure of police systems, the outcomes of decentralization vary depending on the indicator chosen. Assuming that one structure is best to achieve all outcomes will result in policy failures.

Conceptual framework

This study draws on three theories – new institutionalism, decentralization, and fiscal federalism. North (1990, 1991) argues that institutions provide information that reduces individuals' uncertainties and risks and, as a result, shape individuals' behavior and performance. Degrees of centralization and decentralization of government result in different institutions that in turn result in different behaviors and performances.

Decentralization theory argues that decentralizing responsibilities to lower-level governments increases accountability, responsiveness, timeliness of decision-making, and enhances the relationship between government and citizens (Ahmad and Brosio, 2006; Pollitt, 2007; Smith, 1985). For the purposes of this study, in a decentralized government authority, responsibility, and resources for provision of some public services reside at one or more of the subordinate levels of government (Rondinelli *et al.*, 1983).

Fiscal federalism argues that decentralized provision of public services results in increased efficiency because local governments have more accurate information about citizens' preferences (Oates, 1972, 1977, 1999; Tiebout, 1956, 1961). On the other hand, if there are economies of scale and jurisdictional spillovers, decentralized provision may be less efficient. This suggests that decentralization is not a panacea and different levels of government might be appropriate depending on the characteristics of the public goods and services being provided.

Given the variety of government structures, Rondinelli, Nellis, and Cheema (1983) classified decentralization into forms – the objectives of decentralization – and types – the degree to which responsibility and discretion is transferred. The major forms of decentralization are political, administrative, and fiscal.

Political decentralization is the distribution of at least limited autonomy for some decision-making to other levels of government and/or to citizens (Cohen and Peterson, 1997; Rondinelli, 1990; Smith, 1985). Political decentralization is the basis for different levels of government. The transfer to citizens implies public participation and open election of governing bodies and, perhaps, implementation by non-government civil groups (Rondinelli, 1990; Smith, 1985).

Administrative decentralization is the distribution of managerial authority among levels of government, semi-autonomous agencies, or even to the private sector, via contracting. Administrative decentralization is expected to result in smaller and less hierarchical bureaucracies and more rapid decision-making. The efficiency of public services is expected to increase due to the smaller bureaucracy, increased responsiveness to citizens, and innovation based on the local context (Pollitt, 2007). Administrative decentralization is not synonymous with citizen participation as it refers to managerial authority only.

Fiscal decentralization can include (1) authority to self-finance through taxation; (2) co-financing or co-production arrangements with other levels of government; (3) intergovernmental transfers for general or specific purposes; or (4) authority to incur debt (World Bank, 2001). Fiscal decentralization often occurs with either political or administrative decentralization because decision authority over some revenues and expenditures is often needed for that authority to be exercised.

Beyond government decentralization is the additional issue of whether a particular policy is decentralized, which has efficiency and equity implications. Jurisdictional spillovers occur when the actions of one government create external costs, external benefits, common-pool resources, and/or public goods for other jurisdictions. Public finance and public economics argue that for efficiency policy should be assigned to the level of government that encompasses the full costs and benefits of the good or service that is provided (Stiglitz, 2000). However, the spillovers between jurisdictions will not always correspond to existing legally defined jurisdictions. In this case, local jurisdictions may collaborate on an issue, higher levels of government may set rules for what jurisdictions must take into account or may provide the good or service.

In addition to efficiency, an important role for government is equity or distribution. Tiebout (1956, 1961) shows that citizens may sort themselves among jurisdictions based on their preferences for the public goods and services and the tax price of those goods. Sorting into jurisdictions will lead to resource disparities among jurisdictions and over time could negatively affect the ability of some jurisdictions to provide basic public goods and services. At the same time, if a jurisdiction engages in redistribution, perhaps taxing some and reallocating to others, those who are being taxed may perceive that they are receiving no benefit and move to another jurisdiction, increasing resource disparities between jurisdictions. A higher level of government may (1) set minimum standards for the provision of goods and services (Tiebout, 1961) or (2) tax to provide additional resources to jurisdictions where resources are limited. Taxes imposed by a higher level of government require longer moves in order to avoid the tax, which likely are not feasible for most tax payers.

School districts in the US illustrate the issue of equity among decentralized jurisdictions. Primary and secondary education is provided at the local level in the US, and there are large disparities in tax bases and income among the thousands of school districts. All states set minimum standards for education but do not directly provide education services. Most states provide additional resources to jurisdictions with limited resources. The states address the issue of financing in several ways. (1) Some states require school districts to make a minimum effort to tax, an example of Tiebout's minimum standard, in order to receive additional state funding. (2) In several states, districts with more resources must provide revenue to districts with lower resources, rather than the state providing the funding. (3) One state fully finances education; the state collects taxes and distributes the revenues to the schools (Verstegen, 2014). (4) Districts have been reluctant to collaborate and some states have forced consolidation of school districts, mainly rural districts, a fourth way of addressing the resource issue. Lackey, Freshwater, and Rupasingha (2002) find that collaboration among jurisdictions is impeded when jurisdictions have different levels of resources.

The above issues raised by decentralization of education in the US are addressed differently in Canada. The provinces are in charge of education and set educational standards and the curriculum, and allocate the vast majority of the funding. Local school boards hire teachers and manage the budget and the schools.

Descriptive comparison of decentralized rural policy implementation

This section discusses programs to increase economic activity in rural areas. LEADER (Liaison Entre Actions de Développement de l'Économie Rurale) is a program in the European Union and the Community Futures Program is in Canada. Both are supranational or national programs to address local priorities and include public and private partnerships and multi-level governance with major control and implementation at the local level. Then the discussion will turn to local economic development in the US, which does not have such an overarching national program.

In the EU the main rural development program is LEADER. LEADER "promotes sustainable development in Europe's rural areas addressing economic, social and environmental concerns" (European Commission, 2006, p. 5). It uses multi-level governance and public–private partnerships to address rural issues at the local level, political decentralization. Financing is provided by a higher level of government but implementation is by local groups, which are not under the control of local governments. The local groups are a mixture of private business, civic organizations, and local agencies. Development Authorities provide professional assistance, particularly for financial management. Research finds that LEADER has achieved results in the Northern European countries that have a long history of participatory and local democracy, social discussion and consensual decision-making, volunteer work and trust between levels of state and local institutions (Nemes *et al.*, 2014). In these countries the local groups do not rely heavily on the Development Authorities, which have few employees. The program also has had success in the Mediterranean countries, without as long a history of participatory democracy. The authors point to the importance of the professional assistance provided by Development Authorities and their intermediary role between the local groups and higher levels of government. The program has been less successful in the post-socialist countries because the state lacks capacity to implement, insufficient resources at every level of government, and lack of trust at the local level towards higher levels of government (Nemes *et al.*, 2014). This suggests that path dependency affects the success of decentralized programs and that professional assistance can be an important component of success.

The Community Futures Program (CFP) of Canada is built on many local antecedents and also bears similarities to LEADER (Fuller *et al.*, 2010). Federal funding is provided but the implementation is based on local priorities (Réseau des SADC et CAE, 2015). Oversight has been transferred to six regional agencies, decentralizing administrative control. CFP is not a completely rural program as it is based on labor markets which include both rural and urban areas (Fuller *et al.*, 2010). Given the existing fiscal decentralization, municipalities levy property taxes, therefore, they have an incentive to increase economic activity to increase property values (Slack, 2003). Because CFP is locally driven, the range of activities makes complete reporting difficult. At the same time the flexibility to meet local needs has been found to be a strength of the program (Réseau des SADC et CAE, 2015). Statistics Canada provides performance reports of the CFP. "Businesses that have been supported by the CFDCs and CBDCs show a better economic performance when compared with businesses without CFP support" (Réseau des SADC et CAE, 2015, p. 10).

In the US there are no federal programs with a national reach that are both oriented to the development of rural areas and at the same time decentralized in approach. There was a limited federal program that offered incentives for firms to locate in federal enterprise zones in depressed areas (urban and rural). Communities competed for federal enterprise zones but the program for creating new zones ended in 2016. The federal government also provides some competitively awarded grants, such as for infrastructure development.

In the US local economic development is almost completely decentralized, with overarching rules and programs set by each of the 50 states. State oversight is mainly auditing. Local economic development is largely the option of local governments if they choose to exercise that power. Many people, civic organizations, and a variety of economic development organizations are active in local economic development and they most often turn to the local governments for financing. Local governments have the ability to tax and to set their own local policies. Thus, they may decide to use local revenues to provide a program or provide tax breaks for companies that wish to locate or expand in the jurisdiction. Many states also have limited economic development incentive programs and often work with local governments to create a package of incentives.

Examples of multi-community collaboration are rare, although the state can be thought of as a multi-community. Some states work to keep communities within the state from competing against each other. Federal funds cannot be used by states and local governments to provide incentives directly to firms, which tends to take the federal government out of any coordinating role among the states. As a result there is often competition among local governments and among states, leading to larger incentives to firms. Decentralization theory suggests that use of local tax funds would be subject to close citizen oversight and public finance theory suggests that decentralization should result in efficient use of public funds. Yet research shows that tax incentive programs do not lead to increased numbers of jobs and local incomes (Stallmann and Johnson, 2011).

Which raises the question of why tax incentives, which have existed in the US since the late 1950s, continue to exist when research shows they are not effective? Stallmann and Johnson (2011) argue that the continued use of tax incentives as a major economic development strategy is due both to lack of evaluation criteria in contracts and information asymmetries. Local governments may not have the sophistication to write contracts that require firm performance, monitor the contacts, and have sanctions that are enforceable. In addition there are important information asymmetries. Many rural communities are desperate for jobs and willing to attain them at nearly any cost. Firms negotiating with local governments have more information about their costs at various locations than do the local governments. As a result it is likely that local governments are providing incentives for firms to locate where they were planning to anyway (Stallmann and Johnson, 2011). The local government cannot know this and the location of a new firm seems to indicate that the program is successful. Deller (1998) points out that there is a survival bias in the evaluation literature. Because successful programs endure, they are more likely to be studied while the unsuccessful ones often do not last long enough to be studied.

Comparative summary

LEADER in the EU and CFP in Canada are examples of a decentralized administrative structure with funding from higher levels of government. The programs require coordination across levels of government, across economic sectors, and with nongovernmental civil groups in response to local priorities.

The success of LEADER varies by the historical circumstances of EU countries. In addition, for some countries the existence of professional assistance in Development Authorities appears to have been substituted for lack of a long history of participatory democracy (Nemes *et al.*, 2014). Successful outcomes in the former socialist countries are due to the lack of a democratic history and distrust of government.

The CFP in Canada is based on labor markets which may include urban areas. Canadian communities have a history of participatory democracy and trust in government. CFP also makes professional assistance available to local groups. Firms that participated in the program performed better than those that were not part of the program (Réseau des SADC et CAE, 2015).

Successes in the EU and Canada may be due to a higher level of government or administration setting an overarching framework for local action when it provides funding. The implementation is at the local level – objectives are set and actions taken to meet those objectives. The higher levels of government also set up a structure that requires cooperation between many sectors of the local community and provides professional assistance to the local groups. Such professional assistance may not otherwise be available in rural communities.

Local economic development in the US presents a contrasting highly decentralized case with no overarching framework from the national level, and often only a limited one from the state. There are a few federal programs, such as enterprise zones, but the number is small, the funding is limited, and communities must compete for the funding. Many rural communities do not have the resources and expertise to apply. There is no national program in the US similar to LEADER and CFP for comparison.

Each state provides a general policy framework and some funding but the majority of the funding and the implementation is at the local level. This provides wide authority for rural areas to implement policies and programs of their choosing. The majority of financing for local economic development is from local governments. The most common mechanism is providing tax incentives to firms on an ad hoc basis, with "packages" developed for the specific case. Without the overarching framework provided to LEADER and CFP, which encourages cooperation across many sectors in the community, there is competition for resources both within and between communities; one business may receive an advantage over others or incentives to the private sector may result in lower funding of public services for the general population.

Without an overarching structure adjoining communities (rural and rural or rural and urban) can pursue conflicting goals and/or compete against each other, particularly in the area of firm location. The lack of professional support, particularly for rural communities with limited or no professional staff, means that firms have more information than the community, which firms can use to their advantage. Firms often insist on secret negotiations, further limiting information that governments and citizens have and communities accede because they are desperate for jobs. This allows the firm to encourage competition among communities and overbidding on their part resulting in firms receiving tax incentives in excess of the net tax benefits they bring to the community. Lack of evaluation criteria in contracts means that public funds may be spent with limited impact.

Research shows that these incentives do not increase jobs and incomes, yet the programs have been in existence for 50 years or more. This is contrary to the predictions of both decentralization theory and public finance theory. Lack of expertise on the part of local officials in writing and monitoring contracts and information asymmetries that firms can exploit may explain why these programs continue to exist. In addition, as Deller (1998) points out, the successes survive while the failures disappear, creating biased perceptions of the results.

A shortcoming of the discussion of the programs in the EU, Canada, and the US, is that there is no good set of similar programs implemented in a centralized manner.

Box 7.1 Decentralization of police systems and outcomes

A recent cross-national study of 72 countries addressed the issue of the outcomes of centralized or decentralized provision of public services by focusing on a particular public service – general-purpose policing. This eliminates special- or limited-purpose police forces such as border police, park police, etc. The research created an index to control for the degree of decentralization of police services and used multivariate analysis to test for the association of decentralization with various outcome measures (Lowatcharin, 2016). The following discussion summarizes this study and does not continue to cite it in each instance.

The decentralization index integrates theories of new institutionalism and decentralization to measure varying degrees of police decentralization across countries. Based on the concept of political decentralization the number of tiers of government with some autonomy, power for policy- and decision-making within its realm of authority as granted to it from a higher level were counted. Based on the concept of administrative decentralization a government was defined as having administrative control over the police if it is: (1) responsible for the administration, supervision, and/or evaluation of the police; or (2) responsible for recruiting and/or appointing police executives and/or officers.

The decentralization index is a measure of vertical decentralization of general police services based on the number of tiers of government that have administrative control over the police divided by the total number of tiers of government. Because there is no country with more than five tiers of government, the highest possible code for each component is 5, the lowest 1. The index ranges from 0.25 to 1. A higher score is a more decentralized police system.

Two hypotheses were tested. A more decentralized police system was hypothesized to be positively associated with higher levels of citizen trust in the police. Second, a more decentralized police system was hypothesized to be inversely associated with homicide, robbery, and theft rates. The study estimated four random effects, multivariate models testing the association of decentralization with the outcomes of citizen trust in the police, homicide, robbery, and theft rates.

Of the four models in the study, only thefts demonstrated the expected relationship between decentralization and police performance – decentralization of police is associated with lower rates of theft. Contrary to expectations, higher homicide rates are associated with more decentralized governments. Decentralization is not significantly associated with the robbery rate, nor with citizen trust in police. The findings suggest that decentralization by itself (holding all else constant) generally is not associated with improved outcomes for this public service.

While the discussion of decentralization in this study is not explicitly rural, in decentralized countries a large percentage, and in many cases the majority, of governments at the lowest tier are rural and small. One control variable merits discussion. Holding decentralization constant, population density is positively associated with both higher robbery and theft rates, or alternatively that lower density (more rural) is associated with lower robbery and theft rates. However, lower population density (more rural) is associated with higher homicide rates. Population density is not associated with trust in the police.

Decentralization by itself is not sufficient. The significance of control variables, such as surrounding institutions, demographics, economic and geographic conditions and cultural norms demonstrate that the context of decentralization is also important. In addition, many policies have multiple objectives. Given that it is impossible to optimize several outcomes simultaneously, the differential findings of the association between decentralization and the outcomes are not surprising. Further research is needed to determine if these findings are specific to police services.

Further reflections on decentralization

The World Bank (2001) is a proponent of decentralizing government to increase oversight at the local level to reduce corruption and provide more effective delivery of government services (Rondinelli *et al.*, 1983). In addition, it is argued that centralized governments often have one-size-fits-all policies that do not fit the diversity of areas, both between and within urban and rural, leading to lower effectiveness. More decentralized systems provide a larger voice for rural areas as many of the units at the lowest layer of government will be rural.

Decentralization is not a panacea in the face of economies of scale, jurisdictional spillovers (Oates, 1972), information asymmetries (Stiglitz, 2000), and Tiebout-moves (1956, 1961) that increase inequality between jurisdictions. Yet the research literature on the performance of centralized and decentralized systems of government is limited.

A further concern is that the literature does not acknowledge the governance issues that can arise with decentralization. The discussion of the US provides some examples. With decentralization, horizontal relations between governments of equal power, local governments with no hierarchical relations among them, and thus no powers of oversight of the actions of each other, create the potential for competition between local governments or decentralized programs. Competition between governments, as with competition in the private market, can lead to lower prices, in terms of taxes and government fees, and innovations in new goods and processes.

On the other hand, decentralization and competition can cause policy failures because they can create jurisdictional spillovers. The most common types of jurisdictional spillovers are the same as those for which the private market is not efficient: negative externalities, positive externalities, public goods, common-pool resources, and information. Institutional economics and new institutionalism in both economics and political science are concerned with the design of incentives and institutions to address these cases in the market. Much less attention has been given to these issues when it comes to government performance. Examples of decentralized government failures due to common-pool resources and information asymmetries are discussed below

Common-pool resources are rivalrous but non-excludable. Non-excludable means it is cost-prohibitive to limit access to or use of the good. Because the good is rivalrous, if one acquires it, it is not available to another or its value in use by another is decreased. The combination provides an incentive for an economic actor to acquire or use as much of the rival good as possible before another actor can acquire or use it. Common examples include ocean fisheries, common grazing grounds, and use of water resources. Ostrom won a Nobel Prize in Economics for her work on common-pool resources and their governance (Ostrom *et al.*, 1999).

In the case of economic development, mobile tax bases are a common-pool resource for which decentralized jurisdictions often compete. In the case of the US and Canada (Slack, 2003; Brett and Pinkse, 2000), actions by local governments and local programs can increase the value of their property tax bases and more local government revenues. This may set up competition among jurisdictions to increase the tax base by offering preferential loans, quicker approval times, lower tax rates, etc. to firms, depending on the country. It is in the interest of the firm to encourage competition between jurisdictions and programs and not uncommon in the US for the firm to be offered more incentives than the increased tax revenues they will provide while little or no economic growth may be created (Peters and Fisher, 2004).

If jurisdictions can choose from a variety of taxes, they may choose those that are easier to impose on people from outside the jurisdiction, commonly called tax exporting. Examples in the US include the common "tourism taxes", basically a higher rate of sales tax on hotel rooms, tickets for sports events, rental car contracts, etc. because they are paid by people who do not live in the jurisdiction.

As another example, jurisdictions where consumers cross into the nearby jurisdiction to shop compete for the taxable sales. Jurisdictions could compete for taxable sales by lowering their tax rates (Walsh and Jones, 1988), but the elasticity may not provide enough increased sales to increase revenues. Alternatively, jurisdictions may attempt to increase total sales with incentives to attract retailers to their jurisdictions. But incentives to retail firms may cannibalize retail sales from other stores in the area, resulting in limited net gain (Ingraham *et al.*, 2005). Competition for local sales taxes led to sprawl in the St. Louis Metropolitan region (the region crosses the state lines of Missouri and Illinois) (The Brookings Institution, 2002). Governments within the region do not try to attract just new retailers to the region; instead they often offer incentives for retailers to move into their jurisdiction from another within the urban region. It is common to see abandoned retail space as the retailer moved just across the jurisdictional boundary, resulting in no net growth in the region.

Compounding the competition for a common-pool resource is the asymmetric information between the firm and the local government, noted in the case of the US above. Information may be difficult/costly for local governments to obtain for a variety of reasons. It is costly to do the research necessary to create new information, but it is also costly to search for information that already exists. For example, there is an extensive literature on the use of tax incentives, but local governments, and often state governments, do not have the personnel that can evaluate that literature. These problems are compounded where elected officials are volunteer, part-time, lack training in management and budgeting, or information technology. They may not know what information is needed; what questions to ask. The LEADER and CFP programs provide technical assistance that may alleviate this problem.

Citizens and businesses may use this information asymmetry (Stiglitz, 2000) to their benefit at the expense of the other citizens and businesses in the jurisdiction. An example is the use of tax incentives to attract or retain a business whereas other businesses do not receive the same benefit. The research shows that the majority of the promised jobs does not materialize (Peters and Fisher, 2004) and suggests that it may be firms that are only marginally feasible that receive the incentives (Gabe and Kraybill, 2002). An additional concern is that by concealing information firms are able to receive incentives for an action they would have taken anyway. In which case, the net effect for the jurisdiction is negative.

Costs of information might explain why jurisdictions follow what neighboring jurisdictions do (referred in the literature as strategic interactions). If one jurisdiction implements a new policy or program, other jurisdictions may assume that it has information that they do not have (asymmetric information between jurisdictions). To avoid that jurisdiction using the information to its advantage at their expense, other jurisdictions may simply copy the policy or program without seeking other information, such as asking why the other jurisdiction implemented the policy or program, waiting to see the results or analyzing how it fits the jurisdiction (Case *et al.*, 1993; Brueckner, 1998). In addition, local governments may feel they must offer incentives to be competitive.

Decentralization has the two-sided issue of how to encourage the competition among decentralized local governments that lowers costs and increases innovation and how to manage competition that leads to inefficient outcomes due to jurisdictional spillovers and resource imbalances between jurisdictions. This suggests that governance systems between jurisdictions are needed. Yet most decentralized programs or government structures do not make provisions for such structures. Some may develop organically, such as the regional associations of municipalities in Quebec, but often they do not. CFP addresses the issue by being based on a labor market rather than a single community.

Decentralization is promoted as a means for more local voice and control of policy and implementation. Decentralization is expected to allow rural areas to design and implement policies and programs that fit local objectives. The case of the US suggests that a high degree of decentralization is not a guarantee of successful policy outcomes. Lack of professional capacity, information asymmetries, lack of performance criteria in contracts, and perception bias (because only the successful projects survive) may lead to persistence of programs that do not provide public benefit. The LEADER and CFP suggest that an overarching framework may be an important element for the successful decentralized implementation of rural programs. Evaluation of LEADER suggests path dependency but that professional assistance to communities lacking implementation capacity or historical experience in citizen participation may ameliorate some of the lack of history and capacity.

References

Ahmad, E., Brosio, G., 2006. *Handbook of fiscal federalism.* Edward Elgar, Cheltenham.
Brett, C., Pinkse, J., 2000. *The determinants of municipal tax rates in British Columbia.* Canadian Journal of Economics 33, 695–714.

Brookings Institution, 2002. *Growth in the heartland: Challenges and opportunities for Missouri.*

Brueckner, J., 1998. *Testing for strategic interaction among local governments: The case of growth controls.* Journal of Urban Economics 44, 438–467.

Case, A.C., Rosen, H.S., Hines, J.R., 1993. *Budget spillovers and fiscal policy interdependence: Evidence from the states.* Journal of Public Economics 52, 285–307. https://doi.org/10.1016/0047-2727(93)90036-S.

Cohen, J.M., Peterson, S.B., 1997. *Administrative decentralization: a new framework for improved governance, accountability, and performance.* Harvard Institute for International Development, Harvard University, Cambridge, MA.

Deller, S.C., 1998. *Local government structure, devolution, and privatization.* Review of Agricultural Economics 20, 135–154.

European Commission, 2006. *The LEADER approach: A basic guide.* European Communities, Brussels.

Fuller, A.M., Larsson, L., Pletsch, C., 2010. *Insights from comparing the Community Futures Program in Ontario with LEADER in Sweden.* Industry Canada/FedNor, Sudbury, Ont.

Gabe, T.M., Kraybill, D.S., 2002. *The effect of state economic development incentives on employment growth of establishments.* Journal of Regional Science 42, 703–730. https://doi.org/10.1111/1467-9787.00278.

Ingraham, A.T., Singer, H.J., Thibodeau, T.G., 2005. *Inter-city competition for retail trade: Can tax increment financing generate incremental tax receipts?* (SSRN Scholarly Paper No. ID 766925). Social Science Research Network, Rochester, NY.

Lackey, S.B., Freshwater, D., Rupasingha, A., 2002. *Factors influencing local government cooperation in rural areas: Evidence from the Tennessee Valley.* Economic Development Quarterly 16, 138–154.

Lowatcharin, G., 2016. *Centralized and decentralized police systems: A cross-national mixed-methods study of the effects of policing structures with lessons for Thailand* (PhD Dissertation). Truman School of Public Affairs, University of Missouri, Columbia, MO.

Nemes, G., High, C., Augustyn, A., 2014. *Beyond the new rural paradigm: Project state and reflexive agency,* in: Copus, A.K., De Lima, P. (Eds.), *Territorial cohesion in rural Europe: The relational turn in rural development.* Routledge, Abingdon, pp. 212–235.

North, D.C., 1990. *Institutions, institutional change, and economic performance.* Cambridge University Press, New York.

North, D.C., 1991. *Institutions.* Journal of Economic Perspectives 5, 97–112. https://doi.org/10.1257/jep.5.1.97.

Oates, W.E., 1972. *Fiscal federalism.* Harcourt Brace Jovanovich, New York.

Oates, W.E., International Institute of Management, International Seminar in Public Economics (Eds.), 1977. *The political economy of fiscal federalism.* Lexington Books, Lexington, MA.

Oates, W., 1999. *An essay on fiscal federalism.* Journal of Economic Literature 37, 1120–1149.

Ostrom, E., Burger, J., Field, C.B., Norgaard, R.B., Policansky, D., 1999. *Revisiting the commons: Local lessons, global challenges.* Science 284, 278–282. https://doi.org/10.1126/science.284.5412.278.

Peters, A., Fisher, P., 2004. *The failures of economic development incentives.* Journal of the American Planning Association 70, 27–37. https://doi.org/10.1080/01944360408976336.

Pollitt, C., 2007. *Decentralization: A central concept in contemporary public management,* in: Ferlie, E., Jr, L.E.L., Pollitt, C. (Eds.), *The Oxford handbook of public management.* Oxford University Press, Oxford; New York, pp. 371–397.

Réseau des SADC et CAE, 2015. *The CFDCs and CBDCs: A winning approach for community futures.* The Canadian CED Network.

Rondinelli, D., 1990. *Decentralizing urban development programs: A framework for analyzing policy.* Office of Housing and Urban Programs of the US Agency for International Development, Washington, DC.

Rondinelli, D., Nellis, J., Cheema, G., 1983. *Decentralization in developing countries: A review of recent experience.* No. SWP581. The World Bank.

Slack, E., 2003. *Property taxation in Canada.* World Bank.

Smith, B.C., 1985. *Decentralization: The territorial dimension of the state.* George Allen & Unwin, London. http://dx.doi.org/10.1017/S0008423900054238.

Stallmann, J., Johnson, T.G., 2011. *Economic development incentive programs: Some best practices.* No. Report 13–2011. Institute of Public Policy, Harry S. Truman School of Public Affairs, Columbia, MO.

Stiglitz, J.E., 2000. *Economics of the public sector,* third edition. W.W. Norton & Company, New York.

Tiebout, C.M., 1956. *A pure theory of local expenditures.* Journal of Political Economy 64, 416–424.

Tiebout, C.M., 1961. *An economic theory of fiscal decentralization,* in: *Public finances: Needs, sources, and utilization.* Princeton University Press, Princeton, NJ, pp. 79–96.

Verstegen, D., 2014. *How do states pay for schools? An update of a 50-state survey of finance policies and programs.* Association for Education Finance and Policy Annual Conference, San Antonio, TX.

Walsh, M.J., Jones, J.D., 1988. *More Evidence on the "border tax" effect: The case of West Virginia, 1979–84.* National Tax Journal 41, 261–265.

World Bank, 2001. *Decentralization topics.* www1.worldbank.org/publicsector/decentralization/what.htm (accessed 2.27.19).

Zimring, F.E., 2006. *The necessity and value of transnational comparative study: Some preaching from a recent convert.* Criminology and Public Policy 5, 615–622. https://doi.org/10.1111/j.1745-9133.2006.00407.x.

8

CO-CONSTRUCTING RURAL FUTURES

Understanding place-based development and policy

Sean Markey, Greg Halseth, and Laura Ryser

Introduction

Since the early 1980s, rural and small-town places across all OECD states have been challenged by change. Principal among these changes have been those associated with economic restructuring as many places struggle with the transition from natural-resource- or single-industry-dependent economies into more diversified and sustainable economies. The challenge of adjusting to significant globally driven economic change has been exacerbated by a companion shift in public policy approaches to rural and small-town support and renewal. This policy shift, from a Keynesian public policy framework to a neoliberal public policy framework, has witnessed state withdrawal and disinvestment at precisely the time when these rural and small-town places require new tools and new investments.

With a rural focus, this chapter outlines and describes the concept of place-based development and place-based policy as it relates to the critical need for supporting more sustainable economies and resilient communities. It first outlines the macro policy transition from a Keynesian to neoliberal public policy framework. This includes a thumbnail description of the general implications of this policy shift for rural and small-town places since the end of World War II. The chapter then defines both place-based development and place-based policy, including the advantages and disadvantages associated with this approach. The chapter closes with observations about implementing place-based policy and development.

Macro policy transition and rural places

At the close of World War II, states looked desperately for policy tools or a policy framework that could smooth out the dramatic economic swings from boom to depression that had fueled great suffering and much of the unrest leading into the war. As an economic theory, Keynesianism sought to deploy state interventions in the market to help smooth excesses and level an economy's most dramatic fluctuations (Harvey, 2005). As described by Halseth and Ryser (2018), the adoption of a Keynesian public policy framework coincided with state needs to put demobilized soldiers to work in a productive economy and to modernize critical national infrastructure that had been left to languish through 15 years of depression and war.

The investment aspect of Keynesian public policy helped to support and direct the long boom that took shape in the postwar years. As massive wartime industrial capacity was turned to the peacetime production of consumer goods, public policy investments helped to boost both production and consumption. On the consumption side, investments in infrastructure such as national highway and transportation systems hoped to spur and support suburbanization – itself a generator of massive consumer demand for household goods, appliances, and services. National pension, employment insurance, health care, and other programs across OECD states supported people, while investments in state service provision supported communities no matter their geography (Halseth and Ryser, 2006).

On the production side, the massive expansion in productive capacity witnessed during the war needed to be accompanied by a massive increase in the supply of natural resources and energy inputs. State investments were needed to develop existing natural resource supplies or to access more remote regions so as to develop new resource supplies. In Sweden, Norway, Finland, Canada, the United States, Australia, New Zealand, and elsewhere, massive state investments provided access to potential resource development regions along what at the time were seen as natural resource "frontiers" (Halseth, 2017). State investments including transportation, services, infrastructure such as schools and hospitals, together with a range of public policies helped to support global-scale industrial resource development.

An unfortunate long-term consequence of these investments is that they acted to cement single-industry dependence into many rural and small-town places – a dependence that has been difficult to shake. Most such investments were directed at overcoming the costs of distance in getting a resource commodity to market. Additional investments were aimed at supporting the workforces and businesses that could mobilize those resources. Public policy during this era was of the "one-size-fits-all" type that did not differentiate by place.

The long postwar economic boom encountered challenges beginning in the 1970s. State experiments with significant deficit budgets and the growth of debt were straining national economies. These challenges were brought to a head with the global economic recession of the early 1980s. In a counterpoint to the state-focused Keynesian public policy framework, an alternative market-focused framework was described and soon gained widespread application. This neoliberal public policy framework argued "that the social good will be maximized by maximizing the reach and frequency of market transactions, and it seeks to bring all human action into the domain of the market" (Harvey, 2005, p. 3). As noted by Tennberg *et al.* (2014, p. 42), "the role of the neoliberal state is [therefore] to secure proper conditions for markets to function".

The adoption of a neoliberal public policy framework and its belief in market mechanisms for economic and social benefit had a number of wide-ranging implications for rural and small-town places. One of the first, and most critical, was the transformation from an "investment" mindset to an "expense" mindset for government expenditures. In the previous era, the state made significant investments in services and infrastructure with an expectation that the economic and social paybacks would take place over decades, if not generations. Under a neoliberal policy framework, efforts to battle deficits and debt meant that new funding was increasingly viewed as an expense that needed to be paid off in a certain and short-term period. A second has been the application of market-based, especially urban-modeled market-based, metrics for the evaluation of service efficiencies. For rural and small-town places, with their smaller population numbers and larger distances between settlements, both of these implications have been significant. Needed investments in critical infrastructure have not been forthcoming because the payback period does not align with electoral cycles and services have been increasingly closed or regionalized in the name of efficiency (Sullivan *et al.*, 2014). As noted, when confronted with a need to transform communities and economies, rural and small-town places have been hindered by state withdrawal and disinvestment at precisely the time when they require new tools and investments.

Place-based development

Against this backdrop of decline in rural investment, and the recent dominance of a market-oriented approach to public policy, a renovated approach to rural development and policy has emerged. This new, place-based approach is both driven in a reactionary manner by the restructuring impacts associated with the market fundamentalism of neoliberalism, while also seeking to institute new values and different, more resilient approaches to rural development and supportive rural policy frameworks. This turn towards a more contextualized understanding of community development is grounded conceptually and theoretically in Massey's observation that "'General processes' never work themselves out in pure form. There are always specific circumstances, a particular history, a particular place or location. What is at issue is the articulation of the general *and* the local" (Massey and Allen, 1984, p. 9, emphasis in original). Recognition that the matrix of place, with its combinations of assets, populations, histories, and circumstances, influences how global economic and social forces act upon small communities underscores the need for place-based approaches and policies.

Definitions of place and place-based development span a range of core focus areas, including economic dynamics, functional governance, the role of identity in fostering a commitment to place from rural residents, among others (Bollman, 2007; Bradford, 2004; OECD, 2006; Paasi, 2013; Markey *et al.*, 2008). Markey *et al.* (2015) define place-based development as a holistic and targeted intervention that seeks to leverage the natural, physical, cultural, or human capacity endowments of a particular location. As this definition implies, a place-centric approach to rural development seeks to integrate and leverage a greater variety of local assets for the purpose of rural development, and to fundamentally shift the orientation concerning the purpose of development, i.e. that the rural locality or region itself is very much a (if not *the*) beneficiary of the development process. Both of these changes, therefore, also require a departure from traditional policy approaches which tend to view rural regions in simplistic terms, as resource banks for the extraction of natural resources, as lagging areas requiring assistance, or more cynically, as declining areas left behind by the trajectories and forces of urbanism (Markey *et al.*, 2012).

From space to place

Both periods of postwar Keynesian investment and post-1980s neoliberalism outlined above rely upon space-based policy to manage rural areas. In the former, rural policy was driven by issues of distance, the creation or improvement of transportation networks to access resources and populate national space, and the challenges of service delivery across that space. In the latter, neoliberal policy has sought (and seeks) to facilitate market access to rural regions. As Halseth *et al.* (2010, p. 4) articulate, however:

> Both space and place approaches are useful for analysis and policy-making. A space-based approach provides useful insights for identifying the general patterns of community change and separating the relative contribution of economic, social, and political factors to those changes. A place-based approach on the other hand, helps us

see and understand the local responses to those changes – emphasizing how the historically specific conjuncture of key factors and the particular perceptions and identities of local people and groups create new conditions that can significantly modify the general trends they share. Place-based approaches highlight local conditions, the roles of local actors, and agency – of individuals and groups.

A key point of differentiation, however, concerns the process of both policy formulation and implementation. In the space-based approach of both Keynesianism and neoliberalism, policies are implemented in a top-down manner, relying upon centralized experts and macro interpretation of standards and metrics. Neoliberalism takes this even further with the relative abandonment of state oversight and management, yielding instead to a deregulated policy environment and market-based mechanisms (Young, 2008). This contrasts quite fundamentally with a *co-constructed* approach to policy and development in which rural regions themselves seek to influence and direct policy and development processes, (Bryant, 2010; Markey *et al.*, 2015; Mayes, 2014). A co-constructed policy model demands both top-down intervention, investment, and, crucially, bottom-up participation, and shared direction and responsibility for policy development and the subsequent implementation (i.e. how and where policy actually hits the ground). Concerning the interface between communities and regions and senior governments, place-based development is not possible outside of a co-constructed approach (unless as an outcome of oppositional advocacy).

Place-based policy orientation

A co-constructed approach to rural policy in pursuit of place-based development requires a shift in policy orientation. Most importantly, policy may be seen as a facilitative mechanism of local initiative, a convener of territorial interests, and a flexible arbiter of investment and policy standards, allowing for local differentiation. The rural place-based literature provides a variety of concepts and practices for how to frame a place-based policy approach, including discussion surrounding the shift from sectoral to territorial development, the need to shift from a comparative to a competitive stance within the new rural economy, and the need to build rural governance capacity. These represent strategic conceptual foundations for pursuing a place-based policy agenda for rural development.

Territorial development

The ascendancy of territorial development over sectoral development (which conflates rural development policy with isolated programs and policies aimed at different industrial sectors or service areas) is inherent within the place-based approach and offers a variety of benefits for addressing impacts associated with rural restructuring (Barca *et al.*, 2012; Pezzini, 2001; O'Brien *et al.*, 2017; OECD, 2006; Zasada *et al.*, 2015). Territorial development seeks an integrated approach to rural development policy and offers a number of advantages. First, the model can allow for the integration of economic, environmental, social, and cultural dynamics in planning at more manageable scales. Second, a territorial approach recognizes the importance of contextual specificity to the process of development, and how sector-based policy approaches can create inconsistencies and unintended barriers, and even work at cross-purposes to rural development. Third, a sense of territoriality facilitates consideration of local and regional assets – which is also referred to as "territorial capital" in Chapter 9 of this volume. For example, within a resource region, territorial planning may allow regional decision-makers and planners to view primary resources as integral assets of the regional economy rather than as isolated sector-based activities. Political and economic restructuring may have reduced or removed industry–town linkages (economic and social), but territorial planning can provide a foundation for re-linking and re-imagining resource activity in an integrated way for surrounding communities. Finally, a territorial approach to policy-making may help to overcome traditional siloed patterns of senior government operation. A place-based policy orientation challenges the traditional institutional structures of senior governments. Sectoral divisions of responsibility within different siloed ministries and other entities of government keep policy-makers separated from one another as intersectoral issues arise (Jonas, 2012).

From comparative to competitive advantage

The increasing mobility of both capital and labor should cause all policy-makers and local decision-makers to reconcile the question: "if capital and labor can locate 'anywhere', why would it/they locate 'here'?" The answer to this question lies in the characteristics of places in terms of regulations, connectivity to the world economy, available labor supply, supportive industries and skills, quality-of-life services and amenities, natural environment, safety, political stability, and a host of other inputs to production and reproduction systems. In other words, this partial list of place-based variables shows that space is becoming less important in the global economy, while place is becoming more important, perhaps no more so than for rural places that clearly need to state their case in a rapidly urbanizing, mobile world (Porter *et al.*, 2004).

In development terms, it is possible to speak of rural policy needing to shift from seeking to facilitate comparative advantage to competitive advantage in rural places. Comparative advantage follows the principle whereby territories "produce those goods or services for which they have the greatest cost or efficiency advantage over others, or for which they have the least disadvantage" (Gregory *et al.*, 2009, p. 105). When combined with a space-based policy and planning approach, the mobilization of comparative advantage helps to explain the patterns of regional specialization (i.e. mining, forestry, fishing, etc.) found within many peripheral and resource-dependent regions of developed states (Gunton, 2003). By comparison, competitive advantage is a more complex and nuanced concept. Linking better to a place-based policy and planning approach, it is dependent on the assets and decisions (to capitalize on those assets) of particular places in order to attract and retain both capital and labor (Kitson *et al.*, 2004). One of the challenges is a more nuanced approach that demands much more of places and policy-makers. Consideration must now be given to a wider variety of both quantitative (i.e. physical infrastructure, production, location, etc.) and qualitative (i.e. social capital, innovation, institutions) variables in development planning (Porter *et al.*, 2004; Bristow, 2010; Florida *et al.*, 2010).

Governance and co-construction capacity

Another key feature of the place-based policy process concerns efforts to build local and regional capacity to effectively engage in co-constructed policy processes and implement the development decisions that follow. The past 30 years of rural restructuring has weakened place-based governance foundations for policy and planning. When you consider that this most recent neoliberal phase was preceded by 30 years of heavy-handed top-down planning, the task of building robust place-based governance and implementation capacity is considerable (Aarsæther and Bærenholdt, 2001; Reddel, 2002).

Despite complexity within the literature on place-based development, one area of convergence regarding the efficacy of the place-based approach concerns the need to build the capacity of local actors and organizations to manage and implement co-construction objectives (Douglas, 2005; Reimer, 2010). A place-based governance approach that engages the cooperation of many local and regional stakeholders can generate quick decision-making and mobilization of resources that was not always possible under previous top-down regimes. Such attention to "place" reveals a greater variety of assets and fosters an awareness that those assets are local and may be used for local purposes (Markey *et al.*, 2012). In this context, new governance arrangements seeking to understand collective capacities as roles and responsibilities for community development are redefined and redistributed. The transformation of governance as regions experiment with different institutional structures and relationships in an attempt to compensate for government withdrawal may lead to innovations that establish better local participation, competitive advantage, and economies of scale (Shucksmith, 2010; Uyarra, 2010). The effectiveness of these new arrangements, however, can be impacted by varied participation, unequal power relationships, and conflict across stakeholders (Peterson *et al.*, 2010; Zirul *et al.*, 2015). Other capacity barriers, such as access to information, limited staff resources, small pools of expertise, and limited financial resources can place an extra burden on innovative development processes. In response, Halseth *et al.* (2010) argue that new governance regimes will only be effective if accompanied by sufficient resources and allowed time to develop mature leadership, trust, and structures capable of sustaining momentum.

Implementing rural place-based policy

Being strategic in place-based policy requires efficient and effective models of facilitating the co-construction process that links senior governments with rural communities and regions. The tolerance and willingness of both community and state actors involved in the policy transition process to engage in discussion, experiment with different models, and accommodate to shifting external forces depends on good process. Good process and models of governance will lead to more effective implementation.

A first step towards implementing place-based policy concerns authentic efforts to *listen to rural voices*. Place-based policy demands the robust inclusion of rural perspectives. This is particularly critical considering that policy-makers are often located in urban centers. This presents challenges for how to engage with rural citizens (Farmer *et al.*, 2010).

Effective rural engagement does not simply consist of linking rural residents with urban policy-makers. Senior governments should re-invest in having a more robust presence in rural regions. Having these *"boots on the ground"* will enable them to be more active and continuing participants in rural development processes and to generate first-hand information of rural conditions that can inform broader policy goals and directions (Halseth and Ryser, 2016).

In seeking to implement place-based policy, senior governments should reconsider the need to (re)create their own delivery infrastructure. There may be opportunities to *leverage existing local and regional institutions*, which have the local knowledge and trust of local residents to manage policy development and implementation. This point links with the observations above concerning the need to support and enhance rural governance capacity.

Finally, the literature offers a *caution against idealizing place-based strategies*. The demand for greater local control and broader policy objectives related to participation and buy-in are worthy objectives within a place-based policy framework. However, the complexity associated with mixing place- and people-based strategies, combined with concerns about the capacity of rural communities to sustain policy processes and to achieve a semblance of equity means that this localist enthusiasm must be tempered (particularly early on in a place-based policy strategy). A number of researchers have highlighted a variety of cautions associated with implementing place-based approaches at community and regional scales (MacLeod, 2001; Lovering, 1999; Polèse, 1999), including: creating a democratic deficit, avoiding the dangers of elitism and parochialism, managing the challenges of interpersonal conflict which may be more concentrated under local conditions, and ignoring established jurisdictions that may limit local or regional development possibilities. In other words, place-based policy and development should not be conflated with, or used as cover for, senior government abandonment. There are still critical roles for senior governments and senior government policy to support place-based development. Senior government responses require a comprehensive vision and coordinated policy approach through strategic investments in human capital, networks, and community infrastructure (Markey *et al.*, 2008).

Conclusions and research agenda

Place-based rural development has emerged as both a negative reaction and a positive response to the restructuring and transition from a Keynesian to a neoliberal policy orientation by senior governments and accordant systems of flexible production within a rapidly globalizing economy. Negatively, rural communities have struggled with declining senior government and industrial investments, a drawdown and failure to maintain or replace critical infrastructure, the erosion of regulatory frameworks that serve to defend and protect the broader public interest, and the offloading of serious governance responsibilities in the absence of adequate resources. This has prompted bottom-up responses to deal with impacts and identify alternative strategies for maintaining community survival and resilience. More positively, researchers around the world, working with and learning from communities, have been documenting positive development features associated with greater agency being exerted by rural communities and regions concerning their own developing futures. The tension between these two dynamics and the extent to which senior governments may be reconsidering what the appropriate roles are that they can play to foster greater resilience, has led to a current period that Halseth and Ryser (2018) describe as a period of reactionary incoherence.

It is within this period of incoherence that a co-constructed place-based policy approach may offer appropriate pathways to support rural communities without returning to the nostalgia of the past, or the false promises of market fundamentalism. Within the place-based approach a revealing of a greater diversity of values and perspectives, including those of long-ignored and suppressed Indigenous communities, can be seen. It offers the hope for reconsidering development assets, and a sense of ownership within rural regions for capturing a greater local/regional share of rural wealth. And, within the dynamics of a mobile global economy, a place-based approach may allow rural communities to leverage their assets as attractive features for the attraction and retention of capital and labor.

Place-based development requires a reconsideration of rural policy, both in process and outcome. It also demands a greater level of investment by senior governments, although not delivered via the traditional top-down modes of the past. It is important to also note the considerable responsibility that rural communities and regions have to build up their own capacity, and to actively engage in their own planning and development to pursue a place-based agenda (and to participate in co-constructed policy arenas). If rural communities are passive recipients of government priorities and programs, or remain internally or regionally divided, their prospects for robust, appropriate development, of which they are the main beneficiaries, will be limited (Douglas, 2010). More likely, passive communities will experience economic and population decline (or unmanaged growth), while being exploited for any surrounding or remaining resource-related wealth.

In closing, the current period of incoherence presents exciting opportunities to further a place-based research agenda, and to contribute greater coherence to both policy and practice. Four suggestions are offered. *First*, research is needed to better understand the dynamics associated with the co-constructed policy approach. What are appropriate roles for senior governments and communities within the process? How can rural participation be best engaged? *Second*, emerging patterns and structures of rural governance need to be tracked and documented. What types of governance regimes best support a co-constructed approach? *Third*, research will be needed on innovative models concerning the renewal of both physical and social infrastructure, which are outcomes of more appropriate co-constructed policies. Relatedly, as noted above, a hypothesis may be considered which makes a connection between the renewal of critical infrastructure and services with a more robust rural capacity, both for development and engagement with policy processes. *Finally*, there is a gap in the literature associated with robust comparative policy. People are simply not learning well enough from each other about successful models and their potential adaptation to other jurisdictions (thus, the importance of this volume). This presents a challenge to both the research community and policymakers to better interact and communicate with each other, and to work together to better understand successful models to support and facilitate place-based development in rural communities.

References

Aarsæther, N., Bærenholdt, J.O., 2001. *Understanding local dynamics and governance in northern regions*, in: Ukendt , A., Ukendt, B. (Eds.), *Transforming the local: Coping strategies and regional policies*. Roskilde University, Roskilde, Denmark.

Barca, F., McCann, P., Rodriguez-Pose, A., 2012. *The case for regional development intervention: Place-based versus place-neutral approaches*. Journal of Regional Science 52, 134–152. https://doi.org/10.1111/j.1467-9787.2011.00756.x.

Bollman, R., 2007. *Factors driving Canada's rural economy: 1914–2006*. Statistics Canada, Ottawa, Ont.

Bradford, N., 2004. *Place matters and multi-level governance: Perspectives on a new urban policy paradigm*. Policy Options 25(2), 39–45.

Bristow, G., 2010. *Resilient regions: Re-"place"ing regional competitiveness*. Cambridge Journal of Regions, Economy and Society 3, 153–167.

Bryant, C., 2010. *Co-constructing rural communities in the 21st century: Challenges for central governments and the research community in working effectively with local and regional actors*, in: Halseth, G., Markey, S., Bruce, D. (Eds.), *The next rural economies: Constructing rural place in a global economy*. CAB International, Oxfordshire, pp. 142–154.

Douglas, D.J.A., 2005. *The restructuring of local government in rural regions: A rural development perspective*. Journal of Rural Studies 21, 231–246. https://doi.org/10.1016/j.jrurstud.2005.01.003.

Douglas, D., 2010. *Rural planning and development in Canada*. Nelson College Indigenous, Toronto, Ont.

Farmer, J., Philip, L., King, G., Farrington, J., Macleod, M., 2010. *Territorial tensions: Misaligned management and community perspectives on health services for older people in remote rural areas*. Health Place 16, 275–283. https://doi.org/10.1016/j.healthplace.2009.10.010.

Florida, R., Mellander, C.P.A., Stolarick, K.M., 2010. *Talent, technology and tolerance in Canadian regional development*. The Canadian Geographer/Le Géographe canadien 54, 277–304. https://doi.org/10.1111/j.1541-0064.2009.00293.x.

Gregory, D., Johnston, R., Pratt, G., Watts, M., Whatmore, S. (Eds.), 2009. *The dictionary of human geography*, fifth edition. Wiley-Blackwell, Malden, MA.

Gunton, T., 2003. *Natural resources and regional development: An assessment of dependency and comparative advantage paradigms*. Economic Geography 79, 67–94. https://doi.org/10.1111/j.1944-8287.2003.tb00202.x.

Halseth, G. (Ed.), 2017. *Transformation of resource towns and peripheries*. Routledge, Abingdon.

Halseth, G., Ryser, L., 2006. *Trends in service delivery: Examples from rural and small town Canada, 1998 to 2005*. Journal of Rural and Community Development 1, 69–90.

Halseth, G., Ryser, L., 2016. *Rapid change in small towns: when social capital collides with political/bureaucratic inertia.* Community Development 47, 106–121. https://doi.org/10.1080/15575330.2015.1105271.

Halseth, G., Ryser, L., 2018. *Towards a political economy of resource-dependent regions.* Routledge, Abingdon.

Halseth, G., Markey, S., Bruce, D. (Eds.), 2010. *The next rural economies: Constructing rural place in a global economy.* CAB International, Oxfordshire.

Harvey, D., 2005. *A brief history of neoliberalism.* Oxford University Press, Oxford; New York.

Jonas, A.E.G., 2012. *Region and place: Regionalism in question.* Progress in Human Geography 36, 263–272.

Kitson, M., Martin, R., Tyler, P., 2004. *Regional competitiveness: An elusive yet key concept?* Regional Studies 38, 991–999.

Lovering, J., 1999. *Theory led by policy: The inadequacies of the "new regionalism" (illustrated from the case of Wales).* International Journal of Urban and Regional Research 23, 379–395. https://doi.org/10.1111/1468-2427.00202.

MacLeod, G., 2001. *New regionalism reconsidered: Globalization and the remaking of political economic space.* International Journal of Urban and Regional Research 25, 804–829. https://doi.org/10.1111/1468-2427.00345.

Markey, S., Halseth, G., Manson, D., 2008. *Challenging the inevitability of rural decline: Advancing the policy of place in northern British Columbia.* Journal of Rural Studies 24, 409–421. https://doi.org/10.1016/j.jrurstud.2008.03.012.

Markey, S., Halseth, G., Manson, D., 2012. *Investing in place: Economic renewal in northern British Columbia.* UBC Press, Vancouver.

Markey, S., Breen, S.-P., Vodden, K., Daniels, J., 2015. *Evidence of place: Becoming a region in rural Canada.* International Journal of Urban and Regional Research 39, 874–891. https://doi.org/10.1111/1468-2427.12298.

Massey, D., Allen, J. (Eds.), 1984. *Geography matters!: A reader.* Cambridge University Press, Cambridge; New York.

Mayes, R., 2014. *Mining and (sustainable) local communities: Transforming Ravensthorpe, Western Australia,* in: Brueckner, M., Durey, A., Mayes, R., Pforr, C. (Eds.), *Resource curse or cure?: On the sustainability of development in Western Australia.* CSR, Sustainability, Ethics and Governance. Springer-Verlag, Berlin; Heidelberg, pp. 223–238.

O'Brien, P., Sykes, O., Shaw, D., 2017. *Evolving conceptions of regional policy in Europe and their influence across different territorial scales,* in: Deas, I., Hincks, S. (Eds.), *Territorial policy and governance: Alternative paths.* Routledge, Abingdon, pp. 35–52.

OECD, 2006. *The new rural paradigm: Policies and governance.* OECD, Paris.

Paasi, A., 2013. *Regional planning and the mobilization of "regional identity": From bounded spaces to relational complexity.* Regional Studies 47, 1206–1219. https://doi.org/10.1080/00343404.2012.661410.

Peterson, A., Walker, M., Maher, M., Hoverman, S., Eberhard, R., 2010. *New regionalism and planning for water quality improvement in the Great Barrier Reef.* Australia. Geographical Research 48, 297–313. https://doi.org/10.1111/j.1745-5871.2009.00634.x.

Pezzini, M., 2001. *Rural policy lessons from OECD countries.* International Regional Science Review 24, 134–145.

Polèse, M., 1999. *From regional development to local development: On the life, death, and rebirth of regional science as a policy relevant science.* Canadian Journal of Regional Science/Revue canadienne des sciences régionales – Archives 22, 299–314.

Porter, M.E., Ketels, C.H.M., Miller, K.K., Bryden, R., 2004. *Competitiveness in rural U.S. regions: Learning and research agenda.* US Economic Development Administration, Washington, DC.

Reddel, T., 2002. *Beyond participation, hierarchies, management and markets: "New" governance and place policies.* Australian Journal of Public Administration 61, 50–63. https://doi.org/10.1111/1467-8500.00258.

Reimer, B., 2010. *Space to place: Bridging the gap,* in: Halseth, G., Markey, S., Bruce, D. (Eds.), *The next rural economies: Constructing rural place in a global economy.* University of Northern British Columbia. CAB International, Oxfordshire, pp. 263–274.

Shucksmith, M., 2010. *Disintegrated rural development? Neo-endogenous rural development, planning and place-shaping in diffused power contexts.* Sociologia Ruralis 50, 1–14. https://doi.org/10.1111/j.1467-9523.2009.00497.x.

Sullivan, L., Ryser, L., Halseth, G., 2014. *Recognizing change, recognizing rural: The new rural economy and towards a new model of rural service.* Journal of Rural and Community Development 9, 219–245.

Tennberg, M., Vola, J., Espiritu, A.A., Fors, B.S., Ejdemo, T., Riabova, L., Korchak, E., Tonkova, E., Nosova, T., 2014. *Neoliberal governance, sustainable development and local communities in the Barents Region.* Peoples, Economies and Politics 1(1), 41–72.

Uyarra, E., 2010. *What is evolutionary about "regional systems of innovation"? Implications for regional policy.* Journal of Evolutionary Economics 20, 115–137.

Young, N., 2008. *Radical neoliberalism in British Columbia: Remaking rural geographies.* Canadian Journal of Sociology 33, 1–36. https://doi.org/10.29173/cjs1525.

Zasada, I., Reutter, M., Piorr, A., Lefebvre, M., Gomez y Paloma, S., 2015. *Between capital investments and capacity building: Development and application of a conceptual framework towards a place-based rural development policy.* Land Use Policy 46, 178–188.

Zirul, C., Halseth, G., Markey, S., Ryser, L., 2015. *Struggling with new regionalism: Government trumps governance in northern British Columbia, Canada.* Journal of Rural and Community Development 10, 136–165.

9

TERRITORIAL CAPITAL IN RURAL POLICY DEVELOPMENT

Francesca Regoli, Dezső Kovács, Natalija Bogdanov,
William H. Meyers, and Matteo Vittuari

Introduction

Rural policy is oriented towards a long-term perspective for agricultural and rural areas and aims to contribute to the satisfaction of societal needs. Farmers and rural entrepreneurs represent the center of the system having to deal with the market, in terms of opportunities and constraints, and acting as providers of services (e.g. energy, environmental, tourism) since they are engaged in the preservation and management of public goods. Those assets are crucial for conservation and enhancement of agricultural landscapes, biodiversity, heritage sites, water quality, climate stability, air quality, resilience to flooding and fire, and as the overall providers of rural vitality, food security, and animal farm health and welfare (Cooper *et al.*, 2009).

In this framework, rural areas are characterized by the combination of their endogenous resources in what can be defined as territorial capital (TC): a social construction shaped by the relationships among cultural, economic, human, institutional, natural, and social assets (Bourdieu, 1987; Brunori and Rossi, 2007; Ambrosio-Albala and Delgado, 2008; van der Ploeg *et al.*, 2008; Camagni, 2009; Belletti and Marescotti, 2011; Segrè *et al.*, 2011; Servillo *et al.*, 2012; Atkinson, 2013; Bogdanov and Nikolić, 2013).

This chapter develops the theoretical approach of the territorial capital concept and its connection with the rural diversification process. The territorial approach is applied to two case studies from Serbia and Hungary (Central and Southeastern Europe) to show different applications of the TC analysis for the enhancement of local resources. The chapter concludes with considerations on how TC is a tool for strategic policy development.

Territorial capital: endogenous approaches to local development policy

The definitions of rural and rurality are not as obvious as they might appear, as clearly outlined in Chapter 1. They refer to a complex set of cultural, institutional, physical, and social elements, often identified according to their diversity and their interconnections with "urban" areas (OECD, 2018; OECD, 2013; Tacoli, 1998). The European Charter for Rural Areas, a report by the Parliamentary Assembly of the Council of Europe (EC, 1996), defines a rural area as

> a stretch of inland or coastal countryside, including small towns and villages, where
> the main part of the area is used for: agriculture, forestry, aquaculture and fisheries;

economic and cultural activities of country-dwellers (crafts, industry, services, etc.); non-urban recreation and leisure areas (or natural reserves); other purposes, such as for housing.

While this definition emphasizes a geographic dimension and a localized system of productive activities, a territory should also be seen as the product of knowledge, specific skills and traditions, social and political relations, values and cultural elements, rules and practices, and sense of belonging (Brunori and Rossi, 2007; van der Ploeg *et al.*, 2008; Camagni, 2009; Belletti and Marescotti, 2011; Segrè *et al.*, 2011; Servillo *et al.*, 2012; **Bogdanov and Nikoli**, 2013; **Tóth,** 2014). Looking at governance processes and collective actions, a territory can be seen as a social and political construction (Bourdieu, 2009), where joint initiatives emerge from the negotiations between local groups and institutions. Governance is "sustaining coordination and coherence among a wide variety of actors with different purposes and objectives" (Pierre, 2000); it implies the capacity of the involved actors to create a local consensus and a shared vision for the development of the area starting from the organization and shaping of local endogenous resources to create new assets. OECD defines this process as territorial capital: "a specific capital that is distinct from that of other areas and is determined by different factors … that include the area's geographical location, size, factor of production endowment, climate, traditions, natural resources, quality of life" (OECD, 2001). Additionally, territorial capital can be identified as the interaction among all the material and non-material, private and public assets characterizing a territory; territorial governance is the process of combining the interactions and the interests of the different actors and their ability to use, combine, and transform those assets (Bourdieu, 1987; Brunori, 2006; Brunori and Rossi, 2007).

The multidimensional framework composing territorial capital favors the elaboration of different definitions of the concept (see Table 9.1). For example, the "assets pentagon" includes the natural, financial, human, social, and physical assets (UN – ESCWA, 2009), while other definitions consider institutional and cultural dimensions rather than the financial and physical ones (Brunori, 2006). Another meaning identifies rural territory as social constructions (Ambrosio-Albala and Delgado, 2008), outlined by the combination of policy settings, politics, history, socio-economic, and agro-ecology contexts. The concept of "countryside capital" focuses on the need for a reshaping of rural resources as a capital asset that can be "invested in and from" and which can lead to several benefits, but it should not be overstretched by the demands upon those resources (Garrod *et al.*, 2006).

Moreover, the territorial capital concept is changing and transforming itself with the historical evolution of the relations among its components, placing a key emphasis on this adaptive capacity of rural economies and of the agricultural sectors (Knickel *et al.*, 2018). Rural systems, viewed as agrarian ones, can be perceived as the way farmers exploit the environment that has been historically created by all the relations and interactions that occur between all of its social, economic, and physical components (Mazoyer and Roudart, 2006). It is a complex system characterized by present dynamics, socio-economic structures, and the mode of exploitation of the ecosystem.

Furthermore, the observation of territorial assets results functionally in understanding a territory, its resources, and which actions should be implemented to adapt to changes and challenges affecting a specific region. Often these actions have global effects as well. In addition, the multidimensional character of an area determines peoples' well-being, since the concept of welfare is increasingly associated with not only economic conditions, but also social and environmental factors. Thus, the interconnections among human, social, economic, and natural capitals require the idea of policy complementarity (OECD, 2016).

Table 9.1 Territorial capital analytical framework

Capital dimension	Concept definition and adaptation	Main authors
Human	Focus on education Personal abilities and skills	A – B – C – D – E – F – G
Social	Ability to work collectively Mutual trust and connection among groups	A – B – C – D – E – F – G – H – I
Institutional	Trust in local institutions (participation in administrative election) Public services development Public and private connection/networks	A – B – D – F – H – I
Economic	Entrepreneurial activities and related development in the territory Financial services Synergies among the economics and the specificities of the area	A – B – E – F – G – H
Cultural	Forms of knowledge specifically linked to the area; local heritage	A – B – C – D – F – G – H – I
Natural	Natural resources (water, air, soil, biodiversity) Human pressure on natural resources and waste management	A – B – C – D – F – H – I

Sources: A: Atkinson (2013); B: Bogdanov and Nikolić (2013); C: Camagni (2014); D: Mazzola *et al.* (2018); E: Perucca (2014); F: Servillo *et al.* (2012); G: van der Ploeg *et al.* (2008); H: Belletti and Marescotti (2011); I: Camagni (2009).

The *Rural Policy 3.0* – the extension of the *New Rural Paradigm* – underlines the need for engaging a number of different actors and involving multi-level governance mechanisms to guarantee effective rural policies (OECD, 2018). Therefore, an endogenous approach implies a focus on a co-participation and a bottom-up approach, which means the need for the active involvement of citizens as local stakeholders alongside government actors. Meanwhile, local resources represent a bridge to external enterprises and new initiatives: the territory perceived as "a space of flows" (investments, public funding, new entrepreneurial and/or external actors, tourists). Those processes focus on establishing partnerships among different local stakeholders around a common objective (e.g. the enhancement of the territory and its capital), as well as bringing outside actors (tourists, consumers, citizens) within the projects implemented by the local community (Brunori, 2006). Nevertheless, this cycle implies a certain level of awareness of the territory by local actors and knowledge of the endogenous assets of an area. To guarantee competitiveness and novelty in rural areas, local assets (territorial capital) should be enhanced while unused resources should be properly exploited (OECD, 2006):

> Dealing with complexity requires the harnessing of all available knowledge sources, including tacit knowledge at (the) farm and business level and requires the involvement of all relevant actors (farmers, foresters, cooperative and industry, advisors and knowledge brokers, etc.) in a process of knowledge co-creation and appropriation. This is what we refer to as the interactive innovation model.
>
> *(EC, 2016a)*

Hence, territory and local resources are at the center of policy discourses, with a shift from a sectoral to a territorial approach and towards effective rural policies and practices. Chapter 8 of this volume outlines the relevance of a shift in policy orientation towards a place-based approach. With this shift comes a change from emphasis on government to the governance of rural areas, with local communities as one of the leading actors and as one of the main policy trend orientations (Table 9.2).

Table 9.2 Shift to a territorial approach: Rural Policy 3.0

Variable	Old approach	New approach	Rural Policy 3.0
General objective	Production and economic growth	Sustainable management of local resources	Well-being composed of economy, society, and environment dimensions
Specific objectives	Farm income, farm competitiveness	Competitiveness of rural areas, enhancement of local assets	Aspects to be targeted (for low-density economy): 1. physical distance from major markets; 2. economic competitiveness; 3. specific economic structures
Key target sectors	Agriculture	Various sectors of rural economy	Approach differentiated by type of rural area
Main tools	Subsidies	Investments	A range of support measures addressed to public sector, firms, and third sector
Key actors (individual)	Farmers	Rural entrepreneurs	Interaction of public, private, and third sectors
Strategic competencies of individual actors	Farm management and farming methods	Entrepreneurial vision, integration of agriculture with other activities, networking, improving awareness on local resources and skills	Focuses on mechanisms for the implementation of effective rural policies and practices
Key actors (institutional)	National governments	All levels (supra-national; national; regional; local)	Multi-level governance with support to social enterprise and voluntary sector
Institutional approach	Top-down (government)	Bottom-up (governance)	Multiple policy domains – functional region
Changes and challenges	Passive role of farmers: application of equal top-down decisions	Active roles of rural entrepreneurs through innovative and inclusive approaches	Interactive approach

Source: Authors' elaboration from OECD (2006) and OECD (2016 and 2018).

In this framework, government refers to the institutions and processes by which rules are made and enforced for all members of society, while governance implies new forms of integration, consolidation of new territorial coalitions and groups, and inclusion of local communities in policy and decision-making processes aimed at supporting rural economic development. The spirit of *Rural Policy 3.0* intends to frame the effective capacity of governments to address and leverage both opportunities and challenges characterizing rural areas (OECD, 2018). The challenge is to make those statements effective and operative. In some cases, informal networks and multi-actor cooperatives have provided a useful tool to balance different interests and reinforce medium- to long-term perspectives or realize opportunities (Brunori and Rossi, 2007; Knickel et al., 2018; Stoker, 2011). Different case studies suggest that considering the management of network as a "service of public interest" could represent an important asset for rural development programs (Knickel et al., 2018), a "soft power" which allows the creation of partnerships among local governments (Stoker, 2011).

Methodology

The differences which stand out from the various definitions of the dimensions of territorial capital lead to a highly diversified set of applied methodological approaches. These methods range from the use of several territorial indicators based on multidimensional datasets (Mazzola et al., 2018), quantitive methods including principal component analysis (Brasili, 2012; Perucca, 2014), other multivariate statistics (Pompili and Martinoia, 2011), and some mixed methodologies integrating qualitative analysis with the use of selected indicators (Bogdanov and Nikolić, 2013; Segrè et al., 2011).

This chapter analyzes territorial capital through a mixed methodology based on the use of a specific set of indicators identified according to the different dimensions of TC and the analysis of secondary data (academic literature and policy documents). The aim of this examination is to extend the analysis to the use of territorial-based resources and the role of local policy approaches. Therefore this chapter proposes the utilization of the TC concept for understanding a territory through its local assets and formulating resources-based policy intervention.

The following territorial capital analysis is applied to two case studies from Central and Southeastern Europe, where agriculture and rural development represent crucial assets for the promotion of economic development and social stability. The first case study focuses on raspberry production in the region of Arilje in southwestern Serbia, while the second investigates the apiculture sector in Hungary where, due to its peculiar "transhumance" character, the whole national sector has been analyzed. The selected sectors do not belong to the mainstream branches of the rural economy, instead representing niche products which have particular significance to these countries and are based on the engagement of a large number of small rural producers.

The two case studies are organized following a common structure (Territorial capital characterization; Challenges; Actions taken; Results; Lessons learned) that informs the comparative analysis carried out in the last section of the chapter. Final considerations are elaborated as the analysis moves from the specific cases to broader concluding reflections, exploring how territorial capital analysis can contribute to facilitating the design of policy interventions coherent with the *Rural Policy 3.0* framework. Emphasis is placed on policy design that focuses both on opportunities and challenges in rural areas and on the role of national governments in supporting their development efforts (OECD, 2018).

Raspberry production in the Arilje region

Territorial capital characterization

In terms of natural capital (see Table 9.3), Serbia is a country of rich ecosystems and biodiversity and great potential for diversified agricultural production. The variety of ecosystems is mostly reflected in its vegetation. There are over 1200 varieties of agricultural plants and over 700 species of medicinal plants (of which 280 are traded) (RS MESP, 2010). The mixture of cultures and historical heritage of nations living in this region has led to the presence of a number of specific food products based on a specific natural resource.

Arilje municipality is located in the hilly, mountainous area of Western Serbia (Valjevo region) with fertile land, springs, streams and rivers, and a favorable microclimate for fruit cultivation. Planted on sloping grounds with advantageous agro-ecological conditions and non-polluted surroundings, raspberry farms in the area of Arilje have unique characteristics such as a clearly expressed aroma, specific taste, high content of antioxidants, and medicinal properties (Sredojević et al., 2015).

Since 1950, the production of raspberries has characterized the Arilje region, including several villages from surrounding municipalities – such as Arilje, Ivanjica, Pozega, Lucani, Uzice, Cajetina, Nova Varos – encompassing a total area of around 930 km². The rapid expansion of production for the export market started with the establishment of the first freezing warehouse in the mid-1970s. Raspberry production was an innovative adaptive response mechanism introduced by small farms as a form of structural adjustment towards niche market formation which has enabled resilient rural communities (Battaglini *et al.*, 2016). This cultivation stimulated the enhancement of institutional capital since not only manufacturers, but also local governments, advisory services, producers' associations, and cooperatives invested in tailor-made trainings aimed to strengthen the competencies of producers.

Raspberry cultivation is very labor intensive, especially during the harvest season when mid-sized farms often hire two to three seasonal workers, placing high requirements on skilled human resources in the region. The fragility of the raspberries requires that picking be handled with care, leading to a limited use of mechanical harvesting. Local labor is highly skilled, well trained, and educated in various disciplines relevant for post-harvest activities (sorting, packing, storage, transport). However, producers face the threat of shortages of available skilled seasonal workers. To maintain the regional raspberry industry's unique quality standards, employees are required to make an ongoing commitment, which is not easy to achieve with low-skilled seasonal workers. This phenomenon exposes raspberry growers to risks, such as labor shortages leading to harvests of fruit left unpicked, and leads to increased costs of hired labor or financial losses due to inability to meet quality standards.

These risks are relevant in terms of economic capital since raspberry production has great impact on the local economy of the whole region (see Table 9.3). Furthermore, the Serbian raspberry industry is concentrated primarily around Arilje, making the region important for national production. Raspberry plantations in Arilje municipality cover an area of over 1200 ha, with an average total production of 15,000 tons. Ninety-five percent of total production is managed by over 4500 family farms on small plots averaging about 0.3 ha. As a labor-intensive activity, raspberry production engages about 15,000 workers during the harvest season, an estimated 5500 of these consisting of non-local workers (Paraušić and Simeunović, 2016). The expansion of raspberry production has contributed to the development of other interrelated industries in the area, including over 100 cold storage facilities as well as large fruit-based processed food manufacturing industries with different levels of technology and product innovation. Thanks to a market trend

Table 9.3 Summary table case study 1: raspberry production in the Arilje region

Territorial capital	Raspberry production Arilje region – Serbian case study	Implemented practices, challenges and visions
Natural capital	Hilly – mountainous area of Western Serbia. Fertile land, springs, streams and rivers, and favorable microclimate for fruit growing, non-polluted surrounding. Raspberry: clearly expressed aroma, specific taste, high content of antioxidants and medicinal properties. Raspberry production: an area of over 1200 ha.	Since 1950 rapid growth of the production of raspberries.
Human capital	Skilled human resources, trained and educated in disciplines for post-harvest manipulation of raspberries. Labor intensive, especially for the harvest season. About 15,000 workers during the harvest season, around 5500 hired non-local workers. Dominant chain actors: intermediaries. Threat of shortage of available skilled seasonal workers.	Farmers' education and provision of high-level expertise.
Economic capital	Middle-size farmers are hiring two to three seasonal workers. Innovative adaptive response and mechanism introduced by small farms. Average production of 15,000 t. 95 percent of tot. production by over 4500 family farms, on plots of 0.3 ha. Development of other interrelated industries in the area. Expansion of production: further fragmentation and recomposition of the value chain, more difficult to ensure quality and safety standards. 49 PGI products, only 10 PGI products have authorized users.	Strategy for structural adjustment in niche markets, to enable resilient rural communities. PGI of food products recognized as a valuable marketing tool to improve market access and promote niche products.
Social capital	Twenty farmers' groups, numerous scientific and advisory institutions, certification bodies and agricultural extension providers.	Farmers' protest and dissatisfaction with their position in the value chain. No research studies on quality of local social networks. 2016: the General Association of Entrepreneurs and Innovation Centre for Agriculture obtained the recognition of PGI for fresh, frozen, and dried raspberry: "Ariljska malina" ("Raspberry from the Arilje").

Territorial capital	Raspberry production Arilje region – Serbian case study	Implemented practices, challenges and visions
Institutional capital	Local governments, advisory service, producers' associations and cooperatives invested in tailor-made trainings to strengthen competencies of producers. Inter-municipal collaboration to expand existing social networks and to join new ones.	Lack of vertical integration, mistrust and antagonism between and among producers and buyers, resulted in price and production volatility. Initiatives, i.e. Measure "On-farm investment support for agricultural holdings" for quality standards within national RDP. Support of Ministry of Agriculture, donor projects, development agencies, certification providers, and extension service, to adopt HACCP, GLOBALGAP, and ISO standards adopted by most of the actors in value chain. Further activities on strengthening business sector involved in the value chain or marketing of GI products. To promote and encourage geographical indication concept (vision). Local governments and stakeholders an important role to enhance the competitive advantage of promoting local food quality product and collaborating with other local actors to realize their potential (vision).
Cultural capital	Long tradition. Mixture of cultures and historical heritage.	Cultural and historical heritage led to a number of typical food products, based on natural resources.

Source: Authors' elaboration.

towards greater demand for healthy food products, raspberry producers have benefited from a significant growth in demand for their products (CBI website, n.d.). However, dominant value chain actors including intermediaries, cold storage operators, and retailers often benefit disproportionately from these trends, while producers – particularly small growers – are not able to meet the strict quality requirements of the sector or take advantage of the profitable niche market.

Due to the high concentration of producers, suppliers, processors, and institutions engaged in the production within the raspberry-growing region of Arilje, social capital has been established around the raspberry market through a critical mass of stakeholders (see Table 9.3). These stakeholders include 20 farmers' groups, numerous scientific and advisory institutions, certification bodies, and agricultural extension providers. In addition, the presence of supportive and proactive networks, local authorities, and a well-established history of inter-municipal collaboration contribute to expand existing social networks and facilitate local actors in joining new ones. The well-developed social networks and close ties between producers and processors contribute to knowledge generation and increase the bargaining power of actors in the sector.

However, there are no research studies on the quality of local social networks or the attitudes of raspberry growers about their position in the value chain. Nevertheless, frequent farmers' protests and dissatisfaction with their circumstances suggest a low level of trust between primary producers, cold storage operators, and wholesalers, as well as the existence of potential incoherence within the network. The lack of vertical integration, as well as mistrust and antagonism between and among producers and buyers, has resulted in price and production volatility.

Challenges

New challenges emerged in the course of growing competition and the appearance of new risks. Export growth was a major driver of the expansion of raspberry production to other regions in Serbia, but also to neighboring countries. In addition, the emergence of new exporters (Chile, Hungary, and Poland) also affected the leading position of Serbia in export markets. The expansion of production has caused further fragmentation and recomposition of the value chain, making it more difficult to ensure quality and safety standards. Among these challenges, Phytophtora (root rot), to which the predominant Serbian cultivar (*Willamette*) is susceptible, affected the raspberry orchards at the end of the 1990s, and infected areas have been increasing in consecutive years.

Actions taken

In terms of institutional capital, a wide range of initiatives and activities have been launched in Serbia aimed at strengthening institutional, legal, and administrative capacities related to food quality standards (see Table 9.3). The focus was on farmers' education and provision of high-level expertise. At the primary producer level, apart from the support for strengthening human capacities, the measure "On-farm investment support for agricultural holdings" was provided by the national Rural Development Programme, with the aim to meet quality standards.

In the circumstances of increased competition, export-oriented and large-scale growers have been forced to improve technology and maintain the traditional quality of Arilje raspberries. The institutional and social dimensions in Arilje region were successful: with the support of the Ministry of Agriculture, donor projects, development agencies, certification providers, and extension services, the HACCP, GLOBALGAP, and ISO food safety standards were adopted by most of the actors in the value chain. Furthermore, the General Association of Entrepreneurs – cold storages sections, with the support of the Innovation Centre for Agriculture (both from Arilje), launched an initiative to obtain Protected Geographical Indications (PGI) for fresh, frozen, and dried raspberry. In 2016, The Intellectual Property Office of the Republic of Serbia recognized "*Ariljska malina*" ("Raspberry from the Arilje") as a product with PGI (RS IPO website).

Results

Not just Arilje municipality, but the whole region benefits from the reputation embedded in the specific quality of raspberries grown in this area. For the raspberry growers and small and medium-sized companies that operate in the region, the standardization and differentiation of the product implies an opportunity to benefit from the consistent quality of their product.

Currently Serbia has 49 products with registered PGI, including a variety of food products (processed meat, cheeses, wine, honey, fruits, and vegetables). However, the fact that only ten products with geographical indications have authorized users indicates the necessity for further activities on strengthening the business sector involved in the value chain or marketing of GI products. Introduction and maintenance of quality standards within small farms and companies implies slow progress due to the low level of investment, lack of knowledge, and vertical integration. Besides, a lack of processed products and added value to raw raspberry exports still limits export income increases. At the institutional level, stakeholders and policy-makers must continue to work together to further harmonize with EU legislation, strengthen control systems, develop other optional quality schemes, and promote budgetary support measures for GI products.

Lessons learned

During the last decade, with the liberalization and internationalization of the agro-food market, Serbian farmers have become more exposed to competition and new risks and have been forced to find new markets for their commodities through value-added marketing. The wider benefits of geographical indication of food products have been recognized as a valuable marketing tool through which to improve market access and promote niche products. However, implementation of such an enhancement strategy in a developing country context largely depends on whether there are a set of policies, institutions (producer associations, quality control agencies, enforcement bodies), and technical and financial services in place to promote and encourage the geographical indication concept.

The local governments and other stakeholders should play an important role in launching initiatives to enhance the competitive advantage of local food products and collaborate with other local actors to realize their potential. However, the weak capacity of municipal staffs, coupled with the lack of financial resources, pose a serious obstacle. The key challenges for rural communities in transition countries is the lack of regulatory expertise and entrepreneurial and marketing capacity, which are key factors hampering them from securing a fair market value for their products.

The Hungarian apiculture sector

Territorial capital characterization

In terms of natural capital (see Table 9.4), Hungary is a Central European country in the Carpathian Basin. Due to climatic and soil conditions, the agricultural sector can produce excellent quality products such as honey, wine, jams, fruits, vegetables, and meat. Acacia (locust) honey is the main product of the Hungarian apiculture sector, and the country is one of the main producers of locust honey for the European market (Kovács, 2017). There are about 460 thousand hectares of locust honey-plant forests in the country, representing nearly 25 percent of the forest coverage. Besides acacia, the country has several special varieties of honey like bear's (wild) garlic, chestnut, rosemary, lavender, goldenrod, linden, hawthorn, and others. The main bee forage in the country is canola (rape), acacia, and sunflower.

The apiculture sector is important not only for honey production but for pollination and contribution to biodiversity. EU sources claim that the value of pollination is 10–20 times higher than the value of honey and other beekeeping material. The estimated value of pollination in Europe is around €20 billion (OPERA Research Center, 2011). The behavior of bees is also an excellent indicator to assess the environmental conditions of an area.

More than 60 percent of the beekeepers migrate their bees from one place to another, shipping them across hundreds of kilometers, because there is two to three weeks' difference in the blossoming of locust and other plants in the northern and southern parts of the country. Due to this "transhumance process", the focus on the whole apiculture sector is more appropriate than just on a specific Hungarian region. Thus, the country can be seen as a unified "commons" from an apiculture perspective.

The professional knowledge and experience of beekeeping is significant in Hungary (see Table 9.4). While the number of beekeepers is decreasing in several Western European countries, the trend is different in Hungary. Especially in remote rural areas, where employment and income possibilities have declined, beekeeping has grown as a subsistence activity. Beekeeping is a minor agricultural sector with strong handicraft features. The beekeeping sector is unique in that it can be started and pursued without land or a big investment. It can be managed as a hobby or a professional activity for subsistence. Between 2004 and 2006 there were 15,302 beekeepers in the country; 12 years later the number of beekeepers had increased by 25 percent (EU Beekeeping Sector, 2016). The Hungarian apiculture sector represents 1 percent of the agricultural GDP and 3 percent of the animal husbandry GDP of the country. In 2015, there were 21,565 beekeepers with 1,191,851 beehives in Hungary (Hungarian National Apiculture Programme, 2016).

Concerning the economic dimension of the honey sector (see Table 9.4), Hungary is the only country in Europe where honey production is almost three times higher than national honey consumption. According to estimates of the National Hungarian Beekeeping Association (NHBA), total honey production was 24,400 tons in 2014, and 30,700 tons in 2015. The average yearly honey yield per beehive was 21.94 kg in 2014 and 25.76 kg in 2015 (Hungarian National Apiculture Programme, 2016).

The honey from beekeepers is collected by eight to ten big honey packers and traders, plus more than 400 hundred small local/regional honey processors via their territorial representatives. Around 70 percent of beekeepers rely only on representatives from packers who act as middlemen, buying up honey from beekeepers in barrels. The big honey packers and traders are interested in bulk sales and export, not in the creation of quality products, local brands, or territorial products. More than two-thirds of honey is exported, mainly to the EU member states as raw material in barrels. The special variety honeys are usually mixed together as flower honey, leading to the loss of potential value-added resulting from the individual varieties. This blended honey mix from several beekeepers is used to improve the quality of Asian import honeys as well. The "label" of this honey is called "quality improver". This special euphemistic term is proudly used by politicians and traders, but results in a very unfortunate practice and expression, since the meaning implies that the good quality Hungarian honey is mixed with poor quality honey originating from other countries without the same commitment to quality.

On the contrary, national consumption of honey is low, with estimates varying between 700–1000 gr/capita/year. One of the reasons for this low per capita consumption is the persistent lack of an overall marketing strategy for honey within Hungary. The institutional dimension of the honey sector demonstrates that during the past 50–60 years it was never a priority to promote Hungarian honey as a healthy, natural food and to encourage honey consumption. The specialty honeys are mainly unknown to Hungarian customers.

Social capital among beekeepers exists (see Table 9.4), but connections are focused mainly towards the beekeepers, while customers, social partners, and policy-makers get much less attention. The NHBA is an umbrella organization with 13,000 members in 113 local beekeeping associations. Two-thirds of all the beekeepers are organized in local associations and from fall to spring in the out-season period they usually organize different trainings, local fairs, and other events. For certain tasks, one to two beekeepers help each other in work, but overall cooperation for the whole local beekeepers' community hardly exists. In spite of the global challenges in climate, market, and environment, they try to keep their "independent" position. They act more as competitors than cooperating partners. A longstanding tradition persists in the personal rivalry and conflicts in the national leadership of the organization. Relationships to civil society, policy-makers, and other actors in the government sector are relatively limited. The strategy of the association is not clear and ranking of the tasks is not evident. Overall, the approach is strongly production oriented. Recent leaders are not in favor of direct sales of beekeepers to consumers, rather favoring the wholesale market.

Challenges

In terms of institutional and economic capital (see Table 9.4), numerous changes have affected the national honey sector over the decades. During the socialist period, honey was an important export good and the country earned hard currency for it. After the political changes of the 1990s, the former monopolist state-owned trading company went bankrupt and smaller private trading companies emerged from its ruins, continuing the previous buying practices of the state-run system. After testing the honey, the traders pay in cash on site or transfer the price immediately to the beekeeper.

The European Union's honey self-sufficiency level is around 60 percent (European Commission, 2016b). The other 40 percent is imported from major producer regions including China, Latin America, and more recently Ukraine. Since honey is a product of the demand market, in essence the EU Common Agricultural Policy (CAP) market regulation for honey defines only the rules of subsidies of the three-year National Apiculture programs (Regulation (EU) No. 1308/2013).[1] Since the surplus of honey is channeled out from the country with a price similar to low-quality Chinese honey, the economic and overall significance related to this sector is not appropriately valued within the national economy, leading to a permanent crisis in the apiculture sector.

The challenges for the Hungarian beekeeping sector are enormous, given that no national medium-to-long-term strategy for the sector is currently being promoted. It would be necessary to increase the national consumption of honey significantly, diminish the surplus for export and get a better price from retail trade and via direct sales. These changes would require a paradigm shift at the institutional level and among multiple stakeholder groups including beekeepers, beekeeping associations, and politicians. This shift would be oriented towards re-formulating existing practices and placing a greater focus on marketing, local branding, and honey sales in local markets or the establishment of local beekeepers' cooperatives.

Actions taken

In terms of social capital (see Table 9.4), several actions have occurred to improve the market position of honey and beekeepers, mainly in the framework of the NHBA. The first attempt to organize a kind of national cooperative owned by beekeepers occurred in 1989. It was called Mellifera and became the market leader in the country, with 3000 tons of annual exports. After this initial success, it was privatized in 1992. Other attempts to improve honey's market position in the 1990s also failed for various reasons. The first attempt at beekeepers' self-organization through the NHBA also included cases where honey shipments were not paid for, leading to lack of trust among beekeepers within the large trade organization, as well as mistrust towards organizers. The last initiative to organize a nationwide shareholding company of beekeepers occurred in 2006, but only 29 percent of the beekeepers signed a contract to participate, while the expected threshold was 90 percent. As a result, this organization was also not established

Table 9.4 Summary table case study 2: the Hungarian apiculture sector

Territorial capital	Apiculture sector – Hungarian case study	Implemented practices, challenges and visions
Natural capital	About 460,000 ha of locust honey-plant forest, One-quarter of the forest coverage. Relevance for pollination and contribution to biodiversity at the EU level. Nectare producing agricultural crops like sunflower and rapeseed.	Difference in the blossoming of locust and other plants within the country: the apiculture sector develops a "transhumance process" approach.
Human capital	Beekeeping: strong handcraft feature. Eight to ten honey packers and traders as main actors in the apiculture market chain.	Packers and traders: interested in bulk sales and export, not in quality products, local brands, *terroir*[1] product. Beekeepers: to express their interests and professional values and create supporting network with consumers, school systems, and also among decision makers and politicians (vision).
Economic capital	Apiculture sector 1% agricultural GDP and 3% animal husbandry GDP. 21,565 beekeepers with 1,191,851 beehives (2015). Honey production 24,400 tons (2014), 30,700 tons (2015). The average yearly honey yield by beehive 21.94 kg (2014) and 25.76 kg (2015). One of the main producers of locust honey for the EU market. "Quality improver": export to improve the quality of Asian import honeys. Low price for honey sector. Low national consumption: 700–1000 gr/capita/year.	Never a priority to promote Hungarian honey. A successful sector with significant export achievements. Undervalued quality product. To increase the national consumption of honey and diminish the surplus for export (vision). To get better price from retail trade and via direct sales (vision).
Social capital	National Hungarian Beekeeping Association (NHBA): focused on beekeepers, less on: customers, social partners, and policy.	Not a high level of cooperation among beekeepers, more competitors than cooperating partners.
Institutional capital	After the 1990s, the state trade company went bankrupt, and smaller private trade companies emerged. Weak EU market regulation, just for subsidies: national programmes, if approved, 50 percent CAP support for the selected measures (bee-health, modernization of beekeeping equipment, knowledge of beekeepers, and support for advisory service and research).	2016–2019 Hungarian National Beekeeping Programme: no implementation of "market monitoring" and "enhancement of product quality to exploit the potential on the market". No effective coordination force and lobbying power for marketing strategy and to increase the national consumption, neither at ministry level nor within NHBA.

Territorial capital	Apiculture sector – Hungarian case study	Implemented practices, challenges and visions
		Need to switch from wholesale market to retail and quality market (vision). To pay attention to marketing, create brands and sell honey on the local markets or establish local cooperatives for beekeeping and honey (vision). Government to adequately represent the problems of beekeepers in front of EU bodies (vision).
Cultural capital	Long tradition, handicraft heritage in beekeeping sector.	It can be managed as a hobby or professional activity.

Source: Authors' elaboration.

Note

1 Terroir: "a delimited geographic space where a human community has developed a collective knowledge of production through a historical path. This process is based on the interaction of both physical and biological environment and an ensemble of human factors. In these relations the socio-technical components play a determinant role in generating a reputation, awarding the typical character and revealing the uniqueness of a product originated by that specific 'terroir'. National Institute of Origin and Quality (INAO, 2007)" Institut national de l'origine et de la qualité (INAO). Proposition de définition "terroir et typicité" Document de synthèse du groupe de travail INRA/INAO. Letter dated 05/18/2007.

(Bross, 2006). Nevertheless, five to six smaller cooperatives do exist today based on Hungarian and EU laws. They collect honey from their members and sell it to the processing companies. Their profit comes from the price advantage of economies of scale derived from the ability to trade in larger quantities of honey.

A formative moment in Hungarian beekeepers' social action, both as a networking initiative in conflict with EU institutional bodies and without the support of the national government, was the protest against "Chinese honey" at the dawn of EU accession. Hungarian beekeepers went to Brussels in 2004, and again in 2015, to protest against the import of "Chinese honey" to Europe and the failed labeling system which allowed the mixing of EU and non-EU honey. However, these protests did not lead to substantive changes in the criticized practice.

A so-called "acacia coalition" was formed in 2014 to protect acacia, which is not a native plant and is considered an invasive species in the country. In this case, institutional capital was enhanced, since several organizations among others, the NHBA, and politicians worked together to "protect" acacia trees against the planned EU regulation to remove this species. Ironically, acacia honey, which gained a special quality label "Hungaricum", is sold mainly as a bulk product.

Concerning the economic dimension (see Table 9.4), honey inspection on the shelves of supermarkets is an important activity that was initiated by the NHBA in 2007. Due to these regular inspections, the quality of honey sold in supermarkets improved. Another economic and institutional opportunity for the modernization of beekeeping and knowledge transfer for beekeepers that has existed since 1997 is the three-year National Beekeeping Programme, based on EU market regulation (institutional dimension). After EU approval, this program can get 50 percent CAP support for selected measures implemented at the national level. The other 50 percent of support is provided by the member state. Nevertheless, the EU measures of "market monitoring" and "enhancement of product quality with a view to exploiting the potential of products on the market" are not included in the 2016–2019 Hungarian National Beekeeping Programme. In light of the great surplus in Hungarian apiculture, it is hard to understand why this opportunity has been neglected.[2]

Results

In economic terms, Hungarian apiculture and its adjoining sectors (e.g. tool manufactures, glass companies, special cloth makers) employ 50,000–60,000 people nationwide. By formal measures, it is a successful sector with significant export activity. Yet from the perspective of value and quality, it is still an undervalued quality product which is sold in bulk. Instead of targeting the value-added, high-quality honey market, Hungary still delivers raw material to international honey packers and traders. Thirteen years after EU accession, Hungarian apiculture follows a "colonial position" in its sales of honey on the wholesale market.

From institutional and social perspectives (see Table 9.4), there is no effective coordinating force or lobbying power which could initiate a marketing strategy and measures for the benefit of beekeepers and apiculture. Due to the recent crisis in the honey market, more and more beekeepers try to sell their honey at local markets and festivals, as well as at home. These are small individual escape routes. Most of these new market players do not have experience in selling their honey efficiently and there are no national or regional honey marketing efforts behind these individual actions. In fact, the Hungarian apiculture sector exists in a contradictory market environment featuring overproduction within the country but shortage at the wider European Union level. This overproduction is channeled out via trade companies in the form of bulk product, and the price is adjusted to the import prices from developing countries that purchase it. These low prices create permanent tension and complaints among beekeepers. Neither honey packers nor traders are willing to recognize that the country should move from the wholesale market to a retail and quality market. Furthermore, the national agricultural policy is not committed to this kind of structural change or capable of enabling the positive effects that could be felt both in terms of beekeeper livelihoods and the health of the people.

Lessons learned

An important (and old) lesson for beekeepers is that it is not enough to have a good product. To achieve market success, it is necessary to implement appropriate marketing at international, national, sub-regional and individual levels. Beekeepers should cooperate with all the other stakeholders involved in the honey value chain. Unfortunately, beekeeping is a hidden and isolated profession, in which beekeepers are required to cover their face and body and warn others to the dangers of their work. Nevertheless, beekeepers should have an inherent interest in creating a wide supportive network among consumers, school children and their parents, health-conscious people, and civic organizations. The government should also take its own responsibility for helping resolve the problems identified in the sector, such as adequately representing the problems of beekeepers in front of EU bodies and recognizing the importance of the sector outside of its contribution to agricultural GDP.

Comparative policy analysis

In both of the cases examined, the success of the product is possible firstly due to the presence of specific natural resources and conditions: a particular microclimate for fruit growing, which facilitates the growth of raspberry in Arilje area (Serbia), and a large expanse of locust honey-plant forest in the case of honey production in Hungary. These natural assets have allowed for the development of specific economic activities for decades by small and medium-sized farms, managed by skilled producers with specific expertise to collect raspberries or manage beehives and bees to get a good quality and quantity of honey. The human capital employed to harvest these products is key for processing a high-quality product. However, the examination of these case studies has highlighted that it is not enough to be successful in the market chain of these products. In fact, the main role in these value chains is played by intermediaries, packers, and traders, who are mainly interested in selling big quantities, especially in the Hungarian case. Serbian traders are also aware of the importance of quality schemes due to increased competition.

Social networks as they currently exist suffer from weak ties, corruption, and poor organization, resulting in the ineffective representation of the real interests of producers. This poor social capital negatively affects the farmers, who have become dependent on the choices made by other external players. This dynamic is exemplified in the case of the Hungarian apiculture sector, in which the price is determined by those who influence the EU market by mixing low-quality and high-quality products.

Institutional collaboration in Hungary, including the involvement of the government (at different levels) and government partnerships with local producers and associations, is only focused on production and not on quality products or improving awareness among the local population about the value of the products from different perspectives. To date, an inclusive approach to promoting the sector has not been taken. On the contrary, in Serbian raspberry production there has been collaboration with government in favor of the recognition of Production of Geographical Indication for raspberry from Arilje. This quality identification implies a stronger role of the region's raspberry sector in the national and international market, if properly managed. Effective policy strategies, when developed in partnership with local producers, local associations, and local government, could contribute to improved awareness of the value of products, as well as enhanced methods for managing and enhancing them at the regional, national, and international levels.

The analysis of the different dimensions of territorial capital can create the basis for the elaboration of such integrated and efficient local development strategies, while taking into consideration all the different local assets and identifying strategies for their preservation and enhancement. The two case studies examined here show a lack of effective environmental strategies for the protection of these natural assets, neglecting the contributions that these resources make to the relevant economic sectors in both countries, as well as their importance for preserving biodiversity, pollination, and human well-being. The case studies also reveal a lack of enhancement of specific human capital for the development of regional or national agricultural sectors in the development strategies examined. Even if training activities have been organized, farmers feel they and their products are undervalued. Furthermore, due to dysfunctions within regional and national value chains, producers consider themselves at the mercy of other actors. The implemented policy actions also negatively affect the countries examined by diminishing their negotiating power at the international level. This challenge is due to the fact that governments are not able to promote quality products (in the Hungarian case) or recruit enough farmers to participate in the PGI labeling system (in the case of Serbia).

One of the key challenges for rural communities is the lack of regulatory expertise – including at the institutional level – as well as the lack of entrepreneurial and marketing capacity, which significantly hamper the achievement of market value for regional agricultural products. The transfer of best practices from other successful sectors, such as vineyards in Hungary, and awareness-raising about local territorial capital can lead to spillover effects that help contribute to responsible development strategies. This approach could be focused on an interdisciplinary strategy and be aimed at creating new opportunities at the economic, social (e.g. active associations, groups of farmers, groups of entrepreneurs), and cultural (e.g. promotion of local products and traditions) levels.

Through the analysis of different dimensions of territorial capital, a number of important policy actions can be outlined. The first of these is the need for a practical tool to identify strategies and improve awareness of local assets to foster the well-being of rural inhabitants. This approach is especially important considering how rural policies are often more focused on integrated approaches based on local resources to facilitate competitiveness and innovation within areas of intervention. These avenues can also strengthen interactions among public, private (including for-profit firms and social enterprises), and third sectors to guarantee a cohesive and supportive local society.

Notes

1 In the 1308/2013 EU market regulation text the term "honey" appears only 11 times, while the term "wine" appears 423 times and "milk" 296 times.
2 In March 2018, The EU Parliament adopted a "Report on Prospects and Challenges for the EU Apiculture Sector", initiated by a Hungarian prime minister, Erdős Norbert (www.europarl.europa.eu/sides/getDoc.do?pubRef=-//EP//TEXT+REPORT+A8-2018-0014+0+DOC+XML+V0//EN#title5, accessed August 2018).

References

Ambrosio-Albala, M., Delgado, M., 2008. *Understanding rural areas dynamics from a complex perspective: An application of prospective structural analysis*, in: 12th EAAE Congress, People, food and environment: Global trends and European strategies, Ghent, Belgium.

Atkinson, R., 2013. *Territorial capital, attractiveness and the place-based approach: The potential implications for territorial development*, in: Pálné Kovács, I., Scott, J., Gál, Z. (Eds.), *Territorial cohesion in Europe: For the 70th anniversary of the Transdanubian Research Institute*. HAS IRS, Pécs, pp. 297–308.

Battaglini, E., Babović, M., Bogdanov, N., 2016. *Framing resilience by territorialisation*, in: Palovita, A., Jarvela, M. (Eds.), *Climate adaptation, policy and food supply chain management in Europe*. Routledge, London, pp. 119–131.

Belletti, G., Marescotti, A., 2011. *Monitoring and evaluating the effects of the protection of geographical indications: A methodological proposal*, in: Belletti, G., Marescotti, A., Paus, M., Reviron, S., Deppeler, A., Stamm, H., Thévenod-Mottet, E. (Eds.), *The effects of protecting geographical indications ways and means of their evaluation*. Swiss Federal Institute of Intellectual Property, Bern, pp. 31–122.

Bogdanov, N., Nikolić, A., 2013. *Area based development approach: Evidence from border rural region Drina-Sava*, in: Bogdanov, N., Stevanović, S. (Eds.), *Agriculture and rural development: Challenges of transition and integration processes*. Department of Agricultural Economics, Belgrade, pp. 101–111.

Bourdieu, P., 1987. *The forms of capital*, in: Richardson, J.G. (Ed.), *Handbook of theory and research for the sociology of education*. Greenwood Press, New York, pp. 241–258.

Bourdieu, P., 2009. *Ragioni pratiche*. Il Mulino, Bologna.

Brasili, C., Saguatti, A., Benni F., Marchese, A., Gandolfo, D. 2012. *The impacts of the economic crisis on the territorial capital of Italian regions*. www-sre.wu.ac.at/ersa/ersaconfs/ersa12/e120821aFinal00646.pdf (accessed August 2018).

Bross, P., 2006. *Véget ért egy történet. Magyar Méhész Zrt. (The end of a story: Hungarian Beekeepers Shareholding Co.)*, Méhészet 5, 10–11.

Brunori, G., 2006. *Post-rural processes in wealthy rural areas: Hybrid networks and symbolic capital*. Research in Rural Sociology and Development 12, 125–152.

Brunori, G., Rossi, A., 2007. *Differentiating countryside: Social representations and governance pattern in rural areas with high social density: The case of Chianti, Italy*. Journal of Rural Studies 23, 183–205.

Camagni, R., 2009. *Territorial impact assessment for European regions: A methodological proposal and an application to EU transport policy.* Evaluation and Program Planning 32(4), 342–350.

Camagni, R. 2014. *The regional policy debate: A territorial, place-based and proximity approach,* in: Torre, A., Wallet, F. (Eds.), *Regional development and proximity relations.* Edward Elgar, Cheltenham, pp. 317–332.

CBI – Ministry of Foreign Affairs, n.d. *Exporting fresh berries to Europe.* www.cbi.eu/market-information/fresh-fruit-vegetables/berries/europe/ (accessed August 2017).

Cooper, T., Hart, K., Baldock, D., 2009. *The provision of public goods through agriculture in the European Union.* Report Prepared for DG Agriculture and Rural Development. Institute for European Environmental Policy, London.

EC – European Commission, 1996. *European Charter for Rural Areas, a report by the Parliamentary Assembly of the Council of Europe.* European Commission, Brussels.

EC – European Commission, 2016a. *A strategic approach to EU agricultural research and innovation.* Paper Prepared for the European Conference: Designing the Path: a Strategic Approach to EU Agricultural Research and Innovation, 26–28 January 2016. European Commission, Brussels.

EC – European Commission, 2016b. *Report from the Commission to the European Parliament and the Council on the implementation of the measures concerning the apiculture sector of Regulation (EU) No 1308/2013 of the European Parliament and of the Council establishing a common organisation of the markets in agricultural products.* http://eur-lex.europa.eu/legal-content/EN-HU/TXT/?uri=CELEX:52016DC0776&from=EN (accessed July 2017).

EC – European Commission, 2017. *Report from the Commission to the European Parliament, the Council, the European Economic and Social Committee and the Committee of the Regions on the implementation of the Circular Economy Action Plan and related Annex.* http://ec.europa.eu/environment/circular-economy/index_en.htm-http://ec.europa.eu/environment/circular-economy/implementation_report_annex.pdf (accessed April 2017).

EU Beekeeping Sector, 2016. *National apiculture programmes 2016.* https://ec.europa.eu/agriculture/honey/programmes_hu (accessed July 2017).

European Parliament, 2013. *Regulation (EU) No. 1308/2013 of the European Parliament and of the Council establishing a common organisation of the markets in agricultural products and replacing Council Regulations (EEC) No 922/72, (EEC) No 234/79, (EC) No 1037/2001 and (EC) No 1234/2007,* paras. 55–57. http://eur-lex.europa.eu/legal-content/EN/ALL/?uri=CELEX%3A32013R1308 (accessed April 2017).

Garrod, B., Wornell, R., Youell, R., 2006. *Re-conceptualising rural resources as countryside capital: The case of rural tourism.* Journal of Rural Studies 22, 117–128.

Hungarian National Apiculture Programme, 2016. Hungarian National Apiculture Programme 2016–2019 Földművelési Minisztérium. Március. https://ec.europa.eu/agriculture/sites/agriculture/files/honey/programmes/national-apiculture/nap-hu_hu.pdf (accessed August 2017).

Knickel, K., Redman, M., Darnhofer, I., Ashkenazy, A., Calvao Chebach, T., Sumane, S., Tisenkopfs, T., Zemeckis, R., Atkociuniene, V., Rivera, M., Strauss, A., Kristensen, L.S., Schiller, S., Koopmans, M.E., Rogge, E., 2018. *Between aspirations and reality: Making farming, food systems and rural areas more resilient, sustainable and equitable.* Journal of Rural Studies 59, 197–210.

Kovács, D., 2017. *Méhészkönyv. Eladjuk vagy értékesítjük? (Beekeepers' book: Do we sell or valorize?).* Baja és Körzete Méhész Klub Egyesület, Baja, Hungary.

Mazoyer, M., Roudart, L., 2006. *A history of world agriculture: From the Neolithic age to the current crisis.* Monthly Review Press, New York.

Mazzola, F., Lo Cascio, I., Epifanio, R., Di Giacomo, G., 2018. *Territorial capital and growth over the Great Recession: A local analysis for Italy.* The Annals of Regional Science 60, 411–441. https://doi.org/10.1007/s00168-017-0853-2.

OECD, 2001. *Multifunctionality towards an analytical framework.* OECD Publications, Paris.

OECD, 2006. *Coherence of agricultural and rural development policies.* OECD Publications, Paris.

OECD, 2013. *Rural–urban partnerships: An integrated approach to economic development.* OECD Publishing, Paris.

OECD, 2016. *Rural policy 3.0,* in: OECD Regional Outlook 2016, Productive Regions for Inclusive Societies. OECD Publishing, Paris.

OECD, 2018. *Rural 3.0: A framework for rural development, Policy note.* www.oecd.org/regional/regional-policy/oecdworkonruraldevelopment.htm (accessed April 2018).

OECD, n.d. *Understanding rural economies, Rural Policy 3.0 information note.* www.oecd.org/cfe/regional-policy/understanding-rural-economies.htm (accessed April 2018).

OPERA Research Center, 2011. *Bee Health in Europe – Facts and Figures – 2011.*

Paraušić, V., Simeunović, I., 2016. *Market analysis of Serbia's raspberry sector and cluster development initiatives.* Economics of Agriculture 63(4), 1417–1432.

Perucca, G., 2014. *The role of territorial capital in local economic growth: Evidence from Italy.* European Planning Studies 22(3), 537–562.

Pierre, J., 2000. *Debating governance: Authority, steering, and democracy.* Oxford University Press, New York.

Pompili, T., Martinoia, M., 2011. *Building synthetic indicators for aspects of territorial capital towards their impact on regional performance.* European Regional Science Association 51st European Congress, pp. 1–30.

RS IPO, n.d. Republic of Serbia Intellectual Property Office website. www.zis.gov.rs/intellectual-property-rights/inidications-of-geographical-origin/list-of-igo.91.html (accessed August 2017).

RS MESP (The Republic of Serbia Ministry of Environment and Spatial Planning), 2010. *Fourth national report to the United Nations Convention on Biological Diversity.*

Segrè, A., Vittuari, M., Regoli F., 2011. *Can rural tourism boost green livelihoods? Empirical evidence from Maramureş.* Romanian Review of Regional Studies 7(1), 107–122.

Servillo, L., Atkinson, R., Russo, A.P., 2012. *Territorial attractiveness in EU urban and spatial policy: A critical review and future research agenda.* European Urban and Regional Studies 20(4), 349–365.

Sredojević, Z., Vlahović, B., Maksimović, A., 2015. *Economic indicators of different types of raspberry production on family farms.* Agroekonomika 66, 114–124.

Stoker, G., 2011. *Was local governance such a good idea? A global comparative perspective.* Public Administration 89(1), 15–31.

Tacoli, C., 1998. *Rural–urban interactions: A guide to the literature.* Environment and Urbanization 10(1), 147–166.

Tóth, B.I., 2014. *Territorial capital: Theory, empirics and critical remarks.* European Planning Studies 23(7), 1327–1344.

UN – ESCWA, 2009. *Indicators on rural development and agriculture household income.* Expert Group Meeting on Adopting the Sustainable Livelihoods Approach for Promoting Rural Development in the ESCWA Region. United Nations, Beirut.

van der Ploeg, J.D., van Broekhuizen, R., Brunori, G., Sonnino, R., Knickel, K., Tisenkopfs, T., Oost-indie, H., 2008. *Towards a framework for understanding regional rural development,* in: van der Ploeg, J.D., Marsden, T. (Eds.), *Unfolding webs: The dynamics of regional rural development.* Van Gorcum, Assen, pp. 1–28.

PART II

People and society

10

INTERNATIONAL MIGRATION

Sustaining rural communities

Philomena De Lima and Lidia Carvajal

Introduction

Transport, technological innovations, demographic trends, globalization, geo-politics, and climate change have intensified the pace and diversity of mobilities and migrants in urban and rural areas. These trends are disrupting the distinctions between emigration (sending), immigration (receiving), and transit countries as migratory routes and categories of migrants become increasingly diverse, leading to the extension of the geographical scope and spread of countries implicated in migration globally (Czaika and de Haas, 2014). Despite an overwhelming focus on international migration, the majority (97.6 percent) of the world's population chooses not to cross international borders (UN, 2017a, p. 3). Internal migration associated with international migration is estimated to be approximately 763 million (FAO, 2016, p. 6). Most of those who migrate, including those crossing international borders, are moving to cities, and for this reason scholarship has privileged an urban focus. However, this preoccupation with urban migration has been challenged by a growing body of literature on international labor migration in rural regions of the North which have little or no previous history of extensive international immigration. Recognizing there is no ideal nomenclature for categorizing countries, for the purposes of this chapter the authors use the terms South ("low income" countries) and North ("high income" countries), except when citing literature where the terms utilized by the authors are used (for further information refer to IOM, 2013, Table 1, pp. 44, 41–47).

Long-term demographic trends associated with declining fertility rates and aging societies characterize most countries in the North. Globalization, the restructuring of rural economies interacting with challenges posed by aging populations, declining birth rates, youth out-migration, and shortages of labor and skills have led to the production of "uneven spatial development" in rural areas, which has affected the survival of some rural communities (Brown and Shucksmith, 2016). Consequently, policy-makers have turned to international migrants as a strategy to address these challenges. However, the reliance of rural sectors such as agriculture on seasonal and/or temporary migrant workers to address shortages of labor during certain times of the year is not a new phenomenon (e.g. Collins, 1976). What is different in the twenty-first century is that the tendency to employ international migrant labor has intensified and expanded, incorporating a wider range of rural sectors (e.g. food processing, tourism, services) in the context of deregulated labor markets and changing geo-politics. Associated with these trends is a tendency towards "3D jobs" (dirty, dangerous, and demeaning/demanding), seasonality, insecurity, and low pay (Otero and Preibisch, 2014; Preibisch, 2011). As suggested in the Canadian agricultural context, which applies equally to countries in the North in general, "cheap labor is exchanged for cheap food" (Read *et al.*, 2013, p. 4). This trend is not only restricted to food or specific products but also applies to service sectors such as tourism and social care.

This chapter provides an overview of international labor migrants and their role in sustaining rural communities. This examination draws on the experiences of a sending country (Mexico) and a receiving country (Scotland, United Kingdom). The following three sections set the context by addressing three questions: (i) who is a migrant?; (ii) what are the trends in international migration; and (iii) what is the relationship between migration and development? Followed by a discussion of two countries and ending with a concluding section identifying key emerging themes, the chapter offers overarching policy implications and further research questions.

Who is a "migrant"?

Despite the considerable public gaze on "migrants" globally, there is no internationally agreed definition. At an international level for data gathering purposes, most countries tend to employ the United Nations (UN) (2017a, p. 3) definition: "An international migrant is a person who is living in a country other than his or her country of birth", which does not capture the diverse forms of migration. The Organization on Migration (IOM) (2018) adopts an inclusive definition:

> ...as any person who is moving or has moved across an international border or within a State away from his/her habitual place of residence, regardless of (1) the person's legal status; (2) whether the movement is voluntary or involuntary; (3) what the causes for the movement are; or (4) what the length of the stay is.

This definition acknowledges that migrants are diverse, encompassing movement within or across national borders (spatiality, e.g. internal, international migration), characterized by four dimensions which are interrelated and dynamic. These are: (i) legal status (e.g. labor migrant, skilled/unskilled, tourist, student, asylum seekers/refugees, undocumented/"illegal"); (ii) migration choices (e.g. forced, voluntary); (iii) motivations (e.g. work, poverty, lifestyle, leisure, study, wars, natural disaster, persecution); and (iv) temporality (e.g. temporary, permanent, circular).

Trends in migration

The tasks of counting migrants and plotting trends are challenging. This is associated with the diversity of migrants and countries involved, and the varied definitions of international migrants and proxies employed in data collection by countries (Cangiano, 2018). The UN (2017b, p. 1) estimated that in 2017 there were 258 million international migrants, constituting 3.4 percent of the global population, which increased from 2.8 percent (173 million) in 2000. The North and the South experienced a 50 percent increase each, reflecting the growing role of the South in global migration. However, given that the total population growth rate in the North is lower than the South, it is estimated that international migrant share of the total population is likely to grow faster in the North than in the South (for more detailed information see UN, 2017a, 2017b).

The demographic characteristics of international migrants are complex and changing, but broadly in 2017, the median age was 39.2 years, with females constituting just under half (48.4 percent) with 74 percent being of working age. The evidence on the contribution of international migration to long-term population change is equivocal. However, it has been identified as contributing to population growth (e.g. North America) and slowing down or even reversing population decline (e.g. Europe), as well as reducing the old-age dependency ratio in more developed regions (UN, 2017a, pp. 15–20).

Migration and development

A detailed discussion on the intersections between international migration and development is beyond the scope of this chapter. However, since the 1950s, debates have veered between narratives of "developmentalist optimism in the 1950s and 1960s, to neo-Marxist pessimism over the 1970s and 1980s, towards more optimistic views in the 1990s and 2000s" (de Haas, 2010, p. 227). The migration-development discourses have foregrounded the contribution of migration to economic growth and poverty alleviation in countries of the South motivated by concerns about reducing and/or managing migration to the North (see Fratzke and Salant, 2018; Newland, 2017). In addition to focusing on drivers and motivations for migration, the impacts of remittances (financial transfers and investment) occupy a central place in migrant-development scholarship (discussed further in relation to Mexico below). Empirical evidence on the impacts of remittances, however, remains equivocal and contested across countries (IFAD, 2007).

While evidence abounds of the impacts – both positive and negative – of migration on development, the reasons why policy-makers should integrate migration into development planning still lack empirical foundations (OECD, 2017, p. 22). The situation is exacerbated as "development" is rarely defined or operationalized in policy discussions (Fratzke and Salant, 2018; Russell, 2003) – rather drawing from universalist assumptions of "development" (Raghuram, 2009) – and migration impacts for heterogeneous groups and settings are contingent on context, which are rarely researched in this field. Migration-development scholarship is fragmented and has been extensively criticized on the following grounds: the causes and drivers of migration are researched separately from its impacts; the impact of international migration on economic growth and poverty alleviation in sending countries is privileged at the expense of a focus on receiving countries; migration is rarely discussed as intrinsic to "wider social and development processes"; and there is a lack of attention to human rights and the well-being of migrants (de Haas, 2010, p. 228; see also Fratzke and Salant, 2018; Preibisch and Su, 2016; Castles, 2010, 2009; Russell, 2003). At the international level, there is a growing policy emphasis on the relationship between migration and development policies as dynamic interactive processes because "[when] supported by appropriate policies migration can contribute to inclusive and sustainable economic growth and development in both home and host communities" (UN, 2017a, p. 1). This trend is also evident in the context of rural development, where it is recognized that rural sectors (such as agriculture) require global solutions and approaches that include an emphasis on the social impacts with a commitment to the well-being and human rights of migrants (FAO, 2016; Preibisch and Su, 2016). There has also been an increasing interest in development beyond economic remittances to social and cultural remittances (e.g. new ideas, know-how, etc.) (Levitt and Lamba-Nieves, 2011).

Moving from migration-development debates in general to addressing the evidence base regarding the extent to which migration contributes to rural development is unsurprisingly weak and discussed mainly in relation to the South. The Food and Agricultural Organization (FAO) has been attempting to address some of the gaps, nevertheless the focus continues to be the South. In addition to the general challenges highlighted previously, the heterogeneity in definitions of "rural" and rural development makes the task of measuring impacts in rural areas challenging. Approximately 40 percent of international remittances are sent to rural areas, reflecting the rural origin of migrants (FAO, 2016, p. 6). The evidence for the impact of remittances on rural areas and sectors in sending countries (e.g. agriculture) remains mixed, with some research suggesting that remittances may exacerbate inequalities between households in sending countries (OECD, 2017; FAO, 2018, 2016). By contrast, much of the literature in the North has focused on the reliance of sectors such as agriculture on international migrants, as well as a more general focus on international migrants for addressing gaps in skills and labor shortages because of changing demographic trends (discussed further in relation to Scotland/UK).

USA, Canada, and Mexico: impact of remittances

In North America, the US and Canada are mainly migrant receiving countries, whereas Mexico is identified as a sending country or as a migrant route for those from elsewhere in Latin America, Africa, or Asia, whose final destination is the US (UN, 2017a). Given that the US has a population of 49.7 million immigrants, it is unsurprising that this is the most important remittance-sending country globally, with total remittances estimated at almost US $66.6 billion (World Bank, 2017). In the context of North America, the discussion focuses on international labor migrants from rural Mexico and the impacts of remittances on countries of origin. The majority of these workers enter the US either as undocumented workers or through a temporary guest worker program, and to Canada mainly through the latter.

Migration and remittances

According to the World Bank (2017), Mexico occupies the fourth place in the top ten remittance-receiving countries, after India, China, and the Philippines. A well-known migration/remittances corridor exists between Mexico and the US that has enabled more than 13 million Mexicans to reach "the other side" where they have found paid jobs and from where Mexico receives the majority (95 percent) of remittances of more than US $28.77 billion (Banco de Mexico, 2018). Furthermore, in 2016 Mexico received US $0.15 billion in remittances from Canada (World Bank, 2016), mainly from Canada's Seasonal Agricultural Workers Program (CSAWP).

At the macro level, remittances have been identified as an important source of foreign exchange for national accounts, playing an important role in promoting macro-economic stability. For example, remittances can contribute to a surplus in some quarters in the national accounts of recipient countries, enabling them to negotiate international loans. For Mexico, remittances are much more stable than foreign direct investment or foreign portfolio investments, given that they enable the receiving country to avoid future financial obligations. At the micro level, remittances can increase household income with the multiplier effect of its impact on household savings and investment (Romero González, 2016). Each dollar raised becomes $1.05 of an effect on income, which means a multiplier effect of remittances that translates into higher consumption of services and increases in secondary activity, potentially leading to greater demand for manufactured products (Woodruff and Zenteno, 2001). At the social level, remittances may be a mechanism to reduce social and economic inequalities, given that they are channeled directly without diversion of resources. Initially during the migration process, there are likely to be negative demographic and economic effects due to increased social inequality. However, this is reduced as more migrants move (the "migrant chain" effect) due to the fact that the families of the new migrants can access levels of consumption that only the families of previous migrants could (Canales, 2006).

Mexico–USA migration

Mexico and the US have a long and complicated history with respect to immigration, particularly regarding agricultural workers. The Mexican international migration experience through the guest worker started with the Bracero Program that was established between the two world wars and was extended until 1922 and lasted until 1964, allowing approximately five million people to work temporarily in the US agricultural sector. The main objective was to break with the old migratory pattern known as "indentured labor" controlled by contractor companies that supplied Mexican laborers to the agriculture sector, mines, rail companies, and other industries which was established in response to the scarcity of low-skilled labor during World War II (Durand, 2006).

After having no guest worker program for more than two decades, the Immigration Reform and Control Act in 1986 was passed in the US to enable Mexico to send workers once again through the H2 visa programs with the purpose of admitting agricultural workers to carry out a specific, temporary activity to face the scarcity of national labor force. The obligations on US employers employing workers under the program are: (1) payment of the same salary that US residents receive; (2) a document/contract that sets out in detail the total income of the worker, working conditions, and hours of work; (3) transportation from the worker's home to his or her work, when workers live far from the farm, and then to the next place of employment when the contract ends; (4) suitable accommodation with the minimums established at the federal level; (5) agricultural tools and implements; (6) food or facilities for them to prepare their own food; (7) compensation insurance; and (8) guarantee at least three-quarters of the total work offered (Wassem and Collver, 2001). In 2016, 332,445 Mexican workers participated in the H2A, which represents 95.5 percent of the total number of workers that the United States receives through this program (Homeland Security, 2016).

According to Escobar-Latapi (1999), the H2A program is the subject of strong criticism as it violates human rights, and it diverts resources from workers to agencies and middlemen recruiting the workforce.

As in H2A visas, the maximum period for H2B is one year, which can be extended by a total of three; however, in this case there is a cap of 66,000 workers per year. The application and eligibility process is similar to the H2A program. Both qualified and unskilled workers are eligible, with the exception of doctors and agricultural workers. In 2016, however, 90,301 Mexican workers participated in this program (Homeland Security, 2016)

Mexico–Canada migration

In contrast to the US, guest worker programs in Canada are relatively new with regard to agricultural labor migration. Successive Canadian governments implemented various internal and international programs to alleviate the lack of a reliable labor force willing to work on Canadian farms (Basok, 2002; Satzewich, 1991; Verduzco, 2000). However, these efforts failed to solve the problem. Few Canadians are willing to undertake agricultural activities (temporarily or permanently) due to low wages, difficult and dangerous jobs, and the exclusion of agriculture from provincial labor legislation that covers working conditions. Over the last four decades, this labor market disequilibrium has been addressed through Canada's Seasonal Agricultural Workers Program (CSAWP) to meet farmers' requirements for reliable workers. It is suggested that the program also can help maintain Canada's economic prosperity and global agricultural trade competitiveness, therefore expanding job prospects for Canadian citizens in sectors that depend on agriculture and other related activities (Preibisch, 2007).

The main objective for Mexico, as stated in the International Labour Organization (ILO) agreement framework, flows from the principle that every government should seek to provide people with employment in order to improve their standard of living (STyPS, Mexican Ministry of Labor and Social Welfare, 2006). As there is insufficient labor demand in rural areas of Mexico, the Mexican government signed in 1974 a Memorandum of Understanding (MoU) with the Canadian government to establish a program for seasonal employment in the Canadian agricultural sector by facilitating the granting of temporary work permits to Mexican agricultural workers.

The number of participants has grown significantly, from 203 in 1974 to 25,344 in 2017 (STyPS, 2018), While over the 42 years of the program's existence, 326,525 workers have been placed in Canadian farms, most of whom are male. Female participants account for approximately 3 percent of the total Mexican workers in the program and work mainly selecting plants and fruits in greenhouses, nurseries, or the field. There are two relevant policy objectives in the CSAWP regulations and immigration laws which go some way to ensuring that differences between migrant workers and Canadian citizens are minimized: (1) migrant workers are to be afforded the same treatment as Canadian workers; and (2) the hiring of migrant agricultural workers should not result in depressed wages and working conditions that are unattractive to Canadian workers.

These programs not only assist in providing migrants a secure income and support families in rural areas due to the spillover effects they create, but also provide financial stability at the macro-economic level for national governments, as highlighted above. A managed international labor migration program is increasingly identified internationally as being a "win–win" situation, with positive effects on both the communities of origin and the communities of destination. However, research has also highlighted that guest worker programs potentially limit the bond migrants would like to have or could build with the community where they live temporarily.

Impacts of remittances in rural Mexico

There is an ongoing debate in the literature about the uses of remittances and the consequent economic impacts.[1] There is significant evidence that remittances are used primarily for daily consumption, leaving almost nothing for the purchase of productive assets (Reichert, 1981; Rubenstein, 1992). Other researchers, however, argue that remittances are used for more than just consumption and can have spillover effects on extended families and the local economy, as well as on community development more broadly (Canales, 2016; Sander, 2003; Durand et al., 1996b, for Mexican migration to United States; Basok, 2003; Wiggins et al., 2000; Verduzco and Lozano, 2003; Taylor and Yunez-Naude, 1999; Taylor and Fletcher, 2002; Binford, 2003, for the case of Mexican migration to Canada).

Durand et al. (1996a, 1996b) make a strong case for the argument that "migradollar" consumer spending yields substantial and varied multiplier effects in a wide range of Mexican communities. In turn, there is evidence that remittances can represent a way out of poverty by improving human, physical, and financial assets (Canales, 2016; Verduzco and Lozano, 2003; Goldring, 2004; Preibisch, 2000; Sandoval and Vanegas, 2001; Basok, 1999; Alcaraz, 2012). Remittances have both indirect short-term effects and long-term asset accumulation effects on the level and distribution of household farm incomes; furthermore, where credit and insurance markets are missing or are imperfect, migrant remittances may promote the growth of non-remittance incomes by enabling households to overcome liquidity and risk constraints (Taylor, 1992; Canales, 2016; Carvajal and Johnson, 2016). Remittances create multiplier effects on household production and consumption, increase input demand that in turn enhances local production, and therefore the community income in general. Some families increase livestock production and other economic activities, therefore increasing household and community income (Yunez-Naude, 2001; Taylor, 2003).

Remittances follow a seasonal pattern throughout the course of a year, increasing significantly during summer and decreasing at Christmas vacation times when Mexican migrants tend to return home. August is the month that remittances reach the highest annual peak, corresponding to the month just before students start a new academic year. Migrant parents tend to send more money at this time to pay tuition and buy school supplies, uniforms, and shoes. May is also one of the most important months for sending remittances, in part because Mother's Day occurs in this month. According to Arroyo and Berumen (2000), remittances represent an average of 54 percent of income for 5 percent of Mexican households; for many economically impoverished rural communities, remittances constitute 75–90 percent of local income (cited in Binford, 2003). In addition, in urban Mexico, remittances represent an important source of financing for micro-enterprises. An increase in the share of external remittances by 1 percent significantly decreases the share devoted to food (-0.10%) and business (-0.24%) and increases that devoted to health (0.007%), durable goods (0.01%), nondurable goods (0.02%), patrimony (0.1%), and savings (0.02%). External remittances have a positive impact on household savings and stimulate investments in durable goods (Canales, 2016). One of the hypotheses of migration is that it has negative impacts on agricultural activity due to the abandonment of sending communities' agricultural assets that is assumed to be generated because of migration. However, in countries like Mexico where the labor force in rural areas is abundant, remittances can economically counteract this effect through allowing other agricultural laborers to work the land belonging to those who have migrated (Carvajal and Johnson, 2016).

Sustaining rural communities in Scotland/UK: international migration

In contrast to the characterization of Canada and the US as countries of immigration, the UK has been described as "[a] reluctant country of immigration" (Somerville *et al.*, 2009). Contemporary Scottish/UK policy interests in international labor migration in particular are driven by similar concerns to a number of countries in the North, although the geo-political, socio-cultural, and institutional contexts (e.g. governance, legislation) vary. The rural Scottish example focuses on the experiences of a receiving country associated with the migration of EU nationals from Central and Eastern Europe[2] (A8 and A2 nationals) since 2004, primarily for work purposes. Free movement, including labor mobility between regions and countries that constitute the EU/EEA, is a fundamental right of being an EU national, and is not subject to the immigration rules applied to non-EU/EEA nationals. The eventual withdrawal of the UK from the EU may of course change this scenario. The rationale for focusing on intra-EU mobility is because of the diverse spatial trends in migration that followed the entry of the A8 nationals to the UK since 2004, which was not confined to the usual urban destinations. Although most of these immigrants migrated to cities, many also moved to rural areas on a scale not experienced previously, working in sectors such as agriculture, horticulture, food processing, and services (MAC, 2018a; de Lima *et al.*, 2012; McCollum *et al.*, 2012).

In 2015, Scotland's rural population accounted for 18 percent of the population and occupied 98 percent of its landmass; of this, 70 percent is defined as "remote rural" with population sparsity a particular feature (Scottish Government, 2015b, p. 8; definitions of rural/urban, pp. 6–7). The extent to which international migration might counter the impacts (especially labor supply) of population decline and an aging population has been a major preoccupation in Scotland. The discussion focuses on two of a number of recurrent issues which are closely related: migration as a contributor to population change and migrant engagement in rural labor markets.

Contribution of migration to demographic changes

Successive Scottish governments have consistently emphasized population growth as critical to their economic strategy, featuring prominently as one of four priorities in achieving economic growth: "A country with an international outlook and focus, open to trade, migration and new ideas" (Scottish Government, 2015b, p. 11). This emphasis contrasts with the rest of the UK and has led the Scottish government to argue for a more tailored immigration policy to suit its economic needs (Scottish Government, 2018).[3] This difference has become more pronounced in the context of the UK vote to leave the EU (Boswell *et al.*, 2017).

For decades, Scotland's population has hovered just above 5 million – in 2016, it was estimated at 5.4 million (NRS, 2016, p. 6) with variations across and within different regions. A projected increase of residents over age 60 by 60–68 percent is predicted by 2033, as well as a rising old-age dependency ratio (i.e. "number of pensionable age people per 100 working age people") and below-replacement fertility rates. These demographic trends are identified as having a significant impact on the Scottish economy. Aging population trends have a significant "strong urban/rural dimension", with 21 percent of the population in some rural areas over 60 years of age, in contrast to 17 percent in urban locations (Scottish Government, 2010, p. 13). These trends are exacerbated further in rural communities due to the out-migration of youth and the economically active seeking post-school education opportunities and better employment, resulting in a shortage of labor and skills in a range of sectors.

Although EU migration, and particularly that of A8 nationals, has been a significant contributor of net migration in the UK, the situation is dynamic in the context of Brexit, with less people arriving and more leaving the UK (MAC, 2018b; ONS, 2018). In Scotland, internal and international migration are identified as significant contributors to population gain, with A8 nationals being the major contributors to population growth since 2004 (SPICe, 2016). Mid-year 2017 population statistics estimated the presence of 219,000 EU nationals in Scotland; 130,000 of these were A8 nationals. (Scottish Government, 2018, p. 7). Some rural areas (including local authority areas in the predominantly rural Scottish Highlands and Islands region) and particularly those defined as "accessible rural" recorded net population gains. A8 nationals have been present in most, if not every, local authority area since 2004 (Jentsch *et al.*, 2007). However, some of the population gains in rural areas could be associated with the internal migration of older people for lifestyle reasons (Scottish Government, 2010).

The migration of A8 nationals to Scotland is viewed positively by policy-makers concerned with the impacts of changing demographic circumstances on the goal of sustaining remote rural communities. However, there are concerns that migration policy discourses continue to be framed in the context of demographic considerations at the expense of evidence of defined labor market needs (Boswell *et al.*, 2017). Furthermore, obtaining accurate data on migrants, let alone the contribution of migration to population change in Scotland more generally and in rural areas in particular, is a persistent challenge given the lack of a comprehensive system for registering migrants in the UK (NRS, 2018).

EU nationals generally, but those from A8 countries in particular, have a younger age profile: 80 percent of this group is of working age, compared to 65 percent of the overall

Scottish population (SPICe, 2016, p. 3). This, therefore, has helped offset population decline across Scotland in the short term, but the gains might be less evident in rural areas due to the higher numbers of older people. The population gain has been facilitated by the provision within the EU for young migrants to settle and have/bring their families in/to their new homes. However, the extent to which migration can be relied upon to contribute to population growth and mitigate the impacts of an aging population in the long term is recognized as limited. Not only will migrants age, but evidence from demographic studies in general suggests that high birth rates tend not to be sustained beyond the first generation as migrants' birth rates come to match the birth rate of the host population. Furthermore, the number of migrants required to compensate for the decline in the working-age population is estimated to be higher than that required for offsetting population decline and would require "extremely high" and ongoing levels of migration much more pronounced than is currently the case or is potentially feasible. In this context, there have been calls for a reassessment of social and public policies related to retirement, involving the state, employers, and civil society (UN Population Division, 2001), a focus on addressing the reasons why people leave (MAC, 2018b), and the retention/attraction of economically active people.

EU labor migration

Aging and declining rural populations have led to a heightened need for migrants. For example, in the Highlands and Islands, the combination of lower levels of unemployment with growth in sectors such as tourism, food, and drink have attracted migrants to live and work in rural areas (Scottish Government, 2018, p. 17). The relationship between demographic changes and economic needs are intertwined as changes in age structure (discussed above) can result in poor economic performance in sectors experiencing labor shortages. Although reasons for labor shortages are complex and varied, they can be exacerbated if unemployment rates are low, as is reported to be the case in the Scottish economy. Migrant labor has the potential to counter poor economic performance by enabling businesses to meet demands for their products and increasing demand for products through the contribution of new skills and contacts (see Boswell *et al.*, 2017). Immigration is a UK government responsibility and, given Scotland's relatively recent experience of international migration compared in particular to England, evidence on the macro-economic impact of migration tends to be UK-wide. Consequently, assessing the impact of migrants on the Scottish economy, let alone on rural development, is problematic. Much of the evidence on the impact of migrants on rural areas and their role in local labor markets in Scotland relies on local studies focusing on views of employers, migrant workers, and service providers.

Recent UK evidence identified employment and study as the two most common reasons why people migrate to the UK (ONS, 2018). EU nationals employed in Scotland represented 4 percent (115,000) of the Scottish workforce in employment, with the majority (79,000) from Eastern European countries (SPICe, 2016, p. 11). The evidence in Scotland persistently highlights that EU nationals generally, but particularly A8 nationals act as a flexible labor supply where demand exceeds local labor supply but also meets demands for low-skilled labor, despite some having relatively high levels of qualifications (Scottish Government, 2016). The drive towards segmentation of the labor market where sectors, including agriculture and food processing, hospitality, and catering, rely on migrant labor in preference to local labor is extensively documented (de Lima, 2015; McCollum and Findlay, 2015; Rolfe and Metcalfe, 2009).

Despite efforts to diversify the rural economy in Scotland, the narrow "economic base" continues to present challenges (Roberts and Newlands, 2010). The two main sectors of employment in rural Scotland are the "tertiary sector" (comprising services) and the "primary sector" (agriculture, forestry, and fishing). The primary sector employs more people in remote rural areas (16%) and accessible rural areas (12%) than in the rest of Scotland (0.2%). (Scottish Government, 2015b, pp. 49–53). Against this backdrop, remote rural labor markets are identified as having two interrelated constraints which make them unattractive for local workers and migrants in the long term: limited types of employment and poor conditions of employment (e.g. seasonality, low pay, lack of progression, and "3-D" jobs). From employers' perspectives, especially in sectors such as agriculture, horticulture, and food processing, migrant workers are perceived as "reliable and good workers" and as vital to the survival of their businesses (MAC, 2018a).

In making sense of migrants and their impacts on rural communities, it is important to consider "place effects", given that the opportunities (e.g. socio-economic, educational, cultural, environmental) and resources that particular places can mobilize will vary. Despite espousing the value of migrant labor, in general evidence suggests that labor migrants in rural areas have limited opportunities for professional development and career progression and are more likely to experience poor access to services such as language classes, as well as strong pressures to assimilate (Scottish Government, 2016; Netto *et al.*, 2015). The predictions of labor market need in the UK and Scotland suggest that the occupations likely to face shortages will tend to be relatively low-skilled and low-status in sectors such as agriculture, horticulture, social care, and hospitality. If post-Brexit Britain opts for immigration controls for EU nationals, labor shortages may have to be met by the introduction of temporary worker programs that were prevalent previously for specific sectors, as well as on the robotization of some of the jobs currently undertaken by migrants.

Conclusions

A migration and mobility lens serves to highlight rural areas as dynamic and intrinsically embedded in global, national, and regional relations. The chapter has provided an overview of some of the contemporary issues related to migration generally and on labor migration and "development".

The migration-development relationship and emphasis on remittances is a contested terrain with varied perspectives and possible policy options. Evidence of the impact of remittances on development, let alone on rural development, is acknowledged as equivocal and open to multiple interpretations and country-specific implications. The emphasis on migrant remittances has facilitated states implicitly and explicitly to place the onus on individuals and households as agents of "development" and redistribution at the expense of their human rights. More recently, this trend has indeed been addressed by agencies such as the UN, which have argued for adopting a broader concept of development beyond economic remittances to include the human rights and well-being of migrants. Migration cuts across all policy areas clearly cannot be addressed by migration policies in isolation from prevailing policies related to employment, health, social welfare, safety, education, and so on. A prerequisite for effective policies on international migration generally, including rural contexts, is independent rigorous transdisciplinary research to help inform transversal policies.

The chapter has focused on the Mexican–North American labor migration corridor from a sending country perspective and EU nationals migrating to rural Scotland from a receiving country perspective. The North American and Scottish examples reveal a similar rationale for the employment of international labor migrants in particular sectors in rural areas of receiving countries. In the North American context, temporary foreign worker programs have been well-established, particularly in the Mexico–Canada case. By contrast, the approach to labor migration in the UK has tended to be piecemeal and is increasingly uncertain in the context of Brexit. Against the background of the latter, temporary foreign worker programs in the context of sectors such as agriculture and horticulture are once again on the policy agenda. For the US and Canada, as for Scotland, it meets labor shortages particularly in the agricultural sector; for Mexico, migration provides employment for its citizens and enables it to negotiate external debts with the support of remittances. The recent turn in the discussion on international migration globally has focused on "migrant well-being" and "managed migration", where temporary worker programs are seen as a "win–win" for receiving and sending countries and where "return" migration is being encouraged.

In the context of globalization, changing geo-politics, and demographic trends, appropriate policy developments are predicated on further research to address the economic, cultural, social, and human rights consequences of international and internal migration on rural development in particular. Research is also needed to understand the implications for policy at different scalar levels (local to global) for both sending and receiving rural communities. Much of the research on rural migration has tended to privilege the perspectives of employers and migrants in the North. Equally important is developing an understanding of how long-term/host communities (as well as sending communities) view labor market changes impacting on their livelihoods and their prospects for staying in or leaving rural communities. This imperative has become more urgent in the context of so-called "populist" politics and "anti-immigrant" discourses in the US and Brexit Britain (England in particular), both of which have had a strong rural dimension. Research and policies on labor migration to rural areas of the North need to take a whole-community perspective where migration both into and out of rural areas are conceptualized as two sides of the same coin if appropriate policy solutions are to be devised.

Notes

1 The empirical results presented in this section are drawn from a variety of academic works. Most of these are related to remittances sending from the US in general because there is no specific registration for remittances from the H2A or H2B programs; therefore, results include documented and undocumented Mexican migrants in the US. On the other hand, the remittances from Canada include mainly those sent through CSAWP because more than 90 percent of remittances coming from that country are sent by SAW participants.

2 Accession 8 (A8) countries refers to the Czech Republic, Estonia, Hungary, Latvia, Lithuania, Poland, Slovakia, and Slovenia, countries which joined the EU in May 2004. The A8 were joined by Bulgaria and Romania (Accession 2, A2) in January 2007 (https://europa.eu/european-union/about-eu/countries_en).

3 For more detailed information on the UK immigration policy and how it operates within a devolved context at present, see the UK government website, *Devolution of Powers to Scotland, Wales and Northern Ireland* at: www.gov.uk/guidance/devolution-of-powers-to-scotland-wales-and-northern-ireland/.

References

Alcaraz, C., Chiquiar, D., Salcedo, A., 2012. *Remittances, schooling and child labor in Mexico*. Journal of Development Economics 97(1), 156–165.

Arroyo, A., Berumen, S., 2000. *Efectos sub-regionales de las remesas de emigrantes mexicanos en Estados Unidos*. Comercio Exterior 50(4), 340–349.

Banco de Mexico, 2018. *Estadísticas*. www.banxico.org.mx/SieInternet/consultarDirectorioInternetAction.do?sector=1&accion=consultarCuadroAnalitico&idCuadro=CA11&locale=es (accessed 3.15.18).

Basok, T., 1999. *Free to be unfree: Mexican guest workers in Canada*. Labour, Capital, and Society 32(2), 192–221.

Basok, T., 2002. *Tortillas and tomatoes: Transmigrant Mexican harvesters in Canada.* McGill-Queen's University Press, Montreal.

Basok, T., 2003. *Mexican seasonal migration to Canada and development: A community-based comparison.* International Migration 41(2), 3–26.

Binford, L., 2003. *Migrant remittances and (under) development in Mexico.* Critique of Anthropology 23(3), 305–336.

Boswell, C., Kyambi, S., Smellie, S., 2017. *Scottish immigration policy after Brexit: Evaluating options for a differentiated approach.* www.research.ed.ac.uk/portal/files/38000389/SIPafterBrexit0617.pdf (accessed 1.2.18).

Brown, D., Shucksmith, M., 2016. *A new lens for examining social change.* European Countryside 2, 183–188. DOI: 10.1515/euco-2016-0015.

Canales, A., 2006. *Remesas y desarrollo en México. Una visión crítica desde la macroeconomía.* Papeles de población 12(50), 171–196. www.scielo.org.mx/scielo.php?script=sci_arttext&pid=S1405-7425200600040 0009.

Canales, A., 2016. *Remittances as expenditure drivers in rural Mexico.* Estudios Fronterizos, nueva época 17(33), 231–259.

Cangiano, A., 2018. *Briefing: The impact of migration on UK population growth.* https://migrationobservatory. ox.ac.uk/wp-content/uploads/2016/04/Briefing-Impact-on-Population-Growth.pdf.

Carvajal, L., Johnson, T., 2016. *The impact of remittances from Canada's seasonal workers programme on Mexican farms.* International Labour Review 155(2), 297–314.

Castles, S., 2009. *Development and migration – migration and development: What comes first? Global perspective and African experiences.* Theoria: A Journal of Social and Political Theory 56(121), 1–31.

Castles, S., 2010. *Understanding global migration: A social transformation perspective.* Journal of Ethnic and Migration Studies 36, 1565–1586. https://doi.org/10.1080/1369183X.2010.489381.

Collins, E., 1976. *Migrant labour in British agriculture in the nineteenth century.* The Economic History Review 29(1), 38–59.

Czaika, M., de Haas, H., 2014. *The globalization of migration: Has the world become more migratory?* International Migration Review 48, 283–323. DOI: 10.1111/imre.1209.

de Haas, H., 2010. *Migration and development: A theoretical perspective.* International Migration Review 44(1), 227–264. DOI: 10.1111/j.1747-7379.2009.00804.x.

de Lima, P., 2015. *Reconciling labour mobility and cohesion policies: The rural experience,* in: Copus, A.K., De Lima, P. (Eds.), *Territorial cohesion in rural Europe.* Routledge, New York, pp. 126–150.

de Lima, P., Para, P.A., Pfeffer, M.J., 2012. *Conceptualizing contemporary immigrant integration in the rural United States and United Kingdom,* in: Shucksmith, M., Brown, D., Shortall, S., Vergunst, J., Warner, M.E. (Eds.), *Rural Transformations and Rural Polices in the UK and US.* Routledge, London, 62–83.

Durand, J., 2006. *Programas de trabajadores temporales Evaluación y análisis del caso mexicano.* CONAPO, Mexico.

Durand, J., Kandel, W., Parrado, E., Massey, D., 1996a. *International migration and development in Mexican communities.* Demography 33(2), 249–264.

Durand, J., Parrado, A., Massey, D., 1996b. *Migradollars and development: A reconsideration of the Mexican case.* International Migration Review 30(2), 423–444.

Escobar-Latapi, A., 1999. *Low-skill emigration from Mexico to the United States: Current situation prospects and government policy.* International Migration 37(1), 153–182.

FAO (Food and Agriculture Organization), 2016. *Migration, agriculture and rural development.* www.fao.org/3/a-i6064e.pdf (accessed 2.22.18).

FAO (Food and Agriculture Organization), 2018. *Rural migration, agriculture and rural development. In Brief.* FSN. www.fao.org/3/I8722EN/i8722en.pdf. (accessed 3.2.18).

Fratzke, S., Salant, B., 2018. *Moving beyond "root causes": The complicated relationship between migration and development.* Global Compact for Migration: A Development Perspective, No. 2. www.migrationpolicy.org/sites/default/files/publications/DevelopmentAssistanceMigration_FINAL.pdf (accessed 1.24.18).

Goldring, L., 2004. Family and *Collective remittances to Mexico: A multi-dimensional typology.* Development and Change 35(4), 799–840.

Homeland Security, 2016. *Table 32. Nonimmigrant temporary worker admissions (I-94 only) by region and country of citizenship: Fiscal year 2016.* www.dhs.gov/immigration-statistics/yearbook/2016/table32.

IFAD (International Fund for Agricultural Development), 2007. *Proceedings of the Round Table on Migration and Rural Employment.* www.ifad.org/documents/10180/599ac33e-987f-432a-a4df-3ddea216bf4f (accessed 2.20.18).

International Organization for Migration (IOM), 2013. *World migration report 2013: Migrant well-being and development*. International Organization for Migration, Geneva. https://publications.iom.int/system/files/pdf/wmr2013_en.pdf

International Organization on Migration (IOM), 2018. *Who is a migrant?* www.iom.int/who-is-a-migrant (accessed 1.19.18).

Jentsch, B., de Lima, P., Macdonald, B., 2007. *Migrant workers in rural Scotland: "Going to the middle of nowhere"*. International Journal on Multicultural Societies 9(1), 35–53.

Levitt, P., Lamba-Nieves, D., 2011. *Social remittances revisited.* Journal of Ethnic and Migration Studies 37(1), 1–22.

McCollum, D., Findlay, F., 2015. *"Flexible" workers for "flexible" jobs? The labour market function of A8 migrant labour in the UK.* Work, Employment and Society 29(3), 427–443.

McCollum, D., Cook, L., Chiroro, C., Platts, A., MacLeod, F., Findlay, A., 2012. *Spatial, sectoral and temporal trends in A8 migration to the UK 2004–2011: Evidence from the worker registration scheme.* CPC Working Paper No. 17. ESRC Centre for Population Change, Southampton.

Migration Advisory Group (MAC), 2018a. *EEA-workers in the UK labour market: Annexes.* March 2018. https://assets.publishing.service.gov.uk/government/uploads/system/uploads/attachment_data/file/695111/MAC_ANNEXES__FINAL_-_Interim_Update_v4.pdf (accessed 4.4.18).

Migration Advisory Group (MAC), 2018b. *EEA-workers in the UK labour market: Interim update.* March 2018. https://assets.publishing.service.gov.uk/government/uploads/system/uploads/attachment_data/file/694494/eea-workers-uk-labour-market-interim-update.pdf (accessed 4.4.18).

Netto, G., Hudson, M., Noon, M., Sosenko, F., de Lima, P., Kamenou-Aigbekaen, N., 2015. *Migration, ethnicity and progression from low-paid work: Implications for skills policy.* Social Policy and Society 14(4), 509–522.

Newland, K., 2017. *The global compact for migration: How does development fit in?* Policy Brief, November. Migration Policy Institute. www.migrationpolicy.org/research/global-compact-migration-how-does-development-fit.

NRS (National Records of Scotland), 2016. *Annual report of the Registrar General of Births, Deaths and Marriages for Scotland 2016*, 162nd edition. www.nrscotland.gov.uk/files//statistics/rgar/16/16rgar.pdf (accessed 2.14.18).

NRS (National Records of Scotland), 2018. *Migration-methodology.* www.nrscotland.gov.uk/statistics-and-data/statistics/statistics-by-theme/migration/methodology.

OECD, 2017. *Interrelations between public policies, migration and development.* OECD Publishing, Paris. http://dx.doi.org/10.1787/9789264265615-en.

Office for National Statistics (ONS), 2018. *Migration statistics quarterly report: November 2018.* www.ons.gov.uk/releases/migrationstatisticsquarterlyreportnovember2018.

Otero, G., Preibisch, K., 2014. *Does citizenship status matter in Canadian agriculture? Workplace health and safety for migrant and immigrant laborers.* Rural Sociology 79(2), 174–199. DOI: 10.1111/ruso.12043.

Preibisch, K., 2000. *La tierra de los (no) libres: migración temporal Mexico–Canada y dos campos de reestructuración económica neoliberal*, in: Binford, L., D'Aubeterre, M.E. (Eds.), *Conflictos migratorios transnacionales y respuestas comunitarias.* Benemérita Universidad Autónoma de Puebla, Puebla, pp. 45–65.

Preibisch, K., 2007. *Local produce, foreign labor: Labor mobility programs and global trade competitiveness in Canada.* Rural Sociology 72(3), 418–449.

Preibisch, K., 2011. *Migrant workers and changing work-place regimes in contemporary agricultural production in Canada.* International Journal of Sociology of Agriculture and Food 19(1), 62–82.

Preibisch, K., Su, Y., 2016. *Pursuing the capabilities approach within the migration–development nexus.* Journal of Ethnic and Migration Studies 42(13), 1–17. DOI: 10.1080/1369183X.2016.1176523.

Raghuram, P., 2009. *Which migration, what development? Unsettling the edifice of migration and development.* Population, Space and Place 15, 103–117.

Read, J., Zwell, S., Fernandez, L., 2013. *Migrant voices: Stories of agricultural migrant workers in Manitoba.* CCPA. http://ccrweb.ca/files/migrant_voices_mb_report.pdf (accessed 2.1.18).

Reichert, J.S., 1981. *The migrant syndrome: Seasonal U.S. wage labor and rural development in central Mexico.* Human Organization 40(1), 56–66.

Roberts, D., Newlands, D., 2010. *The economic integration of new sectors in rural areas: A case study of the Shetland economy.* Environment and Planning A 42, 2687–2704.

Rolfe, H., Metcalf, H., 2009. *Recent migration into Scotland: The evidence base.* Scottish Government, 2009. www.gov.scot/Resource/Doc/261996/0078342.pdf (accessed 2.28.18).

Romero González, M., 2016. *El significado de las remesas socioculturales en la migración indígena internacional de la Sierra Zongolica.* Veracruz. Huellas de la migración 1(2), 41–71.

Rubenstein, H., 1992. *Migration, development and remittances in rural Mexico.* International Migration 30(2), 127–153.

Russell, S., 2003. *Migration and development: Reframing the international policy agenda.* www.migrationpolicy. org/article/migration-and-development-reframing-international-policy-agenda (accessed 11.12.17).

Sander, C., 2003. *Migrant remittances to developing countries.* Bannock Consulting. UK Department of International Development (DFID).

Sandoval, J., Vanegas, R., 2001. *Migracion laboral y agricola mexicana temporal hacia Estos Unidos y Canada: Viejos-nuevos problemas.* INAH 21. Dimension Antropologica, Mexico.

Satzewich, V., 1991. *Racism and the incorporation of foreign labour: Farm labour migration to Canada since 1945.* Routledge, London.

Scottish Government, 2010. *Demographic change in Scotland.* www.gov.scot/Publications/2010/11/24111237/0.

Scottish Government, 2015a. *Scotland's economic strategy.* www.gov.scot/Resource/0047/00472389.pdf (accessed 1.2.18).

Scottish Government, 2015b. *Rural Scotland key facts 2015.* www.gov.scot/Resource/0047/00473312.pdf (accessed 2.19.18).

Scottish Government, 2016. *The impacts of migrants and migration into Scotland.* https://beta.gov.scot/publications/impacts-migrants-migration-scotland/pages/2/ (accessed 1.2.18).

Scottish Government, 2018. *Migration discussion paper on new powers for the Scottish Parliament: Scotland's population needs and migration policy: Discussion paper on evidence, policy and powers for the Scottish Parliament.* www.gov.scot/Resource/0053/00531087.pdf (accessed 2.7.18).

Somerville, W., Sriskandarajah, D., Latoree, M., 2009. *United Kingdom: A reluctant country of immigration.* Migratin Policy Institute. www.migrationpolicy.org/article/united-kingdom-reluctant-country-immigration

SPICe, 2016. *EU nationals living in Scotland.* Scottish Parliament, Edinburgh. www.parliament.scot/Research-BriefingsAndFactsheets/S5/SB_16-86_EU_nationals_living_in_Scotland.pdf (accessed 2.19.18).

STyPS (Secretaría del Trabajo y Previsión Social), 2006. *Dirección General de Empleo.* www.dgec.df.gob.mx/programas/snedf/capacitacion.html#migratorios.

STyPS (Secretaría del Trabajo y Previsión Social), 2018. *Temporada 2018.* www.gob.mx/stps/videos/temporada-2018-programa-de-trabajadores-agricolas-temporales-mexico-canada-ptat (accessed 2.20.18).

Taylor, E., 1992. *Remittances and inequality reconsidered: Direct, indirect and intertemporal effects.* Journal of Policy Modeling 14(2), 187–208.

Taylor, E., 2003. *The microeconomics of globalization: Evidence from China and Mexico,* in: *Agricultural trade and poverty: Making policy analysis count.* OECD.

Taylor, E., Fletcher, P., 2002. *Remittances and development in Mexico, Part one: The new labor economics of migration: A critical review.* Rural Mexico Research Review 2, Davis: University of California.

Taylor, E., Yunez-Naude, A., 1999. *Education, migration and productivity: An analytic approach and evidence from rural Mexico.* OECD.

UN, 2017a. *International migration report 2017.* www.un.org/en/development/desa/population/migration/publications/migrationreport/docs/MigrationReport2017_Highlights.pdf (accessed 1.24.18).

UN, 2017b. *Population facts.* No. 2017/5. www.un.org/en/development/desa/population/migration/publications/migrationreport/docs/MigrationReport2017_Highlights.pdf (accessed 1.24.18).

UN Population Division, 2001. *Replacement migration: Is it a solution to declining and ageing populations?* www.un.org/esa/population/publications/migration/migration.htm (accessed 2.19.18).

Verduzco, G., 2000. *El programa de trabajadores agricolas Mexicanos con Canada: Aprendizaje de una nueva experiencia.* Canada un Estado Posmoderno, 327–346.

Verduzco, G., Lozano, M.I., 2003. *Mexican farm worker's participations in Canada's seasonal agricultural labour market and development consequences in their rural home communities.* Unpublished document.

Wassem, R., Collver, G., 2001. *Immigration of agricultural guest workers: Policy, trends and legislative issues.* www.ncseonline.org/NLE/CRSreports/Agriculture/ag-102.cfm.

Wiggins, S., Otiendo, O., Proctor, S., Upton, M., 2000. *Population, migration and rural diversification: The implications for the crop post-harvest sector.* Crop Post-Harvest Programme (CPHP), Issues paper 1, December.

Woodruff, C., Zenteno, R., 2001. *Remittances and micro-enterprises in Mexico.* University of California at San Diego, Mimeo.

World Bank, 2016. *Migration and remittances factbook 2016.* www.knomad.org/sites/default/files/2017-11/bilateralremittancematrix2016_Nov2017.xlsx.

World Bank, 2017. *Migration and remittances data.* www.worldbank.org/en/topic/migrationremittances diasporaissues/brief/migration-remittances-data.

Yunez-Naude, A., 2001. *The determinants of non-farm activities and incomes of rural households in Mexico.* World Development 29(3), 561–572.

11

RURAL IMMIGRATION AND WELCOMING COMMUNITIES

Ryan Gibson and Robert Annis

Introduction

Migration and immigration have historically been urban phenomena. The global cities of London, Paris, and New York, among others, have been primary destinations of immigrants for the past centuries. These large urban centers often boasted large ethnic communities, ample immigrant service provisions, and most importantly employment opportunities. Over the past two decades, however, rural communities and governments have actively explored immigration strategies as options to address local challenges and opportunities, such as labor shortages and population growth. The attraction, settlement, integration, and retention of immigrants represents substantial planning requirements for rural communities, health and social service providers, government services, and community-based organizations. To facilitate rural immigration many rural areas are adopting a welcoming community strategy – a strategy whereby multi-sectoral partnerships are created to facilitate the immigration process. For many rural areas, unfortunately, there is limited experience and capacity to build and sustain these partnerships.

The reframing of rural as a viable locale for new immigrants is not unique to any one country. In fact, Canada, the European Union, and the United States of America have all witnessed a rural immigration phenomenon. Through a series of different policies, governments encourage immigration into rural communities to achieve labor force replacements, economic development opportunities, and population growth. Each country, and in fact each rural community, has different experiences. This highlights the diversity and nuances associated with rural immigration.

This chapter provides an overview of key concepts related to immigration, multiculturalism, and welcoming communities as it applies to rural communities. This contribution is developed on the theory of multiculturalism (Berry, 2006) and the welcoming communities' characteristics (Esses *et al.*, 2010). These central tenets provide a platform for understanding immigration to rural regions. The concepts of immigration, multiculturalism, and welcoming communities are applied in two case studies, one in Canada and the second in Scotland. The experience of these rural areas with an influx of new immigration and the areas' responses are discussed. From these cases implications for local development, policy, and research are explored.

The rise of the rural as a destination for immigrants

The migration of people into rural areas runs counter to most people's thinking and what has been observed throughout the past decades. Illustrative media reports throughout Canada, Ireland, Italy, and the United States paint the pictures of rural out-migration, rural exoduses, and in some cases rural "ghost towns" (Bundale, 2017; Cohen, 2013; Melia, 2017; Squires, 2017). Rural communities are often depicted as areas "losing people", frequently young people and skilled labor migrating to urban environments (Corbett, 2005; Mclaughlin *et al.*, 2014; Rauhut and Littke, 2016; Stockdale, 2002). The motivations for this migration focus on employment prospects, educational opportunities, lifestyle, and amenities. Other reasons for rural out-migration focus on health-care needs, family, and quality of life factors.

Historically, rural communities throughout Europe and North America have not been "hot spots", or popular destinations, for new immigrants. Most new immigrants were attracted to large urban cities for their employment, cultural diversity, and social services. The experiences of rural communities with immigration have often been reserved for a small number of specialized and required services, such as health-care practitioners. This phenomenon changed in the 1990s, when rural communities became a focus, but also popular destinations for immigrants.

With a backdrop of rural out-migration of young people and skilled labor, community leaders and governments turned to immigration as a potential mechanism to shift these historical patterns. Policies and programs have been enacted by various levels of government focused on three main strategies: (i) to replenish local labor forces, (ii) to generate economic development opportunities, and (iii) to re-populate rural communities and regions.

The out-migration of young people and skilled labor has created difficulty for rural employers to find appropriate labor to continue the operation of their industries. To ensure a viable labor force, governments in Canada and the United States have created policies and programs to facilitate immigrant attraction to address these labor shortages (Ashton *et al.*, 2015; Broadway, 2000, 2007; Silvius, 2005). Immigrant attraction programs are typically only implemented after exhaustive internal searches for labor have taken place. Typically, industries seeking new labor include agricultural processing industries, manufacturing, and other low-skilled industries. As a result of the labor force replacement strategy many rural communities, such as Garden City (US), Olds and Neepawa (Canada), have witnessed large increases in immigration. In Europe, similar situations have emerged whereby immigrants are taking up employment in hospitality, agriculture, and food-processing industries (Jentsch *et al.*, 2007).

In addition to labor force replacement strategies, governments view immigrant attraction as a potential opportunity for rural economic development revitalization. In the Canadian province of New Brunswick, the Business Immigrant Mentorship program was created to provide new immigrants a six-month transition period to facilitate learning about the provincial business climate, rules, regulations, and policies. In the Canadian province of Ontario, the Community Immigrant Retention in Rural Ontario program was created as a toolkit to facilitate immigrant attraction and economic development (Ontario Ministry of Agriculture, Food, and Rural Affairs, 2011). In the European Union, the European Agricultural Fund for Rural Development offers support for rural immigration through rural economic development and employment (Juan, 2017). These programs recognize the potential impact of new immigrants on rural economies, in terms of both labor and entrepreneurs.

Rural immigration is also viewed as a strategy for population growth by governments across North America and Europe. For many rural regions, the past decades are characterized by population stagnation and decline. Immigration to rural areas is an opportunity to change the story on rural population. To that end, governments have enacted policies and strategies for population growth built on immigration, such as Scotland's Fresh Talent Initiative (Danson, 2007), Sweden's National Strategy for Sustainable Regional Growth and Attractiveness (Ministry of Enterprise and Innovation, 2015), and New Brunswick's "Be Our Future" (Government of New Brunswick, 2014).

It should be noted the success of each of these rural immigration strategies (labor force replacement, rural economic development, and population re-growth) are yet to be determined on a long-term basis. A number of case studies have indicated initial successes; however, it is unclear if these successes can be translated into long-term, systemic change (Hedlund *et al.*, 2017).

Key concepts for understanding rural immigration

Migration is taking place today at unprecedented levels. Not only are there increases in the number of people migrating, there are also increases in the distances moved and new migration patterns. Castles and Miller (2009) suggest this is the "Age of Migration" based on these new migration dynamics. To understand these migration dynamics, a number of key concepts need to be clarified.

An *immigrant* is an individual who moves from one country to take up residency in another country. An immigrant can move as an individual or as a member of a family. Often immigrants are in search of better quality of life. Within the European Union, the terms immigrant and migrant need to be differentiated. Since the signing of the Citizens' Rights Directive in 2004, the European Union grants its citizens the freedom to move between member states (Bauböck, 2006). A European Union citizen who moves from one member country to another member country is referred to as a *migrant*. An individual who moves into a country of the European Union from a non-EU country is referred to as an immigrant. It is important to note that for some places in the European Union rural areas are experiencing higher levels of European Union migrants than immigrants (de Lima and Wright, 2009).

Influencing whether an individual or family chooses to remain in the current location or migrate to a new place are a series of *push and pull factors*. Push factors encourage an individual to move from their current location. Push factors may include lack of employment opportunities, low quality of life conditions, unstable social conditions, and low personal or family safety. Pull factors work in the opposite direction, attracting people to the new location (King, 2012; Lee, 1966). Potential pull factors may include employment opportunities, high quality of life, high safety and security (Parkins, 2010). Rural communities need to consider what pull factors they embody to attract new immigrants.

Attraction, settlement, and integration are often described as processes involved in enticing and retaining rural immigrants. *Attraction* refers to activities conducted by the host community or region to invite people to re-locate to their area. The host community may advertise a series of pull factors to get the attention of immigrants, such as job opportunities, high-quality education and health services, and low cost of living. *Settlement* refers to a suite of services in the host community to help new immigrants get established. This may include services to assist in locating appropriate and affordable housing, information on community and public services (i.e. public transit, library services, recreational facilities), details on immigrant services in the community, or material for family members. *Integration* refers to activities or processes that facilitate immigrants to feel a part of the host community. This may include participation in civic activities, recreation teams, or religious events. Attraction, settlement, and integration taken as a whole are often seen as a linear process which will result in long-term residency by immigrants.

Acculturation is the process of cultural change that takes place from contact between cultural groups, particularly long-term rural residents and new immigrants (Sam and Berry, 2010). The outcome from the contact between cultural groups is either assimilation (immigrants engage with the host community and do not maintain their cultural identity), separation (immigrants maintain their identity and avoid interacting with the host community), integration (immigrants maintain their cultural identity while pursuing engagement with the larger society), or marginalization (immigrants have no interest in maintaining their culture and do not wish to engage with the host community) (Berry, 2006; Gibson *et al.*, 2016). When immigrants choose integration strategies for interacting with the rural host community it is usually described as multiculturalism. When immigrants choose assimilation strategies for interacting with the rural host community it is usually described as a "melting pot" (Bossman, 2000).

A *welcoming community* is one that embraces diversity, encourages civic participation among all residents, provides a range of appropriate service provisions, and offers meaningful employment (Gibson *et al.*, 2017). Welcoming communities build on the strengths that are achieved through integration strategies of acculturation previously described. The history and characteristics of a welcoming community are explored in the next section.

Welcoming communities: a strategy for immigrant attraction and integration

Leaders in rural communities and among multiple levels of government have turned to welcoming community strategies to facilitate the attraction, settlement, and integration into rural areas. The welcoming communities concept implies that all residents, whether long-term or newcomers, have the ability to fully engage in all aspects of community life (Belkhodja, 2009; Gibson *et al.*, 2017; National Working Group on Small Centre Strategies, 2007). The notion of welcoming communities incorporates the concepts of social cohesion (Rajulton *et al.*, 2006; Shragge and Toye, 2006), community capital (Flora and Flora, 2013), and place-based development (Bellefontaine and Wisener, 2011; Vodden *et al.*, 2015). Since the 1990s, the term has been utilized by all levels of government and across multiple countries (Belkhodja, 2009; Bourhis *et al.*, 2009; Massey, 2008).

While there is no universally agreed definition of welcoming communities, common components include diversity, civic participation, access to service provisions, and employment (Gibson *et al.*, 2017). Furthermore, welcoming community initiatives should identify and remove barriers for newcomers, promote a sense of belonging to the host community, meet the diverse needs of individual newcomers, and offer services to promote successful integration into the host community (Esses *et al.*, 2010).

Welcoming communities can be viewed as both a local development practice and a policy approach. At the local level, a variety of stakeholders can be engaged in proactive measures to facilitate the settlement and integration of newcomers. Stakeholders may include local governments, health-care service providers, educational service providers, employers, language training centers, religious organizations, and other levels of government. At a policy level, welcoming communities have been embraced by numerous governments as a mechanism to direct a government's investment and programming surrounding immigration. Both the local development practice and policy approaches to welcoming communities are complicated by the fact that immigration is often a shared responsibility among multiple levels of government (Bruce and Lister, 2005; Caldwell *et al.*, 2017; Carter *et al.*, 2008).

Based on a review of immigration literature, Esses *et al.* (2010) compiled a series of characteristics of welcoming communities. The 17 ranked characteristics of a welcoming community facilitate discussions and planning by all levels of government, immigrant-serving organizations, and host rural communities. These characteristics also provide a framework by which short-term and long-term evaluations can be conducted. The importance of any characteristic is an output of place. The local context, local processes, local partners, and local dynamics are funda-mental and may alter the ranking. How communities choose to identify, understand, and imple-ment actions on these 17 welcoming community characteristics differs by place.

Box 11.1 17 characteristics of a welcoming community

1   employment opportunities
2   social capital
3   affordable and social housing
4   positive attitudes towards immigrants and newcomers
5   presence of newcomer-serving agencies
6   links between main actors working towards welcoming communities
7   municipal features and services sensitive to the presence and needs of newcomers
8   educational opportunities
9   accessible and suitable health care
10   available and accessible public transit
11   presence of diverse religious organizations
12   social engagement opportunities
13   political participation opportunities
14   positive relationships with policy and justice system
15   safety
16   opportunities for use of public space and recreation facilities
17   favorable media coverage

(Esses *et al.*, 2010)

Rural immigration in action

To illustrate the key concepts of rural immigration and welcoming communities two case studies are highlighted: (i) Brandon, Canada and (ii) Highlands and Islands, Scotland. Each case study uncovers the rationale for turning to immigration as a viable solution for the local context, how each community/region strived to attract, settle, and integrate new immigrants, and the general success demonstrated to date.

Brandon, Manitoba, Canada

Located on the Canadian prairies (Figure 11.1), the community of Brandon (population 48,859) is a regional hub for surrounding rural communities. Prior to 2001, Brandon's previous experi-ence with immigration was reserved for high-skilled professionals in the health-care fields and international students to the local university. Driven by labor market factors the community's experience with immigration fundamentally changed. As a result of rapid rates of immigration, the community embarked on a welcoming communities initiative to facilitate the arrival, settle-ment, and integration of new immigrants.

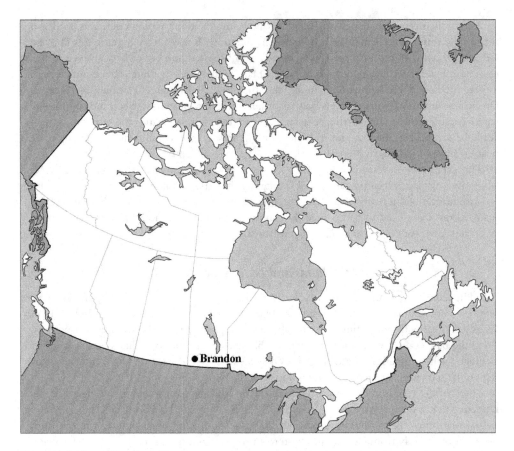

Figure 11.1 Map of Brandon, Canada

The catalyst for immigration to Brandon was a combination of labor shortages combined with industrial expansion in the community. In particular, one meat processing facility drove the need for labor force expansion. From 2001 to 2009, this meat processing company hired over 1700 immigrants to continue their operations. The number of annual immigrants to Brandon peaked in 2010 at 1433 (Manitoba Labor and Immigration, 2012). During this period, the provincial government actively pursued rural immigration policies and programs focused on labor force replacement, economic development, and population growth (Carter *et al.*, 2008). Through government policies, the number of new immigrants quickly rose from 1700 to 5100 after family member reunification took place.

Prior to the influx of new immigrants, Brandon witnessed a stable and largely homogenous population. In response to the rapidly changing population dynamics the community organized a collaborative, multi-stakeholder strategy to allow for a planned series of actions addressing attraction, settlement, and integration. In 2007, the Brandon Welcoming Communities Dialogue Group was convened. The group consisted of local government departments, industry, immigrant-serving organizations, government departments, health services, education providers, and community-based organizations (Bucklaschuk, 2008). The mandate of the group was to coordinate communication, share information on planning activities, and advise local research.

A key dilemma associated with Brandon's new immigration phenomenon was predicting when new immigrants would be arriving. The Brandon Welcoming Communities Dialogue Group worked with industry partners to assess the anticipated number of new immigrant hires each month along with the potential number of family members that might be reunified in the future. Sharing these estimations among the Brandon Welcoming Communities Dialogue Group allowed immigrant-serving organizations, health and education services, and community-based organizations to make the necessary preparations before immigrants arrived. Services could be prepared to meet the needs of new immigrants. Likewise, estimations of family reunification allowed schools to prepare for the arrival of new students.

The experience in Brandon demonstrated the need and value of a multi-stakeholder, collaborative organization in preparing and facilitating the arrival of new immigrants. In building an organization of this nature it was also recognized that substantial amounts of both human and financial resources need to be invested. For more information on the Brandon rural immigration case study, see Gibson *et al.* (2017) and Bucklaschuk (2008, 2009).

Highlands and Islands, Scotland

The Highlands and Islands region is located in the northwest of Scotland (Figure 11.2) and represents approximately 361,000 residents. Like many other rural regions, the Highlands and Islands struggle with population growth, labor force replacement, and economic restructuring. Over the past years, the Scottish government has enacted a series of policies and strategies to facilitate further migration to rural regions. Over the past two decades the Highlands and Islands region has witnessed an increase in rural migration.

Much of the recent migration to the rural region is facilitated through the Citizens' Rights Directive that was approved in 2004 (Bauböck, 2006). Through this European Union initiative migrants are moving to the Highlands and Islands region from other countries in the European Union, mostly from Central and Eastern European countries, such as Estonia, Lithuania, and Poland. The key pull factors attracting people to the Highlands and Islands region include family ties, job opportunities, the environment, access to affordable housing, and a perceived higher quality of life (Crow, 2010). De Lima *et al.* (2005) confirmed pull factors of employment opportunities in interviews with migrant workers. Their work also noted the role of similarities in culture between Central/Eastern Europe and Scotland and the role of social networks.

Similar to the Brandon case, the retention of migrants in the Highlands and Islands region is based on the ability to settle and integrate. A number of key initiatives have been undertaken to promote the settlement and integration of new migrants. Employers are increasing their engagement in providing accommodation services for new migrants (Jentsch *et al.*, 2007). Community-based organizations are creating "welcome packs" for new migrants. These packages include key information about settlement services for new migrants and are available in multiple languages. The settlement and integration of new migrants has not been without hiccups along the way. New migrants struggle to find appropriate and culturally sensitive health and social services, gain recognition of qualifications from outside Scotland, and be engaged in local planning forums.

It is clear from the experiences in the Highlands and Islands region there is a role for businesses, government, public services, and community leaders in attracting, settling, and integrating new migrants in the region. For more information on the Scottish rural immigration case study, see Crow (2010), de Lima *et al.* (2005), and Jentsch *et al.* (2007).

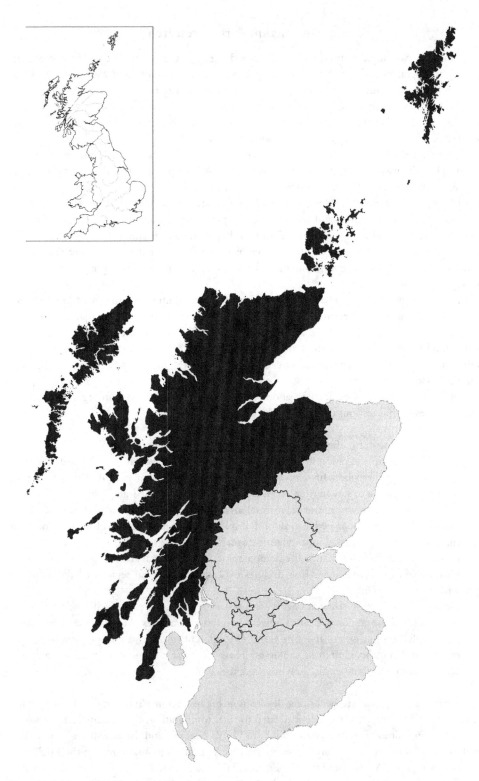

Figure 11.2 Map of Highlands and Islands Region, Scotland

Conclusions and further research

Over the past two decades, rural communities and regions have emerged as viable destinations for new immigrants/migrants, bucking the trend whereby immigrants only went to urban areas. The attraction of immigrants to rural areas has had an immediate positive impact on labor force replacement, economic development, and population growth strategies. Although these strategies are often established by government, it is community-level stakeholders that are increasingly responsible for settlement and integration processes and programs.

The Brandon case study illustrated the value and need for multi-stakeholder engagement forums. The discussion among industry, government, service providers, and community-based organizations facilitates planning processes and enhances the ability to deliver key programs required by new immigrants. Multi-stakeholder forums require a substantial investment of time on behalf of all organizations and require a level of trust among all the stakeholders. Time to build relationships and trust is required. From the Highlands and Islands case study it is possible to see a similar story in the value of proactive planning. Whether it be businesses engaged in housing settlement for new migrants or community-based organizations preparing welcome packages, planning matters.

In both instances, it is important to recognize immigrants/migrants still wished for services that neither community currently provided. It is also important to recognize that new immigrants/migrants are not necessarily a homogenous group when it comes to attraction, settlement, and integration. New immigrants/migrants from different home countries may require different services. Rural communities need to understand the unique differences among new immigrants/migrants.

There is still much to be learned about rural immigration and welcoming communities. Three key research questions that need to be explored are:

1 What is the long-term effectiveness of rural immigration programs?
  Successful rural immigration initiatives have been recorded over the past 20 years. What is unknown is if these benefits can be recognized over a longer period. Do new/recent immigrants choose to stay in rural areas? Do the children of these immigrants follow similar trajectories as other youth and leave rural areas at the completion of high school in the pursuit of post-secondary education and employment opportunities? How will the next rural recession impact rural immigration efforts?
2 Does rural immigration change the demographic trends of rural areas?
  Can the historical stagnations and declines experienced by rural regions be discontinued with new immigrants?
3 How do acculturation strategies evolve in rural areas over long periods of time?
  Although the case studies appear to suggest integration strategies of acculturation are taking place, will this continue in the long term? Do different immigrant groups (or sub-groups) employ different acculturation strategies? How do rural communities plan for multiple acculturation strategies among new immigrants?

It is clear that rural areas are becoming destinations for immigrants/migrants. This chapter has delivered an overview of key concepts related to rural immigration, multiculturalism, and welcoming communities, from the context of both North America and the European Union. The application of these concepts can be clearly seen in application in Brandon and the Highlands and Islands regions. At the same time, there are many unanswered questions in rural immigration from policy, practice, and academic perspectives.

References

Ashton, B., LaBelle, S., Mealy, R., Wuttunee, W., 2015. *Manitoba*, in: Markey, S., Breen, S., Gibson, R., Lauzon, A., Mealy, R., and Ryser. L (Eds.), *The state of rural Canada*. Canadian Rural Revitalization Foundation/Fondation canadienne pour la revitalisation rurale, Camrose, AB, pp. 31–38.

Bauböck, R., 2006. *Migration and citizenship: Legal status, rights, and political participation*. Amsterdam University Press, Amsterdam. https://doi.org/978-90-5356-888-0.

Belkhodja, C., 2009. *Toward a more welcoming community? Observations on the Greater Moncton Area*. Plan Canada 2(2), 96–98.

Bellefontaine, T., Wisener, R., 2011. *The evaluation of place-based approaches: Questions for further research*. Policy Horizons Canada. https://ccednet-rdec.ca/sites/ccednet-rdec.ca/files/the_evaluation_of_place-based_approaches_questions_for_further_research.pdf.

Berry, J., 2006. *Mutual attitudes among immigrants and ethnocultural groups in Canada*. International Journal of Intercultural Relations 30(6), 719–734. https://doi.org/10.1016/j.ijintrel.2006.06.004.

Bossman, D., 2000. *Teaching pluralism: Values to cross-cultural barriers*, in: Kelley, M., Fitzsimmons, V. (Eds.), *Understanding cultural diversity: Culture, curriculum, and community in nursing*. Jones and Bartlett, Sudbury, MA, pp. 55–66.

Bourhis, R., Montreuil, A., Barrette, G., Montaruli, E., 2009. *Acculturation and immigrant–host community relations in multicultural settings*, in: Demoulin, S., Leyens, J., Dovidio, J. (Eds.), *Intergroup misunderstandings: Impact of divergent social realities*. Psychology Press, New York, pp. 39–62.

Broadway, M., 2000. *Planning for change in small towns or trying to avoid the slaughterhouse blues*. Journal of Rural Studies 16(1), 37–46. https://doi.org/10.1016/S0743-0167(99)00038-8.

Broadway, M., 2007. *Meatpacking and the transformation of rural communities: A comparison of Brooks, Alberta and Garden City, Kansas*. Rural Sociology 72(4), 560–582. https://doi.org/10.1526/0036011 07782638701.

Bruce, D., Lister, G., 2005. *Rural repopulation in Atlantic Canada: A discussion paper*. Agriculture and Agri-Food Canada, Ottawa, Ont.

Bucklaschuk, J., 2008. *Settlement: Considerations for temporary foreign workers in Brandon and area*. Rural Development Institute, Brandon University, Brandon, MB.

Bucklaschuk, J., 2009. *Enhancing and linking ethnocultural organizations and communities in rural Manitoba: A focus on Brandon and Steinbach*. Rural Development Institute, Brandon University, Brandon, MB.

Bundale, B., 2017. *Where have all the East Coast's kids gone? Census shows a rapidly greying Atlantic Canada*. The Toronto Star, May.

Caldwell, W., Labute, B., Khan, B., D'Souza, N., 2017. *Attracting and retaining newcomers in rural communities and small towns*. Municipal World, Union, Ont.

Carter, T., Morrish, M., Amoyaw, B., 2008. *Attracting immigrants to smaller urban and rural communities: Lessons learned from the Manitoba Provincial Nominee Program*. Journal of International Migration and Integration/Revue de L'integration et de La Migration Internationale 9(2), 161–183. https://doi.org/10.1007/s12134-008-0051-2.

Castles, S., Miller, M., 2009. *The age of migration: International population movements in the modern world*. Palgrave Macmillan, Basingstoke.

Cohen, N., 2013. *Rural US shrinks as young flee for cities*. Financial Times, June.

Corbett, M., 2005. *Rural education and out-migration: The case of a coastal community*. Canadian Journal of Education 28(1–2), 52–72. https://doi.org/10.2307/1602153.

Crow, H., 2010. *Factors influencing rural migration decisions in Scotland: An analysis of the evidence*. Scottish Government, Edinburgh.

Danson, M., 2007. *Fresh or refreshed talent: Exploring population change in Europe and some policy initiatives*. International Journal on Multicultural Societies 9(1), 13–34.

de Lima, P., Wright, S., 2009. *Welcoming migrants? Migrant labor in rural Scotland*. Social Policy and Society 8(3), 391–404.

de Lima, P., Jentsch, B., Whelton, R., 2005. *Migrant workers in the Highlands and Islands: Research report*. PolicyWeb, University of Highlands and Islands, Inverness.

Esses, V., Hamilton, L., Bennett-AbuAyyash, C., Burstein, M., 2010. *Characteristics of a welcoming community*. University of Western Ontario, London, Ont. http://p2pcanada.ca/wp-content/uploads/2011/09/Characteristics-of-a-Welcoming-Community-11.pdf.

Flora, C.B., Flora, J.L., 2013. *Rural communities: Legacy and change*. Westview Press, Boulder, CO.

Gibson, R., Racher, F., Annis, R., 2016. *Negotiating the culture of care*, in: Vollman, A., Anderson, E., McFarlene, J. (Eds.), *Canadian community as partner: Theory and multidisciplinary practice*, 3rd edition.

Lippincott, Williams, and Wilkins, Philadelphia, pp. 154–176. https://shop.lww.com/Canadian-Community-As-Partner/p/9781496339980.

Gibson, R., Bucklaschuk, J., Annis, R., 2017. *Working together: Collaborative response to welcoming newcomers in Brandon, Manitoba*, in: Bonifacio, G., Drolet, J. (Eds.), *Canadian perspectives on immigration in small cities*. Springer International Publishing, Cham, pp. 35–53. https://link.springer.com/chapter/10.1007/978-3-319-40424-0_3.

Government of New Brunswick, 2014. *Be our future: New Brunswick's population growth strategy*. Government of New Brunswick, Fredrickton, NB.

Hedlund, M., Carson, D., Eimermann, M., Lundmark, L., 2017. *Repopulating and revitalising rural Sweden? Re-examining immigration as a solution to rural decline*. The Geographical Journal 183(4), 400–413.

Jentsch, B., de Lima, P., MacDonald, B., 2007. *Migrant workers in rural Scotland: "Going to the middle of nowhere"*. International Journal on Multicultural Societies 9(1), 35–53.

Juan, A., 2017. *EU rural development policy and the integration of migrants*. European Parliament, Brussels.

King, R., 2012. *Theories and typologies of migration: An overview and a primer*. Institute for Studies of Migration, Diversity, and Welfare, Malmö University, Malmö.

Lee, E., 1966. *A theory of migration*. Demography 3(1), 47–57.

Manitoba Labor and Immigration, 2012. *Manitoba immigration facts: 2012 statistical report*. Manitoba Labor and Immigration, Winnipeg, MB.

Massey, D. (Ed.), 2008. *New faces in new places: The changing geography of American immigration*. Russell Sage Foundation, New York.

Mclaughlin, D.K., Shoff, C.M., Demi, M.A., 2014. *Influence of perceptions of current and future community on residential aspirations of rural youth*. Rural Sociology 79(4), 453–477. https://doi.org/10.1111/ruso.12044.

Melia, P., 2017. *Deserted Ireland: Census reveals daily rural exodus*. Irish News, June.

Ministry of Enterprise and Innovation, 2015. *National strategy for sustainable regional growth and attractiveness 2015–2020*. Government Offices of Sweden, Stockholm.

National Working Group on Small Centre Strategies, 2007. *Attracting and retaining immigrants: A tool box for ideas for smaller centres*. Government of Canada, Ottawa, Ont.

Ontario Ministry of Agriculture Food and Rural Affairs, 2011. *Community immigrant retention in rural Ontario*. Government of Ontario, Toronto, Ont.

Parkins, N., 2010. *Push and pull factors of migration*. American Review of Political Economy 8(2), 6–24.

Rajulton, F., Ravanera, Z.R., Beaujot, R., 2006. *Measuring social cohesion: An experiment using the Canadian National Survey of Giving, Volunteering, and Participating*. Social Indicators Research 80(3), 461–492.

Rauhut, D., Littke, H., 2016. *"A one way ticket to the city, please!" On young women leaving the Swedish peripheral region Västernorrland*. Journal of Rural Studies 43, 301–310. https://doi.org/10.1016/j.jrurstud.2015.05.003.

Sam, D.L., Berry, J.W., 2010. *Acculturation: When individuals and groups of different cultural backgrounds meet*. Perspectives on Psychological Science 5(4), 472–481. https://doi.org/10.1177/1745691610373075.

Shragge, E., Toye, M. (Eds.), 2006. *Community economic development: Building for social change*. Cape Breton University Press, Sydney, NS.

Silvius, R., 2005. *Immigration and rural Canada: Research and practice*. Canadian Rural Revitalization Foundation and Rural Development Institute, Brandon, MB.

Squires, N., 2017. *And then there was one: Paolina, 90, the sole resident of a village highlighting Italy's rural exodus*. The Telegram, June.

Stockdale, A., 2002. *Out-migration from rural Scotland: The importance of family and social networks*. Sociologia Ruralis 42(1), 41–64. https://doi.org/10.1111/1467-9523.00201.

Vodden, K., Gibson, R., Baldacchino, G. (Eds.), 2015. *Place peripheral*. Festival 500. ISER Books, Memorial University, St John's, NL.

12

THE ROLE OF WOMEN IN RURAL AREAS

Patricia T. Fernandez-Guajardo, Denise Lach, and
Allison Davis-White Eyes

Introduction

The roles of women in rural communities vary widely across the world; regardless of location, however, women tend to have less access than men to resources, services, and opportunities including land and livestock, financial services, and education. It is increasingly recognized that if rural communities are going to be vital over the long term, opportunities for women to succeed are a necessity. This chapter looks at three major impediments for the integration of women into rural development: unequal participation in the rural economy, unequal access to benefits and services, and unequal participation in local decision-making, as well as long-term strategies for women's empowerment, and recommendations for future research. Of necessity, the chapter will take a broad-brush and comparative approach, using the latest data from international and national organizations as well as recent research on the roles of women in rural development.

The World Bank estimates that approximately 46 percent of the world lives in rural areas, of which about half are women (World Bank, 2016). Of course, that number covers a wide range of urbanization in the world, ranging from 100 percent in some countries like Hong Kong and Singapore to less than 15 percent in others like Papua New Guinea and Lichtenstein. And, the roles of the approximately 1.7 billion women in rural communities vary widely. Regardless of location, however, women tend to have less access than men to resources, services, and opportunities. It is increasingly recognized that if rural communities are going to be vital over the long term, opportunities for women to succeed are a necessity, not a luxury.

Many international organizations, conferences, and reports have acknowledged the contribution of women to rural communities and have emphasized the need for gender mainstreaming in public policies. The first World Conference on Women was held in Mexico City in 1975. Since then there have been numerous international conferences and efforts by the United Nations (UN) and other international organizations, including promotion of the Millennial Development Goals focusing on gender equality and empowerment of women over the decades (UN Women, 2016). However, as the Food and Agriculture Organization (FAO) of the UN noted,

> With few exceptions, every gender, and development indicator for which data are available reveals that rural women fare worse than rural men and urban residents and

that they disproportionately experience poverty, exclusion, and the effects of climate change.

(FAO, 2016, p. 49)

Public policies aimed at bridging these gaps for women in rural areas seek to transform institutions and laws that restrict women's rights and constrain full participation in rural life.

One of the main challenges to advancing gender participation is having accurate information about the complicated lives of women in rural areas. Only with good data will it be possible to better understand the full range of women's experiences and the challenges they face today. The limitations of data availability were addressed by relying on information for this chapter primarily from international organizations like the UN, the FAO, Organization for Co-operation and Economic Development (OECD), and the World Bank.

While women play a critical role in all rural activities, it is possible to identify three major areas blocking the full integration of women into rural success including unequal participation in the rural economy, limited access to benefits and services, and lack of participation in local decision-making. Of necessity, the chapter takes a broad-brush and comparative approach, relying on limited and somewhat dated cases and data. After providing a brief overview of the issues, social and cultural constructions that promote gender inequality in rural areas are explored, and different policies that have been implemented to address these issues are discussed. The chapter is concluded by identifying various long-term strategies for empowering women to participate in and actively build robust rural communities.

Integrating women into robust rural communities: reducing unequal participation in the rural economy

Women represent a significant share of the labor force in rural areas around the world. This is particularly evident in developing countries, where women "comprise 43 percent of the agricultural labor force, ranging from about 20 percent in Latin America to almost 50 percent in East and South-east Asia and Sub-Saharan Africa" (FAO, 2011, p. 22). The contribution of women in the crop, livestock, fishery, and forestry sectors is crucial, not only because of their participation in the production and marketing of goods, but also for women's involvement through informal labor providing food, water, and wood for fuel, as well as caregiving tasks. Despite this, the participation of women in the rural economy faces structural inequalities in access to productive resources, inputs, and services.

One of the many limitations that women face is unequal access to and control over land. Ownership of land defines social status and power relationships within many rural communities, and is of particular importance to Indigenous communities who struggle with issues of sovereignty, subsistence, and cultural preservation (Besra, 2014). UN Women (2019) estimates that globally women represent 20 percent of landowners and yet constitute 43 percent of the agricultural labor force. As a result, there is a significant gap between the total number of women farmers and the proportion of women who manage an agricultural holding in both the developed and developing worlds. For example, in Sub-Saharan Africa, while more than 53 percent of women are self-employed in agriculture, only 15 percent of farm owners are women. The regions where this is most acute include the Middle East and North Africa, while in Europe this relationship is reversed and women are more likely to own a farm than work on the land. Cultural norms dictate land tenure rules in many rural communities and create stressors that disproportionately affect women's access to subsistence, customary practices, and inheritance laws (Besra, 2014).

When women do own land, it is lower in productivity compared to land owned by men, smaller than those farms owned by men, and worked with less hired labor than men's farms (Croppenstedt *et al.*, 2013). In addition, rural women are constrained by limited access to inputs such as seeds and fertilizers; they often use low-cost equipment and have less access to new technologies and infrastructure. Women also have restricted access to credit, extension, and advisory services (GIZ-BMZ, 2013; UN Women, 2016). It is common in some countries to deny women the right to hold bank accounts or to sign contracts without their husband or another male relative (FAO *et al.*, 2013).

An illustrative example is women livestock breeders. The FAO (2011) estimates that two-thirds of the world's poorest livestock farmers are women. Their farms are as productive as farms operated by men when measured by the income generated by their animals. However, on average, women tend to own fewer animals. Furthermore, in the distribution of chores on livestock farms, it is common for men to "Keep and market large animals such as cattle, horses, and camels, while women tend to control smaller animals, such as goats, sheep, pigs and poultry" (FAO, 2011, pp. 25–26). The complex interactions of land tenure, farming, and agricultural production reflect how rural women's life chances are affected by government policy and laws as well as cultural practices and norms.

Another aspect that places women at a disadvantage compared to men in rural areas is the gendered division of labor; women often have a greater workload than rural men as they spend more time on unpaid activities. In rural areas, women are usually the primary providers of the basic needs of their families (GIZ-BMZ, 2013). They spend a higher proportion than men of their income and time in procuring and taking care of other household members, which prevents women from fully participating in employment opportunities (Inter-Agency Task Force on Rural Women, n.d.). This difference between women and men is even larger in developing countries (Figure 12.1). Unpaid activities are usually not reflected in official statistics, so this work performed by women is often "invisible" and not considered when designing public policies.

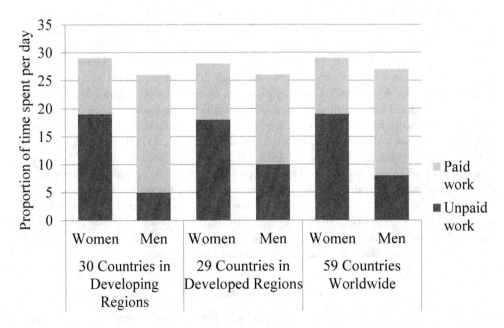

Figure 12.1 Amount of time spent daily by women and men on unpaid and paid work in selected countries, 2000–2014

Source: United Nations (2016, p. 21).

Finally, rural women are more likely than men to be employed in the informal economy, so their share in rural wage employment is much lower than that of men (Inter-Agency Task Force on Rural Women, n.d.). When women take part in economic activities outside the household or their own farm, they are more likely to engage in "shorter term, more precarious and less protected [jobs] than those of rural men and urban people" (Inter-Agency Task Force on Rural Women, n.d., p. 2), even when they are equally or even more qualified than male counterparts (GIZ-BMZ, 2013).

Because rural women often engage in informal and subsistence rather than commercial farming and have limited mobility compared to men, they are less integrated into value chains that increase the value of products and have less access to markets than men (GIZ-BMZ, 2013). When women participate in value chains, they tend to do it through low-skill activities with low-cost equipment, while men are more likely to engage in managerial roles. The FAO (2011) has suggested that if women had the same access as their male counterparts to resources and services needed, they would increase field productivity and have a significant impact on nutrition and food security. The economics of both the formal and informal economies raise questions of "what is *value* and what is *valuable* to society" (Benería *et al.*, 2003, p. 159). Himmelweit (1995), for example, argues that a shift is needed in policy-making to render unpaid labor as "work", thus allowing the work of women in the informal economy to be more visible.

Roles, images, and social constructions underlying gender inequalities

At the root of these unequal opportunities for women participating in the rural economy are legal and cultural systems that are in turn sustained by social images and gender roles. In some countries, for example, land inheritance follows a patriarchal line: only sons inherit land from their father (Charatsari and Černič, 2016). In other cultures, women's rights over land are subject to their marital status; they hold the right only through their husband and lose it in the case of divorce or a spouse's death (GIZ-BMZ, 2013). The difference between women and men in access and control over assets (including land, livestock, equipment, credit, but also human and social capital) is explained not only by regulatory frameworks but also because, "Through socialization, men and women are taught to value assets differently" (Quisumbing *et al.*, 2015, p. 15). For example, women are less likely than men to engage in entrepreneurial farming activities due to gendered images of their responsibilities within the household. The idea of entrepreneurship is associated with ideas of "power, control, aggressiveness, competitiveness", more commonly associated with men than women (Little, 2016, p. 361). In some societies, for example, women "entrepreneurs are judged as bad mothers" (Shortall, 2016, p. 349). It is common that when women do decide to undertake some activity outside the home or to engage in paid work, they do it in part-time or temporary jobs, to be able to fulfill their childcare and household responsibilities (Little, 2016). Such arrangements create an understanding of labor such that the unpaid labor of rural women is considered of lesser value than that done by men, reinforcing and reproducing economic disparities between women and men as well as creating systemic inequalities (Ling, 2002; Marlow and McAdam, 2013).

Recommendations and examples

In order to overcome these gender-specific barriers, international organizations have urged countries to create regulatory frameworks sensitive to women's rights, such as land tenure rights of rural women, particularly those of widows and divorcees (GIZ-BMZ, 2013). They have also recommended developing programs that allow women to have more equitable access to different kinds of services, especially banking and financial services (OECD, 2012). Article 14 of the Convention on the Elimination of All Forms of Discrimination Against Women (CEDAW) recommends investing in infrastructure and care services for children, the elderly, and people with disabilities as time-saving strategies that would relieve the workload of rural women (Pruitt, 2011). An example of a gender-sensitive regulatory framework is the Namibian Communal Land Reform Act No. 5 (2002), which grants equal land rights to women and men in communal areas. In addition to the removal of restrictions for women to register their land, the Namibian government created Communal Land Boards in charge of land rights registration. Each board includes at least two women and has issued more than 40 percent of land use certificates to women (GIZ-BMZ, 2013).

Integrating women into robust rural communities: increasing access to benefits and services

In general, rural communities over the world face a lower quality of services such as health and education, ensuring that, "Places left behind are disproportionally rural" (Brown and Schafft, 2011, p. 11). Policies often allocate resources to areas with higher concentrations of people, in detriment to rural, remote areas. These allocation strategies contribute directly to unequal access to potable water, sanitation, education, health, and justice, thereby creating what the FAO has termed "the feminization of poverty amongst rural women" (FAO *et al.*, 2013, p. 5).

For example, there is a gap between urban and rural children's school attendance: rural children are more likely than urban children to be out of school (Inter-Agency Task Force on Rural Women, n.d.). Girls in rural areas fare worse than both urban girls and rural boys because in many places, the education of girls is considered less important than that of boys (Figure 12.2). The same trend is observed in adult women, who commonly receive less "formal and non-formal education (short training, farmer field schools, extension, etc.) and informal education (media, community gatherings, etc.)" than men (FAO *et al.*, 2013, p. 3).

The lack of educational opportunities for women has significant repercussions for the women, their families, and their communities. The UN estimates that an additional year of elementary education for girls translates into a 10 to 20 percent increase in wages, a delay in the age at which women marry and become mothers, and a decrease in the risk of becoming victims of violence. Women's education is also decisive in determining "whether or not [their] children will survive the first five years of life" (Inter-Agency Task Force on Rural Women, n.d., p. 6)

The *Sustainable Development Goals Report* (UN, 2016) estimates that people in rural areas are at a disadvantage in comparison to urban populations regarding access to health-care services. The International Labour Organization (ILO) 2015 Report calculates that while 22 percent of the urban people in the world do not have access to basic health services, in rural areas this number reaches 56 percent. The situation is particularly acute in developing countries, where the deficit in health coverage of the rural population exceeds the urban by more than 50 percent. Africa and Latin America are the two most affected regions, while the gap is narrower in Europe and the Middle East (ILO, 2015).

Any lack of access to health and sanitation services particularly affects rural women. They face many limitations in accessing health services including affordability, restrictions on mobility, and lack of transport. For example, rural women are less likely than urban women to be assisted by health professionals during birth (Figure 12.3), resulting in disproportionately higher rates of maternal mortality in rural areas compared to urban areas. The UN Report on the Sustainable Development Goals reports that, "Almost all maternal deaths occur in low-resource settings and can be prevented, including by expanding access to appropriate sexual and reproductive health

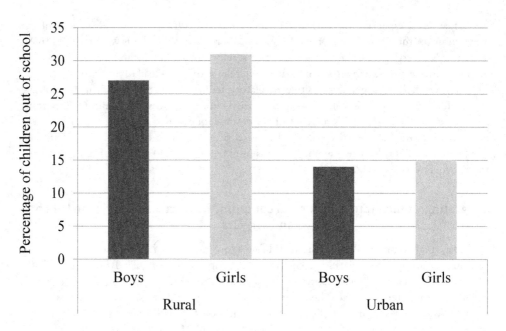

Figure 12.2 Percentage of children out of school by gender and rural/urban residence, 42 countries, 2000/2008 (%)

Source: Inter-Agency Task Force on Rural Women (n.d., p. 3).

services" (2016, p. 16). Complications in childbirth are often the result of factors such as malnutrition, early pregnancy, and difficult working conditions, all of these prevalent among rural women (FAO *et al.*, 2013).

As with education, "Access to overall health care of the girl child, who is usually neglected due to prevailing patriarchal attitudes in many traditional rural settings, is often very poor" (FAO *et al.*, 2013, pp. 3–4). For example, the UN Report on the Sustainable Development Goals (2016) highlights that in rural areas, women are less aware than urban women of how HIV/AIDS is spread and how to prevent it. This is particularly true in East and Southern Africa, where 4500 young women (15–24 years old) developed HIV *every* week in 2015, double the number of new infections in young men (UN AIDS, 2016).

The proportion of rural households with improved drinking water and sanitation facilities is usually lower than urban households (Figure 12.3). The UN (2016) estimates that only onethird of the rural population has water piped to their homes in contrast to almost 80 percent of urban households. As mentioned before, women are usually responsible for bringing water to their family; this translates into heavier workloads for rural women as they often have to travel long distances to collect water. For example,

> In a single day in 25 sub-Saharan African countries, women spend 16 million hours collecting water, often to the detriment of schooling or paid work, and with potential health risks from repeatedly carrying heavy burdens over long distances.
>
> *(UN Women, 2016, p. 14)*

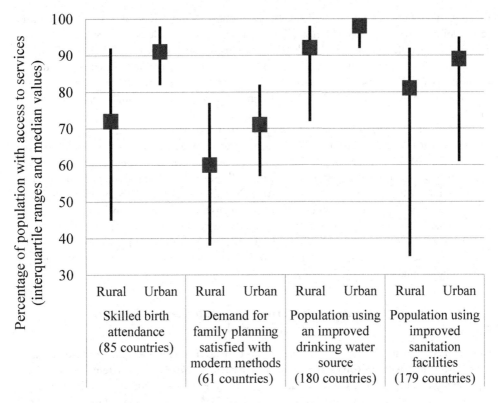

Figure 12.3 Percentage of rural and urban populations with access to selected services, 2015

Source: United Nations (2016, p. 49).

Roles, images, and social constructions underlying gender inequalities

Cultural and tradition systems may explain some of the difference in access to services between women and men. For example, some cultures follow post-nuptial residence norms known as "patrilocal". That is, after marriage, a woman becomes part of the family of her husband and resides with them. This gives families fewer incentives to invest in daughters' education and health, compared to sons who will remain in the family even after marriage. According to Jayachandran (2014), "The financial mindset about investing in daughters is encapsulated in an often-quoted Indian saying that 'raising a daughter is like watering your neighbors' garden'" (p. 11). Social and cultural norms translate into laws that limit the autonomy of women to make choices about their education and their own health. For example, more than 80 percent of married 15–19-year-old women in Senegal, Niger, Burkina Faso, Côte d'Ivoire, and Cameroon do not have the final say in their own health care (UN AIDS, 2014). And, in 29 countries, women need the consent of a spouse or partner to access sexual and reproductive health services (UN AIDS, 2017).

Recommendations and examples

Examples of strategies that have been identified as effective measures to remove barriers to education and health services include eliminating school fees for girls and providing incentives for attending school (OECD, 2012) as well as adopting a re-admission policy so girls can return to school after pregnancy (FAO *et al.*, 2013). In the case of health care, organizations have recommended making sure skilled birth attendants are available (OECD, 2012, p. 87). Investing in building schools and health centers near remote areas, creating mobile clinics that provide free medical services (FAO *et al.*, 2013), providing transportation to school, and ensuring that schools have enough sanitary facilities (OECD, 2012) are all ways to increase rural women's access to those services.

A group of international organizations has recommended promoting farmers' groups as an effective means to share information and facilitate technology adoption among rural women (FAO *et al.*, 2013). An example practice of this and its potential impacts beyond training is the Agricultural Development Project and Agricultural Sector Investment Program in Zambia. This initiative included seminars to train both women and men on the distribution of seeds and effects on protein supply and malnutrition. The seminars also provided an opportunity to discuss gender relationships. "Women were taught to articulate their knowledge, experiences, and concerns, while men learned to listen" (GIZ-BMZ, 2013, p. 6). This participatory extension approach has been adopted in other districts in Zambia and has motivated women to participate in community meetings.

Integrating women into robust rural communities: participating in local decision-making

Gender inequities are also reflected in unequal participation and representation in forums where issues that affect women's lives are debated and decided. Rural women tend to be under-represented and marginalized in community organizations such as producer organizations, agricultural cooperatives, water user associations (GIZ-BMZ, 2013), land administration, and judicial organizations (Inter-Agency Task Force on Rural Women, n.d.).

Exclusion from these decision-making processes means that women's concerns, perspectives, and expertise are not taken into account when designing public policies and deciding resource allocation. The unequal access to goods and services discussed above may to a large extent be the result of marginalization from decision processes. Underrepresentation also exacerbates women's vulnerability to poverty and the impacts of climate change (UN Women, 2008). It is widely acknowledged that greater and meaningful participation of women is associated with better access to productive resources and markets (GIZ-BMZ, 2013).

In many countries in Central and South America, for example, men frequently hold leadership positions in grassroots organizations while women participate only as members (UN Women, 2008). A similar trend can be observed in the European Union. The LEADER program (LEADER is a French acronym for Links between Actions for the Development of the Rural Economy), which promotes rural development from a bottom-up and local area-based approach through Local Action Groups (LAGs), also exhibits overall limited participation of women. For example, there are 892 LAGs across 15 European Union countries. In about 420 LAGs, less than 25 percent of members are women. In only 196 LAGs is female membership more than 50 percent (Bock, 2010).

Both external and internal reasons may prevent women from participating (Thuesen, 2016). Rural women may be unfamiliar with the policies and norms of community organizations and are often unaware of their own rights. In addition, as mentioned above, given child-care responsibilities, mobility restrictions, and security concerns, possibilities for participation may be limited (FAO *et al.*, 2013; GIZ-BMZ, 2013). Bock (2015), referring to women's participation in the LAGs in the European Union, indicates that a masculine culture dominates politics in such a way that, "Women who do enter the new political structures report their difficulty with the male political culture that may even motivate them to resign" (p. 737).

Roles, images, and social constructions underlying gender inequalities

In addition to these external constraints to participation, women also face internal constraints. Bock (2015) found that the most common reasons that rural women self-exclude from formal political activities are because they consider themselves inexperienced, not qualified, and/or lack time to get involved. Women leaders who were surveyed in Asian and Pacific countries described their approach to politics and decision-making as very different from that of their male colleagues (UN Women, 2008). For example, McVay (2016) explains the many ways in which gender role stereotypes, which typically assign women caregiving tasks, shape the idea of leadership as associated with the exercise of power. She found that many rural women, even when they exert leadership positions with a high level of responsibility, do not identify themselves as leaders; they consider the activities they participate in as a service to their families and communities or fulfillment of what is expected from them. Furthermore, many women prefer to participate in informal activities with less exposure to public opinion; "These [informal] community groups, however, are rarely invited to participate in decision making on rural development plans" (Bock, 2015, p. 737), so that in the end they are excluded from these processes.

Recommendations and examples

Among the recommendations to strengthen women's participation in decision-making processes are providing training and information about women's rights, relevant regulations, and decision-making processes to both women and men; offering financial and advisory support to rural women who are part of farmers' organizations and other local leadership efforts; and creating spaces or venues in which women can formulate concerns as well as inform policy-makers about interests and needs (GIZ–BMZ, 2013). Incorporating a gender equality perspective into public financial systems, so that budget allocations equally meet the needs of both women and men, has also been identified as critical (OECD, 2012). Some countries have promoted women to be elected or appointed to leadership positions by decentralizing decision-making processes since it is easier for women to participate at the community or local level. In addition, they have created gender quotas in decision-making bodies. For example, a constitutional reform in India in 1993 mandated that one-third of seats be reserved for women in *panchayats*, the local governing councils. Pakistan and other countries have undertaken similar measures (UN Women, 2008). The experience from women councilors in India demonstrated the impact of women in leadership positions on policies that benefit other women. "Their presence has also made women citizens more likely to take advantage of state services and demand their rights" (UN Women, 2008, p. 36).

Long-term policies for engaging women in building robust rural communities

While rural women across the world face a wide variety of life experiences and opportunities, they share in common an inequality of access to resources, services, and benefits due not just to limited infrastructure but also to gender and cultural inequality. Many organizations and individuals have been working for decades to change opportunities for rural women to succeed and there have been improvements. However, work remains because achieving gender equality requires transformative policy changes. Several suggestions for improving women's participation in rural communities are described below. While many of these suggestions have been integrated in some efforts around the world, none of them are widely used or recognized as best practices in policy development or project planning.

Because local, national, and international decisions about resource allocation affect women and men differently, policy- and decision-makers need to learn how to integrate a gender analysis into public planning and policy-making. This can include collecting information from affected women and clearly articulating women's needs and priorities as well as reporting on context-specific constraints and vulnerabilities.

It is increasingly common to train and use women as facilitators in community efforts along with setting quotas for women's participation in decision-making bodies. Moving forward, these practices can be enhanced by training both women and men about the role of women in robust communities, especially for those in decision-making roles including religious leaders. Engaging existing women's groups to help create optimal spaces for women to participate can draw on existing capacity and knowledge about location, timing, and child-care needs that may be different for women than men.

As described above, even when women do get involved in decision-making, their voices are often subdued. While there has been success with separate meetings and voting procedures for women, more creative ways for expressing preferences may be needed for women who do not read or write, or feel uncomfortable speaking in public. Requiring that a certain amount of resources always be allocated to women's priorities may help ensure that projects and services address women's livelihoods and constraints.

However, until women are treated equally under the law, many of these important implementation activities may not lead to permanent and widespread change in the conditions of rural women. So, in addition to these "ground-up" and local efforts, it is critical that laws and regulations be developed and enforced from the "top-down" in order to prevent discriminatory practices against women. Grassroots efforts to involve rural women will be more effective in the long run when coupled with legal reforms and justice systems that reflect gender equality (International Development Law Organization, 2013). However, legal reforms designed to increase women's access to services and benefits need to be context-specific as there aren't any universal solutions. New practices should intentionally examine where opportunities for women's engagement and integration of priorities can be found in the given context, whether that be in formal or informal systems and initiatives. One way to improve the likelihood of success is to engage a multidisciplinary or multi-organizational approach that includes partners such as those working on common women's issues such as income generation, legal reform, domestic violence counseling and reproductive services, microcredit access, and improved educational opportunities for children and adults.

While none of these suggestions or approaches is a guarantee of success everywhere all the time, the fate of rural communities in an increasingly urban world requires the successful integration of women into all aspects of community. Increasing women's success increases the productivity of land and livestock, educational attainment of children, and human and environmental health. All of these tend to deteriorate over time when half the population is limited in its opportunities to contribute.

Conclusions and recommendations for future research

It is somewhat disingenuous to separate gender from all other issues facing rural communities because, as noted early in this chapter, women play critical roles in rural communities; without their effective participation, rural communities are unlikely to be vibrant places where people thrive. The most critical priority for future research is to ensure that gender issues are considered holistically in studying rural communities. There are several areas where new research can be effectively targeted and are described briefly below. For the most part, these recommendations are similar for both OECD countries and the Global South.

One of the main challenges to understanding the lives of rural women is the lack of regularly updated information disaggregated by gender and geographic area. The research agenda on rural women for the next ten years should articulate critical indicators for understanding rural women's lives in both OECD countries and the Global South, and begin collecting longitudinal data disaggregated by gender and rural/urban settings that is consistent across geographic areas to allow comparisons over time, and within and between countries.

Research on gender issues in rural areas will benefit from empirical data about the cost of women's marginalization from the economic life of their communities as well as the impact of gender violence, lack of education and health services. Research undertaken with this multi-issue approach will inform the understanding of how social and cultural systems reinforce structural inequalities for rural women.

International organizations have compiled a record of practices and policies designed to promote gender equality. Future research should focus on finding empirical evidence of the long-term effects of such gendered policies. Especially important is an identification of policies that can transform social, institutional, and legal barriers to advance full inclusion of women in rural communities.

Very little information is available on the political participation of rural women in decision-making bodies at any level from the most local to the most global. Critical questions include understanding the incentives and barriers for rural women participating in both formal and informal decision processes.

Very little information can be found about the impact of minority status on the experiences of rural women. The Inter-American Commission on Human Rights (2017) suggests that the confluence of various discriminatory factors such as sexism, racism, and rural poverty exacerbates the possibility of human rights being violated. These factors act as "overlapping layers" that reinforce each other and make it even more difficult to eliminate the forms of discrimination generated. Future research can help articulate the types and impacts of overlapping discrimination affecting Indigenous and minority women in rural communities.

References

Benería, L., Berik, G., Floro, M., 2003. *Gender, development and globalization: economics as if all people mattered*. Routledge, London; New York.

Besra, L., 2014. *Do indigenous women have right to inherit land? A critical review of customary practices of land inheritance with reference to gender justice in Bangladesh*. International Journal of Social Science and Humanity 4(5), 339–343.

Bock, B.B., 2010. *Personal and social development of women in rural areas of Europe*. European Parliament. http://library.wur.nl/WebQuery/wurpubs/fulltext/163660.

Bock, B.B. 2015. *Gender mainstreaming and rural development policy: The trivialization of rural gender issues*. Gender, Place and Culture 22(5), 731–745.

Brown, D.L., Schafft, K.A., 2011. *Rural people and communities in the 21st Century: Resilience and transformation*. Polity Press, Malden, MA.

Charatsari, C., Černič Istenič, M., 2016. *Gender, farming and rural social research: A relationship in flux*, in: Shucksmith, M., Brown, D.L. (Eds.), *Routledge international handbook of rural studies*. Routledge, London; New York, pp. 389–398.

Croppenstedt, A., Goldstein, M., Rosas, N., 2013. *Gender and agriculture: Inefficiencies, segregation, and low productivity traps*. The World Bank Research Observer 28(1), 79–109.

FAO (Food and Agriculture Organization), 2011. *The state of food and agriculture*. www.fao.org/docrep/013/i2050e/i2050e.pdf.

FAO (Food and Agriculture Organization), 2016. *The state of food and agriculture: Climate change, agriculture, and food security.* www.fao.org/publications/sofa/2016/en/.

Food and Agriculture Organization, International Fund for Agriculture Development, World Food Program, and UN Women, 2013. *Concept note for the general recommendation on Article 14 of the Committee on the Elimination of Discrimination Against Women (CEDAW).* www.ohchr.org/EN/HRBodies/CEDAW/Pages/RuralWomen.aspx.

GIZ-BMZ, 2013. *Gender and rural development: Aspects, approaches and good practices.* www.gender-in-german-development.net/custom/images/contentBilderGalerie/bilderGalerie1000508/GIZ-BMZ-Gender-and-rural-development-2013-EN.pdf.

Himmelweit, S., 1995. *The discovery of "unpaid work": the social consequences of the expansion of "work".* Feminist Economics 1(2), 1–19.

Inter-Agency Task Force on Rural Women, n.d. *Rural women and the millennium development goals. Fact sheet.* www.un.org/womenwatch/feature/ruralwomen/documents/En-Rural-Women-MDGs-web.pdf.

Inter-American Commission on Human Rights (IACHR), 2017. *Las mujeres indígenas y sus derechos humanos en las Américas.* https://oig.cepal.org/sites/default/files/mujeresindigenascidh.pdf.

International Development Law Organization (IDLO), 2013. *Assessing justice: Models, strategies, and best practices on women's empowerment.* www.idlo.int/publications/accessing-justice-models-strategies-and-best-practices-womens-empowerment.

International Labour Organization (ILO), 2015. *Global evidence on inequities in rural health protection: New data on rural deficits in health coverage for 174 countries.* www.socialprotection.org/gimi/gess/ShowRessource.action?ressource.ressourceId=51297.

Jayachandran, S., 2014. *The roots of gender inequality in developing countries.* Annual Review of Economics 7(1), 63–88.

Ling, L.H., 2002. *Postcolonial international relations: Conquest and desire between Asia and the West.* Palgrave Macmillan, London.

Little, J., 2016. *Gender and entrepreneurship,* in: Shucksmith, M., Brown, D.L (Eds.), *Routledge international handbook of rural studies.* Routledge, London; New York, pp. 357–366.

Marlow, S., McAdam, M., 2013. *Gender and entrepreneurship: Advancing debate and challenging myths; exploring the mystery of the under-performing female entrepreneur.* International Journal of Entrepreneurial Behavior and Research 19(1), 114–124.

McVay, L., 2016. *Leadership and gender,* in: Shucksmith, M., Brown, D.L. (Eds.), *Routledge international handbook of rural studies.* Routledge, London; New York, pp. 367–378.

Organisation for Economic Co-operation and Development (OECD), 2012. *Women's economic empowerment,* in: OECD, *Poverty reduction and pro-poor growth: The role of empowerment.* www.oecd-ilibrary.org/development/poverty-reduction-and-pro-poor-growth_9789264168350-en.

Pruitt, L., 2011, *Deconstructing CEDAW's Article 14: Naming and explaining rural difference.* William and Mary Journal of Women and Law 17(2), 347–394.

Quisumbing, A.R., Meinzen-Dick, R.S., Johnson, N.L., Njuki, J., Julia, B., Gilligan, D.O., Kovarik, C., Peterman, A., Roy, S., Waithanji, E., Rubin, D., Manfre, C., 2015. *Reducing the gender asset gap through agricultural development: A technical resource guide.* www.ifpri.org/publication/reducing-gender-asset-gap-through-agricultural-development-technical-resource-guide.

Shortall, S., 2016. *Changing configurations of gender and rural society,* in: Shucksmith, M., Brown, D.L. (Eds.), *Routledge international handbook of rural studies.* Routledge, London; New York, pp. 349–356.

Thuesen, A.A., 2016. *Gender and rural governance,* in: Shucksmith, M., Brown, D.L. (Eds.), *Routledge international handbook of rural studies.* Routledge, London; New York, pp. 379–388.

United Nations, 2016. *The Sustainable Development Goals report.* www.un.org.lb/Library/Assets/The-Sustainable-Development-Goals-Report-2016-Global.pdf.

United Nations AIDS, 2014. *Prevention gap report.* http://files.unaids.org/en/media/unaids/contentassets/documents/unaidspublication/2014/UNAIDS_Gap_report_en.pdf.

United Nations AIDS, 2016. *Prevention gap report.* www.unaids.org/sites/default/files/media_asset/2016-prevention-gap-report_en.pdf.

United Nations AIDS, 2017. *When women lead, change happens.* www.unaids.org/sites/default/files/media_asset/when-women-lead-change-happens_en.pdf.

United Nations Women, 2008. *Rural women in a changing world: Opportunities and challenges. Women 2000 and Beyond.* www.un.org/womenwatch/daw/public/Women%202000%20-%20Rural%20Women%20web%20English.pdf.

United Nations Women, 2019. *Facts and figures*. www.unwomen.org/en/news/in-focus/commission-on-the-status-of-women-2012/facts-and-figures.

United Nations Women, 2016. *Women and Sustainable Development Goals*. https://sustainabledevelopment.un.org/content/documents/2322UN%20Women%20Analysis%20on%20Women%20and%20SDGs.pdf.

World Bank, 2016. *Urban population (% of total)*. https://data.worldbank.org/indicator/SP.URB.TOTL.IN.ZS?end=2016&start=2016&view=map.

13

RURAL POVERTY IN A COMPARATIVE CONTEXT

Bill Reimer[1]

Poverty: the state of one who lacks a usual or socially acceptable amount of money or material possessions.

(Merriam-Webster)

Introduction

The analysis and interpretation of poverty is an important focus for both policy and social action because it concerns the treatment of the most vulnerable in society. Its different manifestations in rural and urban places also justify attention to the dynamics supporting those differences. This chapter outlines some of the key conceptual and operational issues implicated in the analysis of poverty as a basis for conducting such research. It begins with a description of various conceptual frameworks which have guided poverty definitions and some of the dominant ways in which it has been operationalized among OECD countries before turning to the issue of rural and urban differences. After a brief outline of various explanations for poverty the chapter concludes with six suggestions regarding rural poverty research.

Poverty and inequality are about how assets and resources are shared. Given the sensitive nature of such an issue, it is no wonder that definitions and interpretations vary considerably by time, nation, location, advocate, and analyst. Equally varied are the judgements regarding the justification for the distribution, ranging from those who argue that inequality is necessary for motivating industriousness (Davis and Moore, 1945) to those who suggest it is at the root of a wide range of social, political, and economic ills (Sharing, 2018).

Research and policy analysis of poverty and inequality, therefore, require considerable reflection regarding their objectives, appropriate definitions for those objectives, the types of measures which are consistent with those definitions, and the value judgements regarding each. Given their ideological connections, some consideration of the historical, social, and political contexts for various approaches is also in order.

This chapter identifies some of the major ways in which poverty has been conceptualized and analyzed. In keeping with the ICRPS framework the focus will be on OECD countries although many revisions of poverty and income analysis have been influenced by research in the Third World. The objective is to direct attention to key issues and questions relating to this analysis as these issues are addressed in the context of rural and remote places.

What is poverty?

Poverty is not a rural indicator but its prevalence and organization vary by distance and distance-to-density (cf. Chapter 1). This chapter, therefore, begins with a general discussion of poverty before considering its particular manifestations in rural areas.

Poverty has been defined in multiple ways, reflecting the broad range of objectives and approaches within the research and policy domains. In his report to the Food and Agriculture Organization of the UN, Favareto (2017, p. 7) identifies three major "stages" through which poverty has been defined by analysts and policy-makers. Approaches reflected in all of the stages can be seen in current scholarship, policy, and media discussions.

Emerging from the late nineteenth century and used in the twentieth century, during the first stage, poverty was considered to be the absence of a minimum amount necessary to conduct life with dignity. Proponents also assumed that this was best reflected in a minimum monetary income and eventually the identification of poverty lines for analysis and policy. Rather than treat income as one way to operationalize a more abstract definition of poverty, low income was often used as if it were the defining characteristic itself, curtailing discussions regarding definitions which include a wider range of assets.

If low income is the defining characteristic of poverty, it is little wonder that the search for causes and policy options focus on improving incomes alone. Such an approach runs the risk of missing important dynamics of poverty which are necessary to include for effective solutions or overlooking features of poverty which are related to contextual factors such as local community or neighborhood conditions. Increasing incomes, for example, may be the result of people taking on more jobs to make ends meet. By doing so, however, they will have less time to repair the roof, maintain a kitchen garden, prepare preserves from its bounty, or fix the car. They will also have less time to spend with their children, get more training, or visit with family members and neighbors who will serve as backup in times of crisis. In short, increasing incomes may result in the diminution of other assets critical to survival under conditions of poverty (Reimer, 2006, 2011).

The second stage emerged from analysis questioning poverty as the absence of minimum income. Nobel Prize winner Amartya Sen (1982, 1992, 1999) summarized this analysis using three arguments: income does not include all relevant contributions to a dignified life; a minimum level varies considerably across space, time, and culture; and people make trade-offs among dimensions (including, but not limited to income) in order to seek personal and family opportunities.

Advocates of this multidimensional approach argued that poverty is better defined as the "deprivation of the capability to make choices". They elaborated this definition to consider how different individuals and social groups may value different types of achievements, activities, and contextual supports related to those achievements, and capabilities to take advantage of them. In this way, poverty was redefined in relational terms with the unequal distribution of opportunities available to individuals and groups playing an important part of its formulation (Favareto, 2017; Shucksmith, 2016). The research altered the definition of poverty by interpreting its more restricted economic focus as one dimension of "social exclusion" (Shucksmith and Schafft, 2012; Shucksmith, 2016; Tickamyer and Wornell, 2017).

From this perspective, living with low incomes is just one way in which individuals, households, or groups may face exclusion from the benefits of their society. It highlights the point that material poverty is often associated with disenfranchisement of people via access to education, health care, housing, legal due process, and many other resources which are necessary for full participation in the society. The UN definition of poverty (see Box 13.1) and its Human

Development Index are examples constructed on the basis of this multidimensional approach – synthesizing income, education, and health indicators (UNDP, 2016).

Box 13.1

Poverty is more than the lack of income and resources to ensure a sustainable livelihood. Its manifestations include hunger and malnutrition, limited access to education and other basic services, social discrimination and exclusion as well as the lack of participation in decision-making. Economic growth must be inclusive to provide sustainable jobs and promote equality.

(UN, 2018)

Favareto argues that the limitations of this multidimensional approach led to a third stage in which quality of life and well-being play a more central role in the definition of poverty (2017, pp. 10–11). It introduces the use of subjective measures of welfare along with objectives, conditions, and opportunities such as health, education, social connections, and environmental conditions into the analysis. Such definitions and their related operationalization can become more sensitive to rural conditions, where people are less likely to participate in markets and more likely to combine their financial, material, and social assets in different ways from those in urban locations. This approach was reinforced by the "rural livelihoods" concept and research of the late twentieth century (Ellis, 1993).

In 1988, Hagenaars and De Vos (1988) identified three characteristics of poverty definitions that still stand as relevant today.

The first (*Absolute Poverty*) refers to having less than an objectively defined, absolute minimum amount of material resources. Such definitions usually focus on the cost of basic needs such as food, shelter, and clothing as the point of reference for identifying the poor. The UN Development Program, for example, established this type of definition in 1995 (see Box 13.2). A major limitation of this approach becomes clear when comparisons are attempted. The nature and costs of those basic needs vary considerably by country, region, and scale.

Box 13.2

Poverty is a condition characterized by severe deprivation of basic human needs, including food, safe drinking water, sanitation facilities, health, shelter, education and information. It depends not only on income but also on access to services.

(UNDP, 2016)

The second category (*Relative Poverty*) identifies the poor by comparing them to the country, region, or social group in which they are located. The OECD uses such an approach for calculating the poverty rate. By establishing a particular population as a point of reference, the definition adjusts the significance relative to the distribution of incomes within that population or social group (OECD, 2013) (see Box 13.3).

Box 13.3

The poverty line is an income level that is considered minimally sufficient to sustain a family in terms of food, housing, clothing, medical needs, and so on (OECD, 2005). Operationally, poverty is measured by the ratio of the number of people (in a given age group) whose income falls below the poverty line; taken as half the median household income of the total population.

(OECD, 2018)

The third category (*Subjective Poverty*) uses a subjective standard for the identification of poverty – often measured by individuals' self-assessment of their condition. The assumption is that if people feel they have inadequate resources to function as individuals or households, they are likely to experience the negative effects of poverty, no matter what more objective indicators might reflect (Goedhart *et al.*, 1977; Hagenaars and de Vos, 1988) (see Box 13.4).

Box 13.4

In everyday usage, poverty commonly means lack of money resources and of social respect to the levels demonstrably required to achieve the minimum standards of … respect for human dignity and full social participation or inclusion.

(Veit-Wilson, 2006, p. 318)

How is poverty measured?

Many of the debates regarding the definition of poverty emerged as researchers grappled with its operationalization in a variety of locations and for a variety of objectives. What assets should be considered? How much scarcity is required? Scarcity of what? What reference group should be considered? What comparisons are being made? Addressing these questions has produced a variety of indicators that are used by researchers today.

The question regarding assets usually includes income, but it often goes beyond to consider physical assets such as property or household goods along with pensions and financial assets. Recognizing the value of other forms of capital (human, social, political, or cultural) for adequate functioning within society, some researchers have included indicators for these assets within their definition and measurement of poverty (Young, 2016).

Several details of the assets considered can also significantly affect the results of these measures. Considering incomes before or after taxes, for example, will change the poverty estimates significantly, especially within societies with extensive social support programs. Similarly, focusing on consumption indicators as opposed to incomes will alter the meaning and implications of poverty in the resulting analysis.

The question regarding scarcity has also produced a wide variety of approaches – most often in absolute terms. Using this approach, researchers frequently justify the levels selected on the basis of costs estimated from surveys regarding expenditures for food, clothing, shelter, and sometimes the cost of incidentals such as transportation or services which are necessary for employment.

Implicit in both absolute and relative measures of poverty is the selection of the basic and reference units of analysis. Largely due to the data available, the individual is most often identified as the basic unit. In some cases, family units are considered, but rarer still is the identification of groups, networks, or types of people as such units. Each of these selections implies different characteristics and dynamics of poverty, however.

One of the most important decisions concerns the nature of any comparisons being made. If, for example, countries are the primary units of comparison, it is necessary to choose indicators which are equivalent across countries with respect to the definition of poverty being chosen. In some cases, incomes may be comparable on their own, but such incomes rarely reflect differential opportunities without adjustments for cost of living or access to employment across countries or regions.

The specific decisions made regarding the measurement of poverty should be guided by two important considerations. First, is the objective and understanding of the research or policy issue being considered. This should be provided in a clear conceptual definition of poverty. For example, if poverty is understood as an economic phenomenon alone, the definition and subsequent indicators should identify and justify the relevant assets in those terms. If it is considered to be a feature of lifestyle or culture, the key elements should be made clear.

The second consideration is the claim being made for poverty – whether as a cause, consequence, or program outcome. If the analysis includes a claim for such causes or outcomes, the definition and measurement of poverty should carefully exclude indicators that are likely to be related to those causes or outcomes. In order to test hypotheses about such a relationship, the indicators for poverty must be independent from those for any causes or consequences being investigated. Even the UNDP definition (Box 13.2), for example, remains equivocal in its inclusion of nutrition, health, and access to services as characteristics of poverty. If indicators of these characteristics are included as necessary or sufficient conditions of poverty, then research regarding their relative importance is excluded. On the other hand, if poverty is independently defined from these characteristics, such research can be justified.

Poverty and inequality in the EU

Most of the countries in the EU use relative indicators of poverty. The movement away from a narrow interpretation of poverty was encouraged in 1979 by the publication of a major study in Britain (Townsend, 1979) and many follow-up analyses focusing on the meaning and dynamics of the broader concepts of deprivation and social exclusion (Bock, 2016) (see Box 13.5). Since poverty reduction is a key goal of the EU's Europe 2020 strategy (European Commission, 2010), a common set of poverty and social exclusion indicators have been produced by each country since that time (the Laeken Indicators). These indicators include several income-related measures as well as indicators of regional cohesion, unemployment, lack of education or training, life expectancy, and self-defined health (Dennis and Guio, 2004; European Commission, 2017). The primary source of collective statistics for the European Commission (Eurostat, 2018) reflects the way in which such broad approaches have been adopted, leading to the specification of 18 common indicators (Dennis and Guio, 2004).

Box 13.5 EU definitions of poverty and inequality

The Joint report by the Commission and the Council on social inclusion (March 2004) defines people as living in poverty if "their income and resources are so inadequate as to preclude them from having a standard of living considered acceptable in the society in which they live. Because of their poverty they may experience multiple disadvantage through unemployment, low income, poor housing, inadequate health care and barriers to lifelong learning, culture, sport and recreation".

Poverty is interrelated with social exclusion, a condition defined by the joint report as "a process whereby certain individuals are pushed to the edge of society and prevented from participating fully by virtue of their poverty, or lack of basic competencies and lifelong learning opportunities, or as a result of discrimination. This distances them from job, income and education opportunities as well as social and community networks and activities".

(EU Commission Member Services, 2016)

Rural poverty and inequality have received considerable attention in Europe as a result of several initiatives addressing economic and social development challenges (European Commission Member Services, 2016). The LEADER programs beginning in 1991 (Paneva, 2014), the importance of poverty in the Europe 2020 strategy, several member state initiatives, and the more recent Multidimensional Poverty Assessment Tool (European Commission, 2014) have all contributed to continued monitoring and development of attention to rural places. Although still largely limited to demographic and economic indicators, the research and political agendas reflect a vision of both poverty and inclusion which creates pressure to develop a broader framework. This is an explicit feature of the OECD's recent exploration of concepts such as social exclusion, vulnerability, and well-being (OECD, 2017).

Poverty and inequality in the US

Public discussion and policy regarding poverty and inequality in the US has been heavily influenced by three main historical and social events: the Great Depression of the 1930s, the War on Poverty initiative of President Johnson in the early 1960s, and the dismantling of those welfare initiatives during the Nixon, Ford, Reagan, and Clinton eras (1969 to 2015) (Weber and Miller, 2017).

The War on Poverty, for example, required standards to drive its political justification, the allocation of benefits, and the monitoring of results. Using a standard developed in the Social Security Administration, the US Census Bureau established an official poverty rate from 1959 (Center for Poverty Research, 2016). This rate is an absolute measure – based on an assessment of the income needed for various-sized families to meet their food and housing demands. It uses money income before taxes and public income supports like cash welfare without including capital gains or in-kind social programs such as public housing, Medicaid, or Food Stamps (US Census Bureau, 2017). In 2011, a new poverty estimate was released as an alternative indicator to the official poverty line. Entitled a "supplemental poverty measure" (SPM) this indicator adjusted for regional cost-of-living differences and included in-kind government benefits and tax credits and required expenses like health care, child care, and other work-related expenses and taxes (Fox, 2017).

Clinton's Welfare Reform (Personal Responsibility and Work Opportunity Reconciliation Act of 1996), turned the Aid to Families with Dependent Children (AFDC) entitlement established in 1935 into a time-limited block grant to states that attempted to move poor people into work and marriage but without considering whether adequate jobs were available. It has been credited with moving many single mothers into work (Weber *et al.*, 2004) but also pushing those without skills and social support into deep poverty (Edin and Shaefer, 2016). It also included the expansion of another work-oriented income transfer (the Earned Income Tax Credit). This program was greatly expanded in 1993, and, along with Food Stamps, is credited as being the program most effective in reducing poverty in recent decades (as measured by the Supplemental Poverty Measure).

Rural poverty has received specific attention in the US – at particular times and as a result of government programs. The establishment of the land-grant universities and colleges in the 1860s with their agricultural and outreach missions provided an institutional basis for sustained research and social action with a rural focus. Weber and Miller (2017) point to the Tennessee Valley Authority Act of 1933, rural electrification, resettlement initiatives, and the Farm Security Act of 1937 as some of the earliest poverty-related programs targeting rural places and people as a result of the Great Depression. During the War on Poverty period, President Johnson created a National Advisory Commission on Rural Poverty. Its 1967 report not only demonstrated that rural people were at higher risk than urban but introduced a theme which was to be found in many subsequent studies: that rural poverty has an important regional and place-focused dimension. Since this period, however, Weber and Miller note that, "federal policy shifted away from a concern about the effects of poverty on people and communities, and toward a concern about work behaviour and marital and child-bearing decisions of low-income households" (Tickamyer and Wornell, 2017).

In spite of the policy reliance on a limited range of indicators for poverty, US researchers have continued to document the complexity and geographical relevance of poverty in rural places. Case studies such as those by Fitchen (1991), Duncan (2000), and Sherman (2006, 2013), along with national studies (President's National Advisory Commission on Rural Poverty, 1967) continue to highlight the extent and complexity of the issues – often moving beyond the narrow focus on income to highlight the specific challenges facing poor people and communities in rural places (Duncan, 1992; Rural Sociological Society Task Force on Persistent Rural Poverty, 1993; Tickamyer *et al.*, 2017).

Poverty and inequality in Canada

Unlike the US there are few programs in Canada which require a common threshold for poverty. Since health, education, welfare, labor, and natural resource production are provincial responsibilities, the responses to poverty and inequality vary across the country. The federal government is involved in these issues primarily through its constitutional mandate to monitor and manage fiscal inequities across the provinces and regions. As a result, the national focus is on regional inequities (see Chapter 35).

On the other hand, poverty-related issues in Canada have been significantly affected by broad-based financial and social programs that emerge from this focus on regional equality. Foremost among them are the employment insurance, pension, health, and education initiatives that ensure labor and population mobility across the country without loss of eligibility. The first old age pension program was introduced in 1927, unemployment insurance in 1940, and universal health care between 1962 and 1971 (Reimer, 2010; The Canadian Encyclopedia, 2013).

These programs had significant impacts on populations that were overrepresented in rural regions (e.g. elderly and seasonal workers) or on services that were difficult to access (e.g. health). Since their establishment, the programs have undergone many changes as the neoliberal pressures of the 1980s and beyond have eroded some of the more universal aspects of the programs and re-introduced the discourse of the "deserving poor".

Policies and programs relating to Indigenous Peoples in Canada are also relevant to rural poverty since most of the reserves are located in non-urban regions. Programs for First Nations People are primarily delivered by the federal government through the provisions of the Indian Act of 1876. It has been strongly criticized for its colonial framework, contributions to cultural genocide, and abysmal record regarding poverty, education, and health. Fortunately, many Indigenous Peoples in Canada are currently negotiating or renegotiating land and governance claims as a result of court challenges and policy changes. The implications of the various outcomes will have important impacts on poverty programs for both individuals and communities.

Canada does not have an official indicator for poverty. On the other hand, Statistics Canada maintains a record of three different measures related to low incomes (Government of Canada, 2016). The low-income cut-offs (LICO) were established in 1967 as relative income thresholds for families sharing income (economic families). Two sets of indicators (before and after taxes) are maintained for seven family sizes – all of them estimating the average proportion of income that families spend on food, shelter, and clothing (Government of Canada, 2016). In 2000, an absolute Market Basket Measure (MBM) was included as an alternative – based on the cost of a pre-determined set of goods and services appropriate to their family size and area of residence. Statistics Canada also provides an indicator of the low-income gap: the difference between a family's income and its appropriate low-income line.

Although regional issues take precedence over rural ones, there have been occasional federal initiatives with a specific rural poverty focus. The most recent is a study by the Senate Standing Committee on Agriculture and Forestry (Fairbairn, 2006; Fairbairn and Gustafson, 2008).

Poverty and inequality in Mexico

Mexico makes use of a multidimensional index of marginalization in its approach to poverty and inequality measurement. Marginalization is associated with a lack of accessibility to basic goods and services (including welfare), opportunities, social networks, and the inability to acquire them (Hernandez *et al.*, 2013).

This index is constructed using sophisticated structural equation techniques to integrate information regarding such elements as access to basic services (electricity and drinking water), the quality of dwellings, education, and the proportion of the working population that is poorly paid. The index is calculated for various geographical entities, including federal districts and municipalities – in both absolute and relative forms (Flores-Jimenez *et al.*, 2010; Hernandez *et al.*, 2013; World Bank, 2008, p. 79).

The index stands as an interesting contrast with the poverty-level approach found in most other countries. By assessing and including indicators sensitive to a wide variety of demographic, social, and employment characteristics it moves the focus from the economic definition of income poverty alone to include many of the conditions contributing to it. Although the index precludes subsequent analysis regarding those contributing conditions, it provides a more sophisticated approach to the context of income poverty and points to potential policy and program initiatives which might affect those outcomes.

Poverty and inequality in the OECD

Since its origin in 1960, the OECD has monitored the level of poverty and inequality among its member states. As a multinational organization, it is also faced with the difficult challenge of comparing poverty and inequality among very different national partners. Under these circumstances, absolute indicators are problematic since the standards of need are often different according to each nation. Although relative measures take these differences into account, the challenge of identifying adequate living conditions within different countries remains (see Figure 13.1).

Figure 13.1 makes clear that relative income poverty varies greatly across OECD countries.

In spite of its economic focus, OECD analysts have also explored more general meanings and interpretations of "material deprivation" (OECD, 2008, Ch. 7). Surveys regarding the ability to adequately heat homes, have a healthy diet, or get access to health care have been used along with information regarding the ownership of consumer durables, quality of the housing, financial stress, and the ability to get help from others. Using a summary measure across these variables a 2008 study found only weak correlations with income poverty (OECD, 2008, p. 184). Some of the individual country territorial reviews also provide extensive discussions regarding issues of "well-being" which expand the income focus of the key indicators (OECD, 2007, 2010).

Other sources for poverty and inequality analysis

In addition to the national sources for information and analysis about poverty and inequality, there are several other organizations which provide useful material for understanding and analysis.

The World Bank group was created out of the European devastation of World War II in 1944. Since 1970, it has included poverty reduction or eradication on its primary agenda – with

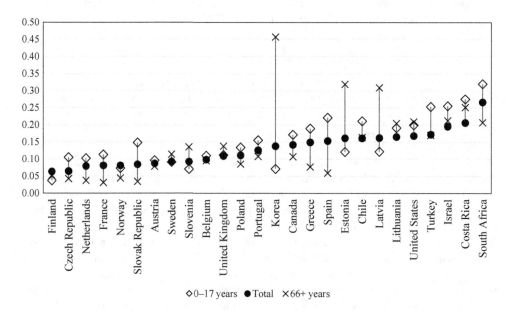

◇0–17 years ●Total ✕66+ years

Figure 13.1 Poverty rate, ratio of the number of people whose income falls below the poverty line for total, 0–17-year-olds, and 66+-year-olds by OECD countries

Source: OECD (2015).

a wide range of initiatives related to food production, rural and urban development, health, and nutrition. Originally conceived in relatively limited economic and financial terms, their understanding of poverty and inequality has expanded to include social development issues such as education, communications, cultural heritage, and governance (World Bank, 2018).

The Third World focus of the World Bank has meant that it has taken an absolute approach to poverty – defining poverty in terms of the purchasing power of individuals. Through an analysis of spending on basic needs, the Bank has identified an international poverty line as $1.90 USD per day in income or consumption expenditure and maintained a record of country-level rates since 1990. Their primary indicator of inequality is the growth in the average income or consumption of the bottom 40 percent of the population (World Bank, 2016b). Their most recent estimates from 2013 suggest that about 10.7 percent of the world's population lived on less than $1.90 USD a day, compared to 12.4 percent in 2012. Half of the extreme poor live in Sub-Saharan Africa and the vast majority live in rural areas, are poorly educated, mostly employed in agriculture, and are less than 18 years of age (World Bank, 2016a).

One of the primary Sustainable Development Goals of the United Nations is to "End poverty in all its forms everywhere" (United Nations, 2018). Its international focus means that the UN also focuses on extreme poverty (less than $1.90 USD per day). As shown in Box 13.1, it has adopted a broad definition of poverty (United Nations, 2018). Its 2018–2021 Strategic Plan identifies rural areas as particularly important, especially where the people in such areas are dependent on agriculture and natural resources (United Nations, 2017, p. 13).

The UN was instrumental in establishing several other organizations that have a strong interest in poverty and inequality. The World Health Organization (http://who.int), for example, and the Food and Agriculture Organization (http://fao.org) both have poverty-related programs that provide useful information for research, analysis, and policy.

In addition to the more formal institutions, there are many NGOs which advocate and conduct anti-poverty research. Some of them, like the Joseph Rowntree Foundation (www.jrf.org.uk/) have been important sources for the conceptualization of poverty in all its forms – from an economic focus to a broader framework including deprivation and social exclusion. Many of them are nationally or regionally focused groups (e.g. www.cwp-csp.ca/, www.poverty.ac.uk/; www.irp.wisc.edu/index.htm; http://cordis.europa.eu/result/rcn/190769_en.html; http://cope-research.eu/) with some of them specifically focusing on rural and regional-related issues (e.g. www.rupri.org/; www.eapn.eu/; www.brandonu.ca/rdi/; www.unbc.ca/community-development-institute).

How is rural different than urban poverty?

Evidence from census, survey, and ethnographic studies makes clear that the nature and experiences of poverty are different in urban and rural areas (Hooks *et al.*, 2016; Lobao *et al.*, 2007; Tickamyer *et al.*, 2017). The details of these relationships remain equivocal, however. Even though rural poverty rates are higher than metro rates in the US, this changes with the indicator used for poverty. If non-cash transfers and cost-of-living differences are considered – as in the US supplemental poverty measure – the relationship reverses, with poverty rates in metro regions generally higher than in rural ones (Weber and Miller, 2017, p. 61). Evidence from other OECD countries reinforces the general principle of rural–urban differences (Copus, 2014, p. 30; Fortin *et al.*, 2008; Rupnik *et al.*, 2001; Singh, 2002). The challenge is to provide explanations for these differences.

How do low density and long distance-to-density structure poverty (cf. Chapter 1)? In some cases, it may be direct (e.g. access to services) whereas in other cases it is likely to have indirect effects (e.g. when long distance-to-density fosters local collaboration, adaptation, identity, and differential access to assets and resources) (Weber and Freshwater, 2016). Reimer (2006) points to the way in which the industrial structures, access to knowledge, skills, social networks, need, and norms of social support differentially structure the informal economies of urban and rural places – thus restructuring the experience of poverty by location. The relationships are complex, however, with spread and backwash economic effects from high-density regions playing an important role in poverty rates (Partridge and Rickman, 2008) and with remoteness possibly providing some protection from competition under specific circumstances (Weber and Freshwater, 2016, p. 162).

Longer distances are likely to limit access to particular assets and resources, capacity-building opportunities, and support services such as employment, training, health, education, welfare, or other government service facilities. In many cases, accessing these resources will involve increased transportation costs and require family or community support to manage additional time requirements (Reimer, 2011). Much of this burden falls on women more than men (Reimer, 2006).

The relative isolation can also create more indirect effects where alternative forms of poverty management take place. This includes more opportunities to participate in the informal economy or make use of social capital. Agriculture, fishing, and forestry in particular have created livelihood arrangements whereby family, housing, and access to property have structured the nature and responses to poverty. Having access to garden plots, renovation skills, or small equipment, for example, provides some of the minimal assets necessary to participate in the informal economy (Reimer, 2006) – assets that may be unavailable in more urban settings. Many of these arrangements have changed radically over the last few decades, however, forcing rural people to live with conditions lacking such assets or move to urban areas.

Income poverty also tends to have place-specific features with persistent poverty being a characteristic of many regions (Copus, 2014; Hooks *et al.*, 2016; Partridge and Rickman, 2008; Weber and Miller, 2017). In addition, rural locations of relatively high poverty tend to have concentrations of racial, ethnic, or Indigenous minorities – in the US (Weber and Miller, 2017, p. 54) and Canada (Poelzer and Coates, 2015).

The lesson here is that although there is plenty of evidence that rural and urban poverty are different, it should not be taken for granted in a simplistic fashion. This includes questioning both the relevance of location and the analytical unit of analysis in comparison to other features of poverty. From a research point of view, it means that rural–urban differences should be considered in research designs (including near-urban and remote distinctions) wherever possible. From a policy perspective it means that made-for urban policies and programs should always be evaluated for their relevance in rural places. Fortunately, there is evidence that government programs directed to poverty-related characteristics and places can have a significant impact on income poverty levels (Partridge and Rickman, 2006).

Characteristics and causes of rural poverty

Answers are often found in the way the questions are asked and the data selected. If poverty is seen as an individual or household-driven phenomenon as reflected in low income, then the answers are likely to be sought among those things that affect an individual's access to and use of income. If it is seen as a condition created and sustained by social forces that constrain and drive individuals' opportunities, then the search will focus on those forces. Occasionally, however, researchers are able to combine multiple frameworks in the same design, thereby addressing the relative importance of these different approaches. International comparisons provide a valuable context in which this can be done (Copus, 2014; Flores-Jimenez *et al.*, 2010; Partridge and Rickman, 2005, 2006).

Tickamyer and Wornell (2017) identify three types of theories used to explain poverty. The first type focuses on individual characteristics and choices that leave them less equipped to prosper in the labor market. These explanations frequently make use of neoclassical economic and rational choice theories combining human capital, status attainment, and culture of poverty variations to account for the characteristics and persistence of poverty in both urban and rural contexts. By focusing on human capital, such theories provide a basis for expecting rural and urban differences to emerge. If education, training, and experience opportunities are different or weaker in rural areas, higher levels of poverty are expected in those regions.

The second type of explanation focuses on structural, institutional, or spatial characteristics that limit the opportunities, beliefs, behavior, and outcomes of individuals. These explanations use theories regarding social class, race, gender, and social and economic development to explain how social structures and institutions disadvantage certain persons or types of persons over others. Processes of economic development, stratification, or social exclusion, especially via gender and sexuality, age, "race", and ethnic minority status are most often used in the US context (Tickamyer and Wornell, 2017).

The third type of explanation combines the first two in ways that are sensitive to people, places, individual, and structural characteristics. Intersectionality approaches, for example, propose that marginalization can be compounded by sharing status and place characteristics. Being an African-American woman living in the American South or an Indigenous person in Canada, for example, combines status characteristics which are likely to increase the person's marginalization over each of these statuses alone.

The social exclusion frameworks developed in the EU provide other intersectionality examples. From this perspective, poverty is seen as the result of exclusion from the benefits of a person's society, including access to incomes and other personal assets (Shucksmith, 2012, 2016). Such exclusion can take place within a variety of normative domains (market, bureaucratic, associative, or communal[2]), sometimes reinforcing and sometimes offsetting each other (Reimer, 2011). This perspective has been used by the EU to expand the range of poverty indicators to include a wide variety of assets – economic, health, education, housing, social, and political.

Tickamyer and Wornell (2017) conclude that although complex, the intersectionality approaches provide the best hope for developing adequate understandings of rural poverty in all its forms. Intersectionality approaches promise to bridge micro and macro frameworks along with individual and structural ones – thereby providing an opportunity to explain some of the apparent contradictions found in the current literature. Such approaches also provide frameworks for policy and programs that can adequately represent the complexity of rural poverty.

Conclusions: what does this mean for rural poverty research?

As researchers and policy analysts, what can be learned from this extensive and diverse body of work on rural poverty? In spite of the fact that there are many points of divergence in the conceptualizations, measurements, types of analysis, and conclusions of this research, it is possible to identify several consistent themes and use them to direct future work and approaches. Research is farther ahead than previous century works, not only because of the more extensive available data, but also because of the development of more sophisticated explanations and perspectives emerging from the analysis.

First, caution must be used when adopting income poverty as a primary indicator. Even within an economic definition of poverty, income is a limited indicator of assets for both absolute and relative interpretations. Approaches focusing on the processes and norms of social exclusion, for example, hold greater promise for dealing with the challenges of comparing poverty across regions and countries (Reimer, 2004; Shucksmith, 2016).

Second, given the potential variation in understanding poverty, it is important to be as explicit as possible about the conceptual definition, its justification, and the meaning of poverty being used. Not only will this help to situate the discussion with respect to the variation of approaches, but it will provide a clear point of reference for subsequent decisions regarding indicators and research designs.

Third, care must be taken to define and measure poverty independently from the various causes, consequences, or associated characteristics. In order to develop a dependable case for its origins and impacts, designs must ensure that possible contributing factors are not conflated in the conceptualization and measurement of poverty itself.

Fourth, the definition and measurement of poverty is in need of theoretical and operational multidimensional analysis. It is clear from the existing research that the concept is multi-dimensional and sensitive to the level of analysis, but the relative importance of each dimension for particular issues is not sufficiently established. This type of work is now possible with the expansion of data collection beyond income. Combined with greater attention to the independent measurement of its elements, the techniques of multidimensional analysis, index development, and complex systems modeling hold promise for assessing the relative importance and relationships among those elements.

Fifth, research on rural poverty must integrate, if possible, appropriate comparisons with both rural and non-rural places. Since current research makes clear that location (geographic or social) matters, it behooves us to anticipate such differences, build appropriate limits to claims, design research accordingly, and learn more about the important features of different places.

Sixth, the expansion of research approaches holds promise for bridging the gap between research and policy domains. Social experiments such as MINCOM (Forget, 2011) and the Community Employment Innovation Project (Gyarmati et al., 2008) not only put theories to test, but by doing so in natural settings they serve to address some of the most politically sensitive issues with demonstrable results so long as thorough evaluation is included.

Key questions for the future of rural poverty research and policy

Key messages

- Rural poverty is a complex phenomenon, requiring a clear definition and justification, appropriate measurement, and multidimensional analysis.
- Relative income poverty varies greatly across OECD countries. It is also a limited indicator for most conceptual definitions of poverty.
- By most indicators (but not all) rural poverty is higher than urban.
- Intersectionality and relational approaches provide the most promise for understanding rural poverty.

Future research questions and opportunities

- Why is (rural) poverty an important focus of (your) research? Which conceptual definitions are appropriate for this focus?
- Which operational definitions and indicators are appropriate for the conceptual definition(s) identified? What is the most appropriate way to combine multidimensional indicators? In

what ways do the definitions of poverty exclude or distort the unique features or processes of poverty in rural places?

• What are the most effective ways in which insights from poverty-related research influence policies and programs (in OECD countries)?

Notes

1 The author would like to thank Greg Halseth, Laura Ryser, Bruce Weber, and an anonymous reviewer for the materials and comments they have provided to facilitate the production of this chapter.
2 These domains dominate respectively in economic exchanges, corporations and governments, voluntary associations, and family relationships.

References

Bock, B., 2016. *Social and economic equality: A territorial and relational perspective*, in: Shucksmith, M., Brown, D.L. (Eds.), *Routledge international handbook of rural studies*. Routledge, London; New York, pp. 427–432.

Center for Poverty Research, 2016. *How is poverty measured in the United States?* September 13. https://poverty.ucdavis.edu/faq/how-poverty-measured-united-states (accessed 1.15.18).

Copus, A., 2014. *The territorial dimension of poverty and social exclusion in Europe*. ESPON, Aberdeen, pp. 1–63. www.espon.eu/programme/projects/espon-2013/applied-research/tipse-territorial-dimension-poverty-and-social.

Davis, K., Moore, W.E., 1945. *Some principles of stratification*. American Sociological Review 10(2), 242–249. https://doi.org/10.2307/2085643.

Dennis, I., Guio, A.C., 2004. *Poverty and social exclusion in the EU*. Statistics in focus: Population and social conditions 16/2004.

Duncan, C.M., 1992. *Rural poverty in America*. Greenwood Publishing, Westport, CT. https://books.google.ca/books?id=05Eb3GCllhYC&pg=PA112&lpg=PA112&dq=book+rural+poverty+appalachian&source=bl&ots=xYtJNu5DNR&sig=S1O2iipNbajAudRjczi3rzkAkjg&hl=en&sa=X&ved=0ahUKEwj4wbO_nNvYAhUh0oMKHYuFC_cQ6AEIWDAK#v=onepage&q=book%20rural%20poverty%20appalachian&f=false.

Duncan, C.M., 2000. *Worlds apart: Why poverty persists in rural America*, New edition. Yale University Press, New Haven, CT.

Edin, K.J., Shaefer, H.L., 2016. *$2.00 a day: Living on almost nothing in America*, Reprint edition. Mariner Books, Boston, MA.

Ellis, F., 1993. *Peasant economics: Farm households in agrarian development*. Cambridge University Press, Cambridge.

European Commission, 2010. *Europe 2020: A strategy for smart, sustainable and inclusive growth*. European Commission, Brussels. http://eur-lex.europa.eu/LexUriServ/LexUriServ.do?uri=COM:2010:2020:FIN:EN:PDF.

European Commission, 2014. *New tool to address rural poverty*. https://ec.europa.eu/jrc/en/news/new-tool-address-rural-poverty (accessed 1.14.18).

European Commission, 2017. *Europe 2020 strategy*. https://ec.europa.eu/info/business-economy-euro/economic-and-fiscal-policy-coordination/eu-economic-governance-monitoring-prevention-correction/european-semester/framework/europe-2020-strategy_en (accessed 1.14.18).

European Commission Member Services, 2016. *Rural areas and poverty*. https://epthinktank.eu/2016/12/16/rural-areas-and-poverty/ (accessed 1.14.18).

Eurostat, 2018. *Eurostat: Your key to European statistics*. http://ec.europa.eu/eurostat/.

Fairbairn, J., 2006. *Understanding freefall: The challenge of the rural poor. Interim report of the Standing Senate Committee on Agriculture and Forestry [Electronic resource]*. Standing Senate Committee on Agriculture and Forestry, Ottawa, Ont. www.parl.gc.ca/39/1/parlbus/commbus/senate/com-e/agri-e/rep-e/repintdec06-e.pdf.

Fairbairn, J., Gustafson, L.J., 2008. *Beyond freefall: Halting rural poverty*. Standing Senate Committee on Agriculture and Forestry, Ottawa, Ont. http://publications.gc.ca/collections/collection_2011/sen/yc27-0/YC27-0-392-9-eng.pdf.

Favareto, A. da S., 2017. *The social dimension of rural statistics.* Global Strategy Technical Report No. 17, Technical Report Series GO-17-2017. FAO, Rome. http://gsars.org/wp-content/uploads/2017/02/TR-27.01.2017-The-Social-Dimension-of-Rural-Statistics.pdf.

Fitchen, J.M., 1991. *Endangered places, enduring places.* Westview Press, Boulder, CO.

Flores-Jimenez, P., Tejeida-Padilla, R., Morales-Matamoros, O., 2010. *Structural equation model for the multidimensional measurement of the poverty in Mexico,* in: *Proceedings of the 54th Annual Meeting of the ISSS-2010, Waterloo, Canada* (Vol. 54). ISSS.

Forget, E.L., 2011. *The town with no poverty: The health effects of a Canadian guaranteed annual income field experiment.* Canadian Public Policy 37(3), 283–305. https://doi.org/10.3138/cpp. 37.3.283.

Fortin, M., Statistics Canada, Agriculture Division, 2008. *A comparison of rural and urban workers living in low income.* Statistics Canada/Statistique Canada, Ottawa, Ont. www.deslibris.ca/ID/210389.

Fox, L., 2017. *The supplemental poverty measure: 2016.* Current Population Reports, P60–261 (RV). US Census Bureau. www.census.gov/content/dam/Census/library/publications/2017/demo/p60-261.pdf.

Goedhart, T., Halnerstadt, V., Kapteyn, A., van Praag, B.M.S., 1977. *The poverty line: Concept and measurement.* Journal of Human Resources 12, 503–520.

Government of Canada, Statistics Canada, 2016. *Low income lines: What they are and how they are created.* July 8. www.statcan.gc.ca/pub/75f0002m/75f0002m2016002-eng.htm (accessed 1.16.18).

Gyarmati, D., Raaf, S.D., Palameta, B., Nicholson, C., Hui, T.S., Wagner, R.A., … Shek-Wai Hui, T., 2008. *Encouraging work and supporting communities: Final results of the community employment innovation project.* November. Social Research and Demonstration Corporation, Ottawa, Ont. www.srdc.org/uploads/CEIP_finalrpt_ENG.pdf.

Hagenaars, A., de Vos, K., 1988. *The definition and measurement of poverty.* The Journal of Human Resources 23(2), 211–221. https://doi.org/10.2307/145776.

Hernandez, R.A., Vazquez, Y.T., Ramirez, J.L., 2013. *Índice absoluto de marginación 2000–2010.* Consejo Nacional de Poblacion, Mexico, D.F. www.conapo.gob.mx/work/models/CONAPO/Resource/1755/1/images/IAM_00-04.pdf.

Hooks, G., Lobao, L., Tickamyer, A.R., 2016. *Spatial inequality and rural areas,* in: Shucksmith, M., Brown, D.L. (Eds.), *Routledge international handbook of rural studies.* Routledge, London; New York, pp. 462–476.

Lobao, L.M., Hooks, G., Tickamyer, A.R., 2007. *The sociology of spatial inequality.* State University of New York Press, Albany, NY.

OECD, 2005. *Glossary of statistical terms.* Poverty line. http://stats.oecd.org/glossary/detail.asp?ID=6337.

OECD, 2007. *OECD rural policy reviews: Germany* (2007a); *Mexico* (2007b); *Finland* (2008a); *Netherlands* (2008b); *Scotland* (2008c); *China* (2009a); *Italy* (2009b); *Spain* (2009c); *Québec* (2010a); *England* (2011).

OECD, 2008. *Growing unequal?* OECD, Paris. www.oecd-ilibrary.org/content/book/9789264044197-en.

OECD, 2010. *OECD Rural policy reviews: Québec, Canada 2010.* OECD, Paris. www.oecd-ilibrary.org/content/book/9789264082151-en.

OECD, 2013. *OECD framework for statistics on the distribution of household income, consumption and wealth.* OECD Publishing, Paris. https://doi.org/10.1787/9789264194830-en.

OECD, 2015. *Poverty rate.* https://data.oecd.org/inequality/poverty-rate.htm.

OECD, 2017. *How's life? 2017.* OECD Publishing, Paris. https://doi.org/10.1787/how_life-2017-en.

OECD, 2018. *Poverty rate.* https://data.oecd.org/inequality/poverty-rate.htm.

Paneva, V. 2014. *LEADER/CLLD.* October 27. https://enrd.ec.europa.eu/leader-clld_en (accessed 1.14.18).

Partridge, M.D., Rickman, D.S., 2005. *High-poverty nonmetropolitan counties in America: Can economic development help?* International Regional Science Review 28(4), 415–440.

Partridge, M.D., Rickman, D.S., 2006. *The geography of American poverty: Is there a need for place-based policies?* W.E. Upjohn Institute, Kalamazoo, MI.

Partridge, M.D., Rickman, D.S., 2008. *Distance from urban agglomeration economies and rural poverty.* Journal of Regional Science 48(2), 285–310. https://doi.org/10.1111/j.1467-9787.2008.00552.x.

Poelzer, G., Coates, K.S., 2015. *From treaty peoples to treaty nation: A road map for all Canadians.* UBC Press, Vancouver, BC; Toronto, Ont. www.ubcpress.ca/search/title_book.asp?BookID=299174418.

President's National Advisory Commission on Rural Poverty, 1967. *The people left behind.* Washington, DC. https://files.eric.ed.gov/fulltext/ED016543.pdf.

Reimer, B., 2004. *Social exclusion in a comparative context.* Sociologia Ruralis 44(1), 76–94.

Reimer, B., 2006. *The informal economy in non-metropolitan Canada.* The Canadian Review of Sociology and Anthropology 43(1), 23–49.

Reimer, B., 2010. *Social welfare policies in rural Canada,* in: Milbourne, P. (Ed.), *Welfare reform in rural places: Comparative perspectives* (Vol. 15). Emerald Publishing, Bingley, pp. 81–110. http://billreimer.ca/research/files/ReimerInMilbourneRuralWelfare2010.pdf.

Reimer, B., 2011. *Social exclusion through lack of access to social support in rural areas,* in: Fréchet, G., Gauvreau, D., Poirer, J. (Eds.), *Social statistics, poverty and social exclusion: Perspectives Québecoises, Canadiennes et internationals.* Les Presses de l'Université de Montréal, Montreal, PQ, pp. 152–160.

Rupnik, C., Thompson-James, M., Bollman, R., 2001. *Measuring economic well-being of rural Canadians using income indicators.* Statistics Canada, Ottawa, Ont.

Rural Sociological Society Task Force on Persistent Rural Poverty, 1993. *Persistent poverty in rural America.* Westview Press, Boulder, CO.

Sen, A., 1982. *Poverty and famines: An essay on entitlement and deprivation.* Clarendon Press, Oxford.

Sen, A., 1992. *Inequality reexamined.* Clarendon Press, Oxford.

Sen, A., 1999. *Development as freedom.* Oxford University Press, New York.

Sharing, 2018. *Share the world's resources.* www.sharing.org/.

Sherman, J., 2006. *Coping with rural poverty: Economic survival and moral capital in rural America.* Social Forces 85(2), 891–913. https://doi.org/10.1353/sof.2007.0026.

Sherman, J., 2013. *Surviving the Great Recession: Growing need and the stigmatized safety net.* Social Problems 60(4), 409–432. https://doi.org/10.1525/sp.2013.60.4.409.

Shucksmith, M., 2012. *Class, power and inequality in rural areas: Beyond social exclusion?* Sociologia Ruralis 52(4), 377–397

Shucksmith, M., 2016. *Social exclusion in rural places,* in: Shucksmith, M., Brown, D.L. (Eds.), *Routledge international handbook of rural studies.* Routle dge, London; New York, pp. 433–449.

Shucksmith, M., Schafft, K., 2012. *Rural poverty and social exclusion in the United States and the United Kingdom,* in: Shucksmith, M., Brown, D., Shortall, S., Vergunst, J., Warner, M. (Eds.), *Rural transformation and rural policies in the US and UK.* Routledge, New York, pp. 100–116.

Singh, V., 2002. *Rural income disparities in Canada: A comparison across the Provinces.* Minister of Industry, Ottawa, Ont.

The Canadian Encyclopedia, 2013. *Social security.* December 16. www.thecanadianencyclopedia.com/index.cfm?PgNm=TCE&Params=A1ARTA0007530 (accessed 1.16.18).

Tickamyer, A.R., Wornell, E.J., 2017. *How to explain poverty?,* in: Tickamyer, A.R., Sherman, J., Warlick, J. (Eds.), *Rural poverty in the United States.* Columbia University Press, New York; Chichester, West Sussex, pp. 84–114.

Tickamyer, A.R., Sherman, J., Warlick, J., 2017. *Rural poverty in the United States.* Columbia University Press, New York. https://cup.columbia.edu/book/rural-poverty-in-the-united-states/9780231172233.

Townsend, P., 1979. *Poverty in the United Kingdom: A survey of household resources and standards of living.* University of California Press, Berkeley, CA. www.poverty.ac.uk/system/files/townsend-book-pdfs/PIUK/piuk-whole.pdf.

UNDP, 2016. *Human development for everyone.* United Nations Development Programme, New York.

United Nations, 2017. *UNDP strategic plan, 2018–2021.* United Nations, New York. http://undocs.org/DP/2017/38.

United Nations, 2018. *Poverty.* www.un.org/sustainabledevelopment/poverty/ (accessed 1.14.18).

US Census Bureau, 2017. *How the Census Bureau measures poverty.* August 11. www.census.gov/topics/income-poverty/poverty/guidance/poverty-measures.html (accessed 1.15.18).

Veit-Wilson, J., 2006. *No rights without remedies: Necessary conditions for abolishing child poverty.* European Journal of Social Security 8(3), 317–337.

Weber, B.A., Freshwater, D., 2016. The death of distance? Networks, the costs of distance and urban–rural interdependence, in: Shucksmith, M, Brown, D.L. (Eds.), *Routledge international handbook of rural studies.* Routledge, London; New York, pp. 154–164.

Weber, B., Miller, K., 2017. *Poverty in rural America then and now,* in: Tickamyer, A.R., Sherman, J., Warlick, J. (Eds.), *Rural poverty in the United States.* Columbia University Press, New York, pp. 28–64. www.jstor.org/stable/10.7312/tick17222.7.

Weber, B., Edwards, M., Duncan, G., 2004. *Single mother work and poverty under welfare reform: Are policy impacts different in rural areas?* Eastern Economic Journal 30(1), 31–51.

World Bank, 2008. *World development report 2009: Reshaping economic geography.* World Bank Publications. https://openknowledge.worldbank.org/handle/10986/5991.

World Bank, 2016a. *Overview*. October 2. www.worldbank.org/en/topic/poverty/overview (accessed 1.13.18).

World Bank, 2016b. *Poverty and shared prosperity 2016: Taking on inequality*. World Bank. https://doi.org/10.1596/978-1-4648-0958-3.

World Bank, 2018. *History of the World Bank*. www.worldbank.org/en/about/archives/history (accessed 1.17.18).

Young, N., 2016. *Responding to rural change: Adaptation, resilience and community action*, in: Shucksmith, M., Brown, D.L. (Eds.), *Routledge international handbook of rural studies*. Routledge, London; New York, pp. 638–649.

14

UNDERSTANDING THE DIMENSIONS OF AGING AND OLD AGE IN RURAL AREAS

Philipp Kneis and Keith Baker

Aging is a complex multifaceted policy problem that is compounded by a growing and potentially frail elderly population. Existing policy approaches are embedded in a medical conception of aging and modernist forms of political economy. The multifaceted nature of aging as a policy problem challenges this approach, and in rural areas many aspects of the problem are magnified. If aging is approached in cultural terms, a deeper understanding of aging can be developed, and the dimensions of the problem exposed, and it is shown that collaborative approaches may offer a way forward. The new public governance offers a way of incorporating collaborative approaches into public decision-making to address complex problems. The chapter concludes by making some policy recommendations as to how the problems highlighted can be addressed within the framework of the new public governance.

Introduction

From time to time, the question of aging and old age surfaces in discussions of culture, society, and politics. Recently, these discussions have attracted a great deal of academic interest and are framed as something relevant to policy-makers. This is driven by the realization that a significant percentage of the population is growing older. As of 2016, the US Census indicates that people aged 65 and over account for about 15 percent of the population. This figure will increase to 25 percent by 2060 (US Census, 2016). Many of those aged 65 and over remain fit and healthy throughout their lives. From a cultural or a policy perspective, this group is relatively unproblematic. Indeed, many of the spritely elderly will continue to work, pay taxes, and otherwise lead fulfilling, socially-rich lives. However, an equally significant proportion can be described as the "frail" elderly. The frail elderly are less likely to work, are more likely to be socially isolated, and are far more likely to require significant (and costly) medical interventions or support. This is compounded by the fact that many long-term degenerative diseases such as dementia disproportionately affect older people (see Reitz and Mayeux, 2014). Throughout this chapter, the terms aged or elderly will be used interchangeably to refer specifically to those over 65 requiring some form of support or intervention.

A key problem in the analysis of policy impact of an elderly population is the question of old age in rural areas. This is sometimes referred to as "aging in place" (Schroeder, 2016). In rural areas, populations may be dispersed, service delivery becomes difficult and inefficient, and access to necessary services and care may be haphazard. Rural populations may also be comparatively deprived or economically disadvantaged. However, the discussion of aging in rural areas is remarkably reductive in that it often focuses on access to quality health care and support in old age. This may result from an applied focus within rural studies as an emergent discipline, or from the tendency to see aging as a health problem rather than a complex, interconnected social issue.

This chapter critically explores core assumptions and suggests areas for research and policy work. Much of the terminology used in the second section may be unfamiliar to students of aging, so terminology will be defined upon first use. However, this terminology is technical or is a term-of-art and is necessary for discussion and analysis. The chapter has four sections. In the first, the notion of aging itself is considered. In the second section, it is argued that managing the problems of the frail elderly can be understood as a wicked problem – a complex and hard-to-solve policy problem that cuts across the remits of multiple organizations and administrative entities. This is then linked to the idea of the "new public governance" which argues for an administrative regime that is prefaced around collaborative solutions. In the third section, the key dimensions of the problem of aging in rural areas are highlighted. Finally, some conclusions that will help guide policy-makers and scholars in discussing aging in rural areas are presented.

Conceptual approaches to aging and old age

The cultural and social construction of aging

The social roles that people inhabit at different ages vary within cultures and societies. "Aging" and "old age" are culturally and socially constructed (Gullette, 2015; and for constructivism see Searle, 1995). Frequently, the aged would be construed as sources of culture and knowledge, and even hold some political, social, or cultural power. There have also been social models that exclude the aged, normalize leaving them behind, or accept seeing them in poverty or on the margins of society (Kneis, 2013). However, differences within a culture can be just as great as those between cultures (cf. Keith *et al.*, 1994).

The modern socio-economic framework has led to a reduction of such differences and a convergence of problems related to aging in many "Westernized" or "modernized" societies. The current understanding of aging and old age is closely connected to changes in the model of social organization that resulted from industrialization (Katz, 1996, p. 30; Thane, 2007). In that model, productive work is central to how people understand their social identity. However, at a certain age, a worker's productivity lessens, so that the notion of retirement was introduced with the intention of permitting workers to enjoy a short period of time free of work commitments. As standards of living have risen, people can reasonably expect to survive a long time after they formally retire from work. In the 1950s, David Riesman described the "roleless role" that would be the consequence of retirement for older Americans (in Bauman, 2013). The absence of a clearly defined social or cultural role for older people, now outside of work, can have negative impacts on their social and psychological well-being.

In OECD countries, most work is found in urban areas. These economic changes have had significant impact on the social composition of populations in rural areas. Rural places have seen a decline of working-age populations. It is this change of the social composition of rural populations which, due to a variety of factors, impacts aging and old age in characteristic ways that are different from urban aging. Aging has profound financial impacts as people may or may not have sufficient savings to live comfortably in old age. Credit and debt are manageable when incomes are high, but in retirement, debts and cost of living may become hard to manage. Moreover, social security and retirement systems were designed and funded in a period when life expectancies were significantly lower. To continue to fund such systems may ultimately entail a considerable transfer of wealth through the taxation system from wage earners to the aged. Rubin (2007) comments that as the aged retain and use property and capital for longer, inheritances will diminish. These sums may become tempting targets for taxation or means-tests imposed by governments determined to avoid raising the overall tax burden. However, older people and their heirs are a significant electoral constituency.

Aging also has social impacts. As of 2014, the average American woman births her first child at age 26 (National Centre for Health Statistics, 2016), but this raises questions as to whether or not 70-year-old persons will be caring for their near centennial parents (Rubin, 2007). As people live longer, the possibility that they may outlive a spouse or partner increases. But as people age, meeting others becomes difficult – a problem particularly acute in rural areas. Others may come to realize that they no longer wish to remain in an existing relationship and will divorce but are faced with the prospect of seeking remarriage in later life. Rurality plays a role in all these considerations, mainly as a factor that influences how an aging person interacts with the world in which they live. Social isolation may also aggravate degenerative conditions and increase stress levels. Baker and Irving (2016) observed in their study of social prescribing that people who experienced the early stages of dementia were taking part in social activities, they reported a greater sense of well-being and lower stress. There is some evidence that continued social activity helps to improve physical and mental health due to the close connection between the two (see Todd, 2017).

Understanding and analyzing aging as a wicked problem

The traditional understanding of aging as a "collection of diseases" (Gullette, 2011, p. 34) lends itself to an understanding of aged populations that revolves around questions of medical and palliative care, assisted living, overall health, and quality of life. This "biomedicalization" of aging is appealing to public sector professionals as they become the central agency involved in managing an aging population (Estes and Binney, 1989, p. 587). Moreover, medicalized models provide public bureaucracies with quantifiable information about the aged that can be used to aggregate people in manageable categories or simply to justify a particular policy decision. The classical administrative approach to aging populations focuses on securing the legal rights of people to a particular standard of care and services that is equally available.

The medicalized model that informs both the administrative and managerial approaches results from "systems theory" in which process is emphasized. This approach is inadequate as a focus on process is reductive in that it can only recognize and respond to issues in one way and prefers solutions that meet the needs or capabilities of the administrating agencies rather than the needs of the aged. Systems thinking is frequently confounded by the fact that many issues in social policy are complex and multifaceted. These issues are often described as "wicked" in that they are cross-cutting, intractable, and only manageable through cooperation and collaboration between a range of different agencies and actors (Rittel and Webber, 1973; Weber and Khademian, 2008; Ney, 2012).

Aging in rural places can be understood as a wicked problem in that it can never truly be resolved as people will continue to age, will face a variety of physical health issues that will impact on their well-being, and as the tyranny of distance will make it expensive to deliver services to aged populations in rural areas. These matters must be managed and will require multiple different actors who bring different perspectives and capacities to policy-making and implementation and problems that involve human well-being. Osborne's (2006, 2010) concept of the new public governance offers a way forward. Public sector professionals who are informed by new public governance will focus on the quality of life and well-being of the citizens. Bryson *et al.* (2014) would argue this will require public bureaucracies to place a premium on shared citizenship, democracy, humanism and to be open to the variety of perspectives that are brought to bear on a range of different actors. Osborne (2006, p. 384) comments that this will cause public bureaus to become both plural and pluralist. The public sector is now plural in that it is comfortable with complexity and the involvement of "multiple inter-dependent actors [who] contribute to the delivery of public services" (Osborne, 2006, p. 384), and pluralist in that policy-making will involve many different actors who engage in a negotiated and collaborative process. The new public governance has the potential to develop solutions to the wicked issues created by frail and aged populations. It is necessary to take one additional step in the analysis and identify the range of factors that must be considered when examining rural aging from a policy perspective.

Aging and rural spaces

A key, if under-remarked, element of the discussion of the new public governance is the relationship between service delivery and space. However, the ability of social actors to engage in the interactions necessary to define space is shaped by physical distance, or remoteness. The process and the outcomes of democratically engaged citizenship are greatly affected by distance. If aging is, as Rüdiger Kunow has proposed, "the difference that time makes" (Kunow, 2009, p. 295), then rurality can be seen as the difference that spatial remoteness makes. Put boldly, the further away from services and the customary social spaces a person is, the harder it is for that person to take part in society and enjoy the rights of citizenship.

Distance/remoteness/mobility infrastructure

Most definitions of rurality highlight distance from urban areas as a key marker of difference. "Rural" is oftentimes used as a synonym for remoteness, geographical and cultural. The above-mentioned split between industry and agriculture comes to mind, and it can carry even further cultural connotations (see Chapter 16).

Distance to urban areas is also often understood as distance from culture, specifically with regard to concerts, museums, movie theaters, academic talks, regular large-scale political and social gatherings, etc. The more remote the area, the less likely it is that a person would find easily accessible round-the-clock cultural and intellectual engagement. Access to such institutions or events requires mobility. This is the area where challenges frequently arise. In several OECD countries, once functioning public transport systems have had to face deterioration due to budget cuts. Train or bus services may have been thinned out or discontinued, or development of further public transport is continuously prevented. In addition, privatization programs have eroded services in rural areas as these are often unprofitable. Without individual mobility, typically in the form of automobiles, rural areas will not easily be able to access urban-centered services.

There are further challenges to come. Several cities have already banned, or are in the process of banning, access to inner cities by cars. Parking has been made more difficult. Bicycle use is encouraged, oftentimes by heavy investments in bicycling infrastructure. However, this makes access to city centers by commuters from rural areas more difficult, especially for the elderly. Once convenient access to services, which includes public offices, is now made more difficult. The focus on bicycling could very well be seen as promoting ableism and a focus on youth. Within rural areas themselves, public transportation is typically spotty and less reliable than in urban centers. Driving remains a central skill. Health challenges that could impede driving thus may automatically turn into preventers of mobility, and may limit access to institutions, cultural engagement, and services.

Service and subsistence infrastructure

The organization of daily life can be more difficult in rural areas. Yet "rural" is always a matter of degree, and more remote areas of course may make subsistence and service infrastructure more difficult. Rural northern Saskatchewan is different from rural Bavaria, for example. This may affect quality of life, ease of shopping, repair services, etc. In many cases, the availability and reliability of phone and broadband internet services are affected as well. For older populations, a lack of physical mobility could combine with a lack of shopping and support opportunities, especially with regard to health choices.

Food may very well be available, yet healthier food choices may be more difficult to obtain. So-called "food deserts" are found more typically in rural than in urban areas. A lack of administrative and business structures can also translate into a lack of employment and service opportunities. Private companies may consider the expenses of traveling vast distances to be uneconomical and charge higher rates or simply restrict services. This not only affects the possibility of seniors to improve their financial situation, but also limits their possible social engagement and ability to enjoy the comforts of society.

Family structures, social cohesion, and integration

The scarcity of employment opportunities in some rural areas has also led to increased mobility among the working population, which means that family structures in rural areas may be less intact. Aging parents and grandparents may be far away from their children and friends, whether they choose to remain in their rural home, or whether they retire in rural areas. This can lead to increased isolation. Conversely, an oftentimes tighter social cohesion within rural communities may compensate for this. Should broadband internet or reliable cell phone coverage with inexpensive data plans be available, audiovisual communication can be of help as well.

Health and (dis)ability

The largest focus of research on aging in rural areas is directed at health and well-being (cf. Hash *et al.*, 2014). This is based, of course, on the assumption that aging and deteriorating health are deeply connected. A singular focus on health has been criticized as promoting a merely biomedical paradigm of aging (Estes and Binney, 1989), as remarked earlier. Such admonishment not to limit the discussion of aging and old age to merely questions of health is important. Nevertheless, questions of health care do arise frequently in old age, especially when they pertain to a general access to care. However, such access may be limited in rural areas, and even if health care exists, there may not be enough of an affordable and adequate selection of services to cater to everyone's needs. This is especially important when it comes to questions of retirement and nursing homes. Quality standards of such care facilities are not equal across the board, and especially in rural areas, the lack of competition may allow lower standards to persist.

The ideal of living in one's own place may be more prevalent in rural areas, especially due to long-term home ownership and an elderly person's attachment to the family home. The maintenance of independence would again depend on the availability of home care services. Life alert systems may help in emergencies, yet continuous care may not be guaranteed in remoter locations. Offerings of assisted living providers may be limited as well. An additional problem compounded by remoteness is the potential lack of social and family connections, and potential loneliness of older persons. This may lead to a need of psychological care, but rural areas may not be able to support this.

Cultural activity and cultural-social engagement

Rural areas may offer less access to the traditional forms of entertainment and cultural expression such as theaters, operas, art galleries, museums etc. Yet conversely, they may also frequently allow for more social engagement, expressions of folk art, and community engagement. Ideally, such forms of more direct involvement also incorporate elders, who frequently form the backbone of the volunteering personnel. This may contribute to better overall psychological health and may even offset some of the negative effects of remoteness (cf. Helseth, 2014). Such engagement still relies on infrastructure, oftentimes provided through public libraries, community centers, churches, schools, or even casinos. Although it must be noted that while public sector organizations may be obligated to provide such opportunities, private or not-for-profit sector organizations carry no such obligations. Reliance on a sense of social responsibility on the part of communities or businesses may produce significant variation in access or availability.

Cultural preservation and vulnerable communities

Real or perceived remoteness from urban areas oftentimes allows the possibility for distinct cultural communities, especially Indigenous cultures, to maintain a sense of cultural distinctiveness and preserve more traditional ways of living. Examples would be First Nations in Canada, American Indian, Alaska Native, and Pacific Islander populations in the United States, Sorbs in Germany, Saami populations in Norway, Ladino populations in Italy, but also oftentimes autonomous regions with a history of independence movements within European countries such as South Tyrol/Alto Adige, Cornwall, Catalonia, and others. Rural settings can also compound problems of otherwise already vulnerable communities. This considers a lack of access to health care specifically for oftentimes undocumented immigrant farm worker populations in the United States, but also for remote Indigenous communities with a severe lack of health and services infrastructure.

Nature and quality of life

Finally, the remoteness of some rural regions may also have a distinct positive effect on psychological and spiritual health. Distance from large urban centers ideally also correlates with closeness to nature and a quieter and less hectic lifestyle. This may only be desirable though if subsistence, service, and health-care demands are met, especially in old age.

Discussion and conclusions

This chapter has argued that challenges associated with aging in rural areas are considerable. Like a magnifying glass, the topic of aging and old age can serve as a lens or focal point for the discussion of culturally, socially, and politically relevant topics. This multifaceted approach has distinct implications for policy-makers and scholarly researchers. It is useful to offer some suggestions to hopefully guide policy and research in the future.

In general, as the construction of aging and old age during modernity has become similar in all Western countries, the following aspects can be seen to apply to all OECD countries. Some countries may or may not seem comparably better prepared than others, but that will mainly be due to the availability of affordable quality health care. The main factor, when speaking about rurality, is distance, and its related problems – clearly, vast rural areas in the United States, Canada, or Scandinavia will pose different challenges than you would find in Luxemburg or San Marino, for comparison. Otherwise, this policy complex is seen as a pressing matter in all OECD countries.

Policy considerations and recommendations

Aging and health are topics that are intimately intertwined. It is correct to address these policy topics together, and especially in rural areas, access to health care for aging populations is a key to well-being. Yet a good life requires more than health, and is not necessarily limited by markers of health, not even in old age. An incessant policy focus on health and physical fitness may even prove counterproductive: An avalanche of pictures of physically fit 90-year-olds ready to run the marathon may actually make a mockery of the real-life fitness of seniors, and prove more discouraging, even insulting, rather than inspiring. Several factors come together that work to define well-being. Health is only one parameter, yet it continues to dominate the discussion. This needs to be remedied and there is a need to consider the broader spectrum of issues discussed above which are relevant to increasing the quality of life in old age in rural areas.

Specifically, policy-makers and other stakeholders must consider – at the very least – matters of distance, the nature of services themselves, the physical and administrative infrastructure, family relationships, health and well-being, and the cultural mores of a given society or social group. This list is not exhaustive but offers a first step in identifying the different issues. Nevertheless, different policy-makers, facing different circumstances and different stakeholders, will arrive at different policies. This variation should be regarded as problematic. A key insight of the new public governance (Osborne, 2010) is that variation is to be expected and that policy-makers should be encouraged to respond to local contingencies. Moreover, policy-makers must recognize that government is not the only actor involved and must be prepared to share the stage with others.

In many areas access to health care often varies considerably across the population. Vulnerable, minority or migrant communities often have difficulty in accessing high-quality services. These groups are often socially constructed as marginal and may have a difficult understanding of the role of aged in Western societies. In combination, these factors may make it hard to develop the collaborative relations that new public governance envisages. In addition, policy-makers must be cautious of working only with self-appointed representatives who make themselves readily available. These problems, however, are not insurmountable. Building relationships with communities takes time and effort and requires local representatives and officials who are embedded within a community. This not only helps to develop the relationships upon which new public governance depends, but also strengthens democratic accountability.

Issues of transportation and urban design are also critical. Cooperating with and involving others in decision-making or delivering services is relatively easy if communication and travel are relatively straightforward. Across vast distances or in poorly designed urban areas where travel depends on private cars, it becomes much harder to work with a range of stakeholders and to develop the robust community-centric connection suggested above. There are a number of possible solutions. One – albeit politically difficult – is for government to subsidize extensive transportation options. A second option is investment in local community centers, which can serve as hubs for engagement and a point of contact between governments and the community at large. A community center also cuts the distance traveled and helps to address some issues of geography.

A further point concerns affordable access to quality health care in general, and to elder care specifically. The profit motive has reshaped the caregiving landscapes even of once admirably performing countries like Germany and the United Kingdom (which are frequently cited as models). Across-the-board cost-cutting has had devastating results for staffing and monitoring, and this affects the aged worst of all, especially in "structurally weak" rural areas. In Germany and the UK, an emerging debate is beginning to reject the demands for austerity, but other countries have not followed suit.

Finally, from comparisons with traditional cultures or with Western cultural models in the past, it becomes clear that the changes in the cultural construction of aging in modern, industrialized society have emphasized functioning and productivity over introspection, wisdom, and guidance, which is leading to confusion, frustration, oftentimes anger, and isolation (Hall, 1922; Moody, 1992; Woodward, 2003; Kneis, 2013). It would appear important to work to change the positionality of society towards seniors to imbue them with culturally relevant roles. "To feel needed" is, anecdotally, the most common request made by seniors, typically.

Rural areas may be more promising in this respect, actually, and hold the promise of what Thomas (2004) has termed "Eldertopia". Given the trope of smaller rural towns not being attractive anymore for younger inhabitants, this might give a chance to create elder-centric communities. Perhaps this could resemble a version of the gerontocratic model in use in historical Venice, in today's Vatican, but also within contemporary politics.

Considerations for future research

Traditionally, the discussion of aging is dominated by medicalized, administrative and managerial approaches which tend to understand aging as a problem that is to be treated or organized away. Furthermore, in the case of aging in rural areas, matters of space and distance are problematic, and this is compounded by the fact that aging itself is a wicked issue and such issues are difficult to address through a single agency. A more humanistic approach is found by approaching the topic through the lens of the new public governance, which is a research agenda that is growing in popularity (see Osborne, 2010; Pestoff et al., 2013). This approach also has the advantage that it emphasizes precisely the pluralist engagement of many different actors necessary to tackle wicked issues. At a more theoretical level, Torfing and Triantafillou (2013) observe that new public governance represents an emerging research agenda and that considerably more studies are necessary to advance the concept.

In conclusion, the study of aging offers numerous opportunities for such socially relevant research as this is a problem that will become increasingly important in coming years. Rural areas may feel the need of addressing the topic most urgently but are also equipped to take charge of it due to their own aging populations. Hopefully, a sensible mixture of solutions, old and new, will make it possible to create a society in which "being old" is not any longer merely felt with the dread of an abandoned King Lear, but with some form of appreciation of new-found possibilities and new positive challenges in later life.

References

Baker, K., Irving, A., 2016. *Co-producing approaches to the management of dementia through social prescribing.* Social Policy and Administration 50(3), 379–397.

Bauman, Z., 2013. *Liquid modernity.* John Wiley & Sons, New York.

Bryson, J.M., Crosby, B.C., Bloomberg, L., 2014. *Public value governance: Moving beyond traditional public administration and the new public management.* Public Administration Review 74(4), 445–456.

Estes, C.L., Binney, E.A., 1989. *The biomedicalization of aging: Dangers and dilemmas.* The Gerontologist 29(5), 587–596.

Gullette, M.M., 2011. *Agewise: Fighting the new ageism in America.* University of Chicago Press, Chicago, IL.

Gullette, M.M., 2015. *Aged by culture,* in: Twigg, J., Martin, W. (Eds.), *Routledge handbook of cultural gerontology.* Routledge, Abingdon, pp. 43–50.

Hall, G.S., 1922. *Senescence: The last half of life.* Appleton, New York.

Hash, K.M., Jurkowski, E.T., Krout, J., 2014. *Aging in rural places: Programs, policies, and professional practice.* Springer, Berlin.

Helseth, C., 2014. *Volunteering a win–win for seniors and rural communities.* The Rural Monitor, November 18. www.ruralhealthinfo.org/rural-monitor/volunteering-seniors/.

Katz, S., 1996. *Disciplining old age: The formation of gerontological knowledge.* University of Virginia Press, Charlottesville, VA.

Keith, J., Fry, C.L., Glascock, A.P., Ikels, C., Dickerson-Putman, J., Harpending, H.C., Draper, P., 1994. *The aging experience: Diversity and commonality across cultures.* Sage, Thousand Oaks, CA.

Kneis, P., 2013. *(S)aged by culture: Representations of old age in American Indian literature and culture.* Peter Lang, Frankfurt.

Kunow, R., 2009. *The coming of age: The descriptive organization of later life,* in: Hornung, A., Kunow, R. (Eds.), *Representation and decoration in a postmodern age.* Winter, Heidelberg, pp. 295–309.

Moody, H.R., 1992. *Ethics in an aging society.* Johns Hopkins University Press, Baltimore, MD.

National Centre for Health Statistics, 2016. *Mean age of mothers is on the rise: United States, 2000–2014.* NCHS Data Brief No. 232, January 2016. www.cdc.gov/nchs/data/databriefs/db232.htm.

Ney, S., 2012. *Resolving messy policy problems: Handling conflict in environmental, transport, health and ageing policy.* Routledge, London.

Osborne, S.P., 2006. *The new public governance?* Public Management Review 6(3): 377–378.

Osborne, S.P., 2010. *The new public governance?* Routledge, New York.

Pestoff, V., Brandsen, T., Verschuere, B. (Eds.), 2013. *New public governance, the third sector, and co-production.* Routledge, London.

Reitz, C., Mayeux, R., 2014. *Alzheimer disease: Epidemiology, diagnostic criteria, risk factors and biomarkers.* Biochemical Pharmacology, 88(4), 640–651.

Riesman, D., Glazer, N., Denney, R., 2001. *The lonely crowd.* Yale University Press, New Haven, CT.

Rittel, H.W., Webber, M.M., 1973. *Dilemmas in a general theory of planning.* Policy Sciences, 4(2), 155–169.

Rubin, L.B., 2007. *60 on up: The truth about aging in America.* Beacon Press, Boston, MA.

Schroeder, M.O., 2016. *Safely aging in place in rural America.* US Health News, December 8. https://health.usnews.com/wellness/aging-well/articles/2016-12-08/safely-aging-in-place-in-rural-america.

Searle, J.R., 1995. *The construction of social reality.* Simon and Schuster, New York.

Thane, P., 2007. *The long history of old age.* Thames and Hudson, London.

Thomas, W.H., 2004. *What are old people for?: How elders will save the world.* VanderWyk and Burnham, St. Louis, MO.

Todd, C., 2017. *Exploring the role of museums for socially isolated older people* (Doctoral dissertation). Canterbury Christ Church University, Canterbury.

Torfing, J., Triantafillou, P., 2013. *What's in a name? Grasping new public governance as a political-administrative system.* International Review of Public Administration, 18(2), 9–25.

US Census, 2016. *Facts For Features: Older Americans Month: May 2016.* CB16-FF.08. April 15. www.census.gov/newsroom/facts-for-features/2016/cb16-ff08.html.

Weber, E.P., Khademian, A.M., 2008. *Wicked problems, knowledge challenges, and collaborative capacity builders in network settings.* Public Administration Review, 68(2), 334–349.

Woodward, K., 2003. *Against wisdom: The social politics of anger and aging.* Journal of Aging Studies, 17(1), pp. 55–67.

15

RURAL HEALTH AND WELL-BEING

Kathleen Kevany and Maya Fromstein

Rural living is complex, dynamic, and intertwined with impacts of actions by local actors as well as policies and practices imposed from beyond the region. Efforts to address concerns in rural health and well-being necessarily consider systems perspectives like attending to social inclusion, economic stability, personal security, and human health along with environmental sustainability, among other quality-of-life indicators. Recommendations to enhance rural well-being arise from successful examples derived from diverse rural settings.

Introduction

This chapter discusses the complex nature of the challenges and the opportunities for increasing well-being in rural contexts. A geographic interpretation of "rural" is adopted: rural areas are defined by their spatial characteristics and are typified by relatively long distances to access markets and services, as well as relatively low population density (Anriquez and Stamoulis, 2007). Opportunities and challenges in rural communities need to be considered as multi-dimensional, complex, and technical, cultural, political, social, ethical, economic, historical, and environmental.

The understanding of "rural well-being" is informed by several formal measurements of well-being – Genuine Progress Indicator, Canadian Index of Well-being, and Gross National Happiness in Bhutan, and work by Kevany et al. (2017). According to Fahey et al. (2004) "well-being then reflects not only living conditions and control over resources across the full spectrum of life domains, but also the ways in which people respond and feel about their lives in those domains" (p. 14). Several explorations of community well-being in European contexts (Brereton et al., 2011; Glendinning et al., 2003) align with Kevany et al. (2017) who outlined community well-being from a Canadian viewpoint. These studies revealed that youth engagement in, and motivation to return to, rural settings were aided by youth perceiving they were respected, valued, and their talents utilized (MacMichael et al., 2015), and they were actively connected to vibrant individuals and communities (e.g. Glendinning et al., 2003). Brereton et al. (2011) identified the ability to enjoy the natural environment and fresh air was fundamental to rural health and prosperity. Kevany et al. (2017) blended their field studies with patterns in the well-being literature to encapsulate four broad categories constituting well-being: vibrancy, including community health; prosperity, including economic adaptiveness and entrepreneurship;

individual and community resiliency; and sustainability of all types. These four overarching and interrelated categories form part of the theoretical framing applied to health and well-being in rural contexts in subsequent sections. This theory includes a holistic and systems thinking framing, to offer analyses that consider internalities and externalities of rural communities, be they positive or negative. These analyses may be applied to different scenarios and rural settings. This short study does not lend itself to comprehensive inquiry but affords consideration of links and causalities, of individual and community actions and external actor inputs to rural health and well-being.

Challenges with rural health and well-being

Much of the previous research on quality of life emphasized a dichotomy between rural and urban characteristics, often suggesting the superiority of one over the other and many of these differences were refuted and revised over time. Urban and rural settings each offer many advantages and disadvantages (Shucksmith *et al.*, 2009). For example, no support was found in the reviewed literature that supported a romantic notion that work–life balance is more satisfactory in rural areas or that access to work and school is more difficult in rural areas. Work–life balance and time to work and school were similar between urban and rural areas (the average round trip commuting time was 39 minutes per day in both urban and rural areas) (Shucksmith *et al.*, 2009).

While rurality is associated with many challenges as well as opportunities, rural communities may face more external and internal stresses (Aked *et al.*, 2008; Cox *et al.*, 2010). Some scholars have suggested that rural regions have been disproportionately subjected to deleterious neoliberal policies with their social, economic, and environmental impacts (Holden and Bourke, 2014). Some health professionals have observed health inequalities that contribute to disproportionally poorer health in rural settings (Coady and Cameron, 2012). The decline in community infrastructure has been found to lead to poorer access to health and social services (Collins *et al.*, 2017), and greater geographic remoteness and seclusion that often engenders debilitating, social isolation and loneliness (Kelly *et al.*, 2011). Consequently, greater socio-economic disadvantages were identified with rural areas (Holden and Bourke, 2014) as well as greater vulnerability from exposure to and trauma from environmental adversity (e.g. severe drought, fires, water contamination, and unprecedented climate change) (Fraser *et al.*, 2005). In their reporting on findings from an array of studies, Meng *et al.* (2009), found that aging adults who live in rural areas, compared with their urban counterparts, are more likely to engage in poor health behaviors (such as smoking and physical inactivity), suffer from chronic illnesses, and experience limitations in functional abilities. Rural residents also live longer in remote areas without accessing the care for medical conditions that their urban counterparts might more easily seek out and utilize (Meng *et al.*, 2009). Rural residents often experienced greater prevalence of diabetes, heart disease, cancers, and non-communicable diseases, economic disparity, and social exclusion (WHO, 2003; Hanlon and Halseth, 2005; Marsden, 2009).

Efforts made by countries to improve health care, educate about public health, and allocate financial support to programs to improve socio-economic conditions may be influenced by a country's political environment, financial abilities, or priorities of the government. But most health outcomes are found to improve with betterment to socio-economic conditions and public health efforts (Yasin and Helms, 2010).

In a Canadian study of health inequalities in urban and rural Canada, social inequalities in health were found to be similar but also distinct types arose in rural and urban Canada, often fueled by social or economic deprivation. In such studies social inequalities were measured differently. "In urban areas, social inequalities are generally measured through neighbourhood income whereas in rural areas distance or remoteness from urban centres is mainly considered" (Pampalon *et al.*, 2010, p. 416). Consequently, in rural areas social health inequalities appear smaller than in urban areas. But when people's social conditions are estimated at a small-area or household level, greater variability is found, and greater deprivation is identified in rural areas and particularly in remote settings. While urban areas experience greater socio-economic variations, rural areas also produce conditions of significant inequalities. These differences may be underestimated with the use of measurement tools used in demographic studies such as distance or remoteness from urban centers. More work is needed to disaggregate rural area data into meaningful entities.

Research in 2014 of rural–urban differences in health-care expenditures by US households found that rural populations spent more money on prescription drugs than urban populations (rural: $1278.3; urban: $1061.4). Urban populations ($1636.4) spent more than rural populations ($1167.4) on emergency room services (Lee *et al.*, 2014). Their findings revealed that less than 2 percent of rural or urban populations accounted for half of hospital inpatient care and emergency room service expenditures. In these two areas, expenditures were slightly more concentrated in urban versus rural areas. In spite of the authors hypothesizing that

> expenditures would be higher for rural populations than for urban populations, possibly due to a greater prevalence of poor health status in rural populations, or due to inferior access to (or quality of) preventative care in rural areas, based on the findings … there was no difference in total health expenditures between rural–urban residents.
>
> *(Lee et al., 2014, p. 6)*

Newcomers or immigrants to a rural region may contend with economic burdens and language and cultural barriers (Hanlon and Halseth, 2005). Minority populations too may be challenged with achieving a suitable sense of integration and belonging in rural contexts. They may encounter unique disadvantages in accessing needed services and may face more anxiety and depression. When these obstacles are compounded by experiences of discrimination or perceptions of mistreatment, immigrants could be at a greater risk of developing mental disorders (Caxaj and Gill, 2017). The health and mental issues for immigrants need serious consideration as they may be compromised and their sense of well-being in the community may jeopardize their state of mental health and happiness.

Smaller-scale agricultural producers, and the rural regions in which they operate, experienced "volatile commodity prices brought about by movements in global capital, and the growing power of transnational agribusiness" (Holden and Bourke, 2014, p. 209). Smallholder farmers' livelihoods have been undermined by food manufacturers with a range of options for the global sourcing of cheap inputs, thereby increasing competition and lowering prices paid for these commodities (Scrinis, 2016). Transdisciplinary research has indicated that countries with resource-intensive agriculture and those that support concentrated production were more wed to these industrial methods and less inclined to consider alternative modernization trajectories (Knickel *et al.*, 2017). Agricultural education institutions and research bodies appeared to be deeply attached to the model of technologically driven agricultural industrialization. Research that may challenge the conventional approach was less frequently funded and thus insufficiently explored and tested and thereby less likely to be adopted to enhance resilience (Pretty, 1997). Then over decades the default focus for investments become technologically driven agricultural industrialization.

Table 15.1 Obstacles to rural well-being

Prosperity – Economic	Vibrancy – Social	Resiliency – Human	Sustainability – Natural
Deleterious neoliberal policies	Declining rural infrastructure	Inaccessibility of or lack of services	Environmental adversity
Dominance of transnational agribusiness	Remoteness, seclusion, social exclusion	Isolation and loneliness	Extensive resource extraction and consumption
Pressure for increasing concentrated production and yield	Cultural and language barriers	Vulnerable to anxiety and depression	Resource intensive agriculture
Volatile commodity prices		More non-communicable diseases	Growing rainfall, pests, storms
More poverty, more disparity	Desire to relocate	Disproportionately poorer health	Vulnerable to drought, fires, water contamination, climate change
Funding for resource intensive growth	Disempowerment	Exogenous influence, external decisions	Less funding for sustainability measures

These centralized, industrial investments led to frustration among rural residents that "their community's prospects were dependent upon decisions made in distant parliaments and boardrooms" (Holden and Bourke, 2014, p. 209). Such constraints felt by rural communities (EU-SCAR, 2015 as cited by Knickel *et al.*, 2017) could fuel growing despair, alienation, and disempowerment and ignite a desire for relocation. The findings related to challenges with rural well-being are summarized in Table 15.1.

Enhancing rural well-being

Table 15.2 summarizes the well-being indicators from a range of studies of rural well-being.

In studies of rural well-being an array of considerations is included. The OECD Better Life Initiative report for quality of life in Ireland (2017) distilled well-being down into economic, social, human, and natural capital. Dimensions of physical location, features, assets, proximity to services, community dynamics and demographics were qualities, among others, that led to a sense of shared identity involving the place (Collins *et al.*, 2017). Other factors examined included perceptions of residents of their health and well-being status, employment opportunities, availability of housing, community norms and practices, sense of social cohesion, inclusion practices, and friendly climate (WHO, 2003; Mondelez, 2014). Other attributes were family life, friendships, standard of living, sex life, and relationships, as well as recreational opportunities and places and the time for leisure and freedom (Diener and Suh, 2000).

In examining Sen's (1984) definition of prosperity, de los Ríos *et al.* (2016) found properties of social cohesion and engagement lead to social vibrancy. They further emphasized the need to satisfy one's material needs through financial prosperity (de los Ríos *et al.*, 2016). The third element of Sen's approach to prosperity underscored sustainability by focusing on life conditions by appreciating the quality of, benefits from, and durability of material belongings. With the

Table 15.2 Enhancing rural well-being

Prosperity – Economic	Vibrancy – Social	Resiliency – Human	Sustainability – Natural
Gainful employment, maintaining livelihoods	Diversity in ages, community companions	Sense of shared identity	Desirable physical features, i.e. seaside, countryside, woodlots
Availability of affordable housing	Social inclusion, friendliness, and familiarity	Feel satisfied, fulfilled and community attachment	Places to enjoy leisure
Economic control over resources	Family nearby, friends also accessible for meaningful connections and reciprocity	Sex life and social supports	Appreciation of natural beauty and quality of life
Funds that enable self-directedness and freedom of choice	Time and resources for socializing and relaxing	Enjoying ease and pleasure	Durable material belongings
Places like pubs add support for friends and community convening	Trust, shared values, cohesion and conviviality	Sense of safety and security	Fresh air, clean water, protected spaces
Abilities to leverage local talents, technology, and tolerance	Youth attracted to and retained by rural areas	Diversity of ages, including youth, adds to community longevity and vitality	Nurture present and future generations to support local infrastructure
Devise shared plans for business development	Active roles for youth leaders	Youth and all citizens feeling valued, useful, and respected	Eco-tourism, sustainable development
Quality businesses, future investment mentality	Community appreciation and cooperation	Endogenous decision-making and sense of shared ownership and responsibility	Systematic enhancement and protection of human and natural assets
Increase local trading, strengthen community bonds, increase regional autonomy, bolster urban–rural partnerships, adopt progressive standards, expand export markets	Share benefits through cooperation, and expand direct consumer connections through technology	Redesign supply chains include alternative supply chains, and support the provision of public goods	Support eco-services and countryside amenities
Co-innovation efforts to build local capacities	Culture of learning together and sharing triumphs and trials	Collectively identify issues and plan strategies	Apply best science and strategies to protect environment
Invest in extension services and government programs	Build upon the capacity of citizens and self-reliance	Assess the impact of policies, projects, and programs on health and well-being	
Support entrepreneurship and economic adaptability	Tools and technology for connectivity, communications, and innovations	Increase transparency, public trust and system resiliency	

increasing recognition of community influences on individual health, researchers have also considered the impact of social capital including elements like trust, shared values, sense of security and safety, ability and willingness to participate in community events, and access to resources and amenities (Kelly *et al.*, 2011). Others measured structural social capital by organizational membership and cognitive social capital by a composite index of trust, reciprocity, and mutual help (Yip *et al.*, 2007). Studies have shown that meaningful connections, community belonging, and substantial social supports helped to alleviate challenges from lower states of mental health and perceptions of exogenous influence on the future of one's rural area (Collins *et al.*, 2017; Romans *et al.*, 2010). In 2014 the topic of rural community well-being was of such significance to the community of scholars that a special issue of the journal *Rural Society* was devoted to it. This collection emphasized the importance of individual indicators, as well as the essential nature of the quality of community features and relations along with the perceptions of self-in-community (physical, social, mental, and emotional) as being pivotal to well-being. Studies found that individual and community well-being were assessed by more than physical location alone; social capital combined with personal life experiences like marital status, life events, and sense of support and connections were also important to perceptions of well-being (Kelly *et al.*, 2011). Place and facilities also mattered. Findings from examinations of rural pubs in Ireland showed how pubs shaped community cohesion and economic development, while they also enhanced social capital and well-being (Cabras and Mount, 2017). However, Stain *et al.* (2008) found that community support was more strongly associated with decreased levels of distress for non-farming rural residents than for those living or working on the farm.

Other research showed the positive benefits of rural life and spillover effects from individuals' sense of satisfaction with dwelling characteristics and their assessments of the resources in the public community; Auh and Cook (2009) found a connection between housing satisfaction and community attachment and satisfaction. In another case study in rural Ireland, Brereton *et al.* (2011) found that long-term social and economic well-being in rural communities were dependent upon their ability to attract and retain youth, as an indicator contributing to community longevity and vitality, a point also raised by Kevany *et al.* (2017) and Glendinning *et al.* (2003).

Florida (2002) emphasized the importance of placing greater attention on quality of life than on economic development alone. He stressed the importance of leveraging talent, technology, and tolerance to systemically identify and enhance assets rather than deploy resources to solve separate community problems. Research conducted and posted by The Heartland Center for Leadership Development revealed many factors or "clues" to rural surviving and thriving. Ten of these were: community pride, quality in business and community life, future investment mentality, deliberative community decision-making, spirit of community cooperation, realistic future orientation, appreciation of competitive stance, mapping of local assets and protection of physical environment, active economic development programs, and active roles for younger leaders (The Heartland Center, 2009). Addressing concerns in rural health and well-being necessarily consider systems perspectives like attending to social inclusion, economic stability, personal security, and human health along with environmental sustainability, among other quality-of-life indicators as noted above (Flora *et al.*, 2015; Mondelez, 2014).

Farming communities and rural regions seek a wide range of economic and social strategies to bolster resiliency and prosperity. Some examples from case studies demonstrated in Belgian, Danish, and Swedish proposed helpful strategies to bolster rural well-being. They recommended emphasizing new markets with different consumers to buy agricultural produce, expand export markets, devise strategies to increase regional autonomy, devise new urban–rural partnerships, provide non-food eco-services and countryside amenities, expand beyond economic limitations and boundaries by adopting more progressive standards, foster local trading systems to strengthen community bonds, and pay more attention to quality of life and the provision of public goods and ecosystem services (RETHINK, n.d.). Knickel *et al.* (2017) also cited effective approaches involving the redesign of supply chains as strategies for enhancing resiliency. Forging alternative supply chains decreased dependency on retailers, helped producers retain more value added along the chain, and more evenly shared benefits through cooperation among chain partners. The use of direct marketing and customer engagement through internet connections allowed rural businesses and farmers to engage directly with consumers. This appears to have increased transparency and built consumer trust in local brands and produce (RETHINK, n.d.).

"What is largely neglected in many analyses is that learning, adaptation and realignment are critically important in maintaining livelihoods" (Knickel *et al.*, 2017, p. 5). Improved health and well-being are more likely to arise when individuals and communities come together to learn from one another, identify issues impacting health and well-being, and together decide on plans and actions to address the issues (Coady and Cameron, 2012). Encouraging the support of collective initiatives, co-learning, and co-innovation processes that lead to more local capacity building may be valuable. Agencies, like extension services, can fill pivotal roles in building the capacity of citizens to design programs and then assess the impact of policies, projects, and programs on their health and that of their community (Coady and Cameron, 2012; Flora *et al.*, 2015). In addition, support from local government's public services, including ensuring housing standards were maintained and community spaces were accessible and enjoyable, added to satisfaction with and attachment to community (Auh and Cook, 2009). These findings suggest that different groups within rural communities may experience community and social networks differently and may respond in diverse ways to efforts around social connectedness and inclusion.

Further research

More research is needed on health spending that describes the range of health and well-being impacts on rural communities along with illustrations of communities that have thrived with the level of supports while others have suffered. More investigation may be needed into the confluence and impact of history, land, place, identity, spirituality on collective notions of well-being. In addition, small-scale qualitative research would aid in more effectively and respectfully investigating individual and community lifestyles and their impact on well-being, that is measures of prosperity, sustainability, resiliency, and vibrancy.

Recommendations

These interventions are not promoted as a panacea but as strategies to address a range of issues. The development of suitable policies and programs would consider the demographics of the area – considering who lives there – what the area offers in natural, social, and cultural capital, as well as the array of socio-cultural and historical qualities shared by residents in their values, practices, and a sense of social cohesion and reputation of the area (Collins *et al.*, 2017). Sustainable visions for well-being must include workable strategies for enhancing prosperity, human flourishing, social cohesion, and improving levels of well-being, with minimal adverse impact on the environment (Jackson *et al.*, 2009). As forces for strengthening rural communities, planners and policy-makers should also consider efforts to build community attachment and the quality and availability of housing in community development efforts, accessibility of social service and family welfare programs, along with the quality of local government services (Auh and Cook, 2009).

Building the resilience and health of rural areas might take many forms: targeted interventions to increase prosperity and well-being; purposeful knowledge sharing and innovation supports; and a greater sense of efficacy through increased involvement of people of all ages in local governance, decision-making, and community visioning. In an inquiry into rural well-being, Anderson (2015) considered aspects distinct from their urban counterparts and found that rural community health and vibrancy were impacted by public infrastructure investments particularly around accessibility of services and facilities. Marsden (2009) found that improving physical and technological infrastructure helped to regenerate rural communities and improve the capacity for increased communications between interested groups and individuals. Increasing the quantity and quality of community meeting spaces for more effective organizing also added to community reserves and community empowerment. Knickel *et al.* (2017) found mismatches between visions and strategies about prosperity and well-being on the one hand and market developments, policy instruments, and outcomes on the other. It is recommended that greater alignment be achieved between policies from public officials and citizen-led community strategies and plans. Forging ways to work together across disciplines to enhance rural well-being are called for. In addition to attention to the physical location, housing availability, and environmental features, fostering a sense of connectedness must become a dominating feature of healthier, more robust rural communities (Collins *et al.*, 2017; Auh and Cook, 2009; Fraser *et al.*, 2005). Interventions to strengthen connectedness would require accessibility to transport services and the availability of youth activities and physical and mental health services. Engaging community members in learning about and developing strategies to improve health and well-being empowers citizens to play more active roles in decision-making, designing, and action planning around health. These efforts strengthen community capacity to take action to improve health and well-being (Coady and Cameron, 2012).

Market solutions also play a role to increase public access to healthy options. Businesses may consider innovative opportunities in the bioeconomy and circularity to improve prosperity while also supporting biodiversity and sustainability (Kitchen and Marsden, 2009). Lang (2009) offers many helpful strategies to improve economic prosperity, environmental well-being, and ecological public health through enhancements to more sustainable food systems. The Dutch Council for Rural Areas (Council for Rural Areas, 1998) identified the capacity to regain consumer trust as a major factor driving value-added opportunities. The creation, operation, and evolution of alternative food supply chains can be instrumental in emerging rural development (Van der Ploeg *et al.*, 2000). Additionally, expanding markets can be seen in the provision of more thoughtful, healthful, humane, and sustainable food choices (Baur, 2008; Innova Market Insights, 2017).

To increase rural health and well-being sustainable development and sustainable consumption have gained more attention as key parts of the solution. Full cost accounting in agricultural production would effectively calculate the societal and environmental costs that often are externalized for soil, water, and biodiversity. Policies and practices that sustain and protect ecosystem services should be incentivized to replace unsustainable practices. In rural contexts in particular, agro-ecological initiatives that emphasize more nutritious crop varieties and crop diversification can play an important role in improving diet quality (Scrinis, 2016; Fanzo *et al.*, 2013) and overall health of residents. The re-valuing of whole and minimally processed foods, the demand for "real", fresh, local, and organic foods, and the need to develop cooking and gardening skills are advocated by various food movements (Scrinis, 2016; Lang, 2009). Food sovereignty movements also call for the protection and valuing of local and rural food cultures as an alternative to the onslaught of cheap and imported processed foods. Social marketing and creative agro-tourism may be helpful to include active promotion of natural assets, cultural landscapes, and agritourism and ecotourism.

Policy-makers are advised to recognize that policies and market mechanisms shape much of the outcomes for rural and agricultural communities and these can be advantageous or unfavorable. Policy-makers might systematically assess the effects of market mechanisms, the poignancy of place and history, and the impact personal power or efficacy plays within relationships and abilities to implement desired visions. Building on results that improved conditions for rural Chinese populations, policies should produce an environment that enhances social networks and facilitates the exchange of social support to improve health and well-being (Yip *et al.*, 2007). Attention should also be given to the importance of nuances emphasized by Aboriginal Australians when they strive for increasing understanding of and practices around individual health and well-being as intertwined with the collective, the physical place, the larger environment, and the sense of connection with all beings

> …not just the physical well-being of an individual but the social, emotional and cultural well-being of the whole Community in which each individual is able to achieve their full potential as a human being thereby bringing about the total well-being of their Community.
>
> *(National Aboriginal Community Controlled Health Organisation, 2014 as cited by*
> *Holden and Bourke, 2014, p. 211)*

Interventions to enhance rural health and well-being should strive to be agriculture-supporting, health-enhancing, damage-preventing, environmentally sustaining, and community rejuvenating.

References

Aked, J., Marks, N., Cordon, C., Thompson, S., 2008. *Five ways to wellbeing: The evidence.* New Economics Foundation, London.

Anderson, M., 2015. *Roles of rural areas in sustainable food system transformations.* Development 58(2–3), 256–262.

Anriquez, G. and Stamoulis, K., 2007. *Rural development and poverty reduction: Is agriculture still the key?* ESA Working Paper No. 07-02. June. FAO.

Auh, S., Cook, C.C., 2009. *Quality of community life among rural residents: An integrated model.* Social Indicators Research, 94(3), 377–389.

Baur, G., 2008. *Farm Sanctuary: Changing hearts and minds about animals and food.* Simon & Schuster, New York.

Brereton, F., Bullock, C., Clinch, J.P., Scott, M., 2011. *Rural change and individual well-being: The case of Ireland and rural quality of life.* European Urban and Regional Studies 18(2), 203–227.

Cabras, I., Mount, M.P., 2017. *How third places foster and shape community cohesion, economic development and social capital: The case of pubs in rural Ireland.* Journal of Rural Studies 55, 71–82.

Caxaj, C.S., Gill, N.K., 2017. *Belonging and mental wellbeing among a rural Indian-Canadian diaspora: Navigating tensions in "Finding a Space of Our Own".* Qualitative Health Research 27(8), 1119–1132.

Coady, M., Cameron, C., 2012. *Community health impact assessment: Fostering community learning and healthy public policy at the local level,* in English, L.M. (Ed.), *Adult education and health.* University of Toronto Press, Toronto, Ont., 29–45.

Collins, J., Ward, B.M., Snow, P., Kippen, S., Judd, F., 2017. *Compositional, contextual, and collective community factors in mental health and well-being in Australian rural communities.* Qualitative Health Research 27(5), pp. 677–687.

Council for Rural Areas, 1998. *Trust and care: Food production in the 21st century.* Council for Rural areas, Amersfoort (in Dutch).

Cox, D., Frere, M., West, S., Wiseman, J., 2010. *Developing and using local community wellbeing indicators: Learning from the experience of Community Indicators Victoria.* Australian Journal of Social Issues, https://doi.org/10.1002/j.1839-4655.2010.tb00164.x.

de los Ríos, I., Rivera, M., García, C., 2016. *Redefining rural prosperity through social learning in the cooperative sector: 25 years of experience from organic agriculture in Spain.* Land Use Policy 54(Supplement C), 85–94. https://doi.org/10.1016/j.landusepol.2016.02.009.

Diener, E., Suh, E.M. (Eds.), 2000. *Culture and subjective well-being.* MIT Press, Cambridge, MA.

Fahey, T., Whelan, C., Maitre, B., 2004. *Quality of life in Europe: First European quality of life survey 2003.* Office for Official Publications of the European Communities. European Foundation for the Improvement of Living and Working Conditions, Luxembourg.

Fanzo, J., Hunter, D., Borelli, T., Mattei, F. (Eds.), 2013. *Diversifying food and diets: Using agricultural biodiversity to improve nutrition and health.* Routledge, Abingdon.

Flora, C.B., Flora, J.L., Gasteyer, S.P., 2015. *Rural communities: Legacy + change.* Westview Press, Boulder, CO.

Florida, R., 2002. *The rise of the creative class – and how it's transforming work, leisure, community and every day life.* Basic Books, New York.

Fraser, C., Jackson, H., Judd, F., Komiti, A., Robins, G., Murray, G., Humphreys, J., Pattison, P., Hodgins, G., 2005. *Changing places: The impact of rural restructuring on mental health in Australia.* Health Place 11, 157–171.

Glendinning, A., Nuttall, M., Hendry, L., Kloep, M., Wood, S., 2003. *Rural communities and well-being: A good place to grow up?,* The Sociological Review 51(1), 129–156.

Hanlon, N., Halseth, G., 2005. *The greying of resource communities in northern British Columbia: Implications for health care delivery in already-underserviced communities.* The Canadian Geographer/Le Geographe Canadien 49(1), 1–24.

Holden, T., Bourke, L., 2014. *Rural community wellbeing.* Rural Society 23(3), 208–216.

Innova Market Insights, 2017. *Food ingredients.* www.foodingredientsfirst.com/Supplier-Profiles/Innova-Market-Insights.html.

Jackson, R.J., Minjares, R., Naumoff, K.S., Shrimali, B.P., Martin, L.K., 2009. *Agriculture policy is health policy.* Journal of Hunger and Environmental Nutrition 4(3–4), 393–408.

Kelly, B.J., Lewin, T.J., Stain, H.J., Coleman, C., Fitzgerald, M., Perkins, D., Carr, V.J., Fragar, L., Fuller, J., Lyle, D., Beard, J.R., 2011. *Determinants of mental health and well-being within rural and remote communities.* Social Psychiatry and Psychiatric Epidemiology 46(12), 1331–1342.

Kevany, K., Ma, J., Biggs, J., MacMichael, M., 2017. *Appreciating Living Well in Two Rural Nova Scotian Communities.* Journal of Community Practice 25(1), 1–19.

Kitchen, L., Marsden, T., 2009. *Creating sustainable rural development through stimulating the eco-economy: Beyond the eco-economic paradox?* Sociologia Ruralis 49(3), 273–294.

Knickel, K., Redman, M., Darnhofer, I., Ashkenazy, A., Chebach, T.C., Šūmane, S., Tisenkopfs, T., Zemeckis, R., Atkociuniene, V., Rivera, M., Strauss, A., 2017. *Between aspirations and reality: Making farming, food systems and rural areas more resilient, sustainable and equitable.* Journal of Rural Studies 59(April), 197–210. http://dx.doi.org/10.1016/j.jrurstud.2017.04.012.

Lang, T., 2009. *Reshaping the food system for ecological public health.* Journal of Hunger and Environmental Nutrition 4(3–4), 315–335. http://doi.org/10.1080/19320240903321227.

Lee, W., Jiang, L., Phillips, C., Ohsfeldt, R., 2014. *Rural–urban differences in health care expenditures: Empirical data from US households.* Advances in Public Health 2014, 435780.

MacMichael, M., Beazley, K., Kevany, K., Looker, D., Stiles, D., 2015. *Motivations, experiences, and community contributions of young in-migrants in the Maitland Area, Nova Scotia.* Journal of Rural and Community Development 10(4), 36–53. http://journals.brandonu.ca/jrcd/article/view/1214.

Marsden, T., 2009. *Mobilities, vulnerabilities and sustainabilities: Exploring pathways from denial to sustainable rural development.* Sociologia Ruralis 49(2), 113–131. https://doi.org/10.1111/j.1467-9523.2009.00479.x.

Meng, H., Wamsley, B., Liebel, D., Dixon, D., Eggert, G., Van Nostrand, J., 2009. *Urban–rural differences in the effect of a Medicare health promotion and disease self management program on physical function and health care expenditures.* Gerontologist 49(3), 407–417.

Mondelez, 2014. *The call for well-being: 2013 progress report.* Mondelez International, East Hanover, NJ.

OECD, 2017. *How's life in Ireland?* www.oecd.org/statistics/Better-Life-Initiative-country-note-Ireland.pdf.

Pampalon, R., Hamel, D., Gamache, P., 2010. *Health inequalities in urban and rural Canada: Comparing inequalities in survival according to an individual and area-based deprivation index.* Health and Place 16(2), 416–420.

Pretty, J., 1997. *The sustainable intensification of agriculture.* Natural Resources Forum 21, 247–256.

RETHINK, n.d. *Farm modernization and rural resilience.* Institute for Rural Development Research at the J.W. Goethe University of Frankfurt/Main. www.rethink-net.eu/case-studies.html.

Romans, S., Cohen, M., Forte, T., 2010. *Rates of depression and anxiety in urban and rural Canada.* Social Psychiatry and Psychiatric Epidemiology 46(7), 567–575. DOI: 10.1007/s00127-010-0222-2.

Scrinis, G., 2016. *Reformulation, fortification and functionalization: Big food corporations' nutritional engineering and marketing strategies.* The Journal of Peasant Studies 43(1), 17–37.

Sen, A., 1984. *The living standard,* Oxford Economic Papers 36, 74–90.

Shucksmith, M., Cameron, S., Merridew, T., Pichler, F., 2009. *Urban–rural differences in quality of life across the European Union.* Regional Studies 43(10), 1275–1289.

Stain, H.J., Kelly, B., Lewin, T.J., Higginbotham, N., Beard, J.R., Hourihan, F., 2008. *Social networks and mental health among a farming population.* Social Psychiatry and Psychiatric Epidemiology 43(10), 843–849. https://doi.org/10.1007/s00127-008-0374-5.

The Heartland Center, 2009. *20 Clues to Rural Community Survival,* new edition. http://heartlandcenter. info.

Van Der Ploeg, J.D., Renting, H., Brunori, G., Knickel, K., Mannion, J., Marsden, T., De Roest, K., Sevilla-Guzmán, E., Ventura, F., 2000. *Rural development: From practices and policies towards theory,* Sociologia Ruralis 40(4), 391–408.

WHO (World Health Organization), 2003. *Social determinants of health: The solid facts,* ed. R. Wilkinson and M. Marmot. Copenhagen.

Yasin, J., Helms, M., 2010. *A comparison of health-related expenditures: A multi-country comparison.* Academy of Health Care Management Journal 6(2), 1–19.

Yip, W., Subramanian, S.V., Mitchell, A.D., Lee, D.T., Wang, J., Kawachi, I., 2007. *Does social capital enhance health and well-being? Evidence from rural China.* Social Science and Medicine 64(1), 35–49.

16

RURAL POLICY AND THE CULTURAL CONSTRUCTION OF THE URBAN/RURAL DIVIDE IN THE UNITED STATES AND EUROPE

Philipp Kneis

The cultural construction of the urban/rural divide as a challenge for policy

The cultural and social construction of the urban/rural divide has been very influential in shaping rural and urban policy in both Europe and North America. While recent years have seen an increased polarization between rural and urban areas, fueled by modernization, globalization, and digitalization, such a divide has a long cultural history. In providing a brief sketch of this history, and of the complex cultural construction of both urbanity and rurality, this chapter aims to provide some clues also to contemporary political and social challenges.

Cultural and social constructivism points out that social reality is constructed by human beings, and that there is a distinction between what Searle calls "brute facts" and "social facts" (Searle, 1995). Natural geography may be a brute fact, but how social beings label, describe, understand, and utilize geography would count as a social fact. Such a perspective allows for the assumption, implicit or explicit, that space itself is not neutral. "Space" is culturally and socially produced (Lefebvre, 1974), it reflects the underlying cultural concepts of the respective culture. Especially in response to theories of planetary urbanization and "cityism" (Angelo and Wachsmuth, 2015), and discussions of new urbanism (Soja, 2016; Smith, 2002; Soja, 1999), discussions of the divide between urban and rural spaces have become more urgent.

Recently, this divide has become apparent politically and electorally in the United States. The political division is fueled by cultural just as much as by geographic and demographic factors. Political actors appear unable to repair the rift, which is not surprising given the long cultural history of the problem.

On the one hand, pastoral ideas of society in conjunction with idyllic and utopian notions of small towns and farms, with their associated value systems, are transposed against depictions of cities as industrialized and anti-human conflict zones. On the other hand, post-industrial cities see themselves as progressive islands in a more conservative landscape.

This chapter investigates how these contrasting visions have been informing political reality and influencing policy in the United States. After a brief overview of the cultural history of this divide, the article will sketch how policy has succeeded or failed in addressing the problem, and what might need to be done to solve or ameliorate problems that have arisen.

A brief trans-Atlantic cultural history of the urban/rural divide

From antiquity to the Middle Ages: the city and agriculture

Since the days of Aristotle, a human being has been defined as a *zôon politikón* – an animal which is connected to the polis, the city; a political (and/or social) animal.

The Polis is the Greek city-state, so a human is an animal defined by the city. A Polis includes a city and its hinterland, so even a farmer within that city-state must be seen in relation to the city, as farming happened to feed city dwellers, as the rural area serves the urban. This service to the city delivered by rural areas is primarily seen in three ways – first, as the location of agriculture, second, as the location of spiritual renewal, and third as the locus for the preservation of nature itself.

The dominant line of tradition that has shaped American conceptions of rurality is the idealization of agricultural life celebrated, for instance, by Roman senators like Marcus Porcius Cato, the Elder. An agrarian society was understood to be an honest society living up to traditional values; all culture was derived from agriculture (Porcius, 160 BCE).

In Europe, Roman pastoral ideas are upheld in the Middle Ages, especially in Monastic culture. Yet the decline of the Roman order in the Middle Ages brings back notions of wilderness in fairy tales, where especially the woods feature as a motif. Frequent warfare and the continuing political and social fragmentation of Europe in Renaissance and Early Modern times, especially after the Reformation (1517), the German Peasant's War (1524–1525) and the Thirty Years War (1618–1648) – both wars having affected rural regions drastically – led to increased reflections on nature as wild, especially with regard to human nature. Not coincidentally, Hobbes revives the Roman proverb *homo hominis lupus* – man is to man like a wolf – *bellum omnium contra omnes* – the war of all against all – in his reflection on *The Citizen* (*De Cive*) in 1651. Both the views of nature proper and of human nature seem to stress wilderness, and a skepticism towards the social and political ideal that Aristotle was diagnosing. Rather than believe that human beings are by nature social or fit for political (city) life, some guiding Renaissance ideas focused on the improvement of both the land (Locke, 1689) and the people (Rousseau, 1762).

Renaissance and early modernity: wilderness and the pastoral

European perceptions of nature and politics are further influenced by ideological descriptions of contact with Indigenous civilizations in the Americas. The traditional Aristotelian perception of human beings as – by nature – political animals gives rise to conceptions of a "state of nature" (Rousseau, 1755/1964), which are fueled by colonialist imaginations of Indigenous populations as primitive, casting Indigenous claims to American land thus as null and void. John Locke's definition of property as land that has to be improved upon (Locke, 1689) deliberately ignored proof of Native agricultural achievements (cf. Mann, 2005; Denevan, 1992), and misrepresentations of Indigenous peoples (cf. Gilroy, 2014, pp. 31, 39) and their societies (like in the influential Morgan, 1877, and Engels, 1884).

Such colonial imaginations contributed further to the perspective of seeing rural areas merely as land to be utilized. This view has not been alien to Europe either, as can be seen in Thomas More's criticism in *Utopia* (1516) of the practice of enclosures in England that transformed communally used land into privately owned land. Similar criticism returns in the American context in the struggle between rangers and farmers, and contemporary opposition to the Bureau of Land Management.

Back in the beginnings of the United States, Roman ideas about the virtue of agriculture return with the Jeffersonian ideal of agricultural society. In his *Notes on the State of Virginia*, Jefferson writes "Those who labour in the earth are the chosen people of God", and

> It is the focus in which he keeps alive that sacred fire, which otherwise might escape from the face of the earth. Corruption of morals in the mass of cultivators is a phenomenon of which no age nor nation has furnished an example.

Conversely, it is the city that is seen as the site of moral corruption:

> The mobs of great cities add just so much to the support of pure government, as sores do to the strength of the human body. It is the manners and spirit of a people which preserve a republic in vigour. A degeneracy in these is a canker which soon eats to the heart of its laws and constitution.
>
> *(Jefferson, 1802, pp. 226–227)*

These values return in discourses idealizing the so-called "American Heartland" as the alleged location of moral values, especially in contemporary Republican politics.

Other than as the locations of agriculture, rural areas are also the locations of nature. Agriculture subordinates nature for the sake of civilization. Inherent in its practice in rural areas is the idea that nature is being made useful, purposeful, cultured, tamed, pastoral (Marx, 1964; Nye, 1996).

Yet that means that "nature", of course, primarily exists untamed, as wilderness. Located within rural areas, there is indeed wilderness – forests, prairies, deserts, mountains, etc. Frequently, these are areas equated with the sacred, as spheres beyond human control that dwarf any human endeavor in the presence of transcendental sublimity, as Ralph Waldo Emerson ("Nature", 1836) frequently describes.

This romantic understanding of nature, however, frequently builds upon the aforementioned colonial mis-framings of Indigenous lands as wilderness, as in depictions of upstate New York (the territory of the League of the Haudenosaunee or Iroquois) by the Hudson River School in the US, mirroring European Romanticism in paintings by Caspar David Friedrich and others.

Transcendentalism and early environmentalism

These romantic and wild natural spaces are not places of material production, yet they hold importance as places of spiritual production, specifically as locations of refuge, of inspiration, for retreat and inspiration-seeking. Even here, a utility function of nature can be assumed. There exists a long history of this spiritual utility of nature. For example, in Biblical texts, Moses, Jonah, John the Baptist, and Jesus undergo transformative experiences in the loneliness of nature. Their individual encounters with the majesty of nature and the divine, be it on a mountain, in the belly of a whale, or in the desert, are catalysts for spiritual growth. Edmund Burke speaks of encounters with the Sublime in these cases (Burke, 1757). This is a motif that returns in America as the "Errand into the Wilderness" (Danforth, 1670), and is key to any understanding of early American culture (Miller, 2009). The "errand" motif describes a purposeful trip into nature in order to seek enlightenment. It sees nature itself as a test of moral steadfastness. In iconic texts like Hawthorne's *Young Goodman Brown* (1835) or Melville's *Moby Dick* (1851), nature is seen as the space of temptation where that which is typically suppressed by culture is manifested to test one's character; yet there is also Thoreau's *Walden* (1854), which provides a view of nature as inspirational and grounding.

This view of nature has, in many ways, been the inspiration for the environmentalist movement, which draws on both understandings – nature as sublime, but also as nurturing; needing both reverence and protection, for the sake of human survival (Carson, 1962). Romantic notions of nature as the antidote to civilization have certainly been influential also in the shaping of an understanding of rural areas as the location of nature.

Today's awareness of the necessity for the protection of rural landscapes and nature is built on such traditions of American Romanticism, which may tie in with Indigenous ideas of land stewardship, but also with concepts of the rural as resource, specifically with regard to natural resources, relaxation, and a commodification of rural landscapes for tourism.

The spread of the city

There has, of course, always been a distinction between "city" and "country" ever since human beings began forming cities, as laid out before. Yet the Industrial Revolution leads to an overall transformation of society from an agrarian to an industrial and then to a service-based economy. This changes the dynamics between rural vs. urban spaces in important ways and has increasingly challenged modern understandings of rurality.

The idealization of the city in the United States emerges as a contrast between the industry-driven areas first in the Northeast and the Midwest, and later in the rural South and West. The industrialization of the South was fueled by the invention the cotton gin in the nineteenth century, but its rise may be due to air conditioning (Glaeser and Tobio, 2007).

The key driver of change was technology, which also challenged typically agrarian definitions of rural life once automobile use became widespread and challenged geographies that were previously more clear-cut: gentrification processes, for instance, can be found in rural areas just as in urban areas, in the form of urban sprawl (Ghose, 2004). Yet urban sprawl and suburbanization must seem unthinkable, or least very difficult, without an increasingly motorized populace. Related to the rise of the automobile is also the mechanization of agricultural production. Manpower increasingly is replaced by the power of heavy machinery.

Increasingly, the distinction between urban and rural has been becoming fuzzier, as cities have been spreading into the countryside. Where cities were once surrounded by fields, they are now surrounded by suburbs, exurbs, which then transition seamlessly into the next city. Even nature, through parks, greenbelts, and nature areas, can be part of a city, and agriculture typically is pushed into more and more remote areas. Remoteness from the city may have become the best indicator for rurality now.

Let us consider the European context. In Europe, rurality may appear different than in the American context, as distances between cities are typically closer, and rural areas appear less remote geographically. Remoteness, however, is relative. What counts as an acceptable driving and commuting distance differs starkly between the American and European settings. In addition, remoteness, from a European perspective, oftentimes means a diminished availability of public transport, high-speed internet, and access to services.

With regard to the association of rurality and nature, in Europe, "wilderness" is limited to a few remote and oftentimes less accessible mountainous areas. The few remaining vestiges of old growth forests – mostly located in former Communist countries – are increasingly harvested – both legally and illegally – like Romania's Carpathian forests, or under threat, like Poland's

Bialowieza Forest. What remains of "nature" within rural areas is oftentimes pastoralized. Environmentalism, originally an American idea, nevertheless has become influential since the mid-twentieth century, fueled by the danger of the dying off of forests (The "Waldsterben") and the Chernobyl accident.

Yet arguably, the connection between rurality and wilderness is not as strong as in the US. "Rural" typically is associated with agriculture, or merely with a certain degree of remoteness from urban life. Rurality in Europe is also a driver of regionalism, which becomes clearer also in connection with the *terroire* movement, the "copyrighting" of local food traditions like Champagne, Parmeggiano Reggiano, etc. Rural identity is commodified, and this commodified identity has increasingly also become a marker of cultural regional identity in Europe.

Cultural representations

In cultural representations, rural areas can be depicted just as much as an idyllic paradise (like the shire in *Lord of the Rings* – as contrasted with the industrial hellscape of Mordor), as much as a site of backwardness (as in *Deliverance*), or sometimes even as an unexpected site of promise and scientific progress (*Interstellar*). Rural innocence is typically seen as standing in clear contrast with the mechanized city (*Metropolis*), but is also seen frequently as "flyover country", even as colonized and gentrified by urban elites (again, *Deliverance*, and also *Avatar*).

Examples in culture abound, and without going into further detail, it can be stated that there is a clear perception that "rural" and "urban" are connected to two distinct and different cultural modes of being, with longstanding traditions from within the earliest times of Western culture. The political mobilization of that cultural difference has come full force in American politics. In the following, the political dimension of that cultural divide will be further explored.

The divide and (post-)modern discontent

The cultural construction of "space" in (post-)modernity

How does the cultural discourse and history of the rural/urban divide in America relate to policy? Are there easily definable variables, or even constants, that culturally measure this problem?

As mentioned at the outset, "Space" is culturally and socially produced (Lefebvre, 1974) – thus the very divide is (re)produced in the cultural constructions. Cultural discourse can indeed be prescriptive, or to some degree determinative – in that it can prime how a topic is approached, and set the agenda for political discourse, and how an idea can become reified. Yet cultural discourse can also be descriptive, and thus provide us with data that chronicles a given phenomenon. Both modes – prescriptive or descriptive – are inherent in all media and cultural discourse.

Policy-makers increasingly seek clearly quantifiable parameters and variables yielding data that can be objectively measured, compared, and tracked – in order to argue for policy change. Ideally, the motivation behind the proposed change would be fueled by such data, rather than be informed by ideology or socio-cultural constructions. This positivist perspective is challenged in such an interdisciplinary context where literary and cultural theory, history, social science, political science, and policy theory intersect. To make matters worse, especially in theories of culture and society, the governing post-modern paradigm does not believe in governing paradigms – as the challenge of (post-)modernity, or its very condition (Lyotard, 1984), is the breakdown and questioning of so-called grand narratives, or, in other words, of measurable constants.

What post-modern theory expresses in its very idiosyncratic terminology is indeed visible in reality: that which used to be a constant (city, rural, nature) now has a high variability, a condition of modernity characterized by Marshall Berman as "a maelstrom of perpetual disintegration and renewal" (Berman, 1982, p. 15), or as a form of liquidity (Bauman, 2013). These descriptions, of course, echo Marx's (1848/1978) (materialist) critique from the time of the Industrial Revolution, which inaugurated a process of economic and social changes that have not lost anything of their transformative force, but rather have intensified by creating a unifying condition that is global. Economic globalization does come with the promise of opportunity, but also, in the end, is a force of disintegration. It is this sense of disintegration that has resulted in a push-back in both rhetoric and practice by constituencies that see themselves at the losing end of this process. In recent years, the combined forces of (post-)modernity, globalization, and digitalization have led to a dramatic increase in support for those politics that emphasize this feeling of disintegration, of loss, of uncertainty and insecurity.

The economic colonization of rural America

Rural areas, whether in America, Germany, France, the United Kingdom, or Italy, have oftentimes felt the force of change more drastically. Urban areas are typically confronted with change regularly, whereas rural areas tend to value stability, and align with conservative values (in the best sense of "conserving" and "preserving"). The disruptions of rural areas for the sake of the cities have prompted some critics, such as John Ikerd, to speak of a form of "Economic Colonization of Rural America" (Ikerd, 2017), specifically in the context of industrial-scale animal production. This is just one example of a deep structural change undergoing rural areas. Suburbanization or even renewable energy production and the transformation of the pastoral or natural landscape play a critical role in the perception of disruption as well. These changes are oftentimes obscured culturally, for example when food products are typically advertised by appealing to depictions of rural small farm bliss, rather than with realistic portrayals of industrial food production. Such advertisement is a key indicator for the role cultural constructions play in defining what it means to be rural or urban. Despite often drastic changes in what constitutes urbanity and rurality in recent decades, past cultural depictions of rural and city life continue to exert their influence, not least through religion and traditional values.

These traditional values exert political power. Almost perplexingly to some demographers, constituencies tend to have real and substantial cultural voting interests beyond their assumed material self-interest. Researchers can keep asking "What's the Matter with Kansas" (Frank, 2004), but can also just accept that cultural factors play just as much a role as material ones in shaping consciousness.

As to material and measurable factors, several policy actors up to the level of the United Nations Department of Economic and Social Affairs (2015) have provided clear definitions and guidelines of rural and urban density, development, infrastructure, and the delivery of services. Some researchers, such as Scott et al. (2007), have argued that aspects of the divide may be overplayed in an ever-interdependent world, but they still see clear problems, especially with regard to rural development.

Yet the rural/urban divide is not merely a question of infrastructure or services. It addresses oftentimes fundamental differences in perceptions, values, political philosophy, and conceptions of the good life. In a democratic society, these differences need to be addressed, whether they are in alignment with personal philosophies or not, and whether they can be easily measured or not. In recent years, such differences have had clear political consequences.

Discussion: implications of cultural discourse for policy

Political polarization in the United States

It is no coincidence that in the United States, the reaction to globalization and the perceived post-modern disintegration of values has been framed in terms following a rural/urban divide. The Tea Party movement of 2009 welcomed as its iconic figure Sarah Palin – who made frequent references to rural America as the "real America". Donald Trump was able to capitalize on this movement in 2016 by appealing to voters in rural and formerly industrial areas who feared the political process of globalization and its assumed cultural implications.

Rural poverty – such as in states like Alabama (McKenna *et al.*, 2017), but not limited to it – has been one of the underestimated drivers of political change. The 2016 election can be seen as the clearest example of the political actualization of the cultural split between rural and urban areas.

It appears that the strongest manifestation of the rural/urban divide can be found in the United States currently. Here, the divide clearly follows the patterns described above, with rural traditions frequently framed in Catonian and Jeffersonian terms.

Yet the US is not the only country displaying such a split; similar observations can be made in Europe as well.

Political polarization in Europe

Within Europe, political polarization does not always seem to neatly fit within the urban/rural paradigm at first glance. While in the American context, rural areas are frequently idealized as the "heartland", in Europe, references to "farmers", "villages", and "structurally weak areas" may not immediately bring up the same ideologically charged associations as across the Atlantic. Yet despite a less impressive rhetoric, metropolitan areas oftentimes are seen in opposition to rural areas – which can include small and medium-sized towns, even bigger cities in otherwise "structurally weak" regions. Each of these regions can have complex histories, such as the legacy of failed economies in former Communist states (most of East Germany, rural Poland, and Hungary), extreme centralization and focus on the capital (which has left rural regions in France and the United Kingdom, for instance, feeling left out), or the recent influx of immigrants that has left many citizens in receiving countries increasingly anxious of the future – especially those fearing a decline in their already fragile economic situation. Increasingly multicultural cities with more plentiful job opportunities provide a stark contrast to an increasingly nativist rural areas and small- and mid-sized cities.

The "great regression" (Geiselberger, 2017), however, is not necessarily just the result of immigration. Populations in structurally disadvantaged regions already feel economically and culturally stressed. Parameters of life once thought stable and reliable are increasingly under change, mostly due to processes of digitalization and economic globalization. These stresses are, of course, not limited to rural regions – but these spaces increasingly are proclaimed by extremist political agitators as spaces of last refuge for a diminishing native (German, British, Finnish, Polish, French, Italian, Hungarian, Greek, etc.) population. Xenophobia is a political tool used deliberately to benefit new populist parties like the Alternative for Germany, UKIP or Tory factions in favor of Brexit, the True Fins, Law and Justice, Front National, Five Stars and Northern League, Fidesz and Jobbik, Golden Dawn, etc. These movements are linked internationally, with support from Putin's Russia (Brownstein, 2017; Noack, 2017; Polyakova, 2016; Snyder, 2018).

The real answer to the increased polarization cannot lie in support for nativism, xenophobia, and political separatism. None of these answers are providing sustainable solutions that would actually help the populations that feel disadvantaged. What could be possible solutions?

Recommendations for policy and further research

The rural/urban divide has a long history, and its cultural representations have been a source for identification and ideological competition. In current times, this competition has been at the center of increasing political fragmentation and polarization. Globally digitally networked political extremists are setting out to counteract globalization in an increasingly digital age. As a result, there is a "democracy fatigue" (Appadurai, 2017) that threatens democratic, tolerant, and multicultural societies mainly in the West (but also beyond) and promotes nativist, xenophobic, and anti-Western rhetoric and policies. Yet the underlying factors that fuel such polarization can and need to be addressed. In the following, some suggestions will be provided.

Politics needs to seek a real dialogue. Currently disenfranchised populations may not be the same as typically addressed by politics. Traditional middle-class populations are increasingly feeling at risk of failure. Working-class populations – including agricultural workers – seem to have resigned themselves to have been abandoned by traditional social democrat and labor parties. Poor immigrant populations, whether documented or undocumented, typically are at the bottom rung of the social ladder. Both middle and working-class populations fear imminent or prospective economic decline. Digitalization and artificial intelligence, but also immigration, are seen – rightly or wrongly – as threats to available jobs, whether correctly or incorrectly.

Political actors, but also the media, need to address the fears as real. Typically, such fears are downplayed and dismissed. Citizens who expressed concerns are regularly ridiculed or derided as fringe or "deplorable". Yet perceptions matter, and not addressing real-existing feelings will lead to further feelings of disenfranchisement. Actual policy problems need to be addressed. This concerns housing prices, job availability, living wages, health care, aging care, infrastructure, and physical safety. These concerns hold true for both urban and rural populations. Are there specific points to be made with reference to rural areas?

The main concern all over rural areas is the preservation of their very existence, their way of life, the viability of their home. "Ghost towns" are scattered all over the American West, but also throughout areas in Europe, increasingly so. Rural areas typically lack employment possibilities since the advent and intensification of industrial-style farming. Machines do the work, and people tend to leave. With people, services leave as well, and infrastructure investments are seen as an undue burden.

It appears that from the long history of the cultural construction of what it means to be urban or rural respectively, such an outcome – from the presumed position of the city – would only be natural. If rural areas are only seen as good for either agriculture, relaxation, spiritual growth, or wilderness, and if agriculture can be automated, or even moved into the cities in the form of urban farming, is that not the course of history? With the majority of the people living in cities, why do rural areas matter? Why – in the American example – even allow for the construct of federalism, which gives disproportional power to rural, less densely populated areas, especially when considering the electoral college? This system was devised in Jeffersonian times – when the leadership of the young Republic stylized itself after Roman senators. This very attitude is intensely felt in rural areas in the United States, and in other countries that have seen the needs of the city prioritized over that of rural or so-called "structurally weak" areas. It has arguably bred part of the resentment that saw recent electoral shifts in Western countries.

Yet structural weakness is a result, and not merely a given. It is a result of policies that have accepted that some areas thrive, and others do not. Yet the price paid by democracy is too high if entire populations are deemed unredeemable.

South Tyrol may prove a counter-example (Haimann, 2018) showing the way for some policy suggestions. As rural areas are faced with compounding problems and are less reliably equipped to face future challenges, structural issues need to be addressed, and they pertain to infrastructure including functioning roads, public communication, high-speed internet, schools, health-care providers, and shopping opportunities. The depopulation of rural areas can only be stopped by investing in the future of rural communities.

Cultural representations matter even more in an increasingly media-driven world. Deliberately distorting information, especially on social media networks, can have extremely deleterious effects on the political education of the population. These problems need to be addressed without endangering civil liberties.

Conclusions

To a certain degree, the urban/rural division is fueled by the above-mentioned perception that rural areas are increasingly urbanized, or, in other words, colonized by urban paradigms of both development and culture. That is not to say that rural areas shun development and modernization – but there is a sense of having lost sovereignty over one's own fate, leading to a politics of resentment (cf. Engels, 2015). This is reflected in political discourse and has led to clear differences in voting patterns between densely populated urban areas and rural and suburban areas (Scala and Johnson, 2017; Hochschild, 2016; Haidt, 2012).

Such a divide can only be overcome once its cultural roots have been better understood. What I have been arguing is the following: rather than merely consider measurable parameters such as rural development, access to services, etc. – which are all important in their own right – it is important to consider the very notion of development itself as something that is being perceived as a colonizing tool. More development, in the sense of reshaping the rural as quasi-urban, may contribute to more political dissonance, not less.

Cultural studies, especially postcolonial studies, has long addressed the problem of colonialism as not principally a problem of a lack of development but as a lack of participation and recognition (Honneth, 1996; Appiah *et al.*, 1994). It has also stressed the narrative elements of nationhood (Bhabha, 2013). Gayatri Spivak's famous question "Can the Subaltern Speak?" (Spivak, 1988) already addressed a rural/urban divide, albeit in India. "Can the Rural Speak?" might as well be asked. Is the rural allowed to speak, to participate in shaping its own destiny? More importantly, does the city listen?

References

Angelo, H., Wachsmuth, D., 2015. *Urbanizing urban political ecology: A critique of methodological cityism.* International Journal of Urban and Regional Research 39(1), 16–27.

Appadurai, A., 2017. *Democracy fatigue*, in: Geiselberger, H, *The Great Regression*. Polity Press, London, 1–12.

Appiah, K.A., Taylor, C., Habermas, J., Rockefeller, S.C., Walzer, M., Wolf, S., 1994. *Multiculturalism.* Princeton University Press, Princeton, NJ.

Bauman, Z., 2013. *Liquid modernity*. John Wiley & Sons, Hoboken, NJ.

Berman, M., 1982. *All that is solid melts into air: The experience of modernity*. Verso, New York.

Bhabha, H.K., 2013. *Nation and narration*. Routledge, Abingdon.

Brenner, N., Schmid, C., 2014. *The "urban age" in question.* International Journal of Urban and Regional Research 38(3), 731–755.

Brownstein, R., 2017. *Putin and the Populists: The Roots of Russia's political appeal in Europe and the United States.* The Atlantic, January. www.theatlantic.com/international/archive/2017/01/putin-trump-le-pen-hungary-france-populist-bannon/512303/.

Burke, E., 1757. *A philosophical enquiry into the origin of our ideas of the sublime and beautiful.* R. and J. Dodsley, London.

Carson, R., 1962. *Silent spring.* Houghton Mifflin, Boston, MA.

Danforth, S., 1670. *A brief recognition of New England's errand into wilderness.* Printed by S.G. and M.F., Cambrdige, MA.

Denevan, W.M., 1992. *The pristine myth: The landscape of the Americas in 1492.* Annals of the Association of American Geographers 82(3), 369–385.

Emerson, R.W., 1836, *Nature.* James Munroe and Company, Boston, MA.

Engels, F., Morgan, L.H., 1978 (1884). *The origin of the family, private property and the state.* Foreign Languages Publishing House, Moscow.

Engels, J., 2015. *The politics of resentment: A genealogy.* Penn State University Press, University Park, PA.

Frank, T., 2004. *What's the matter with Kansas?: How conservatives won the heart of America.* Henry Holt, New York.

Friedmann, J., 1996. *Modular cities: Beyond the rural–urban divide.* Environment and Urbanization 8(1), 129–131.

Geiselberger, H., 2017. *The great regression.* Polity Press, London.

Ghose, R., 2004. *Big sky or big sprawl? Rural gentrification and the changing cultural landscape of Missoula, Montana.* Urban Geography 25(6), 528–549.

Gilroy, P., 2014. *Lecture I. Suffering and Infrahumanity; Lecture II. Humanities and a New Humanism.* The Tanner Lectures on Human Values, Yale University, New Haven CT, February 21.

Glaeser, E.L., Tobio, K., 2007. *The rise of the sunbelt.* No. w13071. National Bureau of Economic Research.

Haidt, J., 2012. *The righteous mind: Why good people are divided by politics and religion.* Vintage, New York.

Haimann, R., 2018. *Seit 1972 konnten wir verhindern, dass auch nur ein Dorf sterben musste.* Die Welt. www.welt.de/finanzen/immobilien/plus176697605/Landflucht-So-rettet-Suedtirol-seine-Doerfer.html (accessed 5.26.18).

Hawthorne, N., 2012 (1835). *Young Goodman Brown.* Simon and Schuster, New York.

Hobbes, T., 1651. *Philosophical rudiments concerning government and society.* n.p., London. First modern edtion: John Bohn, London.

Hochschild, A.R., 2016. *Strangers in their own land: Anger and mourning on the American right.* New Press, New York.

Honneth, A., 1996. *The struggle for recognition: The moral grammar of social conflicts.* MIT Press, Cambridge, MA.

Ikerd, J., 2017. *The economic colonization of rural America: Increasing vulnerability in a volatile world.* Prepared for presentation at the Rural Sociology Society Annual Meeting, Columbus, OH, June 23–27. http://web.missouri.edu/ikerdj/papers/OhioRSSConference2017.pdf.

Jefferson, T., 1802. *Notes on the state of Virginia, with an appendix.* H. Sprague, New York.

Lefebvre, H., 1974. *La production de l'espace.* Anthropos, Paris.

Locke, J. 1689. *Two treatises on civil government.* Churchill, London.

Lyotard, J.F., 1984. *The postmodern condition: A report on knowledge* (Vol. 10). University of Minnesota Press, Minneapolis, MN.

Mann, C.C., 2005. *1491: New revelations of the Americas before Columbus.* Alfred A. Knopf, New York.

Marx, K., Engels, F., 1978 (1848). *The communist manifesto,* in: Tucker, R.C. (Ed.). *The Marx-Engels Reader,* 2nd edition. W.W. Norton, New York, pp. 469–500.

Marx, L., 1964. *The machine in the garden: Technology and the pastoral ideal in America.* Oxford University Press, New York.

McKenna, M.L., McAtee, S., Bryan, P.E., Jeun, R., Ward, T., Kraus, J., Bottazzi, M.E., Hotez, P.J., Flowers, C.C., Mejia, R., 2017. *Human intestinal parasite burden and poor sanitation in rural Alabama.* The American Journal of Tropical Medicine and Hygiene 97(5), 1623–1628.

Melville, H., 2002 (1851). *Moby-Dick,* ed. Hershel Parker and Harrison Hayford. Norton and Company, New York.

Miller, P., 2009. *Errand into the wilderness.* Harvard University Press, Cambridge, MA.

More, T., 1516. *Libellus vere aureus, nec minus salutaris quam festivus, de optimo rei publicae statu deque nova insula Utopia.* More, London.

Morgan, L.H., 1877. *Ancient society; or, researches in the lines of human progress from savagery, through barbarism to civilization*. H. Holt, New York.

Noack, R., 2017. *The European parties accused of being influenced by Russia*. The Washington Post, November 17. www.washingtonpost.com/news/worldviews/wp/2017/11/17/the-european-parties-accused-of-being-influenced-by-russia/?utm_term=.ce03c3dca182.

Nye, D.E., 1996. *American technological sublime*. MIT Press, Cambridge, MA.

Polyakova, A., 2016. *Why Europe is right to fear Putin's useful idiots*. Foreign Policy, February 23. http://foreignpolicy.com/2016/02/23/why-europe-is-right-to-fear-putins-useful-idiots/.

Porcius, C.M., 160 BCE. *De agri cultura. On Agriculture*.

Rousseau, J.J., 1964 (1755). *Discours sur l'origine et les fondements de l'inégalité parmi les hommes*, in: *Œuvres complètes*. Gallimard, Paris, vol. 3, p. 161.

Scala, D.J., Johnson, K.M., 2017. *Political polarization along the rural–urban continuum? The geography of the presidential vote, 2000–2016*. The ANNALS of the American Academy of Political and Social Science 672(1), 162–184.

Scott, A., Gilbert, A., Gelan, A., 2007. *The urban–rural divide: Myth or reality?*. Macaulay Institute, Aberdeen.

Searle, J.R., 1995. *The construction of social reality*. Simon and Schuster, New York.

Smith, N., 2002. *New globalism, new urbanism: Gentrification as global urban strategy*. Antipode 34(3), 427–450.

Snyder, T. 2018. *America lost a cyberwar to Russia in 2016: When will we have truth?* The Guardian, February 12. www.theguardian.com/commentisfree/2018/feb/12/america-cyberwar-russia-2016-memo-truth.

Soja, E.W., 1999. *In different spaces: The cultural turn in urban and regional political economy*. European Planning Studies 7(1), 65–75.

Soja, E.W., 2016. *Regional urbanization and the end of the metropolis era*, in: Nello, O., Mele, R. (Eds.), *Cities in the 21st century*. Routledge, London, pp. 41–56.

Spivak, G.C., 1988. *Can the subaltern speak?*, in: Morris, R.C. (Ed.), *Can the subaltern speak? Reflections on the history of an idea*. Columbia University Press, New York, pp. 21–78.

Thoreau, H.D., 1971 (1854). *Walden*. Princeton University Press, Princeton, NJ.

United Nations Department of Economic and Social Affairs, 2015. *Definitions of Policy Variables*, in: *World Population Policies 2015*. https://esa.un.org/poppolicy/img/Definitions_Policy_Variables.pdf (accessed 9.7.17).

PART III

Resources and environment

17

ENVIRONMENTAL POLICY

What are the options?

John Devlin and Brennan Chapman Lowery

Introduction

Rural regions hold the stock of environmental resources and host the majority of environmental services. They also suffer the depletion of environmental resources through extraction activities leading to consequences such as deforestation, soil erosion, and biodiversity decline. Rural regions are subject to downstream effects from industrial and urban activity such as water pollution, falling water tables, and local air pollution. Rural areas are also vulnerable to specific kinds of climate change impacts and contribute to greenhouse gas emissions in different ways than cities, such as through greater personal vehicle dependence and the presence of high-emitting sectors like agriculture. Environmental policies might target specific rural causes and impacts, but many environmental policies affect both rural and urban areas and communities. Furthermore, the role of the state in crafting and enforcing environmental policy tools often implies that policies must be equally applicable to rural and urban areas.

This chapter reviews environmental policy options beginning with a discussion of high-level environmental policy goals: conservation, sustainable development, and environmental justice. The second section surveys the policy instruments available to environmental policy-makers and the third exemplifies these by reviewing sample international and national climate change policies. The chapter ends with some conclusions about the range of environmental problems faced in rural areas, the potential for effective policy responses, and some suggestions for policy research.

Environmental policy goals

Early environmental policy in the North American context focused on conservation and the protection of wilderness and wildlife (Leopold, 1949). Conservation management set aside parks and reserves and employed the concept of maximum sustainable yield to identify how much of a renewable resource could be harvested (Tsikliras and Froese, 2019). Rachel Carson (1962) drew international attention to biodiversity decline resulting from new chemical technologies and their pollution of air and water systems. Later, Hardin (1968) offered a theoretical frame for environmental policy by suggesting that either state management or private ownership were required to achieve effective resource management and avoid the tragedy of the commons created by a laissez-faire approach to the exploitation or pollution of shared natural resources. This policy orientation informed natural resource management actions in areas such as fisheries and grasslands, which tended to view rural resource users as shortsighted exploiters whose actions would inevitably lead to depletion without intervention by either state or market institutions.

The First Earth Day was celebrated in 1970. In 1972 the Club of Rome's *Limits to Growth* and the global oil crisis called into question the sustainability of the prevailing economic development pattern (Meadows *et al.*, 1972; Mebratu, 1998). In 1980 the International Union for the Conservation of Nature introduced the term "sustainable development" (IUCN, 1980). The concept was later popularized by the World Commission on Environment and Development (WCED) in 1987, which suggested it was possible to have "development that meets the needs of the present without compromising the ability of future generations to meet their own needs" (WCED, 1987, p. 43). This seminal report tried to reconcile environmental protection with human development, with a particular focus on poverty eradication (WCED, 1987). Considering that roughly 70 percent of people in poverty in the Global South continue to live in rural areas (Dasgupta *et al.*, 2014), the linking of environmental and human development goals remains a salient rural policy priority.

In 1992, the United Nations Conference on Environment and Development (or Earth Summit) released Agenda 21, a global call to action to implement sustainable development (UNCED, 1992). By aspiring for a long-term balance between environmental, economic, and social outcomes, sustainable development remains the most widely accepted environmental policy goal. Evidence of the abiding attraction of the concept is indicated by the adoption in 2015 of the Sustainable Development Goals (SDGs) (United Nations General Assembly, 2015). This framework sets out 17 goals, 169 targets, and over 240 indicators which have been accepted by 193 countries (Biermann *et al.*, 2017). However, this range of goals, targets, and indicators also reflects significant disagreement about how sustainable development (SD) should be interpreted (Lele, 1991; Devlin and Yap, 1994; Dobson, 1996; Carruthers, 2001; Daly and Farley, 2004; Du Pisani, 2006). The strong sustainability interpretation maintains that essential stocks of natural capital (e.g. clean air, forests, biodiversity) should not be depleted for the sake of growing financial or built capital (Serageldin, 1996). This position is countered by the concept of weak sustainability, which accepts such substitutions and suggests optimistically that environmental modernization will achieve SD through technological change and market strategies such as the payment for ecological services (Dietz and Neumayer, 2007). This interpretive issue remains the subject of heated debate.

In the wake of the wide acceptance of SD, the key distributional issue of environmental justice (EJ) has emerged as an independent environmental policy goal. Concern over EJ arose in response to the uneven distribution of environmental costs which tend to hurt weaker and marginalized, often rural, communities more severely than privileged groups. The location of chemical plants, incinerators, sewage treatment plants, landfills, and other environmentally impactful industries has had disproportionate effects on low-income and often minority communities in terms of public health and neighborhood deterioration. EJ has expanded from an initial focus on inner-city neighborhoods to examine distributional environmental harms in other contexts such as rural areas. For example, Indigenous communities have been adversely affected by uranium mining in remote parts of the southwestern United States (Voyles, 2015), and rural communities in the Niger Delta have been negatively affected by oil extraction activities (Obi, 2009). EJ includes the impact of extreme weather events on poorer communities, most importantly in the Global South (Baber and Bartlett, 2007; Thorp, 2014). EJ also engages with the SD debate over concerns with intergenerational impacts and intergenerational equity (Forrest and Lawrence, 2018).

Environmental policy instruments

In order to pursue these abstract goals, national governments cannot act alone in creating environmental policy. Multi-level governance recognizes a policy role for international, national, sub-national, and local public authorities (Bache *et al.*, 2017; Mavrot and Sager, 2018). Multi-stakeholder governance goes even further by recognizing the role of private and civil society actors in making and implementing policy (Peters and Pierre, 2016). These actor assemblages are argued to be more effective for managing diverse systems across territorially heterogeneous areas (Hooghe and Marks, 2003). Collaborative governance highlights the potential for state and non-state actors to work together to provide novel public policy solutions to challenges that have vexed unilateral state action (Ansell and Gash, 2008). These challenges persist in areas such as watershed governance, which rural residents depend on for food security and economic livelihoods, requiring that these values be considered alongside conservation goals by including local civil society organizations in management decisions (Vodden, 2015). Often it is difficult for government agencies to cede partial control to nongovernmental bodies in arrangements such as co-management of fisheries resources in which fishers actively participate in decision-making about the resource (Chuenpagdee and Jentoft, 2007). These dynamics can be heightened when resource users are located in remote areas that are geographically and socio-economically removed from centers of formal authority located in large cities.

Despite the range of potential participants in environmental governance, public authorities remain the central actors in translating environmental policy goals into operational programs. Such programs are built using a variety of policy instruments, for which several typologies have been suggested. Table 17.1 presents the main typologies that have been proposed for classifying such policy instruments.

Considering these typologies, a basic set of core policy instruments can be identified: regulation, spending, taxation, and organization. The instruments of symbolism and laissez-faire need to be added to capture much of what is offered as policy in the environmental policy debate. These typologies can all subsume a wide range of more specific instruments which a given program may combine in many ways to achieve outcomes consistent with conservation, sustainability, and environmental justice goals.

Over the last few decades, particular attention has been given to economic instruments which combine regulation, taxation, spending, and organization with a degree of laissez-faire.

Table 17.1 Typologies of policy instruments

Source	More laissez-faire						More coercive
Lowi (1972)	Constituent		Regulatory		Redistributive	Distributive	
Doern and Phidd (1983)	Self-regulation	Expenditure		Regulation (incl. taxation)	Exhortation	Public ownership	
Hood (1986)	Information		Finance		Organization	Authority	
Linder and Peters (1989)	Contract	Subsidy	Tax	Regulation	Authority	Exhortation	Direct provision
Sterner and Coria (2013)	Informational policies	Tradable permits	Spending	Taxes	Property rights	Legal instruments	Regulation
Cochran and Malone (2014)	Promotional		Regulatory		Redistributive		

Economic instruments are considered by some to be more efficient because they rely on self-interest to shape behavior. However, Damon and Sterner (2012) suggest that a focus on efficiency does not address political feasibility or the distribution of costs. Linder and Peters (1990, p. 47) argue that, while governments may consider resource intensiveness in selecting or designing policies, they must also pay attention to targeting capacity, political risk, and ideological constraints. Arguments for these market-based instruments also tend to overlook social justice considerations such as the equitable distribution of benefits or the exacerbation of inequities in access to resources or exposure to risks. To provide some examples, the next section reviews climate change policies in several OECD countries.

Climate change policy

There have been an impressive series of international meetings and agreements on climate change. The First World Climate Conference took place in 1979. In 1988 the first UN General Assembly Resolution on climate change was passed and the Intergovernmental Panel on Climate Change (IPCC) was established. Over the next three decades, UN bodies reconvened numerous times and attempted several forms of multilateral agreements to curb greenhouse gas (GHG) emissions. This action culminated with the 2015 Paris Accord, in which 195 countries committed to limit global warming to 2° C above pre-industrial levels (UNFCCC, 2015). Table 17.2 shows the progression of international climate change accords to date.

These accords suggest sustained intergovernmental concern about climate change but, despite their complexity, constitute primarily symbolic policy-making. Globally, there are still no binding regulatory or taxation programs to curb climate change. Neither the Kyoto Protocol nor the Paris Accord generated binding international rules. The Paris Agreement only requires signatories to set national targets and report on their progress, omitting any enforcement mechanisms (Parker *et al.*, 2017). While the cost of meetings and the funding of IPCC research and publications represent some expenditures and organizational efforts, international climate change policy is primarily symbolic and laissez-faire. National governments are left to make their own decisions with little other than moral pressure to create effective programs. Additionally, the climate justice principle of "common but differentiated responsibilities" between the Global North and South remains contentious and unresolved (McCauley and Heffron, 2018).

Table 17.2 Timeline of international climate change accords

1979	First World Climate Conference
1988	Creation of IPCC
1990	Second World Climate Conference; first IPCC Assessment Report
1992	Earth Summit, adoption of Climate Change Convention
1996	Second IPCC Assessment Report
1997	Kyoto Protocol initiated
2000	Third IPCC Assessment Report
2004	Kyoto Protocol ratified
2005	Kyoto Protocol enters into force
2007	Fourth IPCC Assessment Report
2009	Copenhagen Convention
2012	Kyoto Protocol ends
2015	Paris Agreement Signed

Climate change policy in different contexts

European Union

European Union (EU) programs that do move beyond symbolic policy can be found in many other jurisdictions and exemplify some of the programmatic options available. The EU was an early climate leader, exhorting member countries to adopt climate change policy and signing all symbolic international agreements. Today, the EU continues to set ambitious targets in its strategic long-term vision (European Commission, 2018). The centerpiece of the bloc's climate policy has been the EU Emissions Trading Scheme (EU ETS), initiated in 2005. The EU ETS sets and allocates emissions targets across member states, creates emission certificates, and regulates the emissions market (Spencer and Fazekas, 2013). The program operates in all member states plus Iceland, Liechtenstein, and Norway; it covers about 11,000 GHG-emitting operations and about 45 percent of the jurisdiction's emissions (Narassimhan *et al.*, 2018). Emissions allowances were initially distributed without charge based on historical emissions reported by affected operations. Later iterations have introduced an auction for allowances. About US $17 billion was earned in auctions between 2012 and 2016 (Narassimhan *et al.*, 2018). This "cap-and-trade" approach combines regulatory, spending, and organizational instruments while leaving substantial space for laissez-faire decision-making by national governments and affected entities. By 2017 similar programs had been taken up in 20 national or sub-national jurisdictions (Haites *et al.*, 2018). However, in the EU an initial oversupply of allowances set a weak "cap", hampering the effectiveness of the system (Narassimhan *et al.*, 2018). In 2017 the effective price of carbon per tonne in the EU ETS was only US $6, while the highest price per tonne under an emissions trading system has been reported in Alberta, Canada at $24 (Haites *et al.*, 2018, p. 4). Another example from an EU member state which uses taxation is Italy's Landfill Tax and Waste Management Tariffs (Antonioli *et al.*, 2014), which are designed to reduce GHGs other than CO_2, such as methane.

Sweden

Sweden exemplifies how carbon taxes are another approach for putting a price on carbon. The country has been a carbon tax leader, initially introducing a carbon tax in 1991 and gradually increasing it since (Government of Sweden, 2018). In 2017 the Swedish tax per tonne of carbon was $140 (Haites *et al.*, 2018, p. 4). The tax helps to reduce emissions not included in the EU ETS and the tax level is proportionate to the amount of net CO_2 in the fuel, which makes biofuels exempt from this tax (Ministry of the Environment and Energy, 2017). Sweden has among the lowest GHG emissions per capita among OECD countries at 3.8 tonnes per capita (OECD, 2018). However, Sweden also has an energy tax which was first introduced in 1924. This energy tax also supports renewability and energy efficiency targets (Ministry of the Environment and Energy, 2017). As of 2017, 20 other jurisdictions have introduced a carbon tax, but the Swedish carbon tax is substantially higher than in any other jurisdiction (Haites *et al.*, 2018). Notably, despite this high price for carbon the Swedish economy remains robust (Pierrehumbert, 2016).

Spain

Spain has used the spending instrument to generate financial incentives (Zane, 2013). For example, the Environmental Promotion Plan for hotel sectors – PIMA SOL – purchases direct

GHG reduction from hotels through energy-related renovations projects (Gobierno de España, 2015). The Spanish government also spends in the agricultural sector to encourage more efficient vehicles through the PIMA TIERRA Plan to renew old tractors. The more efficient the tractor, the greater the financial incentives available (Gobierno de España, 2015). The government also subsidizes people who renovate their windows, use a more efficient lighting system, or install efficient air conditioning systems (Zane, 2013).

Germany

Germany has pioneered the regulatory instrument of feed-in-tariffs (FIT) for renewable energy. Beginning in 1990, the Feed-In Law required utilities to buy electricity from all renewable energy generators at fixed rates. Between 1990 and 2000, wind power increased by a factor of almost 100, growing from 68 MW to over 6000. In 1999, the new Social Democratic and Green Party alliance introduced the Renewable Energy Law which made several FIT improvements. Rates were fixed for 20 years giving investors long-term planning reliability, and there were different tariffs depending on the renewable energy source and size and location of the energy plant. The new rates tremendously increased the premium for solar energy. While solar energy produced only 1 GWh electricity in 1990, by 2017 some 40,000 GWh were produced (Wirth and Schneider, 2018). Despite its success, the German FIT has come under steady pressure from large energy suppliers and the European Commission, who wished to promote the energy auctions and emissions trading system. Although in 2001 the European Court of Justice decided that feed-in laws did not constitute state-aid, by 2016 pressure from the European Commission has led to a substantial reduction of the FIT program (Leiren and Reimer, 2018).

Canada

Canada is currently experimenting with a carbon tax. The Pan-Canadian Framework on Clean Growth and Climate Change (Government of Canada, 2017) introduced a federal carbon pricing benchmark in 2016 (Maciunas and Saint-Geniès, 2018). Although the pricing benchmark was nationally mandated, the specifics of carbon pricing have been left to each province and territory, which were required to submit provincial carbon pricing plans by 2018. Each jurisdiction was left with the choice of a price-based measure (e.g. a tax of at least CAD \$10/tonne of carbon emitted across all sectors) or a cap-and-trade system. There is also an implicit regulatory element in that the provinces which fail to meet the federal benchmark will be required to adopt a federal pricing backstop, or counter-measure to discourage provinces from non-compliance (Maciunas and Saint-Geniès, 2018). This backstop will consist of a levy on fossil fuel industries and a tax on industrial emitters above a particular threshold (Department of Environment and Climate Change Canada, 2017). This program has met with resistance from several provinces, including Manitoba, Saskatchewan, New Brunswick, and Ontario, whose conservative governments have refused to adopt a provincial carbon pricing plan (Lum, 2018). At this point, it is unclear how Ottawa will be able to enforce the backstop against these provinces and enforce taxation on the politically powerful oil and gas sector. It has also not been discussed how rural residents who commute long distances to work due to distressed local economies – such as in the Atlantic provinces recovering from fisheries moratoria – will be considered in the application of the carbon tax on fuel.

United States

The United States has perhaps the most politicized climate change policy context of any juris-diction examined here. Among the OECD countries, only the US refused to ratify the Kyoto Protocol, and Washington has invited recent ire from the international community for the Trump administration's withdrawal from the Paris Agreement. Nonetheless, the US offers an example of a sustained regulatory program targeting vehicle efficiency standards. Transportation accounts for over 28 percent of overall GHG emissions in the US, with over half of these emis-sions coming from passenger vehicles and light-duty trucks (EPA, 2018). This figure reflects the staggering level of private vehicle dependence which affects rural and urban parts of the country alike. Long before climate change was a political issue in the US, transportation-related emis-sions began to be regulated in 1963 under the Clean Air Act (US Code, 1963), which, since its foundation in 1970, gave the Environmental Protection Agency the authority to regulate vehic-ular pollution (EPA, 1970). In 1975, Congress passed the Corporate Average Fuel Economy (CAFE) standards, entrusting the Department of Transportation with enforcement (US DOT, 2011). In 1977, the Carter administration introduced additional measures including a tax on inefficient vehicles and a rebate for purchases of high-efficiency cars (Milton, 1977). These standards rose gradually from 18 miles per gallon (MPG) for passenger cars in 1978 to 32.7 MPG in 2016 (US DOT, 2011; NHTSA, 2018). This regulatory approach has been sustained despite partisan shifts in Washington. The Obama administration proposed a ramp up of efficiency standards to an ambitious 54 MPG by 2025. However, the Trump administration proposes to freeze CAFE standards at 37 MPG and forbid states such as California from setting higher stand-ards for fuel economy (Davenport, 2018).

Mexico

Mexico has a unique climate change policy context in its response to short-lived climate pol-lutants. The country emits a large amount of black carbon, a particulate pollutant emitted by the incomplete burning of fossil fuels such as diesel and coal (Ramanathan and Carmichael, 2008). Black carbon poses serious threats to public health in urban and rural areas alike, such as cardiovascular disease and lung cancer, and contributes to climate change and localized warming (UNFCCC, 2015). In its Paris Accord commitments, Mexico vowed to reduce black carbon emissions by 51 percent by 2030 (UNFCCC, 2015). These reductions would help the country bring its particulate matter emissions closer to World Health Organization standards, which national regulatory standards currently do not meet (Altamirano *et al.*, 2016). Mexico has had comprehensive climate change legislation since 2012 through its General Law on Climate Change. However, this document does not mention black carbon or short-lived climate pollutants (Government of Mexico, 2012). Mexico has shown a symbolic commit-ment to improving industrial efficiency standards by endorsing the North American Leaders Summit declaration in 2016 (US International Trade Administration, 2016). Within this dec-laration, each North American government endorsed the adoption of voluntary ISO energy standards in industry (Altamirano *et al.*, 2016). Although these measures are largely symbolic and based on voluntary measures, spending has occurred at the municipal level in cities such as Mexico City and Guadalajara to reduce vehicle emissions by investing in the moderniza-tion of public transit infrastructure, thereby reducing GHGs and black carbon emissions (Altamirano *et al.*, 2016). Unfortunately, the prevalence of organic carbon – which occurs disproportionately in rural areas through biomass burning for domestic use – has not been addressed by these measures (Altamirano *et al.*, 2016).

This brief review of some climate change programs demonstrates the wide range of options available to policy-makers. Many of the initiatives reviewed are purely symbolic, as well as showing a strong element of laissez-faire, reflecting the continuing reluctance of public authorities to mandate behavioral change. The result is that overall climate change policy is failing on a global level. The instruments used have not been equal to the task. In 2018 the International Energy Agency reported that if all commitments made in relation to the 2015 Paris Agreement were met there would still be an increase in energy demand of 25 percent over 2017 levels by 2040 (IEA, 2018). Furthermore, the IPCC's most recent report estimates that even if the global emissions commitments under the Paris Agreement are met, global GHG emissions in 2030 would not limit global warming to 1.5° C. To avoid levels above this target will require global CO_2 emissions to start to decline well before 2030 (IPCC, 2018, p. 24).

These grim figures highlight that much more effective climate change programs are required. They also highlight the inherent limitations of global agreements due to the anarchic nature of the international system under the primacy of national sovereignty. With no effective mechanism to coerce national governments to enforce climate change commitments – even the relatively strong ones adopted within the Paris Agreement – many states will fail to act in the best interest of their citizens and planetary survival.

The resulting impacts have cross-cutting implications for all geographies, but will also affect rural areas in specific ways. The IPCC in 2014 identified impacts such as greater vulnerability for rain-fed agriculture, small-scale farms, resource-based livelihoods such as pastoralism and small-scale fisheries, and potential long-term declines in staple crop yields as only a few of the changes that rural areas can expect. Environmental conflict and migration, including the incidence of environmental refugees, are also projected to increase as a result of climate change, as well as disproportionately high impacts on women (Dasgupta *et al.*, 2014). Governments must consider the appropriateness of both mitigation and adaptation policies for rural areas, considering factors such as the vulnerabilities highlighted above and rural-specific emissions sources that must be addressed in unique ways. For example, private vehicle dependence in rural North America cannot be reduced by applying urban strategies for multi-modal transit wholesale, but other models for car-sharing and mobile service delivery can be explored to develop appropriate solutions to reduce vehicle use. Rural areas may also hold tremendous assets for renewable energy production due to the availability of open space where solar, wind, or bio-based energy can be harnessed and the ability for off-grid communities to convert from dirty sources such as diesel to renewables. National and local governments must work with partners in civil society and the private sector to explore such solutions and craft appropriate policy measures using the right mix of instruments for the problem at hand.

Conclusions

Climate change is only one example of a long list of environmental problems affecting rural and urban areas alike, ranging from particulate pollution to deforestation. Every one of these issues presents policy-makers with a conflicted terrain of environmental, social, and economic interests which makes the design and implementation of effective policy extremely difficult. Furthermore, many environmental problems have specific causes and impacts related to rural areas that must be addressed in context, as noted with climate change. Nonetheless, there are examples where such conflicts have been overcome. In 1987 the international community effectively responded to an environmental threat with the Montreal Protocol, which banned chlorofluorocarbons (CFCs) to preserve the threatened ozone layer (DeSombre, 2000). In this case, national governments mobilized the necessary regulatory programs. Another example outside the environmental policy space was the creation of the Trade Disputes Settlement Mechanism under the World Trade Organization. In this case, governments have given up autonomy to an international adjudication body whose judgements are binding on national governments and whose decisions have resulted in significant sanctions (Li, 2018). Such rare agreements indicate that effective policy instruments are available. What is missing for effective environmental policy is agreement on the interpretation of goals and the distribution of costs. The principle of common but differentiated responsibilities within global climate change negotiations highlights these distributional issues, necessitating greater onus on the part of high-emitting countries and their most GHG-intensive sectors. In the Global North, rural areas are both implicated in these justice issues through the high-emitting nature of industrialized agriculture and ill-served by local mitigation strategies designed for cities. Both international coordination to push states to adopt binding environmental policies and local efforts to rural-proof such measures are needed.

The environmental policy research agenda should adopt a positive deviance approach by seeking to identify cases of success at international, national, and sub-national levels and determine how these policies have been reached and sustained (Herington and van de Fliert, 2018). It is also important for policy analysts to explain why so many environmental problems continue to be unresolved and question the contemporary approach that espouses the retreat of the state in favor of laissez-faire approaches. Instead of advocating this retrenchment, environmental policy research should further examine multi-level and multi-stakeholder governance arrangements that demonstrate effective coordination between international, national, and local policy arenas with an emphasis on the best use of available instruments to suit the problem at hand and to fit the rural context. Conservation, sustainable development, and environmental justice remain at the center of the environmental policy agenda. A wide range of effective policy instruments are available. The effective employment of these options must go hand in hand with the generation of multi-stakeholder consensus and the acknowledgment of limitations to both national and international authority to provide the necessary policy leadership.

References

Altamirano, J.C., Sanchez, E.O., Rissman, J., Ross, K., Fransen, T., Sola, C.B., and Martinez, J., 2016. *Achieving Mexico's climate goals: An eight-point action plan.* World Resources Institute. https://energy innovation.org/wp-content/uploads/2016/11/WRI_OCN_Mexico_final.pdf.

Ansell, C., Gash, A., 2008. *Collaborative governance in theory and practice.* Journal of Public Administration Research and Theory 18(4), 543–571. DOI: 10.1093/jopart/mum032.

Antonioli, D., Borghesi, S., D'Amato, A., Gilli, M., Mazzanti, M., Nicolli, F., 2014. *Analysing the interactions of energy and climate policies in a broad policy "optimality" framework: The Italian case study.* Journal of Integrative Environmental Sciences 11(3–4), 205–224.

Baber, W.F., Bartlett, R.V., 2007. *Problematic participants in deliberative democracy: Experts, social movements, and environmental justice.* International Journal of Public Administration 30(1), 5–22.

Bache, I., Bartle, I., Flinders, M., 2017. *Multi-level governance,* in: Ansell, C., Torfing, J. (Eds.), *Handbook on theories of governance.* Edward Elgar, Cheltenham, pp. 486–498.

Biermann, F., Kanie, N., Kim, R.E., 2017. *Global governance by goal-setting: The novel approach of the UN Sustainable Development Goals.* Current Opinion in Environmental Sustainability. Elsevier, Amsterdam. DOI: 10.1016/j.cosust.2017.01.010.

Carruthers, D., 2001. *From opposition to orthodoxy: The remaking of sustainable development.* Journal of Third World Studies 18(2), 93–112.

Carson, R., 1962. *Silent spring.* Houghton Mifflin, New York.

Chuenpagdee, R., Jentoft, S., 2007. *Step zero for fisheries co-management: What precedes implementation.* Marine Policy 31(6), 657–668. DOI: 10.1016/j.marpol.2007.03.013.

Daly, H.E., Farley, J., 2004. *Ecological economics: Principles and applications.* Island Press, Washington, DC.

Damon, M., Sterner, T., 2012. *Policy instruments for sustainable development at Rio+ 20.* The Journal of Environment and Development 21(2), 143–151.

Dasgupta, P., Morton, J.F., Dodman, D., Karapinar, B., Meza, F., Rivera-Ferre, M.G., Toure Sarr, A., Vincent, K.E., 2014. *Rural areas,* in: Field, C.B., Barros, V.R., Dokken, D.J., Mach, K.J., Mastrandrea, M.D., Bilir, T.E., Chatterjee, M., Ebi, K.L., Estrada, Y.O., Genova, R.C., Girma, B., Kissel, E.S., Levy, A.N., MacCracken, S., Mastrandrea, P.R., White, L.L. (Eds.), *Climate Change 2014: Impacts, adaptation, and vulnerability. Part A: Global and sectoral aspects. Contribution of Working Group II to the Fifth Assessment Report of the Intergovernmental Panel on Climate Change.* Cambridge University Press, Cambridge; New York, pp. 613–657.

Davenport, C., 2018. *Trump administration unveils its plan to relax car pollution rules.* The New York Times, August 2. www.nytimes.com/2018/08/02/climate/trump-auto-emissions-california.html.

Department of Environment and Climate Change Canada, 2017. *Technical paper: Federal carbon pricing backstop.* www.canada.ca/en/services/environment/weather/climatechange/technical-paper-federal-carbon-pricing-backstop.html.

DeSombre, E.R., 2000. *Experience of the Montreal Protocol: Particularly remarkable, and remarkably particular.* UCLA Journal of Environmental Law and Policy 19(1), 49–81.

Devlin, J.F., Yap, N.T., 1994. *Sustainable development and the NICS: Cautionary tales for the South in the New World (Dis) Order.* Third World Quarterly 15(1), 49–62.

Dietz, S., Neumayer, E., 2007. *Weak and strong sustainability in the SEEA: Concepts and measurement.* Ecological Economics 61(4), 617–626. DOI: 10.1016/j.ecolecon.2006.09.007.

Dobson, A., 1996. *Environment sustainabilities: An analysis and a typology.* Environmental Politics 5(3), 401–428. DOI:10.1080/09644019608414280.

Du Pisani, J.A., 2006. *Sustainable development: Historical roots of the concept.* Environmental Sciences 3(2), pp. 83–96. DOI: 10.1080/15693430600688831.

EPA – Environmental Protection Agency, 1970. *Reorganization plan No. 3 of 1970. July 9. Special message from the president to the Congress about reorganization plans to establish the Environmental Protection Agency and the National Oceanic and Atmospheric Administration.* https://archive.epa.gov/epa/aboutepa/reorganization-plan-no-3-1970.html.

EPA – Environmental Protection Agency, 2018. *Sources of greenhouse gas emissions.* www.epa.gov/ghgemissions/sources-greenhouse-gas-emissions.

European Commission, 2018. *Communication from the Commission to the European Parliament, the European Council, the Council, the European Economic and Social Committee, the Committee of the Regions and the European Investment Bank. A clean planet for all: A European strategic long-term vision for a prosperous, modern, competitive and climate neutral economy.* Brussels, 28.11.2018. Com(2018) 773 Final.

Forrest, H.A., Lawrence, P., 2018. *Intergenerational justice: A framework for addressing intellectual property rights and climate change,* in: Rimmer, M. (Ed.), *Intellectual Property and Clean Energy.* Springer-Verlag, Switzerland, pp. 151–175.

Gobierno de España. 2015. *Environmental policy.* www.lamoncloa.gob.es/lang/en/espana/stpv/spainto-day2015/environment/Paginas/index.aspx.

Government of Canada, 2017. *Pan-Canadian framework on clean growth and climate change.* www.canada.ca/en/services/environment/weather/climatechange/pan-canadian-framework/introduction.html#1_1.

Government of Mexico, 2012. *General law on climate change.* www.lse.ac.uk/GranthamInstitute/law/general-law-on-climate-change/.

Government of Sweden, 2018. *Sweden's carbon tax.* www.government.se/government-policy/taxes-and-tariffs/swedens-carbon-tax/.

Haites, E., Maosheng, D., Gallagher, K.S., Mascher, S., Narassimhan, E., Richards, K.R., Wakabayashi, M., 2018. *Experience with carbon taxes and greenhouse gas emissions trading systems (January 2018).* https://ssrn.com/abstract=3119241.

Hardin, G., 1968. *The tragedy of the commons.* Science 162(3859), 1243–1248.

Herington, M.J., van de Fliert, E., 2018. *Positive deviance in theory and practice: A conceptual review.* Deviant Behavior, 39(5), 664–678.

Hooghe, L., Marks, G., 2003. *Unraveling the central state, but how? Types of multi-level governance.* American Political Science Review 97(2), 233–243. DOI: 10.2307/3118206.

IEA – International Energy Agency. 2018. *World energy outlook 2018.* IEA, Paris.

IPCC, 2018. *Summary for policymakers,* in: Masson-Delmotte, V., Zhai, P., Pörtner, H.O., Roberts, D., Skea, J., Shukla, P.R., Pirani, A., Moufouma-Okia, W., Péan, C., Pidcock, R., Connors, S., Matthews, J.B.R., Chen, Y., Zhou, X., Gomis, M.I., Lonnoy, E., Maycock, T., Tignor, M., Waterfield,

T. (Eds.), *Global warming of 1.5°C: An IPCC special report on the impacts of global warming of 1.5°C above pre-industrial levels and related global greenhouse gas emission pathways, in the context of strengthening the global response to the threat of climate change, sustainable development, and efforts to eradicate poverty.* World Meteorological Organization, Geneva.

IUCN – International Union for the Conservation of Nature, 1980. *World conservation strategy: Living resource conservation for sustainable development.* Gland, Switzerland.

Leiren, M.D., Reimer, I., 2018. *Historical institutionalist perspective on the shift from feed-in tariffs towards auctioning in German renewable energy policy.* Energy Research and Social Science 43, 33–40.

Lele, S.M., 1991. *Sustainable development: A critical review.* World Development 19(6), 607–621.

Leopold, A., 1949. *A Sand County almanac.* Oxford University Press, Oxford.

Li, F., 2018. *The driving forces of the convergence of WTO dispute settlement mechanism and international investment arbitration.* Journal of World Trade 52(3), 479–503.

Linder, S.H., Peters, B.G., 1990. *Research perspectives on the design of public policy: Implementation, formulation and design,* in: Palumbo, D.J., Calista, D.J. (Eds.), *Implementation and the policy process.* Greenwood Press, Westport, CT, pp. 51–66.

Lum, Z.-A., 2018. *Carbon tax rebates coming to provinces that rejected federal plan.* The Huffington Post, October 23. www.huffingtonpost.ca/2018/10/23/carbon-tax-rebates-canada_a_23569556/.

Maciunas, S., Saint-Geniès, G. de L., 2018. *The evolution of Canada's international and domestic climate policy: From divergence to consistency?* Canada in International Law at 150 and Beyond No. 21. www.cigionline.org/publications/evolution-canadas-international-and-domestic-climate-policy-divergence-consistency.

Mavrot, C., Sager, F., 2018. *Vertical epistemic communities in multilevel governance.* Policy and Politics 46(3), 391–407.

McCauley, D., Heffron, R., 2018. *Just transition: Integrating climate, energy and environmental justice.* Energy Policy 119 (August), 1–7. https://doi.org/10.1016/j.enpol.2018.04.014.

Meadows, D.H., Meadows, D.L., Randers, J.B., 1972. *The limits to growth: A report for the Club of Rome's Project on the Predicament of Mankind.* Universe Books, New York.

Mebratu, D., 1998. *Sustainability and sustainable development: Historical and conceptual review.* Environmental Impact Assessment Review 18(6), 493–520. DOI: 10.1016/S0195-9255(98)00019-5.

Milton, R., 1977. *Carter's energy program.* www.heritage.org/environment/report/carters-energy-program.

Ministry of the Environment and Energy, 2017. *Sweden's seventh national communication on climate change.* Sweden. https://unfccc.int/files/national_reports/annex_i_natcom_/application/pdf/6950713_sweden-nc7-1-swe_nc7_20171222.pdf.

Narassimhan, E., Gallagher, K.S., Koester, S., Alejo, J.R., 2018. *Carbon pricing in practice: A review of existing emissions trading systems.* Climate Policy 1–25.

NHTSA, 2018. CAFE public information center. https://one.nhtsa.gov/cafe_pic/CAFE_PIC_fleet_LIVE.html.

Obi, C., 2009. *Nigeria' s Niger Delta : Understanding the complex drivers of violent oil-related conflict.* Africa Development 34(2), 103–128.

OECD, 2018. *Air and GHG emissions (indicator).* DOI: 10.1787/93d10cf7-en (accessed 12.2.18).

Parker, C.F., Karlsson, C., Hjerpe, M., 2017. *Assessing the European Union's global climate change leadership: From Copenhagen to the Paris Agreement.* Journal of European Integration 39(2), 239–252.

Peters, B.G., Pierre, J., 2016. *Comparative governance: Rediscovering the functional dimension of governing.* Cambridge University Press, Cambridge.

Pierrehumbert, R., 2016. *How to decarbonize? Look to Sweden.* Bulletin of the Atomic Scientists 72(2), 105–111.

Ramanathan, V., Carmichael, G., 2008. *Global and regional climate changes due to black carbon.* Nature Geoscience 1(4), 221–227. https://doi.org/10.1038/ngeo156.

Serageldin, I., 1996. *Sustainability and the wealth of nations: first steps in an ongoing journey.* Report No. 15910. World Bank. http://documents.worldbank.org/curated/en/839711468741391920/Sustainability-and-the-wealth-of-nations-first-steps-in-an-ongoing-journey.

Spencer, T., Fazekas, D., 2013. *Distributional choices in EU climate policy: 20 years of policy practice.* Climate Policy 13(2), 240–258.

Thorp, T.M., 2014. *Climate justice: A voice for the future.* Palgrave Macmillan, Basingstoke.

Tsikliras, A.C., Froese, R., 2019. *Maximum sustainable yield,* in: Fath, B. (Ed.), *Encyclopedia of Ecology,* 2nd edition, Volume 1. Elsevier, Oxford, pp. 108–115.

UNCED, 1992. *Agenda 21.* Rio de Janeiro. https://sustainabledevelopment.un.org/content/documents/Agenda21.pdf.

UNFCCC, United Nations Framework Convention on Climate Change, 2015. *Paris Climate Change Conference – November 2015,* https://unfccc.int/process-and-meetings/conferences/past-conferences/paris-climate-change-conference-november-2015/paris-climate-change-conference-november-2015.

United Nations General Assembly, 2015. *Transforming our world: The 2030 agenda for sustainable development.* https://sustainabledevelopment.un.org/post2015/transformingourworld.

US Code, 1963. Title 42. The public health and welfare, Chapter 85. Air pollution prevention and control Subchapter I. Programs and activities Part A. Air quality and emission limitations section 7401. Congressional findings and declaration of purpose. www.law.cornell.edu/uscode/text/42/7401

US DOT – US Department of Transportation, 2011. *Summary of fuel economy performance.* Washington, DC. www.nhtsa.gov/staticfiles/rulemaking/pdf/cafe/2011_Summary_Report.pdf.

US International Trade Administration, 2016. *North American Leader Summit.* www.trade.gov/nacp/nals.asp.

Vodden, K., 2015. *Governing sustainable coastal development: The promise and challenge of collaborative governance in Canadian coastal watersheds.* Canadian Geographer 59(2), 167–180.

Voyles, T.B., 2015. *Introduction: Sacrificial land,* in: Voyles, T.B. (Ed.), *Wastelanding: Legacies of uranium mining in Navajo country.* University of Minnesota Press, Minneapolis, MN, pp. 1–26.

WCED – World Commission on Environment and Development, 1987. *Our common future: Report of the World Commission on Environment and Development.* Geneva.

Wirth, H., Schneider, K., 2018. *Recent facts about photovoltaics in Germany.* Fraunhofer Institut. www.ise.fraunhofer.de/content/dam/ise/en/documents/publications/studies/recent-facts-about-photovoltaics-in-germany.pdf.

Zane, E., 2013. *Assessment of climate change policies in the context of the European semester: Spain.* Eclareon. https://ec.europa.eu/clima/sites/clima/files/strategies/progress/reporting/docs/es_2013_en. pdf.

18

THE INEFFICIENCY OF RESOURCE POLICY AS A MECHANISM TO DELIVER RURAL POLICY

Ray D. Bollman

Introduction

The historical tight overlap between "rural" and "resources" no longer exists – at least in a demographic (or "jobs") sense. The purpose of this paper is to document the present status of the nature of this overlap, using agriculture as a specific example. This chapter is an update of Bollman (2006).

The "people-scape" (i.e. the people that one meets on the ground) of predominantly rural regions in OECD countries is not agricultural, nor forestry, nor mining, nor oil and gas – even though the landscape (i.e. what one can see on the land) may be agricultural or forestry. Hence, a resource policy does not provide an efficient mechanism to deliver policy to rural residents. This is based on the view that the objective of "policy" is to improve the well-being of individuals in the population.

This chapter starts with a discussion of the meaning of "resource policy". Then, using agricultural policy as an example:

- the overlap between agriculture and rural is presented for each OECD country; and then,
- within rural, the role of agriculture within rural society is shown for each OECD country.

There is a wide range in these measures across OECD countries.

On average, about one-half of agricultural policy is delivered to predominantly rural regions. For the agricultural policy that is delivered to predominantly rural regions, it is received by about 13 percent of the workforce of these regions. Thus, "agriculture" and agricultural policy would appear to have a weak (jobs) overlap with "rural" and rural development policy.

In general, a focus on "resource policy" would not be expected to provide an efficient path to deliver policy for the rural population.

What is resource policy?

A resource policy is focused on the resource. Typically, the focus of policy is to ensure the resource can contribute to the GDP and the GDP growth of the country. Typically, initiatives include improving the productivity of harvesting or extracting the resource.

What is rural?

Rural is density and distance-to-density (Reimer and Bollman, 2010; World Bank, 2009; Bollman and Reimer, Chapter 1 in this volume) Thus, individuals are "more" rural if they live in a low(er)-density locality and/or if they live in a locality with a long(er) distance to a high(er)-density locality. Localities with a low(er) population density (i.e. localities with a smaller population) lack "agglomeration economies", which implies production systems will be smaller and generally less diversified (due to the availability of a smaller workforce). Also, individuals are "more rural" if they must travel long(er) distances to a high(er)-density locality.

Thus, since rurality is defined by density and distance-to-density, *rural policy* will focus on the implications (advantages or disadvantages or prices[1]) of density and distance-to-density for each and every policy proposal.

What is development?

In many short(er)-run policy discussions, one key policy focus of "development" is growth in the number of jobs.[2] This implies that rural development is the creation of jobs in areas with a low(er) population density and/or in areas with a long(er) distance to localities with a high(er) density. Thus, *rural development policy* is a focus on policy initiatives that enhance the creation of jobs in areas which have a low(er) population density and/or in areas that are a long(er) distance from density.[3]

What is agriculture?

Agriculture is the process of producing (i.e. husbandry) food and fiber products. Hence, *agricultural policy* will focus on the efficient production of food and fiber in order to ensure food and fiber production remains competitive. Given the variability in agricultural production due to weather and international price shocks, agricultural policy in some countries also attempts to stabilize the returns to resources employed in certain lines of production so that resources stay in their long-run competitive line of production, rather than suffering short-run transactions costs of switching from one line of production to another. In other countries, some commodities receive a price subsidy – sometimes to ensure national self-sufficiency of the commodity, sometimes to ensure an adequate supply of the commodity for the processing sector, and sometimes with the stated objective of ensuring a "fair standard of living for farmers".

Where is the overlap or intersection of agriculture and rural?

When many observers view an agricultural vista, they see rural. And, when many observers think of "rural", they envision an agricultural landscape. Historically, this was a reasonable set of observations. However, over time, there have been more and more non-agricultural jobs within rural areas. At the same time, transportation technology has allowed individuals in rural-metro-adjacent regions to access city jobs, including members of farming families. Many farming families are not nearly as "rural" as they used to be. As a consequence of the improvements in transportation technology and the relative decline in the price of transportation (Bollman and Prud'homme, 2006), a considerable share of agricultural production now takes place in areas that are not rural – i.e. in areas with a lower price of distance to cities. For example, about 20 percent of Canadian agricultural production occurred within "Larger Urban Centers"[4] in 1996 (Lonmo, 1999) and there is "more than just farming" outside "Larger Urban Centers" (Keith, 2003).

The changing share of Canada's census-rural population that lives on a census-farm

Using the "census-rural" definition (du Plessis et al., 2001), which classifies residents as "rural" if they reside outside centers of 1000 or more, Canada's rural population has remained at about 6 million inhabitants since World War II. In 1931, two-thirds (67 percent) of the census-rural population lived on a census-farm (Table 18.1). (A census-farm is any agricultural holding with products for sale.)

A two-thirds share of the rural population residing on a census-farm is a large share in a Canadian context where rural also encompasses many communities associated with fishing, lumbering, and mining. By 2011, 9 percent of Canada's census-rural population lived on a census-farm. Thus, in 1931, agricultural policy would potentially be received by two-thirds of rural Canadians – today, agricultural policy is received by, at most, only 9 percent of rural Canadians.

In Canada, a major focus of agricultural policy in recent decades has been revenue stabilization support for farms. From 1991 to 2016, about one-half of Canadian census-farms generated less than CAN $50,000[5] of gross farm revenue. Families associated with these census-farms would have received very small program payments because the payments are generally based on the level of farm output.[6] Therefore, only about one-half of the census-farms would be big enough to receive a significant agricultural program payment.

The fact that only about one-half of census-farms receive (a very minor) share of agricultural policy emphasizes that the demographic overlap of agriculture and rural now involves less than 9 percent of the rural population.

The declining share of the rural population that resides on a census-farm documents the significant structural change in the "people-scape" of Canada's rural areas in the last 70 years.

Table 18.1 Canada rural population and rural population living in a farm, 2011

Year	Total population (million)	Census rural* population (million)	Census rural* population living in a census-farm operator household	
			Number (million)	Percent of census rural population
1931	10.4	4.4	3.2	67
2011	33.4	6.3	0.6	9.0

Source: Statistics Canada. Census of Population, 1931 and 2011.

Note
* The census rural population refers to individuals living outside population centers of 1,000 or more.

Across OECD countries, what share of the agricultural workforce is employed in predominantly rural regions?

In the OECD countries for which there are data on employment by sector by region, in 2013, about one-half (47 percent) of the agricultural[7] workforce is employed in predominantly rural regions,[8] (see Box 18.1 for definitions) (Table 18.2). In other words, about one-half the agricultural workforce across OECD countries resides in intermediate or predominantly urban regions. Thus, not all agricultural policy goes to predominantly rural regions. About one-half of agricultural policy across the OECD is delivered to intermediate or predominantly urban regions.

Box 18.1 Definition of geographic regions

Regions are classified at the Territorial Level 3 (OECD, 1994) to three types of regions:

Predominantly Rural Regions: more than 50 percent of the population lives in a "rural community".

Intermediate Regions: 15–50 percent of the population lives in a "rural community".

Predominantly Urban Regions: less than 15 percent of the population lives in a "rural community".

A *rural community* is a community with a population density of less than 150 people per square kilometer (and, in Japan, less than 500 persons per square kilometer).

There is considerable variation across OECD countries in the share of their agricultural workforce being employed in predominantly rural regions. For example, there are five countries (Estonia, Ireland, Slovenia, Austria, and Australia) where more than 70 percent of the agricultural workforce is located in predominantly rural regions (Figure 18.1 and Table 18.3). At the other end of the scale, there are three OECD countries (Spain, Switzerland, and Netherlands) with less than 10 percent of their agricultural workforce residing in predominantly rural regions.

Across OECD countries, what share of the workforce in predominantly rural regions is employed in agriculture?

Within OECD predominantly rural regions, only 13 percent of the workforce is employed in agriculture (Figure 18.2). Thus, from above,

- 47 percent of agricultural policy reaches predominantly rural regions; and
- this directly impacts, at most, 13 percent of the predominantly rural workforce.

Again, there is a wide variation across OECD member countries in terms of the share of the predominantly rural workforce that is employed in agriculture. Only two OECD countries have more than one-third of their workforce in predominantly rural regions employed in agriculture (Romania and Bulgaria) (Figure 18.2). However, eight countries have less than 6 percent

Table 18.2 Employment distribution by sector and type of region in selected OECD countries,[1] 2013[2]

Regional type	Sector		
	Agriculture, forestry and fishing (ISIC=1)	All other (non-agricultural) sectors	All sectors
	Number employed (million)		
Predominantly urban or intermediate regions	9	275	284
Predominantly rural regions	8	51	58
All types of regions	16	326	342
	Percent distribution of employment within each type of region (row percent)		
Predominantly urban or intermediate regions	3	97	100
Predominantly rural regions	13	87	100
All types of regions	5	95	100
	Percent distribution of employment across regions (column percent)		
Predominantly urban or intermediate regions	53	84	83
Predominantly rural regions	47	16	17
All types of regions	100	100	100

Source: OECD Territorial Database; 2011 National Household Survey for Canada.

Notes

Due to rounding, figures may not sum to totals.

1 The OECD countries for which data are available are Australia, Austria, Bulgaria, Canada (2011), Czech Republic, Denmark, Estonia, Finland, France, Germany, Greece, Hungary, Ireland, Israel, Italy, Japan (2012), Korea, Latvia, Lithuania, Luxembourg, Netherlands, New Zealand (2012), Norway, Poland, Portugal, Romania, Slovak Republic, Slovenia, Spain, Sweden, Switzerland, and the United Kingdom.

2 Data related to 2013 except for Japan (2010), Canada (2011), and New Zealand (2012).

of their predominantly rural workforce being employed in agriculture (Germany, Netherlands, Slovak Republic, Norway, Denmark, Switzerland, France, Sweden).

Also, note that the share of the predominantly rural workforce employed in agriculture has been declining in almost every OECD country.

These observations suggest that a focus on agricultural policy is missing the vast majority of rural residents.[9]

The interest of rural in agriculture

Rural development, as conceptualized here, is the growth of jobs in localities with a low(er) population density (e.g. a small(er) population) and/or in localities with a long(er) distance to localities with a high(er) density. Thus, the interest that proponents of "rural" development policy would have regarding "agriculture" would be the ability of "agriculture" to create rural jobs. Across the OECD, the agriculture workforce is declining. Within predominantly rural

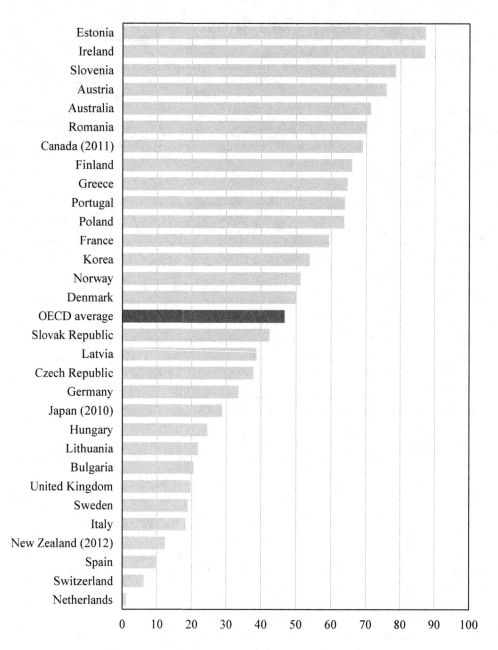

Figure 18.1 Percent of national employment in agriculture, forestry, and fishing in predominantly rural regions, 2013

Source: OECD Territorial Database (data are not available for all countries). Data for Canada are from the 2011 National Household Survey.

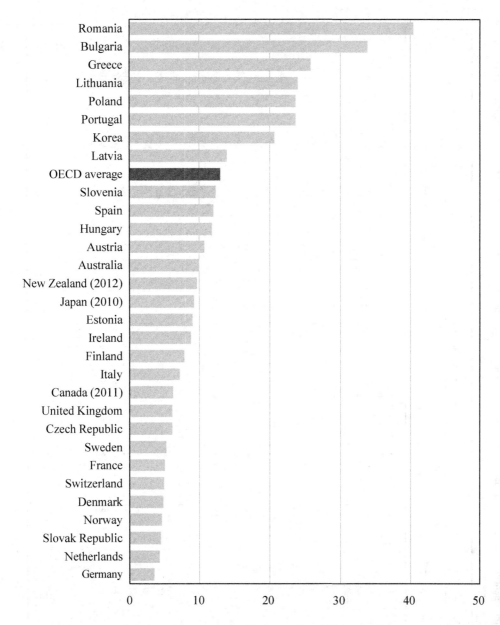

Figure 18.2 Percent of total employment engaged in agriculture, forestry, and fishing in predominantly rural regions, 2013

Source: OECD Territorial Database (data are not available for all countries). Data for Canada are from the 2011 National Household Survey.

Table 18.3 Employment in agriculture, forestry, and fishing (AFF) by type of region in selected OECD countries, 2013. Population values in thousands. R 1 is the ratio of total AFF employment located in predominantly rural regions to the total population; R 2 is the ratio of AFF employment to the population within predominantly rural regions

OECD member country	Predominantly urban regions		Intermediate regions		Predominantly rural regions		All regions		R 1	R 2
	All sectors	AFF	All sectors	AFF	All sectors	AFF	All sectors	AFF		
	A	B	C	D	E	F	G	H	F/H	F/E
Australia	8185	48	1103	38	2152	214	11,440	300	71%	10%
Austria	1446	15	1352	41	1655	176	4453	232	76%	11%
Bulgaria	867	12	2157	510	398	135	3422	657	21%	34%
Canada (2011)	9525	60	2643	63	4428	274	16,596	397	69%	6%
Czech Republic	1472	28	2565	76	1044	63	5081	167	38%	6%
Denmark	783	–	1228	35	726	35	2737	70	50%	5%
Estonia	304	2	57	1	240	22	601	25	88%	9%
Finland	846	7	722	31	950	74	2518	112	66%	8%
France	10,938	80	8373	186	7713	389	27,024	655	59%	5%
Germany	19,700	97	16,429	332	6183	217	42,312	646	34%	4%
Greece	1885	25	850	148	1223	316	3958	489	65%	26%
Hungary	1310	5	2151	207	585	69	4046	281	25%	12%
Ireland	645	4	172	10	1065	93	1882	107	87%	9%
Israel	1718	7	729	15	–	–	2447	22	–	–
Italy	11,639	265	10,420	465	2256	163	24,315	893	18%	7%
Japan (2010)	33,003	552	19,134	1144	7471	688	59,608	2384	29%	9%
Korea	17,622	334	3356	475	4568	944	25,546	1753	54%	21%
Latvia	474	14	227	28	188	26	889	68	38%	14%
Lithuania	385	10	808	74	99	34	1292	118	29%	34%
Luxembourg	–	–	386	5	–	–	386	5	–	–
Netherlands	6551	113	2146	81	50	2	8747	196	1%	4%
New Zealand (2012)	979	15	1044	116	193	19	2216	150	13%	10%
Norway	882	7	1024	23	696	32	2602	62	52%	5%
Poland	5112	79	5381	594	4971	1180	15,464	1853	64%	24%
Portugal	2122	82	954	102	1372	325	4448	509	64%	24%
Romania	1256	76	2818	696	4496	1819	8570	2591	70%	40%
Slovak Republic	419	5	1067	38	706	31	2192	74	42%	4%
Slovenia	–	–	431	17	493	61	924	78	78%	12%
Spain	11,537	263	5650	401	599	72	17,786	736	10%	12%
Sweden	2474	29	1794	61	405	21	4673	111	19%	5%
Switzerland	2534	47	1579	60	142	7	4255	114	6%	5%
United Kingdom	21,932	120	6624	143	1065	64	29,621	327	20%	6%
Total	178,545	2401	105,374	6216	58,132	7565	342,051	16,182	47%	13%

Source: OECD Territorial database; 2011 National Household Survey for Canada.

regions, the agriculture workforce declined 2.3 percent per year during the 1990s (Bollman, 2006; Table 18.3). This trend is continuing. Thus, the agriculture sector is not creating jobs in farming.

However, some families who operate census-farms are also involved in non-farm enterprises. Vogel and Bollman (2016) (see also Bollman, 1998) note that, over more than a decade, about 18 percent of census-farm operator families in Canada and the US also operate a non-farm business. Rural development policy (i.e. the creation of rural jobs) would thus have an interest in farming families which create jobs in non-farm enterprises.

> We found that for both the U.S. and Canada the share of local employment linked to these off-farm businesses is higher for rural counties that are more distant from an urban core. In these rural areas with limited resources, local communities increasingly rely on the FPEs [farm portfolio entrepreneurs] as place-based contributors to its economic resilience. We found that the smaller shares of nonfarm employment supported by FPEs in Canadian rural counties relative to the U.S. were accounted for low population densities resulting further in thin markets and limited nonfarm entrepreneurial opportunities.
>
> *(Vogel and Bollman, 2016, p. 8)*

According to the OECD (2001, 2006, 2016), strategies for regional development should look to invest in, or to valorize, under-utilized assets. One potential asset is the agricultural landscape. Thus, one possible interest of "rural" in "agriculture" is the enhancement of an agricultural landscape that can be valorized to create rural jobs in tourism. However, in some countries, the asset of the agricultural landscape is a relatively small share of all rural assets. In Canada, for example, tourists are more likely to be drawn to mountains, tundra, icebergs, northern lights, whale watching, pristine lakes, polar bears, and white-water rapids and are less likely to be drawn to an agricultural vista. Thus, in some countries, to focus on the asset of the agricultural landscape is to focus on only a small portion of all rural assets.

Arguably, the agricultural landscape near cities (recall that this is *not* a "rural" agricultural landscape because it is not distant from "density" and thus not distant from the (potential) urban consumers of the agricultural landscape) would be expected to be more valuable (i.e. valorized at a higher rate per hectare) because the demand for this landscape would be expected to come from large numbers of urban consumers with relatively easy access.

In some countries, agricultural policy is moving from a focus on agricultural production towards a focus on the agricultural landscape. However, Diakosavvas (2005) has indicated that, across the OECD, about 90 percent of the PSE (Producer Support Estimate) is tied to the level of agricultural production.[10] Thus, although there is a shift towards supporting the landscape for possible valorization by rural development initiatives, this policy shift has a long way to go. Moreover, as suggested earlier, the agricultural landscape is only one of a myriad of rural assets that may be valorized by rural development policy.

Jobs generated from the valorization of an agricultural landscape may be classified to the farming sector (for example, in the case of a farming operation that adds a bed and breakfast enterprise to the farming operation) or the jobs may be classified to another sector (for example, if a tour operator offers weekend bicycle tours through the agricultural landscape). Regardless of the sector, these jobs are generated from the agricultural landscape. The jobs generated in predominantly rural regions will appear as rural jobs and jobs in predominantly urban and intermediate regions will be urban jobs.

The interest of agriculture in rural

"Agriculture", as the competitive production of commodities, relates to rural in two possible dimensions:

1   being less rural would imply that commodities are produced closer to a market; and
2   being more rural would imply that commodities are produced at lower costs because of lower land prices and less attention would need to be paid to the externalities of pollution (noise pollution, odor pollution, water pollution, light from greenhouses, etc.).

Moving past the definition of "agriculture" as being the efficient production of commodities, it might be noted that farming families have an interest in rural. Specifically, some efficient farming enterprises do not require a full-year full-time operator. Thus, some operators choose an off-farm job rather than a secondary farming enterprise to maximize their own labor returns. Similarly, not all farms have full-year full-time work for all family members who wish to work. Thus, some choose an off-farm job.

Typically, farm operators with some off-farm work have higher incomes.[11] Interestingly, in the 1980s, Canadian farmers appeared to have made this adjustment more than US farmers who, in turn, appeared to have made this adjustment more than European farmers. For operators of farms classified to each size class of standard gross margin (i.e. gross farm revenues minus selected expenses), operators of Canadian farms were more likely to work off the farm than operators of US farms.[12] In turn, for farms of each size, operators of US farms were more likely to work off the farm than operators of EU farms (Fuller and Bollman, 1992). Operators with larger farms were less likely to work off the farm (or, individuals with off-farm jobs were more likely to operate smaller farms).

The same general conclusion held for the spouses of farm operators. The spouses of Canadian census-farm operators were more likely to work off the farm than the spouses of US farm operators who, in turn, were more likely to work off the farm than the spouses of European farm operators. However, in Canada, the US, and Europe, the participation in off-farm work by the spouse of the farm operator appeared to be independent of the size of the farm.

Over time, the increasing share of farm family income derived from off-farm sources has been due to the increased participation in off-farm work by the spouse of the farm operator (Bollman, 2009).

In 1972, Smith and Martin (1972) noted that farming families were more dependent on the local community (due to the income derived from off-farm jobs) compared to the level of dependency of the local community on the farming sector.

If the focus is shifted from agriculture and agricultural policy to the socio-economic well-being of families associated with farming, then farming families do have an interest in rural development and rural development policies and the generation of rural jobs. Recall, however, that the demographic count of farming families in predominantly rural regions is small.

Conclusions

Today, in predominantly rural regions across OECD countries, the resource sectors are not the major providers of jobs. This chapter focuses on whether resource policy is an effective mechanism to deliver rural policy.

The analysis focuses on agriculture as an example, but the results would be expected to apply to all resource sectors. The first observation is that agriculture is not solely a rural enterprise. In fact, about one-half of OECD agricultural workers are employed in intermediate and predominantly urban regions. Thus, agriculture extends beyond rural. Agricultural policy is not solely focused on predominantly rural regions (although spin-off effects to other people in related services and the community may occur). One-half of agricultural policy leaks to intermediate and predominantly urban regions. Once agricultural policy arrives in predominantly rural regions, it directly impacts only 13 percent of the workforce in predominantly rural regions. In fact, a large majority of the rural workforce is employed in sectors other than agriculture. In 2013, only two OECD countries had over one-third of their predominantly rural population employed in agriculture. Thus, the agricultural policy that does arrive in predominantly rural regions is directly received by a minority of the rural workforce.

These calculated impacts of agricultural policy as a means to deliver rural policy vary across OECD member countries. However, the general conclusion remains – agricultural policy is an inefficient mechanism to deliver rural policy. These observations would be expected to apply, generally, to all resource policy.

Notes

1 The price of distance would include the money cost and the time cost of moving goods, services, and people across space. As an alternative to the term "price of distance", one might speak of the advantages and disadvantages of distance-to-density. A health price of distance could be estimated by comparing the probability of dying if one skips a health examination versus the probability of dying from an auto accident on an icy winter road if one drives to the health examination.

2 The choice of the indicator of community success is important. Examples of indicators are job growth, income growth, population growth, or wage growth. The choice will depend, in part, to whom one is speaking. The school teacher may prefer population growth from an influx of young families whereas the swimming pool salesperson may prefer a growth in community wages. Different factors are associated with different measures of community success (Bollman, 1999).

3 In the long(er)-run, "ideas" are, arguably, the driver of development (jobs, or other desired development outcomes). Thus, rural development would be the generation of constructive ideas (that would generate desired outcomes) in areas that are a long(er) distance from localities with a high(er) density and/or have a low(er) population density. Rural development policy would be the focus on policy initiatives to enhance the creation of new ideas in areas that are a long(er) distance from high(er)-density localities and/or localities which have a low(er) population density.

4 "Larger Urban Centers" refers to "Census Metropolitan Areas" (CMAs) and "Census Agglomerations" (CAs) which are functional labor markets with a population of 100,000 or more for CMAs and a population of 10,000 to 99,999 for CAs. CMAs and CAs also include the residents of surrounding incorporated towns and incorporated municipalities where 50 percent or more of the workforce commutes to the CMA or CA.

5 See Canadian Census of Agriculture CANSIM Tables 004-0006 and 004-0233. Using 2016 exchange rates, CAN $50,000 was about US $38,000 or about 34,000 euro.

6 In 2004, the Farm Financial Survey showed that 7 percent of government program payments was paid to farms with gross revenue less than CAN $50,000 (calculated from Table 9 in Statistics Canada (2006)). Program payments are generally proportional to the size of gross farm revenue because program payments are based on the size of farm production. Interestingly, since program payments are larger (per unit of gross revenue) for grain farms and since grain farms are more likely to appear in the middle of the farm size distribution, program payments per dollar of gross revenue are smaller on the larger farms (because farms with higher gross farm revenue are more likely to be livestock farms and livestock farms are less likely to receive program payments) (Bollman, 1989; Statistics Canada, 2006).

7 "Agriculture" refers to International Standard Industrial Classification (ISIC)=1, which includes employment in agriculture (i.e. on farms) plus employment in forestry, fishing, and hunting. Although the term "agriculture" is used in this paper to refer to ISIC=1, this will somewhat overstate the importance of agriculture in countries with a significant forestry and fishing workforce, such as Canada. However, overstating the importance of "agriculture" will bias the results against the argument that there is a small and declining demographic overlap of agriculture and rural.

8 To keep the tables simpler, predominantly urban and intermediate (PUI) regions have been combined into one category (see Box 18.1). There is, admittedly, a lot of agricultural countryside in PUI regions. This "countryside" may be agricultural but these areas are not rural – they are *not* distant from high(er)-density localities (i.e. they are relatively adjacent to urban services and urban markets). For some issues (e.g. the supply of clean drinking water), the countryside dwellers in PUI regions may share concerns with rural residents. However, the residents of PUI regions are not rural – because they are not distant from urban services and they are not distant from urban markets.

9 It is acknowledged that the agriculture sector may generate positive spin-off effects for rural residents. Also, payments to the farm sector may not be wholly captured by the farm sector. As the extensive literature in public finance has documented, the (final) incidence of a tax or a subsidy depends upon the demand and supply elasticities for the sector. Thus, for example, suppliers of inputs to the farm sector would be expected to "capture" some of the subsidy and owners of farm land (37 percent of farmland in Canada in 2016 was not owned by the operator) would be expected to "capture" some of the subsidy. In this chapter, the focus is simple (and narrow) – the (initial) impact of agricultural subsidies is assigned by observing the geographic location of people working in agriculture.

10 This includes market price supports plus payments based on output plus payments based on input use plus payments based on area planted and animal numbers.

11 Bollman (1991) showed that operators who receive one-half of their labor earnings from farming and one-half of their labor earnings from off-farm work have lower total labor earnings than operators with a small amount of farm earnings or operators with a small amount of off-farm earnings. In this sense, a 50:50 mix of farm and off-farm work appears to be a less efficient allocation of the time of the operator (in the sense that overall labor returns are smaller).

12 Agriculture and Agri-Food Canada (2005, p. 75) show that, in Canada, less than 50 percent of operators of one-operator census-farms were engaged in some off-farm work and US principal operators of all census-farms were more likely (more than 50 percent) to report some off-farm work. We suspect that the higher share of US census-farm operators reporting some off-farm work is due, at least in part, to the fact that operators associated with smaller census-farms are more likely to report off-farm work and a higher share of US census-farms are "small". About one-half of US census-farms have gross revenue less than US $10,000 whereas only about one-quarter of Canadian census-farms have gross revenue less than US $10,000 (Whitener *et al.*, 1995). Even today, the share of US census-farms that are "small" is much higher than the share of Canadian census-farms that are "small".

References

Agriculture and Agri-Food Canada, 2005. *Farm income issues data source book*. Agriculture and Agri-Food Canada, Ottawa, Ont.

Bollman, R.D., 1989. *Who receives farm government payments?* Canadian Journal of Agricultural Economics 37(3), 351–378.

Bollman, R.D., 1991. *Efficiency aspects of part-time farming*, in: Hallberg, M.C., Findeis, J.L., Lass, D.A. (Eds.), *Multiple jobholding among farm families*. Iowa State University Press, Ames, IA, pp. 112–139.

Bollman, R.D., 1998. *Agricultural statistics for rural development*, in: Holland, T.E., Van den Broecke, M.P.R. (Eds.), *Agricultural Statistics 2000: An international conference on agricultural statistics*. International Statistical Institute, Voorburg, the Netherlands, pp. 29–41.

Bollman, R.D., 1999. *Factors associated with local economic growth*. Rural and Small Town Canada Analysis Bulletin 1(6). Statistics Canada, Ottawa, Ont., Catalogue No. 21-006-XIE.

Bollman, R.D., 2006. *The demographic overlap of agriculture and the rural economy: Implications for the coherence of agricultural and rural policies*, in: Diakosavvas, D. (Ed.), *Coherence of Agricultural and Rural Development Policies*. OECD, Paris, pp. 95–112.

Bollman, R.D., 2009. *Households associated with agricultural holdings: Socio-economic dimensions*. Paper presented to the Second Meeting of the Wye City Group on Statistics on Rural Development and Agriculture Household Income, June 11–12, Rome, Italy.

Bollman, R.D., Prud'homme, M., 2006. *Trends in the prices of rurality*. Rural and Small Town Canada Analysis Bulletin 6(7). Statistics Canada, Ottawa. Ont., Catalogue No. 21-006-XIE.

Diakosavvas, D., 2005. *Evolution of agricultural policies in OECD countries and implications for rural development*. Paper presented to the OECD Workshop on The Coherence of Agricultural and Rural Development Policies, October 24–26, Bratislava.

du Plessis, V., Beshiri, R., Bollman, R.D., Clemenson, H., 2001. *Definitions of rural*. Rural and Small Town Canada Analysis Bulletin 3(3). Statistics Canada, Ottawa, Ont., Catalogue No. 21-006-XIE.

Fuller, A., Bollman, R., 1992. *Pluriactivity among farm families: Some West European, US and Canadian comparisons*, in: Bowler, I.R., Bryant, C.F., Nellis, M.D. (Eds.), *Contemporary rural systems in transition: Volume 2, Economy and society*. CAB International, Wallingford, pp. 201–212.

Keith, B., 2003. *More than just farming: Employment in agriculture and agri-food in rural and urban Canada*. Rural and Small Town Canada Analysis Bulletin 4(8). Statistics Canada, Ottawa, Ont., Catalogue No. 21-006-XIE.

Lonmo, C., 1999. *Cattle, crops and city living*. Canadian Agriculture at a Glance. Statistics Canada, Ottawa, Ont., Catalogue No. 96-325, pp. 245–250.

OECD, 1994. *Creating rural indicators for shaping territorial policy*. OECD, Paris.

OECD, 2001. *OECD territorial outlook 2001*. OECD, Paris.

OECD, 2006. *The new rural paradigm: Policies and governance*. OECD, Paris.

OECD, 2016. *OECD regional outlook 2016: Productive regions for inclusive societies*. OECD, Paris.

Reimer, B., Bollman, R.D., 2010. *Understanding rural Canada: Implications for rural development policy and rural planning policy*, in: Douglas, D.J.A. (Ed.), *Rural planning and development in Canada*. Nelson Education, Toronto, Ont.

Smith, A.H., Martin, W.E., 1972. *Socioeconomic behavior of cattle ranchers, with implications for rural community development in the West*. American Journal of Agricultural Economics (May), 217–225.

Statistics Canada, 2006. *Farm financial survey – 2005*. Statistics Canada, Ottawa, Ont., Catalogue No. 21F0008.

Vogel, S., Bollman, R.D., 2016. *The multifunctional farm household enterprise: Using farm microdata to assess the rural economy impacts generated by farmer-operated off-farm business*. Paper presented to the Seventh International Conference of Agricultural Statistics, October 26–28, Rome.

Whitener, L., Bollman, R.D., Tung, F.L., 1995. *Trends and patterns in farm structural change: A Canada–U.S. Comparison*. Canadian Journal of Agricultural Economics (Special Issue on Farms, Farm Families and Farming Communities), 15–28.

World Bank, 2009. *Reshaping economic geography*. World Bank, World Development Report, Washington, DC.

19

THE WATER–ENERGY–FOOD–CLIMATE NEXUS

John Devlin and Sarah Minnes

Introduction

A nexus is a set of systemic interactions between multiple factors. The water–energy–food–climate (WEFC) nexus focuses attention on three factors basic to the sustainability of biological and social systems (food, energy, and water) and one cross-cutting condition that threatens them (climate change). In 2011 the World Economic Forum published *Water Security: The Water–Energy–Food–Climate Nexus* which drew attention to the looming global crisis of water supply. That document suggested that within two decades, the collective demand of humans for water could exceed supply by about 40 percent with associated escalations in food prices, disruptions of energy supply, constrictions in trade, increased refugee populations, and disrupted authority structures. Since 2011 there have been multiple conferences discussing the nexus and growing investigation of the concept by analysts (Bizikova *et al.*, 2013; Dodds and Bartram, 2014; Leck *et al.*, 2015).

This chapter surveys analytic and policy work revolving around the WEFC nexus. The next section provides projections for growing global demands for food, energy, and water. This is followed by a discussion of nexus interactions: the food–water relationship, the food–energy relationship, and the water–energy relationship. Then climate change is discussed as a cross-cutting factor which will exacerbate the challenge of meeting future food, energy, and water demands. This is followed by a consideration of the policy challenge. It is suggested that the WEFC nexus presents wicked policy problems for which there is no optimization formula. The best policy-makers can do is seek to balance outcomes on each factor while recognizing the potential impact on the other factors. Effective policy will be difficult to manage politically and will require strong leadership from public authorities. A focus on the costs of WEFC inter-actions can offer a justification for the politically difficult and potentially contentious policies that will be required of public authorities at multiple geographic, administrative, and temporal scales.

Trends in global food, energy, and water demand

Projections of food demand are largely linked to a growing population and shifting food quality choices. Annual growth of 1.10 percent adds roughly 83 million people to the global population each year. The world's population is projected to reach 9.8 billion by 2050 (UNDESA, 2017) an increase of 29 percent over the 2017 population of 7.6 billion. Gouel and Guimbard (2018) estimate that, if current consumption trends continue, by 2050 there will be a 47 percent increase in food demand mainly in lower-middle-income and low-income countries. They project a 100 percent increase in demand for animal-based calories and a smaller 19 percent increase in demand for starchy staples.

The International Energy Agency reports that in 2017 world primary energy demand reached 13,972 million tons of oil equivalent (Mtoe) and of this 81 percent was supplied by fossil fuels. With current policies in place the IEA projects that by 2040 world primary energy demand would increase to 19,328 million tons of oil equivalent (Mtoe), an increase of 38 percent over 2017 levels. Even with implementation of the national policies promised following the Paris 2015 agreement, world primary energy demand would increase to 17,715 Mtoe, which is roughly a 25 percent increase over 2017 demand, and fossil fuels would still be contributing 78 percent of the larger energy demand by 2040. The IEA also projects a "sustainable develop-ment" scenario which could see energy demand remain at about 2017 levels in 2040 with a drop in the fossil fuel component to 60 percent of supply (IEA, 2018, p. 38). But this scenario assumes radical shifts in energy policy.

Burek *et al.* (2016) estimate that total water demand will reach 5500 to 6000 km^3/year by 2050, an increase of between 20 and 30 percent over the estimated 4600 km^3 average water demand in the early 2010s. Globally, 2.1 billion people currently do not have access to safe drinking water, and more than a third of the world's population is affected by water scarcity (IEA, 2018). If current water demand trends continue, by 2030, two-thirds of the population on earth will live in areas of high-water stress (World Economic Forum, 2011). Beck and Vil-larroel Walker (2013) argue that water is unique because insecurity can arise from both too much and too little water.

Several frameworks have been offered to describe these relationships (Hoff, 2011; World Economic Forum, 2011; ICIMOD, 2012; Bizkova *et al.*, 2013; Scott *et al.*, 2015). All recognize that meeting the increasing demand for any one of the factors may make it more difficult to meet the increasing demand for the other two factors (see Figure 19.1). The following section considers some of the potential interactions between food, energy, and water supply and demand. To simplify the presentation current technology is assumed throughout. Technological change will be considered briefly in the discussion of policy responses to the nexus challenges.

Nexus interactions

The food–energy relationship

Meeting increasing food demand will require more energy. Energy is required for fertilizer production, the pumping of water for irrigation and livestock, the operation of farm equipment, the processing, packaging, refrigeration, transportation, and storage of food. Furthermore, as globalization increases, the length of food supply chains may increase requiring more energy for transportation and storage. Rising energy costs will thus put upward pressure on food costs as they did during the food price spike in 2008 (Headey and Fan, 2008; Tadasse *et al.*, 2016).

In turn meeting increased energy demand can also reduce food production. Productive agri-cultural land is finite, potentially putting food and energy production into competition (Hanes *et al.*, 2018). The production of biofuels has substituted for some production of food grains (Bazilian *et al.*, 2011) and the food price spike in 2008 was in part a result of increased produc-tion of biofuels (Headey and Fan, 2008). As food demand increases it will be difficult to justify

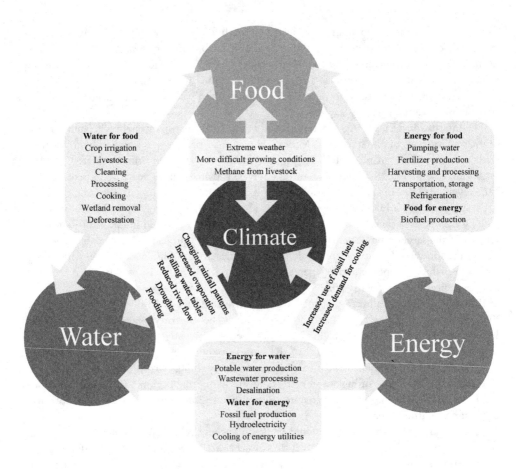

Figure 19.1 Food–energy–water–climate nexus relationships

Sources: Adapted from: Hoff (2011); Bizkova *et al.* (2013); Scott *et al.* (2015); Bieber *et al.* (2018).

continued production of biofuels, especially when alternative energy technologies such as wind and solar are available (Hanes *et al.*, 2018).

The food–water relationship

Meeting increasing food demand will increase demand for fresh and potable water. Water is needed for crop irrigation, livestock, food processing, and cooking. Globally, 70 percent of all freshwater withdrawals are used for agricultural purposes, with that percentage increasing to 90 percent in some fast-growing economies (Bazilian *et al.*, 2011). Averaged globally it takes 1334 liters of water to produce one kilogram of wheat and 15,500 liters of water to grow one kilogram of beef (Hoekstra and Chapagain, 2006). As the world demand for food and water grows, so too will the potential for water scarcity in many food-producing countries (Grafton *et al.*, 2017). Food importing countries are importers of virtual water (i.e. the water it takes to produce a product) (Hoekstra and Chapagain, 2006; Wang *et al.*, 2015; Water Footprint Network, n.d.). Food importers are thus vulnerable to water supply problems outside their borders.

Global water supply is relatively fixed, but food production may reduce the local and regional supply of potable water. For example, a portion of water withdrawn for food production is lost to leaks and evaporation (Pillot *et al.*, 2016). In addition, if not managed properly agriculture can pollute water resources with surface runoff or field drainage of fertilizers and pesticides, thereby reducing potable surface and groundwater. Conversion of more wetlands to cropland will reduce local capacity for surface and groundwater retention (Bartzen *et al.*, 2015). Clearing of forest for food production can also affect surface water yield and the distribution of precipitation in site-specific ways (Filoso *et al.*, 2017).

The water–energy relationship

The supply of potable water requires energy. Energy is required for the collection, distribution, and transport of fresh water particularly for the pumping of groundwater (Laves *et al.*, 2014). Energy is also required for water and wastewater treatment. Between 30 and 50 percent of municipal energy costs are associated with water and wastewater utilities (OECD/IEA, 2018). Water desalination also demands energy and is a major constraint on the use of desalination in water-scarce regions (Abdelkareem *et al.*, 2018).

The supply of energy is in turn linked to the availability of water (Fan *et al.*, 2018). Hydropower generation provides 16 percent of the world's electricity supply. The use of water for irrigation can reduce flows for hydroelectric generation (Bazilian *et al.*, 2011). The extraction and preparation of fossil fuels consumes significant quantities of water in coal mining, petroleum refining, oil extraction from tar sands, and natural gas extraction from shale (Wang *et al.*, 2015). Generating energy from fossil fuel and nuclear plants also requires water for cooling and in drought episodes the lack of water can reduce the production of energy in power plants and make energy availability precarious (Wang *et al.*, 2015). Using water for cooling in fossil fuel plants raises the temperature of water resources which can reduce water quality. Hence as energy demand increases, so does the demand on water (De Loë and Patterson, 2017).

Climate change

Climate and food

The food–energy–water interactions surveyed above are made more complex by the overarching process of climate change. Climate change can reduce food production through extreme weather events such as hurricanes, wind storms, and floods, which destroy crops and livestock. Droughts can reduce crop production over extended periods. Lesk *et al.* (2016) show, using global extreme weather data from 1964 to 2007, that during a drought cereal production was reduced by nearly 10.0 percent and extreme heat led to a production deficit of nearly 9.0 percent. Milder winters can increase pest survival putting downward pressure on yields (Taylor *et al.*, 2018). The negative effects of climate change on food production are likely to be nonlinear with yields increasing up to a temperature threshold and then declining sharply beyond this limit (Grafton *et al.*, 2017). In turn food production contributes to climate change through N_2O emissions from nitrogen fertilizer applications and CO_2 emissions from the use of fossil fuels for agricultural purposes and food processing, transporting, and storage (Frank *et al.*, 2019). Livestock production generates an estimated 37 percent of human-induced methane (CH_4) emissions and 65 percent of N_2O emissions from feed-related fertilizers (Steinfeld *et al.*, 2006). These emissions levels will only increase if diets continue to shift towards increased meat consumption. Deforestation to expand land for livestock, grains, and oil crops such as palm oil will add to CO_2 releases and reduce the capacity for carbon sequestration in the future (UNCTAD, 2013).

Climate and energy

Climate change will lead to increased energy demands in several sectors. Energy for air conditioning is already an important drain on electricity grids and this will increase as temperatures rise in urban areas (Isaac and Van Vuuren, 2009) Energy demand for refrigeration of food and for pumping of water will increase as discussed earlier. In turn climate change can reduce energy supply. Declining water flows in rivers will reduce the output of hydroelectricity. This can be exacerbated by siltation owing to increasing soil erosion which can increase with extreme weather events. It is important to manage ecosystem service degradation in order to maintain both energy and food productivity (Hanes *et al.*, 2018). However, climate change continues to be driven by emissions from the burning of fossil fuels for energy production (IEA, 2018).

Climate and water

Climate change will reduce the availability of fresh and potable water. Rising temperatures will increase surface water evaporation and also threaten snowfall and mountain glaciers, which feed major river systems providing water to billions around the world (World Economic Forum, 2011). Climate-related water loss, as well as issues with more intense weather events such as flooding and rising sea levels, will create further conditions of water scarcity (Liu, 2016). Heavier and more intense rain events are increasing surface water runoffs and reducing the rate at which aquifers are replenished. Rivers with periodic low flows may begin to dry up completely, affecting production and increasing the use of ground water, which in turn will lower groundwater levels and increase the need for groundwater pumping (De Loë and Patterson, 2017). As sea levels rise, low-lying coastal areas are increasingly being inundated with saltwater, gradually contaminating the soil and potentially disrupting food production at the local level (Chen and Mueller, 2018)

The policy challenge

Rising demands for food, energy, and water in a context of accelerating climate change present complex policy challenges. There is also the need for nexus policies to be interconnected administratively and spatially. In the absence of effective international frameworks, unilateral or bilateral responses could increase competition for nexus resources while allowing free riding on climate change policy (Märker *et al.*, 2018). Similar tensions may arise within individual countries where policy responsibility cascades downward from national to local levels. These challenges are increased by a multitude of additional factors including population growth, demographic shifts, income changes, urbanization, industrialization, economic growth, shifts in social and cultural values, global trade patterns, environmental protection, public health, community well-being, defense, and geo-politics (De Loë and Patterson, 2017; Fan *et al.*, 2018).

Rasul and Sharma (2016, p. 682) call for an integrated policy approach that "uses knowledge of the interlinkages to maximize gain, optimize trade-offs, and avoid negative impacts". Scott *et al.* (2015) also stress adaptive capacity to be able to respond to nexus policies. Nexus thinking is contributing to the analysis of trade-offs and interconnections in governance and sustainable development (Kurian, 2017). Efforts to model WEFC interactions will help suggest options (Garcia and You, 2016; Howarth and Monasterolo, 2016). But despite the realization of the nexus interdependencies, there are few examples of co-management of the resources (Loring *et al.*, 2013; Laves *et al.*, 2014). Several existing resource management approaches seek to deal with high levels of complexity. For example, integrated natural resources management (INRM);

integrated water resources management (IWRM); systems analysis; and the circular economy (Wichelns, 2017; Dell'Angelo, 2018). A key constraint for all these approaches is sectoral thinking (Liu, 2016; Märker *et al.*, 2018).

For all these reasons policy-making in any part of the WEFC nexus will be "wicked" implying problems with no clear solutions where policy failure is chronic (Rittel and Webber, 1973). Ackoff (1974) would describe them as "messy" because of the extensive interdependencies and policy ripples that occur when governance decisions about wicked problems are made. Such problems are "complex, unpredictable, open ended, or intractable" (Head and Alford, 2015, p. 712). Levin *et al.* (2012, p. 123) add that limited response time, absence of a central authority, and a tendency to discount the future create "super-wicked problems ... where traditional analytical techniques are ill equipped to identify solutions, even when it is well recognized that actions must take place soon to avoid catastrophic future impacts". Technological responses can be important. Technology is a mediating variable in most nexus relationships. Technological change can make food production and distribution more efficient, reduce and de-fossilize energy production, and reduce water consumption (Rogers and Daines, 2014; Pillot *et al.*, 2016; Liu, 2016). Renewable energy technologies (wind, hydro, and solar), will reduce greenhouse gas emissions and water demand (Fan *et al.*, 2018). But climate change policy provides an important caution to any assumption of a technological fix for nexus challenges. Alternative energy technologies exist but their adoption has been slow owing to path dependencies, costs, and efficiency arguments. Cooperation across sectors to incentivize the use of renewable energy needs to occur in order to achieve climate and energy targets (Märker *et al.*, 2018).

In addition to the science and technology challenges, political pressure plays an important role. Sarni (2017) asks why water-intensive crops are subsidized in water-scarce regions? Parry (2018) asks why fossil fuels are subsidized? These are political issues. De Loë and Patterson (2017, p. 91) suggest that the nexus discourse has been "strongly apolitical, focusing largely on resource efficiency and technical and market-based responses to scarcity, while downplaying issues of equity, access, and power". Allouche *et al.* (2015, p. 610) suggest that the politics are hidden by the "market-technical framing of the nexus". WEFC nexus politics will be made even more intractable by normative and value-based "frames" which express different preferences for the policy roles of civil society, business, and public authorities. These frames are deeply entrenched and largely immune to the impact of facts on decision-making (Ney, 2009). As the climate change policy debate has demonstrated, more science and more technological innovation will not guarantee the effective formation and implementation of nexus policies (Kurian, 2017), particularly when influential groups can use uncertainty to justify policy vetoes (Ney, 2009). Policy approaches noted by Reisch *et al.* (2013) are the support of the consumption of less animal products, to increase the consumption of organic products, and to favor local products (particularly avoiding food requiring air travel as part of their food system). Kevany *et al.* (2019) stress the importance of whole-food, plant-based diets, as they are associated with using less water and lowering greenhouse gas emissions, resulting in cleaner air, and increasing human health.

Improved stakeholder cooperation is generally recommended as a response to uneven policy influence (Bizkova *et al.*, 2013; Hanlon *et al.*, 2013). Palmer (2012) suggests the "extended peer community" promoted by Funtowicz and Ravetz (1993) will help make agreement more likely. Levin *et al.* (2012) suggest that short-term gains can entrench support and be expanded over time. Larcom and van Gevelt (2017) are optimistic that stakeholder engagement through procedural justice can improve policy decisions. But Head and Alford (2015) caution that for wicked problems only provisional solutions are possible and the approach must be incremental. Peters (2017, p. 387) warns that "promising to solve problems, wicked or otherwise, may ultimately weaken already diminished faith in government". Despite best efforts policy outcomes will remain uncertain (Farber, 2015; Pezzey, 2019). Trade-offs will be necessary and negative impacts cannot be avoided.

The suggested approach is to focus policy discussion on risk and cost (see Figure 19.2). The costs of WEFC interactions are accelerating. For example, in the US in 2018, there were 14 weather and climate disaster events with losses exceeding $1 billion each. These events included drought, severe storms, tropical cyclones, wildfires, and winter storms. The average number of such events from 1980–2018 was 6.2 per annum but the annual average for the most recent five years (2014–2018) has doubled to 12.6 events. The cost of such events since 1980 has reached $1.6 trillion (NOAA, 2019). Globally the costs are many times greater. In addition, the human costs of food, energy, and water shortages or price spikes are substantial, are difficult to quantify (Field, 2016), and potentially unquantifiable. These costs will continue to escalate (Rojas *et al.*, 2013; Moore *et al.*, 2017) and there will be no consensus on who pays. Public authorities must reassert their responsibility to act. It will be necessary to move away from currently popular market-oriented and voluntaristic options which give priority to shorter-term, sectoral, and local concerns. To affect larger geographic, administrative, and temporal scales strong public authority will be needed.

Conclusions

The WEFC nexus presents rural policy-makers with an extremely long list of challenges. Some rural areas may gain as rising food and energy prices generate income and employment. Many will lose as food production becomes more difficult, energy costs rise, water supplies decline, and destructive climate events become more frequent. Science and technology research will provide an array of options for policy-makers. However, contending interests and frames will make the design and implementation of effective rural policy extremely difficult.

The comparative rural policy research agenda can supplement science and technology research and contribute to successful adaptation by adopting a positive deviance approach which identifies cases of successful WEFC policy at international, national, or sub-national levels to

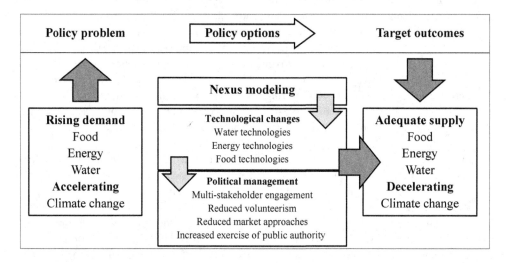

Figure 19.2 FEWC nexus policy implications

determine how these policies have been reached and sustained (LeMahieu *et al.*, 2017; Herington and van de Fliert, 2018; Albanna and Heeks, 2019). For example, Germany's efforts to create a holistic integrated nexus framework deserve attention (Märker *et al.*, 2018). It is also important for rural policy analysts to question the contemporary approach that espouses the retreat of the state in favor of voluntaristic and market-oriented approaches. There will be no immediate multi-stakeholder consensus and few "win–win" short-term solutions to the challenges presented to rural communities and regions by the WEFC nexus. Public authorities will have to provide strong leadership to distribute the current costs with a degree of equity across current and future rural and urban stakeholders.

References

Abdelkareem, M.A., Assad, M.E.H., Sayed, E.T., Soudan, B, 2018. *Recent progress in the use of renewable energy sources to power water desalination plants.* Desalination 435, 97–113.

Ackoff, R.L., 1974. *Redesigning the future.* Wiley, New York.

Albanna, B., Heeks, R., 2019. *Positive deviance, big data, and development: A systematic literature review.* The Electronic Journal of Information Systems in Developing Countries 85(1), 12063. https://doi.org/10.1002/isd2.12063.

Allouche, J., Middleton, C., Gyawali, D., 2015. *Technical veil, hidden politics: Interrogating the power linkages behind the nexus.* Water Alternatives 8(1), 610–626.

Bartzen, B.A., Dufour, K.W., Clark, R.G., Caswell, F.D., Dale, F., 2015. *Trends in agricultural impact and recovery of wetlands in prairie Canada.* Ecological Society of America 20(2), 525–538. DOI: 10.1890/08-1650.1.

Bazilian, M., Rogner, H., Howells, M., Hermann, S., Arent, D., Gielen, D., Steduto, P., Mueller, A., Komor, P., Tol, R.S.J., Yumkella, K.K., 2011. *Considering the energy, water and food nexus: Towards an integrated modelling approach.* Energy Policy 39(12), 7896–7906. DOI: 10.1016/j.enpol.2011.09.039.

Beck, M.B., Villarroel Walker, R., 2013. *On water security, sustainability, and the water–food–energy–climate nexus.* Frontiers of Environmental Science and Engineering 7(5), 626–639. DOI: 10.1007/s11783-013-0548-6.

Bieber, N., Ker, J.H., Wang, X., Triantafyllidis, C., van Dam, K.H., Koppelaar, R.H., Shah, N., 2018. *Sustainable planning of the energy–water–food nexus using decision making tools.* Energy Policy 113, 584–607.

Bizikova, L., Roy, D., Swanson, S., Venema, H.D., McCandless, M., 2013. *The water–energy–food security nexus: Towards a practical planning and decision-support framework for landscape investment and risk management.* International Institute for Sustainable Development, Winnipeg, MB.

Burek, P., Satoh, Y., Fischer, G., Kahil, M.T., Scherzer, A., Tramberend, S., Nava, L.F., Wada, Y., 2016. *Water futures and solution: Fast track initiative (Final report).* IIASA Working Paper WP-16-006. IIASA, Laxenburg, Austria. http://pure.iiasa.ac.at/id/eprint/13008/.

Chen, J., Mueller, V., 2018. *Coastal climate change, soil salinity and human migration in Bangladesh.* Nature Climate Change 8, 981–985.

De Loë, R.C., Patterson, J.J., 2017. *Rethinking water governance: Moving beyond water-centric perspectives in a connected and changing world.* Natural Resources Journal 57(1), 75–99.

Dell'Angelo, J., 2018. *The global food–energy–water nexus.* Reviews of Geophysics 56(3), 456–531.

Dodds, F., Bartram, J., 2014. *Building integrated approaches into the sustainable development goals.* A declaration from the Nexus 2014: Water, Food, Climate and Energy conference, University of North Carolina at Chapel Hill, March 5–8. http://nexusconference.web.unc.edu/files/2014/08/nexus-declaration.pdf.

Fan, J.L., Kong, L.S, Zhang, X., 2018. *Synergetic effects of water and climate policy on energy–water nexus in China: A computable general equilibrium analysis.* Energy Policy 123, 308–317. DOI: 10.1016/j.enpol.2018.09.002.

Farber, D.A., 2015. *Coping with uncertainty: Cost–benefit analysis, the precautionary principle, and climate change.* Washington Law Review 90, 1659–1725.

Field, S., 2016. *The financialization of food and the 2008–2011 food price spikes.* Environment and Planning A: Economy and Space 48(11), 2272–2290.

Filoso, S., Bezerra, M.O., Weiss, K.C.B., Palmer, M.A., 2017. *Impacts of forest restoration on water yield: A systematic review.* PLOS ONE 12(8), 1–26. https://doi.org/10.1371/journal.pone.0183210.

Frank, S., Havlík, P., Stehfest, E., van Meijl, H., Witzke, P., Pérez-Domínguez, I., van Dijk, M., Doelman, J.C., Fellmann, T., Koopman, J.F., Tabeau, A., 2019. *Agricultural non-CO2 emission reduction potential in the context of the 1.5° C target.* Nature Climate Change 9(1), 66–72.

Funtowicz, S.O., Ravetz, J.R., 1993. *Science for the post-normal age.* Futures 25(7), 739–755.

Garcia, D.J., You, F., 2016. *The water–energy–food nexus and process systems engineering: A new focus.* Computers and Chemical Engineering 91, 49–67.

Gouel, C., Guimbard, H., 2018. *Nutrition transition and the structure of global food demand.* American Journal of Agricultural Economics 101(2), 383–403. https://doi.org/10.1093/ajae/aay030.

Grafton, R.Q., Williams, J., Jiang, Q., 2017. *Possible pathways and tensions in the food and water nexus.* Earth's Future 5(5), 449–462. DOI: 10.1002/2016EF000506.

Hanes, R.J., Gopalakrishnan, V., Bakshi, B.R., 2018. *Including nature in the food–energy–water nexus can improve sustainability across multiple ecosystem services.* Resources, Conservation and Recycling 37(June), 214–228. DOI: 10.1016/j.resconrec.2018.06.003.

Hanlon, P., Madel, R., Olson-Sawyer, K., Rabin, K., Rose, J., 2013. *Food, water and energy: Know the nexus.* GRACE Communications Foundation, New York.

Head, B.W., Alford, J., 2015. *Wicked problems: Implications for public policy and management.* Administration and Society 47(6), 711–739.

Headey, D., Fan, S., 2008. *Anatomy of a crisis: The causes and consequences of surging food prices.* Agricultural Economics 39, 375–391.

Herington, M.J., van de Fliert, E., 2018. *Positive deviance in theory and practice: A conceptual review.* Deviant Behavior 39(5), 664–678.

Hoekstra, A.Y., Chapagain, A.K., 2006. *Water footprints of nations: Water use by people as a function of their consumption pattern,* in: Craswell, E., Bonnell, M., Bossio, D., Demuth, S., van de Giesen, N. (Eds.), *Integrated assessment of water resources and global change.* Springer, Dordrecht, pp. 35–48.

Hoff, H., 2011. *Understanding the nexus: Background paper for the Bonn 2011 Nexus Conference: The water, energy and food security nexus.* Stockholm Environmental Institute, Stockholm.

Howarth, C., Monasterolo, I., 2016. *Understanding barriers to decision making in the UK energy–food–water nexus: The added value of interdisciplinary approaches.* Environmental Science and Policy 61, 53–60.

ICIMOD – International Centre for Integrated Mountain Development, 2012. *Contribution of Himalayan ecosystems to water, energy, and food security in South Asia: A nexus approach.* International Centre for Integrated Mountain Development, Kathmandu, Nepal.

IEA – International Energy Agency, 2018. *World energy outlook 2018.* IEA, Paris. www.iea.org/weo2018/ (accessed 2.15.19).

Isaac, M., Van Vuuren, D.P., 2009. *Modeling global residential sector energy demand for heating and air conditioning in the context of climate change.* Energy Policy 37(2), 507–521.

Kevany, K.M., Baur, G., Wang, G.C., 2019. *Transitioning to sustainable food choices: A course design,* in: Filho, W.L., McCrea, A.C. (Eds.), *Sustainability and the Humanities.* Springer, Cham. https://doi.org/10.1007/978-3-319-95336-6_10.

Kurian, M., 2017. *The water–energy–food nexus: Trade-offs, thresholds and transdisciplinary approaches to sustainable development.* Environmental Science and Policy 68, 97–106. DOI: 10.1016/j.envsci.2016.11.006.

Larcom, S., van Gevelt, T., 2017. *Regulating the water–energy–food nexus: Interdependencies, transaction costs and procedural justice.* Environmental Science and Policy 72, 55–64.

Laves, G., Kenway, S., Begbie, D., Roiko, A., Carter, R.W., Waterman, P., 2014. *The research–policy nexus in climate change adaptation: Experience from the urban water sector in South East Queensland, Australia.* Regional Environmental Change 14(2), 449–461.

Leck, H., Conway, D., Bradshaw, M., Rees, J., 2015. *Tracing the water–energy–food nexus: Description, theory and practice.* Geography Compass 9(8), 445–460.

LeMahieu, P.G., Nordstrum, L.E., Gale, D., 2017. *Positive deviance: Learning from positive anomalie.* Quality Assurance in Education 25(1), 109–124.

Lesk, C., Rowhani, P., Ramankutty, N., 2016. *Influence of extreme weather disasters on global crop production.* Nature 529, 84–87.

Levin, K., Cashore, B., Bernstein, S., Auld, G., 2012. *Overcoming the tragedy of super wicked problems: Constraining our future selves to ameliorate global climate change.* Policy Sciences 45(2), 123–152.

Liu, Q., 2016. *Interlinking climate change with water–energy–food nexus and related ecosystem processes in California case studies.* Ecological Processes 5(1), 1–14. DOI: 10.1186/s13717-016-0058-0.

Loring, P., Gerlach, S.C., Huntington, H., 2013. *The new environmental security: Linking food, water, and energy for integrative and diagnostic social-ecological research.* Journal of Agriculture, Food Systems, and Community Development 3(4), 1–7. DOI: 10.5304/jafscd.2013.034.005.

Märker, C., Venghaus, S., Hake, J.F., 2018. *Integrated governance for the food–energy–water nexus: The scope of action for institutional change.* Renewable and Sustainable Energy Reviews 97(C), 290–300. DOI: 10.1016/j.rser.2018.08.020.

Moore, F.C., Baldos, U., Hertel, T., Diaz, D., 2017. *New science of climate change impacts on agriculture implies higher social cost of carbon.* Nature Communications 8(1), article 1607.

Ney, S., 2009. *Resolving messy policy problems: Handling conflict in environmental, transport, health and ageing policy.* Earthscan, London.

NOAA National Centers for Environmental Information (NCEI), 2019. *U.S. billion-dollar weather and climate disasters.* www.ncdc.noaa.gov/billions/ (accessed 2.15.19).

OECD/IEA, 2018. *World energy outlook: Water–energy nexus.* www.iea.org/weo/water/.

Palmer, J., 2012. *Risk governance in an age of wicked problems: Lessons from the European approach to indirect land-use change.* Journal of Risk Research 15(5), 495–513.

Parry, I., 2018. *Fossil-fuel subsidies assessed.* Nature 554, 175–176.

Peters, B.G., 2017. *What is so wicked about wicked problems? A conceptual analysis and a research program.* Policy and Society 36(3), 385–396.

Pezzey, J.C., 2019. *Why the social cost of carbon will always be disputed.* Wiley Interdisciplinary Reviews: Climate Change 10(1), e558.

Pillot, J., Catel, L., Renaud, E., Augeard, B., Roux, P., 2016. *Up to what point is loss reduction environmentally friendly?: The LCA of loss reduction scenarios in drinking water networks.* Water Research 104, 231–241.

Rasul, G., Sharma, B., 2016. *The nexus approach to water–energy–food security: An option for adaptation to climate change.* Climate Policy 16(6), 682–702. DOI: 10.1080/14693062.2015.1029865.

Reisch, L.A., Eberle, U., Lorek, S., 2013. *Sustainable food consumption: An overview of contemporary issues and policies.* Sustainability: Science, Practice, and Policy 9, 7–25. DOI: 10.1080/15487733.2013.11908111.

Rittel, H.W.J., Webber, M.M., 1973. *Dilemmas in a general theory of planning.* Policy Sciences 4(2), 155–169.

Rogers, P., Daines, S., 2014. *A safe space for humanity: The nexus of food, water, energy, and climate.* ADB Brief No. 20. Asian Development Bank, Mandaluyong City, Philippines.

Rojas, R., Feyen, L., Watkiss, P., 2013. *Climate change and river floods in the European Union: Socio-economic consequences and the costs and benefits of adaptation.* Global Environmental Change 23(6), 1737–1751.

Sarni, W., 2017. *Beyond the energy–water–food nexus: New strategies for 21st-century growth.* Routledge, Abingdon.

Scott, C.A., Kurian, M., Wescoat Jr, J.L., 2015. *The water–energy–food nexus: Enhancing adaptive capacity to complex global challenges,* in: Kurian, M., Ardakanian, R. (Eds.), *Governing the nexus.* Springer, Berlin, pp. 15–38.

Steinfeld, H., Gerber, P., Wassenaar, T., Castel, V., Rosales, M., de Haan, C., 2006. *Livestock's long shadow: Environmental issues and options.* Food and Agriculture Organization, Rome.

Tadasse, G., Algieri, B., Kalkuhl, M., von Braun, J., 2016. *Drivers and triggers of international food price spikes and volatility,* in: Kalkuhl, M., von Braun, J., Torero, M. (Eds.), *Food price volatility and its implications for food security and policy.* Springer, Cham, pp. 59–82.

Taylor, R.A.J., Herms, D.A., Cardina, J., Moore, R.H., 2018. *Climate change and pest management: Unanticipated consequences of trophic dislocation.* Agronomy 8(1), p. 7.

UNCTAD, 2013. *Wake up before it is too late: Make agriculture truly sustainable now for food security and changing climate.* Trade and Environment Review. United Nations, Geneva.

UNDESA – United Nations, Department of Economic and Social Affairs, Population Division, 2017. *World population prospects: The 2017 revision, key findings and advance tables.* Working Paper No. ESA/P/WP/248. United Nations, New York.

Wang, Y.D., Lee, J.S., Agbemabiese, L., Zame, K., Kang, S.G., 2015. *Virtual water management and the water–energy nexus: A case study of three Mid-Atlantic states.* Resources, Conservation and Recycling 98, 76–84. DOI: 10.1016/j.resconrec.2015.01.005.

Water Footprint Network, n.d. *Water footprint.* https://waterfootprint.org/en/water-footprint/ (accessed 11.23.18).

Wichelns, D., 2017. *The water–energy–food nexus: Is the increasing attention warranted, from either a research or policy perspective?* Environmental Science and Policy 69, 113–123.

World Economic Forum, 2011. *Water security: The water–food–energy–climate nexus.* Island Press, Washington, DC.

20

GOVERNANCE OF WATERSHEDS IN RURAL AREAS

Karen Refsgaard[1]

This chapter introduces and discusses the issues of governance surrounding watersheds in rural areas, giving examples of how critical challenges are managed in different rural institutional settings. It focuses on rural water resource problems, including access to clean and sufficient water for varying purposes and different stakeholders, how these problems are managed and solved in different rural settings, and what the impacts are for different groups in rural communities. The chapter begins with an outline of contemporary global challenges relating to the demand for and supply of sufficient clean water, arguing that resolving the needs and demands of different users amounts to a governance crisis. The chapter conducts a comparative analysis of the different governance regimes for watershed management in continental Europe, Nordic countries, the UK, Mexico, the US, and Canada – as well as with non-Western countries. This examination can be very useful in understanding how different regimes have varying impacts and outcomes for rural communities and a wide range of stakeholders, illustrated with examples from different rural areas around the world. The chapter has theoretical underpinnings in institutional economics, which lends an analytical framework for analyzing water and watershed issues which can compare the economic, environmental, and social impacts on rural communities under varying regimes. Finally, the integration of watershed management and rural development policies are discussed, flowing from the articulation of specific problems, the challenges facing policy-makers, and residents in managing those issues in rural watersheds.

Historically, humans have always made systems for water management to support basic needs such as food production, drinking water, transport, energy, and eventually as a reservoir for wastewater. An early example of water management under a feudal regime comes from Canada in the sixteenth century, where the *seigneurial system* was introduced in New France in 1627 along the banks of the St. Lawrence River by Cardinal Richelieu, the French secretary of state. Under this system, lands were arranged in long narrow strips, called *seigneuries*, along the banks of the river (Mathieu, 2013). See Figure 20.1 for an illustration. Each piece of land belonged to the king of France and was maintained by the landlord, or *seigneur*. The system was an important colonial project given that the St. Lawrence River at that time was the "Highway of New France", providing water as a means of transportation which enabled French settlement along the St. Lawrence. Land along the river, therefore, was much in demand.

With increasing population and industrialization, access to clean water – either sourced from rivers or from groundwater – became an issue in many societies. In the early nineteenth century,

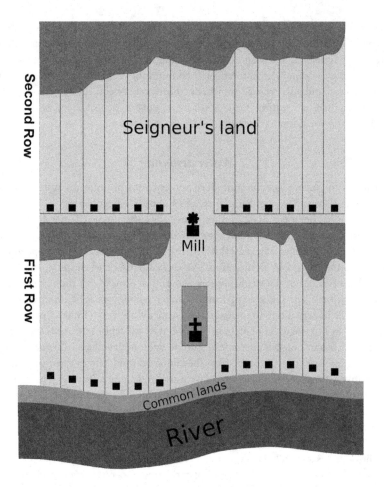

Figure 20.1 A typical layout for a feudal manor in New France

the main causes of water contamination in Western societies were untreated human wastewaters and organic and inorganic pollution from growing industry. In the twentieth century, technological development, economic and population growth, and urban expansion brought new pollution problems from agricultural, road, and urban runoff, and industrial effluents. At the same time, the nineteenth century saw the advancement of public health resulting from improved understanding of waterborne diseases. With the onset of industrialization and urbanization, production and people often became concentrated in towns and cities. This created a need for transportation of clean and sufficient water for growing urban populations. At the same time, the discharge of waterborne and polluting human and industrial wastes increased. Rural areas were directly affected by those changes, as they were commonly the source of the clean water, food, and energy needed to produce and transport them. They were also affected by pollution from cities.

The demand for and supply of enough and clean water

Water is a precondition for human existence and for the sustainability of the planet. However, the complex water cycle also creates externalities (e.g. global trade with food, clothes, or other

273

goods), which affect actors in locations distant from where they are measured and charged. The issue of externalities is very clearly illustrated in the example of a river where discharges of polluted water upstream from a sewage plant may pollute drinking water for rural settlements downstream without compensation to affected communities. Such impacts are not easily capitalized in the market and also cross administrative borders between actors such as municipalities and land owners, thereby creating challenges for the governance of access to sufficient, clean, and affordable water for human existence.

Water demand

Water demand is increasing as economic development puts pressure on water ecosystems and other natural resources, and as population increases and people become richer. Water withdrawal refers to water that has been removed from its source for a specific use. Large differences in water withdrawal exist, both geographically and between different sectors (Food and Agriculture Organization, 2014). Globally, water withdrawal has increased 1.7 times faster than population over the last century. Agriculture, including irrigation, livestock watering and cleaning, and aquaculture is associated with 69 percent of the world's water withdrawal – making it the most water-intensive activity. However, the importance of agricultural water withdrawal is highly dependent on both climate and the role of agriculture in the economy. Agriculture ranges from 21 percent of the total water withdrawal in Europe to 82 percent in Africa and 85 percent in the Arab countries (Bryden, 2017). Most countries in non-Mediterranean Europe dedicate less than 10 percent of their water withdrawal to agriculture, due to the fact that the climate is moderate in these countries and agriculture is a relatively small economic sector. In industrialized nations, however, industries consume more than half of the water available for human use. Belgium, for example, used 88 percent of the water available for industry in 2009 (FAO, 2019). Globally, about 884 million people have inadequate access to safe drinking water and 2.5 billion people have inadequate access to water for sanitation and waste disposal (WHO/UNICEF, 2008).

Although water has always been a contested resource, the contemporary wave of water grabbing is distinct in that the mechanisms for appropriating and converting water resources into private goods are much more advanced and increasingly globalized (Mehta et al., 2012). Water now features prominently within a global resource grab that is driven by processes of commodification, privatization, and large-scale capital accumulation (Mehta et al., 2012). These global changes for the most important resource for humans put water at the heart of conflicts in areas where it is scarce. Water grabbing refers to situations where powerful actors take control of or reallocate water resources to their own benefit at the expense of previous (un)registered local users or the ecosystems on which those users' livelihoods are based. The results are often deprived local communities whose livelihoods depend on these resources and associated ecosystems.

Boelens and Gaybor (2014) identify different "levels of confrontation" and provide some cases on water grabbing, e.g. from Peru on who has the power to grab water resources. In Peru's Ica Valley, the top 0.1 percent of users – powerful agro-exporters – control a third of the total water, while small-scale farmers, 71 percent of the valley's users, have access to only 9 percent. Another example from Turkey illustrates how the power to determine the contents of rules, rights, and laws to govern water distribution and allocation has changed towards privatization of rights to water (Islar, 2012). Hydropower development is made possible through neoliberal reforms that have transferred exclusive access rights to hundreds of rivers and streams to private companies in Turkey.

Water also lies at the heart of key regional conflicts, including the Israel–Palestine–Jordan conflicts (Jordan River) and North–South Sudan conflicts, conflicts between Jordan and Saudi

Arabia over groundwater extraction from the Disi/Saq aquifer, and the Ethiopia–Somalia conflicts (Jubba and Shabele Rivers) (Bryden, 2017). In 1988 then-Egyptian Foreign Minister Boutros Boutros-Ghali, who later became the United Nations' Secretary-General, predicted that the next war in the Middle East would be fought over the waters of the Nile, not politics. The Nile River has been a source of political tensions and low-intensity conflicts among three of its major riparian countries (Ethiopia, Sudan, and Egypt) for several decades (Swain, 2010).

However, since the late 1990s the Nile basin countries – with the encouragement and support of the international community – have made some attempts to establish basin-wide cooperative institutions. This process is presently under severe stress due to increasing demand and decreasing supply of water resources in the basin. Cooperation may be further complicated by global climate change, which is anticipated to result in long-term changes in the volume and pattern of runoff in the Nile River system. Moreover, the emergence of China as a major player in the power politics of the Nile basin has facilitated a number of unilateral initiatives for large-scale water development projects (Swain, 2010).

According to the United Nations (United Nations Economic and Social Council, 2002), "The human right to water is indispensable for leading a life in human dignity. It is a prerequisite for the realization of other human rights". This was then made more explicit in 2010 by the United Nations Assembly in Resolution 64/292, which recognized that clean drinking water and sanitation are essential to the realization of all human rights (United Nations General Assembly, 2010). The Resolution calls upon states and international organizations to provide financial resources, help capacity building and technology transfer to help countries – in particular developing countries – to provide safe, clean, accessible, and affordable drinking water and sanitation for all. The affordability is expressed through a requirement for the water cost not to exceed 3 percent of household income.

Water scarcity

One can distinguish between either physical or economic water scarcity, as illustrated in Figure 20.2. Around one-fifth of the world's population currently live in regions affected by physical water scarcity, implying that there are inadequate water resources to meet a country or region's demand, including the water needed to fulfill the demand of ecosystems to function effectively (United Nations Development Programme, 2006). Many arid regions frequently suffer from physical water scarcity. Physical water scarcity also occurs where water seems abundant but where resources are over-committed, such as with heavy development of hydraulic infrastructure for irrigation. Symptoms of physical water scarcity include environmental degradation and declining groundwater, as well as other forms of exploitation or overuse.

Economic water scarcity is caused by lack of investment in infrastructure or technology to draw water from rivers, aquifers, or other water sources, or poverty leading to insufficient human capacity to satisfy the demand for water. One-quarter of the world's population is affected by economic water scarcity (United Nations World Water Assessment Programme, 2016). Economic water scarcity includes lack of infrastructure, which causes people without reliable access to water to travel long distances to fetch water for domestic and agricultural uses. In addition, the water is often contaminated from upstream sources. Large parts of Africa suffer from economic water scarcity. In countries such as Mozambique, average daily water consumption per capita is below 10 liters, compared to international recommendations of a minimum of 20 liters of water (not including water needed for washing clothes), available no more than 1 km from the household. According to the OECD (2012), water demand is projected to grow by some 55 percent due to growing demand from manufacturing (+400 percent), thermal electricity generation

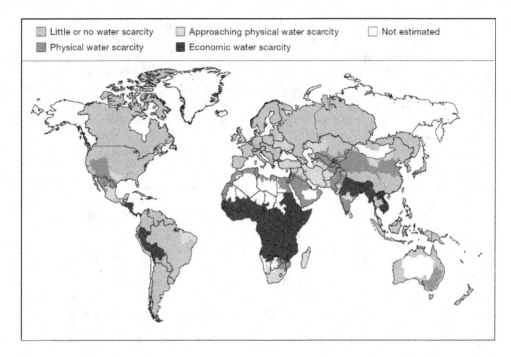

Little or no water scarcity   Approaching physical water scarcity   Not estimated

Physical water scarcity   Economic water scarcity

Figure 20.2 Physical water scarcity and economic water scarcity by country, 2006

(+140 percent), and domestic use (+130 percent) (see Figure 20.3). Regardless the magnitude of future global – and more importantly local – water deficits, water scarcity is likely to limit opportunities for economic growth and creation of decent jobs in the near future (United Nations World Water Assessment Programme, 2016).

Rural areas may in many ways suffer even more from water scarcity. Water used for industrial production and expanding growing areas in cities may result in lack of adequate rural water resources for household needs and agricultural production. Critical conditions often arise for economically poor and politically weak communities. This happens in Africa, but also in industrialized countries such as the US. Sparsely populated, low-income communities across the rural US suffer from polluted water. The New Republic (2018) refers to the case that most health-based violations of drinking water standards occur outside of big cities in the US in small, poor, isolated places. Of the 5000 drinking water systems that racked up health-based violations in 2015, more than 50 percent were systems that served 500 people or fewer. Often, the very industries that provide a community its economic backbone are threatening its water supply with heavy metals, nutrients, or other contaminants from mining, oil, large-scale agriculture, or other industries. Many poorer countries are challenged by not only dry environmental conditions but also large powerful companies engaging in water grabbing. According to *The Independent* (2018), natural water supplies have run out in the Indigenous town of San Felipe Ecatepec in the state of Chiapas, southern Mexico. A nearby bottling plant run by Mexican company FEMSA consumed 1.08 million liters of water. Chiapas has a high level of renewable water per capita among Mexican regions, but one in three people in rural regions reportedly lack safe drinking water, meaning that, according to one local official, people must walk for two hours to fetch drinking water. The implication is that people must walk for hours each day to get water or buy bottled water – an experience mirrored in many other rural regions.

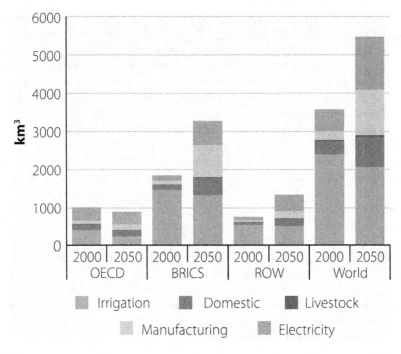

Figure 20.3 Global water demand (freshwater withdrawals): baseline scenario, 2000 and 2050

Supply

There are great differences in the availability of water from region to region – from the extremes of deserts to tropical forests. There is also variability of supply over time as a result both of seasonal variation and inter-annual variation. The magnitude of variability and the timing and duration of periods of high and low supply are not easily predictable, which poses great challenges to water managers in particular, and to societies as a whole. Most developed countries have artificially overcome natural variability by investing in supply-side infrastructure to assure reliable supply and reduce risks, albeit at high cost and often with negative impacts on the environment, and sometimes on human health and livelihoods. Many less developed countries, and some richer countries, now realize that supply-side solutions alone are not adequate to address the ever-increasing demands from demographic, economic, and climatic pressures. Wastewater treatment, water recycling, and demand management measures are being introduced to counter the challenges of inadequate supply. In addition, there are also problems of water quality with pollution of water sources creating major problems for water users as well as for maintaining natural ecosystems.

An institutional economic perspective of water and the watershed

From a natural science point of view, a watershed covers the land area that drains runoff (rain or snow) into a lake, river, or stream. Watershed systems – from those with many small tributaries to large-scale lake systems and river basins – provide direct inputs to economic processes, serve as waste sinks for economic output, and provide ecosystem services that make life possible

(Erickson *et al.*, 2007). For instance, a single watershed may provide water for consumption, transport, energy, and recreational use, being a depository for treated sewage and industrial pollutants, providing flood control services, as well as a multitude of aquatic and terrestrial habitats that form the source of life and sanctuary for diverse species. The use of the watershed as a geographic unit for the planning and management of water supply and flood control in the United States dates to the late nineteenth and early twentieth centuries (Randall and Heberling, 2005), but its use for ecosystem protection is more recent (Cole *et al.*, 2005).

Conflicts arise over the use and allocation of these resources from diverse actors in watershed economies (Erickson *et al.*, 2007). The challenge for social science at the watershed scale is thus to provide an analytical framework for decision support that both describes the system and measures its functioning, while also providing insights to decision-makers on the governance of the watershed. As articulated by Smith and Porter (2009), "[ultimately], any goal for improvement in water quality is socially defined, depending on the desired human use of water (Revenga *et al.*, 2000), or desired attributes of an aquatic ecosystem for which water is conserved".

At the watershed scale, conflicts over water and land resources are inherently multi-attribute, multi-stakeholder, and multi-discipline decision problems. Institutional mechanisms exist to guide activities on a watershed. Laws and customary rights affect a watershed and the water that flows through and from it. Laws, regulations, and policies can help to determine the effectiveness and distribution with which the responses to the demands and needs for water and other natural resources are implemented. A key issue within this is the human right for safe, clean, accessible, and affordable water (Gregersen *et al.*, 2007).

To understand, analyze, and compare the processes and outcomes of watersheds and governance regimes it can be useful to employ insights from institutional economics and its theory on resource regimes. A watershed is a common-pool resource (Ostrom, 1990), according to the standard distinction between exclusion costs and rivalry in use or consumption (Randall, 1983), with high costs of excluding others from using the same resource and rivalry in use (see Table 20.1). A common-pool resource typically consists of a core resource (e.g. a watershed) being the stock variable, while providing a limited quantity of extractable fringe units, being the flow variable. While the core resource is to be protected or nurtured in order to allow for its continuous exploitation, the fringe units can be harvested or consumed. In a watershed the river is such a stock while the industrial use, consumption of drinking water, serving as a pool for discharged polluted water, and a recreational spot for swimming all are flows. These characteristics have implications for allocation as to the rivalry in use creating externalities, implying that the costs of production and use are carried by a person other than the producer. For example, emitting wastewater upstream decreases the quality of the water downstream in the river, while extracting water for bottled water reduces water for downstream communities; similarly, producing energy may imply a decrease in salmon stocks due to obstruction of habitat. Further, the fact that the demarcation or exclusion costs are high implies that there is a danger of the "tragedy of the commons" (Hardin, 1968). In a watershed, it is difficult to exclude cities upstream from discharging polluted water as the city may be located in another municipality or country with no decision-making power over the downstream community. It is costly to pay an industry not to pollute upstream. Such ecological systems need carefully designed governance systems in order to consider the different interests to ensure that resources are both allocated efficiently and distributed fairly. The tragedy of the commons arises because of failed governance systems. To avoid such tragedy, one can establish common property within which the cost of coordination is to be balanced with the cost of exclusion. In the case of a common-pool resource, it may be governed by open access, a common property regime, or by the state. The European Water Framework Direction is an example of a regime that aims to avoid such tragedy.

Table 20.1 Characterization of goods according to costs of exclusion and rivalry in use

		Cost of exclusion	
		Low	*High*
Rivalry in use	Yes	Private goods (e.g. bread)	Common-pool resource (e.g. watershed, fishing ground)
	No	Club goods (e.g. hunting)	Public goods (e.g. air, military defense)

Sources: Derived from Ostrom (1990) and Vatn (2005).

To summarize, the characteristics for a watershed and its water are the following:

- There is rivalry for its use.
- The costs of exclusion are high.
- It is fundamental for human needs.
- It and its related flows (e.g. drinking water) are irreplaceable for humans and their activities.

These characteristics imply that conflicts are liable to occur between users due to the creation of externalities.

The governance of watersheds is not only a matter of allocation, but also a matter of distribution to consider the human rights for water. Therefore, there is a need for institutions to regulate actions of individuals for the common good to ensure that the resource regime is both efficient (considering allocation) and fair (considering distribution). This implies that the privatization of watersheds may become problematic, for example as the human right to safe, accessible, and affordable water is hindered, reduced, or becomes more costly when a private actor reduces the quality or the quantity of the watershed. This occurs through, for example, industrial use changing the water level or polluting the water recipient. An efficient and fair governance regime therefore needs to take into account not only national and transnational (e.g. EU) legislation, but also catchment-specific physical, socio-economic, and cultural characteristics, interests, and needs. In that respect, the required levels for water recipient quality have to be balanced against the need for legitimate solutions across the different stakeholder groups either emitting into or using the common-pool resource.

In practice, water governance is also sensitive to issues of scale because the hydrological scale system with its different scalar levels from small catchments or watersheds to large river basins plays a dominant role. Levels of government and administration typically do not fit the environmentally relevant scales, resulting in inefficiencies, spatial externalities, and spillovers. Tension also exists between the traditional nested hierarchies of national political-administrative systems and trends towards both the up-scaling of governance in the form of multinational agreements or the growing influence of the European Union and downscaling in the form of decentralization of environmental decision-making, involving a diversity of local non-state actors (Moss and Newig, 2010).

Water and watershed governance around the world

Watersheds will most often cover rural as well as urban areas. However, as described earlier in the chapter, rural water resource problems include issues such as access to drinking water, irrigation, right for industrial use, power generation, access to recreational services like boating and swimming, pollution problems from different sources due to population growth, agricultural production, urban sewage, and problems with biodiversity decline (e.g. flooding, timing of available water, plant/fish species disturbances, etc.).

Watershed management and governance differ widely around the world in response to the unique management contexts facing policy-makers. Deficits of water are likely to increase with climate change in many places, while on the other hand new technologies, including digital solutions, may reduce water use through new technological solutions and changed behavior among users.

However, as water is only one of a number of vital natural resources, it is imperative that water issues are not considered in isolation, but that efficient allocation and distribution between different sectors are ensured. With the establishment of the Dublin Principles in 1992, water was recognized as an "economic good", and a global effort was mounted to promote a set of universal principles for good water management enshrined in the concept of Integrated Water Resources Management (IWRM). The rationale for the IWRM approach (United Nations, 1992) is a way forward for efficient, equitable, and sustainable development and management of the world's limited water resources while coping with conflicting demands. IWRM strategies are based on the four Dublin Principles presented at the World Summit in Rio de Janeiro in 1992:

1   Fresh water is a finite and vulnerable resource, essential to sustain life, development, and the environment.
2   Water development and management should be based on a participatory approach, involving users, planners, and policy-makers at all levels.
3   Women play a central part in the provision, management, and safeguarding of water.
4   Water is a public good and has a social and economic value in all its competing uses.
5   Integrated water resources management is based on the equitable and efficient management and sustainable use of water.

According to the UN World Water Assessment Programme (2006), governance is seen as a core of the water crisis. "Water insufficiency is often due to mismanagement, corruption, lack of appropriate institutions, bureaucratic inertia and a shortage of investment in both human capacity and physical infrastructure". It has also been claimed, primarily by economists, that water mismanagement has occurred because of a lack of property rights, government regulations, and subsidies in the water sector, causing prices to be too low and consumption too high.

These aspects are also emphasized by the OECD (2011), which argues that the water crisis is largely a governance crisis – not a crisis of scarcity but a crisis of mismanagement – with strong public governance features. To respond to the unclear, overlapping, and fragmented roles and responsibilities across policy areas and between levels of government within water governance, a survey among 17 OECD member countries was accomplished in 2010. The OECD Water Governance Initiative (WGI) was created in March 2013 as an international network of 100+ public, private, and non-for-profit stakeholders gathering twice a year in a Policy Forum to share experience on water reforms, peer-review analytical work on water governance, and produce bottom-up knowledge and guidance such as the OECD Principles on Water Governance. The reasons for improved water governance are several:

- Access to water trumps the engineering view because disputes over water often are more related to the social, economic, and institutional context than they are to the technical factors governing the availability of water resources.
- Lack of accountability and transparency in water policy.
- Water sector reforms, to be effective, require improvements in water governance systems.
- Ownership of water rights and associated roles and responsibilities have a complex relationship with water governance, since they have an important influence on the organization of the water sector and coordination between its agents.

While the IWRM focuses on sectoral or social system integration among the various water-using sectors, it leaves the spatial organization of water management open. The concept of river basin management (RBM) is a strategy for sustainable resource use within a complex multi-institutional regulatory context. RBM calls for the management of water resources at the catchment or river basin level, and thus mainly refers to a spatial or natural system integration of water management functions. IWRM is a process that:

> promotes coordinated development and management of water, land and related resources, in order to maximize economic and social welfare in an equitable manner without compromising the sustainability of vital systems.
>
> *(Global Water Partnership, 2000, p. 22)*

However according to Franco *et al.* (2014), many processes and policies of the water governance regime beyond IWRM have largely been shaped by global bodies,[2] of which many are under increasing corporate capture and have largely promoted a pro-water privatization agenda, promulgating the concept of water as an economic good. They are also supported by multilateral institutions such as development banks and donor organizations,[3] where development aid is sometimes linked to the privatization of water resources. Finally, the framework intended to defend water as a public good and advance a human rights-based approach to water governance has, up to date, had very limited impact in granting access to water. Although it certainly should be seen as a positive step that a Right to Water and Sanitation has been recognized by the United Nations, the current approach also falls short in certain key aspects (see also Newig and Challies, 2014). Franco *et al.* (2013) argue that in order to maximize economic, equity, and eco-system benefits, the IWRM does not consider the tensions, trade-offs, and difficult political choices that are involved in natural resource management. The result is that more powerful actors can gain and entrench their control over water resources. It has been commented for instance that both the decentralization of water management as well as the licensing of water abstraction – two IWRM-influenced reforms – have been used to enable and legitimize water grabbing. IWRM has also been found to have limited impact on water management in practice. In a 2005 survey by the Global Water Partnership, only 20 out of 95 countries reported formal implementation of IWRM principles.

A recent attempt to implement IWRM and RBM in the European Union is the EU Water Framework Directive (WFD) of December 2000 (European Communities, 2000). The WFD requires its member states to implement a river basin approach in order to reach common environmental objectives for all surface waters and groundwater bodies in the EU (Petry and Dombrowsky, 2007). Earlier the Acts on Water issues in the EU were scattered in separate thematic directives on drinking water, nitrates, sewage, pollution control, swimming water, nature protection, and other. Within the WFD, the member states and Norway (through the EEA agreement) must implement RBM plans and programs of measures according to the planning cycles. The WFD represents the first time in EU environmental policy that economic principles, tools, and instruments have been explicitly integrated into a piece of legislation, thus opening up a unique opportunity to link empirical research and policy-making around water governance (WATECO, 2003).[4]

Examples of watershed management, policies, and governance

Continental Europe, the Nordic countries, the UK, the US, and Canada display different forms of watershed management, policies, and governance. Some examples and more references of existing governance and management regimes for watersheds and water are illustrated below. One such key public regime is the Water Framework Directive being introduced in EU and EEA countries, as discussed above, along with the global IWRM program.

WFD in Norway: bridging the gaps through holistic and local water governance in a rural area

The Morsa watershed, 690 km², is located in the southeast of Norway; it includes eight municipalities, two counties, and 40,000 inhabitants. The watershed is covered by marine sediments, has several lakes, and a hydrology characterized by peak runoff events during autumn and winter periods. The lake Vansjø is a unique recreational area and also serves as a drinking water reservoir for 60,000 people in the region. Until recently, there has not been a central management structure for the river basin, although the water quality problems linked to lake Vansjø have been of major concern for decades. Registration of 2300 households in rural areas showed that most of the wastewater treatment plants were insufficient. A program of upgrading was proposed and is now almost completed, resulting in a reduction of 1.8 tons of phosphorus runoff into the lakes.

Morsa was the first type of cooperation in the watershed that built on consensus and a common knowledge-based structure for decisions across sectors and municipalities, as well as county borders. It started in 1999, following an initiative from four municipalities in the watershed facing particularly poor conditions. The formal decision-making is in the hands of the participating local and county authorities. A governing board heads the project and has responsibility for overall management while acting as a general assembly. The board includes the mayors of the eight municipalities (with leaders of the opposition as deputies), farming representatives, and representatives from each of the county councils and county governor's offices. The findings demonstrate that collective social action in a polycentric network is feasible and cannot be fully explained by rational actor theories (Naustdalslid, 2015). The relative success of Morsa relates to many factors, including openness of practices and active involvement of key actors, strong but including leadership, and a knowledge-based "hybrid" type of multi-level network combining horizontal and vertical network governance. Although the Morsa model is being recommended as a good example of water governance, criticism has also arisen due to a complex multi-level governance network dominated by experts while political anchorage at local and regional levels is needed for further achievements. Political leadership and network managers have important roles in ensuring political anchorage (Hovik and Hanssen, 2016).

Water reform in Mexico: uneven power and capacity relationships between cities and rural communities

Mexico is a country under severe water stress. Over the past 60 years, the amount of water available per capita has declined drastically due to population growth. Furthermore, water is unevenly spread in Mexico, with more than three-quarters of the population living in regions with little water. It is estimated that during the next 20 years, the country will need to provide an additional 35 million inhabitants with drinking water services and 40 million inhabitants with sanitation services. According to the OECD (2013), since 2011 Mexico has had an existing and well-developed policy framework for water resource management, but its implementation has been uneven. This is seen in river basin councils, which are not fully operational, while the regulatory framework for drinking water and sanitation is also scattered across multiple actors, and harmful subsidies in other sectors (e.g. energy, agriculture) work against water policy objectives.

There is no overarching authority or legislative framework at the federal level that sets clear rules for the water operators. Instead, regulatory responsibilities for water and sanitation services are scattered across different levels of government and various instruments. Water and sanitation service are the primary responsibility of municipalities, with various levels of capacity and resources. This generates heterogeneity across the territory in terms of tariffs, technical and operational characteristics, state involvement, and service providers (OECD, 2013). Mexico's regional disparities play an important role in the capacity of these institutions. For example, only 637 of the 2356 water providers in the country are located in larger towns or cities. Almost three-quarters of the utilities are located in small rural communities and areas where resources and capacities are scarce. According to CONAGUA (2011), in 2010 more than 24 million Mexicans lived in communities where 25 percent were without access to drinking water and 40 percent without a sewage system.

New York City's watershed: dependence on cooperation with upstream rural communities

The 1997 New York City Watershed Memorandum of Agreement (MOA) outlines a program of source water protection (Platt *et al.*, 2000). The MOA provides for an extraordinary financial and legal commitment from New York City to prevent existing and potential contaminants from reaching reservoirs; to monitor water quality and drinking parameters; to conduct research on public health and water quality; and to promote sustainable economic development and social well-being in the surrounding watershed communities.

Why did this happen? According to Platt *et al.* (2000), the opposition of upstate interests to any expansion of the city's influence or control over land use in the watersheds was a major obstacle for the city to meet the Environmental Protection Agency's condition for filtration. New York City owned only about 7 percent of the watershed while state and conservation organization ownership controlled another 20 percent, leaving three-quarters in private ownership mostly devoted to agriculture and forestry. The region is scattered with sparsely populated towns and hamlets that have not shared in the economic boom enjoyed by metropolitan New York (Platt *et al.*, 2000).

Finally, balancing watershed regulation with targeted support of watershed community development is a reasonable strategy considering both providers in rural areas as well as the different users in both cities and rural communities. Due to these features, the case study is an example of good IWRM practices according to Hassing *et al.* (2009).

Integrating watershed governance and rural policy

Watersheds provide rural and urban areas with key functions for economic activities, such as agriculture, energy, and industry, and for basic residential needs such as drinking water, sanitation, recreation, and ecological functions. In order to balance these different needs against the

available supply of water and ecosystem services within the watershed, good watershed governance considering the fundamental human right to adequate clean water and sanitation is key to
a sustainable rural development policy framework.

In Figure 20.4, the horizontal coordination across policy areas is shown for a number of
OECD countries. Australia, Chile, France, Israel, Korea, New Zealand, Mexico, Spain, and the
UK show such horizontal coordination (OECD, 2011). In some countries and regions, tools
such as the EU Water Framework Directive (WFD) place attention on multi-level governance
regimes with different sectors involved in the coordination around a watershed. The New York
case shows how urban areas can include the surrounding rural communities in governance while
reimbursing them economically.

However, due to the nature of water and externalities, public regulation is necessary in order
to secure key human rights to water for all groups in society. The tendencies in global development within the use of the IWRM principles show that privatization of rights to water are
increasing, in part because water is becoming an increasingly scarce resource. Rural communities
with low political and economic power are thereby challenged by these changes.

As expressed by Franco *et al.* (2014) and Bryden (2017), a paradigm shift is therefore needed
for the management of transboundary water resources. Official policy discussions are often
dominated by a natural scientific view, leading to bureaucratic regimes that treat rivers simply as
water pipes rather than living ecosystems. A classic example is that of silt. While for hydrologists,
power engineers, and policy-makers silt is a major nuisance that breaks turbine blades and
should be filtered out, it provides the lifeblood for farmers who rely on it to replenish their soil

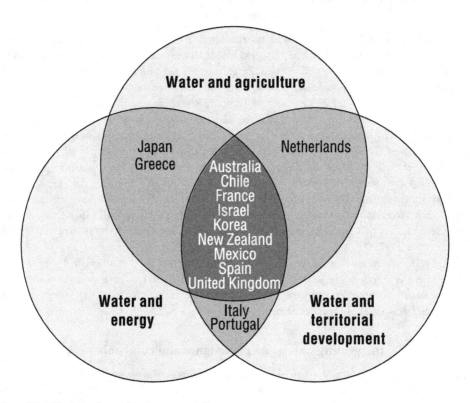

Figure 20.4 Horizontal coordination across policy areas

fertility, or fisherfolk whose fish stocks are fed by it. Yet unless the farming and fishing communities – as well as all those whose lives depend on and are affected by the river system – are included in conversations about their management, these views are unlikely to be heard. A new era of cooperation based on these experiences, voices, and lived knowledge is needed. In much of the world there is much ground to cover to secure human rights to adequate and clean water, as highlighted in this chapter. Furthermore, new governance regimes are needed to establish integrated water management with laws, regulations, and other institutions that provide for both human rights and other water uses that go beyond basic needs to safeguard the diverse values of watersheds for all stakeholders who depend on them.

Notes

1 Thanks to an anonymous reviewer and to John Marshall Bryden, one of the three founders of ICRPS, for providing excellent feedback on the chapter.
2 Such as the World Commission on Dams (WCD), the International Commission on Irrigation and Drainage (ICID), the International Water Resources Associations (IWRA), the World Water Council (WWC), the Global Water Partnership (GWP), or even the Global Water Operators' Partnership Alliance (GWOPA).
3 The World Bank, the International Monetary Fund, and various regional development banks and other large donor organizations.
4 Annex III of the WFD indicates that economic analysis should support the assessment of the most cost-effective combination of measures to be included in the Programme of Measures (Balana *et al.*, 2011; WATECO, 2003; European Communities, 2000). However, to find the economic optimal level for pollution abatement must in principle include all costs and benefits for society. For instance, farmers argue for societal benefits from agriculture to be acknowledged, e.g. food security and survival of rural farm communities. The WFD opens for specific economic interests to obtain exemptions in order to meet societal economic needs. In Norway this is the case for hydropower companies while less the case for agriculture (Bechmann *et al.*, 2016).

References

Balana, B.B., Vinten, A.J., Slee, W., 2011. *A review on cost-effectiveness analysis of agri-environmental measures related to the EU WFD: Key issues, methods, and applications.* Ecological Economics 70, 1021–1031.
Bechmann, M., Collentine, D., Gertz, F., Graversgaard, M., Hasler, B., Helin, J., Jacobsen, B., Rankinen, K., Refsgaard, K., 2016. *Water management for agriculture in the Nordic countries.* NIBIO Report Volume 2, No. 2. https://core.ac.uk/download/pdf/52131987.pdf.
Boelens, R., Gaybor, A., 2014. *Water grabbing in the Andean region: Illustrative cases from Peru and Ecuador,* in: Kaag, M., Zoomers, A. (Eds.), *The global land grab: Beyond the hype.* Zed Books, London, pp. 100–116.
Bryden, J.M., 2017. *Water, energy, and food in the Arab region: Challenges and opportunities, with special emphasis on renewable energy in food production,* in: Amer, K., Adeel, Z., Böer, N., Saleh, W. (Eds.), *The water, energy, and food security nexus in the Arab region.* Springer, New York, pp. 83–103.
Cole, R.A., Feather, T.D., Munch, J.D., 2005. *Watershed planning and management in the United States,* in: Bruins, R.J.F., Heberling, M.T. (Eds.), *Economics and ecological risk assessment: Application to watershed management,* 2nd edition. CRC Press, Boca Raton, FL, pp. 11–42.
CONAGUA, 2011. *2030 water agenda.* National Water Commission of Mexico, Mexico City. www.conagua.gob.mx/CONAGUA07/Publicaciones/Publicaciones/2030-Water-Agenda.pdf.
Erickson, J.D., Messner, F., Ring, I., 2007. *Ecological economics at the watershed scale: Comparing and contrasting the United States and German experiences and approaches.* In Erickson, J.D., Messner, F., Ring, I. (Eds.), *Ecological economics of sustainable watershed management.* Elsevier, Oxford, pp. 3–10.
European Communities, 2000. *Directive 2000/60/EC of the European Parliament and the Council of 23 October 2000 establishing a framework for Community action in the field of water policy.* Official Journal of the European Communities, 1–72. https://eur-lex.europa.eu/resource.html?uri=cellar:5c835afb-2ec6-4577-bdf8-756d3d694eeb.0004.02/DOC_1&format=PDF.

FAO – Food and Agriculture Organization, 2014. *Aquastat: Water withdrawal and pressure on water resources.* www.fao.org/nr/water/aquastat/didyouknow/index2.stm.

FAO – Food and Agriculture Organization, 2019. *Aquastat.* www.fao.org/nr/aquastat.

Franco, J., Mehta, L., Veldwisch, G., 2013. *The global politics of water.* Third World Quarterly 34(9), 1651–1675.

Franco, J., Kishimoto, S., Kay, S., Feodoroff, T., Pracucci, G., 2014. *The global water grab: A primer.* Transnational Institute. www.tni.org/en/publication/the-global-water-grab-a-primer.

Global Water Partnership Technical Advisory Committee, 2000. *Integrated water resources management.* Global Water Partnership, Stockholm. www.gwp.org/globalassets/global/toolbox/publications/background-papers/04-integrated-water-resources-management-2000-english.pdf.

Gregersen, H.M., Ffolliott, P.F., Brooks, K.N., 2007. *Integrated watershed management: Connecting people to their land and water.* CABI, Wallingford.

Hardin, G., 1968. *The tragedy of the commons.* Science 162, 1243–1248.

Hassing, J., Ipsen, N., Clausen, T., Larsen, H., Lindgaard-Jørgensen, P., 2009. *Integrated water resources management in action.* UNESCO. http://unesdoc.unesco.org/images/0018/001818/181891E.pdf.

Hovik, S., Hanssen, G.S., 2016. *Implementing the EU Water Framework Directive in Norway: Bridging the gap between water management networks and elected councils?* Journal of Environmental Policy and Planning 18(4), 535–555.

Islar, M., 2012. *Privatised hydropower development in Turkey: A case of water grabbing?* Water Alternatives 5(2), 376–391.

Mathieu, J., 2013. *Seignurial system,* in: *The Canadian encyclopedia.* www.thecanadianencyclopedia.ca/en/article/seigneurial-system.

Mehta, L., Veldwisch, G., Franco, J., 2012. *Special issue: Water grabbing? Focus on the (re)appropriation of finite water resources.* Water Alternatives 5(2), 193–542.

Moss, T., Newig, J., 2010. *Multilevel water governance and problems of scale: Setting the stage for a broader debate.* Environmental Management 46, 1–6. DOI: 10.1007/s00267-010-9531-1.

Naustdalslid, J., 2015. *Multi-level water governance: The case of the Morsa River Basin in Norway.* Journal of Environmental Planning and Management 58(5), 913–931.

Newig, J., Challies, E., 2014. *Waters, rivers and wetlands,* in: Harris, P. (Ed.), *Handbook of global environmental politics.* Routledge, Oxon and New York, pp. 439–452.

OECD, 2011. *Water governance in OECD countries: A multi-level approach.* OECD Publishing. doi:http://dx.doi.org/10.1787/9789264119284-en.

OECD, 2012. *Meeting the water reform challenge: Executive summary.* OECD. www.oecd.org/env/resources/meetingthewaterreformchallenge.htm.

OECD, 2013. *Making water reform happen in Mexico.* OECD Publishing. doi:http://dx.doi.org/10.1787/9789264187894-en.

Ostrom, E., 1990. *Governing the commons: The evolution of institutions for collective action.* Cambridge University Press, Cambridge.

Petry, D., Dombrowsky, I., 2007. *River basin management in Germany: Past experiences and challenges ahead,* in: Erickson, J.D., Messner, F., Ring, I. (Eds.), *Ecological economics of sustainable watershed management.* Elsevier, Oxford, pp. 11–41.

Platt, R.H., Barten, P.K., Pfeffer, M., 2000. *A full, clean glass? Managing New York City's watersheds.* Environment Science and Policy for Sustainable Development 42(5), 8–20.

Randall, A., 1983. *The problem of market failure.* Natural Resources Journal 23(1), 131–148.

Randall, J., Heberling, M. (2005). *Introduction to ecological risk assessments in watersheds,* in: Randall, J., Heberling, M. (Eds.), *Economic and ecological risk assessment: Applications to watershed management.* CRC Press, Boca Raton, FL, pp. 43–55.

Revenga, C., Brunner, J., Henninger, N., Kassem, K., Payne, R., 2000. *Pilot analysis of global ecosystems: Freshwater systems.* World Resources Institute, Washington, DC. www.wri.org/sites/default/files/pdf/page_freshwater.pdf.

Smith, L.E., Porter, K.S., 2009. *Management of catchments for the protection of water resources: Drawing on the New York City watershed experience.* Regional Environmental Change 10(4), 311–326. DOI: 10.1007/s10113-009-0102-z.

Swain, A., 2010. *Challenges for water sharing in the Nile basin: Changing geo-politics and changing climate.* Hydrological Sciences Journal 687–702. doi:doi.org/10.1080/02626667.2011.577037.

The Independent, 2018. *Coca-Cola sucking wells dry in indigenous Mexican town – forcing residents to buy bottled water.* June 9. www.independent.co.uk/news/world/americas/coca-cola-mexico-wells-dry-bottled-water-sucking-san-felipe-ecatepec-chiapas-a7953026.html.

The New Republic, 2018. *Rural America's drinking-water crisis.* https://newrepublic.com/article/147011/rural-americas-drinking-water-crisis.

United Nations, 1992. *The Dublin Statement on water and sustainable development.* www.un-documents.net/h2o-dub.htm.

United Nations Development Programme, 2006. *Human development report 2006: Beyond scarcity – power, poverty and the global water crisis.* Palgrave Macmillan, Basingstoke. http://hdr.undp.org/en/media/HDR06-complete.pdf.

United Nations Economic and Social Council, 2002. *General comment no. 15. The right to water.* www.unhcr.org/publications/operations/49d095742/committee-economic-social-cultural-rights-general-comment-15-2002-right.html.

United Nations General Assembly, 2010. Resolution A/RES/64/292.

United Nations World Water Assessment Programme, 2006. *Water: A shared responsibility. The United Nations World Water Development Report 2.* https://unesdoc.unesco.org/ark:/48223/pf0000144409.

United Nations World Water Assessment Programme, 2016. *The United Nations human development report 2016: Water and jobs.* UNESCO, Paris.

Vatn, A., 2005. *Rationality, institutions and environmental policy.* Ecological Economics 55, 203–217.

WATECO, 2003. *Common implementation strategy for the Water Framework Directive (2000/60/EC): Economics and environment – the implementation challenge of the WFD.* European Commission, Luxembourg.

WHO/UNICEF, 2008. *Progress in drinking-water and sanitation: Special focus on sanitation.* MDG Assessment Report. www.fao.org/nr/water/aquastat/didyouknow/index2.stm.

21

RETHINKING ENERGY IN AGRICULTURAL AND RURAL AREAS

Marco Pagani, Fabio De Menna, Laura García Herrero, Houston Sudekum, Giuseppe Palladino, and Matteo Vittuari

The industrialization of crop and livestock farming during the twentieth century significantly increased vegetal and animal productivity. Increases in productivity have come at the expense of larger energy intensities, mostly powered by non-renewable fossil fuels. Energy in agriculture is used both directly – as diesel fuel and electricity – and indirectly, embedded in machineries, fertilizers, and pesticides. The high dependence of agriculture on fossil fuels exposes farmers, and rural regions more broadly, to the volatility of energy prices (such as the oil crises of 1973 and 2008). Reducing agriculture demand for fossil fuels will strengthen the resilience of rural regions against future energy crises and liberate resources for local development. This goal can be accomplished by policies that facilitate transitions to renewable energy systems, such as low-input farming systems based on organic agriculture (which can lower energy use intensity by up to one-third), reduced machine power and use, substitution of diesel tractor fuel with bio-methane, and food loss prevention. Furthermore, rural regions have the potential to play a pivotal role in the transition to a new economy based on bioenergy. The full exploitation of natural resources and the development of integrated food–energy systems are the basis for future scenarios where rural areas can be energy independent and have the capacity to export surplus energy to urban regions.

Energy in traditional and modern agricultural systems

For centuries, agriculture relied mainly on human and animal muscular energy. Traditional farming systems in Central America and Asia required between 1100 and 1400 hours of human labor to cultivate one hectare of cereals (equivalent input of 2.4–3.0 GJ/ha) (Pimentel and Pimentel, 2008). See Box 21.1 for energy units. The mechanization of agriculture reduced the working time to about 10–20 hours per hectare but significantly increased fossil fuel consumption (Pimentel and Pimentel, 2008). Other inputs further influence the energy balance of modern agriculture. Machinery, synthetic chemical fertilizers, pesticides, and irrigation add another 21 GJ/ha of energy used for cultivation, leading to a total energy expense of 38 GJ/ha (Table 21.1).

The shift to industrial agriculture was decisive in the history of human societies through its significant increase in crop output, which supplied growing concentrations of people in urban

Table 21.1 Comparison of energy input/output in traditional and industrial cultivation of maize and rice. Unit: GJ/ha, except output/input ratio which is dimensionless

Energy input or output	Agricultural system	
	Traditional (Central America – Asia)	*Industrial (US)*
Human or animal work	3.500	0.002
Mechanical work	–	9.680
Machinery manufacturing	0.012	3.680
Seeds	0.065	2.650
Fertilizer production	–	13.590
Pesticides production	–	2.890
Irrigation	–	5.150
Total input	4.27	37.68
Total output	21.71	115.94
Output/Input	*5.1*	*3.1*

Source: Authors' elaboration from Pimentel and Pimentel (2008).

areas and simultaneously freed human capital to work in other sectors. However, these benefits came at the cost of lower energy efficiency. While traditional systems were yielding 5.1 MJ per MJ invested, modern processes are limited to 3.1. In the following paragraphs, the role of each input category will be briefly discussed to identify the largest hotspots of energy consumption.

Box 21.1 Measuring energy

One megajoule (1 MJ) is the energy contained in 30 cm³ of gasoline, or the nutritional energy available from 65 grams of rice or bread. This energy can be approximatively spent in four-and-a-half hours of full laptop activity, 100 minutes of office work, or 50 minutes of cycling. One gigajoule (GJ) is equivalent to 1000 MJ.

One ton of oil equivalent (toe) is defined as 42 GJ. One kilocalorie is equivalent to 4.18 kJ.

Fertilizers and pesticides

Traditional agricultural systems preserved soil fertility by using locally available organic fertilizers, such as animal and green manure, plant residues, ashes, and human excretion (Hinton, 1966; King, 1911); nitrogen fixing crop rotations and intercropping, such as beans with maize in Central America (Wilken, 1987), and groundnuts with yams and maize in Western Africa (Lagemann, 1977).

Soil fertilization in modern agriculture relies on phosphorous (P), potassium (K), and nitrogen (N), which are supplied by the mining and chemical industries. Global consumption of fertilizers increased six-fold between 1961 and 2011, with the largest growth in Asia and Latin America (FAO, 2018a). Annual fertilizer use surged from an average of 10 kg/capita in 1961 to 26.6 kg/capita in 2015. Annual global consumption of synthetic N alone increased from 11.6 to 112 million tons (Mt), which is equivalent to the annual natural nitrogen fixation of ecosystems around the world (Cleveland *et al.*, 1999).

Fertilizer production requires large amounts of energy, which is primarily fossil fuel-based. N fertilizer production uses between 40 and 50 MJ/kg (Williams *et al.*, 2006), leading to a global input of more than 200 million tons of oil equivalent (Mtoe) per year, which represents 7 percent of global natural gas consumption and nearly 2 percent of global fossil fuel consumption overall. The extraction and processing of phosphate rock and potash to produce P and K fertilizers require 5–8 MJ/kg of nutrient (Williams *et al.*, 2006; Ramirez and Worrel, 2006). Both minerals are quite abundant on the earth's crust, but a significant depletion of reserves is occurring: in 2015, about 40 percent of recoverable phosphate rock and 16 percent of potash had already been extracted (Kelly *et al.*, 2005). Phosphorus reserves may be completely depleted in 50–100 years (Cordell *et al.*, 2009). On the other end of the chain, each year about 9.5 out of 17.5 Mt of mined phosphate are lost to the sea (8 from soil erosion and 1.5 from human excretion), while the other 7.5 Mt are lost in non-arable soil or the atmosphere (Cordell *et al.*, 2009). Leaching of potassium is also common, especially from sandy soils (Kolahchi and Jalali, 2007), and, despite the increasing use, negative mass balances are common in irrigated rice cultivation (Dobermann *et al.*, 1998).

Traditional agriculture systems utilize a large variety of practices that provide crop protection, including: choice of sowing date, determination of optimal plant density, intercropping, and mechanical removals (Abate *et al.*, 2000). The advent of chemical pesticides during the second half of the twentieth century substituted some of these practices. Between 1990 and 2015, the use of fungicides, herbicides, and insecticides increased globally from 1.2 to 3.56 million tons. On average, about 0.5 kg of pesticides per capita are consumed each year, but figures are double that amount in Europe and Latin America and more than five times larger in North America and Oceania (FAO, 2018a). Besides their well-documented toxicity for the environment (Kalliora *et al.*, 2018; Kim *et al.*, 2017; Li, 2018; Machado and Martins, 2018), pesticides also require high energy inputs (between 80 and 580 MJ/kg) for production, packaging, and transportation (Green, 1987; West and Marland, 2002; Helsel, 2006), leading to a global energy consumption of 11 Mtoe per year.

Farming machinery

The intensive use of machinery has increased the energy input in agriculture, in addition to fuel consumption. Machinery production requires a large amount of energy, which has been estimated at approximately 80 MJ/kg of equipment (Stout, 1991; Mikkola and Ahokas, 2010). Machinery also requires repair, service, and maintenance, which raise the total input energy to about 140 MJ/kg (Giampietro and Pimentel, 1994; Mikkola and Ahokas, 2010). This energy input corresponds to an annual specific input of 4.6 MJ/kg year assuming a machinery lifespan of 30 years (ASABE, 2006; Edwards, 2009).

Irrigation

Energy consumption for irrigation originates from well pumps, long distance transportation, and canal maintenance. With regard to irrigation, water management of rice makes it the most energy-intensive crop (8.0–9.0 GJ/ha), followed by wheat (1.5–4.5 GJ/ha, depending on the amount of precipitation), and maize (1.0–2.0 GJ/ha) (Stout, 1991; West and Marland, 2002; Singh *et al.*, 2007; Çiçek *et al.*, 2009; Singh and Mittal, 1992; Pimentel and Pimentel, 2008). In very arid climates, irrigation inputs can reach up to 9.0–22.0 GJ/ha (Sefeedpari *et al.*, 2012, Jackson *et al.*, 2010).

Animal feed

In traditional farming, animals are typically fed vegetal products not suitable for direct human consumption (e.g. pastures and discards from food processing); however, the development of the meat industry in the twentieth century required more rapid animal growth, with a larger share of grains in feed composition. Between 1961 and 2011, the use of cereals and soya cake for animal feed increased from 288 to 816 Mt and from 13 to 150 Mt respectively, whereas land devoted to pasture grew less than 10 percent, from 31 to 33 million square km (FAO, 2018a). The food chain of animal products is characterized by low energy efficiency; 1 MJ of vegetal products fit for human consumption yields on average 0.45 MJ of animal products. The output/input energy ratio is smaller than one in most countries where intensive livestock farming is practiced, with a minimum of 0.31 in the United States. The ratio is larger than one only where extensive farming is prevalent, like India, Pakistan, or Ethiopia. (FAO, 2018a). Consumption of animal products dramatically increased in the last 50 years, from 70 to 280 Mt/year for meat and from 230 to 400 Mt/year for milk, with a parallel enormous growth in energy consumption.

Vulnerability of farmers and rural regions to energy crisis

A production process based entirely on non-renewable fossil fuels is unsustainable over the medium-to-long term (Georgescu-Roegen, 1971; Hall *et al.*, 2014), and may lead to instabilities and poor resilience in the short term. Human civilization is currently facing the problem of *peak oil* (Hubbert, 1956; Pfeiffer, 2006; Pagani and Caporali, 2014), an era in which oil production reaches a maximum and then decreases. As large high-quality oil fields are depleted, the extraction effort shifts towards smaller, remote, and worse quality oil fields, requiring more energy, and more technological and infrastructural inputs, without yielding the same quantities of annual production. Between 2005 and 2015, while conventional oil production only increased by 0.5 percent, overall crude oil production grew by about 9.1 percent, mainly due to lower quality non-conventional oil.

In the same period, energy demand was not saturated, especially in China, which experienced extremely fast industrial and economic growth, and a related increase in energy consumption (+47% oil, +200% gas, + 60% coal). The combination of strong demand and slowly increasing production caused the oil shock of 2007–2009, when prices surged from $54 to $134 per barrel, and then collapsed again to $42. (Hamilton, 2009). The decrease in oil prices in the following couple of years was mainly linked to overproduction in the OPEC countries and reduced demand resulting from the diffusion of renewable energies (Baffes *et al.*, 2015).

The peak of conventional oil and oil prices had a significant effect on world food prices, which are indicated by the FAO food price index (FAO, 2018b). Oil price is strongly correlated (r=0,75) with the food index, as can be seen from Figure 21.1 (EIA, 2018). After the price shocks of 2008 and 2011, the FAO food price index stopped oscillating, but remained relatively high, between 200 and 220. Food revolts, which involved several countries in 2008 and 2011, were triggered when the price index went over the threshold of 210 (Lagi *et al.*, 2011). The strong oil price decline of 2014–2015 was immediately followed by a decrease in the FAO index. It is likely that the overproduction of oil from OPEC countries will not last as long as the time required for a general transition to renewable energies. Thus, it is probable that in the medium-to-long term oil and food prices will rise again.

The high dependence of agriculture on fossil fuels makes farmers and rural regions more vulnerable to high volatility of energy prices (Regnier, 2007), as happened during the oil crises of 1973 (Pimentel *et al.*, 1973) and 2008 (Headey and Fan, 2008). For example, food insecurity

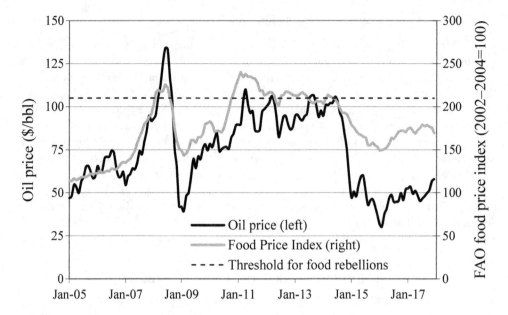

Figure 21.1 Oil price and food price index
Sources: EIA (2018) and FAO (2018b).

significantly increased in rural regions of Ethiopia and other parts of Africa Rift Valley during the 2008 food crisis (Hadley *et al.*, 2011; Richmond *et al.*, 2015).

Rethinking energy in agriculture

The need to restore the positive energy balance that has always characterized traditional agriculture will be one of the crucial challenges for the future of food systems (Heinberg and Bomford, 2009). This transition will require a set of choices that aim to increase self-reliant energy consumption through higher efficiencies and that substitute fossil fuel-based inputs with renewable sources, from animal power and biofuels for mechanized operations, to solar, hydro, bio-power, and bio-heat for other operations (see Figure 21.2). Rethinking the role of energy in agriculture will have the double benefit of making rural regions more resilient to energy crisis and price volatility as well as supporting local development (Sims *et al.*, 2015).

Reducing energy intensity

As in other sectors and areas, the reduction of energy intensity should be prioritized in agriculture and rural areas. One possible option to accomplish this goal is the widespread introduction of organic farming. In fact, while organic farming is generally appreciated for the better quality and sustainability of products, it can also result in a net decrease of energy use. This is mainly due to the reduction of mechanical operations and the exclusions of chemical fertilizers and pesticides, which all contribute significantly to the total energy demand. Organic wheat cultivation requires on average one-third less energy (Refsgaard *et al.*, 1998; MAFF, 2000; Fliessbach and Mäder, 2006) compared to modern conventional agriculture. Similar reductions are true for maize (Bilalis *et al.*, 2013; Klimekova and Lehocka, 2007; McLaughlin *et al.*, 2000), and rice (Pagani *et*

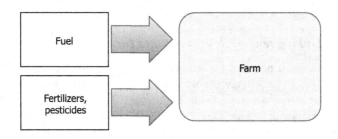

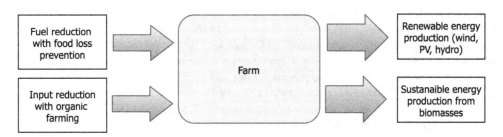

Figure 21.2 Energy diagram of current and sustainable farming systems

al., 2017). Organic farming also reduces energy inputs for the cultivation of roots, tubers, and bulbs (Souza *et al.*, 2008; Fliessbach and Mäder, 2006; MAFF, 2000; Mrini *et al.*, 2002). A significant reduction in input energy can also be achieved in livestock farming by organic farming, reduction of fertilizer use, low-power machinery, and a greater share of forage in animal feed (Pagani *et al.*, 2016).

Preventing food losses

Given the high energy intensity of contemporary food systems, inefficiencies related to food waste should be perceived as a waste of energy and resources. Depending on the nature of products and production systems, a significant amount of embedded inputs, such as water and energy, are wasted alongside food. Cuellar and Webber (2010) estimate that around 2 percent of the annual energy consumption of the United States could be saved if food waste were minimized through appropriate recovery and prevention. In Italy, the amount of energy embedded in food waste has been estimated at about 12 percent of all the energy spent in the food supply chain, and 1.3 percent of the total Italian final energy consumption; moreover, the energy lost in wasted food is equivalent to 2.5 times the energy required by the distribution segment and corresponds to about one-fourth of total Italian production from renewable energy sources (Vittuari *et al.*, 2016). Therefore, higher food chain efficiency can generate substantial energy savings. For example, if losses in the horticultural supply chains alone are reduced, it is possible to save 50 Ktoe (12 Ktoe in greenhouse cultivation and more than 38 Ktoe in open field cultivation), which represent about the 1.6 percent of the total energy consumption in Italian agriculture (Campiotti *et al.*, 2011).

Linking renewable energies and rural development

Rural regions have a great potential for renewable energy production that could help supply local demand and lead to net energy exports towards urban regions, further supporting local development (Bergmann *et al.*, 2006, 2008; Kroll *et al.*, 2012; Zheng *et al.*, 2010). Positive impacts of local development include increases in local revenues and jobs, affordable and reliable energy, capacity building and local empowerment, as well as innovation in products, processes, and policies (OECD, 2012). Among OECD countries, between 30 and 60% of total investments in renewable energy is located in rural areas (OECD, 2012). However, large-scale projects like wind farms may have minimal direct involvement of local people during the design and development phase. In addition, such projects might produce energy for the grid, but not local use, thus generating economic returns for distant shareholders, rather than for the rural communities who host the infrastructure.

By contrast, sustainable rural development is more likely to occur when local communities are involved. In this sense, the emergence of Community Renewable Energy (CRE) schemes in many parts of the world is particularly important. A CRE project is mainly characterized by two key independent factors: (i) the process is open and participatory, directly involving local people in planning, installation, and operations; (ii) the benefits are locally distributed in terms of jobs creation, infrastructure generation, and economic development (Walker and Devine-Wright, 2008). Within this framework, CRE initiatives can be either completely owned by the community or developed in partnership with private or public sectors. CRE schemes are particularly diffused in Germany, where 9% of the total installed renewable energy capacity is owned by energy cooperatives and 12% by citizen participation as shareholders (Trend:research Institut and Leuphana Universität, 2013). Positive effects of community energy include localization of production, cutting off intermediaries, changing of business models, participation of diverse actors, contribution to equity and sustainability, and, last but not least, community building (Rommel *et al.*, 2016). Furthermore, when small-scale projects are realized with community participation and fair distribution of economic benefits, local opposition towards renewable energy projects (the so-called Not-In-My-Back-Yard attitude) can be reduced, and even transformed into support (Rogers *et al.*, 2008; Warren and McFadyen, 2010). There are several instances of local rural communities in Europe that have benefited from small and medium scale CRE, some of which are reported in Box 21.2.

Box 21.2 Examples of community renewable energy in rural areas

Gamblesby, Cumbria, UK, is a small village with a few hundred inhabitants. In 2003 the local community decided to keep their village hall alive by providing heating through a ground source heat pump powered by a 6-kW wind turbine. The installation was partially funded (17 percent) and completely organized by the community and installed primarily by local people. The community was able to preserve a collective resource at the center of village life (Walker and Devine-Wright, 2008; ACT, 2010).

The village of Kobylnica, with little more than 2000 inhabitants, was the first municipality in Poland to take steps to build community support for wind energy. In 2011, 18 turbines were installed with a total power of 41 MW, which later was raised to 130 MW. Farmers obtained extra income from the leasing of their land to the wind developer. Additionally, the taxes from the wind energy installations made up over 10 percent of the community's annual budget. Kobylnica has been ranked as Poland's best commune to live in (EWEA, 2013).

In Hettingen, Baden-Württemberg, Germany, the local community contributed 7 million euros, leveraging an additional 18 million in bank loans, for a total of 25 million euros to invest in five 3.2 MW turbines. This put the total installed capacity of new turbines at 16 MW, with an average annual production of 36 GWh. Spread across roughly 300 shareholders, who were mostly locals, the average citizen invested less than 25,000 euros (EE, 2014).

The local community of Wildpoldsried, Bavaria, Germany has developed an integrated renewable energy network including 11 wind turbines, 5 MW of photovoltaics, 2100 m² of solar thermal systems and several municipal and residential biomass heating systems. As a result, the community is covering most of its energy needs and is selling electrical energy to the grid with revenues of more than 5 million euros per year (Cameron, 2017).

The Integrated Energy Farm is a project of the International Research Centre for Renewable Energy in Germany that aims at realizing a farming model with energy and food autonomy and, possibly, energy export. Farm land is divided in sectors for food production (cereals, oil, and sugar crops, livestock with grazing area) and for energy production from wind turbines, photovoltaic panels, and cultivation of energy crops (both annual and perennial). The project is performed in three farms in Europe, one in Iran and one in Ghana (El Bassam, 2010).

Wood fuel in rural and national economies

The Food and Agricultural Organization of the United Nations (FAO, 2018a) predicts that wood provides around 6 percent of the total global primary energy supply. Wood fuels account for roughly half of global wood removals (FAO, 2015), and around half of the global population rely on wood fuels for all or some of their cooking (AFREA, 2011), while wood fuels are also utilized for heating and increasingly in the electricity production sector (FAO, 2017; Calderon et al., 2016). Various analyses show that wood fuel combustion, production, and/or availability can promote economic development on national and regional levels. Bildirici and Özaksoy (2013, 2016) use econometric models to show that wood energy consumption can promote economic growth on national scales in parts of Sub-Saharan Africa and Europe. Other analyses show that the introduction of various wood energy processing facilities, power plants, or small business can lead to economic benefits in rural parts of the United States and Finland (Aksoy et al., 2011; Huttunen, 2012). Some of the potential benefits include: new employment opportunities, improved air quality, and reduced poverty and oil dependency.

These benefits have prompted some governments to implement policy that promotes rural economic development through forestry and wood energy. In the most recent EU forest strategy, the European Commission listed forests as a key resource in improving the quality of life and creating jobs in rural areas (EC, 2013). Additionally, the European Agricultural Fund for Rural Development allocated between 9 and 10 billion euros for forestry and wood energy-related measures between 2007 and 2013 (EC, 2017). In Sub-Saharan Africa, where per capita consumption of wood energy is two to three times higher than in any other region, governments have worked to promote positive aspects of wood energy (FAO, 2018c). Burkina Faso introduced participatory forest management areas that regulated harvests and marketing of wood fuels and resulted in substantial economic benefits, while Madagascar used a reform that relied on voluntary community participation to spread reforestation and increase wood fuel supply (FAO, 2018c).

Wood fuels also offer an opportunity to reduce carbon emissions. This is especially evident in Europe where many countries have implemented larger shares of woody biomass consumption to meet European Union renewable energy targets (Calderon et al., 2016). Long-term carbon emissions from wood fuels are found to be much lower than fossil fuel alternatives when efficient supply chains and combustion technologies are utilized (Taeroe et al., 2017; Zanachi et al., 2012; Röder et al., 2016). Wood fuels can help shift countries and communities towards energy independence, and aid in the development of local and national economies.

Stimulating a sustainable use of biomasses

Residual biomasses as by-products in the food supply chain can be viewed as assets to rural regions when utilized to power combined heat-electricity generation or biogas production (Herbert and Krishnan, 2016; Singh, 2016). Two examples are considered here, one from animal (manure) and one from vegetal (rice husks) biomass.

According to research conducted in Europe and the US, anaerobic digestion of cattle manure can produce on average about 300 kg of bio-methane, or 17 GJ per cow per year (Ahlgren et al., 2009; El-Mashad and Zhang, 2010). This amount could theoretically satisfy the energy needs of all dairy farms, including fuel for traction (Pagani, 2015). Conventional management of manure, including storage and land spreading, is responsible for significant air emissions of methane (CH_4) and nitrous oxide (N_2O), or about 42 g CO_{2eq} per kg manure or 530 kg CO_{2eq} per cow per year. Biogas production can reduce these GHG emissions by about 86 percent, and it is reasonable to assume that they could be further reduced by proper biogas plant design (Ahlgren et al., 2009). After the extraction of biogas, the digestate product contains virtually the same quantity of N, P, and K, as well as other micronutrients. The carbon content of the digestate is only slightly lower than the original manure, so in the long term the process is sustainable and there is no substantial effect on soil carbon balance (Möller and Müller, 2012). The digestion process can also improve the quality and availability of nutrients (Holm-Nielsen et al., 2009) and generate a pesticide and fungicide effect, which in some cases can be more effective than chemicals (De Groot and Bogdanski, 2013).

Rice husks can be used as a source of renewable fuel, providing about 14.3 MJ/kg (IRRI, 2008), which is lower than other biomass fuels but sufficient to supply renewable energy to many farms. Husks represent approximately 20 percent of paddy rice mass. The annual world rice husk production is about 148 Mt, equivalent to a potential energy production of 35 Mtoe, more than the oil consumption of countries like Malaysia or the Netherlands. Energy from husks could potentially be used for drying rice and/or other farm uses (Van-Hung et al., 2019). Instead of combustion, it is possible to use rice husks for syngas production: from 1 kg of husks it is possible to obtain 2 kg of syngas, whose heating value is about 5 MJ/kg (Ataei et al., 2012; Yoon et al., 2012). Syngas may be used for electrical energy production, while its use for vehicle traction is the subject of research studies (Hagos et al., 2014). Husk ashes produced from burning or gasification may also be used as soil amendment (Rajor et al., 2011).

Despite the potential benefits of biomass, negative externalities and specific trade-offs may arise from an intensification of land for biomass use. Increased pressure from bioenergy production can potentially lead to intensification of management, and a reduction in soil quality; additionally, traditional uses of residues (e.g. soil amending and animal feeding) may be put into direct competition for available biomass. Therefore, as suggested by Bogdanski *et al.* (2010), a sustainable removal rate should be identified according to local conditions, and proper agricultural practices should be used to prevent the degradation of soil health. For these reasons, Bonari *et al.* (2009) argue that synergistic policy approaches are crucial to ensure that the specific conditions of actors ranging from farmers to territories and communities, as well as contextual particularities, are considered. The impacts of energy production on the territorial peculiarities and the ecosystem must be carefully assessed.

In fact, as discussed by Heinberg and Bomford (2009), the transition towards a post-carbon society will pose significant pressure on the agro-food sector to become a net exporter of energy, mainly of solid biomass and biofuels. Therefore, appropriate ecological limits, such as the productive capacity and the fertility of soil, will have to be taken into consideration to prevent a trade-off between society's energy demand and the environmental foundations of food systems. The promotion of decentralized small-scale bioenergy plants could ensure the maintenance of linkages within an area, contribute to the diversification of productive activities, and meet local energy needs (Bonari *et al.*, 2009).

In conclusion, food systems will be increasingly required to satisfy the need for a higher energy efficiency and sustainability. This challenge should be addressed through an ecosystem-based approach and multidimensional perspective aiming at increasing the productivity of land in terms of biomass for food and energy, without endangering soil health. Thus, on one hand, the reduction and/or recovery of food waste can allow societies to reach higher productivity and energy efficiency. On the other hand, the integration of bioenergy generation from residues can reduce the fossil fuel dependence of food systems.

References

Abate, T., Van Hius, A., Ampofo, J.K.O., 2000. *Pest management strategies in traditional agriculture: An African perspective*. Annual Review of Entomology 45, 631–659.

ACT, 2010, *Action with communities in Cumbria. Case study: Gamblesby Village Hall Renewable Energy Project.* December 2010. www.cumbriaaction.org.uk/Portals/0/ACT%20Case%20Studies/CS011%20ACT ACT%20CS%20Gamblesby%20Renewable%20Energy.pdf?ver=2015-04-30-121926-007.

AFREA, 2011. *Wood-based biomass energy development for Sub-Saharan Africa: Issues and approaches.* The International Bank for Reconstruction and Development/The World Bank Group, Washington, DC, 1–46.

Ahlgren, S., Hanson, P., Kimming, M., Aronsson, P., Lundkvist, H., 2009. *Greenhouse gas emissions from cultivation of agricultural crops for biofuels and production of biogas from manure.* Swedish University of Agricultural Sciences. ww.sgc.se/ckfinder/userfiles/files/Greenhousegasemissionsfromcultivation.pdf.

Aksoy, B., Cullinan, H., Webster, D., Gue, K., Sukumaran, S., Eden, M., Sammons, N., 2011. *Woody biomass and mill waste utilization opportunities in Alabama: Transportation cost minimization, optimum facility location, economic feasibility, and impact.* Environmental Progress and Sustainable Energy 30(4), 720–732.

ASABE – American Society of Agricultural and Biological Engineers, 2006. *Agricultural machinery management data.* D497.5 2006.

Ataei, A., Azimi, A., Kalhori, S.B., Abari, M.F., Radnezhad, H., 2012. *Performance analysis of a co-gasifier for organic waste in agriculture.* International Journal of Recycling of Organic Waste in Agriculture 1, Article 6.

Baffes, J., Kose, M.A., Ohnsorge, F., Stocker, M., 2015. *The great plunge in oil prices: Causes, consequences and political responses.* Policy Research Notes, World Bank Group, March 2015. www.worldbank.org/content/dam/Worldbank/Research/PRN01_Mar2015_Oil_Prices.pdf.

Bergmann, A., Hanley, N., Wright, R., 2006. *Valuing the attributes of renewable energy investments.* Energy Policy 34(9), 1004–1014.

Bergmann, A., Colombo, S., Hanley, N., 2008. *Rural versus urban preferences for renewable energy developments.* Ecological Economics 65, 616–625.

Bilalis, D., Kamariari, P.E., Karkanis, A., Efthimiadou, A., Zorpas, A., Kakabouki, I., 2013. *Energy inputs, output and productivity in organic and conventional maize and tomato production, under Mediterranean conditions,* Notulae Botanicae Horti Agrobotanici Cluj-Napoca 41(1), 190–194.

Bildirici, M., Özaksoy, F., 2013. *The relationship between economic growth and biomass energy consumption in some European countries.* Journal of Renewable and Sustainable Energy 5(2). https://doi. org/10.1063/1.4802944.

Bildirici, M., Özaksoy, F., 2016. *Woody biomass energy consumption and economic growth in Sub-Saharan Africa.* Procedia Economics and Finance 38, 287–293.

Bogdanski, A., Dubois, O., Jamieson, C., Krell, R., 2010. *Making integrated food–energy systems work for people and climate: An overview.* Environment and Natural Resources Management Working Paper No. 45. Food and Agriculture Organization of the United Nations (FAO), Rome.

Bonari, E., Jodice, R., Masini, S. (Eds.), 2009. *L'Impresa agroenergetica, ruolo e prospettive nello scenario "2 volte 20 per il 2020".* Edizioni Tellus, Rome.

Calderon, C., Gauthier, G., Jossart, J., 2016. *AEBIOM statistical report 2015: European bioenergy outlook.* European Biomass Association, Brussels.

Cameron C, 2017. *This German village generates 500% more energy than it needs.* Inhabitat. https://inhabitat. com/german-village-produces-500-of-its-energy-from-renewable-sources/.

Campiotti, C., Viola, C., Scoccianti, M., Giagnacovo, G., Lucerti, G., 2011. *Le filiere del sistema agricolo per l'energia e l'efficienza energetica.* RT/2011/11/ENEA. ENEA, Rome.

Çiçek, A., Altintas, G., Erdal, G., 2009. *Energy consumption patterns and economic analysis of irrigated wheat and rain fed wheat production: Case study for Tokat region.* Turkey Journal of Food, Agriculture and Environment 7(3–4), 639–644.

Cleveland, C.C., Townsend, A.R., Schimel, D.S., Fisher, H., Howarth, R.W., Hedin, L.O., Perakis, S.S., Latty, E.F., Von Fischer, J.C., Elseroad, A., Wasson, M.F., 1999. *Global patterns of terrestrial biological nitrogen (N2) fixation in natural ecosystems.* Global Biogeochemical Cycles 13, 623–645.

Cordell, D., Drangert, J., White, S., 2009. *The story of phosphorus: Global food security and food for thought.* Global Environmental Change 19(2), 292–305.

Cuellar, A., Webber, M., 2010. *Wasted food, wasted energy: The embedded energy in food waste in the US.* Environmental Science and Technology 44(16), 6464–6469.

De Groot, L., Bogdanski, A., 2013. *Bioslurry, brown gold? A review of scientific literature on the co-product of biogas production.* Environment and Natural Resources Management Working Paper. FAO, Rome.

Dobermann, A., Cassman, K.G., Mamarila, C.P., Sheehya, J.E., 1998. *Management of phosphorus, potassium, and sulphur in intensive, irrigated lowland rice.* Field Crops Research 56(1–2), 113–138.

EC – European Commission, 2013. *A new EU forest strategy: For forests and the forest-based sector.* Brussels.

EC – European Commission, 2017. *Evaluation study of the forestry measures under rural development: Final report.* Luxembourg.

Edwards, W., 2009. *Estimating farming machinery cost.* Iowa State University Extension and Outreach. www. extension.iastate.edu/agdm/crops/html/a3-29.html.

EE – Erneurbare Energien, 2014. *Biggest community wind farm to open.* April 25. www.erneuerbareenergien. de/biggest-community-wind-farm-to-open/150/434/78385/.

EIA – Energy Information Administration, 2018. *Petroleum and other liquids, spot prices.* www.eia.gov/dnav/ pet/pet_pri_spt_s1_d.htm.

El Bassam, N., 2010. *Integrated energy farming for rural development and poverty alleviation,* in: Behl, R.K., Kubat, J., Kleynhans, T. (Eds.), *Resource management towards sustainable agriculture and development.* Agrobios, New Delhi, pp. 252–262. www.ifeed.org/pdf/Publication_IEF-for-Rural-Development-and-Poverty-Alleviation.pdf.

El-Mashad, H., Zhang, R., 2010. *Biogas production from co-digestion of dairy manure and food waste.* Bioresource Technology 101, 4021–4028.

EWEA – European Wind Energy Association, 2013. *Hitting the jackpot with wind energy in Poland.* The EWEA blog, August 19. www.ewea.org/blog/2013/08/hitting-the-jackpot-with-wind-energy-in-poland/.

FAO – Food and Agriculture Organization of the United Nations, 2017. *Sustainable woodfuel for food security. A smart choice: Green, renewable and affordable.* FAO, Rome.

FAO – Food and Agriculture Organization of the United Nations, 2018a. *Food and agriculture data.* www. fao.org/faostat/en/#home.

FAO – Food and Agriculture Organization of the United Nations, 2018b. *Food price index.* www.fao.org/ worldfoodsituation/foodpricesindex/en/.

FAO – Food and Agriculture Organization of the United Nations, 2018c. *The state of the world's forests – 2018: Forest pathways to sustainable development.* FAO, Rome.

Fliessbach, A., Mäder, P., 2006. *Productivity, soil fertility and biodiversity in organic agriculture.* Paper presented at the Joint Organic Congress, Odense, Denmark, May 30–31. http://orgprints.org/7682/1/Fliessbach_et_al_DOK-trial.doc.

Georgescu-Roegen, N., 1971. *The entropy law and the economic problem.* Distinguished Lectures Series No. 1, Alabama University.

Giampietro, M., Pimentel, D., 1994. *Energy utilization,* in: Arntzen, C.J., Ritter, E.M. (Eds.), *Encyclopedia of agricultural science.* Academic Press, San Diego, CA, Vol. 3, pp. 63–76.

Green, M.B., 1987. *Energy in pesticide manufacture, distribution, and use,* in: Helsel, Z.R. (Ed.), *Energy in plant nutrition and pest control.* Elsevier, Amsterdam, Vol. 2, pp. 165–177.

Hadley, C., Linzer, D.A., Belachew, T., Mariam, A.G., Tessema, F., Lindstrom, D., 2011. *Household capacities, vulnerabilities and food insecurity: Shifts in food insecurity in urban and rural Ethiopia during the 2008 food crisis.* Social Science and Medicine 73, 1534–1542.

Hagos, F.Y., Aziz, A.R.A., Sulaiman, S.A., 2014. *Trends of syngas as a fuel in internal combustion engines.* Advances in Mechanical Engineering, Article 401587.

Hall, C.S., Lambert, J.G., Balogh, S.B., 2014. *EROI of different fuels and the implications for society.* Energy Policy 64, 141–152.

Hamilton, J.D., 2009. *Causes and consequences of the oil shock of 2007–2008.* Brookings Papers on Economic Activity, Spring 2009, pp. 215–259. www.brookings.edu/~/media/projects/bpea/spring%202009/2009a_bpea_hamilton.pdf.

Headey, D., Fan, S., 2008. *Anatomy of a crisis: The causes and consequences of surging food prices.* Agricultural Economics 39, 375–391.

Heinberg, R., Bomford, M., 2009. *The food and farming transition: Toward a post-carbon food system.* Post Carbon Institute, Sebastopol.

Helsel, Z.R., 2006. *Energy in pesticide production and use,* in: Pimentel, D. (Ed.), *Encyclopedia of pest management.* Taylor & Francis, London, Vol. 2, pp. 157–161.

Herbert, G.M.J., Krishnan, A.U., 2016. *Quantifying environmental performance of biomass energy.* Renewable and Sustainable Energy Reviews 59, 292–308.

Hinton, W., 1966. *Fanshen: A documentary of revolution in a Chinese village.* California University Press, Berkeley, CA.

Holm-Nielsen, J.B., Al Seadi, T., Oleskowicz-Popiel, P., 2009. *The future of anaerobic digestion and biogas utilization.* Bioresource Technology 100, 5478–5484.

Hubbert, M.K., 1956. *Nuclear energy and the fossil fuels: Drilling and production practice.* American Petroleum Institute and Shell Development Co. Publication No. 95, pp. 9–11, 21–22.

Huttunen, S., 2012. *Wood energy production, sustainable farming livelihood and multifunctionality in Finland.* Journal of Rural Studies 28(4), 549–558.

IRRI – International Rice Research Institute, 2008. *Rice knowledge bank: Rice husk.* www.knowledgebank.irri.org/step-by-stepproduction/postharvest/milling/what-is-rice-husk.

Jackson, T.M., Khan, S., Hafeez, M., 2010. *A comparative analysis of water application and energy consumption at the irrigated field level.* Agricultural Water Management 97, 1477–1485.

Kalliora, C., Mamoulakis, C., Vasilopoulos, E., Stamatiades, G.A., Kalafati, L., Barouni, R., Karakousi, T., Abdollahi, M., Tsatsakis, A., 2018. *Association of pesticide exposure with human congenital abnormalities.* Toxicology and Applied Pharmacology 346, 58–75.

Kelly, T., Buckingham, D., Di Francesco, C., Porter, E.K., 2005. *Historical statistics for mineral and material commodities in the U.S.* Open File Report 01–006. US Geological Survey, Washington, DC. http://minerals.usgs.gov/ds/2005/140/.

Kim, K., Kabir, E., Jahan, S.A., 2017. *Exposure to pesticides and the associated human health effects.* Science of the Total Environment 575, 525–535.

King, F.H., 1911. *Farmers for forty centuries.* Courier Dover Publications, New York. www.gutenberg.org/cache/epub/5350/pg5350.html.

Klimekova, M., Lehocka, Z., 2007. *Comparison of organic and conventional farming system in terms of energy efficiency.* Wissenschaftstagung Ökologischer Landbau. http://orgprints.org/view/projects/wissenschaftstagung-2007.html.

Kolahchi, Z., Jalali, M., 2007. *Effect of water quality on the leaching of potassium from sandy soil.* Journal of Arid Environments 68(4), 624–639.

Kroll, F., Müller, F., Haase, D., Fohrer, N., 2012. *Rural–urban gradient analysis of ecosystem services supply and demand dynamics.* Land Use Policy 29, 521–535.

Lagemann, J., 1977. *Traditional African farming systems in eastern Nigeria: An analysis of reaction to increasing population pressure.* Weltforum Verlag, Munich. http://pdf.usaid.gov/pdf_docs/PNAAP542.pdf.

Lagi, M., Bertrand, K.Z., Bar-Yam, Y., 2011. *The food crises and political instability in North Africa and the Middle East.* New England Complex Systems Institute, September 2011. http://necsi.edu/research/social/food_crises.pdf.

Li, Z., 2018. *The use of a disability-adjusted life-year (DALY) metric to measure human health damage resulting from pesticide maximum legal exposures.* Science of the Total Environment 639, 438–456.

Machado, S.C., Martins, I, 2018, *Risk assessment of occupational pesticide exposure: Use of endpoints and surrogates.* Regulatory Toxicology and Pharmacology 98, 276–283.

MAFF – Ministry of Agriculture, Fisheries and Food, 2000. *Energy use in organic farming systems.* http://randd.defra.gov.uk/Document.aspx?Document=OF0182_181_FRP.pdf.

McLaughlin, N.B., Hiba, A., Wall, G.J., King, D.J., 2000. *Comparison of energy inputs for inorganic fertilizer and manure-based corn production.* Canadian Agricultural Engineering 42(1), 9–17.

Mikkola, H.J., Ahokas, J., 2010. *Indirect energy input of agricultural machinery in bioenergy production.* Renewable Energy 35(1), 23–28.

Möller, K., Müller, T., 2012. *Effects of anaerobic digestion on digestate nutrient availability and crop growth: A review.* Engineering in Life Sciences 12(3), 242–257.

Mrini, M., Senhaji, F., Pimentel, D., 2002. *Energy analysis of sugar beet production under traditional and intensive farming systems and impacts on sustainable agriculture in Morocco.* Journal of Sustainable Agriculture 20, 5–28.

OECD, 2012. *Linking renewable energy to rural development.* OECD Green Growth Studies. OECD Publications. www.oecd.org/regional/regional-policy/Renewable-rural-energy-summary.pdf.

Pagani, M., 2015. *From fossil to sustainable diets: An assessment of farming energy footprint* (PhD dissertation). University of Bologna, Department of Agro-food Sciences, June.

Pagani, M., Caporali, S, 2014. *The Hubbert model: Looking ahead by looking back,* in: Bardi, U. (Ed.), *Extracted: How the quest for mineral wealth is plundering the planet.* A report of the Club of Rome, Chelsea Publishing, White River Junction, VT, pp. 152–158.

Pagani, M., Vittuari, M., Johnson, T.G., De Menna, F., 2016. *An assessment of the energy footprint of dairy farms in Missouri and Emilia-Romagna.* Agricultural Systems 145, 116–126.

Pagani, M., Johnson, T.G., Vittuari, M., 2017. *Energy input in conventional and organic paddy rice production in Missouri and Italy: A comparative case study.* Journal of Environmental Management 188, 173–182.

Pfeiffer, D.A., 2006. *Eating fossil fuels: Oil, food and the coming crisis in agriculture.* New Society Publishers, Gabriola Island, BC.

Pimentel, D., Pimentel, M.H., 2008. *Food, energy and society,* 3rd edition. CRC Press, Boca Raton, FL.

Pimentel, D., Hurd, L.E., Bellotti, A.C., Forster, N.J., Oka, I.N., Sholes, O.D., Whitman, R.J., 1973. *Food production and the energy crisis.* Science 182(4111), November 2.

Rajor, A., Xaxa, M., Meth, R., Kunal, 2011. *Use of rice husk ash as fertilizer amendment to soil and its effect on crop germination.* National Conference on Emerging Trends in Chemistry-Biology Interface (ETCBI-2011).

Ramirez, C.A., Worrel, E., 2006. *Feeding fossil fuels to the soil: An analysis of energy embedded and technological learning in the fertilizer industry.* Resources, Conservation and Recycling 46(1), 75–93.

Refsgaard, K., Halbergb, N., Kristensen, E.S., 1998. *Energy utilization in crop and dairy production in organic and conventional livestock production systems.* Agricultural Systems 57, 599–630.

Regnier, E., 2007. *Oil and energy price volatility.* Energy Economics 29(3), 405–427.

Richmond, A.K., Malcomb, D., Ringler, K., 2015. *Household vulnerability mapping in Africa's Rift Valley.* Applied Geography 63, 380–395.

Röder, M., Thornley, P., Welfle, A., 2016. *Greenhouse gas emissions from biomass heating systems, 2016.* Presentation at All Energy Glasgow, May 5.

Rogers, J.C., Simmons, E.A., Convery, I., Weatherall, A., 2008. *Public perceptions of opportunities for community-based renewable energy projects.* Energy Policy Special Issue: Transition towards Sustainable Energy Systems 36, 4217–4226.

Rommel, J., Radtke, von Jorck, J.G., Mey, F., Yildiz, Ö., 2016. *Community renewable energy at a crossroads: A think piece on degrowth, technology, and the democratization of the German energy system.* Journal of Cleaner Production, November. https://doi.org/10.1016/j.jclepro.2016.11.114.

Sefeedpari, P., Rafiee, S., Komleh, H.K., Ghahderijani, M., 2012. *A source-wise and operation-wise energy use analysis for corn silage production: A case study of Tehran province, Iran.* International Journal of Sustainable Built Environment 1, 158–166.

Sims, R., Flammini, A., Puri, M., Bracco, S., 2015. *Opportunities for agri-food chains to become energy-smart.* FAO and USAID. www.fao.org/3/a-i5125e.pdf.

Singh, H., Singh, A.K., Kushwaka, H.L., Singh, A., 2007. *Energy consumption pattern of wheat production in India.* Energy 32(10), 1848–1854.

Singh, R., Krishna, B.B., Kumar, J., Bhakar, T., 2016. *Opportunities for utilization of non-conventional energy sources for biomass pretreatment.* Bioresource Technology 199, 398–407.

Singh, S., Mittal, J.P., 1992. *Energy in production agriculture.* Mittal, New Delhi.

Souza, J.L., Casali, V.W.D., Santos, R.H.S., Cecon, P.R., 2008. *Balanço e análise da sustentabilidade energética na produção orgânica de hortaliças.* Horticultura Brasileira 26, 433–440.

Stout, B.A., 1991. *Handbook of energy for world agriculture.* New York, Elsevier.

Taeroe, A., Mustapha, W.F., Stupak, I., Raulund-Rasmussen, K., 2017. *Do forests best mitigate CO2 emissions to the atmosphere by setting them aside for maximization of carbon storage or by management for fossil fuel substitution?* Journal of Environmental Management 197, 117–129.

Trend:research Institut, Leuphana Universität, 2013. *Definition und Marktanalyse von Bürgerenergie in Deutschland.* www.buendnis-buergerenergie.de/fileadmin/user_upload/downloads/Studien/Studie_Definition_und_Marktanalyse_von_Buergerenergie_in_Deutschland_BBEn.pdf.

Van-Hung, N., Van-Thuan, T., Meas, P., Joventino, C., Tado, M., Kyaw, M.A., Gummert, M., 2019. *Best practices for paddy drying: Case studies in Vietnam, Cambodia, Philippines, and Myanmar.* Plant Production Science 22(1), 107–118.

Vittuari, M., De Menna, F., Pagani, M., 2016. *The hidden burden of food waste: The double energy waste in Italy.* Energies 9(8), Article 660.

Walker, G., Devine-Wright, P., 2008. *Community renewable energy: What should it mean?* Energy Policy 36(2), 497–500.

Warren, C.R., McFadyen, M., 2010. *Does community ownership affect public attitudes to wind energy? A case study from south-west Scotland.* Land Use Policy, Forest Transitions 27, 204–213.

West, T.O., Marland, G., 2002. *A synthesis of carbon sequestration, carbon emissions, and net carbon flux in agriculture: Comparing tillage practices in the United States.* Agriculture, Ecosystems and Environment 91, 217–232.

Wilken, C.W., 1987. *Good farmers: Traditional agricultural resource management in Mexico and Central America.* University of California Press, Berkeley, CA.

Williams, A., Audsley, E., Sandars, D., 2006. *Determining the environmental burdens and resource use in the production of agricultural and horticultural commodities.* Defra Project Report IS0205.

Yoon, S.J., Son, Y.-I., Kim, Y.-K., Lee, J.-G., 2012. *Gasification and power generation characteristics of rice husk and rice husk pellet using a downdraft fixed-bed gasifier.* Renewable Energy 42, 163–167.

Zanchi, G., Pena, N., Bird, N., 2012. *Is woody bioenergy carbon neutral? A comparative assessment of emissions from consumption of woody bioenergy and fossil fuel.* GCB Bioenergy 4(6), 761–772.

Zheng, Y.H., Li, Z.F., Fenf, S.F., Lucas, M., Wu, G.L., Li, Y., Li, C., Jang, G.M., 2010. *Biomass energy utilization in rural areas may contribute to alleviating energy crisis and global warming: A case study in a typical agro-village of Shandong, China.* Renewable and Sustainable Energy Reviews 14(9), 3132–3139.

22

CONVENTIONAL AND ALTERNATIVE AGRI-FOOD CHAINS

Victòria Soldevila-Lafon, Lourdes Viladomiu, and Jordi Rosell Foxà

Introduction

Since World War II, farming has faced important changes. Two of the most important ones are the industrialization of agriculture and the globalization of agri-food systems. The industrialization of agriculture refers to the adoption of production practices similar to that in manufacturing, but also includes increasing interlinkages between agriculture and industry. On the one hand, manufacturing and services industries are of increasing importance as technological and input suppliers for farming and, on the other, farm products are no longer final products, but inputs for the food industry. Conceptual approaches have been developed to analyze this new agricultural system. In the 1960s–1970s, the concepts of "agribusiness" (Davis and Goldberg, 1957) and "*filière*" (Malassis, 1979) allowed for a clearer appreciation of the interrelationships between agriculture and industrial sectors. These new approaches have implied an analysis of farming as part of a "long" agri-food value chain which includes all the manufacturing sectors and services taking part in the production and transformation of a farm product into a manufactured food product.

In recent decades, agricultural trade liberalization has contributed to the transformation of most of the agri-food chains into "global agri-food chains". The seminal studies of the Global Commodity Chain (Gereffi, 1994), which later Kaplinsky and Morris (2002) redefined as a Global Value Chain, were first focused on manufacturing industries (apparel, automobile, electronics, etc.) that have segmented their production all over the world. As food and agricultural sectors followed a similar pattern, the Global Value Chain has become a useful tool in the analysis of agribusiness globalization.

Currently, at least in the Global North, these "long" value chains, even "global" ones, are shaping the dominant agri-food model. However, this dominant model has been called into question because of its adverse social, safety, and environmental effects. In recent years, "new" agri-food value chains have appeared (or reappeared in cases when they resemble the resurgence of traditional food chains), encompassed by the term "alternative food networks" (AFNs). They represent another typology of chain and, consequently, their analysis is focused on issues other than those affecting conventional ones.[1] The analytical approach to AFN is based on case studies and, frequently, involves several academic disciplines.

302

This chapter summarizes the main elements included in the analysis of agri-food value chains and their policy implications. This analysis is done with the acknowledgment that this review is limited in scope and does not cover all the approaches and issues regarding agri-food value chains. The first section is based on methodological approaches mainly used to analyze conventional value chains. The seminal works concerning *"filières"* and "agribusiness" and their contribution to conceptualizing agriculture as part of a broader and integrated system are reviewed. Therefore, the "Global Commodity Chain" and/or "Global Value Chain" and the main concepts of this approach ("governance", "upgrading") are introduced. The second section analyzes "alternative food networks" as a critical response to the conventional agri-food chains. In each of the previous sections, a case study selected from the academic literature is given in order to better understand the research approach. The third section summarizes the main political implications of each analysis (agribusiness and *filières*, Global Value Chain, alternative food networks). Finally, a set of suggestions for potential further research is offered.

Conventional agri-food chains

"Agribusiness", *"filières"*, and "Global Value Chain" can be considered conceptual approaches for analyzing "conventional" food chains: the first, the seminal concept that pointed out the incipient agriculture's industrialization process in the 1950s–1960s; the second, more related to the French tradition in agri-food studies and institutional approaches; and the third, more adapted to firm-level organizational changes and internationalization processes resulting from globalization.

"Agribusiness" and "filières"

The development of the agri-food industry and the process of agricultural modernization made it increasingly difficult to isolate agriculture from the rest of economic activity. The previous theoretical frameworks that had been used to study agriculture faced important shortcomings when they tried to analyze the post-World War II agriculture sector.

This increasing interrelation between agriculture and other economic sectors has come about in two different ways. On the one hand, agriculture is no longer a self-sufficient sector, but has become an important buyer of industrial inputs (e.g. fertilizers, pesticides, agricultural machinery, etc.) as well as services (e.g. technical services, financial services, etc.). On the other hand, agriculture is no longer a producer of final goods but a producer of intermediate goods that are later transformed by the manufacturing industry into foods. The distance between the farmer and the ultimate consumer has increased as new intermediary actors have appeared: food processing industries, packagers, transporters, wholesalers, retailers, caterers, etc.

Davis and Goldberg (1957) coined the term "agribusiness". They suggested that agriculture had to be considered as part of a broader and integrated system – the agribusiness – which included all operations and actors involved from the manufacture of farm supplies to the processing and distribution of farm products. Malassis (1979) was one of the first authors to develop the concept of *"filière"* (closely linked to the idea of "agribusiness").[2] The *filière* involves two main methodological aspects: its identification (the product, the flows of inputs and outputs, the agents and the operations performed by them) and the mechanisms of regulation involved (market structures, public regulations, etc.). For example, the pork *filière* includes feed suppliers, pig farmers, slaughterhouses, pig meat processors, wholesalers, and retailers (among others); market structure analysis can highlight the existence of oligopolistic structures in some pig meat production stages or the relevance of contracts and vertical integration between agents. Furthermore, the policies and regulations affecting the pork value chain are of very different types (food safety, animal welfare, environmental regulations, etc.). All these aspects are taken into account in a *filière* analysis (see Box 22.1).

The *filière* visualizes the linkages between farming and all other activities included in the agri-food chain. The main strength of this approach is the focus on power relationships along agri-food chains. Malassis (1979) pointed out how the industrial sectors (upstream and downstream) are the key elements that have promoted the industrialization of agriculture and the marginalization of the farmers within the chain. Thus, the relations between the actors (or linkages) are unequal and asymmetrical. In fact, there are relations of domination and dependence between them. In Latin America and Spain, a close *filière* analysis was introduced under the concept of "sectorial complexes". Under this approach, each "sectorial complex" has a "core". Trajtenberg (1977) defined "core" as the actor who acts as the organizer of domination relations in the chain. The concept of "core" was introduced into the analysis of power relations in *filière* studies as a key insight to better understand agricultural change (Viladomiu, 1985; Soldevila, 2008). Studies of "sectorial complexes" indicate that the "core" of each *filière* is usually in those linkages where there is a highest market concentration (oligopoly). However, there are other elements that must be considered in determining the "core": legal ownership, technology control, and financial power, among others (Viladomiu, 1985). This "core" is not static. In fact, *filière* approaches show how the "core" is changing from one linkage to another, due to changes in regulations or in market structures.

The *filière* analysis, also referred to as "commodity chain analysis" in Anglo-Saxon literature, has been applied in several agri-food studies, especially in the 1970s and 1980s. It has been greatly enriched with theoretical contributions from the field of industrial organization (e.g. vertical integration, transaction costs approach, market power theories) and institutional economics (especially, French regulation school and conventions theory). Today, the *filière* approach continues to be frequently used, especially in French institutions (INRA, CIRAD), but also in publications linked to FAO.

Box 22.1 The pork *filière* in Catalonia and its environmental problems (based on Soldevila, 2008)

Spain is one of the world's main pork producers and exporters. Hog production tends to concentrate in some geographical areas and, in Spain, 25 percent of hog production is based in the Catalonia region. In this case study, the *filière* approach allowed us to analyze the changes in the governance of the pork value chain in Catalonia. The feed producers became the promoters of hog production in Catalonia in the 1950s through "integration" contracts. In these kinds of production contracts, the feed company supplies feed, piglets, and other inputs (medicine, etc.) to the farmer and remains the legal owner of the pigs. The farmer provides facilities, machinery, equipment, and labor. This situation was seen to benefit both groups. For feed firms, the arrangement ensured a market for feed production, while also increasing profits from selling the fattened pigs to the slaughterhouses. On the other hand, small farmers were able to "survive" in a context of agricultural crises through farm diversification by adopting intensive livestock production. For them, contract production was seen as an easy way to increase incomes with low risk: there was no need to buy inputs (feed, piglets, etc.) or worry about selling output (finished pigs). Through integration, contracted hog production expanded quickly in Catalonia. Pig inventories have continuously increased, growing from 1.4

million in 1970 to more than 7.7 million in 2017. Today, more than 80 percent of hog production is done under integration contracts. Integration contracts have become a useful tool for feed producers to control the pork value chain. However, there have been some changes in the pork value chain which have eroded the "core" position of feed producers. After the entrance of Spain into the European Union in 1986, new regulations affecting slaughterhouses induced the closure of small slaughterhouses and increased the size of large ones. This concentration process gave the slaughterhouses greater bargaining power in the Catalonian pork value chain. In recent years, the "core" of the Catalonia pork value chain seems to be moving irreversibly towards the retailers due to the persistence of excess supply, increasing international competition, and higher concentration of supermarkets. This situation is squeezing the margins of the other actors in the chain and generating conflicts among them.

Environmental issues affecting hog production are analyzed through a *filière* approach. Traditional pig manure management is based in spreading manure on crop lands as fertilizer. However, pig farmers have been forced to increase the size of their farms in order to maintain their margins. In so doing, the quantity of manure has increased so much that most pig farmers do not have enough land to manage it properly, resulting in nitrate pollution of both land and groundwater. Nowadays, more than 40 percent of Catalonia's groundwater has excess nitrate content. Environmental regulations are pushing for better manure management, which means increasing costs for farmers, especially since crop farmers in some areas are asking for payments in order to allow pig farmers to spread manure on their lands. From a *filière* perspective, environmental regulations have meant a new linkage (or agent) in the pork value chain: the "crop farms", because of their land base, have become a crucial asset in Catalonian hog production.

"Global Commodity Chains" and "Global Value Chains"

Unlike agribusiness and *filière*, the concepts of Global Commodity Chain (GCC) and/or Global Value Chains (GVC) do not arise from agrarian studies. In fact, these approaches were initially developed to analyze the segmentation of the manufacturing value chain across geographic areas (in particular, the first studies focused on manufactured goods in Southeast Asia). In recent years, these frameworks have become very popular and have proven to be an appropriate analytical tool for agri-food value chain analysis in a globalized context.[3]

The main concepts and research lines of the GCC approach were outlined by Gereffi and Korzeniewicz (1994). GCC reformulates conceptual categories to analyze new patterns of change and global organization. According to the authors, this new approach overcomes some limitations of the analytical frameworks subscribed to at the nation-state level, thus offering a way to integrate theoretical approaches encompassing macro- and micro-economic aspects.

Gereffi (1994) pointed out three dimensions (the "global" or "top-down" ones) on GCC: the flow of inputs and outputs, territoriality, and governance. By integrating these three dimensions, the GCC incorporates some aspects of the *filière* approach (input–output flow) and allows us to analyze the internationalization of the value chain by integrating territoriality. Recently, three new dimensions (the "local" or "bottom-up" ones) have been added to GVC analysis: upgrading, local institutional context, and industry stakeholders (Gereffi and Fernandez-Stark, 2016). Governance and upgrading are the main contributions of the GVC approach.

The concept of "governance" used by the GCC/GVC studies is highly relevant for capturing recent organizational changes in business structures where modern corporations have been externalizing internal tasks to a network of independent firms, some of them overseas. "Governance" refers to how the GVCs are controlled and coordinated by a lead firm (Gereffi and Fernandez-Stark, 2016). There are two main questions in the "governance" analysis in GVC studies. First, who are the "lead" firms, that is, which actors define what the chain requires, and which actors are in charge of the cross-border coordination of the chain? Second, in which way is this "governance" organized, and how are the requirements transmitted to the other actors in the chain?

Regarding the first question, one of the most significant contributions of the GVC studies relates to Gereffi's (1994) distinction between *"producer-driven commodity chains"* and *"buyer-driven commodity chains"*. In the first one, the vertically integrated manufacturing companies are in control of the value chains and coordinate the linkages back and forth. Frequently, this value chain's typology is located in capital- and technology-intensive industries. On the other hand, in the buyer-driven commodity chain, governance is determined either by a large brand name or by retail companies. This happens in labor-intensive consumer goods (textiles, footwear, toys, etc.) production in which the lead companies reserve for themselves the activities of greater value added, linked to design and marketing. In Gereffi's opinion, one of the major transformations in recent decades is the governance shift from producer-driven to buyer-driven production in relevant manufacturing sectors. Several authors have pointed out that this process is also affecting the agri-food value chains (e.g. Pelupessy and Van Kempen, 2005; Burch and Lawrence 2005). Regarding the second question, "governance" in the GCC/GVC approach relates to the coordination relationships between the lead firm and other agents in the chain (mainly, its suppliers). The key insight is to reveal the existence of network forms of organization that go beyond market or vertical integration (Gereffi *et al.*, 2005).

Another important contribution of the GVC studies is the focus on *upgrading*, that is, how an agent (or country or region) can reap a larger share of the surplus in the GVC. As shown in the case study in Box 22.2, small farmers have increasing difficulties in being included in global value chains and, even when they are, have little chance to reach worthwhile incomes. Some of the agri-food studies based on the GVC approach propose upgrading strategies for farmers (mainly from developing countries) within agri-food value chains (e.g. Fold and Larsen, 2011; Staritz *et al.*, 2011, among others).[4]

Box 22.2 Impact of EU supermarkets on African horticulture (Dolan and Humphrey, 2000)

A GCC/GVC approach has been used in order to analyze global agri-food value chains linking developing countries' producers with retailers in developed countries. An interesting case study is the production of fruits and fresh vegetables in African countries destined for European markets. Dolan and Humphrey (2000) explain the case of fresh vegetables produced in Kenya and Zimbabwe destined for UK supermarkets. Fresh vegetables are a non-traditional agricultural export crop for Sub-Saharan African countries and their increasing economic importance is attached to the strategies of supermarket chains in Europe. As noted, supermarkets and major retail chains are playing a decisive role in the governance of agri-food value chains – and fresh fruits and vegetables are no exception. This case study uses a GCC approach to show how changes in the retail sector in the UK have had a great impact on the production of fresh vegetables in Kenya and Zimbabwe.

From the 1980s, there has been an increasing dominance of large supermarkets due to the concentration in the retailing of fresh food in the UK. Fresh fruits and vegetables are a key area of competition among supermarkets because this kind of product attracts high-income customers and offers higher margins to the supermarkets (especially in prepared fresh foods such as pre-washed salads). Imported horticultural products used to be channeled through wholesale markets, but this situation has dramatically changed and nowadays the largest UK retailers control most of the fresh produce imports from Africa. Fresh vegetable imports from Kenya and Zimbabwe have rapidly increased in the last decades, both in volume and product variety. Furthermore, these African suppliers have developed more value-added activities ("upgrading") as UK supermarkets have realized that packaging and labeling activities could be done in the source country at lower costs. Nevertheless, African producers and exporters have faced increasing requirements that they must meet in order to enter European markets. These include legislative requirements (i.e. food safety laws), but other requirements in areas such as labor conditions, environmental management practices, and product quality are imposed by the supermarkets. Inclusion in the Europe-bound chain depends on the supplier's capacity to meet these stringent public and private standards. Supermarkets are increasing their control over the chain by reducing the number of suppliers and implementing monitoring systems over them, usually in collaboration with African exporters and importers. Growers and exporters are pushed to invest in expensive post-harvest facilities, processing systems, and sophisticated logistics. However, only a few of them can afford these expensive investments and the only way to acquire these assets is to be attached to the European supermarket network. As Dolan and Humphrey (2000) pointed out, the consequences of these UK supermarket requirements are the increased concentration in the structure of the industry in Kenya and Zimbabwe, in which a few big exporters control most of the fresh vegetable exports. Similarly, smallholder production is declining since the largest exporters have changed their suppliers from small and medium farms to exporter-owned plantations and large commercial farms.

This case study shows some of the contradictory effects that global agri-food value chains have brought to producers in developing countries due to increased linkages with retailers in developed markets. For developing countries, part of these effects is a rapid increase in export activities. The transfer of technology and knowledge is raising production standards as long as the lead companies are monitoring their suppliers. Support industries have developed in these countries, providing additional employment in complementary sectors. Nevertheless, there is a marked increase in power asymmetries in these value chains, resulting in the exertion of control by retailers who capture most of the value generated across the chain. Small and medium firms are often marginalized and, consequently, there is a higher concentration in the industry due to the exit of many farmers and exporters from the market.

"Alternative food networks" and "short food supply chains"[5]

"Alternative food networks" (AFNs) or "Alternative agri-food networks" (AAFNs) are commonly used as a broad concept to cover all kinds of food supply chains that embody alternatives to the standard model of the industrial food value chain. AFNs include organic production, localized and short food supply chains, community-supported agriculture, farmers' markets, direct selling, box schemes, and similar models.[6]

According to Jarosz (2008), AFNs can be defined in four major ways: first, by shorter distances (proximity) between food producers and final consumers; second, by farm size, scale, and farming methods which differ from conventional agri-food production (e.g. small farms, organic production); third, by the existence of food purchasing venues (e.g. farmers' markets or food cooperatives); fourth, by a commitment to the social, economic, and environmental dimensions of sustainable food production, distribution, and consumption. Brunori *et al.* (2011) go further in the conceptualization of AFNs by defining four of their constitutive elements: (1) a wider conception of food production and consumption including political, ecological, and economic elements; (2) the collective building of new systems of meaning and food provision; (3) a new livelihood strategy for farmers detached from conventional agribusiness; and (4) performance measured in terms that consider not only economic results, but also the capacity to transform existing production and consumption patterns.

"Short food supply chains" (SFSC) has been used synonymously with "alternative food networks" (as well as the concept "local food systems" or "regional food systems"). Nevertheless, "short food supply chains" must be considered a category of AFNs. Marsden *et al.* (2000) consider a key characteristic of SFSC "their capacity to re-socialize or re-spatialize food", in fact, "the ability to engender some form of connection between food consumer and food producer". According to this definition, there are three types of SFSC: (1) "face-to-face" (e.g. direct selling); (2) "spatial proximity", in which products are produced and retailed in a specific region and the consumer is aware of it (e.g. local farm shops); and (3) "spatially extended", where the information about producers is translated to consumers who are outside the region (e.g. certification labels) (Marsden *et al.*, 2000). Other authors consider that the main characteristic of a SFSC is the *proximity* of producers and consumers, which is quite different from the conception proposed by Marsden *et al.* (2000). This proximity could be "relational", that is, there are fewer intermediaries between food producers and consumers, or "physical", meaning shorter geographical distance between them (Aubry and Kebir, 2013; Blasi *et al.*, 2015).

In recent years, there has been an impressive growth in these "short" and "alternative" food supply chains in developed countries resulting from changes in food demand and supply. On the demand side, there has been a decline in consumer trust in the "quality" and safety of food stemming from conventional agriculture (Goodman, 2003), and increasing concern over environmental issues, animal welfare, and social justice. On the supply side, the frequently mentioned continued farm-based "price squeeze" is often the justification, which refers to the diminishing gap between Gross Value of Production (agricultural price stagnation or decline) and costs (growing use of external inputs, technologies, increasing energy costs, etc.) resulting in the fall in agrarian income in real terms (Van der Ploeg *et al.*, 2000; Renting *et al.*, 2003). In this sense, AFNs are seen as an adequate response to farmers' difficulties in capturing a reasonable proportion of total value added in conventional food chains or challenges associated with upgrading in these chains, as the *filières* and GVC perspectives have pointed out.

As a result of this global proliferation of AFNs (see Milone *et al.*, 2015) there is an increasing number of publications based on AFNs. Most of them are case studies that point out the potential positive external effects of these value chains, especially on rural development. Nevertheless, it is also noted that AFNs could be "problematic", with Tregear (2011) arguing that AFNs could be protectionist and exclusionary or do not have a positive effect on regional economies. Furthermore, Ilbery and Maye (2005) question the "sustainability" of AFNs. See Box 22.3 for some other critiques of AFNs and the case study of one initiative – GAS – that tries to overcome some of them.

From a methodological perspective, Tregear (2011) identifies three theoretical perspectives in the AFN literature: political economy, rural development sociology, and network theory or modes of governance. She has also pointed out four main problematic features in AFN research: (1) insufficient clarity and consistency in usage of key concepts (including the concept of "AFNs" itself), (2) conflation of spatial/structural characteristics of AFNs with desirable outcomes, actor behaviors, and food properties, (3) insufficient acknowledgment of the problems of marketplace trading (especially regarding case studies of farmers' markets), and (4) a lack of a consumer perspective (e.g. the consumer welfare implications of significant engagement in local food).

Box 22.3 The Solidarity Purchase Groups (GAS) in Italy: a more "alternative" AFN (Brunori *et al.*, 2011; and Grasseni, 2014)

The AFN denomination includes a wide range of agri-food chains where the "alternative" aspect could be in production systems and/or in distribution channels. However, it is difficult to assess the degree of "alternativeness" in AFNs as well as its real potential to change the current farm techno-economic paradigm. In fact, there is a risk of "conventionalization" in successful AFNs. That is, being in some way captured by "conventional" forms (i.e. organic production produced on large farms and commercialized by supermarkets). Another critique of some AFNs arises from the exclusion of medium- and low-income consumers: the strategy based on organic and high-quality products implies higher production costs and prices that not all consumers can afford. Some AFNs have become a kind of hedonistic association of "foodies" focused on health and quality products, but much less concerned about the income of farmers and the environmental impacts of production.

GAS, the acronym for *Gruppi di Acquisto Solidale* (Solidarity-based Purchase Groups), tries to overcome these criticisms. They can be characterized as grassroots groups of consumers who select their providers and organize distribution by voluntary work (Grasseni, 2014). GAS presents some singularities with respect to other models of box schemes or community-supported agriculture. Voluntary work is crucial and takes part of the concept of "solidarity" embedded in GAS. In order to select their providers, the GAS members hold regular meetings where they discuss the preferences and criteria to contact a farmer or, eventually, to finish a partnership. Mainly they look for small local farmers and there is great concern for respect of workers' rights and environmentally friendly production. Each GAS member is asked to play an active role in the group, acting as "product referent" for one or more products, that is, being in charge of the provisioning of this product: contacting the farmer, placing the order, negotiating the price, making payments, arranging delivery, collecting bulk inputs, storing the deliveries at his or her home for the other members to come, and so on. This close and direct relationship with farmers allows GAS members to encourage their providers to adopt environmentally sound practices. For example, they could negotiate and agree on a roadmap of "conversion to organic" as a requirement to become a GAS supplier. This "transition" from conventional agri-food chains to a GAS supplier could be challenging for the farmer: it requires new knowledge and skills and the need to improve communication and networking practices, both with GAS consumers and with other farmers, forcing them to "innovate" in all aspects of farming (Brunori *et al.*, 2011). However, GAS rewards their providers with "loyalty" and remunerative prices. This kind of agreement is called a "participatory guarantee system". At some point, many costs have been avoided: packaging, intermediation costs, and, especially, the high costs of certification and labeling. In so doing, GAS members secure quality and organic food at relatively advantageous prices and farmers receive higher prices than they would receive in conventional chains and can take advantage of the opportunities emerging from the network.

According to Grasseni (2014), GAS provisioning goes beyond "ethical consumerism"; it is a political form of food activism that transforms the entire supply chain, fosters active citizenship, and re-embeds the economy in relationships of trust. In fact, she concludes that GAS are "much more a form of political-ecological network than they are 'alternative food networks'" (Grasseni, 2014). Brunori points out that GAS "challenge the dominant food regime by creating a public space where food is thought of, known about, produced and consumed according to alternative norms and rules" (Brunori *et al.*, 2011).

Policy implications

From agribusiness and filière approaches

The "agribusiness" and "*filière*" approaches have taken into account all the activities (or links) involved in food production in order to better understand the dynamics of the agriculture sector. In so doing, these approaches have unveiled the decreasing power of farmers in monitoring agri-food chains. The main policy implications of these frameworks are related to how farmers can regain power in the agri-food value chains. For example, farmers are called to cooperate and associate to increase their bargaining power in the face of the other agents. An alternative strategy is to expand to upstream or downstream activities (vertical integration). In fact, this is one of the strategies that some big farmers' cooperatives are implementing. For example, a successful example of this strategy is Grup Alimentari Guissona (Guissona Food Group) in Spain, which started as a livestock farmers' coop and has expanded to all the stages of the *filière*, from feed production to its own retail stores, its own petrol stations, and its own credit institution (see Amat *et al.*, 2016). This strategy has received much attention from development policy-makers who are trying to promote the transformation of primary products as a way to generate wealth and employment in developing countries.

The *filière* approach aimed at identifying strategic phases (the "core"), which are key in order to ensure a level of control over the whole value chain and capture as much of the value generated as possible. The main regional policy implication is to promote specialization at this stage, helping local firms by providing an adequate environment and sufficient resources (e.g. infrastructures, human capital, innovation systems, etc.). As *filières* become more global, the issue also becomes which stage can be delocalized (offshored) without losing control of the overall chain.

The analysis of *filière* and agribusiness also highlights the importance of the coordination between stages or linkages in the chain in order to reduce transaction costs and favor innovations and increasing quality standards along the chain. In this case, the implementation of *filière* strategies is having a renewed momentum in industrial policies, especially in France. Finally, synergies between different *filières* could be promoted by cluster policies.

From a GVC approach

The governance concept in the GVC approach was essentially developed to provide insights on the relationships between the lead firms and their suppliers. Regarding the upgrading strategies, these are focused on the potential internal resources of firms or farmers in order to capture more value in the chain. There are very few references to public policies in both the governance issues and the upgrading strategies. In fact, until recently, GVC approaches had tended to neglect the role of the state and its local institutions in promoting upgrading among farmers.

Nevertheless, there is increasing concern about the impact of public and private standards (e.g. food safety, quality certifications, etc.) on farmers. It is noted that these standards can make it difficult for small farmers (especially in developing countries) to access global agri-food chains. Challies and Murray (2011) have pointed out the importance of technical assistance programs to assist small farmers to accomplish standards and requirements from GVC. They conclude that the state is crucial in sustaining the viability of small farmers involved in GVCs because of continuous changes in quality demands in buyer-driven agri-food GVCs.

Agri-food global value chains have emerged from agricultural trade liberalization. The World Trade Organization (WTO) firmly believes that agri-food trade and integration in GVCs offer a variety of opportunities to developing countries for expanding their agriculture sectors and thus reducing poverty. In this way, they promote "Aid-for-trade", that is, to focus development assistance on programs and policies that, in a direct or indirect way, could favor trade (e.g. simplification of import/export procedures, transport infrastructures, access to trade finance, etc.). This aid tries to remove the barriers that lead firms face in order to be supplied by producers in developing countries and, thus, to promote their integration in a GVC. In recent years, the importance of aid for trade to the agri-food sector has grown significantly, having almost tripled from 2002 to 2015 when it was US$9700 million (OECD/WTO, 2017). This growth is in a context where total official development assistance is decreasing.

From an AFN approach[7]

The relevance of AFN as a key dimension in the new rural development paradigm has been highlighted in numerous papers and reports (e.g. Van der Ploeg *et al.*, 2000; Monllor and Fuller, 2016). This approach emphasizes the role of AFNs in social, environmental, and economic sustainability in rural areas and, as Galli and Brunori (2013) argued, SFSC can be "policy tools" in themselves because they can foster changes in attitudes and practices around food. Thus, the claim for institutional support for AFNs has been recurrent in the agri-food and rural development literature.

These considerations have had important effects on the design of the EU rural development policies (the second pillar of the Common Agricultural Policy – CAP). In fact, supporting AFN is a key point in LEADER[8] programs in the European Union and in National Rural Networks, especially in the Mediterranean countries in the last decade.

Nevertheless, there are some regulatory constraints to the development of AFNs. Increasing regulations on food safety and hygiene regulations or public and private certification systems can inadvertently increase costs for "alternative" farms or food producers. Often, this kind of regulation is tailored to "conventional" agribusiness and marginalizes AFNs. There is an increasing debate about the benefits of differentiated regulation for "conventional" and "alternative" food chains. Local authorities could have a prominent role in policies affecting AFNs (even more than national or regional-level policies). For example, they could use local planning to facilitate SFSCs, facilitate local sourcing in public procurement (e.g. school meal programs), or implement food safety and hygiene regulations in a more flexible way.

Conclusions and future research

To conclude, these three approaches – agribusiness/*filières*, Global Value Chains, and alternative food networks – have proven to be powerful and illuminating tools for understanding food chain dynamics, especially the role of farmers within them. Policy implications are focused in strategies to retain value added in farming to increase farm incomes and to guarantee economic sustainability in rural areas. AFNs could be seen as an alternative to low valorization of farming in the conventional food value chains and an important tool in current rural development policies.

There is a broad field in future research into *filières* and GVC. There are important changes occurring now in conventional agri-food supply chains, such as increased concentration and greater vertical coordination across the value chain (e.g. contract production), the increasing demand of differentiated products, the proliferation of private certifications and standards, the disappearance of agents in the chain (e.g. middlemen, wholesalers), and the appearance of new ones (e.g. NGOs as certifiers) (Saitone and Sexton, 2017). The impact of these changes can be properly analyzed by the *filière* and GVC tools.

From a methodological perspective, regarding *filières* and GVC there is the challenge for a more unified approach combining aspects of both approaches (Raikes *et al.*, 2001; Soldevila, 2008), as well as a need to better understand governance (internal and external) issues. It would be helpful to complement most of the qualitative analysis in governance with quantitative analysis and re-assess and redefine the concept of power and governance in conventional agri-food value chains (Bonanno *et al.*, 2018).

From an AFN perspective, Marsden *et al.* (2000) highlighted the highly fragmented and untheorized literature on this subject; unfortunately, this is still a reality 18 years later. Tregear (2011) claims that, in order to overcome the "problematic features in AFN research", a "greater cross-fertilisation of ideas" from different theoretical perspectives and disciplines needs to be undertaken. Given that most of the AFN contributions are focused in developed countries, there is a broad research opportunity for assessing the potential of AFNs in the developing world (Maye and Kirwan, 2010). Empirically focused research using these approaches is also required. Case studies must be welcomed into the research program in order to better understand the changing and increasingly complex relationships between agriculture, food systems, and rural and urban societies alike.

This work was supported in part by *Comisión Interministerial de Ciencia y Tecnología* (CICYT) of Spain under project ECO2016-79072-P.

Notes

1 We want to thank Marco Pagani for his valuable comments about the distinction between "conventional" and "alternative" approaches.
2 In fact, "agribusiness" and "*filières*" are often used synonymously.
3 Many contributions based on the use of Global Commodity Chain and Global Value Chain analysis are compiled on the website "Global Value Chains" (https://globalvaluechains.org) from Duke University. The OECD and the WTO are increasingly using these methodologies in their reports (www.oecd.org/sti/ind/global-value-chains.htm) and they have created a database to better quantify trade in value-added items/goods (www.oecd.org/industry/ind/measuringtradeinvalue-addedanoecd-wtojointinitiative.htm).
4 The website "Capturing the gains" (www.capturingthegains.org) shows multiple case studies related to upgrading from a Global Value Chain perspective.
5 In this section we are going to present a brief introduction to the "alternative food networks" perspective since this subject is widely discussed in the next chapter under "Regional food systems".
6 For an extensive analysis of AFN definitions and concepts, see Maye and Kirwan (2010).
7 For a deeper analysis of policies affecting AFN, see Chapter 23 in this volume.
8 The term "LEADER" comes from the French acronym for "Liaison Entre Actions de Développement de l'Économie Rurale" (that is, "Links between the rural economy and development actions"). This is the main European initiative for rural development.

References

Amat, O., Banchieri, L.C., Campa-Planas, F., 2016. *La implantación del cuadro de mando integral en el sector agroalimentario: el caso del Grupo Alimentario Guissona*. Revista Facultad de Ciencias Económicas: Investigación y Reflexión 24(1), 25–36.

Aubry, C., Kebir, L., 2013. *Shortening food supply chains: A means for maintaining agriculture close to urban areas? The case of the French metropolitan area of Paris*. Food Policy 41, 85–93.

Blasi, E., Cicatiello, C., Pancino, B., Franco, S., 2015. *Alternative food chains as a way to embed mountain agriculture in the urban market: The case of Trentino*. Agricultural and Food Economics 3(1), Article 3.

Bonanno, A., Russo, C., Menapace, L., 2018. *Market power and bargaining in agrifood markets: A review of emerging topics and tools*. Agribusiness 34(1), 6–23.

Brunori, G., Rossi, A., Malandrin, V., 2011. *Co-producing transition: Innovation processes in farms adhering to solidarity-based purchase groups (GAS) in Tuscany, Italy*. International Journal of Sociology of Agriculture and Food 18(1), 28–53.

Burch, D., Lawrence, G.A., 2005. *Supermarket own brands, supply chains and the transformation of the agri-food system.* International Journal of Sociology of Agriculture and Food 13(1), 1–18.

Challies, E.R., Murray, W.E., 2011. *The interaction of global value chains and rural livelihoods: The case of small-holder raspberry growers in Chile.* Journal of Agrarian Change 11(1), 29–59.

Davis, J.H., Goldberg, R.A., 1957. *A concept of agribusiness.* Harvard University Press, Boston, MA.

Dolan, C., Humphrey, J., 2000. *Governance and trade in fresh vegetables: The impact of UK supermarkets on the African horticulture industry.* Journal of Development Studies 37(2), 147–176.

Fold, N., Larsen, M.N., 2011. *Upgrading of smallholder agro-food production in Africa: The role of lead firm strategies and new markets.* International Journal of Technological Learning, Innovation and Development 4(1–3), 39–66.

Galli, F., Brunori, G. (Eds.), 2013. *Short food supply chains as drivers of sustainable development,* Seventh Framework Programme, collaborative project ENV.2010.4.2.3–3 FOODLINKS. http://orgprints.org/28858/1/evidence-document-sfsc-cop.pdf (accessed 10.10.17).

Gereffi, G., 1994. *The organization of buyer-driven global commodity chains: How U.S. retailers shape overseas production networks,* in: Gereffi, G., Korzeniewicz, M. (Eds.), *Commodity chains and global capitalism.* Praeger, Westport, CT, 95–122.

Gereffi, G., Fernandez-Stark, K., 2016. *Global value chain analysis: A primer.* Center on Globalization, Governance and Competitiveness (CGGC). Duke University, Durham, NC.

Gereffi, G., Korzeniewicz, M. (Eds.), 1994. *Commodity chains and global capitalism.* Praeger, Westport, CT.

Gereffi, G., Humphrey, J., Sturgeon, T., 2005. *The governance of global value chains.* Review of International Political Economy 12 (1), 78–104.

Goodman, D., 2003. *The quality "turn" and alternative food practices: Reflections and agenda.* Journal of Rural Studies 19(1), 1–7.

Grasseni, C., 2014. *Seeds of trust: Italy's gruppi di acquisto solidale (solidarity purchase groups).* Journal of Political Ecology 21(1), 178–192.

Ilbery, B., Maye, D., 2005. *Alternative (shorter) food supply chains and specialist livestock products in the Scottish–English borders.* Environment and Planning A 37(5), 823–844.

Jarosz, L., 2008. *The city in the country: Growing alternative food networks in Metropolitan areas.* Journal of Rural Studies 24(3), 231–244.

Kaplinsky, R., Morris, M., 2002. *A handbook for value chain research.* IDRC. http://sds.ukzn.ac.za/files/handbook_valuechainresearch.pdf (accessed 9.10.17).

Malassis, L., 1979. *Economie agro-alimentaire.* Cujas, Paris.

Marsden, T., Banks, J., Bristow, G., 2000. *Food supply chain approaches: Exploring their role in rural development.* Sociologia Ruralis 40(4), 424–438.

Maye, D., Kirwan, J., 2010. *Alternative food networks.* Sociology of Agriculture and Food 20, 383–389.

Milone, P., Ventura, F., Ye, J. (Eds.), 2015. *Constructing a new framework for rural development.* Research in Rural Sociology and Development, Vol. 22. Emerald Group Publishing, Bingley.

Monllor, N., Fuller, A., 2016. *Newcomers to farming: Towards a new rurality in Europe.* Documents d'Anàlisi Geogràfica 62(3), 531–551.

OECD/WTO, 2017. *Aid for Trade at a glance 2017: Promoting trade, inclusiveness and connectivity for sustainable development.* WTO, Geneva/OECD Publishing, Paris.

Pelupessy, W., Van Kempen, L., 2005. *The impact of increased consumer-orientation in global agri-food chains on smallholders in developing countries.* Competition and Change 9(4), 357–381.

Raikes, P., Jensen, M., Ponte, S., 2000, *Global commodity chain analysis and the French filière approach: Comparison and critique.* Economy and Society 29(3), 390–417.

Renting, H., Marsden, T.K., Banks, J., 2003. *Understanding alternative food networks: Exploring the role of short food supply chains in rural development.* Environment and Planning A 35(3), 393–411.

Saitone, T.L., Sexton, R.J., 2017. *Agri-food supply chain: Evolution and performance with conflicting consumer and societal demands.* European Review of Agricultural Economics 44(4), 634–657.

Soldevila, V., 2008. *El Impacto de los costes medioambientales en la cadena de porcino. El caso de Catalunya* (PhD Dissertation). Universidad de Barcelona.

Staritz, C., Gereffi, G., Cattaneo, O., 2011. *Shifting end markets and upgrading prospects in global value chains.* International Journal of Technological Learning, Innovation and Development 4(1), 1–12.

Trajtenberg, R., 1977. *Un enfoque sectorial para el estudio de la penetración de las empresas transnacionales en América Latina.* Instituto LatinoAmericano de Estudios sobre Empresas Transnacionales, DEE/D/1, Mexico.

Tregear, A., 2011. *Progressing knowledge in alternative and local food networks: Critical reflections and a research agenda.* Journal of Rural Studies 27(4), 419–430.

Van der Ploeg, J.D., Renting, H., Brunori, G., Knickel, K., Mannion, J., Marsden, T., Ventura, F., 2000. *Rural development: From practices and policies towards theory.* Sociologia Ruralis 40(4), 391–408.

Viladomiu, L., 1985. *La inserción de España en el complejo soja-mundial.* Instituto de Estudios Agrarios, Pesqueros y Alimentarios, Madrid.

23

BUILDING SUSTAINABLE REGIONAL FOOD SYSTEMS

Policies and support

Kathleen Kevany and Maya Fromstein

Sustainable regional food systems hold the potential to increase food security and accessibility, sovereignty, and prosperity, and to support sustainability principles and practices. This chapter provides a definition of sustainable regional food systems and a discussion of the elements involved and recommended policies and supports. The insights uncovered may lead to the value of promoting the development of food system regionalization for increased regional food sovereignty, economic prosperity and environmental sustainability, rural well-being and social equity.

Introduction of sustainable regional food systems

Sustainable regional food systems may offer value for increasing food security and accessibility, sovereignty, and prosperity, in addition to supporting sustainability principles and practices. Sustainable regional food systems require planning efforts that are collaborative, integrated, and enable regions to articulate and implement local and regional sustainability goals. Health, sustainability, conviviality, and prosperity are widely accepted as dimensions needed to define food systems (Lang, 2009). Good agricultural policies ought to serve also as good economic, social, environmental, and health policies. While this chapter does not put forth a definitive model, it does provide a definition of sustainable regional food systems and a discussion of the elements involved and recommended policies and supports. Food systems include the full cycle involved with policies, infrastructure, and practices that contribute to the producing, processing, distributing, selling, purchasing, consuming, and disposing of food. The consumption components of the food systems are influenced by history, culture, policies, economics, environments, preferences, lifestyle, spirituality, and health. Sustainable regional food systems include the logistical and logical geographic management of all the dimensions of a food system in ways that achieve sustainability within the food, ecosystems (soil, air, water, etc.), and for animal and human well-being. An example might be the Los Angeles Regional Food System, which is defined as a healthy, sustainable, and equitable regional food system that is a complex set of activities and relationships related to every aspect of the food cycle, including production, processing, distribution, retail, preparation, consumption, and disposal (Good Food for All Agenda Task Force, 2010).

Problems with food systems

Rural regions have faced a number of challenges in producing and delivering sufficient food. Storms and droughts, for example, have led to food crises. Many farmers are producing in an atmosphere of ever-increasing variable climate and weather patterns, with "limited possibilities for corrective alternatives" (Milestad and Darnhofer, 2003, p. 86). Rural regions are realizing that their communities or regions are ill prepared to demonstrate food security, sovereignty, or sustainability. Many government policies or supports that would help to build more resilience have been missing. Costs of farming and land also loom large. Expensive investments, increased labor costs, and concerns over reliability of price premiums were additional financial concerns noted by Austrian organic farmers (Milestad and Hadatsch, 2003). Accessibility to farm infrastructure for new entrants and affordable farm tax, farm expenses, and food processing are not sufficiently available. Yet many farmers do not have access to needed supports and thus their visions for vibrant farm business are being undermined.

Past debates around food provisioning included many disputes like whether people deserved better food or support for a healthy diet, and how the land and its biology should be reshaped to produce more food (Hamm, 2009; Lang, 2009). These operating beliefs and values lead into modern agriculture whose viability has been brought into question by many scholars (Burlingame and Dernini, 2012; Hamm, 2009; Lang, 2009; Weis, 2007). For example, the industrialization and globalization of the systems that produce and process food have increased the value and price for legumes and grains as feed that goes to animals. These ubiquitous practices of channeling grains and legumes to animals and away from human consumption make it more challenging for small producers to compete in the global supply chain and for the poor to obtain adequate nourishment. The industrialized food system, through producing food and particularly the raising of factory farmed animals, has been contributing to the world's most pressing environmental problems, climate change through greenhouse gas emissions (methane, nitrous oxide, carbon dioxide) as well as contributing to water and air pollution, biodiversity loss, and soil deterioration and land degradation (Burlingame and Dernini, 2012; Weis, 2007). With the intensification of animal production, billions of sentient animals are confined to extreme conditions and a short life before being slaughtered. This also leads to significant amounts of antibiotics being applied to farm animals and contributing antibiotic-resistant bacteria and superbugs that can outpace medical advances. Today policy-makers have enormous environmental and structural challenges to address in food policy: climate change, water stress, energy pressures, demographic change, the nutrition transition (over-, under-, and malnutrition) leading to a host of health concerns with dramatic increases in non-communicable diseases worldwide and social inequity around food access and the burden of environmental contamination and biodiversity loss (Lang, 2009; Weis, 2007).

Alternative food movements contributing to sustainable rural food systems

Rural peoples and places have historically contributed significantly to sustainable local and regional food systems. The advent of the industrialized models of agriculture and food processing have introduced many changes to these processes. If nine billion people are to be adequately fed by 2050, food must be produced more ethically, effectively, and efficiently. Advocates propose the development of food system regionalization and increased regional food sovereignty (Dorward et al., 2016). Sustainable regional food systems are explored here in conjunction with emerging alternative food movements (AFM) and alternative food networks (AFN). Jarosz (2008) indicated that AFNs were commonly defined by spatial proximity between farmers and consumers, the existence of retail venues such as farmers' markets, community-supported agriculture (CSA), and community involvement in supporting regional, sustainable food production and consumption. For the purposes of this chapter AFM will be used with the understanding that it also includes AFN initiatives.

Value-based supply chains and ethical foodscapes (Lang, 2009) are designed out of respect for the systems that support food and the sacred, pleasurable, and life-giving roles food plays in everyone's lives (Broad, 2016). There is a growing focus on the disconnect between distant and homogeneous, industrially produced foods and the desire to live by values around knowing the way food is produced, procured, and consumed. In efforts to rectify the deterioration to environmental, social, economic, and health outcomes arising from an industrialized food system, emphasis is placed more on local, healthy, and fresh foods (Levkoe *et al.*, 2017; Slocum, 2006). It ought to be noted that the literature on food systems often overlooks fisheries and aquaculture. This focus on agricultural rural communities would include fisheries as well as other innovations like hemp and cannabis production to envelope a broader vision of agricultural pathways for sustainable rural communities.

More organizations, actors, and individuals are mobilizing around food as a powerful tool and point of focus for needed systemic shifts to replace unsustainability and inequity (Levkoe *et al.*, 2017; Mason and Lang, 2017). To reclaim rural food systems, AFMs seek to achieve different outcomes of the industrialized agriculture and food systems, including shortening supply chains to more effectively connect consumers with producers and farmers in ways that the corporate model does not afford (Allen and Wilson, 2008; Slocum *et al.*, 2016). Some popular efforts include the campaigns around Slow Food and Buy "Local" and farmers' markets, community-supported agriculture initiatives, and community gardens (Slocum, 2006), as well as food hubs, cooperative storefronts, or depots. Agents engaged in these movements may be motivated by an array of drivers: greater accessibility to foods that adequately and equitably nourish the population, support for farmers and farmworkers to earn adequate income for a desirable quality of life and a commitment to steward the environment, and a desire to know the source of food through shorter supply chains connecting consumers and producers. Citizen-consumers also may become mobilized around disparate but related issues within sustainable food systems discourse but these drivers are less frequently noted as valuable products of engagement. Civic engagement, democratic participation, and strengthened feelings of community have been found to emerge through engagement in AFM (Duarte Alonso and O'Neill, 2010; Franklin *et al.*, 2011; Sumner *et al.*, 2010). Building community and fostering space for deliberations enabled members to mobilize around issues highlighted by the AFM and helped to redirect the pressure placed on individuals to make changes to that of highlighting how conventional food systems are producing unwelcome debilitating results yet are not held to account. Critiques also are directed towards policy-makers and institutions that support profit-driven practices at the expense of other principles and overall well-being (Levkoe *et al.*, 2017; Mason and Lang, 2017). It seems clear as well that the growing interest in AFMs was helped through growing interest in food issues in general.

While involvement in the AFM may be a success for some, fostering community and democratic participation equitably across society through food remains a challenge. Some authors noted that the false binaries of alternative–conventional, local–global, sustainable–unsustainable are not reflective of reality, and obstruct further progress (Allen, 2003; Smithers and Joseph, 2010). These scholars asserted that projects of the AFM existed on a spectrum of "alternative" and "conventional/industrial" as spaces of experimentation and exploration of their transformative capacity as well as from their susceptibility to subordination by the corporate world (Johnston *et al.*, 2009). Where the conventional food system reacts to the uptake of its alternative counterpart by adopting some of its practices (i.e. organic food's increasing availability in large grocery stores) such that it is increasingly difficult to draw a clear line between the "two" food systems and necessitates further attention to practice/praxis (Cadieux and Slocum, 2016). Some advocates have criticized blanket support for AFM without assessing whether they address the underlying issues of justice, race, class, gender, and accessibility that these movements seek to redress (Allen, 2010; Sumner *et al.*, 2010). Some authors have raised concerns around whether the AFM may be more elitist or individualistic rather than focused on changing dysfunctional, if not corrupted, systems (Allen, 2010; Allen *et al.*, 2003; Born and Purcell, 2006).

These questions, motivations, and challenges all call for a deeper exploration of how sustainable food systems may be created, and support sustainable rural regions, through embedding principles of justice and prosperity for everyone, including farmers along with marginalized and vulnerable peoples (Sbicca and Myers, 2017). In urban food studies topics of food justice, democracy, and sovereignty, may focus on racialized, Indigenous, or low-income populations that may be seen as more marginalized. And yet patterns of continued urbanization and declining rural conditions do not adequately include the efficacy, resiliency, innovation, and capacity of rural populations in designing sustainable food regions. Food system redesign could work to empower rural communities by focusing on their experiences and their essential roles of protecting the contexts and processes for good food and good jobs (Sbicca and Myers, 2017). Strategies for bolstering sustainable rural food systems must consider well more than the consumer role. Systems changes, including the influence of farmers and producers, are considered next.

Building regional farming and sustainable food systems

Broad (2016) indicated that issues in food, their distribution across society, and the impacts on health and the environment are mirrored in rural regions and broader society. Equity and inequity in food impact all people, urban and rural, albeit to varying degrees and with varying capacity to redress it and organize around it. From their research, Si and Scott (2016) found a mutually beneficial relationship among sustainable agriculture, regional food systems, and rural development. In a case study they considered how rural development policy focused on creating bottom-up, democratically-run governance structures that played a role in scaling up, and uniting, the fractured elements of an AFM in China. Such rural development campaigns provided a framework, and became a space, for discussing, uniting, and localizing more dislocated AFM initiatives. Their disparate, but related efforts, focused on achieving political, health, social, and economic goals and increasing food security, sovereignty, and sustainability through rejecting the industrialized food systems. Consequently, alternative rural governance structures and food networks helped to reinforce each other's goals (Si and Scott, 2016). Jarosz (2008) contributed similar findings, asserting that not only were rural communities well positioned to affect one another's goals, the quality and characteristics of AFMs were enhanced by rural restructuring and growing desired relationships with urban centers.

With the recognition that rural prosperity was not necessarily realized through modernized agriculture (Rivera *et al.*, 2018), there was growing interest in investigating how sustainable food systems could be instrumental in cultivating sustainable regional and rural development (Deller *et al.*, 2017). Milestad and Darnhofer (2003) found that building resilience required leaders and spaces for collective learning and collaboration among farms and communities. Collaborative efforts increased community flexibility and improved problem solving. Such relations also enabled the formation of some "strategic alliances" and knowledge transfer that motivated cooperation among farmers in ways unique to their success (Halloran and Archer, 2008). Barnes *et al.* (2015) studied the long-term viability of Scottish and Swedish farms and attributed the significantly greater viability of Scottish farms to their emphasis on production diversity in their rural planning policy (as compared to overall productivity and environmental protection in the Swedish rural policies). Research also revealed that off-farm activities appeared helpful for many to balance out modest to low farm income (Milestad and Darnhofer, 2003). However, reliance on off-farm activities added challenges in requiring specialized knowledge, trained labor, and significant time demands (Milestad and Darnhofer, 2003).

Lessons arising from these findings were that rural development and scaling up of AFMs could benefit reciprocally as they drew upon the strengths of each other. Yet the potential for rural development and AFM programs to support one another was a relatively unexplored area (Deller *et al.*, 2017). Leveraging the centrality of food in people's lives as a source of culture, community, employment, health, environmental stewardship, and in democratic participation may give stakeholders that are using food a unique vantage point in the design and dimensions of sustainable regions (Broad, 2016). AFMs may then be seen as contributors to sustainable rural development through their role in shifting paradigms towards ecological, socially just, and community-focused food systems. Si and Scott (2016) and Smithers and Joseph (2010) have noted that it was difficult for AFMs to scale up largely because each AFM was disconnected from others and was separately designed and marketed around how it was uniquely trustworthy, authentic, and local. Furthermore, each AFM's unique rural context, geographic conditions, and production potential, with its embedded barriers and opportunities, would also impact its strategies and partnerships (Mount, 2012).

De Los Ríos *et al.* (2016) connected rural prosperity to agricultural sustainability – which they asserted, from witnessing it in their case study, demanded a collaborative management strategy, with good knowledge and data, shared platforms, skills, and strategies. To form such strong networks requires investments in communication, coordination, and collaboration. For greater rural food system sustainability and prosperity, proactive education around collaboration and cooperation has become essential. Also, creative use of social media and public education may serve to include more actors and farmers in the regional food systems and may foster greater innovation, diversification of products and livelihoods (de Los Ríos *et al.*, 2016). Effective communication tools and electronic platforms and artificial intelligence tools to bolster rural prosperity would be needed. Knickel *et al.* (2018) corroborated the findings of de Los Ríos and colleagues, especially in terms of building capacity through self-organization and improved learning channels. Strategies include ensuring a constant flow of knowledge and learning, informally and formally, and harnessing knowledge, skills, and attitudes to raise awareness of environmental, technical, economic, and social issues that enable farmers to be more competitive and increase their confidence in coping with issues that directly affect their abilities to adapt to new circumstances, to innovate, and to collaborate (de Los Ríos *et al.*, 2016).

The social and environmental movement of Transition Towns is an illustration of communities coming together to plan actions needed for sustainable communities and food sovereignty. And at the farm level, examples of effective teaching farms have emerged like Everdale Farm in Hillsburgh, Ontario, which is a farm-based organization that provides hands-on programs on food and farming to people of all ages and backgrounds, and farming education to build and engage healthy local communities.

Sustainable regional food systems could also be strengthened through farmer-to-farmer collaborations. Halloran and Archer (2008) provide examples of "strategic alliances" (p. 301) between farmers that took advantage of the benefits of diversified production without requiring a dramatic change in knowledge and or land expansion. Such alliances allowed farmers in close proximity to one another, each of whom would typically produce a single type of crop, to introduce crop rotations by "sharing" land with each other. They provided an example of a potato–broccoli alliance, wherein the farmers facilitated crop rotation by planting on the lands of other farmers. This also afforded them multiple environmental benefits of crop rotation, as well as their associated economic insurances, and proved to be economically viable as this rotation was more profitable than introducing a more typical rotation of barley silage, for example. Strategic alliances between farmers not only improved environmental stewardship with immediate economic benefits, they created a more widespread system of "integrated agricultural production" (p. 301) beyond the individual farm unit (Halloran and Archer, 2008). A creative example associated with economically viable rural food production can be found in Pennsylvania where a local wholesale produce auction, a form of food hub, was initiated that allowed farmers to reduce concerns about transportation costs and proximity to markets as well as restrictions associated with selling large amounts of a single crop to grocery stores. Direct marketing strategies also contributed to reduced reliance on powerful procurers (i.e. large grocery stores) and redistributed power and autonomy back to the farmers themselves (Milestad and Darnhofer, 2003).

Strengthening sustainable, regional food systems may necessitate approaching farms and rural areas not as individual, isolated actors but rather as related parts of larger networks and regions that may benefit from accessing spaces and structures to connect to others with broader visions and goals. Marsden (2009) and Lang (2009) have referred to the importance of considering rural agri-development in the context of the global agri-food system and assert it can be helpful to consider regional development in which the local is involved in a long, global food chain. Placing emphasis on local policies within regional systems may be helpful. In addition to considering the established structures and residents within regional food systems, consideration also needs to be extended to those "mobile" elements. These mobilities Marsden (2009) refers to as, "flows of capital, people, and knowledge" (p. 120) that may take the shape of labor, tourism, and/or residential migration. Situating the rural settings into greater regional contexts acknowledges, as well as makes use of, the fact that the rural areas do not exist in a void, nor do the policies and structures that impact them act in isolation from external factors (Marsden, 2009). Efforts may also be needed around strengthening the regional assets, particularly geographic features (like bodies of water, scenic views) and historical legacies and touristic appeal, along with bolstering and adding value to regional culinary identities. Communal kitchens may be another example, if certified for safe food handling, that could enable access to various food actors in the region and could become tremendous assets in bringing together producers of diverse foods, stimulating new partnerships and value-added relations, while contributing to prosperous regional food systems. Now attention needs to be turned to policy supports needed to foster more of these enabling environments and outcomes.

Policy supports and recommendations

Across the US, many large-scale, specialized production systems were able to take advantage of economies of scale and benefit more from technology, farm policy, and changing market conditions and structures (Halloran and Archer, 2008). Technology incentives served to aid in their increasing production size and greater specialization of crops ensued. Farm policy, with a focus on export markets and a heavily influential lobbying base, reinforced the specialized production of specific commodity crops (Halloran and Archer, 2008). Within large, industrial food systems with inaccessible power structures and networks, and with concentration in large agribusinesses, fewer producers benefited from this model. These large-scale, industrialized food systems have served less to advance the interests of the majority, the food system, or rural communities (Lang, 2009; Rivera et al., 2018). Rural settings and food systems encountered obstacles like prohibitive financial costs to enter conventional agriculture, declining youth uptake, and cost impediments that undermine the viability of small operations.

To make needed shifts to more sustainable practices Lang (2009) recommended that governments, citizen-consumers, corporations, and change agents become engaged with policy. Policy-makers may be encouraged to view food policy through an ecological public health lens and to build ecological health into their business model and to inject health and social justice more effectively into the sustainability agenda. Areas to address in policy would be inequities of power and the unequal distribution of ill-health arising from food availability and accessibility (Jackson et al., 2009; Lang, 2009). As noted above many results from food systems are "depressingly inadequate" (Jackson et al., 2009, p. 395). Citizen-consumers are failing to ask why there is not enough healthy, affordable, and sustainable food while public health officials and agricultural and environmental policy-makers are failing to consider the range of policies that are driving detrimental results like increasing climate change, escalating obesity, and premature death, along with inequitable access to healthy food and fair income (Jackson et al., 2009).

Regulators are cautioned against making policy and regulations too oppressive to small-scale producers. They could consider a whole-systems design and the adaptability or scalability of their policy architecture and tools. Following are several policy tools that regulators may employ: the power of *government mandates*, funds collected through *taxes*, suitable *legislation* or *regulations* like environmental protection or waste management, or *zoning*, like farmland preservation, *incentives* to support local producers and processors, possible *subsidies* to support sustainable practices, *education* as well as *local and regional branding*, insightful *research*, and commitment to *data-driven decision-making*. Other tools may include programs to *avoid wasting and instead harvesting* it as an asset within the evolving bioeconomy. Some assistance also may be needed with *investing in infrastructure* like storage facilities for regional food processing or food hubs, among other innovations and structures.

Jackson and colleagues (2009) also advise of many actions for policy-makers in health, environment, and agricultural portfolios. They recommend that these actors *advocate* for sustainable food policies and *communicate* the full cost of current food systems in terms of subsidies, ill-health, environmental costs, and the emotional strain experienced by farmers unable to compete in an oppressive industrial supply chain. These authors further contend that policy actors can positively influence policy and practice when they *create multidisciplinary teams* to research on and *propose practical approaches* to regional food systems and *educate* themselves and their organizations and *become examples* and *establish procurement practices* that *source and support only sustainable food sources*.

Examples of blended policy efforts

Many elements have been incorporated into enhancing regional food systems. A study of some models revealed how sustainable regional food systems could be fashioned through blending the strengths and strategic advantages of AFM and conventional approaches. Farmers and rural communities have worked to develop CSAs and farmers' markets; their efforts are accelerated when they harness the commonalities and synergies of their visions and blend the best of alternative and "conventional" approaches (Good Food for All Agenda Task Force, 2010; Rivera et al., 2018). These innovative partnerships consider structures to support connections between and among policy-makers, funders, producers, marketers, wholesalers, grocers, institutions, citizens, consumers, academics, researchers, extension services, and connections between urban and rural. Programs such as the Good Food Challenge from the Canadian national organization Meal Exchange, and the Charting Growth to Good Food project from the Wallace Center in Virginia, US incorporated system components that paid attention to the contexts and geographic locations that produced the food and thereby enabled food availability that was humane, affordable, fresh, and fair. An example in eastern Ontario was the formation of a Local Food Conference. These sessions have been held since 2011 and have improved business connections and built strong community relations across the food landscape. More rural areas are hosting county fairs and contests designed to foster food literacy and food pedagogy and provide space for sharing and reproducing culture and skills and passing on of traditional knowledge as well. Another example comes from Columbia Basin Trust – Food Security initiatives that have established processing resources on behalf of the diverse needs across the region. Cooperative efforts, including Credit Unions like VanCity Credit Union, have invested in food initiatives and worked to build community through efforts like FarmFolk CityFolk in Vancouver. This is a not-for-profit that works to cultivate a local, sustainable food system by providing access to and protection of farmland, supporting local growers and producers through principled procurement practices, and engaging communities in the celebration of local food. Sustain Ontario provides education around an array of food issues like the value in reduced pesticide use and benefits of supporting farmers' markets like those found in Guelph and Waterloo and strategies incentivize and encourage the regional food system as a whole to make good food more widely available to all Angelenos. The city places emphasis on its "Good Food for All Agenda", which promotes food that is healthy, affordable, fair, and sustainable. By using principles and values like sustainability and equity to direct their food purchases, they encourage greater production of sustainably produced food, healthy eating habits, respect for worker's rights, and support for the local business economy by providing new opportunities for small and mid-sized farmers and job creation along the food supply chain (Good Food for All Agenda Task Force, 2010, p. 20).

Collaboration among producers and policy-makers

This research has revealed a number of blended strategies that may be beneficial and identified regional assets that could be incorporated into visions for sustainable foods and effective policies. Innovative policy involves connecting rural and regional as well as urban and rural areas in new and productive ways. It may call for some reassembling, redefining, and appreciating resources and infrastructures in ways that carve out new, diversified niches to more sustainably produced goods and services (Marsden, 2009; Burlingame and Dernini, 2012). Halloran and Archer (2008) highlighted approaches for diversifying production. These were often downplayed in discussions of farm and food profitability. Polyculture practices can serve to improve "whole farm profitability" by increasing economic buffers in case of certain crop failures, as well as enhance resistance to pest and soil infestations, and contribute to what Halloran and Archer have called "whole farm profitability" (2008, p. 301). Milestad and Darnhofer (2003) noted some financial benefits of diversified, collaborative, and ecological agriculture. Diversification can serve to buffer against fickle market effects on prices, weather and climate influences on yields, and other problems that arise in food businesses. Some benefits were reduced reliance on external inputs and more control over one's seeds and production processes. Approaches to rural and agricultural planning should work to improve resilience, for instance, building or strengthening local nodes and regional food hubs to bolster autonomy and vitality in rural areas. Effective regional food systems would also include building up capacity through governance, shared practice, and community abilities to deal with planned changes and to exercise their resilience in navigating unplanned pressures and demands. Planners could document existing wholesale food system infrastructure and cooperative agricultural clusters as they contribute to the regional economic development and devise ways to better accommodate smaller producers in food distribution regional planning. Collaboration could be encouraged with policy-makers and food safety regulators to foster zoning and regulation that protect public safety and welfare and build the capacity and market access of local food. These features and benefits would then be emphasized in strategic marketing and branding efforts (Day-Farnswortha and Morales, 2011). Examples might be "multifunctional agriculture and agri-food, environmental cooperatives, social and enterprise community initiatives" (Marsden, 2009, p. 120). In his paper, "Principles for Framing a Healthy Food System", Hamm advised of seven components. These may be adapted to or incorporated into sustainable regional food systems. They are: (1) emphasize food security for all, (2) be community based, (3) be locally *(and regionally)* integrated, (4) seek and enjoy seasonal foods and opportunities, (5) frame the situation as an opportunity disguised as a problem, (6) take a systems approach, and (7) emphasize diversity in foods, in peoples, and in practices (2009, p. 243). Based on the findings and principles indicated earlier, it is important to stress the necessity to de-emphasize animal and dairy products for the added health, ethical, and environmental benefits, as well as channel any food wastes to productive purposes.

Such collective management strategies would necessitate engagement with social learning. Social learning has been effective in supporting innovation, building new partnerships and relationships, affording shared management approaches, and learning tools that enable sharing of information and knowledge among a broad range of actors (Hinrichs *et al.*, 2004). Examples might be purposefully designed artificial intelligence, data management, and blockchain. Blockchain is an accessible, technological platform to record transactions and keep track of food at all stages from planting to harvesting to processing, delivering, consuming, and enjoying (Fraser, 2017). By incorporating such platforms, regional food system actors could keep track of inventory and administration and negotiation strategies, fulfilling customer needs as well as harnessing the tools to enhance local, regional goals, networks, and reach. In-person and virtual spaces that help promote and facilitate knowledge sharing and learning become valuable components of successful regional systems. The inclusion of democratic debates, collaborative approaches, and systems analyses are recommended to bolster ecological public health through vibrant, prosperous, and equitable regional food systems designed to foster sustainable food and food systems and inspire rural well-being for generations to come.

Further research

More detailed analysis also would help reveal the essential policy supports for regional food systems and how they were developed along with investigations that illuminate the goals for regional food systems. These food systems also would benefit from checks and balances along with mechanisms and standards for measuring elements of well-being: sustainability, resiliency, vibrancy, and prosperity. Due to the perishable nature of many items in the food system, another interesting field of study is the emergence of technological tools and applications ("apps") that are proving to be cost effective and helpful with data collection, production, planning, timing for delivery of goods, and the return on investment for such strategic and context-specific, time-sensitive decisions.

References

Allen, P., 2003. *Together at the table: Sustainability and sustenance in the American agrifood system.* Penn State University Press, University Park, PA.

Allen, P., 2010. *Realizing justice in local food systems.* Cambridge Journal of Regions, Economy and Society 3, 295–308.

Allen, P., Wilson, A.B., 2008. *Agrifood inequalities: Globalization and localization.* Development 51(4), 534–540.

Allen, P., FitzSimmons, M., Goodman, M., Warner, K., 2003. *Shifting plates in the agrifood landscape: The tectonics of alternative agrifood initiatives in California*. Journal of Rural Studies 19(1), 61–75. https://doi.org/10.1016/S0743-0167(02)00047-5.

Barnes, A.P., Hansson, H., Manevska-Tasevska, G., Shrestha, S.S., Thomson, S.G., 2015. *The influence of diversification on long-term viability of the agricultural sector*. Land Use Policy 49, 402–412.

Born, B., Purcell, M., 2006. *Avoiding the local trap*. Journal of Planning Education and Research 26(2), 195–207. https://doi.org/10.1177/0739456X06291389.

Broad, G.M., 2016. *More than just food: Food justice and community change*. University of California Press, Oakland, CA.

Burlingame, B., Dernini, S., 2012. *Sustainable diets and biodiversity: Directions and solutions for policy, research and action*, in: *Sustainable diets and biodiversity: Directions and solutions for policy, research and action. International scientific symposium, biodiversity and sustainable diets united against hunger, FAO headquarters, Rome, Italy, 3–5 November 2010*. Food and Agriculture Organization of the United Nations (FAO).

Cadieux, K.V., Slocum, R., 2016. *What does it mean to do food justice?* Journal of Political Ecology 22(1), 1–26.

Day-Farnswortha, L., Morales, A., 2011. *Satiating the demand: Planning for alternative models of regional food distribution*. Journal of Agriculture, Food Systems, and Community Development 2(1), 227–247.

de los Ríos, I., Rivera, M., García, C., 2016. *Redefining rural prosperity through social learning in the cooperative sector: 25 years of experience from organic agriculture in Spain*. Land Use Policy, 54(Supplement C), 85–94. https://doi.org/10.1016/j.landusepol.2016.02.009.

Deller, S.C., Lamie, D., Stickel, M., 2017. *Local foods systems and community economic development*. Community Development, 48(5). https://doi.org/10.1080/15575330.2017.1373136.

Dorward, C., Smukler, S., Mullinix, K., 2016. *A novel methodology to assess land-based food self-reliance in the southwest British Columbia bioregion*. Renewable Agriculture and Food Systems 1, 1–19.

Duarte Alonso, A., O'Neill, M., 2010. *Small hospitality enterprises and local produce: A case study*. British Food Journal 112(11), 1175–1189.

Franklin, A., Newton, J., Mcentree, J., 2011. *Moving beyond the alternative: Sustainable communities, rural resilience and the mainstreaming of local food*. Local Environment 16(8), 771–788.

Fraser, E., 2017. *Canada should adopt blockchain technology to meet agri-food goals*. News, University of Guelph, December 8. https://news.uoguelph.ca/2017/12/canada-adopt-blockchain-technology-meet-agri-food-goals/ (accessed 12.21.17).

Good Food for All Agenda Task Force. 2010. *Creating a new regional food system for Los Angeles*. The Harman Press, Los Angeles, CA. https://goodfoodlosangeles.files.wordpress.com/2010/07/good-food-full_report_single_072010.pdf (accessed 9.17.17).

Halloran, J.M., Archer, D.W., 2008. *External economic drivers and US agricultural production systems*. Renewable Agriculture and Food Systems 23(4), 296–303.

Hamm, M.W., 2009. *Principles for framing a healthy food system*. Journal of Hunger and Environmental Nutrition 4(3–4), 241–250.

Hinrichs, C.C., Gulespie, G.W., Feenstra, G.W., 2004. *Social learning and innovation at retail farmers' markets*. Rural Sociology 69(1), 31–58.

Jackson, R.J., Minjares, R., Naumoff, K.S., Shrimali, B.P., Martin, L.K., 2009. *Agriculture policy is health policy*. Journal of Hunger and Environmental Nutrition 4(3–4), 393–408.

Jarosz, L., 2008. *The city in the country: Growing alternative food networks in metropolitan areas*. Journal of Rural Studies 24(3), 231–244.

Johnston, J., Biro, A., MacKendrick, N., 2009. *Lost in the supermarket: The corporate-organic foodscape and the struggle for food democracy*. Antipode 41(3), 509–532.

Knickel, K., Redman, M., Darnhofer, I., Ashkenazy, A., Calvao Chebach, T., Šūmane, S., … Rogge, E., 2018. *Between aspirations and reality: Making farming, food systems and rural areas more resilient, sustainable and equitable*. Journal of Rural Studies, 59, 1–14.

Lang, T., 2009. *Reshaping the food system for ecological public health*. Journal of Hunger and Environmental Nutrition 4(3–4), 315–335.

Levkoe, C., Lefebvre, R., Blay-Palmer, A., 2017. *Food counts: A pan-Canadian sustainable food systems report card*. FLEdGE; Social Sciences and Humanities Research Council of Canada. https://fledgeresearch.files.wordpress.com/2017/05/food-counts-pan-canadian-sustainable-food-systems-report-card2.pdf (accessed 7.27.17).

Marsden, T., 2009. Mobilities, *Vulnerabilities and sustainabilities: Exploring pathways from denial to sustainable rural development*. Sociologia Ruralis 49(2), 113–131. https://doi.org/10.1111/j.1467-9523.2009.00479.x.

Mason, P., Lang, T., 2017. *Sustainable diets: How ecological nutrition can transform consumption and the food system.* Routledge, Abingdon; New York.

Milestad, R., Darnhofer, I., 2003. *Building farm resilience: The prospects and challenges of organic farming.* Journal of Sustainable Agriculture 22(3), 81–97.

Milestad, R., Hadatsch, S., 2003. *Growing out of the niche: Can organic agriculture keep its promises? A study of two Austrian cases.* American Journal of Alternative Agriculture 18(3), 155–163.

Mount, P., 2012. *Growing local food: Scale and local food systems governance.* Agriculture and Human Values 29(1), 107–121. https://doi.org/10.1007/s10460-011-9331-0.

Rivera, M., Knickel, K., de los Ríos, I., Ashkenazy, A., Pears, D.Q., Chebach, T., Šūmane, S., 2018. *Rethinking the connections between agricultural change and rural prosperity: A discussion of insights derived from case studies in seven countries.* Journal of Rural Studies 59, 242–251.

Sbicca, J., Myers, J.S., 2017. *Food justice racial projects: Fighting racial neoliberalism from the Bay to the Big Apple.* Environmental Sociology 3(1), 30–41.

Si, Z., Scott, S., 2016. *The convergence of alternative food networks within "rural development" initiatives: The case of the New Rural Reconstruction Movement in China.* Local Environment 21(9), 1082–1099. https://doi.org/10.1080/13549839.2015.1067190.

Slocum, R., 2006. *Anti-racist practice and the work of community food organizations.* Antipode 38(2), 327–349.

Slocum, R., Cadieux, K.V., Blumberg, R., 2016. *Solidarity, space and race: Toward geographies of agrifood justice.* Spatial Justice 9 (January). www.jssj.org/article/solidarite-espace-et-race-vers-des-geographies-de-la-justice-alimentaire/.

Smithers, J., Joseph, A.E., 2010. *The trouble with authenticity: Separating ideology from practice at the farmers' market.* Agriculture and Human Values 27(2), 239–247. https://doi.org/10.1007/s10460-009-9250-5.

Summer, J., Mair, H., Nelson, E., 2010. *Putting the culture back into agriculture: Civic engagement, community and the celebration of local food.* International Journal of Agricultural Sustainability 8(1–2), 54–61.

Weis, A.J., 2007. *The global food economy: The battle for the future of farming.* Zed Books, London.

24

DRIVERS OF FOOD LOSSES AND THEIR IMPLICATIONS FOR THE AGRO-FOOD CHAIN

SELECTED CASE STUDIES

Matteo Vittuari, Andrea Segrè, Luca Falasconi, Simone Piras, Laura Brenes-Peralta, Laura García Herrero, Marco Pagani, and Fabio De Menna

Food losses and waste: why do they matter?

Food losses and waste (FLW) represent a major challenge for food systems sustainability and a growing concern in the political agendas of national governments and international organizations. This interest derives from the interrelated implications in terms of food security, human health, economic development, and environmental impact. The staggering amount of FLW currently generated at global (Gustavsson *et al.*, 2011) and European Union (EU) levels (Stenmarck *et al.*, 2016) exacerbates the challenges posed by projected world population growth, changing dietary habits, and the reduction in food production capacity due to climate change, soil erosion, and land use change for energy production (FAO, 2013).

In a life-cycle perspective, besides being a missed opportunity to feed the growing world population, FLW create a huge pressure on natural capital in terms of natural resources consumption (energy, minerals, water, fish stocks, agricultural land), environmental pollution (water, air, soil), and biodiversity loss (Scherhaufer *et al.*, 2015). Due to these multifaceted implications, in recent years FLW attracted the interest of an increasing number of stakeholders who have examined its definition and scope boundaries (Östergren *et al.*, 2014), drivers (Canali *et al.*, 2014), quantification and reporting methods (Tostivint *et al.*, 2016), emerging policy proposals, and evaluation methods (Burgos *et al.*, 2016; Vittuari *et al.*, 2015). Based on these premises, in September 2015 the UN General Assembly adopted the Sustainable Development Goals (SDGs) to renew the fight against poverty and hunger, in addition to many other human development and environmental goals. The twelfth of these SDGs aims at "ensuring sustainable consumption and production patterns" and suggests an additional focus (Target 12.3) on reinforcing the fight against food waste: "by 2030, halve per capita global food waste at the retail and consumer levels and reduce food losses along production and supply chains, including postharvest losses" (UN, 2015).

Drawing on the distinction between FLW and the identification of the major causes of food losses (FL) in the production, post-harvest, and processing stages of the food supply chain (FSC), this chapter presents and analyzes a set of related situations to disclose their complexity. The case studies of FL in the field and unfair trading practices (UTPs) along the FSC are investigated, and the policy interventions implemented by local and national governments to mitigate these problems are discussed.

Definitions and estimations of food losses and waste

FAO defines FLW as all the agri-food products allocated for human consumption that are instead discarded, lost, degraded, or consumed by pests at any stage of the food chain (FAO, 1981). More specifically, this definition places losses and waste in different segments of the FSC:

- *food losses* occur during the agricultural production, post-harvest, and processing stages of the FSC, and are mainly related to logistical and infrastructural limitations, like crops destroyed by adverse weather or pests, products that are not properly collected during harvest, or are spoiled after harvest because of improper storing conditions;
- *food waste* occurs during distribution, sale, and final consumption, and is primarily related to institutional, market, or behavioral factors, like unsold food, over preparation, or over serving (Gustavsson *et al.*, 2011).

Besides this characterization, a further distinction can be introduced between *avoidable* and *unavoidable* FLW (WRAP, 2009; Ward, 2018):

- *avoidable* FLW is that which would not exist if the system were managed properly in terms of farm practices, but also market and policy decisions. In other words, FLW generated from inefficient production systems could be related to over-planting or to products remaining in the field since they do not meet the standards imposed by retailers;
- *unavoidable* FLW includes materials that are not edible – typically described as by-products, co-products, or residues, like bones, shells, cores, stems – and cannot be avoided even in efficient production systems; the amount of unavoidable FLW could be reduced if appropriate technologies were available to recover some of the contained nutrients.

Additionally, the concept of *(in)edibility* might have different implications in the different stages of the agri-food supply chain. The "optimal efficiency level" of an agri-food product may not be reached if by-products are considered inedible at all stages. For instance, fish bones, which are a rich source of micronutrients, or fish heads/eyes, which are a valuable source of essential fatty acids, could be used as a raw material to be processed for human consumption with appropriate technology and market acceptance. Another raw material with a high nutritional value is blood. Nutritional deficiencies such as of iron and vitamin A have a great impact on human health. In this sense, the boundaries of what should be considered *inedible* might be revised – in a context of food safety – in function of the available technologies, the consumption trends, and the forecasted innovations.

The distinction between *edible* and *inedible* parts of food is one of the key elements of the definition proposed by the EU project FP7 FUSIONS (Food Use for Social Innovation by Optimizing waste preveNtion Strategies), which focuses on the optimization of food use to achieve resource efficiency. Hence, the definition adopted is more oriented towards how FLW are managed and valorized in the food supply chain. FUSIONS defines food waste as "any food, and inedible parts of food, removed from the food supply chain to be recovered or disposed (including composting, crops ploughed in/not harvested, anaerobic digestion, bio-energy production, co-generation, incineration, disposal to sewer, landfill or discarded to sea)" (Östergren *et al.*, 2014, p. 6). Food or inedible parts of food that are valorized as animal feed or converted to produce bio-based material/biochemical processing are excluded from this definition. The inclusion of inedible parts in the definition of FLW aims to consider them within different management options. Furthermore, capturing information on inedible parts highlights the potential of this fraction for improved food use (e.g. bringing currently "inedible" food into wider food use, such as turning orange peels into marmalade, recovering nutrients from bones, etc.).

This chapter focuses mainly on FL, as they relate to farm practices, decisions made by farmers, and market and policy conditions influencing farm operations. Considering that 80 percent of agricultural products in the EU originate in rural regions (Eurostat, 2010, 2016), FL represent a major rural issue.

Table 24.1 presents available data on FL in some European countries. Pre- and post-harvest losses range from 0.7 to 1.7 percent of primary production, equivalent to 10–30 kg per capita per year. Processing losses present a higher variability, from 0.5 to 4.6 percent of the production, equivalent to 10–60 kg per capita per year. This corresponds to an estimated 9.1 ± 1.5 million tons of FL occurring at production and 16.9 ± 12.7 million tons of FL occurring at processing (the larger standard deviation for the latter reflects the variations among European countries, as shown in Table 24.1).

An aspect of FL at farm level that is often overlooked is *virtual food loss*, or the opportunity cost arising from inefficient on-farm operations. For example, a farmer who fails to operate to best practice due to factors such as inadequate fertilizer application or inappropriate crop variety use may produce lower yield and quality with respect to the farm's potential. While ignored in the usual assessments of losses, this is a real loss to the system that can be measured by the difference between actual and optimal yields (Ward, 2018).

Food losses: drivers at production, post-harvest, and processing levels

According to Canali *et al.* (2017), the drivers of FL may be classified in three principal contexts: technological, economic, and institutional. The *technological context* is related to misuses, failures,

Table 24.1 Food losses during production and processing in selected European countries

Country	Losses during production		Losses during processing	
	Total (1000 t)	Per capita (kg)	Total (1000 t)	Per capita (kg)
Denmark	169	29.8	–	–
Finland	63	11.5	–	–
France	1990	29.9	626	9.4
Germany	1186	14.5	1850	22.7
Italy	1246	20.3	–	–
Sweden	111	11.2	–	–
Lithuania	–	–	105	36.2
United Kingdom	–	–	3900	60.0
Estimation for EU	9100 ± 1500	18 ± 3	16900 ± 12700	33 ± 25

Source: Stenmarck *et al.* (2016).

and limits of current technologies (Table 24.2). Unpredictable adverse weather conditions, pests, and mycotoxins contaminations may cause the failure of 0.5–1 percent of crops (Bhat and Miller, 1991; USDA, 2018a); inadequate control of microbial and physiological activity may cause perishability of products (Raak *et al.*, 2017).

Current technologies may also determine food losses as a collateral effect, like with animal deaths due to stress conditions in industrial livestock farming (St-Pierre *et al.*, 2003) and to a greater extent for fish by-catch, since they occur as externalities (Kelleher, 2005). Mechanical peeling and handling of produce is a high-throughput process, but it causes a significant amount of waste (Willersinn *et al.*, 2015). Sub-optimal processing includes, for instance, cutting and trimming losses (Somsen, 2004), package sealing failures (Whitehead *et al.*, 2011), and cold chain inefficiencies (George *et al.*, 2010).

A second group of drivers is related to the *economic context* (Table 24.3), such as the organization of food businesses and their integration along the chain and management choices determined by economic variables. Some of these problems could be managed by a single FSC operator, like food contaminations, grading and sorting errors, or overfilling of containers (Raak *et al.*, 2017; Lee and Willis, 2010; WRAP, 2012).

Other losses are mainly caused by market power imbalances between different operators of the FSC and could be solved by better cooperation among operators and fairer commercial practices. For example, operators that have more bargaining power may tend to transfer the risks of unsold products and related costs of disposal to suppliers; large retailers frequently impose on suppliers the return of unsold or damaged products for free or the possibility of last minute cancellations of orders (see below case study on unfair trading practices). Consumer demand and related cosmetic standards set by retailers – which are self-reinforcing – may also play a role in FL: food (mainly fruit and vegetables) that does not match these standards cannot usually be marketed.

A third group of drivers relates to the *legislative and policy context* (Table 24.4), such as inefficient legislation in the food sector that may subordinate potential generation of FL to other priorities, like food safety, consumer information, or low cost of disposal. Examples of inefficiencies in legislation are overly strict marketing standards on product shape and appearance or

Table 24.2 Summary of technology-related food loss drivers

Type of driver	Driver description
Limits in technology	Adverse weather conditions
	Mycotoxins and pests
	Perishability of products
Collateral effects of technologies	Non-selective fishing
	Stress-related animal deaths in industrial livestock farming
	Losses caused by mechanical peeling and handling
Sub-optimal processing	Slaughtering and process losses in meat industry
	Cutting and trimming losses
	Packaging sealing failures
	Poor storage and handling conditions
	Cold chain inefficiencies
	Mismarking and mislabeling

Source: Authors' elaboration.

Table 24.3 Summary of economics-related food loss drivers

Type of driver	Driver description
Manageable by a single operator	Production of sub-standard food and food contamination
	Grading and sorting errors
	Overfilling of containers
	Inaccurate storage and incorrect stock turnover
Manageable with coordination among different operators	Overproduction and overstock due to short time imposed to deliver orders
	Reduced tolerance of retailers for errors in delivering
	Return of unsold or damaged products for free
	Last-minute cancelations of orders
Dependent on structural variables and not easily manageable	Low prices of farm may induce unharvesting
	Cosmetic standards and scarce use of by-products

Source: Authors' elaboration.

Table 24.4 Summary of legislation and policy-related food loss drivers

Type of driver	Driver description
Related to agricultural policy and quality standards	EU marketing standards (i.e. product shape)
	Measures within the Common Agricultural or Fishery Policy
	Packaging legislation
Related to food safety, consumer health, and animal welfare policies	Overproduction due to short time imposed to deliver orders
	Too strict food hygiene and safety regulations
	Date marking regulations
Related to waste policy, taxation, and other legislation	Low landfill taxes
	Ban on animal feeding with animal by-products and catering waste

Source: Authors' elaboration.

food safety (Mena *et al.*, 2011), unclear regulations on the expiry date of products (i.e. "best before" vs. "consume by") (European Commission, 2015), and landfill taxes that are too low to discourage the disposal of FL (Fedrigo-Fazio *et al.*, 2013).

This section demonstrates that the drivers of FL are complex and interrelated and addressing them requires a systemic approach involving multiple stakeholders along the FSC and decision-makers at different levels of public administration. Since a large share of food – and thus the actors involved in its production, processing, and distribution – originates from rural areas, the policy mix required to address FL can be properly characterized as a rural policy. The following two case studies illustrate this more in detail.

Case study 1: food losses in the field in Italian and Spanish farms

FL at the pre-harvest level fall into three main categories:

a   non-harvested production due to damage by pests, diseases, or weather;
b   production left in the field because market prices are too low to cover the production cost (sometimes even the cost of harvesting) at the time of harvest;
c   overproduction due to planning errors or to reduce the risk of not meeting buyer requests.

Unharvested products are usually ploughed into the soil, so that some organic matter is recovered. However, they represent a net loss in terms of human nutrition and employed resources, such as water, energy, labor, and chemicals. Italy is one of the primary food producers in the EU, especially in terms of fruits and vegetables, which are highly perishable. In 2017, in Italy about one million tons of food were not harvested and remained in the field – which amounted to 2.6 percent of total agricultural production. Losses are lower for cereals and higher for fruits and vegetables, oil crops, and sugar crops. The highest losses are registered for vegetables grown in greenhouses (see Table 24.5). Some of these figures can be considered normal, since they are relatively consistent with trends from the past decade in terms of losses in the field. They are also consistent with pre-harvest losses in the United States, which amount to around 1 percent of production for cereals (USDA, 2018a), 1–3 percent for fruit (data obtained comparing total and utilized fruit production according to USDA [2018b]), and 6–10 percent for vegetables (Johnson et al., 2018).

Post-harvest losses are due to commercial standards. Products that do not comply with minimum quality standards in terms of shape, size, color, and time to ripeness cannot usually be marketed, and it is not always possible to find alternate uses for them. It has been estimated that every year more than 50 million tons of fresh fruits and vegetables are discarded from on-farm cosmetic grade-out in the European Economic Area (Porter et al., 2018). Based on this figure, it is possible to estimate that, in Italy, 4.5–6.0 million tons of produce are lost every year for cosmetic grade-out, which is ten times the amount of unharvested fruit and vegetables.

Table 24.5 Losses in the field in Italy, 2017

Product	Total production	Harvested production	Absolute loss	Relative loss
	Mt	*Mt*	*Mt*	*%*
Cereals	16.41	16.17	0.23	1.4
Tubers	1.40	1.36	0.04	3.1
Pulses	0.47	0.46	0.01	2.7
Oil crops	4.10	3.90	0.19	4.7
Sugar crops	0.27	0.25	0.03	10.1
Fruit	10.12	9.88	0.24	2.3
Vegetables – field	4.68	4.52	0.15	3.3
Vegetables – greenhouse	1.70	1.56	0.14	8.2
Total	39.14	38.11	1.04	2.6

Source: ISTAT (2018).

In Italy, as detailed in the following case study on UTPs, the agricultural sector is character-ized by a high number of small enterprises that are not in the position of setting the price of the goods they produce, causing power imbalances. This situation, combined with information asymmetries or imperfect information and the mechanism of price transmission, does not allow farmers to predict the exact time of planting or transplanting, and the final production and market price of the crop. The rigid structure of production costs may cause the final price not to be enough to cover harvesting costs. Therefore, in some instances, producers are forced to leave the crop in the field in order to minimize economic losses.

Another EU country that produces (and exports) large quantities of perishable food products is Spain. FLW along the whole FSC represents 20 percent of production, of which 4.4 percent is lost at the production and processing stages. This waste is mainly due to aesthetic reasons or the non-standard weight of agricultural products, with vegetables and fruits representing the highest losses. In 2013, the Spanish government launched a national strategy called "*Más ali-mento, menos desperdicio*" (More food, less waste) with the aim of reducing FLW and maximizing the value of discarded food. This strategy is aligned with the EU's commitment to sustainability through the Action Plan for the Circular Economy (MAPA, 2019). For the first three years, the programs were focused on the quantification of FLW, given that until 2013 Spain had not per-formed any national study to identify how much, how, where, and why FLW were occurring. Parallel actions were taken to raise awareness, review the current legal framework, understand different partnership options for voluntary collaborations, and promote a new technology path to target FLW (MAPAMA, 2017). Table 24.6 shows the results from the first study on FL accomplished under the "More food, less waste" program (MAAMA, 2013).

The study identified the causes of FL in the different stages of food production. Thus:

- *at crop level* most of the losses were due to climate conditions and plagues;
- *at harvesting level* FL were due to machinery inefficiencies, harvesting costs (market prices not covering the production cost), quality standards (mainly cosmetic), and climate conditions;
- *at storage and manipulation level* FL were due to quality standard (mainly cosmetic standards), uncompetitive price, and variation in product demand.

Table 24.6 Losses in the field in Spain, 2013

Product	Total production	Losses[1]	Other losses[2]	Total losses vs production
	Mt	%	%	%
Cereals and legumes	20.57	21.9	4.6	26.5
Citrus	5.04	18.5	3.9	22.4
Rest of fruits	5.13	19.2	3.9	23.1
Vegetables	9.85	21.9	6.5	28.4
Oils and fats	2.69	19.3	3.4	22.7
Wine	4.60	23.4	3.3	26.7

Source: MAAMA (2013) and FAO (2013a).

Notes

1 Percent of production lost due to lack of efficiency, for example climate conditions or pests. It could be avoidable with good practices.

2 Percent of losses which are not able to be avoided with current agricultural techniques.

The products not eligible for commercialization are diverted to industry (to be processed to obtain juice, jam, etc.), animal feed, composting, or landfill (MAAMA, 2013). After a revision of the program, the strategy for 2017–2020 was articulated in eight pillars. Areas requiring changes in regulation to facilitate the donation and distribution of food surpluses between stakeholders were identified. The strategy also embraces agreements among sectors not fully involved in previous periods, such as cooking schools, distribution, or hospitality, and the relationship between the environment, FLW, and climate change (MAPA, 2018).

Some actors in Spain are fighting food losses in the field and for cosmetic reasons. An example of success is the NGO Espigoladors (Gleaners). This NGO, active since 2014, harvests non-tradable food and manages the discarded product with the support of volunteers. About 95 percent of its production goes to social charities in Catalonia, while 5 percent is transformed and commercialized to sustain the project. Commercialized products are mainly prepared using the so-called "ugly fruit or veggies", rejected by the retail markets due to their appearance despite their perfect quality conditions. Espigoladors' activities of recovering food from the fields is linked to different processes of social actions, as it involves volunteers or groups at risk of social exclusion.

In Italian rural areas, gleaning practices have been historically regulated under the power of the Rural Policy (Narducci and Narducci, 2015). Gleaning was a legal practice whenever the landowner allowed it, although this system has not been extended due to controversial issues such as the guarantee that gleaning output is dedicated exclusively for donation and considering gleaners as volunteers and not as unpaid workers. In 2016 Italy implemented Law No. 166/2016, concerning provisions on the donation and distribution of food to limit food waste. Article 3.5 recognizes gleaning, reinforcing the regulatory framework to protect this practice by allowing the free transfer of surpluses of agricultural suitable products in the field for human and animal consumption by donation. The operations of collection of these products are carried out under the responsibility of those who perform the collection, in compliance with the rules on food hygiene and safety. Therefore, the only constraints to glean in Italy are on one hand finding landowners willing to facilitate their agricultural surplus, and on the other hand finding organizations providing volunteers with experience on agricultural practices.

An important cause of FL is represented by UTPs, described in the next section. This cause is not explicitly covered by the 2017–2020 strategy, although it might be targeted under one of the eight areas dealing with regulatory aspects. This area deals with the identification of regulatory barriers to addressing FLW and the development of instruments to overcome them (MAPA, 2018).

Case study 2: unfair trading practices

In the European Commission's (EC) "Green Paper on unfair trading practices in the business-to-business food and non-food supply chain in Europe", UTPs are defined as

> practices that grossly deviate from good commercial conduct and are contrary to good faith and fair dealing. UTPs are typically imposed in a situation of imbalance by a stronger party on a weaker one and can exist from any side of the B2B relationship and at any stage in the supply chain.
>
> *(European Commission, 2013, p. 3)*

UTPs may occur whenever one commercial party:

- shifts its own costs or entrepreneurial risks to another;
- takes benefits of any kind without performing a service;

- makes unilateral and/or retroactive changes to a contract;
- unfairly terminates a contract or threatens termination without justification.

UTPs might occur in the FSC due to significant power imbalances between different sides of the market, particularly between larger buyers, such as the major European retail corporations, and smaller suppliers such as individual farmers or small cooperatives. The concentration of power within the food retail sector varies across the EU: in countries like Germany, the UK, Poland, or Spain the three top retailers control between 40 and 50 percent of the market, while in other countries like Greece or Italy traditional grocery markets are still important (Piras *et al.*, 2018). Where retail markets are highly concentrated, the disproportionate power of retailers over suppliers can result in the imposition of unfair conditions on weaker players (Ghosh and Eriksson, 2019).

The lack of an inhibiting transnational regulatory framework or an adequate system of investigation and redress at the national level allows power imbalances to result in persistent and high levels of UTPs across multiple areas of the FSC. As a reflection of the weak position of farmers, the long-term trend in the distribution of value added in European food chains has been a steady decline in their share, from 31 percent in 1995 to 21 percent in 2011, while the retail sector has increased its share from 38 to 51 percent (Piras *et al.*, 2018). The interpretation of this trend is complex and includes changes in Common Agricultural Policy payments, and a general shift towards a greater share of higher value-added food products (e.g. pre-prepared/convenience foods). However, over this period greater market concentration has also occurred within the retail sector, with most European food purchased by only 110 retailer buying desks from approximately three million farmers (see Figure 24.1). This means that a large redistribution of resources has taken place between rural areas, where most farmers are based, and cities, where large retail companies have their headquarters and the majority of their customer base.

In addition to the commercial impact on smaller food producers, and the resulting social impact in terms of increased uncertainty in rural livelihoods, some UTPs can also generate FLW. Examples of these scenarios are:

- when a buyer makes last minute changes or cancellations to volumes previously ordered, the producer does not have the time to find other buyers before the produce is spoiled, especially in the case of perishable products;
- when farmers overproduce in order not to run the risk of losing business: if they cannot then find a market for their surplus product, FLW may result (Piras *et al.*, 2018);
- when cosmetic specification may be used by retailers to restrict market access when demand is lower than supply, resulting in FLW (Colbert, 2017; Colbert and Stuart, 2015);
- when "minimum life on receipt" (MLoR) criteria are used to grant retailers an appropriate shelf life for fresh products by rejecting those expiring too soon: in some cases, MLoR have been used as an excuse to reject produce that the buyer has decided she cannot sell because of falling demand; this rejection is a net FL (GCA, 2017).

The EU has been discussing UTPs and responses to them since 2009 (European Commission, 2017a). In a 2017 public consultation with stakeholders of the FSC (farmers and their organizations, downstream businesses, public authorities, EU institutions, consumers, and their organizations), it was determined that 90 percent of the respondents agreed or partially agreed that UTPs exist, citing examples related to late payments and unilateral or retroactive changes to contracts (European Commission, 2017b).

The main challenge with UTPs regulation and prevention is the difficulty of translating them into actual infringements of the current competition law (European Parliament, 2016). Thus,

Stage in the value chain	Number of actors
Consumers	160 million
Customers	89 million
Retail outlets	170 000
Supermarket formats	600
Buying desks	110
Manufacturers	8600
Semi-manufacturers	80 000
Suppliers	180 000
Farmers/producers	3 200 000

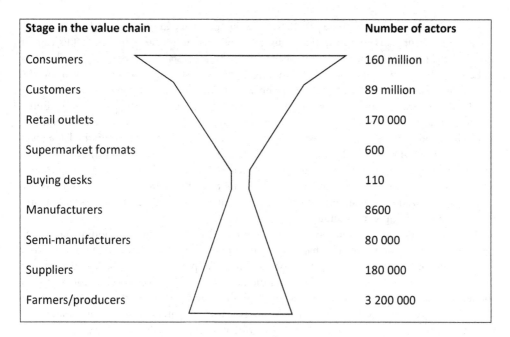

Figure 24.1 The supply-chain funnel in Europe

one of the causes of UTPs is the absence of effective legislative control, stemming in part from differences in definition and responses at the national level, and in part from the unique nature of the FSC (Stefanelli and Marsden, 2012). Currently, as pointed out by Ghosh and Eriksson (2019), exertion of retail power is very difficult to prove and unlikely to be reported. With a view to designing more effective interventions, the remainder of this section compares the different regulatory approaches to UTPs adopted by the UK and Italy, which originate from their contrasting FSC market structures as well as different legal systems.

The UK has a high degree of market concentration, with the top four retailers holding 70 percent of the market and imposing UTPs on producers, including order cancellations, poor communication, inaccurate forecasting, and inconsistent application of cosmetic standards. These practices are exacerbated by a climate of fear generated by the power imbalances between suppliers and retailers (Feedback, 2018). In the UK, the policy intervention in response to UTPs was the establishment in 2013 of the Groceries Supply Code of Practice (GSCOP), which is inspired by a principle of fairness and sets how retailers should manage their relationships with suppliers. The GSCOP states, for example, that there must be no delay in payments to suppliers, no obligation to contribute to marketing cost, no request of payment in case of produce shrinkage, and no retrospective variations to supply agreements, while it foresees compensation to suppliers for forecasting errors (GSCOP, 2009). Respect of the GSCOP is ensured by an independent authority, the Groceries Code Adjudicator (GCA). The GCA has been effective in reducing the prevalence of UTPs between retailers and their direct suppliers, yet 62 percent of the suppliers surveyed in 2016 said that they were still experiencing issues with UTPs. After three years of activity, the GCA found increasing levels of awareness and understanding of the code. For example, there was a rise in the number of suppliers that undertook training in the code, while suppliers also reported an increase in knowledge about how to contact the Code Compliance Officers. There was also a fall in the number of direct suppliers declaring having raised an issue with a retailer in the past 12 months. Despite these improvements, the GCA only protects direct suppliers, meaning that indirect suppliers that are the target of UTPs cannot appeal to the GCA. Therefore, there has been a wide range of stakeholders calling for the code to be extended to indirect suppliers. Furthermore, overseas suppliers lack information on the rights granted by the GSCOP, but there are no actions foreseen to raise their awareness.

The Italian retail sector presents a lower market concentration compared to Western European countries. Nevertheless, the supply is extremely fragmented, and a relative market consolidation has been taking place in the last 15 years: the share of food sales carried out by large retail distributors (GDO) reached 72 percent in 2010 (OECD, 2013). There are two dynamics which strengthen the power of buyers even further: the creation of super-alliances among retail chains, and high concentration at the local level. At the same time, the share of producers who join a producer organization is small (e.g. less than 30 percent for fruit and vegetable producers), and thus their bargaining power is limited.

The European Court of Auditors (2016) recognized that trading practices and market structures can generate food waste. This happens mainly in two ways: either through a disproportion of bargaining power between two parties, or through unfair practices taking place in the context of imbalanced power relations. Given the structure of the Italian agri-food sector described above, both phenomena are likely to occur, as figures reveal. In Italy FLW account for 8.8 million tons every year (CIHEAM and FAO, 2016). It is estimated that UTPs are responsible for between 5 and 10 percent of the losses occurring in primary production (Piras *et al.*, 2018).

Until 2001, the Italian norm used to address UTPs in agri-FSCs was the law on industrial subcontracting (Law 192 of 1998), which introduced a prohibition of *abuse of economic dependence* for the first time in Italy. Law 57 of 2001 further extended the scope of the 1998 law to protect overall market competition, in line with the legislation of other EU member states. To do so, it distinguished between *abuse of dominance* and *abuse of economic dependence*. Competence over the former was attributed to the Italian National Competition Authority (AGCM), an independent authority mainly responsible for introducing antitrust norms, established in 1990. According to the 2001 law, the AGCM can address cases of abuse of dominance that affect a relevant market but cannot sanction the infringer. Instead, cases of abuse of economic dependence are under the jurisdiction of ordinary courts.

Despite a different market structure, the "victims" and "wrongdoers" are the same in both Italy and the UK: small producers or processors of perishable products and large retail companies, respectively. Therefore, "victims" may avoid pursuing legal claims to have their rights respected because of the "fear factor". Another issue is represented by the awareness of rights as, for example, in the UK the "wrongdoers" are based in the country, but the "victims" may be based overseas.

Compared to Italy, the UK presents stronger market concentration, but also farmers' organizations that brought evidence of the impact of UTPs to show that regulation was needed. In contrast, in Italy there is almost exclusively anecdotal evidence of UTPs provided by newspaper reports (see, for instance, Ciconte and Liberti, 2017). The pathway to establishing the GCA in the UK followed a bottom-up approach: a voluntary framework was set up, a survey carried out, and an investigating commission established before moving to a regulatory approach. In Italy the adoption of art. 62 of law January 24, 2012, N.1 was the result of a top-down process, as the country probably aimed at complying with EU criteria.

A strong challenge to the fight against UTPs in Italy was the lack of prior attempts to address UTPs by means of persuasive instruments; hence, information on the phenomenon was poor. In the UK, voluntary tools are usually preferred: in the case of the GCA, these were turned into compulsory regulations due to the serious concerns identified by a 2008 investigation. In Italy, there were limited feedback loops between voluntary and regulatory approaches, and policymakers did not take advantage of civil society monitoring to improve the regulation.

However, addressing UTPs does not mean only sanctioning the wrongdoer and compensating the victim. To mitigate their negative effects in terms of FLW, it is essential to design an organizational structure for redistributing the surplus food generated by UTPs like order cancellations. In this respect, stakeholder involvement and the design of a comprehensive policy mix become crucial.

Conclusions

This chapter illustrates the relevance of FLW in the context of food systems sustainability and its relation with rural areas. It demonstrates the importance of FLW by focusing on food losses, their quantification, drivers, and possible prevention measures. According to available data, the amount of FL occurring during the earlier stages of the FSC is relatively low when compared to the larger quantities of food waste generated at the retail and consumption level. However, FL, including virtual losses, represent a significant net loss for small producers and processors, which are key actors for rural areas. The drivers of FL are complex and interdependent. While some losses are somehow inherent to production processes or linked to external causes such as adverse climate or pests, other factors related to cosmetic standards and price volatility contribute to farmers' decisions not to harvest. In addition, the power asymmetry characterizing the European FSC creates the conditions for UTPs causing FL, and of an "inverse" income redistribution from rural farmers to large urban-based retail companies.

Therefore, interventions on the FL challenge require an effective and multi-sectoral policy mix, and the involvement of food chain stakeholders and institutions, with a special emphasis on stakeholders from rural areas. Specifically, the two case studies presented provide potential examples of bottom-up initiatives, voluntary agreements, and compulsory regulation. The gleaning initiative organized by the Spanish NGO is a success story of how to turn FL into opportunities for rural societies, contributing to poverty reduction. While similar practices are carried out in some countries, in others (like Italy) policy measures might be needed in order to remove over-regulation preventing similar solutions. UTPs can be addressed through either voluntary agreements or compulsory regulation. In any case, market conditions should be properly addressed in order to design effective regulatory policies, but also strong (civil society) organization, such as through farmers' associations, is needed to counterbalance power asymmetries. Through such regulations, farmers, especially small ones, are usually better off and food losses are reduced, leading to positive outcomes for rural areas.

References

Bhat, R.V., Miller, J.D., 1991. *Mycotoxins and food supply.* Food, Nutrition and Agriculture, FAO. www.fao.org/docrep/U3550t/u3550t0e.htm#mycotoxinsandfoodsupply (accessed 9.10.16).

Burgos, S., Gheoldus, M., Vittuari, M., Politano, A., Piras, S., Aramyan, L., Valeeva, N., Wenbon, M., Hanssen, O.J., Scherhaufer, S., Ottner, R., Silvennoinen, K., Paschali, D., Braun, S., Cseh, B., Ujhelyi, K., 2016. *Food waste policy evaluation framework.* FUSIONS project.

Canali, M., Östergren, K., Amani, P., Aramyan, L., Sijtsema, S., Korhonen, O., Silvennoinen, S., Moates, G., Waldron, K., O'Connor, C., 2014. *Drivers of current food waste generation, threats of future increase and opportunities for reduction.* FUSIONS project.

Canali, M., Amani, P., Aramyan, L., Gheoldus, M., Moates, G., Östergren, K., Silvennoinen, K., Waldron, K., Vittuari, M., 2017. *Food waste drivers in Europe, from identification to possible interventions.* Sustainability 9, 37–70.

Centre international de hautes études agronomiques méditerranéennes (CIHEAM) and Food and Agriculture Organization (FAO), 2016. *Mediterra 2016. Zero waste in the Mediterranean: Natural resources, food and knowledge.* Presses de Sciences Po, Paris. www.fao.org/3/a-bq976e.pdf.

Ciconte, F., Liberti, S., 2017. *Supermercati, il grande inganno del sottocosto.* Internazionale. www.internazionale.it/reportage/fabio-ciconte/2017/02/27/supermercati-inganno-sotto-costo.

Colbert, E., 2017. *Causes of food waste in international supply chains.* A report by Feedback Global and funded by the Rockefeller Foundation. https://feedbackglobal.org/wp-content/uploads/2017/05/Causes-of-food-waste-in-international-supply-chains_Feedback.pdf.

Colbert, E., Stuart, T., 2015. *Food waste in Kenya: Uncovering food waste in the horticultural export supply chain.* Report produced by Feedback Global and funded by the Rockefeller Foundation and the Barham Trust. https://feedbackglobal.org/wp-content/uploads/2015/07/Food-Waste-in-Kenya_report-by-Feedback.pdf.

Espigoladors NGO, 2019. www.espigoladors.cat/es/.

European Commission, 2013. *Green paper. Unfair trading practices in the business-to-business food and non-food supply chain in Europe.* COM (2013) 37 final. European Union, Brussels.

European Commission, 2015. *Food waste and date marking.* TSN Political and Social. Flash Eurobarometer 425. European Commission, Directorate-General for Communication, Brussels.

European Commission, 2017a. *Inception impact assessment: Initiative to improve the food supply chain.* Ares (2017) 3735472–25/07/2017.

European Commission, 2017b. *News. Strong majority of stakeholders back European Union action to support farmers in food chain.* https://ec.europa.eu/info/news/strong-majority-stakeholders-back-european-union-action-support-farmers-food-chain_en.

European Court of Auditors, 2016. *Combating food waste: An opportunity for the EU to improve the resource-efficiency of the food supply chain.* Special Report No. 34. European Union, Brussels.

European Parliament, 2016. *Report on unfair trading practices in the food supply chain.* 2015/2065(INI). www.europarl.europa.eu/sides/getDoc.do?pubRef=-//EP//TEXT+REPORT+A8-2016-0173+0+DOC+XML+V0//EN.

Eurostat, 2010. *Overview of the urban/rural type for each NUTS 3 region, based on the 2010 NUTS version and 2006 Geostat population grid.* https://ec.europa.eu/eurostat/web/rural-development/methodology.

Eurostat, 2016. *Crop production in EU standard humidity by NUTS 2 regions.* http://appsso.eurostat.ec.europa.eu/nui/show.do?dataset=apro_cpshr&lang=en.

FAO – Food and Agriculture Organization, 1981. *Food loss prevention in perishable crops.* Agricultural Service Bulletin No. 43. FAO, Rome. www.fao.org/docrep/S8620E/S8620E00.htm.

FAO – Food and Agriculture Organization, 2013. *Food wastage footprint: Impacts on natural resources.* FAO, Rome.

Fedrigo-Fazio, D., Brink, P., Volkery, A., Russi, D., Mazza, L., McKenna, D., Wunder, S., 2013. *DYNAMIX policy mix evaluation: Food waste in the UK.* Ecologic Institut, Berlin.

Feedback, 2018. *Farmers talk food waste: Supermarkets' role in crop waste on UK farms.* https://feedbackglobal.org/wp-content/uploads/2018/08/Farm_waste_report_.pdf.

GCA – Groceries Code Adjudicator, 2017. *Annual report and accounts, 1 April 2016–31 March 2017.*

George, R.M., Burgess, P.J., Thorn, R.D., 2010. *Reducing food waste through the chill chain.* WRAP, Banbury.

Ghosh, R., Eriksson, M., 2019. *Food waste due to retail power in supply chains: Evidence from Sweden.* Global Food Security 20March, 1–8. https://doi.org/10.1016/j.gfs.2018.10.002.

GSCOP – Groceries Supply Code of Practice, 2009. *Guidance.* Department for Business, Energy and Industrial Strategy. www.gov.uk/government/publications/groceries-supply-code-of-practice/groceries-supply-code-of-practice.

Gustavsson, J., Cederberg, C., Sonesson, U., van Otterdijk, R., Meybeck, A., 2011. *Global food losses and food waste: Extent, causes and prevention.* FAO, Rome.

ISTAT, 2018. *Agricoltura e zootecnia. Coltivazioni.* agri.istat.it.

Johnson, L.K., Dunning, R.D., Bloom, J.D., Gunter, C.C., Boyette, M.D., Creamer, N.G., 2018. *Estimating on-farm food loss at the field level: A methodology and applied case study on a North Carolina farm.* Resources, Conservation and Recycling 137, 243–250.

Kelleher, K., 2005. *Discards in the world's marine fisheries: An update.* FAO: Rome.

Lee, P., Willis, P., 2010. *Waste arisings in the supply of food and drink to households in the UK.* WRAP, Banbury.

MAAMA – Ministerio de Agricultura, Alimentación y Medio Ambiente, 2013. *Las pérdidas y el desperdicio alimentario generado por la producción agrícola de alimentos en España.* www.menosdesperdicio.es/sites/default/files/documentos/relacionados/resumen_perdidas_desperdicio_agricolas_2014.pdf.

MAPA – Ministerio de Agricultura, Pesca, y Alimentación, 2018. *More food, less waste strategy 2017–2020.* www.menosdesperdicio.es/sites/default/files/documentos/relacionados/estrategia_2017-2020_en.pdf.

MAPA – Ministerio de Agricultura, Pesca, y Alimentación, 2019. *Más alimento menos desperdicio.* www.menosdesperdicio.es/.

MAPAMA – Ministerio de Agricultura, Pesca, Alimentación y Medio Ambiente, 2017. *Memoria de actuaciones 2013–2016*. www.menosdesperdicio.es/sites/default/files/documentos/relacionados/memoria_estrategia_13-16.pdf.

Mena, C., Adenso-Diaz, B., Yurt, O., 2011. *The causes of food waste in the supplier–retailer interface: Evidences from the UK and Spain*. Resources, Conservation and Recycling 55, 648–658.

Narducci, F., Narducci R., 2015. *Guida normativa per l'amministrazione locale 2015*. Maggioli Editore, Santarcangelo di Romagna.

OECD, 2013. *Competition issues in the food chain industry*. DAF/COMP (2014)16. OECD, Paris.

Östergren, K., Gustavsson, J., Bos Brouwers, H., Timmermans, T., Hansen, O.J., Møller, H., Anderson, G., O'Connor, C., Soethoudt, H., Quested, T., Easteal, S., Politano, A., Bellettato, C., Canali, M., Falasconi, L., Gaiani, G., Vittuari, M., Schneider, F., Moates, G., Waldron, K., Redlingshöfer, B., 2014. *FUSIONS definitional framework for food waste*. FUSIONS project. www.eu-fusions.org/phocadownload/Publications/FUSIONS%20Definitional%20Framework%20for%20Food%20Waste%202014.pdf.

Piras, S., Garcìa Herrero, L., Gheoldus, M., Burgos, S., Colin, F., Parfitt, J., Jarosz, D., Vittuari, M., 2018. *Qualitative policy mix assessment: Unfair trading practices and voluntary agreements in the context of food waste in select EU member states*. Deliverable D3.2. European Union's Horizon 2020 research and innovation programme, grant agreement No. 641933.

Porter, S.D., Reay, D.S., Bomberg, E., Higgins, P., 2018. *Avoidable food losses and associated production-phase greenhouse gas emissions arising from application of cosmetic standards to fresh fruit and vegetables in Europe and the UK*. Journal of Cleaner Production 201, 869–878.

Raak, N., Symmank, C., Zahn, S., Aschemann-Witzel, J., Rohm, H., 2017. *Processing- and product-related causes for food waste and implications for the food supply chain*. Waste Management. 61, 461–472.

Scherhaufer, S., Lebersorger, S., Pertl, A., Obersteiner, G., Schneider, F., Falasconi, L., De Menna, F., Vittuari, M., Hartikainen, H., Katajajuuri, J.M., Joensuu, K., Timonen, K., van der Sluis, A., Bos-Brouwers, H., Moates, M., Waldron, K., Mhlanga, M., Bucatariu, C., Lee, W., James, K., Easteal, S., 2015. *Criteria for and baseline assessment of environmental and socio-economic impacts of food waste*. FUSIONS project.

Somsen, D., 2004. *Production yield analysis in food processing: Applications in the french-fries and the poultry industries*. Journal of American Studies 22, 108–109.

St-Pierre, N.R., Cobanov, B., Schnitkey, G., 2003. *Economic losses from heat stress by US livestock industries*. Journal of Dairy Science 86, E52–E77.

Stefanelli, J., Marsden, P., 2012. *Models of enforcement in Europe for relations in the food supply chain*. British Institute of International and Comparative Law. www.anilact.pt/documentos/hlf001.pdf.

Stenmarck, A., Jensen, C., Quested, T., Moates, G., 2016. *Estimates of European food waste levels*. FUSIONS project. March 31. www.eu-fusions.org/phocadownload/Publications/Estimates%20of%20European%20food%20waste%20levels.pdf.

Tostivint, C., Östergren, K., Quested, T., Soethoudt, H., Stenmarck, A., Svanes, E., O'Connor, C., 2016. *Food waste quantification manual to monitor food waste amounts and progression*. FUSIONS project.

UN – United Nations, 2015. *Transforming our world: The 2030 agenda for sustainable development*. United Nations, New York.

USDA, 2018a. *Crop acreage data*. www.fsa.usda.gov/news-room/efoia/electronic-reading-room/frequently-requested-information/crop-acreage-data/index.

USDA, 2018b. *Fruit and tree nut yearbook tables*. Economic Research Service. www.ers.usda.gov/data-products/fruit-and-tree-nut-data/fruit-and-tree-nut-yearbook-tables/.

Vittuari, M., Politano, A., Gaiani, S., Canali, M., Azzurro, P., Elander, M., Aramyan, L., Gheoldus, M., Easteal, S., 2015. *Review of EU legislation and policies with implications on food waste*. FUSIONS project.

Ward, S., 2018. *Reducing food loss on the farm: A holistic approach. Starting paper for the focus group*. EIP-AGRI Focus Group. European Commission, Brussels.

Whitehead, P., Palmer, M., Mena, C., Williams, A., Walsh, C., 2011. *Resource maps for fresh meat across retail and wholesale supply chains*. WRAP, Banbury.

Willersinn, C., Mack, G., Mouron, P., Keiser, A., Siegrist, M., 2015. *Quantity and quality of food losses along the Swiss potato supply chain: Stepwise investigation and the influence of quality standards on losses*. Waste Management. 46, 120–132.

WRAP – Waste and Resources Action Programme, 2009. *Household food and drink waste in the UK*. www.wrap.org.uk/content/report-household-food-and-drink-waste-uk.

WRAP – Waste and Resources Action Programme, 2012. *Sector guidance note: Preventing waste in the fruit and vegetable supply chain sector*. WRAP, Banbury.

25

FISH AS FOOD

Policies affecting food sovereignty for rural Indigenous communities in North America

David Fazzino, Philip Loring, and Glenna Gannon

Introduction

Today, rural fisherfolk confront a number of challenges in making a sustainable and fulfilling living from aquatic environments, including: climatic shifts which lead to a series of changes in the presence and behavior of marine resources, market fluctuation in the price of supplies and materials necessary to carry out variously scaled fishing operations, market fluctuation in the prices they receive for their products, and what are increasingly viewed as arbitrary and onerous rules which increasingly restrict the tools and timing of operations. It is the last of these that is the primary concern in this chapter.

This chapter focuses on the impacts of the state and its various policies on multi-generation fisherfolk. It begins with a consideration of key anthropological concepts from the anthropological literature that are necessary to any cross-cultural comparison or engagement (cultural relativism and ethnocentrism) and provides background information on the interrelated historical roots and state justification for management of local populations. These conceptual and historical understandings are then applied to the contemporary management of rural, small-scale fisheries and hence peoples/communities in Canada and the United States of America (US). The chapter concludes with potential ramifications of this comparative analysis for contemporary and future fisheries management in both countries given the current political and legislative climate in each.

Cultural relativism and ethnocentrism: a primer

Cultural relativism and ethnocentrism are basic lessons from the discipline of anthropology (Bohannan, 1966; Miner, 1956); cultural relativism describes the notion that, when viewed from the outside, cultural practices that are in fact rational may seem strange and irrational. Cultural relativism is an analytical lens, one that acknowledges that what counts as appropriate, true, and just knowledge and behavior will vary from cultural setting to cultural setting. A related concept, ethnocentrism, describes a tendency by people to focus on, emphasize, or prefer their own culture's way of doing things, often to the point where other ways of being and knowing are considered wrong, backwards, and strange. Together, these ideas underscore the importance of considering cultural differences in values, goals, and broadly, ideology, from the onset of any sort of planning or management project, especially when the people in power (i.e. the governing) are from a different cultural background than those not in power (i.e. the governed).

In the context of the contemporary globalized world of intensified interactions across borders, fisheries are inherently cross-cultural, hence lessons learned and shared on cultural relativism and ethnocentrism by such anthropologists as Miner (1956), Bohannan (1966), and Lee (1969) are invaluable guideposts. First, it is important to recognize that the fundamental values of respect, integrity, and generally being a fully functional member of society vary in different cultural settings (Lee, 1969). Second, and along similar lines, stories and concepts that appeal to logic or aesthetics for one group of people may not be universal or directly translatable to other places or cultures (Bohannan, 1966). Finally, and building on these premises, there is a danger of proceeding from an assumed position of enlightenment, wherein what would otherwise be completely rational actions in each cultural context are viewed as irrational, stupid, and self-degrading to core aspects of humanity (Miner, 1956).

In general, long-term and sustainable solutions must bear in mind these considerations and lessons from anthropology in cultural relativism and ethnocentrism. To do otherwise would, at the minimum, create misunderstandings in cross-cultural interactions and at worst perpetuate injustices through the outcomes of management. In the context of fisheries management, the imposition of policies based on non-local agendas is likely to be resisted through a variety of means, potentially leading to a more deleterious situation than had the policy never been implemented.

In the next sections, encounters between cultures are historicized, discussing the definition of and appropriation of resources, and touch back to these core theoretical concepts as they emerge in practice. The goal is to emphasize how a more robust consideration of culture ultimately enhances the effectiveness of any management or development project implementation (Kottak, 1990).

Fisheries management in a historical context

Prior to the concepts of cultural relativism being developed in the discipline of anthropology, Western powers extended their reach across the globe encountering what they viewed as limitless resources to feed, figuratively and literally, their booming populations. This led to a potential moral and ethical quandary: how to deal with those who already occupied these regions? The solutions were various, but nearly all revolved around ethnocentric assumptions and maintaining a rigid hierarchy of humanity, wherein the needs of some Europeans were greater than the needs of others. Biological differences along the lines of race played a part, in many instances instituting various iterations of the great chain of being to suggest humanity did not comprise a single species with equal capacities but a tiered and hierarchical alignment that necessitated domination of some by others. Also playing a part in justifying the control of some people by others was the attribution of practices and characteristics to specific populations. Among the most insidious of these was the attribution of cannibalistic practices to specific peoples to justify what became a moral imperative in order to control the "heathens" (Moore, 1972, p. 9).

Thus, in defining the Indigenous peoples as something less than human, the need to struggle with the moral conflict of "people-as-people" was eliminated and it became possible to view "people-as-things" or property (Kopytoff, 1982, p. 220). The underlying and ethnocentric assumptions of Columbus and his contemporaries aside, what the above clearly reveals is an earlier view of management of populations to serve supposedly greater ends. This was the first in a series of what have become known as orientalist discourses that maintain a racialized and hierarchical order of humanity (Said, 1979), despite evidence from biological anthropology and archaeology of humanity's shared past. Today, the impacts of this order are evident in a variety of settings, including natural resource management, where a popular mantra is that managing resources is truly a matter of managing people. An unfortunate outcome that this essay seeks to unpack is that certain populations are often marginalized to promote the supposed superiority of some environmental goals, actions, and knowledges.

The globalization of fisheries management

Today, the notion that people need to be "managed" in order to avoid ecological catastrophe is front and center in discussions of nearly any natural resource system, with fisheries being an exemplar. Consider Hardin's (1968) tragedy of the commons, which underpins contemporary fisheries management approaches. The tragedy of the commons suggests that left to their own devices, humans will work to maximize their own self-interests to the harm of common-pool resources. The well-known example from he draws involves cattle in a common grazing area or paddock. The underlying assumption in this model is that individuals will seek to increase their own advantage by putting greater and greater numbers of animals in the common area. Further, these individuals will not be held in check by any social mechanism to curb their selfishness, rather autonomous, individual actors are merely acting unchecked as maximizing their own immediate utility as rational actors, purportedly giving no consideration to future generations. Hence, in Hardin's framework, individuals and the communities within which they live cannot be trusted to manage their resources in the long term. This necessitates outside intervention in the form of "effective" management strategies which are justified and necessary incursions designed specifically to control local resource utilization to avoid this tragedy that, assumedly, would otherwise automatically follow. What this approach does is minimize long-term management strategies, including traditional ecological knowledge, to achieve sustainable utilization of environmental resources through a series of checks and balances wherein individual self-interest is not only curbed but also deemed inappropriate behavior, socially sanctioned with everything from gossiping about to exiling the offending individual. Hence, what it means to be a rational actor varies depending on the particular cultural context and this will, necessarily, impact individual behavior in their everyday lives, including participation in subsistence activities.

Today, Hardin's thesis, which he presented as a basic tenet of human nature, has been widely critiqued by such scholars as Elinor Ostrom, John Acheson, and Bonnie McCay, whose extensive comparative works illustrated that many traditional societies successfully govern common-pool resources without outside intervention, through locally adapted and culturally appropriate rules and norms. To the outsider, these can seem downright irrational; four poignant examples of when outsiders, because of ethnocentric assumptions, misunderstand the logic of local social and cultural systems are detailed by Marvin Harris, *Cows, Pigs, Wars, and Witches* (Harris, 1974). Harris, and others such as Roy Rappaport (1968), show that only when one considers local values, norms regarding sharing and power, and understandings of time and nature, can one read through what seem like cryptic cultural differences to understand the logic at play.

Instead, however, in the history of state-based natural resource management the opposite has been true: ethnocentric assumptions have dominated, that the colonist state's way of doing things is the only true, correct, or rational way of thinking, feeling, and being in the world. Indeed, James Scott (1998) has argued that this is an assumption that is fundamentally necessary for the state to govern at all. He argues that state governance depends on some degree of uniformity or standardization: concepts in policy and regulation that render complex societal and environmental systems more "legible". Weights and measures and environmental quality standards are just two examples of ways the government makes society more legible in order to implement laws that are both enforceable and just (justice here being another state-defined concept that assumes what is "just" is a situation where people have due but not necessarily equal protection under the laws). However, Scott also argues that there are invariably situations where these concepts create problems because of the social and cultural complexity that they mask; as explained by Loring in the context of fisheries (2016):

> In natural resource management, multiple concepts are used to make natural systems and human–environment interactions more legible. Many of these are drawn from science: concepts such as the ecosystem, population and meta-population, and maximum sustainable yield (MSY). In fisheries, MSY is one of the most widely used, but … MSY and the various other quantitative management concepts that accompany it can conceal the significant complexity that is inherent to marine ecosystems; as such, if management regimes focus too narrowly on MSY or some similar single-species benchmark, other fishing-related impacts that threaten the future of a fish population can be overlooked.

To their point, James Acheson and James Wilson (1996) actually reviewed cases of traditionally managed fisheries as well as those where quantitative state-based systems for management were in place, and found that the former generally outperform the latter despite not being concerned with the actual number of fish being taken!

So, while making some level of assumptions regarding legibility or rationality makes sense from the perspective of developing workable policies and management structures, it would be wrong to assume that what works in specific cultural contexts and in subcultures, the everyday experiences that permeate people's lives, are in fact universal, a-cultural, and will work anywhere. Cultural differences are not inherently an impediment or anathema to the effective management of natural resources, or even the conceptualization of human–environment interactions in the first place but can be the very basis of effective natural resources management. Humans have very successfully occupied ecological niches prior to the creation or imposition of written systems and increasing levels of social hierarchy. At the same time, civilizations have risen and fallen due to a variety of factors including unchecked growth and exploitation of both natural and social resources.

Indigenous fisheries policy in the US and Canada and its impacts on food sovereignty

Indigenous fishers in both the US and Canada face a unique and complicated set of policies and practices that influence their ability to make a living with fisheries and other aquatic resources. A comparison of the two contexts is useful for illustrating the issues discussed above – where unchecked (or unacknowledged) ethnocentrism and programs for creating legibility in complex socio-natural systems, diminish local people's ability to achieve food sovereignty. Food sovereignty describes the right of peoples to define their own policies and strategies for the sustainable production, distribution, and consumption of food, in ways informed by their own cultures and their own systems of managing natural resources and rural areas (Schiavoni, 2016).

Alaska, United States

In Alaska, it is important to understand the history of policy-making and state–Indigenous relationships at both the federal (US) and state (Alaska) levels. Federally, early state-driven changes to traditional-use Indigenous fisheries came about with the 1784–1894 land acquisitions known as the US Land Cessions, in which tribes were payed token amounts and promises were made for aid by the US federal government in exchange for large amounts of tribal territory. These deals, called treaties, were made with the federal government's guarantee that fishing rights in traditional territories would be protected, but this guarantee quickly eroded with the proliferation of commercial and sport fisheries developed by settlers (Cohen, 1989). States, likewise, often further diminished Indigenous fishing rights and access in favor of developing the state's fishing economy, whether directly, by disenfranchising Indigenous users of their fishing rights through the introduction of limited-entry permit systems, or indirectly through the resulting degradation of fish stocks and habitat (Cohen, 1989). For US fisheries, landmark court cases such as the 1974 *US v. Washington* Supreme Court case had the potential to be critical turning points in re-affirming (restoring) Indigenous fishing rights and participation in fisheries management. *US v. Washington* created mechanisms by which Indigenous entities (tribes) could have representation and participation in fisheries management, such as in the Pacific Fisheries Management Council, and tribal participation in US–Canadian treaty negotiations (Cohen, 1989). Similarly, the 1976 Magnuson-Stevens Act contains provisions to manage fisheries for the benefit of fishing communities.

Despite these provisions, Indigenous fishers continue to be disenfranchised from their traditional fisheries, largely as a result of the widespread adoption of limited-entry permit and other exclusionary approaches to managing fisheries (Knapp, 2011; Loring, 2013). Unlike Indigenous land tenure systems, Alaska has long considered fisheries to be "common-pool resources" that are open and belong to all. As such, the assumptions of the tragedy of the commons have long informed and justified Alaska's intervention and exclusionary practices. Indeed, limiting access to fisheries through tradable or salable permits or quotas is often called "rationalization" by managers and fisheries scientists, directly implying that such systems without state control are *irrational*, regardless of the sophistication or elegance of any traditional systems of management that exist. Using a market to manage rights in this way has uniformly resulted in the consolidation of fishing rights among a few individuals, invariably moving these rights out of the hands of Indigenous peoples and into the hands of business owners with the capital to invest, and even take losses, in order to consolidate holdings (Carothers, 2010; Knapp, 2011; Loring, 2013). In some cases, Indigenous people would sell their permits or quotas during times of economic hardship, but then no longer be able to buy back into the fishery because permit prices would continue to rise, or because large shareholders simply would not be willing to sell.

No formal treaties exist between the US federal government and Alaska Natives, and Alaska Natives were not considered US citizens until 1929 (after which they were finally allowed to claim land under the Homestead Act). The Indian Reorganization Act (IRA) was passed in 1934, and amended two years later, to protect Alaska Native use of land and subsistence activities, and enabled a process by which tribes could become federally recognized (Gerlach et al., 2011; Norris, 2002). However, Alaska attained statehood in 1959, and later that same year, the newly formed State of Alaska took over the management of fish and wildlife under the jurisdiction of the Alaska Department of Fish and Game and later the Alaska Board of Fisheries (Ebbin, 2004). The new state constitution declared that, "wherever occurring in their natural state, fish wildlife, and waters are reserved to the people for their common use" (Gerlach et al., 2011), meaning equal access rights to all user groups, setting the stage for ongoing conflict between various user groups, for the state's fisheries; this contention is especially fierce between commercial, subsistence, and sport users (Loring et al., 2014). The 1971 Alaska Native Claims Settlement Act (ANCSA) created 13 regional tribal corporations, and payed out US $962.5 million and 375 million acres of land in exchange for the extinguishment of aboriginal title (Thompson,

1993; Chaffee, 2008). Due to the failure of ANCSA to address subsistence rights issues, the US Congress passed the Alaska National Interest Lands Conservation Act (ANILCA) in 1980. ANILCA was passed with the intent to protect Alaska Native hunting and fishing rights and established a "subsistence priority" for activities deemed "customary and traditional", which generally referred, at the time, to practices that existed prior to 1971 (Norris, 2002). However, as noted previously, the State of Alaska's constitution declares that Alaska's natural resources belong equally to all citizens, and in 1989 the Alaska Supreme Court ruled that any rural priority for subsistence for Alaska Natives on state lands was a violation of the Alaska constitution (*McDowell v. State*, 785 P.2d 1, 1989). Nevertheless, the notion of customary and traditional practices persists as a contemporary example of an orientalist discourse, and one that created a "frozen rights" doctrine that continues to limit the adaptability of Alaska Natives (Loring and Gerlach, 2010).

Today, Alaska Natives have very little ability to influence decisions made regarding fisheries. While subsistence fisheries maintain a priority over other sectors (federally, because of ANILCA, and at the state level because of the Alaska state constitution, though the latter applies to all state residents), there are only narrow options for Alaska Natives to contribute to decisions regarding fisheries policy and management. For state-managed fisheries, Alaska Natives must contend with the Board of Fish (BoF), a board of gubernatorial appointees comprising representatives for all fishing sectors: commercial, sport, and subsistence. The BoF is a highly politicized entity and often reflects the political machinations of the day and political leanings of the governor. The BoF has been notoriously unable to govern in a way that does not exacerbate conflict among the sectors.

While the composition of the BoF is appreciable in terms of allowing for an equitable conversation of trade-offs among fishing sectors, the procedural mechanisms in place are, in themselves, deeply problematic. In the everyday processes of the BoF, fisheries managers may view these mechanisms as efficient means to handle the business at hand; however, they often invalidate proper protocols for showing respect and maintaining relationships among Alaska Natives in a variety of ways. BoF's process is highly bureaucratized, conforming to colonialist norms regarding how decisions ought to be deliberated and made. This leaves little space for local practices for sharing, deliberating, and achieving consensus. In brief, the BoF addresses new policy needs only for specific regions of Alaska on a three-year rotating schedule. They release calls for proposals a few months prior to a planned meeting, and these proposals must conform to a specific proposal form that must be submitted online or in person. At the meetings, public testimony on proposals is limited to a few minutes per person. This is hardly enough time for an Alaska Native person to properly introduce themselves and their lineage, which is a customary way of establishing standing and validity, let alone sufficient for relating a traditional story. Storytelling can be essential in communicating a holistic sense of the problem and the solution being discussed. Instead of attempting to understand such testimony many non-Native participants in the process often sigh, act uncomfortable, and treat such sharing as a waste of time. Likewise, BoF decisions are made by simple majority rather than consensus. While this may be the norm in the dominant US bureaucratic culture, this sharply contrasts with the consensus-based decision-making ethic long-held by many Indigenous cultures as a way to maintain positive relationships and a sense of shared stake among bands (Berkes *et al.*, 1991). In consensus-based decision-making, reaching consensus on a decision is at least as important as the decision itself, because the relationship is what is emphasized. In majority-based decision-making, it is the decision that is deemed more important than the relationship.

A final challenge to Indigenous participation and, indeed, sovereignty within the realm of fisheries in Alaska relates to Scott's argument about legibility. At both state and federal levels, fisheries are managed through strict categories – commercial, sport, and subsistence or personal use. That these are distinct spheres is essential to the logic of state-based management. Indigenous rights are (somewhat) protected and maintained for subsistence uses, but not for commercial; the ethnocentric assumption being that Indigenous people have no tradition of commerce and therefore no more or less right than anyone else to use these resources for that purpose. Even small-scale sale of a few "subsistence-caught" fish among friends or neighbors is prohibited in Alaska, with the concern being that this would provide an opening for people to take advantage of their subsistence access and overharvest the resource for profit. The entire system is thus rife with ethnocentrism – subsistence is construed as something historical and primitive, whereas fishing for commerce is modern and civilized (something that primitive people could not possibly have practiced). Likewise, Hardin's tragedy of the commons is also present in this assumption that if commerce is present, people will necessarily overharvest unless the state keeps them from doing so.

British Columbia, Canada

Fisheries in British Columbia (hereafter BC), are similarly shaped by several important and distinct historical events (Turner et al., 2013). While some similarities exist, there are also significant differences in how user groups derive their rights, access to, and participation in fisheries in BC.

Numerous treaties were established across Canada among First Nations and the federal government between the eighteenth and early twentieth centuries. These treaties generally contain specific protection of harvesting rights. For example, Treaty 8 gives First Nations in northeastern BC the "liberty to hunt over unoccupied lands". The so-called "Douglas Treaties" with First Nations on southern Vancouver Island give the right to fish "as formerly", though Douglas Treaties are not uniformly observed by First Nations because signatures were often obtained without full disclosure of the treaty text, and for meager payments. A small number of so-called "modern treaties" also exist for BC's First Nations. For example, the Nisga'a, Tsawwassen, and Maa-nulth First Nations have negotiated Final Agreements that set out explicit harvesting rights. However, 45 First Nations have no settled treaty with the government, so fishing rights remain unclear or inferred through the broader constitutional and case law protections noted above.

Additional protections of aboriginal rights to fisheries and other natural resources are often based on case law. Among the most noteworthy piece of case law is the Sparrow decision (R. v. Sparrow, 1990 S.C.R.1 1075, 1990), which affirmed fishing as an aboriginal right by ruling that the right is protected under section 35 of Canada's constitution, and cannot be imposed upon without valid justification (Allain and Fréchette, 1993). Three recent rulings also deal with commercial fishing rights (R. v. Van der Peet, R. v. Smokehouse, and R. v. Gladstone). These rulings further define how aboriginal rights will be determined. As with Alaska, to assert a right as an aboriginal one that is deserving of legal protection, one must prove that these practices, traditions, and customs existed in North America historically. In Canada, that means that they existed *prior* to contact with Europeans. Likewise, to be recognized as an aboriginal right, the practice must be demonstrably integral to the distinctive culture of aboriginal peoples. However, R. v. Sparrow ruled that aboriginal rights that existed prior to the 1982 signing of Canada's Constitution Act cannot be extinguished, at least not without specific deliberation regarding the impacts of any proposed limitations. Interpretation of these criteria by the courts has been flexible, in order to avoid creating the "frozen rights" doctrine noted above that locks aboriginal people into historical lifeways. Whether or not these rulings achieve this outcome, however, is debated (Allain, 1996).

As noted above, Sparrow creates a venue for the state to impose limits on aboriginal fishing rights. Specifically, a test of three vague provisions must be made:

- Is the limitation reasonable?
- Does the regulation impose undue hardship?
- Does the regulation deny the holders of the right their preferred means of exercising that right?

In interpreting these questions, *Sparrow* makes the following recommendations regarding important considerations (though the court refused to set out a more specific set of guidelines):

- an intent to minimize the infringement of aboriginal rights;
- consultation regarding the specifics of regulations resulting in the loss of rights;
- fair compensation for the loss.

Later, *R. v. Van der Peet* added the following considerations to the accepted calculus for infringing on an aboriginal right:

- the perspective of aboriginal peoples on the change;
- justification for the change (i.e. cost–benefit comparison);
- the central significance of the practice to aboriginal peoples;
- the relationship of aboriginal peoples to the land;
- the distinctiveness of aboriginal culture.

Ultimately, these create a robust protection for aboriginal rights to fisheries and other wild resources, but they do create a noteworthy burden not just for the outsider seeking a policy change that would impact rights, but also for the aboriginal people to prove the history and importance of certain practices. This is especially highlighted in the case of commercial fishing. Generally, the government of Canada has not observed commercial fishing as an existing and integral part of aboriginal culture. In *R. v. Gladstone*, (C.N.L.R.4 65, 1996), the Heiltsuk people sued the crown for a provision banning the commercial sale of herring roe on kelp, and effectively demonstrated that herring spawn trade did exist prior to European contact and that it was not an incidental activity. However, the Supreme Court also made it clear that this was an exceptional case and should not be interpreted as creating precedent that eases the level of proof expected of future claimants. That is, unless otherwise determined, commercial activities are considered by the courts to be distinctly non-Indigenous.

Management of fisheries resources is another activity that Canada considers to be largely non-Indigenous. According to the Indian Act, bands may pass bylaws on reservation territories for the purpose of conserving or managing fisheries resources. However, two rulings (*R. v. Lewis* and *R. v. Nikal*) note that this authority does not extend beyond the boundaries of the reservation, regardless of the ecosystem boundaries. Hence while bands are allowed to regulate harvest activities on reservation, they do not have the right to manage the resource itself, given that rivers generally run through multiple jurisdictions.

The recent conflict among the Canadian government and the Nuu-Chah-Nuth and Haida First Nations over commercial herring fisheries brings nuances of protections and their caveats into greater relief (Jones *et al.*, 2016). In 2014 and 2015, these Nations sought injunctions against commercial fisheries openings, arguing: (1) openings would create irreparable resource harm, and (2) that they had not been sufficiently consulted in the fisheries opening decisions. These fisheries had seen stark decline over the previous decades, causing closures in the 1990s but a brief reopening in the early 2000s. All fisheries, which include large-scale commercial fisheries as well as the traditional commercial spawn-on-kelp fisheries noted above, were closed as of 2005. In 2014, Canada reopened all fisheries, even though the stocks had not recovered, and despite the continued assertion by First Nations that they should remain closed. Their argument for doing so was that the lack of improvement since 2005 indicated that fishing was not the cause of the problem. Some injunctions were successful in stopping commercial fishing, but another regional First Nation, the Heiltsuk, had to resort to creating blockades with their own vessels to stop the commercial fleets from fishing. In 2015, despite widespread opposition, Canada again opened all fisheries, and again the openings were met with petitions for injunction. The Haida successfully argued that fishing would constitute irreparable harm, illustrated by the fact that fishery projections for 2015 were lower than 2014. They also argued lack of sufficient consultation. On this latter point, the court also ruled in their favor, essentially affirming their *de jure* right to management (a right to manage that derives from their right to the resource), but only because they have not, as yet, negotiated a treaty with the Canadian government ceding those rights.

Recognition by Canadian courts of *de jure* management rights has been rare (Jones *et al.*, 2016), and as noted above the Indian Act only provides First Nations with limited ability to pass bylaws within reservation territory. The Haida case has important implications for the future of commercial fisheries policy in British Columbia; several First Nations have unsettled title, and a trend of increasing fisheries privatization, as in Alaska, is evident. With *de jure* rights intact, these First Nations have additional ability to oppose such initiatives.

Finally, co-management, which describes power sharing in environmental governance among the state and local communities, is a newer paradigm in environmental policy-making that has gained prominence in Canada, specifically because of successes in Haida Gwaii (Jones *et al.*, 2016; Pinkerton, 2011). Despite the issue of unsettled title, Haida Gwaii and Canada have a co-management arrangement for Gwaii Haanas, a National Park Reserve, National Marine Conservation Area, and Haida Heritage Site. Gwaii Haanas includes most of the bottom third of islands in the Haida Gwaii archipelago. While not a true power-sharing agreement in the strictest terms, the Gwaii Haanas Agreement (established in 1993) holds both parties to come to decisions only through true consensus. The arrangement allows each party to claim decision-making authority without conceding any power to the other. Gwaii Haanas is widely considered to be a rare co-management success, and indeed the agreement provided some of the precedent for the Haida to assert their *de jure* rights to be involved in decision-making in other areas, such as commercial fisheries in waters in or near Haida Gwaii.

In its ideal, theorized form, co-management has the potential to be a venue to address the ethnocentrism and the pitfalls of centralized governance described by Scott (1998). It is premised on the notion of devolution – the transfer of power from higher to lower levels of organization, and that power involves not just power to make decisions but power to decide how, and with what kinds of information, decisions will be made. This requires that the state acknowledge the legitimacy of other ways of knowing and living before a conversation about true co-management, where other people's categories and systems for making the world legible, even if they seem "primitive" or "irrational" to the Western gaze. In the interim, absent systematic changes, fisheries managers can continue to work within the day-to-day bureaucracy of fisheries management to address procedural issues surrounding consultation, such as protocols of respect, acknowledgment, and relationship-building, which are cross-culturally appropriate for various stakeholders.

Conclusions

This chapter considers a variety of case studies from the United States and Canada to compare and contrast government interactions with Indigenous peoples. While this chapter focuses on the issues of subsistence and fisheries in particular the larger point is that contemporary policies should be considered in the larger colonial legacies of both countries. Hence, when developing policy formulations that directly impact subsistence current and future decision-makers need to give greater weight to the needs of Indigenous populations. Indeed, the goal with this chapter is to unpack some of the cultural values attending to fisheries utilization by diverse actors. The first part of this is to be cognizant of the cultural values present in institutions which motivate and direct action in the context of the organizations. What must be considered is how a meal at a restaurant or cafeteria is fundamentally different than a meal that one has worked to directly attain. Food is not merely a product to fuel bodies and minds, enabling us to craft elaborate frameworks, but it is inherently cultural. It has a location, it has an address, and there are people living their lives out with one another in these various locations. Stakeholder analysis and curt consultation practices do not give proper weight to these considerations, replicating earlier ethnocentric encounters and maintaining the colonial legacies upon which these two countries were forged. In the contemporary, accelerating, and globalized world scientists would do well to view narratives of progress and development with skepticism or otherwise risk replicating some of the same injustices which keep people from living as they properly should; becoming a full human in a specific cultural context.

Although this chapter has focused on rural Indigenous case studies from the US and Canada, with focus on Alaska and BC respectively, the lessons are transferable to those fisherfolk communities with longstanding utilization of resources and should be considered by fisheries managers. Ultimately, this chapter demonstrated the value of greater dialogue and participation for Indigenous peoples which avoid the pitfalls of ethnocentrism. Although not embedded in a place from time immemorial, local communities have extensive knowledge of resources and cultural protocols which should be duly considered in resource management decisions that ultimately manage the lives of individuals and communities.

Three key messages

- Contemporary policies should be considered in the larger colonial legacies of both countries.
- Cultural values are present in institutions. These motivate and direct action.
- Managing resources is about managing people.

Three future research needs and opportunities

- To what extent are orientalist discourses still present in natural resource management regimes?
- In what ways can more progress be made through co-management to address the ethnocentric underpinnings of the state's approach to management?
- Does co-management truly bring communities closer to food sovereignty?

References

Acheson, J.M., Wilson, J.A., 1996. *Order out of chaos: The case for parametric fisheries management.* American Anthropologist, New Series 98, 579–594.

Allain, J.M., 1996. *Aboriginal fishing rights: Supreme Court decisions* (BP428e). Canadian Library of Parliament. Parliament Information Research Services. https://lop.parl.ca/content/lop/researchpublications/bp428-e.htm (accessed 9.7.17).

Allain, J.M., Fréchette, J.-D., 1993. *The Aboriginal fisheries and the Sparrow decision*. Library of Parliament, Research Branch, Ottawa, Ont.

Berkes, F., George, P.J., Preston, R.J., 1991. *Co-management: The evolution of the theory and practice of joint administration of living resources*. Program for Technology Assessment in Subarctic Ontario, McMaster University, Hamilton, Ont.

Bohannan, L., 1966. *Shakespeare in the Bush*. Natural History Magazine, August–September, 1–5.

Carothers, C., 2010. *Tragedy of commodification: Displacements in Alutiiq fishing communities in the Gulf of Alaska*. Mast 9, 95–120.

Chaffee, E.C., 2008, *Business organizations and tribal self-determination: A critical reexamination of the Alaska Native Claims Settlement Act*. Alaska Law Review 25, 107–155.

Cohen, F., 1989. *Treaty Indian tribes and Washington state: The evolution of tribal involvement in fisheries management in the US Pacific Northwest*, in: Pinkerton, E. (Ed.), *Co-operative management of local fisheries: New directions for improved management and community development*. UBC Press, Vancouver, BC, pp. 37–48.

Ebbin, S.A., 2004. *The anatomy of conflict and the politics of identity in two cooperative salmon management regimes*. Policy Sciences 37, 71–87. https://doi.org/10.1023/B:OLIC.0000035464.24471.89.

Gerlach, S.C., Loring, P.A., Turner, A.M., Atkinson, D.E., 2011. *Food systems, climate change, and community needs*, in: Lovecraft, A.L., Eicken, H. (Eds.), *North by 2020*. University of Alaska Press, Fairbanks, AK, pp. 111–134.

Hardin, G., 1968. *The tragedy of the commons*. Science 162, 1243–1248.

Harris, M., 1974. *Cows, pigs, wars, and witches: The riddles of culture*. Random House, New York.

Jones, R., Rigg, C., Pinkerton, E., 2016. *Strategies for assertion of conservation and local management rights: A Haida Gwaii herring story*. Marine Policy. https://doi.org/10.1016/j.marpol.2016.09.031.

Knapp, G., 2011. *Local permit ownership in Alaska salmon fisheries*. Marine Policy 35, 658–666. https://doi.org/10.1016/j.marpol.2011.02.006.

Kopytoff, I., 1982. *Slavery*. Annual Review of Anthropology 11, 207–230.

Kottak, C.P., 1990. *Culture and "economic development"*. American Anthropologist 92, 723–732.

Lee, R.B., 1969. *Eating Christmas in the Kalahari*. Natural History 78(10), 60–63.

Loring, P.A., 2013. *Alternative perspectives on the sustainability of Alaska's commercial fisheries*. Conservation Biology 27, 55–63. https://doi.org/10.1111/j.1523-1739.2012.01938.x.

Loring, P.A., 2016. *The political ecology of gear bans in two fisheries: Florida's net ban and Alaska's salmon wars*. Fish and Fisheries. https://doi.org/10.1111/faf.12169.

Loring, P.A., Gerlach, S.C., 2010. *Outpost gardening in interior Alaska: Food system innovation and the Alaska Native gardens of the 1930s through the 1970s*. Ethnohistory 57, 183–199.

Loring, P.A., Harrison, H.L., Gerlach, S.C., 2014. *Local perceptions of the sustainability of Alaska's highly contested Cook Inlet salmon fisheries*. Society and Natural Resources 27, 185–199. https://doi.org/10.1080/08941920.2013.819955.

Miner, H., 1956. *Body ritual among the Nacirema*. American Anthropologist 58, 503–507.

Moore, R., 1972. *Caribs, cannibals and human relations*. Pathway Publishers, Aylmer, Ont.

Norris, F., 2002. *Alaska subsistence*. National Park Service, Anchorage, AK.

Pinkerton, E., 2011. *Co-operative management of local fisheries: New directions for improved management and community development*. UBC Press, Vancouver, BC.

Rappaport, R.A., 1968. *Pigs for the ancestors: Ritual in the ecology of a New Guinea people*. Yale University, New Haven, CT.

Said, E., 1979. *Orientalism*. Vintage, New York.

Schiavoni, C.M., 2016. *The contested terrain of food sovereignty construction: Toward a historical, relational and interactive approach*. Journal of Peasant Studies. https://doi.org/10.1080/03066150.2016.1234455.

Scott, J.C., 1998. *Seeing like a state: How certain schemes to improve the human condition have failed*. Yale University Press, New Haven, CT.

Thompson, P., 1993. *Recognizing sovereignty in Alaska native villages after the passage of ANSCA*. Washington Law Review 68(2), 373, 390–394.

Turner, N.J., Berkes, F., Stephenson, J., Dick, J., 2013. *Blundering intruders: Extraneous impacts on two Indigenous food systems*. Human Ecology 41, 563–574. https://doi.org/10.1007/s10745-013-9591-y.

26

PUBLIC POLICIES AFFECTING COMMUNITY FOREST MANAGEMENT

Víctor Ávila Akerberg, Luis Angel López Mathamba,
Tanja González Martínez, Sergio Franco-Maass, and
Gabino Nava Bernal

Forests are valuable resources from an economic, political, social, and environmental standpoint. They play an important role in rural development and climate change mitigation. Forests provide employment, energy, food, and other goods and services for the estimated 1.5 billion forest-dependent people around the world (FAO, 2014). Forests are stabilizing elements in soil and water regimes and play an important role in the global carbon balance. Commercially, they are a source of important timber and non-timber products for domestic or international consumption, but they are also essential for communities as a source of a range of subsistence products used by many rural Indigenous and non-Indigenous peoples (Segura, 2000).

This paper provides a historic analysis of the different public policies that affect and have affected the way communities manage their forests in rural areas of Mexico. In developed democracies, public policy by definition considers the participation of different actors in society involved in a given problem; meanwhile, in less advanced democracies, participation of broader societal groups is rather limited, with government tending to rely on expert groups for planning and definition phases in the development of problem-solving mechanisms (Arellano Gault and Blanco, 2013).

Mexican *ejido* and *comunidad,* central elements of community forest management

Mexican *ejidos* and *comunidades* are agrarian communities that represent the most extensive land use tenure system in Mexico, which encompasses more than half of the national territory including the largest forested lands. These land tenure types are exclusive to Mexico and are the result of agrarian reform that started with the Mexican Revolution and ended with the constitutional reforms of 1992 (Orozco-Garibay, 2010). There are 31,873 *ejidos* and *comunidades* in Mexico, distributed all around the country, whose owners are called *ejidatarios* and *comuneros*, respectively. A bit less than half of these (15,584) are settled in areas with silvicultural potential covering an area of 62.5 million hectares; however, only 2207 of these are engaged in some form of forest management, even though most of them only cut trees down without any further transformation of the wood (Morett-Sánchez and Cosío-Ruiz, 2017). The Mexican common property system may be unique in the world due to its distinct characteristics as a massive, state-directed, and regulated system that has emerged and been consolidated since the third decade of the twentieth century (Bray and Merino-Pérez, 2002). As much as 80 percent of Mexican forests may belong to communities as a result of agrarian reforms that have led to these tenure systems (Bray et al., 2003), which is the second highest percentage in the world after Papua New Guinea (White and Martin, 2002).

Agrarian reform in Mexico

Towards the end of the nineteenth century, a big part of the Mexican territory was in the hands of large *latifundia*, or extensive tracts of privately owned agricultural land, which used a large quantity of peasant labor that was kept under poor working conditions. Thanks to the confiscation and alienation of wastelands, the *latifundia* became massive haciendas (large farms) dedicated mainly to exporting agricultural products (DGAH, 2003). Shortly after the Mexican Revolution, an agrarian land reform started which resulted in the fragmentation and distribution of a large part of the national territory. The redistribution of land to the landless began between 1912 and 1934, though there were no structural changes in land tenure during those years. This process was more like an act of popular justice towards some peasant communities than a real mechanism of economic development (Warman, 2003).

In 1925, the Reglementary Act on the Distribution of Ejido Lands and the Establishment of Ejido Lands Heritage (*Ley Reglamentaria Sobre Repartición de Tierras Ejidales y Constitución del Patrimonio Parcelario Ejidal*) was approved, in which rules for *ejidos* were established. It was a corporate form of land tenure, in which grazing and mountain lands were turned over to communal use (Cárcar-Irujo, 2013). From 1934 to 1940 – under President Lázaro Cárdenas' administration – the country experienced a real transformation of its rural structure, during which about 18 million hectares of land were distributed among the Mexican people. The aim of this policy was to eliminate the control of land ownership by the oligarchy while modernizing the countryside and sending labor forces to cities. Such reform involved usufructuary rights in the distribution and delivery of land (Cárcar-Irujo, 2013). An agrarian code was promulgated which stated – among other things – the authorization of government to define the operational rules for forest exploitation. According to Merino-Pérez (2001), at the end of President Lázaro Cárdenas' government, more than 6 million hectares of forest had been distributed, representing 18 percent of the country's forested area. Most of the wood production in these areas, however, was carried out under "rentierism" (rent-seeking) conditions.

By 1992, in response to the need to respond to new realities in the global economy and trade flows, a new agrarian law was enacted and the Program for the Certification of Agrarian Rights and Land Ownership Titles (PROCEDE) was initiated (Cárcar-Irujo, 2013). Due to a change to Article 27 of the constitution, land owners (i.e. *ejidatarios* and *comuneros*) were granted the right to manage and exploit their forests. Strictly speaking, this policy change initiated the privatization process of communally held lands since it allowed – and encouraged – individual land deeding. From that time on, *ejidos* were no longer a communal form of collective land ownership but were transformed into a rough picture of smallholdings or *minifundia* by this and subsequent policies (Trujillo-Bautista, 2009). However, the agrarian law establishes that forests must be of common use and cannot be divided into plots, failing which the new arrangement may be invalidated (Orozco-Garibay, 2010).

As indicated in the current text of the agrarian law, *ejidal* and communal goods belong to the group of people benefiting from the land supply. The *ejido* population centers have legal personality and their own heritage and are owners of the lands they have been endowed or that they have acquired by other kinds of title (DOF, 2017). The management of forest resources within the *ejido* occurs within a common property scheme of restricted access, with clearly recognized owners. Thus, since forests are considered a community asset under communal land tenure, private forest ownership is exercised on the basis of a collective property regime (Bray et al., 2007).

Within this scheme of autonomous community forest management, the state remains in control of forest resources. In other words, it is a form of massive property management structured by the state (Bray et al., 2007). It is the state that establishes the rules for resource management through government policies focused on forest conservation and sustainable use. While forest conservation has been encouraged through programs such as the Payment for Hydrological Environmental Services (Spanish acronym PSAH), the sustainable use of forests has been promoted through the integration of Community-based Forest Enterprises (CFEs). That is how some aspects of the autonomy of *ejidos* and *comunidades* have been strengthened, while maintaining state regulation in many aspects, mainly those related to extraction. Therefore, Mexico's Forest Act and state and federal institutions responsible for environmental management hold a strong, significant influence on forest management and conservation.

Since their inception, Public Forestry Policies (PFPs) were conceived as a key factor for environmental protection and conservation and represent a particular way of making decisions and executing government actions. They also deal with government decisions and actions that define: (a) specific public issues, and (b) particular mechanisms to be used to provide solutions for problems. In this sense, they are not exclusive to developed democracies but can occur in poorly advanced democracies, and even in authoritarian regimes where the government acts unilaterally without consulting broader actors in society or considering alternative solutions (Arellano Gault and Blanco, 2013). In response, federal and state governments have solved forest problems traditionally based on the creation of laws, plans, and programs, which has ultimately led to the implementation of PFPs. Therefore, PFPs have focused on the recognition, legalization, and titling of land tenure of local communities by the government; the possibility within legislation for the national government to grant permits for forest exploitation in favor of *ejidos* and *comunidades;* and the implementation of government programs with two visions: a conservationist vision through the program of Payment for Hydrological Environmental Services (PSAH) and the exploitation of forests through the CFEs program.

The National Forest Commission in Mexico (CONAFOR) first created the program for PSAH in 2003 to complement other policy responses to the crises of high deforestation and water scarcity (Muñoz-Piña et al., 2008). The program is financed by the Mexican Forest Fund via the collection of fees charged to water users to protect watersheds (CONANP, 2012). The initial goal of the program was to provide economic incentives to forested lands' owners (*ejidos, comunidades,* and private owners) to guarantee water supply from aquifers through the conservation of forest cover. Payments were first directed to the conservation of forests and jungles. Currently, the program has a wider range of objectives:

1   to reduce poverty indexes in forested areas through a subsidy that would also allow a sustainable use of natural resources;
2   to promote forest conservation and sustainable use of forest resources;
3   to contribute to the production of forest goods without harming the conservation of biodiversity while also improving the quality of life of their owners.

As a rural public policy, the program of PSAH seeks to revert deforestation through economic incentives that recognize individual efforts to maintain ecosystem services, therefore enhancing environmental benefits for communities.

Forested rural lands in the state of Mexico

The state of Mexico, located at Mexico's geographic center, is one of the 32 Mexican states and the most populated, with 14 percent of the total national population. It covers a total area of 2,235,100 ha (SE, 2018), and around 48 percent of its territory is forested land, of which 31 percent is temperate forests – mainly pines, firs, and oaks (PROBOSQUE, 2018). In 2016, the state of Mexico had a total production of 296,067 m³ of wood, primarily pine (57 percent) and fir (20 percent). This represented about 4.4 percent of total national wood production (SEMARNAT, 2016). Such low production results partly from the high degree of fragmentation of the forest masses, upon which management activities have to be conducted under the communal scheme described above.

Like in the rest of the country, the state of Mexico was divided in big *latifundia* towards the end of the nineteenth century. Haciendas with forested lands gave extensive permits to forest enterprises for the commercial extraction of wood, which allowed the establishment of big sawmills and railway systems for wood transportation (Anastacio-Martínez *et al.*, 2014). After the enactment of the national law declaring the reconstitution and endowment of land to *ejidos* in 1915, landowners desperately tried to save their property. Some landowners in the state, foreseeing the loss of a large part of their lands, subdivided and sold them as small, privately owned ranches. These efforts, however, were reversed years later when in 1936 President Lázaro Cárdenas' government promoted agrarian distribution and the creation of large-scale *ejidos* (Anastacio-Martínez *et al.*, 2014).

Today, there are 1061 *ejidos* in the state of Mexico covering 847,331 ha, and 173 *comunidades* covering about 293,048 ha. The area occupied by *ejidos* and *comunidades* represents 51 percent of the state's area and benefits 323,941 *ejidatarios* and *comuneros* (Morett-Sánchez and Cosío-Ruiz, 2017). Given their large number, mean parcel surface is as small as 3.5 ha per individual – below the national average of 4.2 ha per individual – which subjects these communal lands to intense pressure. The development of CFEs has been carried out in this context, whose viability has been seriously compromised by these conditions.

Are community forest enterprises an alternative for sustainable forest management?

Few examples exist in the common property literature of community-based forestry enterprises (CFEs) operating in competitive markets worldwide. Yet, in Mexico there are hundreds of such examples at varying levels of vertical integration (Antinori and Bray, 2005). Forest exploitation programs are described as central instruments for management because the regulations corresponding to policies, strategies, conservation zones and activities, protection, use, and research are established (Madrid *et al.*, 2009). In the course of the twentieth century, Mexican forest communities, alternately hindered and supported by official policy, have had to struggle against logging bans, concessions, and corruption to achieve more autonomous management of their forests, with CFEs emerging as a significant, initially state-supported sector in the mid-1970s (Bray and Wexler, 1996; Klooster, 2003).

Under its public forest policies, CONAFOR promotes the creation of CFEs as a means to achieve forest ecosystem management and conservation in *ejidos* and *comunidades*, mainly

Indigenous. The program gives funds to *ejidos* and *comunidades* to hire technical supervisors ("professional service providers" and "technical services providers") to accompany and reinforce such forest organizations. The number of CFEs in Mexico is not known, nor is the number of CFEs doing controlled forest exploitations (Bray *et al.*, 2007) and under what kinds of terms. According to Madrid *et al.* (2009), transition towards CFE creation involves abandonment of the idea that peasant communities are incapable of managing their own forestry resources in a sustainable way, but it also implies the development of agrarian governance systems for *ejidatarios* and *comuneros*. Success or failure depends on: the organization and institutionalization capabilities of *ejidos* and *comunidades* (in most of the cases, with a significant educational lagging); the market conditions of forest products; and the public policies related to community forestry development.

The *ejidos* that have been successful in community forest management are characterized by the following attributes (Madrid *et al.*, 2009):

1   management and capacity to link government programs;
2   internal organizational capabilities for managing their natural resources in an equitable way;
3   capacity to connect with the forestry market and meet the demand for forest products with competitive prices.

Although the features of these more effectively managed *ejidos* have given them a certain degree of success in community forest management, they have faced significant barriers. Among the many problems they have faced is the fact that the need to meet wood demand has led peasants to increase forest extraction rates, leading to the serious modification of forest structure and composition. Another serious ecological problem is the partial or total substitution of native species with commercial varieties that typically grow faster. Another barrier to community forest management has been the existence of other public policies that oppose forest conservation (De la Cruz Hernández *et al.*, 2016). A prime example is the suite of governmental programs that promote agricultural production. The economic and environmental value of forests have been traditionally underestimated throughout colonial and postcolonial history. After the constitutional reform of 1917 and the agrarian reforms that followed the Revolution of 1910, government policies to develop rural areas focused on agriculture and livestock activities, ignoring the potential of forestry activities (Segura, 2000).

CFEs have been developed as social enterprises to meet two different production goals. On the one hand, CFEs can be considered either as traditional companies whose by-products and final products bear social value; on the other, they can be regarded as a profitable business. This ambiguity has sparked debate, with some authors arguing that both objectives can be merged into a "hybrid" type of CFE, while others contend that each goal develops independently and under opposing interests that make them virtually irreconcilable. For example, capitalism encourages individualism, ambition, and taking risks, whereas social organizations tend to operate based on values such as loyalty, trust, and overall enhancement of communities' social well-being (CEPAL/FAO/IICA, 2014). Moreover, public policies related to CFEs lack cross-sectoral coordination since different government programs do not pursue the same forest conservation objectives, instead focusing on promoting economic development by subsidizing peasants and farmers. There is a clear lack of transversal agreement in relation to environmental criteria among government offices. Therefore, although significant progress has been made in terms of environmental legislation and regulations, the practical application of these instruments remains limited.

Facing this lack of enforcement, government agencies have set forth other legal practices intended to achieve transparency and improve governance by moving towards "voluntary compliance" schemes that avoid the strict application of rules. These voluntary measures give rise to a misunderstood "tolerance" and "discretional negotiation" – which is ultimately a bargaining practice that often leads not only to an enlarged environmental bureaucracy, but also increases the risk of forest deterioration. Without a doubt, public forestry policies have tended to recognize *ejidos* and *comunidades* as entities in which there is a possibility to integrate conservation and exploitation strategies. However, there are still many barriers to the real participation of different stakeholders in the development of forest policies that can recognize and promote the autonomous organization of CFEs in rural areas without entering into conflict with other development policies.

Future research needs and opportunities

It has been shown that there is a need to extend and promote the Mexican community forest model. However, more research is necessary both nationally and regionally to understand the real dimensions and contributions of community forest management to social well-being and economic productivity, and how the continuing problems that plague some communities and regions can be addressed. Further research is needed to assess the impacts of the coming Forest Legal Framework in Mexican rural areas, especially if private enterprises get involved in forest management in conjunction with communities. The North American Free Trade Agreement (NAFTA) between Mexico, Canada, and the United States was re-negotiated in 2018. It will be interesting to see how the new framework is going to affect the balance of exports and imports in the forest sector between the three countries.

References

Anastacio-Martínez, N.D., Nava-Bernal, G., Franco-Maass, S., 2014. *El desarrollo agropecuario de los pueblos de alta montaña. La Peñuela, Estado de México.* Economía, Sociedad y Territorio 14(45), 397–418.

Antinori, C., Bray, D.B., 2005. *Community forest enterprises as entrepreneurial firms: Economic and institutional perspectives from Mexico.* World Development 33(9), 1529–1543.

Arellano Gault, D., Blanco, F., 2013. *Políticas públicas y democracia.* Instituto Federal Electoral, Mexico City.

Bray, D.B., Merino-Pérez, L., 2002. *The rise of community forestry in Mexico: History, concepts, and lessons learned from twenty-five years of community timber production.* The Ford Foundation, New York.

Bray, D.B., Wexler, B.M., 1996. *Forest policies in Mexico,* in: Randall, L. (Ed.), *Changing structures in Mexico: Political, social, and economic prospects.* M.E. Sharpe, Armonk, NY, pp. 217–228.

Bray, D.B., Merino-Pérez, L., Negreros-Castillo, P., Segura-Warnholtz, G., Torres-Rojo, J.M., Henricus, F.M.V., 2003. *Mexico's community-managed forest as a global model for sustainable landscapes.* Conservation Biology 17(3), 649–942.

Bray, D.B., Merino-Pérez, L., Barry, D., 2007. *El manejo comunitario en sentido estricto: las empresas forestales comunitarias de México,* in: Bray, D.B., Merino-Pérez, L., Barry, D. (Eds.), *Los bosques comunitarios de México. Manejo sustentable de paisajes forestales.* Secretaría de Medio Ambiente y Recursos Naturales, Instituto Nacional de Ecología, Consejo Civil Mexicano para la Silvicultura Sostenible, Instituto de Geografía, UNAM. Florida International Institute, Miami, FL, pp. 21–50.

Cárcar-Irujo, A.I., 2013. *Las reformas agrarias en México y los proyectos de desarrollo rural en un municipio del estado de Veracruz.* Nómadas. Critical Journal of Social and Juridical Sciences 38(2). www.redalyc.org/pdf/181/18128245015.pdf.

CEPAL/FAO/IICA, 2014. *Fomento de circuitos cortos como alternativa para la promoción de la agricultura familiar.* Serie Boletín No. 2 complemento del documento Perspectivas de la Agricultura y del Desarrollo Rural en las Américas: una mirada hacia América Latina y el Caribe. http://repiica.iica.int/docs/b3372e/b3372e.pdf.

Comisión Nacional de Áreas Naturales Protegidas (CONANP), 2012. *Historia*. www.conanp.gob.mx/quienes_somos/historia.php.

De La Cruz Hernández, J.A., Ávila Akerberg, V., Rivera Herrejón, M.G., Vizcarra Bordi, I., 2016. *Áreas naturales protegidas y sistema de uso común de recursos forestales en el Nevado de Toluca*. Revista Mexicana de Ciencias Forestales 7(38), 25–42.

Diario Oficial de la Federación (DOF), 2017. *Ley Agraria. Nueva Ley publicada en el Diario Oficial de la Federación el 26 de febrero de 1992*. Texto Vigente. Últimas reformas publicadas DOF 27-03-2017.

Dirección General del Archivo Histórico (DGAH), 2003. *Boletín informativo y Memoria legislativa*. Año III, número 24, Marzo Abril 2003.

Food and Agriculture Organization of the United Nations (FAO), 2014. *State of the world's forests: Enhancing the socioeconomic benefits from forests*. FAO, Rome.

Klooster, D., 2003. *Campesinos and Mexican forest policy during the twentieth century*. Latin American Research Review 38(2), 94–126.

Madrid, L., Nuñez, J.M., Quiroz, G., Rodríguez, Y., 2009. *La propiedad social forestal en México*. Investigación ambiental 1(2), 179–196.

Merino-Pérez, L., 2001. *Las políticas forestales y de conservación y sus impactos sobre las comunidades forestales*. Estudios Agrarios 2001, 75–115.

Morett-Sánchez, J.C., Cosío-Ruiz, C., 2017. *Panorama de los ejidos y comunidades agrarias en México*. Agricultura, Sociedad y Desarrollo (ASyD) 14, 125–152.

Muñoz-Piña, C., Guevara, A., Torres, J.M., Braña, J., 2008. *Paying for the hydrological services of Mexico's forests: Analysis, negotiations and results*. Ecological Economics 65, 725–736.

Orozco-Garibay, P.A., 2010. *Naturaleza del ejido, de la propiedad ejidal. Características y limitaciones*. Revista Mexicana de Derecho 12, 163–193.

Protectora de Bosques del Estado de México (PROBOSQUE), 2018. *Aprovechamiento forestal maderable*. http://probosque.edomex.gob.mx/aprovechamiento_forestal.

Secretaría de Economía (SE), 2018. *Información económica estatal del Estado de México*. www.gob.mx/cms/uploads/attachment/file/99605/estado_de_mexico.pdf.

Secretaría de Medio Ambiente y Recursos Naturales (SEMARNAT), 2016. *Anuario estadístico de la producción forestal*. Secretaría de Medio Ambiente y Recursos Naturales.

Segura, G., 2000. *Mexico's forest sector and policies: A general perspective*. Paper presented at Constituting the Commons: Crafting Sustainable Commons in the New Millennium, the Eighth Biennial Conference of the International Association for the Study of Common Property. Bloomington, Indiana.

Trujillo-Bautista, J.M., 2009. *El ejido, símbolo de la Revolución Mexicana*, in: Luzón, J.L., Cardim, M. (Eds). *Problemas sociales y regionales en América Latina. Estudio de casos*. Edicions Universitat Barcelona, Barcelona, pp. 101–126.

Warman,, A., 2003. *La Reforma Agraria Mexicana, una visión de largo plazo*, in: FAO, *Land reform, land settlement and cooperatives, 2003/2*. Economic and Social Development Department. http://fao.org/docrep/006/J0415T/j0415t09.htm.

White, A., Martin, A., 2002. *Who owns the world's forest? Forest tenure and public forest in transition*. Center for International Environmental Law, Washington, D.C.

PART IV

Innovation

27

SOCIAL ECONOMY AND ENTREPRENEURSHIP IN RURAL AREAS

Al Lauzon, Mary Ferguson, Catherine Lang, and Barbara Harrison

Introduction

The restructuring of the economy during the 1980s led to a decline of the welfare state and the rise of neoliberalism, facilitating a move from government to governance. As a result, there is an increasing reliance on the non-profit sector to deliver services, and yet it too has seen a decline in support it has historically received from the state, and this is further exacerbated by a decline in charitable giving. As a consequence, activity in the non-profit sector has increased whereby non-profits develop services and produce products to generate revenue to invest in supporting their social mission. These are known as social enterprises. The focus of this chapter is on rural social enterprises, how regional historical forces shape them, and how rural social enterprises develop, to conclude by examining the implications for policy to support rural social enterprise development.

The historian Eric Hobsbawm (1994) has argued that humankind is living through a fundamental shift on par with the Industrial Revolution, concluding that the twentieth century really ended in the 1980s with the new millennium beginning slightly ahead of schedule. During the 1970s and 1980s fundamental changes in the economy began, in addition to the decline of the Keynesian welfare state and the rise of neoliberalism where the market is given priority over people; economic globalization, where increasing free trade creates opportunities for companies to go offshore or outsource labor; and developments in technology, robotics, and artificial intelligence continue to reduce the need for workers across most occupations. All of this is driven by the primacy of the idea of efficiency (Pletsch, 2011) and maximizing profit and return to shareholders. As a result, there is increasing inequity between countries and within countries while stakeholders continue to search for ways of agreeing upon and dealing with global climate change and environmental destruction. All of this is happening while the rate of change accelerates exponentially (Friedman, 2016; Harvey, 1990). The irony in all of this is people become more vulnerable as the social safety net that was part of the welfare state is being increasingly dismantled, leaving individuals and communities in situations of uncertainty, insecurity, and vulnerability. As Teasdale and Dey (2013) argue, what was the state's responsibility has become the responsibility of the individual and/or non-government actors. Simply put, the world has changed in fundamental ways and individuals and communities find themselves increasingly vulnerable in an era of uncertainty.

These changes have facilitated a movement from government to governance, whereby how decisions get made and actions taken no longer depends solely on government direction, but is about independent, self-governing organizations and other actors collaborating and working together to fill in the gaps created by the retreat of the state (Stoker, 1997; Murdoch, 2000; Pletsch, 2011). In many ways, it has become increasingly about endogenous development and community economic development rather than exogenous development. Local initiatives are developed utilizing local resources and knowledge.

These changes have, according to Pletsch (2011), resulted in the non–profit sector in part-nership with municipalities, education, and the health-care sector taking a more active and larger role in the delivery of services and the promotion of development. Despite this larger role, there was a change in the way the non-profit sector was funded with governments redu-cing their financial support along with a decline in charitable giving (Goldenberg *et al.*, 2009). To put it mildly, the financial health of these organizations became increasingly challenged (Pletsch, 2011).

These changes have given "birth" to what has been referred to as the social economy. An example of government's interest in the social economy finds expression in Canada in 2004 under the auspices of the "Social Economy Initiative" whereby the federal government articu-lates its expectations for social enterprises:

> Social economy enterprises are run like businesses, producing goods and services for the market economy, but they manage their operations and redirect their surplus in pursuit of social and community goals ... [these] strategies involve citizens, govern-ments, the voluntary sector, business, learning institutions and others working together.
>
> *(ACOA, n.d., 1)*

As noted, social enterprises could play a role in:

1   stimulating job creation and skills development;
2   enhancing community capacity for social supports;
3   supporting economic growth and neighborhood revitalization;
4   protecting the environment;
5   mobilizing disadvantaged groups (ACOA, n.d., 1).

Thus, there is the emergence of what has become known as social enterprises that engage in revenue generation strategies and streams by producing goods or delivering services and rein-vesting the profits from these revenue streams back into their social mission. In particular, non-profits have seen this strategy as a means to help meet some of their financial challenges (Goldenberg *et al.*, 2009). For example, in a study of Ontario non-profits it was reported that 80 percent earn income to fund their work, although they do not necessarily identify themselves as social enterprises (Chamberlain *et al.*, 2015). In addition, the authors reported that over 45 percent of non-profit revenues in Ontario's 55,000 non-profits come from earned revenue.

The idea of social enterprises is a contested concept, and one on which there is an absence of an agreed-upon definition. This chapter begins with an examination of the idea of social enter-prise and how the regional context gives shape in form to both the understanding of social enterprise and the practice of social enterprise. This will be done by briefly looking at Western Europe, the United States, and Canada. This section is followed by an examination of rurality and social enterprises, arguing that rural is a different context for social enterprises than urban areas, and hence is deserving of being looked at independently of the urban context. The next sections draw on empirical work conducted in the Canadian province of Ontario and examines the development of rural social enterprises. Finally, the implications for policy are examined, arguing there are three tiers of policy that must be considered in the context of social enterprise development and functioning. They are place-based policy, non-profit sector policy, and the sector policy of the individual social enterprise.

Social enterprises

One idea that has been promoted in response to the development of the social economy has been the idea of social innovation whereby communities need to develop the means and ways of meeting community needs that were once met through state provisions (Oosterlynck *et al.*, 2013). There is a need to create communities that are able to create environments that foster social innovation that promotes the well-being of people, communities, and their environments. Furthermore, social innovation draws on two traditions: civic virtue that drives people to engage in activities that promote the well-being of others and the spirit of entrepreneurialism that drives innovation (Maclean *et al.*, 2012). These are social entrepreneurs and it is social entrepreneurs who create social enterprises that combine a social mission with the utilization of commercial revenue generation to support their social mission.

The term social enterprise was first used in the 1990s in Britain (Lang *et al.*, 2016b) and became a focus of greater concern across Western Europe and North America with the beginning of the new millennium. The idea of social enterprise came to be associated with the social economy that emphasizes social well-being and not-for-profits, and that values cooperation and collaboration rather than competition. And despite the newness of the construct of a social enterprise, as a form of social and economic organization it has been around since the Middle Ages originally in the form of artisan and crafters' guilds (Lang *et al.*, 2016b). These organizations were created with the idea of generating income to ensure the social well-being of their membership.

The contemporary understanding of social enterprises lacks conceptual clarity and agreement upon definition. There are multiple definitions and from a practice perspective, many social enterprises do not identify with the idea of social enterprise but often identify as a voluntary organization or a non-profit organization (Lang, *et al.*, 2016b). Lang *et al.* (2016b) further note that social enterprises are varied and operate across a variety of differing corporate forms ranging from charities to non-profits, cooperatives, and even some types of for-profit business. Kerlin (2006, p. 248), in her analysis of difference between social enterprises in Western Europe and the Unites States, argues that the form a social enterprise takes is dependent upon the "contrasting forces shaping and reinforcing the movement in each region". She continues, "Thus, not surprisingly, research has found that while definitions of a social enterprise tend to vary within the regions themselves, even broader divisions exist between the two regions in terms of understanding, use, context, and policy for social enterprise" (2006, p. 248). Table 27.1 provides an overview comparing social enterprises in the United States and Western Europe.

As can be seen from Table 27.1, the nature of social enterprises, their function, and how they are supported vary between the United States and Western Europe. In Western Europe, in general, they are more strategic and focused on human services while government plays a major role in supporting the development of these activities. As there is an increasing emphasis on evidence-based policy, research plays an increasing role in the formation of policy. In Western Europe research on social enterprises is through a social science lens that then constructs the understanding of what a social enterprise is and this informs policy development. Kerlin (2006)

Table 27.1 Comparative overview of social enterprise in the United States and Western Europe

	Unites States	*Western Europe*
Emphasis	Revenue generation	Social benefit
Common organizational type	Non-profit	Association/cooperative
Focus	All non-profit activities	Human services
Type of social enterprise	Many	Few
Recipient involvement	Limited	Common
Strategic development	Foundations	Government/EU
University research	Business and social science	Social science
Context	Market economy	Social economy
Legal framework	Lacking	Underdeveloped but improving

Source: Kerlin (2006, p. 259).

concludes that Western Europe has such a narrow range of services supported by social enterprises that it is an underutilized strategy.

In the United States they are focused on the gamut of activities in which the non-profits are engaged but are dependent predominately on foundations to support those activities. Foundations are known as "social enterprise accelerators". Kerlin (2006) notes that despite healthy social enterprise development the dependence on foundations may lead to a weakening of civil society and lead to the social exclusion of some groups because of minimal government engagement. There is no coordinated strategic development and support for the sector. Furthermore, as a result of the research lens through business and the social sciences, and an emphasis on the market rather than the social economy, there is a greater focus on the business side of social enterprise development and functioning than in Western Europe.

The Canadian experience varies from that of the United States, and to some extent Western Europe, in that Canada has a heritage of deep roots in social citizenship that historically was manifest in the social democracy, social gospel, and cooperative movements (Ferguson and Lang, 2013). These movements provide a foundation on which social citizenship has been built and in the Canadian context social enterprises have more in common with community economic development strategies that focus on community self-reliance than the United States and Western Europe. Quebec and Manitoba are Canadian examples that have developed social enterprise policy frameworks that were co-created among government and engaged stakeholders. Quebec is an exemplary illustration of the values that underlie the development of the Canadian perspective on social enterprises. As Mendell and Neatman wrote (2010, pp. 63–64):

> What distinguishes the social economy in Quebec … is its broad reach, which extends beyond … collective enterprises to include social movements and territorial intermediaries that identify themselves as part of the social economy … the social economy not only challenges the prevailing economic model through its outcomes, but also on the institutional changes that this requires, the processes of re-engaging government in new ways … establishing spaces for dialogue and working towards collective objectives or in the general interest of the many organizations and movements involved.

Comparing Western Europe with its focus on human services, the United States focus on provision of services, and Canada, which focuses on endogenous development, it is possible to see how the national historical context shapes policy, support, and the function of social enterprises.

Rurality and social enterprises

The fundamental changes articulated earlier in this chapter have not left rural areas unscathed. Speaking directly to the economic issues and implications for rural, Lauzon *et al.* (2015) note, the changing rural economies are forcing rural communities to adapt, to become creative and innovative. Markey and Halseth (2015) argue there is a danger of simply running down the capital investments of previous rural generations and a danger of viewing rural infrastructure investment as something that simply cannot be afforded. They argue rural is in danger of being lost in the "cities" agenda with a reduction of government "boots on the ground" resulting in a lack of understanding in and of rural.

While rural faces many economic challenges, it also faces a host of other challenges including: dealing with and meeting the needs of aging populations, out-migration of youth, poor health outcomes, developing human capital, attracting immigrants, a shrinking tax base, and declining resources (Atherton and Hannon, 2006). And while rural communities face similar challenges, they each have their own unique context that both enables and constrains actions and is a product of their own unique development trajectory. As noted by Markey *et al.* (2015), rural communities face their own set of unique challenges that differentiate them from larger urban and metropolitan centers, but also from one another. Economic globalization and other transformative changes challenge rural communities, creating winners and losers.

Much like their urban counterparts, rural communities are increasingly looking to non-profits to help fill the gaps created by the decline of the welfare state and the out-migration of a variety of services. Increasingly, rural non-profits are looking at social enterprise as a means of supporting their missions. As Lang *et al.* (2016a) argue, the challenges and needs of rural social enterprises are different from urban and require made-for rural solutions. Yet even in the context of rural there can be no "cookie-cutter" approaches to supporting the development of rural social enterprises and, as noted by Lauzon *et al.* (2015), if you have seen one rural community you have seen one rural community: they are all different in their own ways. This perspective also applies to social enterprise development in rural areas. Chamberlain *et al.* (2015), in a study of social enterprises, highlights differences between urban and rural social enterprises. Table 27.2 provides an overview of the unique characteristics of rural social enterprises.

Steinerowski and Steinerowska-Streb (2012) also note a number of challenges unique to the rural context: geographic isolation; lack of appropriate human capital; the market size limits enterprise scale; and need to avoid conflict with local businesses while being able to offer something unique and currently unavailable.

There has been little attention paid to and research conducted on rural social enterprises. Ferguson (2018) reports that at the 2013 World Forum on Social Enterprises held in Calgary there were only two sessions devoted to rural social enterprises and they came from the same presenters.

Table 27.2 Unique features of rural social enterprises

- Rural social enterprises are more likely to have a cultural or an environmental mission as opposed to an employment mission
- Rural social enterprises target a particular geographic community
- Rural social enterprises are about half the size of urban social enterprises
- Rural social enterprises have more volunteers per staff member than urban social enterprises

---

Source: Chamberlain *et al.* (2015).

Rural social enterprise development

Lang *et al.* (2016a) have noted that while attention has been paid to social enterprise development, its focus has been on the urban context with little attention being paid to the rural context, a context they argue is significantly different from the urban context. Lang *et al.* (2016a) undertook an action-based research project that sought to support rural non-profit social enterprise development. It was focused on developing an ecosystem to promote rural social enterprise development through social enterprise capacity development, networking, and enhancing rural social enterprise practice. It was an attempt to promote the long-term sustainability of social enterprise development and practice in rural areas. It was argued that the development of an ecosystem is essential to successful social enterprise development in rural areas.

Building upon Lang *et al.* (2016a), Lang *et al.* (2016b) undertook research to examine how rural social enterprises develop through a set of case studies. Given the dearth of research and information on rural social enterprise development, Lang *et al.* (2016b) utilized Flora's community capitals model to explain how they develop. Table 27.3 provides an overview of Flora and Flora's (2008) community capitals.

According to Flora and Flora (2008) these various forms of capital interact, building upon one another to create vibrant and sustainable rural communities. A summary of the findings of Lang *et al.* (2016b) is highlighted below. First, the people engaged with these social enterprises value and utilized collaboration rooted in what is traditionally considered as rural self-reliance. It should be also noted that each case study has a unique context and set of conditions in which each is responding, developing, and operating. Given the uniqueness of each context, the social enterprises are responding to place-based opportunities and challenges. Each of the cases had available to them a cluster of forms of capital that were underutilized or latent and the social enterprise was able to leverage these types of capital in service to their mission.

While the leveraging of existing forms of capital was instrumental to social enterprise development, it required the vision of the founding members of the social enterprise. Thus, human capital was instrumental to the success of the social enterprise as it is through the efforts of the founding members that the other forms of capital could be mobilized. Lang *et al.* (2016b, p. 98) make this point when they state:

> The social enterprises studied began with a small cluster of people who had an innovative idea and took on the role of leadership as community champions and social entrepreneurs. They were able to identify local/regional issues and opportunities and leverage community capital to bring their ideas to life and make positive change in their communities ... Human capital, or the knowledge, talent and skills of core leaders

Table 27.3 Forms of community capital

- *Built capital*: infrastructure that supports the community
- *Political capital*: ability to influence rules, standards, and their enforcement
- *Financial capital*: financial resources such as loans, investments, and available income
- *Social capital*: connections among people and organizations characterized by trust
- *Cultural capital*: the way people know the world and act within it; includes such elements as place, identity, worldview, ethnicity, etc.
- *Human capital*: people's knowledge, skills, abilities, and competencies
- *Natural capital*: natural resources, environment, and ecosystem services

---

Source: Flora and Flora (2008).

of each initiative, was central to idea generation and the initial development of the enterprise.

It is also worth noting that usually those who provided the initial leadership were migrants to the area and characterized by passion, resilience, and a willingness to work through barriers they encountered. In this sense they were tenacious and not afraid to challenge longstanding assumptions about what was possible.

The success of these social enterprises was dependent upon those who were providing leadership and vision to build a network, or in terms of capital, leverage social capital. It was through the development of this network that the enterprise was then able to recruit volunteers to aid in the business development which required a high degree of volunteer effort during the start-up process. As the enterprises moved forward in their development, more formal structures evolved to ensure enterprise sustainability and the movement from vision to reality. This required drawing on local cultural capital such as self-reliance, valuing collaboration, and civic engagement and service. Through developing these formal structures an expansion of the human and social capital was enabled, setting the stage for implementation and impact. It was during this stage too that the enterprise began to secure significant financial capital and built capital. For those requiring natural capital, it was during this phase that they began to secure the necessary natural capital and resources. In examining these case studies, Lang *et al.* (2016b) derived six principles for social enterprise success. Table 27.4 provides a summary of these principles.

In summary, while social enterprise development requires differing forms of capital with an emphasis initially on human and social capital, it also leads to further development of various forms of capital within the region and the development of social capital beyond the region. This provides a further development of the foundation for future social enterprise development.

Policy and social enterprise development

This leaves the question of how policy can best support the development of rural social enterprises. Lang *et al.* (2016b) argue that policy that supports the development of rural social

Table 27.4 Principles for successful rural social enterprise development

- The economic model serves mission goals; revenue generation was not prioritized over the social/environmental mission.
- Access to appropriate business supports leads to successful social enterprise development; the development of these supports was cultivated through social capital and the enterprise's network by drawing into the enterprise those individuals with the required specialized knowledge/skills needed.
- The development of social enterprises is more organic than linear; social enterprise development emerges as a result of the interaction among key figures as opposed to being developed through long-term plans.
- The focus was on the region rather than any one community.
- Success in social enterprise builds resilience and grows social, human, and political capital as the network emerges and encounters success; this is a product of what can be described as serial social enterprise activity and often leads to growth in cultural capital.
- Social enterprise development often leads to networking outside the region, or what can be described as bridging social capital. This bridging social capital can enhance and create further opportunities for development.

Source: Lang *et al.* (2016b).

enterprise must be multi-tiered. The first tier, what is often called place-based policy, relates to ensuring that policy that supports enabling factors are in place, followed by the second tier specific to social enterprise and the non-profit sector, and the third tier which deals with sector-specific policies (i.e. employment, environment, etc.).

The first question is what is place-based policy? A simple and succinct definition is it is policy that *enables* place-based communities to mobilize local resources in response to the unique challenges and opportunities facing a community. Lang *et al.* (2016b) argue that the enabling factors are those factors that are required to develop social enterprises and identify four foundational enablers. Table 27.5 provides an overview of the enablers identified by Lang *et al.*

How can policy support these enablers? The one thing that has become clear from the research conducted by Lang *et al.* (2016b) is that each rural community/region and each rural social enterprise is unique and must respond to particular needs and circumstances, a challenge for policy. Previous Ontario research that focused on the development of community-based organizations to promote and support local/regional telecommunication needs in rural communities sheds some light on these issues.

Ramirez (2001) studied the development of local community-based organizations as they responded to their own unique challenges and opportunities as they related to the provision of telecommunications infrastructure/services in rural and remote communities. Each of the three cases examined focused on their own unique challenges and opportunities with one focusing on economic development, one focusing on community development, and one focusing on cultural production. Ramirez identified the factors outlined in Table 27.6 as critical in the development of these community-based organizations.

And as Ramirez noted, these elements must be *locally grown* and cannot simply be imported. But the critical component was the incentives that allowed groups to access small amounts of capital to facilitate the organizations' development through mobilizing various forms of capital. These organizations emerged rather than being linearly planned. In describing what he calls social emergence, Sawyer (2005) explains it is a means of understanding system behavior, or in this case an organization's behavior, as a result of the actions and interaction among the agents of the system, or as actors engage in self-organizing and are influenced by enablers and barriers in the larger environment.

Lauzon *et al.* (2003), following Ramirez's research of successful community-based telecommunications organizations, asked the question why some communities succeeded and others failed when operating in the same policy environment and having the same opportunities; they

Table 27.5 Enablers for rural social enterprise development

- Necessary human capital: all of the enterprises were launched by entrepreneurial leaders who contributed significant and valuable skills and experience.
- Human capital that leverages and bridges social capital: the founders and their champions exhibited strong bonding social capital and community identity which then bridged to include more stakeholders over time to spread risk, enhance capacity, and grow their social enterprise.
- A capacity to identify underutilized community resources or forms of capital: the enterprise champions identified opportunities that represented gaps in the mainstream economy in their regions and found ways to utilize existing place-based cultural, financial, and built capital to successfully address these gaps through their initiatives.
- The development of securing other forms of capital as needed: all the social enterprises built on and further developed cultural, financial, built, and political capital.

Source: Lang *et al.* (2016b).

Table 27.6 Critical development factors for community-based organizations

---

- A team of champions that offers vision, management and facilitation
- Workable informal relationships between champions and policy-makers
- Community-based organizations that respond to a community vision and services its interest; are flexible to change; are able to take on risks and are willing to review services on an ongoing basis
- Community trust in the organization earned over time
- A continuum of policy incentive programs that a community group or partnership could access as their specific capacities and needs were identified and developed, including small grants to mobilize community resources to do their work (Ramirez called these small grants Lego building blocks).

Source: Ramirez (2001).

chose to examine failed cases. Their analysis led them to answer that question by stating there was sufficient motivation and human capital present in the communities, it was the deficiency of, or the inability to develop or mobilize, sufficient social capital that ultimately led to these communities failing where others had succeeded. In some sense, it was a failure of emergence and despite interactions among various actors they did not move forward because the necessary relationships – social capital – did not exist and could not be developed. It was the ongoing animosity among members of the community and region that proved a barrier that was insurmountable and despite the incentive grants and programs, none were available to work at developing positive relationships among stakeholders that were required for them to experience success.

There are many parallels between Ramirez's (2001) research and that of Lang *et al.* (2016b), and lessons learned have application to rural social enterprise development. Both point out how human capital and social capital are critical for developing and/or mobilizing other forms of capital that allow for social enterprises to develop and then sustain their functioning. As mentioned previously this requires providing investments to create enabling conditions and this is the purview of place-based policy identified as Tier 1.

Yet place-based policy is only one tier. Tier 2 (policy as it relates specifically to non-profits) and Tier 3 (which relates to the particular sector, i.e. environment, health, etc.) can constrain or enable local efforts to develop social enterprises. Table 27.7 provides two examples of the policy complexity that rural social enterprises in rural Ontario had to understand, respond to, and negotiate in their development and ongoing operations at three different levels of government: municipal, provincial, and federal.

What does this mean for policy? It means that social enterprise development is about placed-based development, building on those latent forms of capital that may be unused and looking for ways to develop or secure forms of capital that might not be available. Johnson (2013, p. 47), in his articulation of what the OECD has called the "New Rural Paradigm", focuses on increasing "competitiveness through the valorization of local assets and exploitation of unused assets (think capitals) targeted at various sectors (not just agriculture) through investments (not subsidies) with all key actors, including all levels of government and local stakeholders". In essence, investments must lead to creating the conditions of enablement that allow local actors to articulate a vision and to work towards that vision through mobilizing or developing the necessary forms of capitals to bring it to fruition. This perspective has become known as place-based policy. And while place-based policy is essential to the development and running of social enterprises, they are not immune from Tier 2 and Tier 3 policies which may either enable or constrain the activities and goals of social enterprises. The policy terrain that must be negotiated is

Table 27.7 Examples of Tier 2 and Tier 3 policy complexity governing rural social enterprises

Social enterprise	Relevant policy, programs, regulations
Common Roof: The Common Roof aims to maximize mission impact for tenant organizations by capitalizing on economies of scale, decreasing facility rental and operational costs, and increasing service collaboration opportunities including a single point of service and an enhanced multidisciplinary base of expertise for clients. Its mission is as follows: The Common Roof is a community-based social enterprise providing sustainable and professional work space for human-service non-profit agencies.	• Municipal by-laws: zoning and transit • Provincial Ministry of Municipal Affairs and Housing: Assessment Act Property Tax • Canada Revenue Agency • Policies impacting charities and economic development activities • Local health integration network policies • Federal and provincial infrastructure funds and programs • Ministry of Children and Youth Services
Community Living South Huron: Community Living South Huron (CLSH) is a 40+ year old charitable organization that is dedicated to providing support to people with intellectual challenges through education, advocacy, and innovation. CLSH currently operates three enterprises: a transportation system, non-profit housing, and two social purpose enterprises – a woodworking shop that specializes in building pallets and shipping crates and contracting services to small businesses in the area.	• Municipal by-laws • Municipal and provincial social programming funding priorities • Employment Equity Act • Not for Profit Corporations Act • Various provincial policies of the Ministry of Community and Social Services and Ministry of Education

Source: Lang *et al.* (2016b, p. 94).

complex. While place-based policy is a necessary condition, it is not sufficient and Tier 2 and Tier 3 policies can hinder and undermine the development of rural social enterprises.

Conclusions

First, it needs to be recognized that a nation's/region's historical development will shape the form, role, and functions of social enterprises developed. These differences can be seen when social enterprises from the perspective of Western Europe, the United States, and Canada are compared.

Second, it needs to be understood that rural social enterprise development is different from urban social enterprise development and there is no one-size-fits-all solution to the challenges associated with social enterprise development. Furthermore, there is no one-size-fits-all for rural social enterprise development as they are each unique in their own ways and there is great diversity in rural areas that impacts social enterprise development.

Third, the successful development of rural social enterprises requires adequate human and social capital which then interact to leverage or develop other forms of community capital and to bring the social enterprise from an idea through vision to realization. This requires paying attention to three tiers of policy: Tier 1 or place-based policy, which addresses creating conditions of enablement; Tier 2, which addresses the regulation of the non-profit sector and social enterprise development; and Tier 3, which regulates the specific sector in which the social enterprise is situated. All three are important. Tier 1, however, requires strategic investment in order to create the necessary conditions of enablement which are the foundation of rural social enterprise development. In the absence of enabling conditions, it will be extremely difficult to mobilize local resources and capital. Tiers 2 and 3 are not really relevant in the absence of Tier 1 for there is likely to be little social enterprise development. Lauzon *et al.*'s (2003) research on failed cases bears that out.

In summary, rural social enterprises have a vital role to play as the state secedes responsibility to ensure the integrity of the social safety net as the society moves from a paradigm of government to governance. Increasingly individuals and communities are responsible for their own well-being and futures. Rural social enterprises may play a vital role in ensuring that well-being and the future of rural people and their communities.

References

ACOA – Atlantic Canada Opportunities Agency, n.d. *Government of Canada's social economy initiative.* www.envision.ca/pdf/SocialEconomy/FederalSocialEconomyInitiative.pdf.

Atherton, A., Hannon, P.D., 2006. *Localized strategies for supporting incubation: Strategies arising from a case of rural enterprise development.* Journal of Small Business and Enterprise Development 13, 48–61.

Chamberlain, P., Gillis, K., Prindiville, T., Bechard, O., Ulhaq, M., Elson, P.R., Hall, P.V., 2015. *Enterprising change: Report of the 2015 Social Enterprise Survey for Ontario.* The Canadian CED Network, MaRS Centre for Impact Investing, Simon Fraser University, Mount Royal University. https://ccednet-rcdec.ca/en/toolbox/2015_Ontario_SE_Report.

Ferguson, M., 2018. *Rural and remote municipalities as practitioners and intermediaries in social enterprise development: A case for place-based policy development* (Unpublished PhD Dissertation). University of Guelph, Guelph, Ont.

Ferguson, M., Lang, C., 2013. *Municipal involvement in social enterprise.* Milestones Ontario Good Roads Association 13, 10–13.

Flora, C., Flora, J., 2008. *Rural communities: Legacy and change*, 3rd edition. Westview Press, Boulder, CO.

Friedman, T.L., 2016. *Thank you for being late: An optimist's guide to thriving in the age of accelerations.* Farrar, Straus and Giroux, New York.

Goldenberg, M., Kamoji, W., Orton, L., Williamson, M., 2009. *Social innovation in Canada: An update.* CPRN Research Report.

Harvey, D., 1990. *The condition of postmodernity.* Blackwell Publishing, Malden, MA.

Hobsbawm, E., 1994. *Age of extremes: The short twentieth century 1914–1991.* Abacus, London.

Johnson, T., 2013. *Rural policy*, in: Gree, G.P. (Ed.), *Handbook of rural development.* Edward Elgar, Northampton, MA, pp. 42–55.

Kerlin, J.A., 2006. *Social enterprise in the United States and Western Europe: Understanding and learning from the differences.* Voluntas 17, 247–263.

Lang, C., Ferguson, M., Chamberlain, P., Laird, H., Mitchell, J., 2016a. *Rural social enterprise in Ontario: RSEC learning report.* http://ekonomos.com/wp-content/uploads/2016/04/RSEC-Reflections-Report.pdf.

Lang, C., Ferguson, M., Harrison, B., Gillis, K., Lauzon A., Laird, H., 2016b. *Rural social enterprise and community ecosystem development: Policy leverage points – Executive summary.* http://ekonomos.com/wp-content/uploads/2016/05/New-Directions-Research-Report-_Executive-Summary_16-0511.pdf.

Lauzon, A., Milne, W., McCallum, M., 2003. *PACTS: Setting the research agenda.* Report submitted to SRC Research Program, OMAF.

Lauzon, A., Bollman, R., Ashton, B., 2015. *Introduction*, in: Markey, S., Breen, S., Lauzon, A., Ryser, R., Mealy, R. (Eds.), *State of rural Canada 2015.* Canadian Rural Revitalization Foundation, Brandon, MB, pp. 1–13.

Maclean, M., Harvey, C., Gordon, J., 2012. *Social innovation, social entrepreneurship and the practice of contemporary entrepreneurial philanthropy.* International Small Business Journal 31(7), 747–763.

Markey, S., Halseth, G., 2015. *Discussions and recommendations*, in: Markey, S., Breen, S., Lauzon, A., Ryser, R., Mealy, R. (Eds.), *State of rural Canada 2015.* Canadian Rural Revitalization Foundation, Brandon, MB, pp. 109–118.

Markey, S., Breen, S., Lauzon, A., Ryser, R., Mealy, R. (Eds.), 2015. *State of rural Canada 2015.* Canadian Rural Revitalization Foundation, Brandon, MB.

Mendell, M., Neatman, N., 2010. *The social economy in Quebec: Toward a new political economy*, in: Quarter, J., Mook, L., Ryan, S. (Eds.), *Researching the social economy.* University of Toronto Press, Toronto, Ont., pp. 63–83.

Murdoch, J., 2000. *Networks: A new paradigm of rural development.* Journal of Rural Studies 16, 407–419.

Oosterlynck, S., Kazepov, Y., Novy, A., Cools, P., Barberis, E., Wukovitsch, F., Sarius, T., Leubolt, B., 2013. *The butterfly and the elephant: Local social innovation, the welfare state and new poverty dynamics.* IMPROVE Working Papers, Discussion Paper No. 13/03.

Pletsch, C., 2011. *The promise of partnerships: Local governance and the practice of partnership* (PhD dissertation). University of Guelph, Guelph, Ont.. http://atrium.lib.uoguelph.ca/xmlui/bitstream/handle/10214/3241/Final%20Version%20Pletsch%20Thesis%202011.pdf?sequence=1.

Ramirez, R., 2001. *A model for rural and remote information and communication technologies: A Canadian exploration.* Telecommunications Policy 25(5), 315–330.

Sawyer, R.K., 2005. *Social emergence: Societies as complex systems.* Cambridge University Press, New York.

Steinerowski, A.A., Steinerowska-Streb, I., 2012. *Can social enterprise contribute to creating sustainable rural communities? Using the lens of structuration theory to analyse the emergence of rural social enterprise.* Local Economy 10, 167–182.

Stoker, G., 1997. *Partnerships in urban governance: Western European and American experience.* Macmillan, London.

Teasdale, S., Dey, P., 2013. *Exploring the spatial and temporal dimensions of micro-resistance: The tactical mimicry of social enterprise by English third sector organizations.* Presented to Social Enterprise Research Day, October 1, Calgary. Full text provided by author.

28

GROUNDED INNOVATION IN THE RURAL BIOECONOMY

John M. Bryden and Karen Refsgaard

Introduction

This chapter explores the conceptual basis of innovation in the so-called "bioeconomy", conceived of as a partial alternative to the "fossil fuel economy". Since most bioresources are contained and transformed in rural regions, the notion of a new bioeconomy is closely linked to rural development. This approach differs from that of many in the field of innovation studies, but is rooted in the well-established innovation systems approach of Lundvall, Freeman, Edquist, and Fagerborg, as well as in the work on innovation and development by Freeman, Ely, Smith, and colleagues at Sussex University (Science Policy Research Unit SPRU, IDS, and their collaboration in the STEPS Centre), and on the growing field of the relationship between poverty, exclusion, and innovation developed by Kaplinsky, Cozzens, Sutz, and others in the international Globelics research group.

Although the chapter does not directly report on the comparative research undertaken by the authors and colleagues that underpins the conceptual framework developed, the research is reported in other published articles that should be read along with the chapter. The comparison was undertaken over the period 2013–2017 between the three heavily forested Nordic countries of Norway, Sweden, and Finland, and in the region of Emilia-Romagna in Italy. However, it also drew on recent work in other countries including a comparison between India and Russia, and work in South America and Quebec, Canada.

This chapter is largely based on comparative research undertaken by the authors and colleagues between 2010 and 2017 on grounded innovation practices in the development of the bioeconomy and bioenergy in the rural regions of Norway, Sweden, Finland, and in Emilia-Romagna in Italy. This research is reported in greater detail in other published sources, and especially Refsgaard *et al.* (2017), Cavicchi (2016), Cavicchi *et al.* (2017), and Berlina and Mikkola (2017). However, it also draws on research on grounded and inclusive innovation in other contexts and gathered together in the special issue of *Innovation and Development* published in 2017 (Bryden *et al.*, 2017).

The idea of "grounded innovation" is founded on grounded theory as developed by Glaser and Strauss (1967) and shares with grounded theory the key idea of innovation, research, and the development of theory as a bottom-up, inductive, learning process. In these latter respects it also shares many ideas with the innovation systems approach of Lundvall (1988, 1992), Edquist (2004), and others, but it adds the methods of inclusion and participation that until recently have been largely ignored by the innovation systems literature (Ustyuzhantseva, 2017; Bryden *et al.*,

2017). It also adds the ethical issues concerning justice and fairness considered, for example, by Smith, Ely, and colleagues at Sussex University (STEPS, 2010) and Cozzens and Sutz, among others, and discussed in greater detail in Bryden *et al.* (2017), and below. Since the results of the research on which it is based are published elsewhere in refereed articles, this chapter is therefore conceptual in nature, exploring some of the questions that need to be addressed when undertaking research, comparative or not, on innovation in the context of rural development.

The chapter is framed within the wider discussions of the bioeconomy in the context of the so-called transition from a fossil fuel-based economy to a bio-based economy (OECD, 2001; European Commission, 2012; Bryden *et al.*, 2017). This transition reflects the global agreements on action to halt human impacts on climate change settled at the Kyoto and Paris Conferences of Parties in 1997 and 2015 respectively, as well as discussions about the finite character of non-renewable fossil resources and energy security. All of these discussions and debates are also framed in the context of the desire to move towards a more environmentally, socially, and economically sustainable development at the global level (Brundtland Commission, 1987) as well as towards a more "human" economy (Hart *et al.*, 2010).

To start, some key definitions used in this chapter are laid out, especially the terms "grounded innovation" and "bioeconomy" and connected to the wider notions of territorial rural development, multi-level governance, and policy. Then it is discussed in what respects the "bioeconomy" demands special attention, what is different about it, and what the implications of those differences are for practice and policy. Afterwards what is special about "grounded" innovation is considered, along with why it is a very different concept from most interpretations of "innovation", and what its likely limitations are. Drawing on Bryden *et al.* (2013), Bryden (2015), and the later articles in Bryden *et al.* (2017), a "new paradigm of innovation" is posed, which can be contrasted with the "old paradigm". Subsequently, some real-life examples of grounded innovation in different aspects of the bioeconomy and in a range of countries are considered, assessing how the transition to the bioeconomy is taking place, and what it means for rural areas and people in different settings. Finally, the policy and governance regimes that are likely to be most helpful in ensuring that the transition to the bioeconomy both benefits rural areas and people, and delivers positive outcomes for economic, social, and environmental goals of sustainable development are considered.

What is the "bioeconomy"? Why is it important for rural development and policy?

In 2012, the European Commission published a communication: *Innovating for Sustainable Growth: A Bioeconomy for Europe* (European Commission, 2012). As with other early documents on the topic from the OECD and the US government, this focused on the technological aspects and economic growth, mainly concerning biofuels based on agriculture, and barely considered the social and institutional dimensions. Indeed, a review by an expert group criticized the lack of a clear definition of "bioeconomy" in the 2012 document, and recommended that "A clear, explicit and updated definition of the bioeconomy concept is needed as the basis for a shared policy agenda. This could include concepts such as Ecosystem Services, health and nutrition as well as Sustainable Development Goals" (European Commission, 2017, p. 9).

The mainly technological understanding and debate about bioeconomy was also reflected in early critiques, such as Birch and Tyfield (2012). More recent work discussed below reflects the kind of wider understanding of the EU expert review group cited above but goes beyond that to address normative and ethical dimensions of bioeconomy development explicitly (Bryden *et al.*, 2017). In the latter, the "bioeconomy" is generally conceived as an economy based on land and marine-based natural resources including eco-systems services and bio-waste. The bioeconomy produces the most vital goods: food, drinking water, breathable air, and renewable building materials and energy as well as services like access to recreation. Increasingly, the bioeconomy is also seen as offering a green alternative to the fossil-fuel based economy that is largely responsible for climate change. The transition from the fossil fuel economy to the bioeconomy is a large and growing field for all forms of technical and institutional innovation.

The bioeconomy is not so new; in one sense it is as old as civilization, and with wide scope. This is hardly surprising, since it deals with most of the essentials of human life. However, in another sense which focuses on bio-*technologies*, it is very new and with narrower scope. A definition that includes both of these senses should be adopted. This is necessary because, however advanced the technologies involved, the use of biological raw materials frequently and commonly involves land, water, and marine-based biological resources, all of which are ultimately limited in supply, and usually have alternative uses that impact human rights (e.g. to food and water) and also common property.

Although there is no common agreement on the scope and content of the "bioeconomy", an EC public consultation paper states that

> a bio-based economy integrates the full range of natural and renewable biological resources – land and sea resources, biodiversity and biological material (plant, animal and microbial), through to the processing and the consumption of these bio-resources. The bioeconomy encompasses the agriculture, forestry, fisheries, food, and biotechnology sectors, as well as a wide range of industrial sectors, ranging from the production of energy and chemicals to building and transport.
>
> *(European Commission, 2011)*

Both the earlier OECD definitions (2009) and the slightly later one from the US (White House, 2012) put more stress on biotechnology. More recent official definitions include also at least the related waste streams of bioproducts. There are also good arguments for including services produced from the land and sea such as outdoor recreation and tourism, and ecosystem services (clean water and air) as well as public "bads" associated with all the relevant production systems. The definition used by the Finnish government in their Bioeconomy Strategy (Finland, 2014) comes closest to this:

> Bioeconomy refers to an economy that relies on renewable natural resources to produce food, energy, products and services. The bioeconomy will reduce our dependence on fossil natural resources, prevent biodiversity loss and create new economic growth and jobs in line with the principles of sustainable development.

This broad definition is also reflected in the Icelandic definition illustrated in Figure 28.1.

However, this diagram does not include the important areas of biowaste and ecosystem services. Including these dimensions allows a strong link with the so-called "circular economy" in which biowaste streams from one process are used as resource inputs for other processes and products. In common with most definitions of bioeconomy, it also omits the sun and wind, which are nevertheless important natural sources of renewable energy, if not strictly biological.

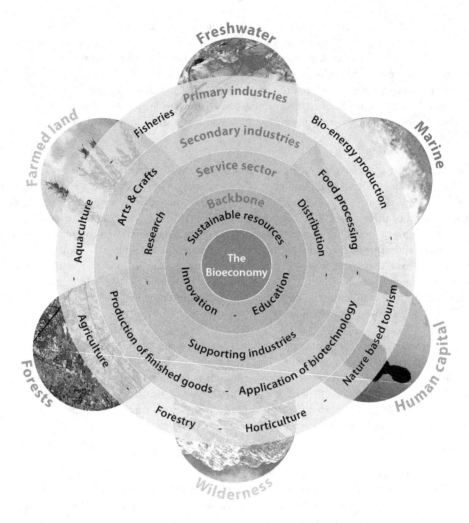

Figure 28.1 Icelandic definition of bioeconomy

According to Mikkola *et al.* (2016), the circular economy has two key interrelated features – retaining resources in the economy for as long as possible and reducing waste. The circular economy challenges traditional linear models of consumption where products are designed, manufactured, consumed, and then discarded. The circular economy aims to maximize use of renewable resources such as bioresources, ensure that they are first used for products of the highest social value,[1] and minimize or eliminate "waste" by incorporating waste streams in other processes. Thus, it is common to find clusters of firms producing different commodities but linked together by their respective waste or by-product streams through industrial symbiosis. Practical examples are to be found in the Kalundborg Symbiosis partnership in Denmark, the Örnsköldsvik cluster in Sweden and in many other similar initiatives (Mikkola *et al.*, 2016). In the circular economy, the by-products of one process or activity become the inputs to another. Thus, organic waste from households becomes bioenergy and fertilizer, or waste energy from industrial processes becomes district heating, to give two small examples.

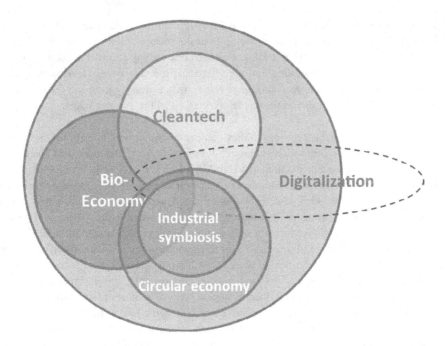

Figure 28.2 Central concepts within green growth

Figure 28.2 shows the overlapping concepts of bioeconomy, circular economy, cleantech, and industrial symbiosis within the frame of green growth

Why is the bioeconomy important for rural regions?

The bioeconomy is already large – especially if taking a wider definition of it – and its raw materials and often related manufacturing and other sectors, as well as the knowledge on management of the bioresources – e.g. among foresters, farmers and fishermen – are mostly located in rural regions. It is estimated that it is worth €2 trillion and provides over 17 million jobs or about 7 percent of the EU labor force (Ronzon *et al.*, 2015).

A recent report estimates that the total turnover of key bioeconomy sectors in the Nordic countries is some €184 billion, or 10 percent of the economy, Iceland being the highest at 18 percent and Norway the lowest at 6 percent (Nordic Innovation, 2014). In Finland, the recent *Bioeconomy Strategy* (Finland, 2014) puts the share of the bioeconomy in the national economy at over 16 percent, with an output currently exceeding €60 billion. In addition, it presently employs over 300,000 people. About half of the Finnish bioeconomy is forest-based. These figures exclude the share of the technology industry that can be classified as belonging to the bioeconomy. However, the objective of the Finnish *Bioeconomy Strategy* is to increase the output of the bioeconomy to €100 billion by 2025 and to create 100,000 jobs. In one rural region of Sweden – Örnsköldsvik – the bioeconomy is reckoned to provide some 25 percent of employment when secondary and tertiary impacts are taken into account (Teras *et al.*, 2014).

Moreover, despite the obvious fact that land and sea bioresources, and even biowastes, are ultimately limited in supply, surprising scope for production and harvesting still exists. According to Lange *et al.* (2015, p. 10).

Upgrade of biomass from waste fractions from agriculture, forestry and fisheries has huge potential for improved use of the biological resources. Globally, approximately 50% of the primary production is still not utilized but wasted. Biomass to bioenergy is already developed for up-scaling and commercialisation. However, development of biobased products into products of higher value, such as healthy food and feed ingredients, speciality chemicals and functional materials is still in its early stages.

Perhaps more important is the long-term policy commitment indicated by national bioeconomy strategies and panels in countries such as Finland, Iceland, Norway, Denmark, and Sweden, and by regional and local arrangements such as VINNVÄXT in Örnsköldsvik, Sweden.

The bioeconomy therefore offers considerable scope for environmentally friendly development in rural regions, producing added value for biological raw materials based on land, forests, and seas and their products and by-products; offering scope for enterprise and employment; and with vast scope for various forms of innovation, not only technological; perhaps above all, in the long run providing the knowledge and institutional means to move from the fossil fuel-based economy to the bioeconomy. However, such a benign transition will not happen without the correct guidance in the form of institutions, regulations, and policies. In particular, the institutional forms for innovation need to actively involve the local as well as national democratic structures, and citizens organizations, to ensure that the many public goods and rights related to the bioeconomy are recognized and respected, and that pathways are chosen that have positive social as well as environmental and economic outcomes. These aspects are considered further below.

Innovation – ideas and practice

This section turns to the ideas around innovation, inclusive innovation, and innovation systems, including modes of learning and ethical dimensions of innovation. It explicitly includes a discussion of the normative premises underpinning ideas of innovation and inclusion.

Bryden *et al.* (2017) argue that "innovation" should be defined generally as "new ways of doing things" (STEPS, 2010, p. 1), and that this perspective also suits the inclusive innovation discourse. "If 'inclusiveness' denotes improved lives for the most needy, 'innovation' should include those new ways of doing things – including technologies, institutions, and other things – that may improve the most needy's lives".

The authors argue that a simple but clear definition of the idea of "inclusive innovation" is "new ways of improving the lives of the most needy". This definition leaves the scope of "new ways" deliberately wide, including things no one has done before (e.g. *tele*-communication), better ways of doing things already done (e.g. the metal plough share replacing wood), and adaptation to contexts (e.g. frugal innovation in the field of vaccines, when resources are scarce) (Srinivas and Sutz, 2008). "New ways" may also include deliberate choices in the direction of research – for example dealing with the health-care problems of the poor, rather than those of the rich. Such deliberate choices can be stimulated by giving "prizes not patents" (Stiglitz, 2007), by research evaluation systems, and by the wording of research programs and related award criteria.

The term "inclusive innovation" reflects a concern among some scholars about how innovation affects, or may be affected by, underprivileged people (Cozzens and Sutz, 2012, 2014; Kaplinsky, 2011; STEPS, 2010). However, the term has several meanings. For example, Guth (2005) regards inclusiveness as a specific *result* of innovation: reduced economic inequality. Alternatively, Foster and Heeks (2013, p. 333) define inclusive innovation as "the means by which new goods and services are developed for and/or by the billions living on lowest incomes", highlighting underlying *intentions* and the *nature of the actors* involved. George *et al.* (2012, pp. 661–663), define inclusive innovation both as "innovation that benefits the disenfranchised" and, mainly, as "the development and implementation of new ideas which aspire to create opportunities that enhance social and economic well-being for disenfranchised members of society". In this way the authors stress both the intentions behind innovation, and the importance of its actual results. Foster and Heeks (2013, p. 335) have summarized the several forms of inclusivity found in the literature, highlighting four key aspects of inclusivity: that innovation agendas include problems relevant to the poor; that the poor participate in innovation; that innovations can be used by the poor; that innovations actually benefit the poor. Heeks *et al.* (2013, 2014) merged these understandings, pointing to the contrast between scholars who regard inclusive innovation as only a matter of outcomes and those who think it is also a matter of process. They propose a multi-level approach to the concept of inclusive innovation, which consists of intentions, consumption practices, impacts on the poor, participation in the innovation process, and structural characteristics of innovation's context.

However, Bryden *et al.* (2017) argue that it may be better to pursue "a concept of inclusive innovation that can be included in research questions, constitute a proper variable, and thus identify the research field clearly". A theory of inclusive innovation must explicate causal relationships and the multidimensional notion cannot do this because the major variables that would otherwise belong to a theory about inclusive innovation are included in the definition itself.

Defining the "inclusiveness" of "inclusive innovation"

Bryden *et al.* (2017) argue that a genuine concept of inclusive innovation must focus on the field's main concern, the concern that makes students of inclusive innovation think they have something in common. They suggest that the "inclusiveness" of inclusive innovation denotes improvements to the lives of the most needy and, further, that this is or should be the independent variable in any study of inclusive innovation. This understanding of inclusiveness accords with Guth's (2005) focus on tangible results of innovation, but it goes beyond improvements in economic equality to include general improvements. It further focuses attention on the third level of the inclusiveness ladder outlined by Heeks *et al.* (2013, p. 7). In this way, the concept is kept clear, simple, and measurable, rather than bundling a whole lot of different criteria together. If it is desired to investigate other criteria, such as the impact of participation of the poor in the innovation process on the most needy, then this can be done.

Bryden *et al.* use the term "the most needy" in a deliberately relative and general way, that may seem vague compared to the widely used "bottom of the pyramid" (BoP) criterion (Prahalad and Fruehauf, 2004; see also George *et al.*, 2012; Kaplinsky, 2011). However, the authors agree with Cozzens and Sutz (2012), and argue that BoP suffers from several defects, including that it "implies a limiting and uncontextualized focus on monetized income". Unlike "BoP", the term "the most needy", requires a contextualization of poverty. Like the UN Sustainable Development Goals, defining inclusion this way means that the question of innovation's inclusiveness also becomes relevant everywhere, even to richer countries where people experience relative rather than absolute deprivation

Given the definition suggested above, and acknowledging the important factors outlined by Heeks *et al.* (2014), major questions of the inclusive innovation discourse would be:

- What *kinds of innovation* may improve the lives of the most needy?
- Which *processes* may generate innovations that improve the lives of the most needy?
- Which *motivations* may generate innovations that improve the lives of the most needy?

- Under *what preconditions* (institutional or other) may innovations emerge that have the capacity to improve the lives of the most needy?
- Under what preconditions (institutional or other) do innovations *actually* improve the lives of the most needy?

This approach places the *institutional* preconditions for innovation's ability to improve the lives of the most needy firmly on the research agenda of inclusive innovation (Bryden *et al.*, 2017; see also Heeks *et al.*, 2013). Thus, new technology that enables poor people to produce more efficiently may not improve these people's lives unless they own their products, their incomes, and their time. The inclusiveness of innovation arguably depends on the institutional context of innovation – people's legal and customary rights, their access to governments, their access to markets, their control of resources such as organization and property – and addressing such contexts is vital to studies of inclusive innovation.

Modes of learning and the ethics of inclusiveness

The innovation discourse has always been shaped by largely tacit value premises, and the discourse on inclusive innovation reflects uneasiness about the most common of those (Bryden and Gezelius, 2017). The foregoing discussion of inclusive innovation partly reflects an ethical concern about innovation's legitimate purposes, raising another link with the design of institutions for innovation. Different groups of actors not only bring different kinds of knowledge and interests to the innovation process, but also different ethical values. For this and other reasons, Bryden and Gezelius hypothesize a causal relationship between structures for participation and innovation's inclusiveness. Two interlinked issues are discussed, and deal with the forms of knowledge that are important for a more inclusive innovation process, and with the notions of triple, quadruple, or n-tuple helices as a way of discussing who is involved, and what they bring to the innovation and learning process.

Until recently empirical and historical research into modes of learning discussed the role of users or customers on the one hand and firms or producers on the other (von Hippel, 1976; Rothwell, 1977; Rosenberg, 1982; Pavitt, 1984). Jensen *et al.* (2007) discuss the creative tension between two modes of innovation – Science, Technology and Innovation (STI) and Doing, Using and Interacting (DUI). However, the focus on interactions between firms/producers on the one hand and users/customers on the other – what Rosenberg (1982) called the "stochastic mode of learning" – may be too narrow in the context of "sustainable development", perhaps especially in relation to the bioeconomy. To develop this argument further, it is necessary to reflect on the ethical implications of the "modes of learning" literature. In his "Nicomachean Ethics", Aristotle considers the intellectual virtues through which knowledge is obtained, and his discussion is relevant here. In Book VI, he lists five types of "hexis" (stable dispositions) that a soul can have and which reveal "truth", truth being the ultimate goal of intellectual activity:

1. Art or "techne", sometimes, "craftsmanship". Making things for a purpose, in a deliberate and rational way, and involving both technical skills and thought. This is the equivalent of "DUI".
2. "Episteme" or scientific knowledge that is "teachable" and "learnable". The equivalent of "STI".
3. "Phronesis" or practical judgement involving skilled deliberation about right, prudent, or correct action, and involving applied "value-rationality" (Weber, 1921, 1978).

4   "Nous" or intellect, developed through experience, and giving aims and direction to "phronesis".
5   Sophia or wisdom – a combination of "nous" and "episteme".

Discussions of Aristotle's approach to knowledge generally focus on the first three of these forms – *techne, episteme,* and *phronesis.* There is a remarkable absence of attention to the third – *phronesis* – in debates on innovation. The inclusion of *phronesis* is important in relation to the inclusion of normative values, and those who have knowledge relating to normative questions, in the innovation process. In terms of the literature on innovation systems, it has important implications for debates on "triple", "quadruple", "quintuple", or "n-tuple" helix forms of innovation systems (see Etzkowitz and Leydensdorff, 1995; Edquist, 2004; Etzkowitz, 2003; Carayannis and Campbell, 2019, 2012).

An innovation systems helix can be characterized as portraying the different types of actor in an innovation system, traditionally portrayed by the triple helix whereby the three types of actor represent Firms, Academia, and Government (Etzkowitz and Leydensdorff, 1995; Etzkowitz, 2003). Carayannis and Campbell (2010) added Civil Society and the Media, to propose a quadruple helix. The focus was mainly on spheres of interest and activity in relation to knowledge production, which was assumed to occur in Academia but more – or less – supported by Government. Governments may also support firms in various ways. Firms translated knowledge and government support into innovations and GDP.

What the discussion of forms of knowledge brings to us is the notion that there are different forms of knowledge that are important in processes and outcomes – manufacturing firms, raw material suppliers, consumers, citizens and civil society organizations, governments, and academics possess – and indeed are responsible for, different kinds of knowledge. Equally, they have – or ought to have – different interests in the outcomes of innovation. To put it simply, firms have responsibility to shareholders; governments to society as a whole; consumers to themselves; civil society to the control of governments and the private sector in the interests of people. Both government and civil society have a large responsibility in relation to that missing partner in the triple helix when viewed as a knowledge system – phronesis, which may be fairly interpreted as "right action", notably what to do, why, what to prioritize, and how to do it in morally and ethically correct ways. Thus the quintuple helix proposed by Refsgaard *et al.* (2017) differs from other formulations such as Carayannis and Campbell (2012) in emphasizing the roles of local authorities and civil society, arguing, "It is through the involvement of authorities and citizens that the ethical values protecting interests of future generations and the underprivileged enter the innovation system and, thereby, increase the capacity of this system to make innovation inclusive and sustainable".

The types of actors involved in an innovation system thus bring different values, interests, capacities, as well as different forms of knowledge and responsibility to the system.

A new paradigm of innovation?

The research on grounded innovation in the bioeconomy (Bryden *et al.*, 2013) hypothesized that the quintuple helix could be an institutional mechanism to better ensure a sustainable "ethical triple bottom line" outcome from innovation and growth, and the research findings tend to support this hypothesis (Refsgaard *et al.*, 2017). Bryden (2015) therefore raised the question of whether one could argue that a "new paradigm" of innovation existed, which contrasted with the old paradigm.

The typical "quintuple helix" structure identified in this research includes five distinct types of actor, notably suppliers of bioresources/raw materials (typically foresters or farmers, but also sawmills, food processors and other sources of "waste" biomass materials); businesses/firms that transform those materials into energy (district heating, electricity, biofuels, biogas, pharmaceuticals, bioplastics, and chemicals etc.); local/regional authorities that create local regulations and so engage in "market-making" as well as being "responsible" to their electorate and therefore concerned with legitimacy, fairness, and other ethical and moral questions as well as local development and employment issues; one or more sources of formal knowledge, in some cases universities and research institutes, in others knowledge intermediaries such as extension agents, consultants, etc.; and finally, the civil society/citizens either as "customers" or through their civil society organizations. Figure 28.3 illustrates such structures.

Many examples of similar structures from around the world exist (e.g. STEPS, 2010; Fressoli *et al.*, 2014; Sheik, 2015; del Valle, 2015; Bortz and Thomas, 2017). The local action groups of the EU LEADER program also had similarities to a Grounded Innovation Platform (GRIP) in its earlier manifestations prior to "mainstreaming" (Bryden, 2011).

The "old paradigm" of innovation is thus primarily characterized as innovation mainly serving the private sector in its quest for international competitiveness through improvements in the productivity of labor and capital. State support for innovation has become almost wholly captured by this normative and largely tacit objective, which is nowadays barely discussed in critical terms. In contrast with Polanyi's notion of the market being "within" the state, the state is now within the market, a very powerful belief in Western market economies, especially the "Anglo-Saxon" and lately neoliberal countries of the UK, the US, Canada, and Australia. The state is seen as "subservient" to capital, serving its needs, rather than protecting citizens from the impacts of capitalism, for example on inequalities and the environment. Capital is in fact directing the focus of R&D through its close relationship with national and transnational policies, and firms and individual entrepreneurs and "innovators" are seen as the main actors and policy targets. The main and often the only indicators used to measure the "strength" of innovation,

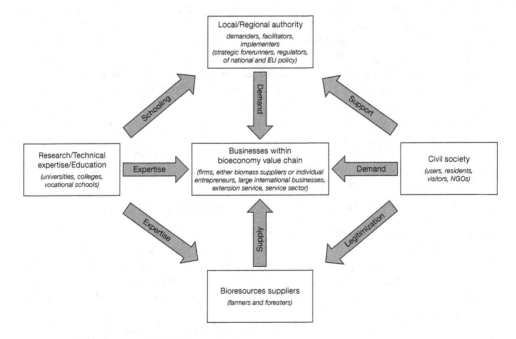

Figure 28.3 The quintuple helix in the Nordic bioeconomy

or the rank order of states, are the number of patents registered and the expenditure on research and development. The outcomes may be evaluated by growth in productivity or GDP.

The "new paradigm" stands in stark contrast to this. Based on the foregoing normative analysis, it is argued that innovation should serve citizens, and the state's activities and policies in relation to innovation should be based on the needs and priorities of citizens as expressed through civil and political society. The market and market actors are of course part of that civil and political society, but Polanyi (1944) argues that the market is within the state, rather than vice versa. Innovation is – or ought to be – thus driven by societal problems and priorities – especially "sustainable development". To summarize, the new innovation paradigm involves:

1   the state serving citizens; the market is within and not above the state;
2   the objectives are first and foremost *social; they are concerned with human well-being and the natural environment that sustains it; where these are codified in human rights they give priority to these;*
3   research and innovation as a *multi-actor collective learning process* which is *inclusive* in the sense that it includes all those with an interest in the outcomes, including those normally excluded from such processes. This is much wider than the notion of "including users" where "users" are considered as "customers";
4   innovation policies target and encourage multi-actor innovation platforms that are inclusive; these are called "Grounded Innovation Platforms" or "GRIPs" (Bryden *et al.*, 2013; Bryden and Gezelius, 2017; Bryden *et al.*, 2017);
5   the outcomes of innovation are assessed by triple bottom line (TBL) and human rights impacts.

The bioeconomy in Nordic countries

Since the scope of the bioeconomy crosses sectors and enterprises, and even involves parts of sectors such as "waste" where disaggregation is difficult, it is not easy to present hard statistics on such things as value-added and labor force. Several studies have been undertaken in the Nordic region, as well as other parts of the world, to assess its importance, and the Nordic and EU estimates have already been mentioned above. In addition, a number of studies have identified case studies that help us to understand how the bioeconomy is unfolding in different contexts. Some of these are summarized in Table 28.1.

Why benefits cannot be assumed to follow from bioeconomy development

As is the case with renewable energy (OECD, 2012), it cannot be taken for granted that any or all expected benefits that will flow from the development of the bioeconomy and related innovation activities will reach rural regions. The competing demands for the bioresources may be too great to allow further development – as where the food production is needed for human nutrition, for example. The prices, or extraction costs, of the raw materials may be too high to allow generation of a surplus. Regulations may be too rigid to allow the commercialization of important by-products (for example, wood ash, or biogas residues as fertilizers). Institutional arrangements, such as long-term private contracts for waste handling, may prevent the utilization of "free" raw materials. There may be opposition to certain processes that produce harmful or smelly particulate emissions. The prices of the end products may be too low because of competing products (chemical pharmaceuticals, oil, etc.). External ownership and property right rents may absorb a high proportion of any surplus. There will also be conflicts with other users

Table 28.1 Highlights in the Nordic bioeconomy

Country	Current situation	Future prospects
Denmark	12 percent of national energy consumption currently comes from agricultural and forest residues. Lolland case study – Community Testing Facility; Green Centre; Algae Innovation Centre. Search for synergy and integrated solutions. "Quadruple helix" approach.	Bioenergy could be at least quadrupled without significant impacts on food production. Considerable scope seen in the bioeconomy through synergy and industrial innovations including waste processing, biogas, new products and processes.
Finland and Åland	Bioeconomy currently provides 16 percent of national economy, with over €60 billion output and 300,000 employed. Importance of regional and municipal activities and policies. Good examples N. Karelia and Forssa regions.	Objective to increase output to €100bn and create 100,000 new jobs by 2025. About 50 percent of the Finnish bioeconomy is forest-based. Regional Strategies, e.g. Forssa Brightgreen Regional Strategy, including eco-industrial park, sees major potential for bioeconomy.
Iceland	Food industry, fishing and aquaculture dominate. 85 percent of the workplaces are outside the Reykjavik region. Food innovation and waste utilization key activities of state-owned Matis Ltd Innovation Centre (est. 2007).	Focus on blue (marine) bioeconomy including new nutrients, biomedicines and pharmaceutical products, and "pink Iceland" (bioeconomy services including bio-based tourism).
Norway	Fisheries and food industry dominate. Bioenergy mainly based on forest resources has increased, and accounts for about 9 percent of stationary energy cons. Targets not yet being met. Advanced biorefinery in southeast Norway – Borregård, with much interest in low cost enzyme production. Local municipal initiatives are also very important in Norway.	Major current research program is BIONÆR, with focus on forest and marine-based bioeconomy. The promotion of interdisciplinary research is seen as important in this context. Key institutional barriers in implementation remain.
Sweden	Bioenergy based on forest, agricultural residues and waste accounts for some 25 percent of total energy production in Sweden, and fossil fuels for heating have been almost totally replaced by bioenergy. 9.8 percent of transport energy is also renewable, mainly based on biofuels and biogas. Innovative bioeconomy projects include the Örnsköldsvik biorefinery cluster, and Inventia (advanced biomaterials).	Swedish R&I strategy for a bio-based economy (2012) uses cross-sectoral and life-cycle approaches. Sees considerable future potential e.g. in transport fuels, chemicals, biomaterials.

Source: Based mainly on Teras *et al.* (2014) and Nordic Council of Ministers (2017).

of natural resources and the land, water bodies, and sea from whence they come. There are common access rights for people in Nordic countries and Scotland, and also rights to take berries, fungi, and related foodstuffs as well as to engage in recreational activities and to camp. There may also be common rights in relation to hunting and fishing. And there are nature lovers. Nor will the intensive exploitation and use of biological resources be without other negative impacts, such as particulate pollution from burning biomass. These and other barriers can prevent or at least slow up or minimize the development of the bioeconomy and affect its local and global impacts.

The crucial role of the public sector

Public policies and governance play a key role in determining the scale, locus, and distribution of such benefits and potential costs. The frequently negative public attitudes towards bioeconomy developments also depend on the related outcomes and processes, and may be such as to prevent any, or further, development of the sector. For these reasons, if for no others, the role of the public authorities is critical. The form this role takes is discussed from the case studies on which this chapter is based. The role of the public sector at national and regional or local levels has been and remains crucial in the Nordic countries, and without active local/regional involvement and active policies the bioeconomy would be much less advanced than it is today.

Public policies in support of locally managed bioeconomy innovation and development in the Nordic countries

Local developments in the Nordic bioeconomy are heavily influenced by both national and EU policies. In this respect, the Nordics are particularly important for EU policies, and vice versa. The Nordic countries account for some one-third of European forest resource. They have also been leaders in renewable energy, CO_2 taxation, bioenergy, and the development of a bioeconomy as a (partial) replacement for fossil fuels. They thus play a crucial role in the development of the European low carbon and circular bioeconomy. Equally, they must ensure that they have an appropriate weight in EU policy development. That makes it important for them to work together and make common cause in EU negotiations. This is especially true for Norway, being an EEA but not an EU member state, and therefore having little say in policy formation on its own.

Forests and forest industries are also very important for Nordic rural and regional development, including in the peripheral regions. The new provisions in the proposed EU Renewable Energy Directive (RED) for the period 2020 on, dealing with the role of bioenergy in local and regional development, and not present in the first RED, are therefore welcomed by those working to combine bioeconomy efforts with rural and regional development and innovation efforts. It is important that policies also consider rural development impacts of the transition to a bioeconomy, and seek to optimize environmental, social, and economic outcomes for rural areas and people. According to the authors' research, Norway lags behind Sweden and Finland with respect to bioenergy development at national and local levels. Norway, although not a member of the EU, is by virtue of its EEA agreement, subject to the EU regulations on renewable energy. The new RED provisions make it important for Norwegian policy-makers to recognize the need for an enabling framework where specific regional and local conditions can be taken into account, local authorities are empowered, and local initiative can flourish. In this respect, Norway could learn much from both Sweden and Finland about such things as how to empower local authorities and encourage quintuple-helix-type structures for bioenergy and bioeconomy developments at local levels, how to ensure a beneficial and synergistic circular bioeconomy, how to apply the cascading principle in locally and regionally sensitive ways, and in many other relevant areas (Bryden *et al.*, 2017).

This research in the Nordic countries shows that the precise nature and level of CO_2 taxes is a key determinant of the switch from fossil fuel-based energy to hydro, bio, wind, and solar energy. These taxes are shown to be much more effective than market-based measures, such as the development of carbon markets. In addition to national carbon taxes there are commonly a set of rules, including those demanding that a certain proportion of fossil-based fuels such as gasoline and diesel comprise liquid biofuels – such rules provide a certainty of a more or less known market in any country or group of countries, such as the EU. Governments and the EU also fund research and set priorities for research over varying periods of time. Renewable energy in general, and more recently the bioeconomy, which has overlaps with the field of energy, has had fairly high priority in the Nordics and at the EU level in recent programming periods. National governments can also do small things to help, such as easing regulations and procedures around the use of wood ash – a by-product from burning waste wood for bioenergy – for purposes of fertilization of soil.

Much of the action in the field of bioeconomy and bioenergy is initiated and developed at local levels by a range of different types of organization, both formal and informal, but most commonly with a quintuple helix form of the type already discussed. National governments can, and some do, support the creation of such groupings. However, most support at present seems to come mainly "in kind" and mostly from local governments. National governments do need to give authority to local governments to take decisions in this area, a process which is sometimes stopped in its tracks by centralization. It is mainly local initiatives that have created the examples of circular bioeconomy, with re-use of former waste streams, clustering of interlinked investments, and so on. Local governments help to make and maintain markets for bioenergy, both by leading the way with their own buildings, and by infrastructure investments – e.g. district heating piping. In many cases local authorities lead the way towards a new more sustainable economy and make this into a selling point for the tourist and visitor economy, for new residents, and so on. Another important finding is that local governments create legitimacy for bioeconomy activities by designing initiatives to meet local needs and conditions, avoid environmental bads, and enabling knowledge transfer and exchange. Local authorities can also ensure that local issues are reflected at regional and national levels when necessary.

Some of the facilitating frameworks for bioeconomy innovation and development in the Nordic countries are summarized in Table 28.2.

Conclusions

Innovation is no longer seen mainly as the act of a single inventor or entrepreneur, but rather as a collective and cooperative process involving a range of different types of actor. These different actors bring different forms of knowledge as well as capital, interests, and power to the innovation process.

All innovation-related policies incorporate overt or hidden values, and this fact, together with the critical impacts that innovation has on different groups in society, including importantly the poor, means that the normative assumptions and their ethical foundations need to be closely examined. It is no longer acceptable, in a world of growing inequalities of wealth and income, to avoid questions of an innovation's purpose, its directions, and its societal impacts.

Some central conclusions about the innovation processes in the bioeconomy from the Nordic experience are:

Table 28.2 Facilitating policy frameworks in select Nordic countries

Country/region	National	Local/regional
Sweden, Örnsköldsvik municipality and wider region	National Bioeconomy Strategy. VINNOVA (Public agency for innovation systems) via VINNVAXT program for regional specialisms.	Biofuel region platform for four northern counties. Local municipal adoption of ethanol buses, and municipal DH. Development of local vision and brand. Municipal and national support for the Biorefinery of the Future Cluster, with quad helix form. Establishment of regional pilot process plants in Umeo and Örnsköldsvik.
Finland, Forssa	National Bioeconomy Strategy 2014. Key national funding support bodies, SITRA and Tekes.	Started in 1990s with new municipal dump and waste management company LHJ. Local company first biogas from waste and food-processing by-products. Envi eco-industrial park; Forssa Envitech club (2006). Forssa cluster cooperation. Brightgreen Forssa concept, as a brand. Bioeconomy and sustainable use of natural resources one of five strategic foci in Hame Regions Strategy 2013–2014.
Denmark, Lolland	Focus on green and sustainable development since the 1990s. Vestas (wind turbines) a world leader.	Lolland Community Testing Facility (CTF) developed 2007. Development of innovative partnerships including community (quadruple helix). Co-creation with culture development, innovation platforms, meetings, and networking. Regional Advisory Group developing ideas for bioeconomy. Membership of national innovation networks. Green Centre, Lolland established 1988, started Algae Innovation Centre with Aalborg and Roskilde Universities.

Source: Based mainly on Teras *et al.* (2014), augmented by interviews in Örnsköldsvik undertaken during the Triborn project.

1   The importance of long-term commitment and policy stability.
2   There are few "low hanging fruits" – as the bioeconomy represents a paradigm shift there are infant industry arguments, and a need to adjust the rules of the game through regulatory and fiscal measures (C and N-taxes etc.) as well as long-term public investments.
3   Need for innovation platforms with quintuple helix form. People – citizens, consumers, inhabitants – must be involved as well as industrial firms, raw materials producers, municipalities, and R&D providers to protect and promote the many societal and public interests involved.

4 Actions at local and regional levels are probably critical for success in the long run, although wider networking, lobbying, involvements are important.

5 There are important roles for national and local (municipal/regional) public policies, including:

    i   public investments in R&D, networks, clusters, innovation platforms, testing and up-scaling facilities;

    ii   stimulating and coordinating synergies between sectors, processes, and actors;

    iii regulations – e.g. for building and planning; energy in buildings; waste management; use of recycled by-products e.g. from bio heat and bio gas, etc.;

    iv tax rules – e.g. carbon taxes and pollution taxes such as N-taxes;

    v   incentives – for R&D, investment in new risky products, collaboration etc.;

    vi branding – green and sustainable products and services.

The quintuple helix as proposed by Refsgaard *et al.* (2017) and Bryden *et al.* (2017), may represent a new paradigm of innovation designed for a more sustainable world and a more human development.

Note

1 Social value is not the same thing as "market price" because it takes into account the value of social goods and services such as employment, environment, fair distribution of costs and rewards as well as the costs of social damage, for example to ecosystem services

References

Berlina, A., Mikkola, N., 2017. *Bioenergy development in Finland and Sweden: The cases of North Karelia, Jämtland, and Västernorrland*. Nordregio Working Paper No. 2017:6. Nordregio, Stockholm. www.diva-portal.org/smash/get/diva2:1147107/FULLTEXT02.pdf.

Birch, K., Tyfield, D., 2012. *Theorizing the bioeconomy: Biovalue, biocapital, bioeconomics or … what?* Science, Technology and Human Values 38(3), 299–327.

Bortz, G., Thomas, H., 2017. *Biotechnologies for inclusive development: Scaling-up, knowledge intensity and empowerment (the case of the probiotic yoghurt "Yogurito" in Argentina)*. Innovation and Development 7(1), 37–61.

Brundtland Commission, 1987. *Report of the World Commission on Environment and Development: Our common future*. United Nations.

Bryden, J., 2015. *New paradigms of innovation in the rural bioeconomy*. Keynote address, VI International Scientific Agriculture Symposium Agro-Sym 2015, October 15–18, Jahorina, Bosnia and Herzegovina.

Bryden, J., Gezelius, S., 2017. *Innovation as if people mattered*. Innovation and Development 7(1), 101–118.

Bryden, J.M., Johnson, T., Thomson, K.J., Ferenczi, T., 2011. *Modelling multifunctionality, territorial development, and policy scenarios in rural Europe: An alternative perspective on CAP reform*. EuroChoices 10(1), 9–16.

Bryden, J., Gezelius, S.S., Refsgaard, K., 2013. *Governing innovation for sustainable development: Designing creative institutions*. NILF Working Paper No. 5-2013. NILF, Oslo.

Bryden, J., Gezelius, S., Refsgaard, K., Sutz, J., 2017. *Inclusive innovation in the bioeconomy: Concepts and directions for research*. Innovation and Development 7(1), 1–16.

Carayannis, E., Campbell, D.F.J., 2009. *"Mode 3" and "Quadruple Helix": Toward a 21st century fractal innovation ecosystem*. International Journal of Technology Management 46(3/4), 201–234.

Carayannis, E.G., Campbell, D.F.J., 2010. *Triple helix, quadruple helix and quintuple helix and how do knowledge, innovation and the environment relate to each other?* International Journal of Social Ecology and Sustainable Development 1(1), 41–69.

Carayannis, E., Campbell, D.F.J., 2012. *Mode 3 knowledge production in quadruple helix innovation systems*. Springer, New York.

Cavicchi, B., 2016. *The burden of sustainability: Obstacles to bioheat development in Norway. Evidence from Hedmark county*. Conference Paper SPRU seminar, Falmer, UK.

Cavicchi, B., Palmieri, S., Odaldi, M., 2017. *The influence of local governance: Effects on the sustainability of bioenergy innovation*. Sustainability 9(3), 406. https://doi.org/10.3390/su9030406.

Cozzens, S., Sutz, J., 2012. *Executive summary – Innovation in informal settings: A research agenda*. https://idl-bnc-idrc.dspacedirect.org/handle/10625/50560.

Cozzens, S., Sutz, J., 2014. *Innovation in informal settings: Reflections and proposals for a research agenda*. Innovation and Development 4(1), 5–31.

del Valle, A., 2015. *Building a rural future in Valparaiso, Chile via "Participatory Innovation": Methodical governance of complexity as a seed for post-neoliberal policy*. Presented at the ESRS Congress, August, Aberdeen.

Edquist, C., 2004. *Systems of innovation: A critical review of the state of the art*, in: Fagerberg, J., Mowery, D., Nelson, R. (Eds.), *Handbook of innovation*. Oxford University Press, Oxford, pp. 181–208.

Etzkowitz, H., 2003. *Innovation in innovation: The triple helix of university–industry–government relations* 42(3), 293–337.

Etzkowitz, H., Leydensdorff, L., 1995. *The triple helix: University–industry–government relations: A laboratory for knowledge based economic development*. EASST Review 14(1), 14–19.

European Commission, 2011. *Public consultation on the bio-based economy for Europe: State of play and future potential*. Parts 1 and 2. https://ec.europa.eu/research/consultations/bioeconomy/bio-based-economy-for-europe-part1.pdf; https://ec.europa.eu/research/consultations/bioeconomy/bio-based-economy-for-europe-part2.pdf (accessed 2.12.18).

European Commission, 2012. *Innovating for sustainable growth: A bioeconomy for Europe*. COM/2012/060final. http://eur-lex.europa.eu/legal-content/EN/TXT/?uri=COM:2012:0060:FIN (accessed 2.12.18).

European Commission, 2017. *Expert group report review of the EU bioeconomy strategy and its action plan*. Directorate-General for Research and Innovation. https://ec.europa.eu/research/bioeconomy/pdf/publications/bioeconomy_expert_group_report.pdf.

Finland, 2014. *Finnish bioeconomy strategy*. Ministry of Employment and Industry. biotalous.fi/wp-content/.../2014/.../The_Finnish_Bioeconomy_Strategy_110620141.p ...

Foster, C., Heeks, R., 2013. *Conceptualising inclusive innovation: Modifying systems of innovation frameworks to understand diffusion of new technology to low-income consumers*. European Journal of Development Research 25(3), 333–355.

Fressoli, M., Arund, E., Abrol, D., Smith, A., Ely, A., 2014. *When grassroots innovation movements encounter mainstream institutions: Implications for models of inclusive innovation*. Innovation and Development 4(2), 277–292.

George, G., McGahan, A.M., Prabhu, J., 2012. *Innovation for inclusive growth: Towards a theoretical framework and a research agenda*. Journal of Management Studies 49(4), 661–683.

Glaser, B.G., Strauss, A.L., 1967. *Grounded theory: Strategies for qualitative research*. Aldine; Transaction Press, London; New Brunswick, NJ.

Guth, M., 2005. *Innovation, social inclusion and coherent regional development: A new diamond for socially inclusive innovation policy in regions*. European Planning Studies 13(2), 333–349.

Hart, J.K., Laville, J.L., Cattani, A.D., 2010. *The human economy*. Polity Press, Cambridge.

Heeks, R., Amalia, M., Kintu, R., Shah, N., 2013. *Inclusive innovation: Definition, conceptualisation and future research priorities*. Development Informatics Working Paper No. 53. Centre for Development Informatics, Manchester.

Heeks, R., Foster, C., Nugroho, Y., 2014. *New models of inclusive innovation for development*. Innovation and Development 4(2), 175–185.

Jensen, M.B., Johnson, B., Lorenz, E., Lundvall, B.A., 2007. *Forms of knowledge and modes of innovation*. Research Policy 36(5), 680–693.

Kaplinsky, R., 2011. *Bottom of the pyramid: Innovation and pro-poor growth*. World Bank, Washington, DC.

Lange, L., Björnsdóttir, B., Brandt, A., Hildén, K., Hreggviðsson, G., Jacobsen, B., Jessen, A., Nordberg Karlsson, E., Lindedam, J., Mäkelä, M., Smáradóttjs, S., Vang, J., Wentzel, A., 2004. *Development of the Nordic bioeconomy NCM reporting: Test centers for green energy solutions: Biorefineries and business needs*. (TemaNord 2017:582). Nordic Council of Ministers, Copenhagen.

Lundvall, B.-A., 1988. *Innovation as an interactive process: From user–producer interaction to the national innovation systems*, in: Lundvall, B.-A., *The Learning Economy and the Economics of Hope*. Anthem Press, London, 61–84.

Lundvall, B.-A., 1992. *National systems of innovation: Towards a theory of innovation and interactive learning*. Pinter Publishers, London.

Mikkola, N., Randall, L., Hagberg, A., 2016. *Green growth in Nordic regions: 50 ways to make it happen.* Nordregio, Stockholm.

Nordic Council of Ministers, 2017. *Nordic bioeconomy: 25 cases for sustainable change.* Copenhagen.

Nordic Innovation, 2014. *Creating value from bioresources: Innovation in Nordic bioeconomy.* Nordic Innovation Publication, Oslo.

OECD, 2001. *The application of biotechnology to industrial sustainability.* OECD, Paris. www.oecd.org/dataoecd/61/13/1947629.pdf.

OECD, 2009. *The bioeconomy to 2030: Designing a policy agenda, main findings.* OECD, Paris.

OECD, 2012. *Linking renewable energy to rural development.* OECD, Paris.

Pavitt, K., 1984. *Sectoral patterns of technical change: Towards a taxonomy and a theory.* Research Policy 13(6), 343–373.

Polanyi, K., 1944 (2001 edition). *The great transformation: The political and economic origins of our time.* Beacon Press, Boston, MA (originally published in New York by Farrar & Reinhart).

Prahalad, C., Fruehauf, H., 2004. *The fortune at the bottom of the pyramid.* Wharton School Publishing, Philadelphia, PA.

Refsgaard, K., Bryden, J., Kvakkestad, 2017. *Towards inclusive innovation praxis in forest-based bioenergy.* Innovation and Development 7(1), 153–173.

Ronzon, T., Santini, F., M'Barek, R., 2015. *The bioeconomy in the European Union in numbers: Facts and figures on biomass, turnover and employment.* European Commission, Joint Research Centre, Institute for Prospective Technological Studies, Spain.

Rosenberg, N., 1982. *Inside the black box: Technology and economics.* University of Illinois at Urbana-Champaign's Academy for Entrepreneurial Leadership Historical Research Reference in Entrepreneurship. Available at SSRN: https://ssrn.com/abstract=1496197.

Rothwell, R., 1977. *The characteristics of successful innovators and technically progressive firms (with some comments on innovation research).* R&D Management 7(3), 191–206.

Sheik, F.A., 2015. *Policymaking for innovations in the informal economy: Insights from National Innovation Foundation and Barefoot College of India.* Paper presented at the Globelics Conference, Havana, Cuba, September 2015.

Srinivas, S., Sutz, J., 2008. *Developing countries and innovation: Searching for a new analytical approach.* Technology in Society 30, 129–140.

STEPS, 2010. *Innovation, sustainability, development: A new manifesto.* STEPS Centre, Brighton.

Stiglitz, J.E., 2007. *Prizes, not patents.* Project Syndicate, March 6. www.project-syndicate.org/commentary/prizes--not-patents?barrier=accesspaylog.

Teras, J., Lindberg, G., Johnsen, I.H.G., Perjo, L., Giacometti, A., 2014. *Bioeconomy in the Nordic region.* Nordregio Working Paper No. 2014:4. Nordregio, Stockholm.

Ustyuzhantseva, O., 2017. *Studies of inclusive innovation in sociotechnical systems: Case studies in Russia and India Special Issue.* Innovation and Development 7(1), 83–100.

Von Hippel, E., 1976. *The dominant role of users in the scientific instrument innovation process.* Research Policy 5(3), 212–239.

Weber, M., 1921. *Gesammelte Politische Schriften,* Drei Masten Verlag, Munich.

Weber, M., 1978. *Economy and society.* University of California Press, Oakland, CA.

White House, 2012. *National bioeconomy blueprint.* April. https://obamawhitehouse.archives.gov/sites/default/files/microsites/ostp/national_bioeconomy_blueprint_april_2012.pdf.

29

INNOVATION, BROADBAND, AND COMMUNITY RESILIENCE

William Ashton and Wayne Kelly

Resilience has emerged as a dynamic community-development concept that is examined here in light of the new digital economy. Resilience is rooted in the ability to remain productive after a dramatic event, like the largest recorded flood in 2011 in the province affecting much of southern Manitoba, Canada. This chapter explores how resilience as a concept might fare with more persistent and vigorous economic and social challenges, rather than a natural disaster. Key characteristics of resilience, as defined by Ashmore *et al.* (2016), form an analytic framework to two critical and contemporary economic drivers in rural communities, namely innovation and broadband. Comparisons between case studies and among nation-states and their respective policies illustrate commonalities and differences in Canada, Europe, and the United States. Each example adds to this analysis of resilience, which is focused on the needs of communities.

Community resilience

Communities need to be increasingly resilient today, as they face significant challenges. Many pressures are exerted beyond these communities' locus of control – from climate change to development of digital technologies and the emerging digital economy – which in turn often create great uncertainty and put many communities in unfamiliar territory. Resilience is the capacity and ability of communities to recover from difficulties and adapt to change, crisis or shock (Besser, 2013; Magis, 2007). Resilient communities do not just survive but continue to evolve with an aim to thrive in change (Magis, 2010). Too often rural communities struggle in their pursuit of specific growth strategies or goals, only to have an uncontrollable event derail their efforts. These events can range from the unexpected closure of an industry, to removal of a regional government office in order to centralize or rationalize services, to a new trade deal with reductions in production and staff; or a catastrophic flood as experienced across southern parts of Manitoba and Saskatchewan in 2011. These events undeniably impact rural communities. In the aftermath, previous plans and established visions can be rendered irrelevant in the face of new realities. As a result, local and regional leaders need the ability to adapt strategies, plans, and projects with the inclusion of flexibility (Steiner *et al.*, 2018).

The concept of resilience is evident across many disciplines, from ecology, health and individual wellness, social sciences, and engineering, to rural and community development. It was adapted from physics to understand how ecosystems adapt and thrive when disturbed, including the upside of forest fires (Holling, 1973). The concept has been applied to individuals, groups, and communities and their ability to recover and move on, which may include a new trajectory under different circumstances (Ashmore *et al.*, 2015; Norris *et al.*, 2008). Community resilience does not refer to the absence of development plans or leadership; it focuses on communities having the ability to adjust and to pursue modified or new challenges and opportunities. In the midst of rapid and devastating change, it is not always communities with more resources or government support that spring back; instead research has found that communities able to adapt in the face of new conditions recover best (Sherrieb *et al.*, 2010; Wilding, 2011).

As the field of community resilience grows, more attention is being given to developing resilience ahead of a possible major event. Magis (2010) provided evidence of community resilience being developed intentionally through planning, collective action, innovation, and learning. Community resilience is part of larger territorial development strategies and policies in Scotland and the UK for building the strength and capacity of rural communities (Sherrieb *et al.*, 2010). Similarly, Infrastructure Canada, a federal government agency, has a goal of resilience with stronger and more inclusive communities, while responding to unique and wide-ranging public infrastructure needs (Government of Canada, 2017). Another suggested characteristic of resilience is manifested in a diverse local economy and business sector (Besser, 2013; Steiner and Atterton, 2014), including the potential of the creative class (Roberts and Townsend, 2015). Strategies and activities will often require revision following an event, which may well emphasize a different trajectory.

Time magazine crowned "resilience" the 2013 term of the year (Walsh, 2013). For some, this recognition serves to illustrate a major concern – while it is a widely used term, resilience as a concept is criticized since it lacks a specific and unifying method of assessing resilience (Anderson, 2015; Scott, 2013). Others critique resilience since it glosses over the power structures in decision-making, and definitions lack specifics about the redistribution of wealth (McKinnon and Derickson, 2012; Roberts *et al.*, 2017a). In short, these and other criticisms point to the need to define who the resilience is for and what the community context is (Côte and Nightingale, 2012). Nevertheless, existing work in the arena of community resilience provides insights into how rural communities prepare for and address development challenges and opportunities, as well as unexpected events (Roberts *et al.*, 2017a). To help illustrate the range and development in definitions of community resilience over the last decade, eight examples are summarized in Table 29.1. These introduce the concept by Ashmore *et al.* (2016) and form the basis for the community resilience framework of this chapter.

Table 29.1 Eight examples that help define community resilience

Resource	Background	Definition	Characteristics of community resilience
Brennan (2008)	Examines community resiliency and agency within a child-care context. Builds on Luloff, Bridger and Wilkson's work on agency and field theory	*The ability to respond or perform positively in the face of adversity, to achieve despite the presence of disadvantages, or to significantly exceed expectations under given negative circumstances*	Community-level resiliency is shaped by a variety of conditions – social controls, local adaptive capacities, networks, and infrastructures and alliances – that allow the community to plan for its needs and build on its strengths

Resource	Background	Definition	Characteristics of community resilience
Norris *et al.* (2008)	Develops a model and strategy for effective disaster readiness and response. This model is based on a literature review that incorporates a wide range of academic fields from psychology to ecology to technology and communications	*A process linking a set of adaptive capacities to a positive trajectory of functioning and adaptation after a disturbance*	Community resilience is based on four adaptive capacities: • economic development • information and communication • community competence • social capital
Magis (2007, 2010)	Conducts a comprehensive and cross-sectoral review of resilience literature for a department of natural resources in the US, which has resulted in one of the more accepted definitions and overviews of community resilience	*Community resilience is the existence, development, and engagement of community resources to thrive in a dynamic environment characterized by change, uncertainty, unpredictability, and surprise. Resilient communities intentionally develop personal and collective capacity to respond to and influence change, to sustain and renew the community, and to develop new trajectories for the community's future*	The community resilience dimensions are: • community resources • development of community resources • engagement of community resources • active agents • collective action • strategic action • equity • impact
Khanlou and Wray (2014)	Conducts a literature review of Canadian-based research in medical disciplines to understand how resilience is connected to child and youth mental health; community and family resilience emerged as one of the key factors in their review	*Resilience is not just a personality trait or attribute of an individual. Rather, resilience is most often viewed as a process that refers to exposure to adversity and "positive" adaptation*	Resilience should be considered as: • a process rather than a single event • a continuum rather than either/or • a global concept with specific local dimensions Factors associated with resilience: • individual or micro-level resilience • family or meso-level resilience • social, environmental, or macro-level resilience

continued

Table 29.1 Continued

Resource	Background	Definition	Characteristics of community resilience
Wilding (2011)	Develops a tool kit and practitioner-focused model of community resilience for Carnegie UK Trust to help communities understand and self-assess their own resilience; a wide range of academic literature and community examples were used to develop the model	*Purposefully avoids defining resilience but cites its importance for responding to social, economic, and environmental disruptions; likens resilience to a muscle which, when exercised, builds both strength and capacity*	Builds on four themes related to resilient communities: • healthy people • inclusive, creative culture • localized economy • cross-community links
Heeks and Ospina (2015)	Adapts Sen's capabilities and the sustainable livelihoods approach to create a comprehensive resilience framework related to community informatics or digital technologies – the emphasis, however, is on urban neighborhoods in developing countries	*Resilience means the ability to withstand and recover from short-term shocks and to adapt to long-term trends*	Foundational properties of community resilience: • robustness • self-organization • learning Enabling sub-properties of community resilience: • redundancy • rapidity • scale • diversity • flexibility • equality
Ashmore *et al.* (2016)	Builds a community resilience framework to better understand rural broadband initiatives and applies this framework in rural and remote regions of the UK	Uses definition from Magis (2010, p. 402): *the existence, development and engagement of community resources by community members to thrive in an environment characterized by change, uncertainty, unpredictability and surprise*	A core framework is developed that is built on: • community capital • agency and leadership • sense of place
Roberts *et al.* (2017a)	Explores three motifs in resilience to better understand rural–digital agendas and related policies	Uses definition from Magis (2010, p. 402): *the existence, development and engagement of community resources by community members ... [who] ... intentionally develop personal and collective capacity to respond to and influence change, to sustain and renew the community and to develop new trajectories for the community's future*	Three key areas of resilience are: • multi-scalar: resilience happens at many levels • normative: resilience takes place within cultural and political contexts • integrated: the need to take a holistic approach based on local context and knowledge

Community resilience framework

Of the community resilience definitions and characteristics in Table 29.1, those of Ashmore *et al.* (2016) are utilized to form an analytic framework for this discussion. Ashmore *et al.* wanted to better understand initiatives in rural and remote UK. Their body of work builds on Magis' (2010) research to engage local resources by local members who are confronted with uncertainty, unpredictability, and surprise. Ashmore *et al.*'s (2016) framework consists of three core elements: community resources or capitals, agency, and sense of place.

- *Community capitals*: community capitals range from human capacity and knowledge to build physical infrastructure, and include political, social, financial, and cultural capital. Each is briefly defined in Table 29.2.
- *Agency*: the capacity to act, also referred to as agency, is detected by evidence of leadership, resourcefulness, and the intent to change (Brennan, 2008; Magis, 2010; Roberts and Townsend, 2015). Acknowledging that power issues and inclusive participation can be a challenge when building resilience, the authors of the framework stress the need for multi-level participation that is inclusive and builds on strong leadership among many rather than relying solely on individuals for decision-making (Ashmore *et al.*, 2016).
- *Sense of place*: given the distinctive realities of rural communities and regions, it is essential to understand resilience within specific place-based contexts, which helps inform local and regional strategies and development (Markey *et al.*, 2015b; Roberts *et al.*, 2015; Wilson, 2012). In turn, for a given place, one can also ask the question of resilience *for whom?* (Côte and Nightingale, 2012; Roberts *et al.*, 2017a).

A fourth important characteristic in community resiliency is a strong and diverse local economy (Bentley and Pugalis, 2013; Noya and Clarence, 2009; Wilding, 2011). Such an economy is defined by initiatives often coming from within the community; by more decentralized, vertical cooperation among government tiers, and horizontal cooperation among public, private, and NGO sectors; by being more place-based on sectoral strategies and investments; by drawing on resources to stimulate progress adjustment; and by creating conditions of balanced economic, social, and environmental development (FCM, 2014). Diverse local economies can

Table 29.2 Seven forms of capital are drawn upon in a community resilience framework

Capital	Description
Human	Population, education, skills, health, creativity, youth, diverse groups
Social	Trust, norms of reciprocity, network structure, group membership, cooperation, common vision and goals, leadership, acceptance of diversity
Political	Level of community organization through the use of government; ability of government to garner resources for the community
Cultural	Values, heritage recognition and celebration
Financial	Tax burden/savings, state and federal tax monies, philanthropic donations, grants, contracts, regulatory exemption, investments, reallocation, loans, poverty rates
Built	Housing, transportation infrastructure, telecommunications infrastructure and hardware, utilities, buildings
Natural	Air, land and water quality, natural resources, biodiversity, scenery

Source: Emery and Flora (2006).

contribute to community resiliency by harnessing and building community resources including human capacity; by ensuring that the community is not reliant on a single industry, so it is less susceptible to the closure of that industry; and by increasing the appeal of a community for both work and tourism (Steiner and Atterton, 2014). At the provincial level, the impact of the 2008–2009 financial crisis was mostly averted because of a diversified mix of primary industries, manufacturing, and services, which made Manitoba largely recession-resistant (Dowell, 2015). Yet, many other provinces were not able to avert the crisis, and this crisis situation repeated in many other countries around the world. The point is that a diversified economy may not grow as quickly, but it may not be subject to rapid downturn, either; hence it is more resilient to the broader ebbs and flows of unpredictable economic conditions and other variables.

Communities can diversify their local and regional economies by emphasizing value-added product development and/or new agriculture crop production, by expanding the variety of local industries or by building knowledge-based local businesses (Steiner and Atterton, 2014). The local business owners can contribute to the leadership and resourcefulness of communities through harnessing the capacity within local businesses to help address community growth and opportunities (Roberts and Townsend, 2015).

Economic drivers are used to better understand these four characteristics of this community resilience framework. Of particular interest are drivers that at times can be disruptive (similar to an unpredicted major event), while at other times they can bring about more incremental growth that if not managed can lead to challenges and missed opportunities. Two such examples of economic drivers that are relevant today and into the future for rural communities are innovation and rural broadband. Both can create sudden change and opportunity, including when a start-up business creates new jobs or a new product line brings in new marketing jobs. Equally impressive is "the last mile" (the final leg or piece of internet infrastructure that connects to homes, businesses, or organizations) as communities connect to broadband and the digital economy door opens. As these economic drivers emerge and become critical for rural communities, it is vital to explore how they relate to resilience and if they improve the capacity and ability of rural communities to withstand future changes. They also provide tools for managing and adapting to ongoing change, mirroring the dual nature of resilience as both a goal and a process. The following sections explore how innovation and digital technologies like rural broadband are related to community resilience and their potential impact.

Innovation and community resilience

In a 2017 analysis, innovation policy was compared across 127 countries. When examined collectively, the countries represented over 90 percent of the world's population and its collective GDP (Gross Domestic Product). Researchers compiled data about the performance of these various economies with 81 innovation indicators that covered critical innovation inputs such as institutions, human capital and research, infrastructure, financial markets, and business sophistication. The critical innovation outputs listed included business sophistication, knowledge, and creative goods and services, and online creativity (Dutta et al., 2017). The five top innovative countries were Switzerland, Sweden, Netherlands, the US, and the United Kingdom. Canada was ranked 18th of 127 countries. This comparative analysis is much like a barometer highlighting policies of top-ranking countries. Each leading country had outstanding investment in human capital, above-average spending on innovation infrastructure, and resource use on creativity, at the individual and collective levels. These countries also emphasize manufacturing sectors, encouraging all-sector involvement and engagement of all innovators. Equally important to innovation is fostering a risk-averse culture across companies, educational systems, government agencies and services, and the broader civil society. The researchers caution countries with little or no investment in innovation and limited proactive engagement of innovators and civil society that they will fall behind. Since 2011, this situation can be seen in Canada, once ranked 11th and now 18th, and it is largely explained by lower government funding for post-secondary education (ranked 65th) and human capital and research (Dutta *et al.*, 2017). Such results are consistent with the policy of a neoliberal federal government, from 2003 to 2015.

It is against this comparative background of innovation across countries the innovations by businesses in a specific location – Manitoba, Canada – are examined. Innovation means that a successful new product or process is generating revenues, and once generating revenues, the innovation is commercialized. Five new food innovations that match this definition are examined to help illustrate the possible contributions from innovation to a more resilient community. Table 29.3 profiles each food innovation.

- *The Canadian Birch Company Ltd* was established to process sap from their own birch trees on the eastern shore of Lake Winnipeg into a variety of 100 percent natural birch syrups. The amber gold syrup is their innovative product, with a unique color and flavor (from the more traditional maple syrup) due to a unique production process.
- *Solberry Incorporated* makes and sells sea buckthorn products. They expanded their range of products to include puree. The proprietary process is their innovation which converts berries into a pure, smooth, naturally brightly colored puree, while retaining the nutrition profile of the berries.
- *Canadian Prairie Garden Puree Products Inc[1]* processes high-quality, locally grown fruit, vegetables, and pulses into non-GMO purees. Their innovative steam injection cooking process results in pure, shelf-stable purees that retain the color, taste, and nutrients of the raw product.
- *Floating Leaf Fine Foods* is a family-owned business involved in harvesting, processing, blending, and packing wild rice. Their innovation is a proprietary process producing quick-cooked wild rice ready to serve in a fraction of the time of traditional wild rice, while retaining taste, texture, and nutritional value.
- *Crik Nutrition* is a premium health food company. Their innovation is a unique ingredient in their protein powders which are crickets, as the major ingredient. It is a nutrient-dense source of protein.

Innovation in the agri-food sector is commonly referred to as product and process development – PPD.[2] To create a new product, a business often has to bring in a new process or modify an existing one, perhaps with new machinery coupled with new technology. In a recent study of 66 innovative initiatives from eight Manitoba companies, 26 percent of the initiatives were PPD (Ashton *et al.*, 2015). Yet, innovation also includes marketing and organizational changes needed to fully realize food innovations. Surprisingly, 74 percent or 41 of the initiatives were marketing (12) and organizational (22) changes, and seven linked marketing with new products, as noted in Figure 29.1.

The five cases on innovation are examined in relation to the four characteristics of resilience – capital, sense of place, leadership, and diversified local economy. In terms of capital, as a characteristic of a resilience framework, the five profiles clearly illustrate that sustained input of resources or forms of capital from many different stakeholders is required over multiple years. Given that the time duration of innovations to the commercialized product ranged from 2 to 12 years, this serves as a proxy of both the amount of resources and the requirement for various kinds of capital. Innovators also attracted significant contributions of capital from outside their

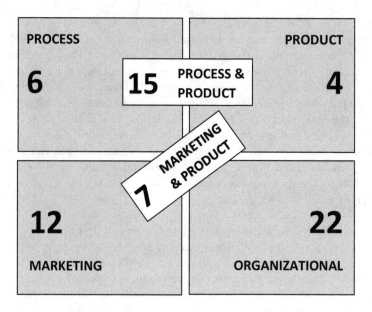

Figure 29.1 Distribution of 66 innovation initiatives across four types of innovation in the food-processing sector in Manitoba, Canada

Table 29.3 Profile of five food innovations and related stakeholders

Profile features	Five food-processing companies in Manitoba and their innovations				
	The Canadian Birch Company	Solberry Incorporated	Floating Leaf Fine Foods	Canadian Prairie Garden	Crik Nutrition
Innovation	Amber Gold Birch Syrup	Sea Buckthorn Puree	Wild Rice in Minutes	Direct Steam Injection Puree Process	Cricket-based Protein Powder
Year Established	2012	2011	1935	2006	2013
Products	Birch Syrup	Sea Buckthorn Puree and Products	Wild Rice	Vegetable, Fruit, and Pulse Purees	Protein Powder
Market	Canada	Canada	International	International	International
Location	Beaconia	Winnipeg/ Portage la Prairie	Winnipeg	Portage la Prairie	Stony Mountain
Website	http://canadian birchcompany. com/	www.solberry. ca/	www.eat wildrice.ca/	http://canadian prairiegarden. com/	https://crik nutrition.com/

Sources: Ashton *et al.* (2017a, 2017b, 2017c, 2017d, 2017e).

business (e.g. human and natural capital of plant breeders and their scientific studies about health benefits; equipment suppliers played essential roles, including their built capital in machinery, along with commodities; and industry specialists and government experts contributed financial, political, and cultural capital). It is evident that many if not all forms of capital contribute to commercializing innovations.

In terms of the place-based characteristic of community resilience, two notions of community emerged from these five cases. Besides the original assumption that communities are place-based, they are also communities of interest. This means that people and businesses share an interest, as they are all part of a supply chain that stretches over a (usually) large geographic area. The five innovation cases drew from many stakeholders within their local and regional communities. While geography was part of what they had in common, they also connected with other people in their working relations over multiple years. Therefore, innovative businesses tap into resources or forms of capital within their local community and attract the involvement of others into their community. These activities in turn bring in outside money and knowledge. Innovation, like resilience, requires a robust effort to access forms of capital that are local or regional (e.g. place-based), while also reaching across the supply chain for knowledge and other valuable resources.

Agency or leadership is another important characteristic of resilient communities. Innovation in the example cases rested on leadership that combined the efforts of the food processor (to initiate activities) and the efforts of many others up and down the supply chain. The innovators clearly demonstrated leadership in terms of attracting resources and carefully allocating them, within a creative enterprise; this is initiated and managed along with their ongoing business operations. The leaders (with others) attract and inject ongoing investments, as they progressively solve problems along their commercialization path. Those involved are reaching beyond their own individual concerns and constraints to pursue an initiative that gradually reveals its value as being greater than any one of them could realize on their own. These five cases demonstrate that successful innovation requires collaboration and collective leadership; innovation is much more of a team effort than a solo act. When innovating, leadership as part of resilience means building and maintaining trusted relations exercised over years and shared among many. This requires frequent deposits by leaders that fill up the "capitals" bank account so it can be drawn upon to overcome countless and often unexpected challenges and setbacks of commercialization.

Diversifying a local economy is a fourth characteristic of community resilience. Locally and regionally, having a range of businesses can diversify the economy, meaning businesses from many sectors. One such sector that communities strive to attract is manufacturing, as these enterprises make a significant contribution to employment and economic diversification. This sector generates demand for raw materials, adds value to goods, and requires numerous professional services. Manufacturing also supplies many businesses with critical products and materials. In 2015, this sector employed 1.7 million people or about 10 percent of Canadians, paid $114 billion in wages (more than any other sector), accounted for $174 billion or 10.5 percent of the national GDP, and 67 percent or $348 billion in Canadian exports, and accounted for 42 percent of investments in all private sector research and development activity (Canadian Manufacturing and Exports, 2017). Looking forward, manufacturing businesses are active partners in realizing such advances as autonomous vehicles, artificial intelligence or self-learning robots, digital production lines, and 3D printing. These and other products and process innovations are rapidly being integrated into standard business operations, which Schwab (2016) calls the fourth industrial revolution. The profiles in Table 29.3 show that diversification of the local economy includes retaining jobs with new products that maintain revenues along with creating new businesses to bring new products to market.

In summary, the five cases of agri-food innovation demonstrate their contributions to resilience. Each case drew extensively upon multiple stakeholders, to access related forms of capital over durations of 2 to 12 years. From a place-based perspective, these innovations added to local geographic communities by bringing together participants along the supply chain, including others that formed a more virtual community. Leadership for innovation focused on building trust among stakeholders, enlarging the circle with expertise, all the while incrementally attracting the necessary resources at the right time. The five cases also contributed directly to diversifying the local economy through new products. The innovations help grow the company and community by maintaining and creating jobs, bringing new resources into the process and community, and adding to overall prosperity.

Broadband and community resilience

Broadband provides rural communities with an increasingly essential tool in today's economy (Conley and Whitacre, 2015). Different technologies are being used to connect rural communities to the internet, including copper lines, fixed wireless, fiber, and satellite; each is considered a form of broadband (Kelly and McCullough, 2016). Being connected to broadband enables rural businesses to benefit from emerging digital technologies like automation, 3D printing, big data, and the internet of things (Gallardo, 2016; Kuttner, 2016; OECD, 2017). Being connected also allows rural communities, organizations, and individuals to participate in social and capacity-building aspects of the blossoming digital society. The definition of broadband and "being connected" varies across countries and, rather than focusing on the type of connection, it typically refers to the quality of connection, ranging from the 25 Mbps download in the United States (FCC, 2017) to the 100 Mbps target in the European Union's Digital Agenda (European Commission, 2016). In Canada, the Canadian Radio-television Telecommunications Commission (CRTC) recently established 50 Mbps as the minimum target for broadband services for all Canadians (CRTC, 2016a). Based on a minimum standard of rural broadband as connectivity with at least 25 Mbps quality, only 50 percent of rural Canadian households have access to the internet at this level; this percentage drops further to 29 percent if the CRTC's target of 50 Mbps is used (CRTC, 2016b).

To further understand the importance of broadband for rural regions, it is necessary to look at how being a "connected" rural community can contribute to its resilience. National policies on rural broadband are examined in Canada, the United States, and Europe, along with links to the four characteristics of resilience.

Governments are recognizing and addressing the importance of rural broadband with policies and initiatives. A recent report by the OECD concludes that G20 countries need to continually invest in digital technologies (especially in rural areas), and they must take advantage of new services applications and business models (OECD, 2017). Internationally, the European Union's Digital Agenda extols the importance of broadband for new economic and social development, regardless of urban or rural location (European Commission, 2016), while the Federal Communications Commission in the United States notes that rural connectivity is needed to stay competitive in the global economy (FCC, 2017). The CRTC and the federal Innovation, Science and Economic Development Canada (ISED) both state that it is essential to connect rural Canada with opportunities in the digital economy (CRTC, 2016a; ISED Connect to Innovate Program, 2019). Thus, rural broadband has become a core economic development tool in public policy within Canada, the US, and Europe.

Smart villages and intelligent communities are two emerging strategies being highlighted in government policy and development networks as part of the new digital economy. The concept of smart villages is being explored and developed by the European Union (ENRD, 2017). Specifically, it outlines a strategy for development in rural communities that builds on digital technologies, innovation, and a knowledge workforce. In a similar fashion, the intelligent communities concept identifies digital technologies, digital equality, innovation, and the knowledge workforce as key indicators of successful communities within the new economy. This concept is put forward by a think tank that anchors a global network of cities and regions, and collectively they make up the Intelligent Community Forum which promotes the need for resilient communities (ICF, n.d.).

In addition to the smart or intelligent community vision for rural communities, CRTC and ISED in Canada, the FCC in the US, and the United Nations' International Telecommunications Union (ITU) all agree that connected rural communities will be more resilient communities with brighter futures. In Canada, the CRTC and ISED agree that rural broadband is fundamental to Canada's economic prosperity, social development, and democratic discourse. The FCC states that rural broadband access is essential in the twenty-first century for economic development (FCC, 2017). Globally, the ITU states that digital technologies and innovations create new opportunities for rural economies and residents (ITU, 2017). Government policies across the OECD have created a direct connection between rural broadband and the resilience and prosperity of rural regions, emphasizing that connectivity is needed for rural communities to survive and thrive in the future.

In terms of the first of Ashmore *et al.*'s (2016) community resilience characteristics, community capital, research has found direct positive impacts from broadband access (Heeks and Arun, 2010). The potential benefits of broadband span multiple economic, social, and environmental arenas (Hupka, 2014; McNally *et al.*, 2016; Zaremohzzabieh *et al.*, 2014). A review of broadband literature offers a long list of various benefits and uses of broadband, as highlighted in Table 29.4.

Sense of place, another key characteristic in Ashmore *et al.*'s (2016) community resilience framework, is vital in relation to rural broadband. Rural places in Canada, the UK, and the US typically fall behind their urban counterparts in terms of broadband access due to lack of adequate market options for such services. These three countries have generally relied on providing financial subsidies to incentivize the private sector to deliver rural broadband in places that are not economically feasible from a business perspective (Ashton and Girard, 2013; Rajabiun and Middleton, 2014; Townsend *et al.*, 2015). This approach has not resulted in wide success, and rural communities that are connected often still lag behind national and international standards (McNally and Trosow, 2013; Rajabiun and Middleton, 2013). With market failure occurring in rural areas of all three regions (Canada, Europe, and the US), communities have undertaken extensive infrastructure projects on their own to develop rural broadband (Dinesg *et al.*, 2017; Ashmore *et al.*, 2016), thereby increasing their resilience. For example, when faced with no viable options for high-speed broadband in their part of northern England, the Broadband 4 the Rural North (B4RN) project was created with local investment and leadership to develop a solution for communities in the region (B4RN, 2017). Established as a community organization, B4RN used local customer and volunteer labor to help trench fiber to more than 1000 properties in their efforts to achieve connectivity. The project works with regional farmers who receive free access in exchange for permission to cross their land with the wires. This project underscores the local and place-based focused solutions sometimes needed to overcome the challenges of deploying a broadband network in rural communities.

The Park West School Division in Manitoba is rolling out more than 300 km of fiber to its schools. As another successful example of place-based broadband development, three of the rural municipalities in this school division formed a fiber-cooperative to build on top of this

Table 29.4 Potential broadband benefits for community forms of capital

Capital	Potential broadband connectivity benefits for capital in rural communities
Human	Connectivity enables building knowledge and improving personal well-being such as: • improved health services through telehealth (Zaremohzzabieh *et al.*, 2014) • access to post-secondary education and certification opportunities online (Hupka, 2014) • increased entertainment options like streaming videos and online gaming (Helsper, 2012)
Social	Connectivity enables more communication and improved social networking such as: • social media engagement with friends, family, and community (Stern and Adams, 2010) • video calling services to bring more people together virtually regardless of distance (Chowdhury and Odame, 2013) • increased participation in community organizations and events (Stern *et al.*, 2011)
Political	Connectivity enables greater civic engagement and accountability of governments: • e-voting, online town halls, or e-surveying (Thakur, 2009) • discussion boards on websites and social media (Svenson, 2016) • information sharing on government websites (Heeks and Arun, 2010)
Cultural	Connectivity enables greater documentation, sharing and discovery of culture, heritage, and values such as: • live-streaming events; creating digital stories and virtual reality experiences (Carpenter *et al.*, 2013) • storing, documenting, and sharing local culture and heritage on websites (Pigg, 2005) • enhancing local tourism through apps and augmented reality (McNally *et al.*, 2016)
Financial	Connectivity enables improved financial services and options such as: • reduced business costs and increased flexibility for employees through teleworking (Hynes, 2014) • access to new markets and products online (Roberts and Townsend, 2015) • access to virtual business services that are not cost-effective or available locally (Beckinsale and Ram, 2006)
Built	Connectivity enables improved built capital such as: • reducing transportation costs and reducing environmental footprint through e-metering of electricity, water, and waste (McNally *et al.*, 2016) • using public wifi to revitalize and attract residents to community spaces and places (Hudson, 2013)

new community fiber loop (CBC, 2017a). These rural municipalities were not satisfied with available broadband and worked with one another and the school division to develop local solutions. As a result, one of the communities is rolling out fiber to the homes of interested residents and to businesses in and out of town, while another is using fiber-connected towers to deliver improved wireless broadband to their residents, creating a highly connected region in rural Manitoba. This sense of place in rural broadband – which focuses on broadband for whom and by whom – mirrors the sense of place in resilience. Building on sense of place is an indispensable characteristic for both community resilience and rural broadband.

Agency or leadership is the third characteristic of community resilience in Ashmore *et al.*'s (2016) framework. There are numerous examples of community-led initiatives that demonstrate community agency in connecting themselves to broadband, knowing the private sector may have already passed them by. In Olds, Alberta, this deliberate action was a community-led initiative to future-proof their region and to ensure a competitive edge. This leadership has given Olds not just a regional advantage but a national one, having perhaps the best internet in Canada, delivering gigabit service to all in their rural community (CBC, 2015). Another great example of leadership is the initiative underway by Manitoba's First Nations Technology Council, which is working to create a network, called Clear Sky Connections, that will connect all 63 of Manitoba's First Nations communities, using 3600 km of fiber optics cable. The Association of Manitoba Chiefs is helping address this connectivity issue on behalf of their communities (CBC, 2017b). Agency was a critical factor in these examples, and such community broadband initiatives – which are manifestations of the intent to act and work collectively – would not occur without deliberate action and *leadership*, an essential characteristic of community resilience.

A diversified economy is the fourth main characteristic of community resilience. The new digital economy is based on harnessing knowledge and digital technology, and broadband is necessary to effectively participate in that economy (OECD, 2012; EU, 2019). Broadband enables rural businesses and individuals to explore a wider variety of options, and it is increasingly essential for business operations and services (Ashmore *et al.*, 2015; Markey *et al.*, 2015a). The creative sector is one example of the diversification of rural economies through broadband. Creative sector businesses focus on making and creating items, art, and culture, and they benefit from rural broadband via increased peer networking and access to new and global markets for their products (Herslund, 2012; Roberts and Townsend, 2015). Broadband brings to these and other rural businesses improved services, a variety of markets, and an entrance into the new economy, which includes access to less obvious benefits such as data-driven decision-making (OECD, 2017).

Community resilience is based on the ability of communities to adapt to change, and in the process to harness agency and leadership to take deliberate action for social and economic development within a specific place or region. Broadband connectivity can enhance resilience in rural communities and increase their ability to adapt and evolve with economic and social change (Magis, 2010), especially as both the economy and society become more digitally focused. Community capital can benefit from harnessing rural broadband, while a sense of place and agency are critical elements for implementation.

Discussion

This chapter examines how two key economic drivers, innovation and rural broadband, relate to community resilience. Ashmore *et al.*'s (2016) community resilience framework provided three significant characteristics, and a diversified local economy constitutes a fourth characteristic. Each was explored in relation to innovation and broadband. Figure 29.2, adapted from Ashmore *et al.* (2016), highlights details of each characteristic of resilience. There is no space or purpose in this chapter to examine the details illustrated in Ashmore *et al.*'s framework, nor to delve into the intersections and overlaps of the characteristics. Yet, this model assisted in examining resilience in the face of two persistent economic drivers common in rural areas – innovation and broadband.

Further research is needed to better understand the intersections among the characteristics and how their combination relates to both innovation and rural broadband. Likewise, a deeper examination of the detailed sub-characteristics in both Ashmore *et al.*'s (2016) framework and the adapted framework would contribute to a more comprehensive understanding of the nuances in each characteristic in terms of rural broadband and innovation.

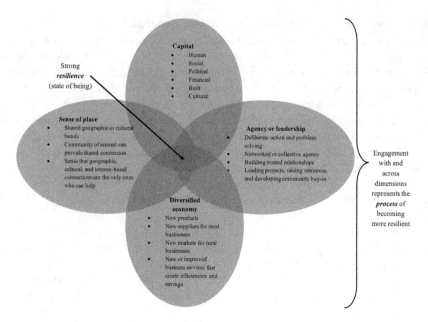

Figure 29.2 Adapted community resilience framework

Ashmore *et al.* (2016) highlighted the issues of power, leadership, and inclusivity in their application of the framework they developed. Specifically, they identified that leadership could actually have a negative impact on broadband initiatives if leaders are not reaching across the community for input and involving others in decision-making and project development. The present exploration of agency and leadership did not examine power and inclusivity issues, but this would be an important item for future research. Broadband has the potential to provide previously unavailable knowledge and services to rural populations and has become essential for individuals and businesses within the digital society. Innovation likewise has the ability to create new economic opportunities. The concept needs to extend to more genuine innovation where community and marginalized populations are invited as well (Mirza *et al.*, 2012). Future research needs to build on the connections between community resilience and key drivers such as innovation and broadband by examining the role of power and leadership and the levels of inclusivity. The aim of the Ashmore *et al.* (2016) study is to better understand if these important economic drivers in the new digital economy are benefiting rural communities as a whole or if their positive impacts are limited to just a few.

Conclusions

Resilience is not a monolithic term with only one definition, but many (Magis, 2010; Roberts *et al.*, 2015). This chapter illustrates, for students and others, that an approach to resilience can be used and adapted, as done by Ashmore *et al.* (2016). Together with various forms of capital, agency, and being more place-based, a fourth characteristic of diversified local economy rounded out this framework to better align with evidence in the literature and the context of rural areas. In addition, two significant drivers of the new digital economy – innovation and broadband – serve to illustrate in a rural context how a modified theoretical framework is used to examine a concept like resilience by exploring key characteristics. It is possible to argue that both innovation and broadband represent key opportunities to build rural capital and resources beyond just financial and built aspects, and that agency and leadership are necessary to bring resources together, including ideas, coupled with a long-term commitment and vision. Equally important is the context, rural communities and regions, which requires respecting a sense of place and involving communities of interest to realize more resilient place-based development. Both innovation and broadband assist in diversifying the economy, and they simultaneously bring about change, be it with innovative products and processes, enlarging client base and market with online ordering, providing employment opportunities (especially for youth), and facilitating broader community engagement via the internet. Equally prevalent, resilience as a concept of local economic development points to the need for rural regions to bring about changes in their favor; otherwise they could easily be drifting further behind, further away from their desired future. As argued in this chapter, practitioners can enhance resilience by involving innovation and commercialization processes and policies in development plans and projects. Furthermore, practitioners can pursue policies resulting in local and regional broadband infrastructure investment and projects to improve the adoption of digital skills. This chapter concludes with a call for further research in terms of understanding the nexus of the four characteristics of resilience and the roles of power and inclusion.

Notes

1 Canadian Prairie Garden Inc validated their case study and during the writing of this report they were placed in receivership.
2 Manitoba Food Development Centre is one of several centers across Canada involved in bringing new food ideas to the market place. The author, Dr. Ashton, holds a ministerial appointment on the FDC in Manitoba.

References

Anderson, B., 2015. *What kind of thing is resilience?* Politics 35(1), 60–66.
Ashmore, F.H., Farrington, J.H., Skerratt, S., 2015. *Superfast broadband and rural community resilience: Examining the rural need for speed.* Scottish Geographical Journal 131(3–4), 265–278.
Ashmore, F., Farrington, J., Skerratt, S., 2016. *Community-led broadband in rural digital infrastructure development: Implications for resilience.* Journal of Rural Studies, 54, 408–425.
Ashton, B., Finesth, N., Galatsanou, E., Gilchrist, J., Richards, G., 2017a. *The Canadian Birch Company Case Study.* Rural Development Institute, Brandon University, Brandon, MB.
Ashton, B., Finesth, N., Galatsanou, E., Gilchrist, J., Richards, G., 2017b. *Floating Leaf Fine Foods: Wild rice in minutes.* Rural Development Institute, Brandon University, Brandon, MB.
Ashton, B., Finesth, N., Galatsanou, E., Gilchrist, J., Richards, G., 2017c. *Crik Nutrition: Cricket protein powder.* Rural Development Institute, Brandon University, Brandon, MB.
Ashton, B., Finesth, N., Galatsanou, E., Gilchrist, J., Richards, G., 2017d. *Solberry Inc.: Sea buckthorn puree.* Rural Development Institute, Brandon University, Brandon, MB.
Ashton, B., Finesth, N., Galatsanou, E., Gilchrist, J., Richards, G., 2017e. *Canadian Prairie Garden Puree.* Rural Development Institute, Brandon University, Brandon, MB.
Ashton, W., Girard, R., 2013. *Reducing the digital divide in Manitoba,* in: Ashton, W., Carson, A.S. (Eds.), Special issue of the Journal of Rural and Community Development 8(2), 62–78.
Ashton, W., Galatsanou, E., Richards, G., Woods, S., 2015. *Innovation in agri-food processing: A study of commercialization of bulk food ingredients in Manitoba with eight case studies.* Rural Development Institute, Brandon University, Brandon, MB.
B4RN – Broadband for the Rural North Ltd, 2017. *The world's fastest rural broadband.* https://b4rn.org.uk/ (accessed 8.13.17).
Beckinsale, M., Ram, M., 2006. *Delivering ICT to ethnic minority businesses: An action-research approach.* Environment and Planning C: Government and Policy 24(6), 847–867.
Bentley, G., Pugalis, L., 2013. *New directions in economic development: Localist policy discourses and the Localism Act.* Local Economy 28(3), 257–274.

Besser, T.L., 2013. *Resilient small rural towns and community shocks.* Journal of Rural and Community Development 8(1), 117–134.

Brennan, M., 2008. *Conceptualizing resiliency: An interactional perspective for community and youth development.* Child Care in Practice 14(1), 55–64.

Canadian Manufacturing and Exports, 2017. *Manufacturing is the bedrock of the Canadian economy.* www.industrie2030.ca/english/actions/actions.html.

Carpenter, P., Gibson, K., Kakekaspan, C., O'Donnell, S., 2013. *How women in remote and rural First Nation communities are using information and communications technologies (ICT),* in: Ashton, W., Carson, A.S. (Eds.), Special issue of the Journal of Rural and Community Development 8(2), 79–97.

CBC – Canadian Broadcasting Corporation, 2015. *Fast fibre-optic internet arrives in many small towns before big cities.* www.cbc.ca/news/technology/fast-fibre-optic-internet-arrives-in-many-small-towns-before-big-cities-1.3174901 (accessed 8.10.17).

CBC – Canadian Broadcasting Corporation, 2017a. *3 Western Manitoba municipalities, school division form their own fibre optic internet service.* www.cbc.ca/news/canada/manitoba/rural-fibre-optic-internet-cooperative-1.4236694 (accessed 8.10.17).

CBC – Canadian Broadcasting Corporation, 2017b. *Connecting communities: First Nations company plans to lay 3,600 km of fibre optics in Manitoba.* www.cbc.ca/news/indigenous/first-nations-high-speed-internet-northern-manitoba-1.4058347 (9.10.17).

Chowdhury, A., Odame, H.H., 2013. *Social media for enhancing innovation in agri-food and rural development: Current dynamics in Ontario, Canada,* in: Ashton, W., Carson, A.S. (Eds.), Special issue of the Journal of Rural and Community Development 8(2), 97–119.

Conley, K., Whitacre, B., 2015. *Does broadband matter for rural entrepreneurs or creative class employees?* The Review of Regional Studies 46(2), 171–190.

Côte, M., Nightingale, A., 2012. *Resilience thinking meets social theory: Situating social change in socio-ecological systems (SES) research.* Progress in Human Geography 36(4), 475–489.

CRTC – Canadian Radio-television and Telecommunications Commission, 2016a. *Closing the Broadband Gap Initiative.* www.crtc.gc.ca/eng/internet/internet.htm (accessed 9.1.17).

CRTC – Canadian Radio-television and Telecommunications Commission, 2016b. *Communications monitoring report.* http://crtc.gc.ca/eng/publications/reports/PolicyMonitoring/2016/cmri.htm (accessed 9.1.17).

Dinesg, R., McMahon, R., McNally, M.B., Prevatt, C., Evaniew, J., Pearce, H., 2016. *Understanding community broadband: The Alberta Broadband Toolkit.* https://era.library.ualberta.ca/items/fb107721-a457-4e96-97cb-fb444ef00377.

Dowell, B., 2015. *Manitoba's economy: Strong growth, modest outlook.* Conference Board of Canada. www.conferenceboard.ca/economics/hot_eco_topics/default/15-03-02/manitoba_s_economy_strong_growth_modest_outlook.aspx.

Dutta, S., Lanvin, B., Wunsch-Vincent, S., 2017. *The global innovation index 2017: Innovation feeding the world.* Cornell University. www.globalinnovationindex.org/gii-2017-report#.

Emery, M., Flora, F., 2006. *Spiraling-up: Mapping community transformation with community capitals framework.* Community Development 37(1), 19–35.

ENRD – European Network for Rural Development, 2017. *ENRD smart villages thematic group: "Revitalising rural services through social and digital innovation".* https://enrd.ec.europa.eu/sites/enrd/files/tg_smart-villages_scoping-work-plan_draft.pdf (accessed 2.16.18).

EU, 2019. *Digital single market policy: Europe 2020 strategy.* https://ec.europa.eu/digital-single-market/en/europe-2020-strategy.

European Commission, 2016. *Connectivity for a European gigabit society.* https://ec.europa.eu/digital-single-market/en/policies/improving-connectivity-and-access (accessed 8.3.17).

FCC – Federal Communications Commission, 2017. *Connect America Fund.* www.fcc.gov/general/connect-america-fund-caf (accessed 8.16.17).

FCM – Federation of Canadian Municipalities, 2014. *The evolution of local economic development in Canada.* Policy Brief. Ottawa, Ont. www.fcm.ca/Documents/tools/International/The_evolution_of_local_economic_development_in_Canada_-_Policy_Brief_EN.pdf.

Gallardo, R., 2016. *Responsive countryside: The digital age and rural communities.* Mississippi State University Extension Service, Starkville, MS.

Government of Canada, 2017. *Infrastructure.* www.budget.gc.ca/2017/docs/themes/infrastructure-en.html.

Heeks, R., Arun, S., 2010. *Social outsourcing as a development tool: The impact of outsourcing IT services to women's social enterprises in Kerala.* Journal of International Development 22(4), 441–454.

Heeks, R., Ospina, A., 2015. *Analysing urban community informatics from a resilience perspective*. The Journal of Community Informatics 11(1), 1108–1135.

Helsper, E., 2012. *A corresponding fields model for the links between social and digital exclusion*. Communication Theory 22(3), 403–426.

Herslund, L., 2012. *The rural creative class: Counterurbanisation and entrepreneurship in the Danish countryside*. Sociologia Ruralis 52(2), 235–255.

Holling, C., 1973. *Resilience and stability of ecological systems*. Annual Review of Ecology and Systematics 4, 1–23.

Hudson, E.E., 2013. *Beyond infrastructure: Broadband for development in remote and Indigenous regions*, in: Ashton, W., Carson, A.S. (Eds.), Special issue of the Journal of Rural and Community Development 8(2), 44–61.

Hupka, Y., 2014. *Findings on the economic benefits of broadband expansion to rural and remote areas*. Centre for Urban and Regional Affairs, University of Minnesota. CAP Report No. 188. www.cura.umn.edu/publications/search.

Hynes, M., 2014. *Telework isn't working: A policy review*. The Economic and Social Review 45(4, Winter), 579–602.

ICF – Intelligent Community Forum, n.d. *What is an intelligent community?* www.intelligentcommunity.org/what_is_an_intelligent_community (accessed 8.22.17).

ISED, 2019. *Connect to innovate*. www.ic.gc.ca/eic/site/119.nsf/eng/home.

ITU – International Telecommunications Union, 2017. *Measuring the information society report 2017*, Vol. 1. www.itu.int/en/ITU-D/Statistics/Pages/publications/mis2017.aspx (accessed 12.18.17).

Kelly, W., McCullough, S., 2016. *Research brief: State of rural information and communication technologies in Manitoba*. Rural Development Institute, Brandon, MB.

Khanlou, N., Wray, R., 2014. *A whole community approach toward child and youth resilience promotion: A review of resilience literature*. International Journal of Mental Health and Addiction 12(1), 64–79.

Kuttner, H., 2016. *The economic impact of rural broadband*. Hudson Institute, Washington, DC.

MacKinnon, D., Derickson, K., 2012. *From resilience to resourcefulness: A critique of resilience policy and activism*. Progress in Human Geography 37(2), 253–270.

Magis, K., 2007. *Indicator 38: Community resilience, literature and practice review*. Submitted to the US Roundtable on Sustainable Forests. http://citeseerx.ist.psu.edu/viewdoc/download?doi=10.1.1.579.7092&rep=rep1&type=pdf.

Magis, K., 2010. *Community resilience: An indicator of social sustainability*. Society and Natural Resources 23(5), 401–416.

Markey, S., Breen, S., Gibson, R., Lauzon, A., Mealy, R. (Eds.), 2015a. *State of rural Canada report*. Canadian Rural Revitalization Foundation.

Markey, S., Breen, S., Vodden, K., Daniels, J., 2015b. *Evidence of place: Becoming a region in rural Canada*. International Journal of Urban and Regional Research 39(5), n.p.

McNally, M.B., Trosow, S.E., 2013. *The new telecommunications sector foreign investment regime and rural broadband*. Journal of Rural and Community Development 8(2), 23–43.

McNally, M., McMahon, R., Rathi, D., Pearce, H., Evaniew, J., Chardelle, P., 2016. *Understanding community broadband: The Alberta toolkit*. University of Alberta, Educational Research Archive, Edmonton, AB.

Mirza, M., Vodden, K., Collins, G., 2012. *Developing innovative approaches for community engagement*. Memorial University, St John's, NL. www.open.gov.nl.ca/collaboration/pdf/community_engagement.pdf.

Norris, F., Stevens, S., Pfefferbaum, B., Wyche, K., Pfefferbaum, R., 2008. *Community resilience as a metaphor, theory, set of capacities, and strategy for disaster readiness*. American Journal of Community Psychology 41(1–2), 127–150.

Noya, A., Clarence, E., 2009. *Community capacity building: Fostering economic and social resilience*. CFE/LEED, OECD.

OECD – Organisation for Economic Co-operation and Development, 2012. *The digital economy*. OECD, Paris.

OECD – Organisation for Economic Co-operation and Development, 2017. *Key issues for digital transformation in the G20*. www.oecd.org/g20/key-issues-for-digital-transformation-in-the-g20.pdf (accessed 8.1.17).

Pigg, K.E., 2005. *Introduction: Community informatics and community development*. Community Development 36(1), 1–8.

Rajabiun, R., Middleton, C.A., 2013. *Multilevel governance and broadband infrastructure development: Evidence from Canada*. Telecommunications Policy 37(9), 702–714.

Rajabiun, R., Middleton, C., 2014. *Rural broadband development in Canada's provinces: An overview of policy approaches*. Journal of Rural and Community Development 8(2), 7–22.

Roberts, E., Townsend, L., 2015. *The contribution of the creative economy to the resilience of rural communities: Exploring cultural and digital capital*. Sociologia Ruralis 56(2), 197–219.

Roberts, E., Farrington, J., Skerratt, S., 2015. *Evaluating new digital technologies through a framework of resilience*. Scottish Geographical Journal 131(3–4), 253–264.

Roberts, E., Anderson, B., Skerrat, S., Farrington, J., 2017a. *A review of the rural-digital policy agenda from a community resilience perspective*. Journal of Rural Studies 54, 372–385. https://doi.org/10.1016/j. jrurstud.2016.03.001.

Schwab, K., 2016. *Fourth industrial revolution*. Harvard Business Review. https://hbr.org/product/the-fourth-industrial-revolution/ROT308-PDF-ENG.

Scott, M., 2013. *Resilience: A conceptual lens for rural studies?* Geography Compass 7(9), 597–610.

Sherrieb, K., Norris, F., Galea, S., 2010. *Measuring capacities for community resilience*. Social Indicators Research 99(2), 227–247.

Steiner, A., Atterton, J., 2014. *The contribution of rural businesses to community resilience*. Local Economy 29(3), 228–244. http://dx.doi.org/10.1177/0269094214528853.

Steiner, A., Woolvin, M., Skerratt, S., 2018. *Measuring community resilience over time: developing and applying a "hybrid evaluation" approach*. Community Development Journal 53(1), 99–118.

Stern, M., Adams, A., 2010. *Do rural residents really use the internet to build social capital? An empirical investigation*. American Behavioral Scientist 53(9), 1389–1422.

Stern, M.J., Adams, A.E., Boase, J., 2011. *Rural community participation, social networks, and broadband use: Examples from localized and national survey data*. Agricultural and Resource Economics Review 40(2), 158–171.

Svenson, L., 2016. *Empowering rural youth with Facebook: Lessons from a local Swedish case-study*. Community Development Journal 51(3), 436–451.

Thakur, D., 2009. *ICTs and community participation: An indicative framework*. The Journal of Community Informatics 5(1), XX–XX.

Townsend, L., Wallace, C., Fairhurst, G., 2015. *"Stuck out here": The critical role of broadband for remote rural places*. Scottish Geographic Journal 131(3–4), 171–180.

Walsh, B., 2013. *Adapt or die: Why the environmental buzzword of 2013 will be Resilience*. Time, January 8. http://science.time.com/2013/01/08/adapt-or-die-why-the-environmental-buzzword-of-2013-will-be-resilience/.

Wilding, N., 2011. *Exploring community resilience. What is it? How are people building it? Why does it matter?* Carnegie UK Trust, UK.

Wilson, G.A., 2012. *Community resilience, globalisation, and transitional pathways of decision-making*. Geoforum 43(6), 1218–1231.

Zaremohzzabieh, Z., Samah, B.A., Omar, S.Z., Bolong, J., Shaffril, H.A.M., 2014. *A Systematic review of qualitative research on the role of ICTs in sustainable livelihood*. The Social Sciences 9(6), 386–401.

30

CLIMATE CHANGE ADAPTATION BY FARMERS

The case of Nepal

Krishna Lal Poudel and Thomas G. Johnson

Introduction

Climate change is posing a serious threat in both low and high-income countries. The IPCC (2007) projects that for every 1°C rise in temperature, agricultural water demand increases by 6 to 10 percent. At the same time increased concentrations of CO_2 tend to increase yields. Overall, climate change is expected to reduce yields by 9 to 22 percent worldwide by 2080 (Parry *et al.*, 2004). Yields are expected to decline most in Africa and South Asia where declines of 8 percent are predicted by 2050 (Knox *et al.*, 2012). Decreased production of this magnitude ultimately will lead to widespread food insecurity and poor living standards especially for the most vulnerable members of society.

Scientists and other concerned individuals have stressed the need for adaptations to changing water availability. Enhancing resilience of families, businesses, and communities requires research-based adaptation strategies designed within the context of development plans. This chapter describes a study intended to determine current adaptation strategies adopted by farmers in Nepal – one of the more vulnerable regions of the world. Results of this research will support policy actions to develop more economically and environmentally sound mountain farming systems, and to improve the living standards of mountain populations and populations living downstream. The rationale for this research was that by identifying early changes in conditions faced by small-hold farmers, and by identifying key vulnerabilities, it would be possible to anticipate some of the most fruitful intervention points for researchers and policy-makers. Furthermore, by identifying current responses of smallholders to these changes, and by documenting the consequences of the responses, better strategies for longer -term adaptation to changing climatic conditions are possible.

Rising average temperatures affect crop and livestock production by altering pests and diseases, soil metabolic processes, soil water content (Liverman, 2008; Sinha, 1997), biotic and abiotic stresses, and soil nutrient cycling (Chaudhari and Aryal, 2009; Schiermeier, 2008; Howden *et al.*, 2007). The resulting changes in crop yields, costs, and revenues have consequences for income distribution and livelihood security of farming communities (Lettenmaier *et al.*, 1994). Most studies of the consequences of climate change on food production predict that crop yields will decline in South America, Africa, and South Asia, while yields in parts of northern Europe and North America could increase (Polley, 2002; Parry *et al.*, 2004; Malla, 2008; Khanal, 2009; Knox *et al.*, 2012). Increased CO_2 concentration and higher temperatures can improve water-use efficiency of crops. Higher temperatures favor higher biomass production (Polley, 2002) and increase the possibility of expanding and diversifying agriculture (Khanal, 2009) at higher altitudes. At the same time, increased CO_2 concentrations will reduce levels of iron, zinc, and proteins in grains and legumes, exacerbating nutritional deficiencies in many populations (Myers *et al.*, 2014).

The goal of climate change adaptation is to reduce expected costs and to enhance opportunities to capture benefits. Conceição and Zhang (2010) frame this as a cost–benefit analysis in which avoiding future losses from climate change is a benefit while current incomes foregone to receive that future benefit are costs.

The consequences of climate change in the Himalayan region are particularly critical owing to the large proportion of the population depending on climate-sensitive agriculture (Pradhan *et al.*, 2012). This paper describes the adaptive responses to climate change observed in a recent study conducted in Nepal (Poudel, 2017).

The study area and data collection

Nepal offers an ideal opportunity to study the potential impacts of climate change and possible adaptive strategies. Water from the Himalayan mountains is essential to food production for millions of residents of South Asia (Immerzeel *et al.*, 2010). The effect of climate change on water flows from the Himalayas, and subsequent adaptation by Nepalese farmers, will have consequences far beyond Nepal.

Nepal is divided into three horizontal ecological belts, namely, Mountain, Hill, and Terai (Figure 30.1). The Koshi River basin was chosen as the study area. The Koshi River is a glacier-fed river which originates on the northern slopes of the Himalayas in Tibet. Its

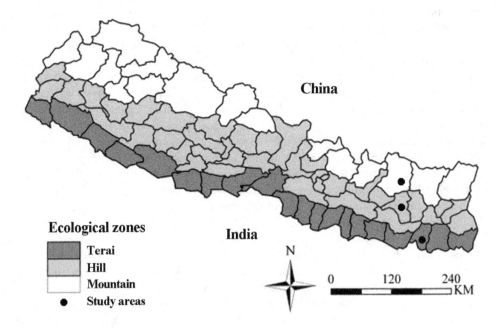

Figure 30.1 Ecological zones of Nepal

drainage system continues through Nepal into northern India (Bihar state) and its confluence with the Ganges.

The three research sites in the Mountain, Hill, and Terai regions were chosen to include freshwater ecosystems, natural disaster-prone regions (e.g. flood, landslide, deforestation, etc.), and farmland.

Primary data were collected through the administration of pre-tested semi-structured face-to-face interviews of 450 households; 150 respondents from each ecological region. In addition, the study involved focus groups and unstructured discussions with farmers. Secondary data on climate variables (rainfall and temperature), macro-economic indicators (GDP, land use patterns, etc.), demographics, area and production of agricultural crops, market prices, water demand, and irrigation were also used.

Farms in Nepal are very small. The average farm sizes are about 0.8, 0.7, and 1.3 hectares in the Mountain, Hill, and Terai regions respectively. Fragmented and terraced land in the Mountain and Hill regions are constraints on adopting mechanized farming. As a result of low incomes and limited local food, only 52 percent of the respondents in the study area have year-round food security whereas 10 percent have less than three months of food security from on-farm activities.

The current situation in the study area

Declining water availability is a problem in all three regions in this study. This has led to additional travel and concomitant time requirements to procure water. Of respondents, 77 percent reported increasing distance to their water source. People in the Terai are facing this problem more than the people in the Hill and the Mountain regions. Residents of the Mountain region suffer because of remoteness and scattered water sources such as natural springs and small rivulets. Residents of the Hill region are constrained by lower water levels in creeks and natural springs, disappearing springs due to deforestation, and the infeasibility of lifting the water from rivers into the high hills. The Terai region is severely impacted by upstream forest degradation, landslides, and rainy-season flooding. Flooding makes surface water unsafe.

There are other threats to the water supplies unrelated to, but confounding, the effects of climate change. Surface water in rivers and reservoirs is becoming more and more polluted. Affluent farmers, businesses, and industries in the Terai region are extracting excessive amounts of ground water, hastening the decline in the water table. The excessive extraction of ground water is leading to land subsidence in the Terai region.

Despite the enormous potential for developing water resources in some areas (Pradhan *et al.*, 2012; Eriksson *et al.*, 2009; WECS, 2011), only a fraction of these water resources are being utilized while in other regions (the Hill region especially) there is a serious shortage of surface water and significant depletion of ground water (WECS, 2011).

Ethnic groups, including the Bote, Majhi, and Tharu, who have traditionally relied on water bodies to harvest fish and other aquatic creatures to sustain their life, are facing substantial reductions in harvests and have largely shifted to other jobs (Kaphle and Dahal, 2014). At the same time, flooding during the rainy season and drought in the winter and summer jeopardize smallholder agriculture. In addition to drought, the flash-floods, landslides (long arid periods followed by intense rainfall), and changing of river courses are prominent problems in the Hill region.

The survey indicated that about 80 percent of respondents have experienced conflicts related to water allocation. The survey and focus group discussions found the following five conflicts:

1   Social group conflict: increased internal migration in search of water has led to displace-
     ment of Indigenous and marginal families which in turn has led to further marginalization
     of vulnerable sections of society.
2   Ethnic group conflict: limited access to water sources by disadvantaged ethnic groups (the
     untouchable caste) especially in the Terai and Hill regions.
3   Political jurisdiction conflict: inter-jurisdictional debate regarding new dams and water
     rights.
4   Intersectoral conflict: competition for water use by agriculture, hydropower, and for indus-
     trial purposes.
5   Physiographic/spatial conflict: upstream–downstream conflict over water use, and between
     communities.

Despite general shortages of water, about 24 percent of respondents in the Mountain region
experienced increased water availability over the period 2000–2015, especially during late
winter through summer. This has been mainly due to increased temperature and glacier retreat.
Other reasons for increased water availability in the Mountain region are ongoing cropping
pattern change (from cereals to non-timber forest products) and decreasing population density
due to out-migration.

Only 14 percent of respondents from the Terai region have installed irrigation pumps to
water cereal crops and vegetables (mostly beans). No one has irrigation pumps in the Mountain
and Hill regions. To date, there is no ground water provision in the Mountain and Hill regions
whereas 100 percent of respondents in the Terai region use ground water for livestock and in-
house activities. Irrigation water in the Terai region includes both surface and ground water.
About a third of respondents use ground water for crop production. Ground water consumption in the Terai region is increasing due to migration from the Hill and Mountain regions and
urbanization.

Ground water users are very diverse. Households who have pumps and access to deep drilling equipment are able to withdraw much more ground water than those having only natural
wells, cemented wells, and shallow tube wells. Ground water extraction is increasing in aggregate,
but decreasing for small holders, marginal households, the landless, and members of lower castes
(untouchables).

Only 46 percent of total water demand by respondents is fulfilled at present (Table 30.1).
Only in the Terai region is more than 50 percent of livestock and household water demand met.
Of the total demand, 68 percent and 76 percent are fulfilled in livestock and in-house uses
respectively in the Terai region. All sectors in the Mountain and Hill regions, and agriculture in
the Terai region are operating with less than 50 percent of water needed (Table 30.1). Respondents in the Mountain, Hill, and Terai regions are willing to pay 78%, 62%, and 76% more than

Table 30.1 Sector-wise water demand fulfillment in study area (percent of sector)

Sectors	Mountain (%)	Hill (%)	Terai (%)	Total (%)
Agriculture	31	27	35	31
Livestock	47	45	68	53
Household	42	43	76	50
Total	40	39	60	46

Source: Field survey, 2015.

the base price of water. This finding is consistent with the conclusion made by Eriksson *et al.* (2009) that insufficient water coupled with inefficiency of variable farm inputs management are the reasons why agricultural productivity in Nepal is very low compared to other South Asian and developing countries.

Climate change and observed changes in precipitation, wind, and temperature

Farmers perceive changes in the climate based on their local knowledge. These perceptions are consistent with the observations and conclusions of other research (Eriksson *et al.*, 2009; Malla, 2008). For example, farmers observe changes in deciduous plant blossoms, crop maturation schedule, animal estrus-cycles, and bird migrations. In addition, phenomena such as lower humidity, ants in creeks and natural springs, drying up of natural springs, and reduced numbers of earthworms are direct experiences of farmers that indicate to them that climate change is having an impact on their environment. This emphasizes the importance of local and indigenous knowledge as inputs in designing place-based adaptation plans.

About 90 percent of respondents have heard of, or personally felt, negative impacts of climate change in their surroundings and livelihoods. In total, 88 percent of respondents noticed less rain with respect to the 2000s. Respondents reported they are experiencing increasingly erratic and intense rainfall as compared to the decade 2000–2010. All respondents in the Terai region reported increased temperatures. People also reported stronger winds in the Hill and Mountain regions. The combined effects of higher winds, erratic rainfall, and higher temperature are serious threats to people's traditional livelihoods. On the other hand, 15 percent of respondents in the Mountain region, most of whom reside on the northern face of the mountain terraces, reported that since they are exposed to just a few hours of sunshine each day, they benefit from increasing temperatures.

Farmers attributed the advantages and disadvantages to increased temperature in their region as outlined in Table 30.2.

While increased glacial melt has resulted in increased flow in major rivers, reduced precipitation has had adverse effects on local streams. All respondents in the Hill and Terai regions, and 90 percent of respondents in the Mountain region reported that water had decreased in creeks. Respondents in the Mountain region reported that snowfall has decreased an average of 6 percent between 2000 and 2015.

Table 30.2 Advantages and disadvantages attributed to increased temperatures by respondents

Advantages	Disadvantages
• Crop production increased by 20–25 percent • Reduced need to melt ice using firewood in summer. That saved about US$21 per year • Vegetable production and consumption increased worth US$44 per year compared to five to seven years ago	• Greater insect-pests prevalence, mosquitos in summer • Foot and mouth disease (FMD) outbreak in goat and sheep • Some medicinal and aromatic plants (MAP) such as Yarsagumba (*Ophiocordyceps sinensis*) are now extinct • Gradual reduction in floral diversity • Early blossoming of rhododendron and hence degraded flavor of its sorbet

Source: Focus group discussions, 2015.

Table 30.3 Average on-farm economic losses from the consequences of climate change, 2008–2013

Climate change effect	Average economic loss (US$/year/family)[1]				
	Mountain (%)	Hill (%)	Terai (%)	Total (%)	Rank
Over precipitation	0	26	24	17	4
Drought	504	522	847	626	1
High temperature	43	63	110	73	3
Flood++	119	47	437	202	2
Landslide	11	34	0	15	5
Total	680	692	1419	931	–

Source: Field Survey 2015 and International Monetary Fund (2017).

Note

1 As per IMF report, per capita income (PPP) in Nepal in 2017 was about US$2,690. Smallholder farm income is much lower than the national average at an estimated US$1,000 per capita.

About 65 percent of respondents have experienced flooding. The highest incidence of flooding (87 percent) was experienced by residents of the Terai region followed by 77 percent and 36 percent in the Hill and Mountain regions respectively.

Respondents reported both dry and wet landslides. Wet landslides, which occur when long dry periods are followed by intense precipitation, significantly affect peoples' lives, the economy, and the environment at lower mountain elevations and the entire Hill region. Landslides in the Mountain and Hill regions and floods in the Hill and Terai regions cause permanent loss of terraced land, siltation of reservoirs, and water stagnation. Respondents reported permanent and temporary land use loss due to extreme climate events (flood, flash flood, intense rain, dry landslide, and wet landslide) is increasing remarkably in the regions. The focus groups revealed that the number of events and magnitude of arable land loss has increased by 8 percent and 5 percent annually, respectively. This may lead to significant economic loss in the region and is especially costly to the smallholders who lack resources to recover and upgrade their land. Permanent land use loss in the Terai region is due to flooding during the rainy season from the Koshi River and its auxiliary rivulets while landslides are the main cause of land loss in the Mountain and Hill areas. Permanent land use loss in the Mountain, Hill, and Terai regions were reported to be 23%, 9%, and 42% respectively.

No one in the Mountain region reported any losses due to excessive precipitation but 12 percent of respondents in the Terai region and 23 percent of respondents in the Hill region reported on-farm economic losses due to intense precipitation with respect to the period 2000–2015. Monetary estimations of economic losses due to droughts, excess precipitation, floods, and landslides are presented in Table 30.3.

Climate change adaptation and land use pattern change

One-third of respondents in the Mountain region and about 50 percent in the Hill and Terai regions are either adapting to climate change impacts or are experiencing some degree of benefits from climate change. Table 30.4 records the number and proportion of respondents who have adopted any of the adaptation measures to develop farming system resiliency related to water resources.

Over 62 percent of respondents have not adopted any measures to adapt to climate change. Reasons for not adopting any measures are presented in Table 30.5. Respondents reported lack

Table 30.4 Adaptation measures in study regions

Adaptation measures	Mountain (%)	Hill (%)	Terai (%)	Total (%)	Rank
Planting time adjustment[1]	13	22	34	23	3
Varietal selection[2]	33	26	47	36	1
Less water technology	17	25	41	28	2
Drought resistant variety	0	1%	0%	<1%	4

Source: Field Survey, 2015.

Notes

1 Farmers change the planting date (usually to an earlier date) to avoid insect infestation, match soil temperature to germination, and to exploit soil moisture in rain-fed areas. Farmers report that planting corn seven to ten days earlier in Terai reduces the probability of maize-stem borer infestation.
2 A majority of smallholders uses local cultivars. Some of these cultivars are drought resistant. The survey indicated that some farmers are choosing Ghaiya and CH-45, two prominent upland rice varieties used in Nepal in expected drought seasons. Both varieties are low yielding but are adopted to avoid total crop failure in the waterless paddy cultivation.

Table 30.5 Reasons for not adopting adaptive measures

Reasons	Mountain (%)	Hill (%)	Terai (%)	Total (%)	Ranks
High cost	33	55	34	41	2
Uncertain output market	10	17	6	11	5
Lack of inputs	67	28	26	40	3
Lack of extension services	67	86	53	68	1
Lack of self confidence	0	23	16	13	4

Source: Field Survey, 2015.

of extension services, high input costs, and lack of reliable farm inputs as the three major reasons for not adopting resiliency measures.

With respect to the first decade of the century, approximately 71 percent of respondents have changed their land use patterns. The underlying reasons behind land use/land cover change are presented in Table 30.6. More than half of the respondents (52 percent) changed their land use due to reduced water levels.

Current extension services provide assistance related only to farming practices such as land preparation, seed rate, fertilizer, and crop protection. There are no extension programs related to climate change information, adaptation practices, and water resource management. Similarly, the forest and soil conservation department of the Nepal government has no specific programs to address the climate, water, and forest nexus.

Access to credit and electricity enhances peoples' capacity for adaptation actions. For example, uninterrupted electricity allows the use of water pumps. However, one-third of the respondents do not have access to power. Similarly, only about 60 percent of respondents have access to formal credit. Those without access to formal credit must rely on informal financial institutions such as landlords, and creditors who charge exorbitantly high interest rates (as high as 40 percent per annum). Credit constraint limits investments in agriculture especially among smallholders and members of marginalized ethnic communities.

Table 30.6 Reasons for adopting land use pattern change

Reasons	Mountain (%)	Hill (%)	Terai (%)	Total (%)	Ranks
Prevalence of pest/disease	13	15	3	10	5
Reduced water level	40	43	73	52	1
Increased water level	18	0	27	15	4
Decreased productivity	30	41	36	36	2
New profit venture	47	25	7	26	3

Source: Field Survey, 2015.

A logistics regression analysis was undertaken to explain the propensity of respondents to make adaptations to climate change. While the analysis found some difference among the three study areas, in general, higher farm income and better access to credit increased the likelihood that farmers had made or were in the process of making adaptations in their farming systems. The age and gender of respondents generally had no effect on people's decision to undertake adaptive strategies. Extension services had a negative effect, suggesting that the service, in fact, discouraged departures from traditional practices.

Conclusions

The findings that only 46 percent of total water demand is fulfilled and that farmers are willing to pay about 73 percent more than the current (base) price of water strongly suggest the need for water resource infrastructure development, and more effective water resource management and allocation. A concerted effort to provide better extension information focused on adaptations to changing climate and water availability, and assistance in the development of institutional arrangements with which farmers are comfortable; greater access to credit and policies to provide more irrigation infrastructure could help close the cropping intensity gap (between adaptive and non-adaptive farmers) and boost the regional economy by expanding agricultural production. If water resource development through investments in reservoirs and irrigation equipment were undertaken to provide adequate water for irrigation of the remaining 76 percent of arable land (MOAD, 2016), livestock, and household uses, the Koshi River basin alone could add as much as 46,958 km² of irrigated crop land, and a 10 percent increment in livestock (herd size) and reduced expenditures of time for household water procurement. A conservative estimate of impacts would be an increase in farm outputs of about 117,000 metric tons of cereal crops (rice, maize, wheat, barley), 20,000 metric tons of vegetables and livestock, worth about NRs.20–25 million to the local economy. This value was calculated on the basis of available cultivable land, productivity difference between irrigated and rain-fed farming, and current market structure (Author's calculation, 2016).

References

Chaudhari, P., Aryal, K., 2009. *Global warming in Nepal: Challenges and policy imperatives.* Journal of Forest and Livelihood 8(1), 4–14.

Conceição, P., Zhang, Y., 2010. *Discounting in the context of climate change economics: The policy implications of uncertainty and global asymmetries.* Environmental Economics and Policy Studies 12, 31–57.

Eriksson, M., Xu, J., Shrestha, A.B., Vaidya, R.A., Nepal, S., Sandstörm, K., 2009. *The changing Himalayas: Impact of climate change on water resources and livelihoods in the greater Himalayas. Perspectives on water and climate change adaptation.* ICIMOD, Kathmandu.

Howden, S.M., Soussana, J.F., Tubiello, F.N., Chhetri, N., Dunlop, M., Meinke, H., 2007. *Adapting agriculture to climate change*. Proceedings of the National Academy of Sciences 104, 19691–19696.

Immerzeel, W.W., Beek, L.P.H., Bierkens, M.F.P., 2010. *Climate change will affect the Asian water towers*. Science 328, 1382–1385. DOI: 10.1126/science.1183188.

Intergovernmental Panel on Climate Change (IPCC), 2007. *Climate change 2007: The physical science basis. Contribution of Working Group I to the Fourth Assessment Report of the Intergovernmental Panel on Climate Change*. Ed. Solomon, S., Qin, D., Manning, M., Chen, Z., Marquis, M., Averyt, K.B., Tignor, M., Miller, H.L. Cambridge University Press, Cambridge; New York.

International Monetary Fund, 2017. *World economic outlook database*. www.imf.org/external/pubs/ft/weo/2017/01/weodata/index.aspx. (accessed 9.29.18).

Kaphle, M., Dahal, K.K., 2014. *Accessing water resources: A case study of ways to improve access of marginalized communities to underutilized lakes for fish farming in Rukum and Kapilbastu Districts, Nepal*. Journal of Forest and Livelihood 12(1), 64–74.

Khanal, R.C., 2009. *Climate change and organic agriculture*. Journal of Agriculture and Environment 10, 100–110.

Knox, J., Hess, T., Daccache, A., Wheeler, T., 2012. *Climate change impacts on crop productivity in Africa and South Asia*. Environmental Research Letters 7(3), 1–8.

Lettenmaier, D.P., Wood, E.F., Wallis, J.R., 1994. *Hydro-climatological trends in continental United States, 1948–1988*. Journal of Climate 7, 586–607.

Liverman, D., 2008. *Assessing impacts, adaptation and vulnerability: Reflections on the Working Group II Report of the Intergovernmental Panel on Climate Change*. Global Environmental Change 18(1), 4–7.

Malla, G., 2008. *Climate change and its implication on Nepalese agriculture*. Journal of Agriculture and Environment 9, 62–71.

MOAD – Ministry of Agricultural Development, Government of Nepal, 2016. *Annual progress report*. Kathmandu.

Myers, S.S., Zanobetti, A., Kloog, I., Huybers, P., Leakey, A.D., Bloom, A.J., Carlisle, E., Dietterich, L.H., Fitzgerald, G., Hasegawa, T., Holbrook, N.M., Nelson, R.L., Ottman, M.J., Raboy, V., Sakai, H., Sartor, K.A., Schwartz, J., Seneweera, S., Tausz, M., Usui, Y., 2014. *Increasing CO2 threatens human nutrition*. Nature 510(7503), 139–142.

Parry, M.L., Rosenzweig, C., Iglesias, A., Livermore, M., Fischer, G., 2004. *Effects of climate change on global food production under SRES emissions and socio-economic scenarios*. Global Environmental Change 14(1), 53–67.

Polley, H.W., 2002. *Implications of atmospheric and climatic change for crop yield and water use efficiency*. Crop Science 42, 131–140.

Poudel, K.L., 2017. *Three essays on economics of water resources management in Nepal* (Unpublished PhD Dissertation). University of Missouri, Columbia, MO.

Pradhan, N.S., Khadgi, V., Schipper, L., Kaur, N., Geoghegan, T., 2012. *Role of policy and institutions in local adaptation to climate change: Case studies on responses to too much and too little water in the Hindu Kush Himalayas*. ICIMOD, Kathmandu.

Schiermeier, Q., 2008. *Water: A long dry summer*. Nature 452, 270–273.

Sinha, S.K., 1997. *Global change scenario: Current and future with references to land cover change and suitable agriculture – South East Asian context*. Current Science 72(11), 846–854.

WECS, 2011. *National water plan*. His Majesty's Government of Nepal, Water and Energy Commission Secretariat (WECS). Kathmandu.

PART V

Rural policy reviews

31

RURAL POLICY IN THE UNITED STATES

Thomas G. Johnson

Introduction

As other authors (including some in this volume) point out, rural policy includes both *narrow rural policies*, those "that have as their stated purpose the improvement in social and economic conditions of rural people and places" (Johnson, 2013, p. 42), and *broad rural policies*, that are of significance to rural people and places, but which are not directly focused on rural issues and problems. While the United States Department of Agriculture (USDA) is the Congressionally mandated lead department for US rural development policy, numerous agencies in most federal departments, including Transportation, Education, Health and Human Services, Housing and Urban Development, and Commerce, contribute significantly to federal rural development efforts. Social Security, Medicare and Medicaid are huge sources of income in many rural communities in the US. A review of US policy affecting rural people and places would be incomplete without acknowledging the important role of programs administered by these agencies. This chapter deals with all types of rural policy but will primarily focus on narrow rural policy.

It is also possible to distinguish *rural policy* from *rural development policy*. While these terms are often used interchangeably, it is useful to define *rural policy* as policy that deals primarily with the provision of services and improvement in quality of life of rural residents and *rural development policy* as policy that aims to improve the performance of rural economies (Johnson, 2013). Clearly rural policy includes rural development policy since economic performance is a critical part of the quality of life in rural communities, but many important programs are not primarily economic in scope.

The issue of US rural policy has been discussed by numerous policy analysts over the years (Bonnen, 1992; Johnson and Fluharty, 2001; Fluharty, 2011; Johnson, 2013; Weber and Kilkenny, 2018). In most cases these articles have decried the lack, or at least weakness, of US rural policy. But a lack of coherent, aggressive public programs to address rural issues and problems is a default form of policy. This chapter briefly reviews the history of rural policy and rural development policy evolution in the US. It then addresses the current and emerging context in which rural policy is made and operationalized and describes and assesses the rural policies in place in 2018. Finally, the chapter looks forward to emerging challenges and possible policy responses.

A brief history of US rural policy

Over the last half century, rural regions of the United States, like most industrialized nations, have been on an economic and social rollercoaster. Prior to the 1970s the status and role of rural America within the larger economy was relatively clear. Urban America manufactured new goods in the early stages of the product cycle, while rural America generated raw materials, food, and energy. In later stages of the product cycle manufacturing plants relocated to rural regions where land and labor were less expensive.

Rural policy in this period included some effort to attract and retain key economic base sectors including agricultural, mining, forestry, and manufacturing. But for the most part, US rural policy, like that in many other countries, was equated with agricultural policy. Government programs designed to financially support agriculture and farmers were assumed to assure a strong and relatively stable engine for rural economies. Non-agricultural rural firms provided inputs, services, and markets for farms and agribusinesses. Farms and agribusinesses provided a strong tax base for local governments in rural areas. In this context, policies designed to increase agricultural productivity and profitability also promoted rural development goals. Rural communities could count on the linkages between their agricultural, mining and manufacturing sectors and their financial, trade, and service sectors.

However, due to the success of public and private investments in productivity-enhancing research, technology, and infrastructure, agriculture, as well as other rural sectors such as mining, forestry, fishing, and manufacturing, shed workers, while producing more commodities than ever. As the traditional rural industries became more capital intensive, rural employment bases shrank and populations declined. The labor released from traditional agriculture sectors eventually found employment in the services, financial, transportation, trade, and other sectors. Some of these new jobs were located in rural areas, but most were located in urban areas where economies of scale and agglomeration economies meant the productivity of both labor and capital was higher.

In the 1970s and briefly in the 1990s rural areas enjoyed population growth and relative prosperity (referred to optimistically as the rural renaissance) but eventually most rural regions fell back into decline. High-amenity and recreation regions were the exception.

The current context for US rural policy

Weber and Kilkenny provide an excellent overview of the current context for rural policy in the US. They describe the rural regions of the US as:

- a geography with extensive low-density and remote territory;
- economies no longer dependent on the agricultural sector;
- economies where agricultural adjustment has led to high incomes for many farm families but to poverty for many other rural residents;
- small rural counties and towns facing out-migration and population loss;
- economies where "market failures have stalled wealth creation and public services in small remote rural counties" (Weber and Kilkenny, 2018, p. 52).

Today the traditional economic bases of rural areas in the US – farming, forestry, fishing, and mining – account for less than 2 percent of total employment, income, and gross domestic product. The indirect economic activities generated by these basic sectors (the multiplier effects) are relatively small especially in rural areas since in many cases these indirect jobs are located in urban areas. Thus, public policy focused on these traditional rural sectors has a small and declining impact on the prosperity and opportunities available to rural residents. In fact, many of these sectoral policies have net negative effects on rural economies. For example, Thompson (2007) speculates that US agricultural policy, which subsidizes farm income and stabilizes agricultural commodity prices, has several deleterious effects on rural communities including farm consolidation and concomitant population losses, higher land values thus reducing competitiveness of rural businesses, and reduced entrepreneurship among farmers and related businesses. In fact, few rural and agricultural policy analysts today would argue, as many did in the past, that good farm policy is good rural policy.

Today, US rural policy is made and executed in an environment of change and uncertainty. Johnson (2001) lists several sources of change and uncertainty faced by rural communities; namely technological change, globalization, localization (the rising importance of local decisions and initiatives), changing industrial structure, changing settlement patterns, aging of the population, and evolving governance (decentralization, e-governance). To this list should be added the need to adapt to climate change. Each of these trends influences the need for, and success of, alternative policy strategies.

Rural regions are not unfamiliar with technological change. Agriculture was arguably the earliest sector to be significantly transformed by technology. More recently, technological change in mining, forestry, and other extractive sectors in the US have continued to create wrenching change in the rural economy. Today, the services, the largest employer in rural economies in the US, are also being transformed by technology. The growing role of information and communication technologies represents both opportunities and threats for rural residents and employers. These opportunities and threats create both efficiency and equity reasons for policy intervention, but require quite different strategies than in the past. Today's technology-related policy challenges include such issues as the rural broadband deficit, telemedicine and distance education, e-commerce, e-governance, and others.

Globalization, the growing integration of the world economy, is related to technology but leads to different stresses and challenges for rural residents and businesses. It has been argued that globalization has accelerated the process of economic agglomeration, by increasing competition and expanding market size for many products (Scott and Storper, 2003). Furthermore, globalization has led to a diversity of responses by regional economies. Some regions have found their niche and adapted to the new competitive realities. Other regions have found it difficult to adapt and experienced various degrees of decline. This growing diversity and specialization makes one-size-fits-all policy even less effective than in the past.

Changes in settlement patterns, especially urbanization, are clearly related to technological change and globalization but have implications of their own. Urbanization has created a political and social gulf between rural and urban areas, even as regional economic specialization has made rural and urban areas more interrelated. Urban voters and politicians in the US are less likely to understand the needs of rural areas and residents, and less likely to appreciate how vulnerable they have become because of their dependence on water, energy, and food that is produced by an ever-declining portion of the population.

Together this policy context requires a different approach to rural policy in the United States but simultaneously makes rural policy-making more difficult and less responsive to these changing needs. The following sections explore the current state of US rural policy in this context.

Current rural policy challenges in the US

Non-farm employment and income

For most farm families in the US, a reasonable level of income and benefits such as health insurance and retirement savings depend on the availability of good off-farm employment and small business opportunities. But given thin local markets and the limited size and diversity of the rural labor force, the scale of many rural firms is insufficient to be competitive. In a world where scale is becoming more and more important this puts rural areas at a distinct disadvantage. However, with a global marketing strategy and intensive use of skilled labor and information technology, the economies of scale necessary to be competitive may still be attainable in certain rural sectors.

Under-investment in human capital

The most depressed rural areas in the US are also those with the lowest levels of educational attainment. A poorly educated workforce and a poor public education system retard employment growth, and low rates of employment growth discourage individuals from investing in education. Those that do are more likely to migrate to other rural, urban, or suburban regions. Similar patterns are evident in other types of human capital – skills development, nutrition, and health.

Infrastructure

The critical public policy trends discussed above highlight the importance of safe, dependable, and affordable infrastructure. Rural economic development requires investment in the traditional forms of infrastructure – roads, airports, housing, water and sewerage, hospitals and schools – and in the new infrastructures – cable, DSL (internet), fiber optics, and wireless systems. Skilled labor will also demand amenities such as parks, recreational facilities, and public safety. The challenge is to provide this infrastructure over large areas and small populations.

Climate change

Both climate change mitigation and adaptation are challenges for US rural policy. The conversion from fossil fuels to renewable energy is an opportunity for rural areas to benefit from a more distributed energy system and an energy comparative advantage (Johnson and Altman, 2014). However, rural areas will face significant disruptions and costs related to climate change adaptation. Referring to the US, Lal *et al.* (2011) conclude that, "rural communities tend to be more vulnerable than their urban counterparts due to factors such as demography, occupations, earnings, literacy, poverty incidence, and dependency on government funds" (p. 819).

US rural policy in 2018

Policy-makers have been aware of these challenges (with the exception of climate change) for many years but little progress has been made at addressing them. A general description of rural policies in 2018 follows.

The Agricultural Act of 2014

The official US rural policy (at least the narrow rural policy) is expressed in the Rural Development Title of the Farm Bill which is periodically amended and reauthorized. Recent farm bills include the Farm Security and Rural Investment Act of 2002; the Food, Conservation, and Energy Act of 2008; and the Agricultural Act of 2014. As of 2018 preparations are being made to write the next Farm Bill which would typically take effect in 2019 or 2020.

Each Farm Bill authorizes program and budget lines. With the exception of expenditures that are mandated by other legislation, specific expenditures require appropriation bills before funds can be committed. Authorization and appropriation bills are the responsibility of the US Congress. The administration (the White House and the many departments including the USDA) have some flexibility in how they work with the authorizing legislation and how they expend appropriated funds. The following discussion describes the administration policy for rural US.

Weber and Kilkenny (2018) describe US rural policy as authorized in the Agricultural Act of 2014, and administered by the Obama administration. They describe the objectives of US rural policy as follows: "(1) improve the quality of life in rural areas; (2) stimulate rural economic development; and (3) reduce rural poverty", and the programs offered to achieve these objectives,

> (1) supporting public services, and public and private infrastructure; (2) stimulating economic development to provide jobs and income for those able to participate economically, and (3) providing a social safety net for those who are not able to fully participate in the economy.
>
> *(p. 56)*

The USDA Rural Development (RD) branch is tasked with delivering most of the programs that fall under these objectives. Over the years USDA RD has developed and maintained numerous grants, loans, loan guarantees, and technical assistance programs to increase and improve rural housing stock, water, sewerage, and other local utilities, community infrastructure including broad band, and to support local efforts to attract agribusiness and non-agricultural related employment. Most of these programs are limited to beneficiaries residing in "rural" areas, although the definition of rural varies significantly from program to program.

During the administration of Barack Obama, an initiative of importance to rural policy was the emphasis placed on interagency collaboration, especially when addressing rural problems and issues. In 2011, President Obama established the White House Rural Council, which included representatives of 25 federal agencies. While the council has had limited direct impact, it did send a signal to federal agencies that interagency coordination and collaboration was encouraged by the administration. Efforts were made to coordinate the programs and activities of USDA with other agencies including, Transportation, Commerce, the Environmental Protection Agency, Housing and Urban Development, various regional authorities such as the Appalachian Regional Commission, and other federal government agencies. As a result, several jointly funded and administered programs were undertaken between 2012 and 2016 (White House, 2015, 2016a).

As of 2018, the US is still transitioning into the administration of President Donald Trump. As in most administration transitions, the policy priorities are expected to change. In early 2017 the Department of Agriculture was reorganized. The position of Undersecretary for Rural Development was abolished but an Assistant to the Secretary for Rural Development position has been established and filled. This reorganization is potentially an elevation of rural development as a policy priority. The White House Rural Council, which was established by President Obama in 2001, has been abolished, but an Inter-agency Task Force on Agriculture and Rural Prosperity was established by President Trump (USDA, 2017). The Task Force final report was released on January 9, 2018 (USDA, 2018). The report identifies e-connectivity, improved rural quality of life, support for the rural workforce, harnessing technological development, and rural economic development as the priorities for agricultural and rural policy.

As noted above, it is often argued that the US has no real rural policy (or even a narrower rural development policy). But there have been various policy themes espoused by the recent administrations. The following section explores the conceptual foundations of some of the themes underlying current US rural policy and how these concepts are being operationalized.

Place-based policy

The first of these ongoing policy themes involves experiments in placed-based programs. Barca (2009) defines place-based policy as,

> a long-term strategy aimed at tackling persistent underutilization of potential and reducing persistent social exclusion in specific places through external interventions and multilevel governance. It promotes the supply of integrated goods and services tailored to contexts, and it triggers institutional changes. In a place-based policy, public interventions rely on local knowledge and are verifiable and submitted to scrutiny, while linkages among places are taken into account.
>
> *(p. vii)*

Unlike many other countries, where place-based rural policy is focused on building on the strengths of rural places, the goal of place-based US rural policy is to redress inefficiencies and inequities by addressing impediments in specific places, especially those places that are lagging more dynamic places. The hope is that by tailoring programs to address a place's weaknesses and exploiting its strengths, higher returns to policy investments can be achieved. It is also hoped that policy will have its greatest impact in lagging regions thus leading to regional convergence. There is reason to believe that such a strategy not only lifts the lagging regions but also boosts the national efficiency and rate of growth (Barca *et al.*, 2012). Thus place-based policies may be one of those cases where complementarities between efficiency and equity can be found.

The theoretical rationale for place-based policy builds upon neoclassical economic concepts of economic efficiency adding a spatial dimension to emphasize the importance of recognizing the role of diverse geographies in the process of economic change and development. Diverse natural resources and spatial, cultural, social, and institutional dimensions, amenities, diverse labor forces, and unique spatial arrays of markets and infrastructure all make flexibility in program implementation an important feature of rural policy.

Cultural and social dimensions of place-based policy introduce the role of preferences, collective societal goals, and interpersonal relationships into the process of prioritizing economic development goals and strategies. Culture introduces numerous, often subtle, effects on behaviors that influence people's response to policy (Guiso *et al.*, 2006). For example, communities and regions with a stronger cultural affinity to natural landscapes will find industrial development less attractive. Communities with a stronger association with land will be less likely to sell, rent, or dramatically change land uses. Attitudes towards education, risk taking, entrepreneurship, women's roles, democratic processes, and many others are both culturally based and economically relevant. Thus, policy that allows for spatial variation in its approach to cultural differences is likely to be more effective.

The institutional dimension of place-based policy is a critical concern for rural and regional policy (Wood and Valler, 2004). The argument here is that institutions are unique to place and historically based. Institutions are critical to economic development because they are the foundation of markets, they establish and protect property rights, and they mediate economic and social interactions. A necessary characteristic of institutions is that they change very slowly to create stability and reduce transactions costs. But development is a process of change, and institutions must also evolve to reflect changing technology, preferences, demographics, and environmental conditions. Institutions must, therefore, reflect the local economic structure, preferences, and demographics of local residents and environments of places. For these reasons, policies and programs are not easily transferred from one place to another because without the necessary institutions in place, the programs will have quite different consequences in a new place than they had in another location.

Because of these spatial, cultural, social, and institutional differences from place to place, effective policies must be place-based. This does not preclude national or state rural policies, but it means that these policies must be flexible enough to adapt to the natural, cultural, social, environmental, and economic conditions of each place. It also means that policy priorities and delivery processes are usually best determined at the local level.

The USDA lists several place-based programs that it participates in (USDA Food and Nutrition Service, 2016). One of the programs listed is the Promise Zone Program which is jointly sponsored with the US Department of Housing and Urban Development (USHUD, 2017). This program, initiated during the Obama administration, has been preserved by the Trump administration. Its goal is to pair, "Federal government partners with local leaders to streamline resources across agencies and deliver comprehensive support" (White House, 2016b). A related program is Promise Neighborhoods sponsored by the US Department of Education (USDoE, 2017). This program provides funding and technical assistance to develop place-based solutions in underperforming school districts. Another notable place-based program of the USDA is the Know Your Farmer, Know Your Food program, which is an element the department's policy to promote local and regional food systems.

Rural wealth creation

The traditional emphasis of US rural development policy has been on increasing the rate of growth in productivity and income of rural residents. In the past, when rural policy was largely equated with agricultural policy, this meant that higher farm incomes equaled rural development. Thus, it was accepted that farm income supports and programs designed to increase the price of agricultural commodities were the most direct paths to rural development. The most common indicator of economic performance, gross domestic product (GDP), could be applied to rural sectors and rural regions to gauge the level of success of the designed rural policy. Measures of median and average family and per capita disposable income were used as indicators of welfare and the distribution of income as an indicator of equity. Disposable income below some level was defined as poverty.

More recently the concept of wealth has reappeared as a goal and as an indicator of progress towards economic development. The distribution of wealth has been suggested as an alternative to distribution of income as an indicator of equity. Why wealth? Surely people's welfare is more dependent on their ability to access and consume goods and services (broadly defined) than it is to their amassed wealth. While this is true it is also true that the sustainability of people's consumption of goods and services depends on their comprehensive wealth including their access to public assets.

At the societal level, aggregate well-being is determined by the flow of benefits from aggregate wealth. A sustainable level of consumption, as Nordhaus (2000) posits, is "the maximum amount that a nation can consume while ensuring that members of all current and future generations can have expected lifetime consumption or utility that is at least as high as current consumption or utility" (p. 259). Nordhaus demonstrates that this constant or growing level of consumption requires constant or rising levels of societal wealth. And this wealth includes more than just financial capital and fixed investments. It includes various non-market and intangible capitals that all must be maintained or enhanced to assure a sustained level of consumption into the future. Hoffer and Levy (2010) identify seven types of capital – intellectual, social, individual, natural, built, financial, and political. These capitals may be individually owned and controlled (human capital for example) or publicly owned and available (built infrastructure, natural capital, and various types of intellectual capital).

GDP is a gross flow measure that ignores changes in (investment in or depreciation of) assets. Wealth is a stock measure that is solely focused on the changing stock of assets. Like GDP, well-being is a flow but one which depends critically on net wealth measured in a number of dimensions in addition to income. During the last two decades, there have been significant advances made in expanding the indicators of economic performance to include various non-market and intangible capitals (especially the natural and environmental capitals) and their associated flows of goods and services to estimate broader indicators of wealth (Nordhaus, 1996).

The policy implications of this focus on wealth are numerous, especially for rural people and places. First, a focus on wealth assures a longer-term perspective, and more sustainable results. Second, rural policy based on a wealth perspective will become more focused on investment and less on income support, a key tenet of the new rural paradigm. Third, a greater policy focus on natural capital is particularly important for rural areas where a majority of a nation's natural capital exists and which represents a very large portion of rural wealth despite its non-market characteristics. The growing focus on rural wealth creation strategies in the United States is evidence that this type of rural policy will have significant visibility for some time.

In the United States, rural wealth creation was adopted as official policy by the USDA. Secretary Tom Vilsack stated that the USDA, "must help rural communities create wealth so they are self-sustaining, repopulating and thriving economically" (Pender *et al.*, 2012, p. 1). The practical implications of adopting wealth creation as a policy goal is that measures of economic performance and assessments of rural policy should then be in terms of changing levels and distributions of net assets (broadly defined). As a result, a number of recent research projects and evaluation exercises have been focused on wealth consequences of policy (Pender *et al.*, 2011; Markley and Low, 2012; Pender *et al.*, 2014; Weber *et al.*, 2013; National Association of Development Organizations, 2016).

Because this policy focus is new, examples of comprehensive rural wealth policies and programs are still rare. One example is the Stronger Economies Together (SET) program which is jointly sponsored by USDA RD and the four regional rural development centers (USDA Rural Development, 2017). The SET program is built around the principles of place-based and wealth creation policy.

Another example is the recently established National Endowment for the Rural Cultural Wealth Lab, which will apply the comprehensive wealth framework to understand the roll of cultural, social, and natural capital in the rural wealth creation process (University of Iowa, 2016).

Conclusions

The process of policy development for rural regions in the United States has generally been slow and ineffective. A number of policy scholars have speculated on why this is the case. The most common conclusion is that US rural policy is difficult to develop because rural people and places lack a well-defined constituency. Unlike sector-based stakeholders, many residents of rural America do not identify common interests with their fellow rural residents as readily as they do with their sectoral cooperators and competitors. Farmers are more likely to recognize their interests in detail in the periodic Farm Bill legislation dealing with agricultural commodities, crop insurance, and even environmental regulation. Rural manufacturers will pay close attention to immigration, taxation, transportation, and regulatory policies. But farmers, rural manufacturers, rural educators, and rural residents in general may not recognize their common interest in policies to encourage the rural services such as education, health care, and economic diversification.

Meanwhile, urban residents in highly urbanized countries like the US have less familiarity with rural problems as they become increasingly distanced from their agrarian origins. Younger generations in the rapidly growing urban areas have fewer familial and social connections to rural people. At the political level members of the US Congress increasingly lack rural constituents or personal experience with rural issues and are thus less likely to give rural issues priority.

Together the lack of a cohesive rural constituency in the US and the declining connection to other constituencies makes rural policy-making more difficult and less likely to be responsive to rural needs unless policy analysts work with policy advocates to increase understanding of the issues and appropriate responses.

Confounding these growing challenges to rural policy-making in the US is the growing criticality of rural vitality and growing dependency of urban populations on the health of rural economies. A common outcome of this policy-making dilemma is a tendency for policy-makers to apply policies designed for urban areas, across the rural–urban spectrum, without regard for the unique needs and constraints of rural regions.

However, as pointed out above, there are promising new policy strategies and tools emerging. Policy theorists, analysts, and educators will play an important role in testing, improving, and implementing the new and future policy strategies for rural areas. Of particular interest to this chapter and this volume are the benefits of comparing the experience of countries around the world.

References

Barca, F., 2009. *An agenda for a reformed cohesion policy: A place-based approach to meeting European Union challenges and expectations.* Independent Report prepared at the request of Danuta Hübner, Commissioner for Regional Policy. European Union Parliament. www.europarl.europa.eu/meetdocs/2009_2014/documents/regi/dv/barca_report_/barca_report_en.pdf.

Barca, F., McCann, P., Rodríguez-Pose, A., 2012. *The case for regional development intervention: Place-based versus place-neutral approaches.* Journal of Regional Science 52, 134–152.

Bonnen, J.T., 1992. *Why is there no coherent US rural policy?* Policy Studies Journal 20(2), 190–201.

Fluharty, C.W., 2011. *Why rural policy now matters to agriculture: Rural development, regional innovation, and the next Farm Bill.* Drake Journal of Agricultural Law 16, 31–67.

Guiso, L., Sapienza, P., Zingales, L., 2006. *Does culture affect economic outcomes?* NBER Working Paper No. 11999. National Bureau of Economic Research. Cambridge, MA. www.nber.org/papers/w11999.

Hoffer, D., Levy, M., 2010. *Measuring community wealth.* A report for the Wealth Creation in Rural Communities Project of the Ford Foundation. www.yellowwood.org/wealthcreation.aspx.

Johnson, T.G., 2001. *The rural economy in a new century.* International Regional Science Review 24(1), 31–37.

Johnson, T.G., 2013. *Rural policy,* in: Green, G. (Ed.), *Handbook of rural development.* Edward Elgar, Cheltenham, 42–55.

Johnson, T.G., Altman, I., 2014. *Rural development opportunities in the bioeconomy.* Biomass and Bioenergy 63(April), 341–344.

Johnson, T.G., Fluharty, C.W., 2001. *Rural development,* in: Outlaw, J.L., Smith, E.G. (Eds.), *The 2002 Farm Bill: Policy options and consequences.* Farm Foundation, pp. 203–208. www.farmfoundation.org/webcontent/The-2002-Farm-Bill-Policy-Options-and-Consequences-816.aspx.

Lal, P., Alavalapati, J.R.R., Mercer, E., 2011. *Socio-economic impacts of climate change on rural United States.* Mitigation and Adaptation Strategies for Global Change 16(7), 819–844.

Markley, D.M., Low, S.A., 2012. *Wealth, entrepreneurship, and rural livelihoods.* Choices 27(1), 6–11.

National Association of Development Organizations, 2016. *Measuring rural wealth creation: A guide for regional development organizations.* www.nado.org/wp-content/uploads/2016/12/MeasuringWealthCreation-RDOsFinal.pdf.

Nordhaus, W.D., 1996. *Budget deficits and national saving.* Challenge 39(2), 45–49.

Nordhaus, W.D., 2000. *New directions in national economic accounting.* American Economic Review 90, 259–263.

Pender, J., Marré, A., Reeder, R., 2011. *Rural wealth creation: Concepts, measures, and strategies.* American Journal of Agricultural Economics 94(2), 535–541.

Pender, J., Weber, B., Fawbush, W., 2012. *Theme overview: Rural wealth creation.* Choices, Quarter 1. http://choicesmagazine.org/choices-magazine/theme-articles/rural-wealth-creation/theme-overview-rural-wealth-creation.

Pender, J.L., Weber, B.A., Johnson, T.G., Fannin, J.M. (Eds.), 2014. *Rural wealth creation.* Routledge, Abingdon.

Scott, A., Storper, M., 2003. *Regions, globalization, development.* Regional Studies 37, 549–578.

Thompson, R.L., 2007. *Globalization and rural America.* Chicago Fed Letter, Federal Reserve Bank of Chicago, Chicago, IL.

United States Department of Agriculture (USDA), 2017. *Interagency Task Force on Agriculture and Rural Prosperity.* www.usda.gov/ruralprosperity.

United States Department of Agriculture (USDA), 2018. *Report to the President of the United States from the Task Force on Agriculture and Rural Prosperity.* www.usda.gov/sites/default/files/documents/rural-prosperity-report.pdf.

United States Department of Agriculture (USDA), Food and Nutrition Service, 2016. *Place based initiatives.* www.fns.usda.gov/sites/default/files/snap/Attachment-C-Place-Based-Initiatives.pdf.

United States Department of Agriculture (USDA), Rural Development, 2017. *Stronger economies together.* www.rd.usda.gov/about-rd/initiatives/stronger-economies-together.

United States Department of Education, 2017. *Promise neighborhoods.* www2.ed.gov/programs/promise-neighborhoods/index.html.

United States Department of Housing and Urban Development (USHUD), 2017. *Promise zones.* https://portal.hud.gov/hudportal/HUD?src=/program_offices/comm_planning/economicdevelopment/programs/pz.

University of Iowa, 2016. *NEA grant to help UI study how art can strengthen rural communities.* https://now.uiowa.edu/2016/12/nea-grant-help-ui-study-how-art-can-strengthen-rural-communities).

Weber, B., Kilkenny, M., 2018. *Rural policy in the United States,* in: Meyers, W.H., Johnson, T.G. (Eds.), *Handbook of international food and agricultural policies, Volume 1: Policies for agricultural markets and rural economic activity.* World Scientific Press, Singapore; New York, pp. 43–70.

Weber, J.G., Brown, J.P., Pender, J., 2013. *Rural wealth creation and emerging energy industries: Lease and royalty payments to farm households and businesses.* Research Working Paper RWP 13–07, The Federal Reserve Bank of Kansas City. www.kansascityfed.org/publicat/reswkpap/pdf/rwp13-07.pdf (accessed 8.11.17).

White House, 2015. *Fact sheet: The Partnerships for Opportunity and Workforce and Economic Revitalization (POWER) initiative.* March 27. https://obamawhitehouse.archives.gov/the-press-office/2015/03/27/fact-sheet-partnerships-opportunity-and-workforce-and-economic-revitaliz.

White House, 2016a. *Rural strategies that work: Lifting up federal policies that are responsive to the assets and challenges of rural America.* October 5. www.whitehouse.gov/sites/whitehouse.gov/files/images/Rural%20Policy%20Learnings%20Memo.pdf.

White House, 2016b. *Obama administration announces final round of promise zone designations to expand access to opportunity in urban, rural and tribal communities.* https://obamawhitehouse.archives.gov/the-press-office/2016/06/06/obama-administration-announces-final-round-promise-zone-designations.

Wood, A., Valler, D., 2004. *Governing local and regional economies: Institutions, politics and economic development.* Ashgate, Aldershot.

32

RURAL POLICY IN CANADA

Bill Reimer[1]

Canada remains heavily influenced by its colonial and mercantile past. Even today the legacy of the relationships among Indigenous peoples, French, and English language and cultural groups as they strove to establish and control an east–west economic and social union in the face of geography favoring north–south trade and relationships is clear. In this chapter are outlined the broad parameters of these initiatives and how they created the context for more narrow-focused policy directed to regional rather than rural concerns. Six eras in which major policies were initiated and promoted are identified. Special attention is also paid to rural policy in Quebec since it stands in contrast to the other provinces and territories. The chapter closes with a discussion of three themes in Canadian regional policy that provide a basis for international comparisons: institutional legacies, vision, and regional governance organization.

Introduction

Canada does not have a rural policy. As discussed below this is largely due to the confluence of a strong sectoral focus supporting trade and the priority of regional issues in the constitutional, governance, and institutional structures of the country. In Canada, regions are exclusively identified as sub-national regions – most often represented by the ten provinces and three northern territories (see Chapter 2) – but sometimes regrouped into five units: British Columbia (BC), Prairies (Alberta [AB], Saskatchewan [SK], and Manitoba [MB]), Ontario (ON), Quebec (QC), Atlantic (New Brunswick [NB], Prince Edward Island [PEI], Nova Scotia [NS], and Newfoundland and Labrador [NL]), Territories (Yukon, Northwest Territories [NT], and Nunavut [NU]).

The analysis of rural policies is often made complex by the ways in which "broad" and "narrow" policies both affect outcomes in rural places. Broad policies are those which may have an impact on rural and remote places but are not specifically directed to such populations. On the other hand, narrow policies specifically target rural populations, groups, or organizations (OECD, 2008). As Fairbairn (1998, p. 20) suggests, it is often the broad policies that dwarf the expenditures of the narrow.

In this chapter the main features of Canadian rural policy will be discussed through an analysis from both broad and narrow points of view. The former identifies some of the key characteristics of Canadian policy (trade, regional focus, and the organization of social supports) that provide important contexts in which the latter are formulated and function. Narrow policies are discussed through an historical analysis of major policy eras. Since Quebec is such an outlier with respect to these trends, a brief section on its history is included before turning to an assessment of rural policies with respect to three themes and some of the limitations in regional policy during the post-World War II period.

The historical and policy context of rural areas in Canada (the broad view)

Rural areas in Canada have been heavily influenced by trends affecting most nations over the last two centuries (Reimer and Bollman, 2010). As a colonial initiative, Canada's formation in 1867 was rooted in a history of economic and social mercantilism with institutionalized monopolies in a staples-based economy (Innis, 1972, 1999). Its transformation to industrial capitalism since then is characterized by a more diverse economy – including a strong services sector.

These changes have had significant impacts on rural areas. The increasing price of labor relative to capital, for example, has driven the mechanization of commodity production and resulted in the continuous decline of workers in rural areas (Reimer and Bollman, 2010; Schultz, 1972). Closely related to globalization, technical developments in communication and transportation have significantly changed the meaning of "distance" both nationally and internationally (Harvey, 1990). It is within the context of these broad trends that Canadian policies have been formed – giving relatively unique qualities to their national manifestations (Reimer and Bollman, 2010; Wallace, 2002).

Three of these national characteristics are particularly relevant for understanding the Canadian rural policy context, especially as a basis for international comparisons: the importance of trade, the regional structure of government, and the organization of social supports. These government and institutional structures interact with demographic transformations such as immigration, the post-World War II baby boom, urbanization, and an aging rural population to produce a complex series of challenges and opportunities for rural places.

The importance of trade

Canadians are, and always have been, a trading people. When Europeans first arrived in these territories, they found it populated with Indigenous peoples who knew how to easily move across its rivers and lakes – and carry with them the tools, materials, and resources that could be bartered for the things they needed (Ray, 1998). In their search for timber, fish, gold, and other materials for their expanding empires, the Europeans added to that trade, created an infrastructure that facilitated it, and left their mark on the society and economy that dominates Canadian life today (Innis, 1972).

Much of this trade is rural-related. The production and export of forest products, grain, fish, minerals, petroleum, and hydroelectricity are all rural products. These goods have sustained the country's economic position ever since confederation and they continue to preserve a positive balance of trade in spite of Canadians' reliance on consumer goods from the rest of the world (see Figure 32.1). The importance of this trade has driven rural and regional policy in some pervasive and fundamental ways.

Canadian scholars have traced the influence of Canadian commodity trade to policies regarding labor, education, health, immigration, land use, transportation, and the treatment of Indigenous peoples (Poelzer and Coates, 2015). Treaty negotiations with Indigenous peoples, military action, and cultural genocide have all been used to control land for the production of tradable resources (Parrott, 2017). In order to facilitate labor mobility, national agreements have been established for the coordination of education credentials and course credits across

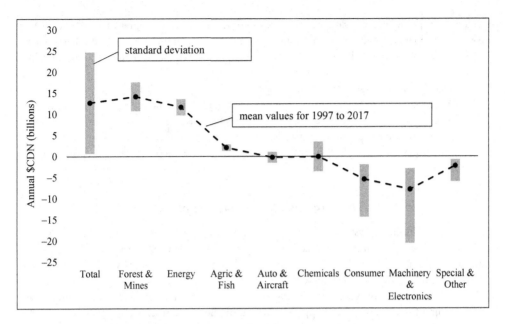

Figure 32.1 Balance of international payments for Canadian goods, 1997 to 2017

Source: CANSIM Table 228–0062.

provinces. Similarly, in spite of the fact that health is a provincial responsibility, the federal government has acted to establish and coordinate a health-care system that is relatively consistent across the country – facilitating mobility without the loss of health-care benefits.

The regional structure of governments

The regional structure of Canada has also strongly conditioned the formulation of rural policy. Canadian confederation was officially launched in 1867 with only four provinces joining. By the turn of the twentieth century, five other provinces and territories had joined but it was not until 1999, when Nunavut was established, that the full complement of 13 provinces and territories was recognized. It was only in 1982 that the Constitution Act was signed – enshrining the Charter of Rights and Freedoms and permitting Canadians to amend the constitution without permission from Britain.

The 1982 Constitution Act included a provision for equalization payments among the provinces. This formalized a system established in 1957 to support the Atlantic provinces who were struggling with low rates of growth and economic hardship relative to the other provinces. Under the Constitution Act, the federal government was given the power to make equalization payments between "have" and "have not" provinces to maintain reasonably consistent levels of public services across the country. The terms and limits of this arrangement have been modified since then, but the regional focus of the payments and the amounts of money involved ensured that attention to regional and provincial issues would be an important feature of Canadian geo-politics.

The result is a confederation where rural-related policies are implicated by a complex web of federal, provincial, and shared responsibilities. Trade, Indigenous peoples, currency, and defense, for example, are under federal jurisdiction; public lands and forests, health, municipal institutions, education, and business licenses are provincially designated; and agriculture, economic development, public works, transportation, communications, and immigration are shared. Over the years, the details of these responsibilities have been challenged – producing a balance of power between the federal and provincial governments which is regularly contested and redefined.

Negotiating and managing the shared responsibilities creates multiple opportunities for the provincial, territorial, and federal governments to test the limits of policy agreements and introduce new issues for discussion. Many of these issues arise as the result of economic or social crises (e.g. youth suicide, pipeline proposals, gas tax arrangements, the homeless, First Nations issues, agricultural topics, or health-care transfers), but the sectoral departments prevail as the most consistent agenda-setting agencies.[2]

The organization of social supports

Canada has established a system of social supports that is generally more collectivist than those in the US, but less so than in Scandinavian countries (Esping-Andersen, 1990). Born out of the hardship of World War I and the 1930s economic depression, the country was primed for government action at the end of World War II (Moscovitch, 2015). The ensuing economic growth of the 1950s and 1960s provided conditions for the expansion of programs supporting pensions, employment insurance, income supports, education, health, and housing (Reimer, 2010b). Unlike the earlier periods, where union and public unrest had been met with harsh suppression, by the mid-1940s the primary social-democrat party in Canada (the Canadian Commonwealth Federation or CCF)[3] had been in official opposition status in three provinces and was the party in power in Saskatchewan. The popularity of its universal hospital insurance, for example, became the inspiration for the national program established in 1961.

Programs supporting old age pensions, unemployment insurance, family allowances, labor-management bargaining, rent controls, regulation of industrial wages, female labor recruitment, and child care were all introduced or expanded before the 1980s (Moscovitch, 2015). Although there were some significant qualifications affecting rural places – such as the exclusion of agricultural labor from many of the labor and wage provisions – many of these programs had special impacts on rural places because of their older populations, lower densities, distance to services, and more seasonal work.

The economic decline of the 1980s and the subsequent imposition of austerity measures have all eroded the welfare state institutions that were established in post-World War II Canada. The individualistic focus of the associated neoliberal ideology has meant that rural and remote places have become particularly vulnerable as their relatively small populations have been used to justify reductions of services and resources (Markey *et al.*, 2013). The legacy of regional institutions established during the welfare state period continue to condition Canadian policies, however, and through them, the rural and more remote places in the country.

A history of federal policies and programs for rural areas (the narrow view)

There are several studies of the history of Canadian policies related to rural and regional issues – each with their own classification of critical periods of policy development. Fairbairn (1998) identifies four eras of Canadian rural-related policies from 1945 to 1995 with a focus on the questions "What works?" and "What doesn't?" – from a community development point of view. Bollman and Ashton (2015) discuss the period up to 2015 with an emphasis on federal policies and programs, their contributions to capacity building, economic development, and governance. Breen *et al.* (2017) identify four eras since the beginning of the twentieth century.

Their focus is on periods of crisis which contributed to the changes in regional policy represented by each of those eras. Their framework is formulated within an analysis of "new regionalism" debates within academic and policy contexts. These three studies are largely consistent
with respect to their representation of Canadian rural and regional policy positions and programs although their particular emphases highlight a variety of interpretations and conclusions
that enhance the following analysis.

Macro-economic Keynesianism (World War II to 1955)

Fairbairn (1998) argues there are four general policy eras represented by Canadian rural and
regional policies from the post-World War II era to about 1995. This classification will be used
with the addition of two other eras to bring the analysis to contemporary conditions (Breen *et
al.*, 2017).

The first he identifies as "Macroeconomic Keynesianism" covering the period up to about
1955. This was a period driven by Keynesian economic policies that welcomed American
capital for building resource infrastructure: including petroleum in Alberta, mining and forestry
in Ontario, Quebec, and BC, and automobile manufacturing in southern Ontario. The assumption was that growth in one region would contribute to growth in all.

This was also the period when Canada initiated several important labor-related programs that
were to have rural and regional implications, although they were not formulated in these terms.
As rural industries became mechanized, surplus labor was retrained and relocated. The general
policy of moving people to jobs and not jobs to people meant that the standardization of services
like health, employment, and education were supported, reinforcing in turn what was to become
a fundamental feature of Canadian national politics: equalization programs among the
provinces.

Populism and regionalism (1955–1965)

Fairbairn identifies the second period as "Populism and Regionalism", lasting from about 1955
to 1965. This was a period in which falling commodity prices and the recession of 1956 combined with the realization that the downturns were not transitory. Western Canada and the
Atlantic provinces were particularly hard hit in comparison to Ontario and Quebec – thus sustaining the articulation of a regional perspective and political agenda (Douglas, 1994). As Fairbairn points out, this approach identified the provinces as locations upon which the policy of
equalization should focus.

It was during this period that the Canadian government embarked on its most aggressive
ever rural policy-making process (Savoie, 2003). Primarily focusing on regional economic
disparities, several programs were initiated, developed, and modified to deal with economically depressed areas across the country (e.g. ARDA, FRED, ADB). The result was the introduction of an array of new programs and agencies specifically designed to support the
economies of predominantly rural regions. The emphasis remained on infrastructure, primary
sector production, labor adjustment, and relocation, however, with little attention given to
community development and capacity building. Rural residents were largely excluded from
the planning (Fairbairn, 1998, p. 20). These policies did not differentiate among the three
types of rural areas – metro-adjacent, non-metro-adjacent, and northern areas – but the consequences of the policy have sometimes been quite different in different types of rural regions.
They also gradually moved the planning focus from populist rural development to regional
planning and industrial incentives.

The rise and fall of technocratic planning (1965–1980)

As the populist rural development rhetoric was transformed to regional development and industrial expansion, it became more centrist in nature: where "rural development was conceptualized as another kind of centralized social program" (Fairbairn, 1998, p. 22). In 1969 the federal government established the Department of Regional Economic Expansion (DREE) to manage the many location-based, human resource development and infrastructure programs. This effectively centralized the decision-making in Ottawa. It also meant that the attention and resources moved from the regions to the urban centers, encouraged by the popularity of growth pole theories of development during this period (Weaver and Gunton, 1982). DREE adopted General Development Agreements (GDAs) around 1974 to manage the variety of relationships that existed between each province and the federal government. Policy control, however, remained with the federal government but they became increasingly unhappy with the little recognition they received for the projects established under the GDAs. This coincided with the ideological shift from Keynesianism to monetary gradualism that was part of the global context of the times.

The rise and fall of megaprojects (1980–1995)

By the end of the 1970s the federal government had lost interest in the rural and regional focus of programs like DREE, so in 1982, it was integrated into the Department of Industry, Trade and Commerce to create the Department of Regional Industrial Expansion (DRIE). Other regional-focused programs were replaced by those of the Ministry of State for Economic and Regional Development (MSERD), and the Industrial and Regional Development Program (IDRP) – all of them with an industrial as opposed to a rural, community, or regional focus (Cummings, 1989; Douglas, 1994; Fairbairn, 1998). The Department of Agriculture was the only one that "retained rural development as a small part of its mandate".

Fairbairn (1998) characterizes the 1980s as a period of megaprojects – where both the federal and provincial governments supported large-scale natural resource developments in energy, forestry, and mining (Douglas, 1994; Lithwick, 1987; Weaver and Gunton, 1982). This was also a period in which funds for business development in the various regions of the country were established, with mandates supporting both large and small-scale enterprises. These included the Western Development Fund in 1980, WD, ACOA, and FEDNOR in 1987, and the Quebec Major Industrial Projects Subsidiary Agreement in 1988.

These initiatives were not without their critics, however (House, 1988). Fairbairn (1998) suggests:

> All of these agencies, though less so ACOA, might be characterized as agencies for development in regions rather than development of regions. They did not attempt regional development in the sense of the comprehensive and integrated (small-) regional planning of FRED or even of ARDA and GDAs.

This was also a period during which the federal and provincial governments were cutting back significantly on social services – in the name of reducing government deficits. To those in rural and remote places the reductions in services felt particularly onerous as post offices, rail lines, military bases, hospitals, and schools were closed or amalgamated – often with little or no public consultation. The reaction was strong, if not particularly effective in shifting the policy direction, but it created sufficient political concern that rural places and people advanced somewhat on the agendas.

One response emerged in the Department of Employment and Immigration Canada (EIC) (now Human Resources and Skills Development Canada – HRSDC). EIC was under considerable pressure to deal with the labor challenges that emerged as Canada underwent the structural and ideological changes of the 1970s and 1980s. The lackluster performance of business development and economic development initiatives in rural and remote places left the department searching for alternatives. In 1986 the department launched the Community Futures program (CFDC) as a job creation and economic development program specifically involving community collaboration. The approach was integrated into many of the provincial programs and provided a tangible set of principles and actions for policy-makers pressing a rural agenda (Donnelly, 1994; Stephens, 1994).

In 1994, Industry Canada launched its Community Access Program (CAP) – with an objective of improving internet access for those in most need. This included a significant component to rural areas in addition to Indigenous peoples, older, low-income, low-education, and francophone Canadians, along with new immigrants. By 2009 it had connected about 3000 rural and remote communities. In that year, it was redesigned as part of Industry Canada's "Broadband Canada" program and eventually terminated in 2012 (OECD, 2010).

The service cutbacks also stimulated several important initiatives among NGOs. In 1988, for example, a group of rural researchers met in Regina to consider appropriate responses to the changing conditions. This was to become the initial meeting of the Agricultural and Rural Research Group (ARRG) – a loosely knit network of researchers, policy-makers, practitioners, and rural citizens who now meet annually as the Canadian Rural Revitalization Foundation (CRRF). This network continues to provide long-term support for the generation of rural-related information, the critical analysis of policy from an international perspective, and venues for collaboration among researchers, policy-makers, practitioners, and citizens interested in rural and northern issues (http://crrf.ca).

The rise and fall of rural policy (1996–2013)

In 1997 a report called "Think Rural" was released by the Senate Standing Committee on Agriculture and Forestry which detailed a plan for the development of a new approach to rural issues for Canada (Mitchell, 1997). In accordance with this plan the federal government created the Rural Secretariat to develop and support rural concerns. The new secretariat was placed within Agriculture and Agri-Food Canada (AAFC), making the Minister of Agriculture and Agri-Food also the Minister Coordinating Rural Affairs. Simultaneously, parliament created the position of Secretary of State for Rural Development at the cabinet level. The secretariat's objectives were to provide leadership and coordination for a new institution called the Canadian Rural Partnership (CRP); to create and liaise with partnerships focused on rural issues and priorities; and to promote dialogue between rural stakeholders and the federal government (Hall and Gibson, 2016).

The Rural Secretariat initiated a number of innovative programs specifically directed to rural people and places. In 1998, they began a program entitled "Rural Dialogue", which consisted of a series of consultations with rural people about the issues they felt were important. The success of the initiative encouraged additional surveys, workshops, online discussion groups, newsletters, and conferences (both regional and national). The program also served as the basis for the Rural Action Plan in 2000 – a set of priorities established through national conferences with considerable citizen participation (see Box 32.1). These priorities were used to establish the "Pilot Projects Initiative" which provided funds for local innovative projects – with preference given to local and not-for-profit groups' engagement. The projects also included an evaluation component.

> ## Box 32.1 Rural Action Plan
>
> 1 Improve access to federal government programs and services for rural Canadians;
> 2 Improve access to financial resources for rural business and community development;
> 3 Provide more targeted opportunities, programs and services for rural youth, including Aboriginal youth;
> 4 Strengthen rural community capacity building, leadership, and skills development;
> 5 Create opportunities for rural communities to maintain and develop infrastructure for community development;
> 6 Connect rural Canadians to the knowledge-based economy and society and help them acquire the skills to use the technology;
> 7 Strengthen economic diversification in rural Canada through more targeted assistance;
> 8 Work with provincial and territorial governments to examine and pilot test new ways to provide rural Canadians with access to health care at reasonable cost;
> 9 Work with provincial and territorial governments to examine and pilot test new ways to provide rural Canadians with access to education at reasonable cost;
> 10 Foster strategic partnerships, within communities, between communities and among governments to facilitate rural community development; and.
> 11 Promote rural Canada as a place to live, work, and raise a family recognizing the value of rural Canada to the identity and well-being of the nation.

In order to address the multi-sectoral and cross-cutting nature of rural and northern issues, the Rural Secretariat developed a "Rural Lens" program and toolkit for the federal government. This program requested all departments to identify and consider any implications of their policies for rural and remote people and places. At the same time, several other federal departments initiated rural-focused programs (e.g. Natural Resources Canada, HRSDC, and AAFC). Most of these initiatives were directed to the agricultural sector alone, but some included an explicit rural focus.

Many of the Rural Secretariat initiatives were supported by NGOs like CRRF. Notable examples can be found in CRRF's call for a rural champion on the federal cabinet as eventually reflected in the Rural Secretary position itself (Apedaile and Reimer, 1996), the 11-year New Rural Economy Project (NRE) (http://nre.concordia.ca), and contributions to the Senate Report on Rural Poverty (Fairbairn, 2006; Fairbairn and Gustafson, 2008). The shift in Rural Secretariat rhetoric to community engagement, capacity building, and asset-based community development can all be found in the presentations, discussions, and research initiated by CRRF.

In 2004, the federal government agreed to transfer a part of its gas tax to municipalities as an element of its new program entitled "New Deal for Cities and Communities". Its focus was primarily on infrastructure but it provided options for municipalities to pool, bank, or borrow against these funds. Initial discussions regarding the allocation of these funds were dominated by large cities, but a concerted effort by the Rural Forum of the Federation of Canadian Municipalities (FCM) (http://fcm.ca) was successful in ensuring that they would have fair access to the pool of funds.

In 2009, however, the CRP was terminated – along with the cabinet position provided by the Rural and Co-operatives Secretariat. The remaining activities and programs regarding rural issues were transferred to the Portfolio Coordination office within Agriculture and Agri-Food Canada (AAFC, 2014). No longer was there a champion for rural Canada on the federal cabinet and most of the interdepartmental activities initiated by the Rural and Co-operatives Secretariat disappeared.

Reactionary negotiation (post-2013)

Breen *et al.* (2017) characterize the most recent regional policy regime as "Reactionary Nego-tiation". Following Halseth and Ryser (2017), they argue that the variety of government responses have been too incoherent and opportunistic to warrant inferences of consistency in policy and that "regions, communities, and organizations are largely left on their own to nego-tiate their fates as best they can … in largely bilateral arrangements" (Breen *et al.*, 2017, p. 6).

Under these circumstances, communities and regions which have developed the capacity to organize their assets, collaborate successfully, and establish strong connections with provincial and federal governments tend to be successful in attracting funders from both the public and private sectors. Those with more limited capacity and assets often fall further behind – creating a bifurcation of wealth and quality of life which exacerbates inequalities.

At the same time, Canadian society has continued to urbanize. Although the rural population has remained steady, its proportion of the population distribution has continued to decline steeply from the 1930s. Since federal, provincial, and territorial governments face increasing demands from urban centers there is little indication that this situation will change in the near future.

Rural policy in Quebec

The federal and Quebec governments in Canada have a long history of different and sometimes antagonistic policy approaches. This is no less the case for rural and regional policies. Quebec faced similar pressures and options as those outlined above, however, in some crucial ways this province responded with programs and policies that are unique in the country and in the world (OECD, 2010).

Quebec governments have consistently given rural places in the province special treatment. During the early part of the last century the high birth rate placed considerable pressure on rural families and communities for access to agricultural land. The Catholic Church and the govern-ment responded by encouraging settlement in rural places as an alternative to out-migration. This was reinforced by cultural, religious, and language characteristics that were blended with rural identity. When the available land became exhausted and rural-based industries decreased their demand for labor, urban industries welcomed the surplus labor in a manner that mirrored the patterns found in most countries.

Up until the 1950s the government and Church were able to maintain the representation of Quebec as rural, Catholic, and French in spite of its industrialization and urbanization, by support-ing a highly stratified society (Guindon *et al.*, 1988). When this ability collapsed with the rejection of the Church and the events of the Quiet Revolution in the 1950s and 1960s[4] this identity began to change as the control over industry and finance shifted to the French-speaking elite. The importance of rural places and people, however, remained, since they provided core elements of the Quebec political identity and a key basis for the independence aspirations of the population.

The parish and county structures established by the Catholic Church were largely replicated by the state when it took over health, education, and social services in the 1950s. The institu-tional structures, familiarity, and social capital of these administrative and political units were reinforced with the establishment of multi-departmental organizations such as community health clinics and social services within each region. These in turn served as the basic regional institutional structures for the councils of mayors and local leaders when regional coordination was legislated. The most important of these were the *municipalités régionales de comté*[5] (MRCs). When the political climate shifted to emphasize economic development over social services, it did not require a large shift to modify the mandate of the MRCs to include business and community development. The result has been a rural and regional structure that is multi-focused, regionally inclusive, and well-integrated into the municipal and provincial political structures.

The multiple foci of the MRC structure have also been conducive to a vision that is rural and territorial in its scope, not just sectoral. It has been reinforced by a number of policies lasting over 25 years, from the *Politique de soutien au développement local et régional* (1991), to the *Politique nationale de la ruralité* (2001–2006), and the *Politique nationale de la ruralité* (2006–2013). This rural focus and its infrastructure survived over nine elections with four government party changes – representing an unusual consistency in Canadian politics.

This consistency is likely to be an important contributing factor to the relative success of the MRCs for the governance of regions (Reimer, 2010a). By requiring municipal representatives to plan and collaborate, giving them the authority to do it across economic and private–public–third sectors, and providing them with resources and accountability requirements to act on those plans, the provincial government created conditions that are conducive to place-appropriate policies. By ensuring that these structures remain in place over the long term, they also made it possible for regional leaders to learn how to collaborate, gave them the time to build trust, and ensured that compromises and deals will be respected even though individuals change.

Quebec rural policies also contained initiatives to support more economically marginal communities within each MRC. First, they ensured marginal communities' representation on the council. Second, they provided extra funding to the MRC for initiatives that addressed the disadvantages of those communities. Third, they provided support for local community development agents to facilitate initiatives to this end. By doing so, they reinforced the benefits of the people and groups within marginal communities and ensured that the MRC treated their improvement as an asset to the region rather than a liability.

In 2014 the Quebec Rural Policy was drastically altered – most likely in response to the increasing pressure from larger urban centers in the face of rising populations and neglected infrastructure. Funding for the Rural Policy program was significantly reduced, the Rural Pacts and Laboratory programs were eliminated, and support for Rural Agents was reduced. Many of the previous functions and support by the provincial government, therefore, became the responsibility of the MRCs. The ability of the MRCs to function well under these new circumstances remains to be seen (Pollett, 2017).

Assessing Canadian policy approaches

In their analysis of new regionalism in the Canadian context, Breen *et al.* (2017) identified three themes reflected in Canadian policy and programs approaches to regional issues.

Institutional legacies

The historical legacies of the various governments (federal, provincial, and municipal) create both opportunities and constraints on the policies envisaged as well as the outcomes of their implementation. For example, Quebec's history with the parish structure, Catholic Church institutions, and language made the organization of MRCs comparatively conflict-free – with its multi-sectoral features relatively intact. Without this legacy, most of the other provinces have experienced changing regional boundaries (often linked to changes in government), single-sector-specific policies, and short-term projects.

Vision as a platform for policy

The existence, scope, and timeframe of a vision for regional development makes important differences to the objectives, organization, and strategies adopted for policies and programs. The Canadian experience outlined above identifies a number of such visions, from land acquisition and settlement in the early years to the Keynesian visions of the welfare state period, and the market-justified perspectives of current laissez-faire approaches. By comparison, Quebec's identification of "rural" in its provincial vision made the emergence of a rural policy unique among the provinces (Trudel and Leclerc, 1989).

Regional governance organization

In the Canadian governance structure, provinces have primary control over the organization of natural resources within their regions. There is little opportunity for municipalities to participate in those decisions, especially for the more remote locations. The Canadian constitution and practice largely reduces municipalities to service delivery agents for local administration, infrastructure, and business development. Federal support for local economic development during the 1966–2013 period met with a variety of obstacles depending on the provincial organization of its regional and municipal relations. Even in those provinces where municipal options were greater, the recession of 2008 and its associated justification for austerity reinforced the pressure to increase administrative boundaries and weaken local autonomy.

Shortcomings associated with the postwar period of regional development

Breen *et al.* (2017) identify the following five policy shortcomings of the postwar period.

*   First, there has been poor coordination of regional development policies and objectives among the different levels of government (Brodie, 1990; Savoie, 1992).
*   Second, the theoretical underpinnings of government policies tend to be overly vague and poorly interpreted (e.g. growth pole theory and narrow economic development foci), with the neglect of human development and capacity and an ignorance of the broader benefits of economic diversification (Fairbairn, 1998; MacNeil, 1997; Savoie, 2003).
*   Third, development policies take on a quasi-environmental determinism by associating common political, social, and cultural characteristics with diverse communities simply because they shared the same geographic or socio-economic characteristics (Savoie, 1992).
*   Fourth, deficiency-based approaches tend to dominate the discussion – focusing more on "needs" and symptoms of community stagnation rather than addressing the underlying conditions, causes, or unique community strengths (Brodie, 1990; Savoie, 1992).
*   Fifth, they argue that the intervention of the state has created a form of dependency among communities and undermined self-reliance (Douglas, 1994; Martin and Sunley, 1998).

These limitations remain evident in the current rural policy context with only slight modifications stimulated by the Rural Secretariat years. During that period, there was a shift to a focus on local capacity building, research, and community consultation within the Secretariat and encouraged by organizations like CRRF and the FCM. The financial and personnel resources supporting this shift have largely been lost with the closure of the Rural Secretariat in 2014, leaving most of the information and policy development up to NGOs.

Conclusions

Narrow policy attention given to rural in Canada has significantly diminished as urbanization has continued and the political agenda for metropolitan centers has come to dominate the attention of policy-makers. The closure of the Rural Secretariat and its infrastructure has left rural, northern, and regional policy development largely up to the provinces and territories with the variety of approaches they reflect. The legacy of neoliberal individualism has meant that low-density regions are left with fewer services, less economic impact, and weakened political power. Even in Quebec, where specific rural policies were most clearly articulated, the financial decimation of those policies in 2014 has undermined some of their most important innovations.

The prospects for rural and regional policy in Canada would be rather bleak were it not for three conditions worthy of exploration. First, the Canadian constitutional and institutional commitments to regional concerns, especially with respect to fiscal and service equality, means that policies will continue to be faced with rural-related issues as reflected in those regions. Inequalities across provinces or regions will always have a rural dimension since Canadian metropoles are not equally located across the provinces and territories. Managing reasonable equity between Nunavut and Ontario, for example, will keep the issues of remoteness, capacity, and differential assets foremost on the policy agenda.

Second, the 20 or so years of attention to community capacity building and modest attempts at subsidiarity have left a legacy where many rural communities, regions, and rural-related groups have taken initiatives to build their capacity in both regional and national contexts. Nowhere is this as dramatic as with Indigenous peoples. Since the Berger Inquiry and its ground-breaking recognition of Indigenous rights and treatment in the Mackenzie Valley (Berger, 1977), Indigenous peoples have rapidly expanded their cultural, legal, social, and political capacity in dealing with land, finances, identity, and rights issues that have driven all levels of government to radically reconsider policies and programs (Coon Come, 2017; Poelzer and Coates, 2015). The 20 years of Rural Policy in Quebec provides another example of regional and community capacity building that may serve as a basis for continued influence – even with the drastic cuts introduced in 2014 (Pollett, 2017). Similar instances of community and regional initiatives can be found which identify a wide variety of approaches to local development – often reflecting the competitive over comparative advantage of place which is currently championed by the OECD and European Union (especially through their LEADER program).

Third, although Canadian rhetoric does not reflect a public or policy recognition of rural places, there is considerable concern and recognition for issues that have a significant rural and northern component (Reimer, 2013). Food, water, energy, economic prosperity, and environmental sustainability are all issues which resonate strongly with urban populations. All of these issues are closely associated with resources and assets of rural places, especially with respect to their production – and all of them have important policy components. If rural and northern people and groups reframe their rural concerns in the language of these issues and seek to form alliances with those currently working on the advancement of policy agendas, they may find that an indirect approach produces more opportunities for affecting policy related to rural than one which articulates the issue in terms of a rural–urban distinction. Such a strategy would also be more consistent with the interdependence between rural and urban places that is such an essential element of Canadian social, economic, and political reality. For rural researchers, this means improving and expanding the analysis of broad rural-related policies over narrow ones.

Key questions for the future of Canadian rural policy

Several important questions emerge from this outline that have important implications for future policy. Some of them are identified below.

1   What is the difference between broad and narrow rural policy? Which are the most strategic approaches to understanding and modifying rural policy in Canada – at the federal, provincial, territorial, and regional levels? How have other countries made this distinction and how effective have the approaches been in affecting rural policies and outcomes?

2   In what ways have the 20 years of rural policies in Quebec created capacity which can sustain regional collaboration, initiatives, and power in the future? What changes have occurred in this capacity since 2014 when the policy funding was reduced?

3   Since the 1990s, there has been an increase in the negotiation and re-negotiation of governance, land, and resource rights of Indigenous peoples in Canada – especially in western and northern regions. What variations in those rights can be found in the negotiations? What have been the social, economic, environmental, and cultural outcomes of the various negotiated settlements? What is it possible to learn about best approaches to such negotiations – both in terms of strategic tactics and proposals for local governance?

4   How do policy-makers at all levels inform themselves about important issues and available research to address those issues (Reimer and Brett, 2013)? Which of these networks of communication and support would be most effective for knowledge mobilization and alliance building?

5   Is rural policy no longer a strategic focus for policy development? Should rural, northern, and remote communities reframe their concerns in terms which have traction for urban populations? Which urban alliances would be most strategic to develop in order to create policies which are more appropriate for rural places?

6   How long have rural-focused institutions, policies, and programs lasted in other countries? What have been the relative advantages or disadvantages of these examples by comparison to short-term initiatives – especially for the development of rural and community capacities?

Notes

1 Details of this paper rely heavily on the research and support of the Canadian Regional Development Project (http://ruraldev.ca). I would like to thank all members of this team for the information, insights, and critical comments they have provided along the way. I would also like to thank Thomas G. Johnson for his initial suggestions for the organization and this chapter and useful comments as the work unfolded.

2 Thanks to David Douglas for this important insight.

3 In 1961 the CCF joined with the Canadian Labour Congress to form the New Democrat Party (NDP). It has become one of the three major parties in the federal government (at one point serving as official opposition). Its provincial counterparts have formed the government on ten occasions in provincial and territorial jurisdictions.

4 The Quiet Revolution in Quebec refers to the decade of change when the dominance of the Catholic Church was rejected and the social services they provided were taken over by the government. It was a period where the influence of the English corporate elite was also challenged as the French public sector grew in power. This change reflected a strong social-democratic ideology.

5 The MRCs are county-level administrative organizations composed of mayors of the municipalities within the county and a prefect – the latter elected from among the mayors or by universal suffrage. They were established in 1979 by the Lois sur l'aménagement et l'urbanisme (Pollett, 2017).

References

AAFC – Agriculture and Agri-Food Canada, 2014. *Report on plans and priorities 2013-14.* Ottawa, Ont.

Apedaile, L.P., Reimer, B., 1996. *Towards a whole rural policy for Canada,* ed. T.A. Group & R. Restructuring. The Canadian Rural Restructuring Foundation, Ottawa, Ont.

Berger, T.R., 1977. *Northern frontier northern homeland: The report of the Mackenzie Valley Pipeline Inquiry* (Vols. 1 and 2). Minister of Supply and Services Canada, Ottawa, Ont. www.pwnhc.ca/extras/berger/report/BergerV1_complete_e.pdf.

Bollman, R.D., Ashton, B., 2015. *Rural policy in Canada,* in: Meyers, W.H., Johnson, T.G. (Eds.), *Handbook of international food and agricultural policies, Volume 1: Policies for agricultural markets and rural economic activity.* Brandon University, Brandon, MB, pp. 149–180.

Breen, S., Markey, S., Reimer, B., Weightman, A., 2017. *Regional development in Canada: Eras and evolution.* Memorial University of Newfoundland, St. John's, NL.

Brodie, M.J., 1990. *The political economy of Canadian regionalism.* Harcourt Brace Jovanovich, Toronto, Ont.

Coon Come, M., 2017. *Opinion: Cree governance accord with Canada is reconciliation in action.* Montreal Gazette, July 20, p. A7.

Cummings, H., 1989. *Rural development and planning in Canada: Some perspectives on federal and provincial roles.* Plan Canada 29(2), 8–18.

Donnelly, K., 1994. *Interdepartmental Committee on Rural and Remote Canada,* in: Bryden, J. (Ed.), *Towards sustainable rural communities: The Guelph seminar series.* University School of Rural Planning and Development, Guelph, Ont., pp. 171–174.

Douglas, D.J.A., 1994. *Community economic development in Canada,* 2 vols. McGraw-Hill Ryerson, Toronto, Ont.

Esping-Andersen, G., 1990. *The three worlds of welfare capitalism.* Princeton University Press, Princeton, NJ.

Fairbairn, B., 1998. *A preliminary history of rural development policy and programmes in Canada, 1945–1995.* New Rural Economy Project, Concordia University, Montreal, PQ. http://nre.concordia.ca/ftproot-Full/rhistory.pdf.

Fairbairn, J., 2006. *Understanding freefall: The challenge of the rural poor. Interim report of the Standing Senate Committee on Agriculture and Forestry [Electronic resource].* Standing Senate Committee on Agriculture and Forestry, Ottawa, Ont. www.parl.gc.ca/39/1/parlbus/commbus/senate/com-e/agri-e/rep-e/repint-dec06-e.pdf.

Fairbairn, J., Gustafson, L.J., 2008. *Beyond freefall: Halting rural poverty.* Standing Senate Committee on Agriculture and Forestry, Ottawa, Ont. http://publications.gc.ca/collections/collection_2011/sen/yc27-0/YC27-0-392-9-eng.pdf.

Guindon, H., Hamilton, R., McMullan, J.L., 1988. *Quebec society: Tradition, modernity, and nationhood.* University of Toronto Press, Toronto, Ont.

Hall, H., Gibson, R., 2016. *Rural proofing in Canada: An examination of the Rural Secretariat and the Rural Lens* (Prepared for the Parliamentary Rural Areas Committee, Sweden). Swedish Agency for Growth Policy Analysis, Guelph, Ont.

Halseth, G., Ryser, L., 2017. *Towards a political economy of resource dependent regions.* Routledge, Abingdon; New York.

Harvey, D., 1990. *The condition of postmodernity: An enquiry into the origins of cultural change.* Blackwell, Oxford.

House, J.D., 1988. *Outports and the microchip: Peripheral regions in a post-industrial age,* in: Fleming, B. (Ed.), *Beyond anger and longing: Community and development in Atlantic Canada. The 1986–87 Winthrop Packard Bell Lectures in Maritime Studies.* Acadiensis Press, Fredericton, NB, pp. 99–118.

Innis, H.A., 1972. *Empire and communication.* University of Toronto Press, Toronto, Ont.

Innis, H.A., 1999. *The fur trade in Canada: An introduction to Canadian economic history.* University of Toronto Press, Toronto, Ont.

Lithwick, N.H., 1987. *Regional development policies: Context and consequences,* in: Coffey, W.J., Pol, M. (Eds.), *Still living together: Recent trends and future directions in Canadian regional development.* Institute for Policy on Public Policy, Montreal, PQ, pp. 21–155.

MacNeil, T., 1997. *Assessing the gap between community development practice and regional development policy*, in: Wharf, B., Clague, M. (Eds.), *Community organizing: Canadian experiences*. Oxford University Press, Toronto, Ont.

Markey, S., Halseth, G., Manson, D., 2013. *Investing in place: Economic renewal in northern British Columbia*, Reprint edition. UBC Press, Vancouver, BC.

Martin, R., Sunley, P., 1998. *The post-Keynesian state and the space economy*, in: Lee, R., Wills, J. (Eds.), *Geographies of economies*. Arnold, New York.

Mitchell, A., 1997. *Think rural!* House of Commons, Ottawa, Ont.

Moscovitch, A., 2015. *Welfare state*. www.thecanadianencyclopedia.ca/en/article/welfare-state.

OECD, 2008. *OECD rural policy reviews: Finland*, OECD Rural Policy Reviews No. 0408021. OECD, Paris. www.oecd.org/gov/oecdruralpolicyreviewsfinland.htm.

OECD, 2010. *OECD rural policy reviews: Québec, Canada*. OECD, Paris.

Parrott, Z., 2017. *Indigenous Peoples in Canada*. May 10. www.thecanadianencyclopedia.ca/en/article/aboriginal-people/ (accessed 3.2.18).

Poelzer, G., Coates, K.S., 2015. *From treaty peoples to treaty nation: A road map for all Canadians*. UBC Press, Vancouver, BC; Toronto, Ont. www.ubcpress.ca/search/title_book.asp?BookID=299174418.

Pollett, C., 2017. *Québec's approach to regional government: An overview and critical reflections*. www.youtube.com/watch?v=5ZjdRc585V8.

Ray, A.J., 1998. *Indians in the fur trade: Their role as trappers, hunters, and middlemen in the lands southwest of Hudson Bay, 1660–1870. With a new introduction*. University of Toronto Press, Toronto, Ont.; Buffalo, NY.

Reimer, B., 2010a. *Rural–urban interdependence as an opportunity for rural revitalization*, in: Beesley, K.B. (Ed.), *The rural–urban fringe in Canada: Conflict and controversy*. Rural Development Institute, Brandon University, Brandon, MB, pp. 10–21.

Reimer, B., 2010b. *Social welfare policies in rural Canada*, in: Milbourne, P., *Welfare reform in rural places: Comparative perspectives*. Emerald Group Publishing, Bingley, Vol. 15, pp. 81–110. http://billreimer.ca/research/files/ReimerInMilbourneRuralWelfare2010.pdf.

Reimer, B., 2013. *Rural–urban interdependence: Understanding our common interests*, in: Parkins, J.R., Reed, M. (Eds.), *Social transformation in rural Canada: Community, cultures, and collective action*. UBC Press, Vancouver, BC, pp. 91–109.

Reimer, B., Bollman, R.D., 2010. *Understanding rural Canada: Implications for rural development policy and rural planning policy*, in: Douglas, D.J.A. (Ed.), *Rural planning and development in Canada*. Nelson Education, Toronto, Ont., pp. 10–52. www.nelsonbrain.com/shop/content/douglas00812_0176500812_02.01_chapter01.pdf.

Reimer, B., Brett, M., 2013. *Scientific knowledge and rural policy: A long distance relationship*. Sociologia Ruralis 53(3), 272–290. https://doi.org/10.1111/soru.12014.

Savoie, D., 1992. *Regional economic development: Canada's search for solutions*. University of Toronto Press, Toronto, Ont.

Savoie, D., 2003. *Reviewing Canada's regional development efforts*. Royal Commission on Renewing and Strengthening Our Place in Canada, St. John's, NL, pp. 147–183. www.gov.nl.ca/publicat/royal-comm/research/savoie.pdf.

Schultz, T.W., 1972. *The increasing economic value of human time*. American Journal of Agricultural Economics 54(5), 843–850.

Stephens, D., 1994. *The Rural Renewal Secretariat in Agriculture and Agri-Food Canada*, in: Bryden, J. (Ed.), *Towards sustainable rural communities: The Guelph Seminar Series*. University School of Rural Planning and Development, Guelph, Ont., pp. 165–170.

Trudel, R., Leclerc, Y., 1989. *Deux Québec dans un: Rapport sur le développement social et démographique*. G. Morin et Québec Conseil des affaires sociales Comité sur le développement, Boucherville, PQ.

Wallace, I., 2002. *A geography of the Canadian economy*. Oxford University Press, Don Mills, Ont.

Weaver, C., Gunton, T.I., 1982. *From drought assistance to megaprojects: Fifty years of regional theory and policy in Canada*. The Canadian Journal of Regional Science 5(1), 5–37.

Acronyms (in order of appearance)

OECD	Organisation for Economic Co-operation and Development
BC	British Columbia
AB	Alberta
SK	Saskatchewan
MB	Manitoba
ON	Ontario
QC	Quebec
NB	New Brunswick
PE	Prince Edward Island
NS	Nova Scotia
NL	Newfoundland and Labrador
YT	Yukon
NT	Northwest Territories
NU	Nunavut
CANSIM	Canadian Socio-Economic Information Management System (Statistics Canada)
CCF	Canadian Commonwealth Federation
NDP	New Democrat Party
ARDA	Agricultural and Rural Development Act
FRED	Fund for Rural Economic Development
ADB	Atlantic Development Board
DREE	Department of Regional and Economic Expansion
GDAs	General Development Agreements
DRIE	Department of Regional Industrial Expansion
MSERD	Minster of State for Economic and Regional Development
IDRP	Industrial and Regional Development Program
WD	Western Diversification Fund
ACOA	Atlantic Canada Opportunities Agency
FEDNOR	Federal Economic Development Initiative
EIC	Employment and Immigration Canada
HRSDC	Human Resources and Skills Development Canada
CFDC	Community Futures Development Corporation
CAP	Community Access Program
NGO	Nongovernmental Organization
ARRG	Agricultural and Rural Restructuring Group
CRRF	Canadian Rural Restructuring Foundation to 1999, then Canadian Rural Revitalization Foundation
AAFC	Agriculture and Agri-Food Canada
CRP	Canadian Rural Partnerships program
NRE	New Rural Economy
FCM	Federation of Canadian Municipalities
MRC	Municipalités régionales de comté (in English: Regional County Municipalities)
LEADER	Liaison entre Actions de Développement de l'Économie Rurale (*Links between actions for the development of the rural economy*) EU program

33

RURAL POLICY IN EUROPE

John M. Bryden

Introduction

This chapter is dedicated to discussing the evolution of rural policy in the European Union[1] (see Figure 33.1) after the Rome Treaty of 1957 through five main periods, each with its own peculiar characteristics:[2]

a   1957–1971: absence of a common rural policy and the dominance of national policies that were mainly agricultural in nature;

b   1972–1984: the productivist modernization of agriculture;

c   1985–1999: the crisis of modernization, recognition of the diminishing role of agriculture in rural development, and the rise of a territorially based rural policy and, largely separately from territorial rural development policies, agro-environmental policies partly in the guise of "multifunctionality";

d   2000–2013: the search for a simpler policy governance and the consolidation of a more environmentally "sustainable" agriculture, the fusion of agro-environmental and territorial rural policies, once again largely under the management of agricultural authorities;

e   2014–2020: a toolkit for generic and multi-purpose strategies, with more limited EU and national budgets, mainly attempting to achieve positive impacts on climate change and ecological balances, and agricultural competitiveness, and, to a lesser extent than formerly, rural economies and societies.

The emergence of agricultural market and structures policies

European agricultural policy was mainly developed at national level as a result of wartime and postwar food shortages in the twentieth century. National agricultural policies developed mainly in the 1930s and 1950s, and were merged and harmonized as one of the first – and most dominant – "common" policies of the European Economic Community after the Treaty of Rome in 1957 (Tracy, 1989).

The Common Agricultural Policy, known popularly as the "CAP", took some time to emerge in practice after 1957 but was originally conceived, and ultimately implemented, in two separate and distinct elements or sections. The first and always the largest section concerned

Figure 33.1 The European Union

markets policy, and the second and smaller part, agricultural structures policy. Markets policy concerned the organization and protection of the European Community's markets through tariffs, quotas, and market intervention. Agricultural structures policy largely aimed at "improving" the farm structures to create "viable" and "modern" farms capable of providing the farmer with an income comparable to other occupations.

The period during which the Common Agricultural Policy (CAP) was formulated was dominated by setting up of market organizations for the most relevant agricultural products and by harmonization of prices between member states (Tracy, 1989). The final resolution of the Stresa Conference (1958) declared that the market policy and the structural policy should be developed in tandem, and also stressed the importance of structural policy much more than was ever realized in practice,[3] the activity of the Guidance Section of the EAGGF (European Agricultural Guarantee and Guidance Fund) started only in 1964. At this time, it supported individual projects to improve production and marketing structures in the six member states,[4] but it was much smaller than the expenditures of the Guarantee Section (market and price stabilization). Moreover, market and price policies were seen to be benefiting north European countries, while the Guidance section was used to compensate Italy to some extent (Tracy, 1993).

The first real structural policy was proposed in the "Memorandum on the Reform of Agriculture", generally known as the Mansholt Plan (Commission of the European Communities, 1968). This was implemented by the first agricultural socio-structural directives in 1972, notably Directives no. 159, 160, and 161 (1972). The logic underpinning these directives was to promote a wide modernization of European agriculture, through investment aids for farms "suitable for development" and understood mainly as mechanisms to reach an income comparable with other occupations for one or two labor units (Dir. 159). This modernization process was accompanied by incentives for early retirement of elderly farmers (in order to facilitate generational change) (Dir. 160) and by specific aid to provide socio-economic advice and training (Dir. 161). Some years later modernization was supported by other schemes concerning agro-industrial firms (Reg. 355/77) and producers' associations and cooperatives (Reg. 1380/78).

The second relevant policy vision was dominated by a redistributive emphasis on the poorer agricultural areas. This vision was to some extent represented by Directive no. 268 (1975) concerning "less favored areas", introduced to provide compensatory allowances to farmers in mountain, hill, or disadvantaged areas, just for keeping farming activities in poorer areas.[5] This scheme was intended to generate social effects rather than structural adjustments. It was a major point of negotiation during the UK accession processes in 1971–1972, since the UK already had such a scheme in place since the 1950s.[6] Importantly, it conceded that some types of region or territory needed special policy arrangements. Rural policy thus first emerged in Western Europe as a derivative of agricultural policy and was initially seen almost entirely as a sectoral agricultural issue (Bryden and Warner, 2012).

These two visions coexisted between 1972 and 1984, with few conflicts or contradictions, under the heading of agricultural structures policy (Bryden and Mantino, 2017). The underlying hypothesis was that they could foster improvements in farm size, agricultural productivity and technological change, and, thereby, parity of incomes with other sectors, while supporting farm family incomes in the "less favored" areas. Tracy (1989, p. 326) argues that these policies did not, however, achieve their goals of land and labor mobility, partly because they were conceived during the postwar economic boom, but implemented in the recession that followed the first oil crisis in 1972–1973. Moreover, implementation was extremely patchy between member states, with 70 percent of expenditure on-farm investments[7] from 1972 to 1986 taking place in the UK, Germany, and France, and only 2 percent in Italy. The attempts to encourage farm enlargement via payments to outgoers was particularly disappointing, with significant expenditure in only two member states up to 1986. Moreover, the context had changed in several important respects: first through economic crises; second the declining significance of agriculture even for farm families, where the persistent importance of off-farm work for farm household incomes was gradually being recognized; and third because intensification of agriculture through "modernization" increased the conflicts with the environment as well as increasing production surpluses.

Increasing concern about the uneven territorial impacts of structural policy was also expressed. The focus on viable farms inspired eligibility criteria that excluded the majority of farms, especially in Mediterranean countries characterized by small farm structures (Henry, 1980; De Benedictis and De Filippis, 1980; Arkleton Trust (Research) Ltd., 1989). The Arkleton longitudinal study of 12,000 farm households in 12 EU countries including Italy,

Spain, Portugal, and Greece between 1986 and 1992 showed that in 1987–1988 the use of all structural policy measures except supply control was strongly related to farm size, and farm business size. Meanwhile the use of modernization and environmental policies was strongly related to the education level of the household, and most heavily used in the northern countries of the UK and Netherlands (Arkleton Trust (Research) Ltd., 1989; van den Bor *et al.*, 1997, Chapter 5 passim).

Although relations with other European policies were not envisaged during most of this period, the Commission conceived three experimental "integrated rural development" programs (IRDPs) as a "sweetener" in the annual policy negotiations at the end of 1978.[8] These were to be implemented in 1981 in the three rural regions of the Western Isles of Scotland, Lozère in France, and the Ardennes in Belgium, a very small and unambitious anticipation of the Mediterranean programs that would be introduced later on.

In conclusion, in this period the European Community introduced structural policy instruments that have in fact remained largely in place for the subsequent periods, even if their initial success was very mixed. However, the policy drivers and visions were changing, and existing instruments had to be adapted and augmented accordingly.

The shift to territorial rural development policies

By the 1980s, the context was changing. In particular, there were growing criticisms both of the budgetary costs of the CAP and of the environmental impacts of modern intensive farming stimulated by the CAP. In addition, the uneven inter-farmer and territorial distribution of CAP payments from both Guidance and Guarantee sections were being noticed. There was also growing external criticism of the CAP from the global food exporting countries, and the GATT Uruguay Round of Trade negotiations included agriculture when it commenced in 1986. Finally, the importance of agriculture and farm families to rural economies and societies, while still important, was diminishing and the environmental lobbies and green political parties were gaining in strength. Added to these general forces, the process of "southern enlargement" started in 1981 with the accession of Greece and continued in 1986 with the accession of Spain and Portugal. To this was added the process of completing the single, border-free, European market through the Single European Act of 1986.

The external and internal pressures on the CAP led to gradual reforms from the mid-1980s, in particular to restraints on guaranteed prices, introduction of quotas for surplus commodities, and the introduction of agro-environmental measures and land set-aside schemes initially within agricultural structures policy.

More importantly for the purposes of this chapter, "southern enlargement"[9] in the 1980s, and the Single European Act of 1986, led to an important reform of the structural funds in 1987, and rural policy became heavily influenced by European regional and cohesion policy. Although there were a few experiments with "integrated rural development" started at the end of the 1970s, this reform led to the emergence of a "territorial" rural policy in the European Union that for the next period at least escaped the narrow confines of the former sector-based policy.[10] The then European Commission president, Jacques Delors, was clear that a larger effort was needed on regional development, especially in weaker regions, and pushed hard for coordinated reform of all the structural funds.[11]

The reform of the structural funds of 1988 was therefore mainly aimed at helping the poorer and more "rural" member countries, including especially the new "southern" countries, with less "efficient" economies to deal with the increased competitive pressures of the single market, and "catch up" with the richer members. The reform was significantly strengthened again in

1994, when the Treaty of Union – known as the "Maastricht Treaty" was signed, paving the way for the single currency – the euro – and further efforts to ensure that this did not add to the problems of the nations and regions with weaker economies.

Reflecting the need for a "territorial rural development policy" within the consequent reforms of structural policies, a key "COM Doc"[12] called "The Future of Rural Society" or "L'avenir *du monde rurale*" was published in 1988. This argued for a cross-sectoral, cross-fund, integrated, decentralized approach involving local interests and democratic organizations (Bryden, 1990, 2010). The director of rural development at the time, Philip Lowe,[13] elaborated what he called the "Ten Commandments" of European rural policy, summarized as follows:

1   Agriculture is still important.
2   Rural diversification is essential.
3   A realistic assessment of opportunities is needed.
4   Initiative and entrepreneurship are crucial.
5   Harmony is needed between economic development, environment, and culture.
6   There should be territorial concentration of public effort in poorer, more vulnerable, regions.
7   The starting point should be a "bottom-up", "partnership" approach.
8   Rural people need improved access to support services.
9   Physical economic and social infrastructure is important.
10 Public policies should support better knowledge, information, and advice relating to new rural initiatives.

The structural funds reform in 1987 involved a significant increase in the budget for economic and social cohesion, and set five priority objectives, including two of major importance for rural regions. These were Objective 1 (development of lagging regions with 75 percent or less of the average Community GDP per head) and Objective 5b (development of rural areas outside Objective 1). Regional development programs were introduced which involved partnership with national and regional authorities, and which involved joint funding from national authorities and the three main EU structural funds – regional and cohesion fund, social fund, and agricultural guidance fund.[14] In addition, a number of "Community Programs"[15] were introduced, one of which was LEADER (Liaisons Entre Actions de Développement de l'Économie Rurale). Of the measures introduced after the 1988 reforms, LEADER was the most visible in the rural localities and the most radical, although the initial budget of 400m ECU[16] was tiny compared with the 30bn ECU budget for agriculture and fisheries (Bryden, 1990, p. 22).

LEADER was first established by the European Commission in 1990 as a pilot program after the reform of the structural funds and linked to the new emerging territorial rural policy. The idea was to form local public–private–civil society partnerships or "Local Action Groups" (LAGs) in the priority rural regions and draw on local cross-sectoral ideas, energy, and talents for economic and social development in innovative ways. Starting with 217 LAGs in 1991–1993, the number of LAGs increased rapidly in subsequent programming periods, and the program was mainstreamed in 2000 and extended to all rural regions, later becoming an "approach", rather than a specific program. This approach implies working with LAGs is the main vehicle for local strategy development and supported activities in rural development and the empowerment of local people (Bryden *et al.*, 2011).

As a policy model, LEADER appeared an anomaly in the context of both the CAP and regional policy, because of its experimental and "bottom-up" character, quite unknown in the previous policy-driven experiences of local development at EU level. LEADER I was followed by LEADER II for the period 1994–2000, with a doubled budget of €800m aimed at increasing the number of Local Action Groups (LAGs) to around 900. This experimental policy provoked many expectations at local level and great participation at the level of local community.

The "rural world" paper of 1988 broke new ground by identifying the need for a territorial rural policy that went beyond agriculture and included local development and environmental concerns as key elements. This and the following decade were the "high point" of European territorial rural policy thinking (Bryden *et al.*, 2011, p. 16; Bryden and Mantino, 2017) with the development of the "bottom-up" LEADER rural development program and the plans and programs for rural regions within the priority Objectives 1 and 5b regions as defined by structural and cohesion policy.

The 1992 CAP reform anticipated the GATT Uruguay Round Agreement (1994),[17] and further boosted rural development policy by de-linking agricultural support from production and increasing support for environmental and economic diversification measures on farms. Moreover, Article 120 of the Treaty of Union ("Maastricht Treaty") of 1994 confirmed rural policy as a part of "cohesion policy", and thus going far beyond the agricultural sector. The cross-sectoral new rural policy was also – importantly – funded by the three main structural funds – agriculture, regional development, and social – and involved coordination between the three relevant directorates-general in the Commission.[18]

The "Northern Enlargement" of the EU in 1996[19] was important for reinforcing the "northern dimension" – in the form of remote and sparsely populated regions – in relation to structural and cohesion policies, and hence adding a new dimension to rural policy.

The fusion of agro-environmental and territorial rural development policies

At the end of the 1990s, the Agenda 2000 reforms of the structural and cohesion funds were introduced to accommodate enlargement to Eastern Europe and the former Soviet Union states in the Baltics from 2004 onward. These reforms influenced EU policy changes in the late 1990s and thereafter.

The 1996 Cork Rural Policy Conference, which preceded these reforms, was intended to highlight the importance of "sustainable rural development" through the "LEADER approach". While it largely succeeded in gaining attention for this, it was only partially adopted due to the opposition of agricultural interests and ministries, especially in Germany and France but also in some of the candidate countries such as Poland. The Agenda 2000 reforms largely abolished the multi-funded structural fund programs outside the top priority Objective 1 regions, thus returning "rural development" to DG Agriculture, and "regional development" to Directorate General for Regional Affairs (DG-Regio). The return to a "single fund" approach to programming led to "territorial rural development" including LEADER reverting to control by the Directorate General for Agriculture and Rural Development ("DG-Agri"), and funding from the Agricultural Fund. This had the added effect of causing DG-Regio to refocus its interests much more on cities and city regions.

The EU enlargement to Central-Eastern European countries introduced new challenges to the CAP as a whole and required the adaptation of both market-related and rural development policies. At the same time, the Doha Round of trade negotiations started in the late 1990s gave prominence to the concept of "multifunctionality" linked to the "European model of farming" considered to be creating environmental and social as well as economic benefits and thereby justifying continued support (Bryden *et al.*, 2011). This was also linked to the vision of "sustainable modernization" and to the new European Agricultural Fund for Rural Development (EAFRD), which perhaps gave rural policy more visibility.

In addition, efforts to improve the governance and simplify the management of policies were focal points of the two reforms implemented in this period (2000–2006 and 2007–2013). However, the territorial vision was weakened in this period and, especially after the financial crisis, has not received the necessary support in Rural Development (RD) programs, added to which the spending on "broad" policies impacting on rural regions has been significantly affected by the crisis and later austerity policies. The LEADER program appears to have become ever more bureaucratic and has lost some of its innovative and experimental capacity, although there are significant regional differences (Bryden, 2006; Bryden and Mantino, 2017). Moreover, the costs of repairing the environmental damage (especially on water courses) done during the postwar intensification of agriculture appear to be increasingly falling on the "rural development program" rather than being dealt with by the environmental budget.

Agenda 2000 reform was conceived as a step towards significant changes in rural development approach and can be thought of as a fundamental change in the governance of EU rural development policies. It introduced Rural Development Programs at national and regional level, broadening the scope of rural development from specific and limited territories (e.g. the previous declining rural areas eligible to Objective 5b of the cohesion policy) to all rural areas, and thus weakening the "cohesion" objectives. This was implemented through re-labeling previous sectoral interventions as rural development policies, eliminating the plethora of specific sectoral programs for different measures, and, finally, creating a new "recipient" (the second pillar) for all measures not included in market support (the first pillar). The governance innovations included simplification of intervention tools, clearer distinction between the institutional actors involved in Rural Development Programs (RDPs), stronger decentralization, and strengthening of monitoring and evaluation, and financial control (Bryden and Mantino, 2017).

During the 2000–2006 programming period, RD policy in Europe was implemented by means of RDPs (at national and more often at regional level) and the continuation of LEADER but now as a "mainstreamed" part of rural policy in the form of LEADER+.

RDPs and LEADER+ programs were implemented in all rural areas. However, in lagging regions (Objective 1) interventions for rural areas were still also defined according to a multi-fund logic. The overall structure of programs implemented under Agenda 2000 is described by Bryden and Mantino (2017, Table 1).

Following the Agenda 2000 reforms, the CAP thus had "two pillars". The first pillar was the reformed "market" policy measures by now increasingly made up of "direct payments" to farmers decoupled from current production. The second was "rural development" and consisted of elements of old agricultural structures policies, the "accompanying measures" of the 1992 CAP reform, the LEADER program (by now "mainstreamed"), and a few elements from Objective 5b regional programs for rural areas in decline. This also consolidated the "green" measures formerly contained in both agricultural structures policy and in the "accompanying measures" to the 1992 CAP reform. Rural development also ceased to be targeted at priority regions, and instead became a program for all regions, rich and poor.

Further reforms for the 2007–2013 period split Pillar 2 into 4 "axes", with axis 1 containing measures to promote agricultural competitiveness, axis 2 agro-environmental measures, axis 3 the agricultural and rural diversification measures, and axis 4 the LEADER method, which could apply to all four axes. The very different proportions of available funds allocated to the different axes by member states and regions indicated very different sets of priorities, with countries such as the UK, Ireland, Finland, Austria, and France allocating more than half to the agro-environmental measures of axis 2.

The rural policy reforms after 2014

After 2014 the main changes can be summarized as follows (Mantino, 2013):

a The introduction of a common programming frame including cohesion policies and rural development, which aims to strengthen integration between them and a more flexible programming system for rural development;
b A new emphasis on innovation in agricultural systems; and
c More space for maneuver for cooperative approaches in specific fields as food chain projects, entrepreneurial networks, and local development projects.

The common programming frame is represented by the Partnership Agreement (PA), seeking the coordination of all European funds to pursue the common set of objectives of Europe 2020. This new emphasis on coordination of funds introduces new challenges for the system introduced in Agenda 2000, which was based on the clear separation of cohesion and rural development policies. The return to a more coordinated frame is linked to a more flexible system of organizing the RDP: six priorities (instead of four) and a menu of measures that can be combined without any restrictions (instead of being ex-ante grouped in four axes), following a more result-oriented logic.

Innovation in the agricultural system is another key issue in the 2014 reforms, and one of the horizontal principles that a new generation of programs should pursue, through a better transfer of the research outputs to the farm system and a more effective use of more traditional policy measures as vocational training and extension services. A new approach to innovation was outlined by the SCAR report in 2012, and basically recommended a co-learning approach through Innovation Platforms involving a range of actors (EU-SCAR, 2012).[20] This approach is enshrined in the European Innovation Platforms (EIPs), also important for Agriculture and part of the Innovation Union.

New Regulations put a strong emphasis on cooperative approaches promoted by farmers, agro-industrial entrepreneurs and local non-farm actors: food chains (short and long), entrepreneurial networks, LEADER-like partnerships, etc. These became new forms of local governance promoted by RD policies in many EU countries (Mantino, 2011). With regard to the LEADER-like approaches, now termed "Community-Led Local Development" (CLLD) in the Regulation, the real novelty concerns the opportunity to use all structural funds to finance rural development projects in all areas, including urban, peri-urban, and coastal areas. In effect, a multi-fund approach could offer more opportunities for mixing funds to cover non-sector interventions and consequently focusing EAFRD on more sector needs in agriculture and agro-industry or even in capacity building of local communities. The multi-fund logic in local development was a feature of the period prior to Agenda 2000, but places new demands on the system at a time when the necessary capabilities seem to be quite unevenly distributed within EU rural areas.

The emergent priorities revealed by the new RD programs have been analyzed in a report for the European Parliament (Dwyer *et al.*, 2016). This reveals five main strategic orientations on the basis of financial shares, notably (a) mainly competitiveness; (b) mainly environmental; (c) mixed environmentally and competitiveness oriented; (d) mixed environmentally oriented; (e) mixed competitiveness oriented; (f) mixed rural diversification oriented. However, no RDP program has a predominantly competitiveness strategy, either in 2007–2013 or in 2014–2020. Eleven countries show stability in their strategy, notably in the prevalence of environmental priorities, these being mainly north European countries (Ireland, UK, Austria, etc.). There is, however, an evident increase of focus upon environment, both moving from mixed environmental strategies to mainly environmental (as in the case of Belgium, Germany, Denmark, Slovenia) and from mixed rural diversification to mainly environmental (Malta and Netherlands). This pattern of change is also evident in some Central-Eastern countries, with a move from rural diversification to an environmental component (Bulgaria, Latvia, Romania). Most of the southern countries seemingly desire to retain their mixed strategy, balancing their allocation essentially between environment and competitiveness, but certainly Spain and Italy would require a sound analysis of their internal regional differences (between less developed regions and the others). Although the role of interest groups and lobbies in these allocations and changes cannot be ignored, the authors of the report note that the EAFRD guidelines and the negotiations during the approval process emphasized sustainability of agri-food processes, climate change issues, food safety, etc. National-level budgetary cuts for the period 2014–2020 countries also strengthened the sector focus of the second pillar in allocation of resources by policy-makers (Mantino, 2013)

The most recent reforms for the 2014–2020 period have discontinued the axes, as proposed in the Communication on the CAP towards 2020.[21] All the reforms for 2014–2020, including those for rural development, reflect the goals of "smart, sustainable and inclusive growth" in line with the EU 2020 Strategy. In particular, the awkwardly named European Agricultural Fund for Rural Development (EAFRD) shall "contribute to a more territorially and environmentally balanced, climate-friendly and resilient and innovative Union agricultural sector" (Article 3) (EAFRD, 2011). However, "sustainable growth" has now come to mean "environmentally sustainable growth", with the social dimensions largely left aside.

There are six priorities and 18 sub-priorities for rural development listed in Article 5 covering innovation, knowledge creation and transfer, training, competitiveness, food chain, ecosystems (biodiversity, water, and soils explicitly), resource efficiency, climate mitigation and renewable energy, diversification of farms and rural economies, local development and ICTs. All of these "shall contribute to the cross-cutting objectives of innovation, environment and climate change mitigation and adaptation".

Conclusions

To sum, in the early years, agricultural structures policy had little linkage with territorial rural development, which was, on the whole, a national and regional matter. In many countries, and especially in northern Europe, the most important measures ensuring balanced and equitable economic and social conditions and territorial development in rural regions were, and mostly remain, linked to social welfare policies, local government policies, regional development policies, and other policies aimed at interpersonal and inter-regional "equivalence" in access to education, health, work, and other public services and public goods. However, such "equivalence" policies were weakened from the 1980s, when neoliberal economic policies became the dominant force (Bryden, 2016). These accompanied greater liberalization of trade and capital movements generally. The related increasing pressures from globalization and the restructuring of economic activity were, however, preceded by the more noticeable and immediate impacts of the extension of free trade, capital movements, and labor mobility. These pressures, along with southern enlargement in the 1980s and partial monetary union in the 1990s, led to a flowering of cohesion policies after the Single European Act of 1986. This gave new emphasis to territorial rural development policies, funded through the multi-fund system, which were in many ways distinct from agricultural policies. This ended with the Eastern Enlargement after 2004, when rural development once again fell back into an "agrarian mode", and the emphasis inside it retreated largely to a confused mix between measures to increase agricultural productivity and those designed to control the effects of agrarian changes resulting from the postwar chemical and machine revolution, and, increasingly, the impacts of climate change – notably agro-environmental measures. The result is that the so-called EU rural development policy is in practice mainly about agricultural ecosystems and agricultural "competitiveness", and very little about territorial development and equivalence of economic and social conditions for people. This shift comes at a time when national and EU neoliberal policies, together with the economic and financial crisis after 2006, have greatly weakened policies for territorial equivalence in general, and leaves many rural regions in a very vulnerable state for the future (Bryden, 2016). Against this rather negative interpretation of policy development, however, greater flexibility has been given to national and regional authorities to design rural development strategies and programs to best meet local conditions and needs, and the kinds of local development promoted by LEADER have again become multi-fund structures, even if these remain much more bureaucratic and less "bottom-up" than was initially the case. Moreover, the support for European Innovation Partnerships opens up the possibilities for collaborative learning groups that offer considerable hope for future development in the land-based bioeconomy.

Discussion

The conception, design, and implementation of rural development policies in Europe have all evolved over time influenced by multiple changing internal and external political forces and visions. External forces include such things as GATT/WTO negotiations and agreements, global security issues, and, most recently, climate agreements. Internal forces include such things as successive enlargements of the EU, economic and fiscal crises, the relative power of agricultural and environmental lobbies, and shifting politics at national and EU levels.

Saraceno (2002) argues that there are two key components in the historical evolution of the RD policy: (a) a sectoral vision, whose main objective is the modernization and transformation of farm structures through a support of agricultural activities; (b) a territorial vision, whose main objective is the diversification of the rural economies, through an integrated and multi-sectoral approach, which is able to address social problems and human capital, the provision of services for rural population (health, education, transport, information and communication technologies, etc.), as well as the development of small and medium-sized enterprises (SMEs). Saraceno argues that each vision has different beneficiaries, contents, and instruments. But both visions are necessary and should be considered, in the evolution of RD policy, as "complementary dimensions of a rural policy". In addition, the importance of agriculture and farm families for the economic and social life of rural regions has diminished greatly since the development of the CAP in 1962.

This chapter has traced how these shifting forces have changed the nature of rural policies in the EU over time, since the founding of the European Community in 1957. However, it is very important to remember that what are called "rural policies", whether territorial or sectoral, are only a part of the story of the overall policy impacts on rural areas and people. Many other policies impact on processes of economic, social, and environmental change in rural regions, especially those concerning local government, education, health, nature parks and reserves, housing and land ownership, public transport, telecommunications and broadband infrastructure, and so on. Both the public spending on such policies and the employment associated with them are crucial for the social and economic health of rural regions and people and must be considered alongside the narrower conception called "rural policy". In Europe this wider set of policies is termed "broad rural policy" and the policies named as "rural policy" are considered to be "narrow rural policy".

Notes

1 The term "European Union" is used in this chapter, although this was not the formal name for the quasi-federated European states involved until after the Treaty of Union in 1994. Previously it was called the European Economic Community, or the European Communities (joining the Economic Community with the Iron and Steel Community and the Community for Peaceful Development and Regulation of Atomic Power, Euratom).

2 The periodization developed by Bryden and Mantino (2017) was used here.

3 The Council agreements of 1962 envisaged that "Structural expenditure would 'as far as possible' constitute one-third of Community expenditure in favour of markets" (Tracy, 1989, p. 256).

4 France, Italy, Netherlands, Belgium, Luxembourg, and the German Federal Republic (GFR).

5 In fact, however, no effort was made to design the LFAD to reflect the relative poverty of rural regions. Rather, the designation was very largely based on land quality. That – and the fact that only farmers were eligible – meant it was hardly a regional development policy. Indeed, the arrangements for co-funding of the structural measures meant that the highest payments were made in the richer member states, such as the UK.

6 It was also supported by Ireland.

7 Under Directives 72/159 and 797/85. The figures are derived from Tracy (1989) Table 14.5, page 327, where data for spending on the other structural Directives and Regulations is also given.

8 "Sweeteners" were often used to persuade one or more member states to agree to the larger package of proposals for markets policy, and led to a large number of small schemes of one kind or another within agricultural structures policies before the era of multi-annual programming.

9 The Single European Act consolidated all national regulations that dealt with tariff and non-tariff barriers to trade in common regulations, thus completing the "single market" in the European Community.

10 Three small experimental "integrated rural development programmes" or "IRDPs" were introduced as a "sweetener" during the 1978–1979 CAP "annual negotiations", in the Western Isles of Scotland, Lozère in France, and Luxembourg province of Belgium, and that these were also multi-fund programs. In some senses, therefore, these can be seen as pre-cursors of the programs that followed the 1988 reforms. See also Bryden *et al.* (2011, p. 15).

11 In a private conversation in 2004, Jacques Delors told one of the authors that he persuaded one of his main opponents at the time (and strong proponent of internal free trade), the then UK Prime Minister Mrs. Margaret Thatcher, by saying that he would accept the totally free internal market only if this reform took place. Mrs. Thatcher apparently did not want higher regional development spending.

12 COM (88)501. A "Com Doc" is a European Commission discussion paper, without legal authority.

13 Philip Lowe was director of rural development from 1991 to 1993 and was formerly Bruce Millan's chef de cabinet dealing with regional policy and ultimately became director general of DG Energy. He retired from the Commission in 2014. Laurent van de Poele remained as director of rural development until he retired from the Commission and returned to the University of Leuven KN as professor of European integration in the Politics Department in 2000. Philip was preceded by Raymond Craps and Graham Avery, also very able directors.

14 There was a fourth, but much smaller, structural fund, the Fisheries Guidance Fund, which was also involved in some regions.

   The reform involved a doubling of three structural funds in real terms between 1988 and 1992. In the 1989 budget, the European Regional Development Fund (ERDF) had ECU 4.5bn, the European Social Fund (ESF) ECU 3.5bn, and the Guidance Section of the Agricultural Guidance and Guarantee Fund had ECU 1.5bn. Following the creation of the European Monetary Union and the creation of the euro in January 1999, the ECU was effectively converted at par to the euro.

15 In this case "Community" referred to European Community.

16 The ECU was the European Currency Unit used prior to the establishment of the euro, mainly for converting farm prices and subsidies into national currencies. It was valued according to a basket of national currencies.

17 Commission officials at the time usually denied this claim, but it is hardly a coincidence that the CAP reforms of 1992 met all the necessary conditions of the URA (1993–1994).

18 Even if this joint funding was severely hampered in practice by the separate and distinctive financial rules and regulations for each of the funds in question, as well as by the usually separate ministries in the member states dealing with each.

19 The accession of Finland, Sweden, and Austria. Norway was also seeking accession, but the population voted against this, and Norway joined the EEA instead. This gave access to the single market, but at a significant cost in terms of contributions to the EU budget and lack of influence over related regulations and their reforms.

20 See also Dwyer (2013).

21 COM (2011)500 final of 29.6.2011.

References

Arkleton Trust (Research) Ltd., 1989. *First report for the Commission of the European Communities on structural change and the use made of structures policies by farm households in the European Community.* The Arkleton Trust (Research) Ltd., Oxford; Nethy Bridge.

Bryden, J.M., 1990. *The impact of 1992 on rural Europe*, in: Tracy, M. (Ed.), *Rural policy issues: Papers presented at Douneside, Aberdeenshire, March 1990.* Arkleton Trust, Oxford; Aspen Institute for Humanistic Studies, Washington, DC.

Bryden, J.M., 2006. *Special focus: From Leader I to Leader + and beyond to the Leader axis.* Leader magazine, 6.

Bryden, J.M., 2010. *Local development*, in: Hart, K., Laville, J.-L., Cattani, A.D. (Eds.), *The Human Economy.* Polity Press, Cambridge, pp. 248–260.

Bryden, J.M. 2016. *Causes and consequences of medium- and long-term territorial inequalities in a European context, with a focus on rural regions.* Working Paper Series No. 182. Rimisp, Santiago, Chile.

Bryden, J.M., Mantino, F., 2017. *Rural policy in Europe*, in: Meyers, W., Johnson, T. (Eds.), *Handbook of international food and agricultural policies, Volume 1: Policies for agricultural markets and rural economic activity.* World Scientific Press, Singapore; New York, pp. 89–119.

Bryden, J.M., Warner, M.E., 2012. *Policy affecting rural people, economies and communities*, in: Shucksmith, M., Brown, D.L., Shortall, S., Vergunst, J., Warner, M.E. (Eds.), *Rural transformations and rural policies in the US and UK.* Routledge, New York, pp. 179–195.

Bryden, J.M., Efstratoglou, S., Ferenczi, T., Johnson, T., Knickel, K., Refsgaard, K., Thomson, K.J., 2011. *Towards sustainable rural regions in Europe.* Routledge, New York; London.

Commission of the European Communities, 1968. *Memorandum on the reform of agriculture in the European Economic Community.* COM (68) 1000, Part A and B, December 18, Bulletin of the European Communities, Supplement to no. 1, 1969. http://ec.europa.eu/agriculture/cap-history/crisis-years-1970s/com68-1000_en.pdf.

De Benedictis, M., De Filippis, F., 1980. *The development of regional agriculture under the common agricultural policy: Regional impact of the Common Agricultural Policy.* Università di Napoli, Centro di specializzazione e ricerche economiche-agrarie per il Mezzogiorno, Naples.

Dwyer, J. 2013. *Transformation for sustainable agriculture: What role for the second pillar of CAP?* Bio-based and Applied Economics 2(1), 29–48. www.fupress.net/index.php/bae/article/view/12174.

Dwyer, J., Kubinakova, K., Lewis, N., Powel, J., Vigani, M., Fährmann, B., Gocht, A., Grajewski, R., Sauras, M.C., Cachinero, P.N., Mantino, F., Berriet-Solliec, M., Pham, H., 2016. *Research for AGRI Committee: Programmes implementing the 2015–2020 Rural Development Policy.* IP/B/AGRI/IC/2015-74. Directorate General for Internal Policies, Policy Department B, Structural and Cohesion Policies, Brussels.

EAFRD, 2011. *Proposal for a Regulation of the European Parliament and of the Council on support for rural development by the European Agricultural Fund for Rural Development (EAFRD).* COM 2011 (627)/2.

EAFRD, 2013. *EU1305/2013. Article 5 – Union priorities for rural development.* https://eur-lex.europa.eu/LexUriServ/LexUriServ.do?uri=OJ:L:2013:347:0487:0548:en:PDF.

EU-SCAR (Standing Committee on Agricultural Structures), 2012. *Agricultural knowledge and innovation systems in transition: A reflection paper.* Brussels.

Henry, P., 1980. *Study on the regional impact of the Common Agricultural Policy.* XVI/44/81-EN. The Directorate General for Regional Policy, European Commission, Brussels.

Mantino, F., 2011. *Developing a territorial approach for the CAP: A discussion paper.* Report prepared for the Institute for European Environmental Policies, London. May. www.ieep.eu/assets/825/Paper_4_-_Final_version_11072011.pdf.

Mantino, F., 2013. *What is going to change in EU rural development policies after 2013? Main implications in different national contexts.* Bio-based and Applied Economics Journal 2(2) 197–207.

Saraceno, E., 2002. *Rural development policies and the "second pillar"*, in: *West European Working Group: Future role of agriculture in Europe.* ARL, Hannover, Germany.

Tracy, M., 1989. *Government and agriculture in Western Europe 1880–1988*, 3rd edition. Harvester Wheatsheaf, London.

Tracy, M., 1993. *Food and agriculture in the European Union and other market economies*. Agricultural Policy Studies, Belgium.

van den Bor, W., Bryden, J.M., Fuller, A.M., 1997. *Restructuring from below: Farm household adjustment in Europe, 1981–91*, in: Bassand, M., Brugger, E., Bryden, J., Friedmann, J., Stuckey, B., *Rethinking rural human resource management*. Mansholt Institute, Wageningen, Netherlands.

34

RURAL POLICY IN THE WESTERN BALKANS

Natalija Bogdanov, Marius Lazdinis,[1] *and Matteo Vittuari*

Introduction

The agricultural sector and the rural areas of the Western Balkans (namely Albania, Bosnia and Herzegovina, Kosovo,[2] North Macedonia, Montenegro, and Serbia) have undergone tremendous changes in the past decades. This transformation has been driven by internal, regional, and international political, economic, social, and environmental forces. Despite these changes, agriculture and rural livelihoods are still at the core of the socio-economic pattern in the Western Balkans. Agriculture and related sectors still contribute up to 22 percent of the Gross Domestic Product (GDP), and 40 percent of total employment is in agriculture, forestry, and fisheries (World Bank, 2017a).

The Western Balkan countries are characterized by a great wealth of natural resources and biodiversity, making the region one of the richest parts of Europe in this respect (Kotevska *et al.*, 2015). Land and natural resources are diverse, ranging from fertile plains and river valleys to the not very productive karst, hilly, and mountainous areas. Regardless of the rich natural resource base, agricultural sectors of all countries in the region face numerous challenges and remain constrained by some deeply rooted structural problems: low average farm size, low productivity, and limited economic opportunities in rural areas. These conditions have a deep impact on the overall economic activity and incomes in rural areas, which cause demographic imbalances and threaten the vitality of rural livelihoods. Many rural areas face decreasing population, which has resulted in a lack of agricultural activity and land abandonment.

Yet, in the face of the low efficiency in production and fragmentation of the sector, the demand for food, both in terms of quantity and quality, is increasing. For example, export opportunities are opening up and an increasing number of middle-class residents in the region want to follow healthier and more nutrient-rich diets.

Addressing structural weaknesses in agriculture and developing rural economies requires a long-term approach, involving considerable investments to increase the efficiency, productivity, safety, and quality in agriculture and food production. During the last few decades, all countries in the region undertook several phases of reforms that streamlined and consolidated their agricultural policies. These reforms were carried out under the pressures caused by internal and regional political instabilities, requirements arising from international agreements, and prolonged economic crisis.

From the region, Slovenia, Croatia, Bulgaria, and Romania joined the European Union (EU) at the beginning of the 2000s. Their agricultural sectors and rural areas are now taking advantage of significant EU support and have already undergone extended transformation processes. Yet, Albania, Bosnia and Herzegovina, Kosovo, North Macedonia, Montenegro, and Serbia are still in the pre-accession state with the EU that has recently identified a more tangible timeframe. The communication issued by the European Commission on February 6, 2018 (European Commission, 2018) has outlined the different elements still to be addressed before any of the Western Balkan countries could join the EU. Even though no exact date for accession of any of the countries is given, an example of "steps required for Montenegro and Serbia to complete the accession process in a 2025 perspective" is provided (European Commission, 2018). After a long period of pre-accession preparations without any obvious target, this is a big change to all of those involved in preparing the region for EU membership. Anyone having been or being involved in development work will know that seven years is not much in terms of carrying out significant institutional reforms, increasing capacities in public and private sectors, and increasing local competitiveness and efficiency.

The Communication outlines a number of actions where the EU intends to significantly enhance its support to the transformation process in the Western Balkans (European Commission, 2018). Agriculture is hardly mentioned, the word "rural" is not. This poses a question about the remaining gap (if any) between the state of development in rural economies of the Western Balkans and those of the EU member states.

This chapter provides a comparative overview of the state of development in the agricultural sector and in overall rural economies in Albania, Bosnia and Herzegovina, Kosovo, North Macedonia, Montenegro, and Serbia (see Figure 34.1). The progress is compared with five reference countries: Slovenia, which shares a common historical and political heritage with most of the Western Balkan countries and joined the EU in 2004; Lithuania, a post-Soviet state that also joined the EU in 2004; Bulgaria and Romania, which are former socialist countries, share similar climatic conditions, and joined the EU in 2008; and Turkey, which is also negotiating accession to the EU.

Having provided an overview of the levels of development in the agricultural sector and overall in rural economies, this chapter also makes a brief comparative analysis of the existing means – policy and budgetary – for interventions in the agri-food sector to facilitate sustainable growth.

Assessing development of rural areas

Is the agri-food sector in the Western Balkans ready to join and compete in the EU internal market on the day of accession? Are rural populations content with living where they are, or are they desperate to migrate to better places? Are rural economies of the Western Balkans ready to find and fill their own niches in the internal market? These questions have no easy answers, in particular in the context of limited statistical information available from the Western Balkan countries.

Moreover, the EU itself is a moving target that has significantly changed with the last waves of enlargement. The new member states (some coming from the Balkan region) have reduced statistical averages in favor of the levels of the Western Balkans. However, disparities between member states within the EU are still significant. Also, the vision and understanding of the type and quality of development in the sector and overall rural economies has evolved. If around 2006, the "New Rural Paradigm" called for increasing competitiveness, support for multiple sectors, bottom-up policies, and local strategies, the new "Rural Policy 3.0" approach advocated by the OECD prioritizes well-being, considering multiple dimensions, low-density economies, and an integrated policy approach with multiple domains (OECD, 2006, 2016a).

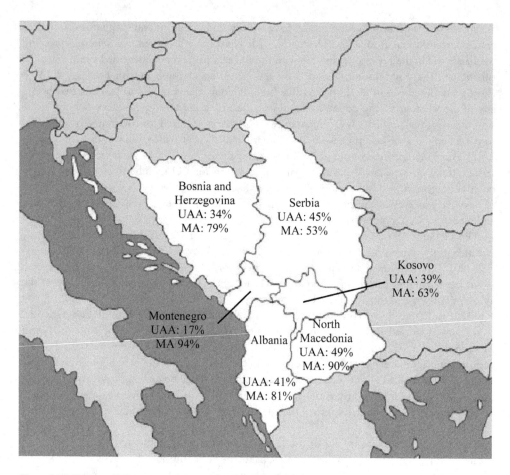

Figure 34.1 Western Balkan countries considered in this chapter. Numbers show percentage of agricultural area (UAA) and percentage of mountain area (MA). The designation of Kosovo is without prejudice to positions on status and is in line with UNSCR 1244/1999 and the ICJ Opinion on the Kosovo declaration of independence

The latest understanding of rural development seems to be holistically focused on increasing well-being. Subsequently, well-being seems to depend on economic efficiency and competitiveness, environmental quality, and social equity, i.e. the three main pillars of sustainable development. In a way this links to a broader discourse addressing inequality and some of the negative consequences of globalization. For example, some economists, like Joseph E. Stiglitz, argue that the last economic crisis has shown that equality and economic performance are complementary, but not mutually exclusive (Stiglitz, 2015). In his report on "agenda for growth and shared prosperity" Stiglitz outlines suggestions on how to "tame the top" (top 1 percent of the wealthiest) and "grow the middle". Some authors go as far as to promote the concept of universal basic income, as an approach and an instrument with a potential to revitalize life and democracy in our societies, and hence to increase well-being (Standing, 2017).

While focusing on economies and societies as a whole, these new approaches are particularly relevant to rural areas. Also, while being just a vision even in many of the advanced economies, some elements of these approaches may serve as a useful framework to assess the state of rural societies and economies of the Western Balkan countries.

While the limited data availability in Western Balkans still poses a major constraint (Kotevska *et al.*, 2015; Bogdanov *et al.*, 2017; Volk *et al.*, 2019), two groups of criteria and indicators are used to assess and compare agricultural sectors and rural livelihoods (Table 34.1). Selected indicators refer to two broad areas covering both a sectoral and a territorial approach: (1) economic performance of the agricultural sector; (2) environmental conditions and quality of life in rural areas.

Economic performance of the agricultural sector depends on household incomes stemming from employment in firms that are productive and competitive or being engaged in a competitive economic activity. As agriculture is still a dominant sector in the rural Balkans, agricultural indicators may provide a good proxy for assessing the overall levels of economic development. For this reason, the indicators selected for this study include employment in agriculture as a share of the total employment and the added value in agriculture as a share of the gross domestic product. Since production and productivity levels could serve as a proxy of the level of modernization of the agricultural sector, as a low labor productivity could be associated with low or insufficient levels of skilled labor, technology, equipment, work organization or infrastructure, gross value added (GVA) per worker is also considered. As an additional index of the structural performances of the agricultural sectors, the number of holdings per size class and the utilized agricultural area per size of holding have been added. Besides sectoral indicators, the analysis includes highlights from some of the major agricultural and livestock production, such as corn, wheat, and milk. While depending on natural conditions, their average yields are a good indicator of productivity and efficiency in the sector. Lastly, agri-food foreign trade was selected to assess the degree of openness of local economies.

Sectoral indicators have been integrated with others to assess quality of life and the condition of rural infrastructures. The share of rural population and population density have been used since they represent rather common indicators to assess the state of the rural area. GDP, which has been analyzed as per capita adjusted by purchasing power parity, has been taken into account

Table 34.1 Criteria and indicators

Economic performances of the agricultural sector	
Added value in agriculture as share of the gross domestic product	
Employment in agriculture as share of the total employment	Table 34.2
Number of holdings (total and per size classes)	
Utilized agricultural area (total and per size classes)	Table 34.3
Maize, wheat, and milk yields	
GVA per worker	Table 34.4
Agri-food foreign trade	Table 34.5
Quality of life and rural infrastructures	
Share of rural population	
Population density in rural areas	
GDP per capita adjusted by purchasing power parity	Table 34.6
Unemployment rates	
Net migration rates	
Self-perceived quality of life	Table 34.7
Rural road networks	
Land lines and mobile penetration	Table 34.8
ICT networks	

as a simplified proxy of the level of economic wealth. Unemployment rates have been included to have a proxy for access to the labor market. For a similar reason also net migration rates have been considered. To assess the quality of life the study has taken advantage of the survey organized by Eurofound in 2016 to estimate the degree of satisfaction of the inhabitants of the Western Balkan countries as well as in the reference countries (Eurofound, 2016).

Additional relevant indicators, mostly aimed at assessing the conditions of rural infrastructures, include rural roads and ICT networks, as they represent enabling conditions facilitating sustainable growth and development. For similar reasons, telephone land lines, and mobile penetration have been included as proxy indicators.

Agriculture and rural areas

Economic performances of the agricultural sector

Agriculture in the Western Balkans remains one of the most important means of livelihood and a key sector in the economy, with a high percentage of economically active people employed and a high contribution to GDP (Table 34.2). In the EU, the primary sector accounts for 1.5 percent of the GDP and employs 4.0 percent of the active work force (Eurostat, 2018), whereas in the Western Balkans the situation shows a very different magnitude – ranging from 7.3 percent (Bosnia and Herzegovina) to 22.9 percent (Albania) of GDP, and from 6.7 percent (Kosovo), to 40.7 percent (Albania) in total employment. Such a wide dispersion across countries in the importance of agriculture in national GDP and employment is the result of the

Table 34.2 Agriculture as a percentage of the gross domestic product and employment in agriculture as a percentage of total employment

Countries	Agriculture as % of the GDP		Employment in agriculture as % of total employment	
	2016	Index 2016/2010 (%)	2016	Index 2016/2010 (%)
Western Balkans				
Albania	22.9	136.3	40.7	92.6
Bosnia-Herzegovina	7.3*	101.9	19.2	97.9
Kosovo	13.4	90.6	6.7	–
Montenegro	9.0	122.0	7.7	123.8
North Macedonia	10.5	91.9	16.6	86.2
Serbia	7.9	90.5	18.6	82.2
Reference countries				
Bulgaria	4.1	69.5	6.8	90.7
Lithuania	3.0	90.9	8.0	98.8
Romania	4.1	65.1	23.1	80.5
Slovenia	1.9	111.8	5.0	58.1
Turkey	6.2	82.7	19.5	82.3

Sources: World Bank (2017a, 2017b).

Note
* Bosnia-Herzegovina data from 2015

interplay of numerous factors, including not just those related to agriculture (natural resources, technology, knowledge), but also the pace of growth in other sectors.

In the Western Balkans land restitution was one of the first transitional reforms, but it had relatively little impact on farm structure according to the ownership and farm sizes. The land reform implemented in the 1990s did not bring significant changes in farm structure in the countries of the former Yugoslavia like in other post-communistic countries, since 85 percent of the total land continued to be farmed by family farms. However, the abolition of restrictions on the maximum farm size allowed in private hands and the liberalization of the land market contributed to create a dual farm structure in the northern part of the region (mostly in Serbia) with a significant number of large commercial farms, established mostly through the privatization of the former kombinats and collective farms (Bogdanov *et al.*, 2017). The rest of the territory is dominated by small-scale and fragmented private farms, which in some regions are subsistence farms lacking the resources for economically viable production. The average farm size ranges from 1 hectare in Albania to 5.4 hectares in Serbia (Table 34.3). In North Macedonia and Bosnia and Herzegovina, small farms represent the dominant share in utilized agricultural area (UAA), whereas in Serbia, with the exception of small family farms, there are also rather large holdings occupying a considerable portion of the total UAA.

In general, the agricultural sector in the region has been experiencing highly volatile yields of main crops, with an upward trend (Table 34.4). While maize and wheat harvests on average are close to those in the reference countries, milk yields are clearly lower in the Western Balkans than in the other new EU member states. Only Serbia has milk yields above those in Romania and Turkey and similar to those in Bulgaria. This comparison should also take into account climatic conditions, which in most instances are more favorable for maize and wheat production in the Western Balkan countries than in most of the reference countries.

Labor productivity in the agricultural sector measured by GVA per worker rapidly increased over the last two decades in all observed counties (Table 34.4). Differences across countries are not easy to assess since they might be driven by differences in multi-factor productivity. Yet, results reveal that labor productivity in the agricultural sector of the Western Balkans is lagging behind and remains lower in comparison with all reference countries, except for Romania. Montenegro is an outlier, with GVA per worker exceeding by far those of the reference countries.

Despite a large agricultural potential, the region is a net food importer, with exports covering only a small fraction of imports, with the exception of Serbia which traditionally has a positive trade balance (Table 34.5). Compared with 2010, in 2015 the highest increases in agri-food exports were recorded in Albania, Kosovo, and Serbia (59%, 38%, and 31%, respectively). At the same time, agri-food imports increased in Serbia (52%), North Macedonia (10%), and Kosovo (9%). In Kosovo and North Macedonia agri-food trade balances are worsening (increasing deficits), whereas in other countries deficits were reduced. Among reference countries, Slovenia and Romania are the only ones with a negative trade balance. Positive developments in trade balance are seen in all countries, except for Slovenia where the trade deficit remained stable.

Quality of life and rural infrastructures

The shares of rural population, as well as rural population density significantly vary across countries. Share of rural in total population and rural population density are lowest in Bulgaria (25.7 percent and 19.7 inhabitants per square kilometer), while Bosnia and Herzegovina and Slovenia are among the most rural countries in terms of size and density of the rural population (Table

Table 34.3 Land use and farm structure in the Western Balkans and target countries. UAA: utilized agricultural area. Areas in hectares (ha)

Country	Holdings			Number of holdings				Utilized agricultural area			
	Number (1000)	UAA	Average area	<2 (%)	2–5 (%)	5–10 (%)	>10 (%)	<2 (%)	2–5 (%)	5–10 (%)	>10 (%)
Western Balkans											
Albania[A]	321.0	333,592	1.0	91	8	1	1	56	21	3	20
Bosnia–Herzegovina[B]	–	–	2.0	49	29	17	5	–	–	–	–
Kosovo[B]	129.2	257,600	2.0	80	16	3	1	45	31	15	10
Montenegro[B]	48.9	221,300	4.5	73	16	6	5	10	11	8	71
North Macedonia[B]	170.9	315,900	1.8	78	16	4	2	8	–	–	–
Serbia[B]	631.6	3,437,400	5.4	48	29	15	8	8	17	18	57
Reference countries											
Bulgaria[C]	254.4	4,650,900	18.3	72	11	4	13	2	2	2	94
Lithuania[C]	171.8	2,861,300	16.7	14	39	22	24	1	8	9	82
Romania[C]	3629.7	13,055,900	3.6	71	19	5	4	12	16	10	62
Slovenia[C]	72.4	485,800	6.7	25	34	24	17	4	17	25	54
Turkey[D]	–	–	1.3	33	32	18	17	6	21	16	57

Sources: (A) Instat (2012); (B) Volk *et al.* (2016); (C) EUROSTAT Farm Structure Survey (2013); (D) OECD (2016b).

Table 34.4 Productivity of agriculture sector – average yields and GVA per worker; for each indicator the 2016 value and the 2008–2016 percent index are given

Country	Maize		Wheat		Milk		GVA per worker	
	2016 (t/ha)	index (%)	2016 (t/ha)	index (%)	2016 (t/anim.)	index (%)	2016 (USD)	index (%)
Western Balkans								
Albania	6.48	129.6	3.90	97.3	2.75	110.4	5442	141.3
Bosnia–Herzegovina	6.14	125.1	4.29	115.0	2.88	112.5	6037	127.0
Kosovo	4.49	–	4.10	–	–	–	–	–
Montenegro	4.21	116.9	3.15	90.0	3.05	104.5	24,238	119.3
North Macedonia	4.62	113.0	3.83	112.3	2.40	115.4	7885	88.3
Serbia	7.30	152.1	4.84	112.8	3.63	128.7	6907	146.2
Reference countries								
Bulgaria	5.47	131.8	4.74	113.9	3.69	108.5	10,199	102.5
Lithuania	6.90	163.9	4.36	102.3	5.40	113.0	5153	130.9
Romania	4.16	129.2	3.94	115.2	3.32	108.5	12,168	119.0
Slovenia	9.51	129.9	5.18	114.6	5.76	100.5	20,790	196.5
Turkey	9.41	130.9	2.70	115.4	3.09	112.0	15,108	121.4

Sources: FAOSTAT (2018); ASK (2017) for Kosovo; Data from database: World Development Indicators, last updated: 07.25.18.

Table 34.5 Agri-food foreign trade (billions of current dollars)

Country	Coverage of imports by exports (%)		Index 2015/2010 (%)	
	2010	2015	Exports	Imports
Western Balkans				
Albania	10.8	21.9	159	76
Bosnia-Herzegovina	21.3	28.0	129	97
Kosovo	5.5	6.7	138	109
Montenegro	11.3	11.5	95	98
North Macedonia	78.6	68.8	96	110
Serbia	215.5	186.5	131	152
Reference countries				
Bulgaria	136.1	140.1	121	117
Lithuania	124.3	126.5	132	129
Romania	80.4	98.5	157	128
Slovenia	46.2	50.6	114	104
Turkey	329.5	148.1	139	310

Sources: WITS (2017) and ASK (2017) for Kosovo.

34.6). Such differences might be explained by variations in natural capital and economic and social conditions, as well as by different criteria utilized to define rural areas.

Despite positive developments in regional economies, the income gap between the Western Balkans and the reference countries is still consistent (Table 34.6). Current GDP per capita in all Western Balkan countries is well below those of the reference countries, with Kosovo, Albania, and Bosnia and Herzegovina at the bottom among European countries.

The trend of population shrinking and aging in the Western Balkans represents at the same time a major characteristic of the region's socio-demographic structure and a key challenge. It is not prominent only in remote and marginalized rural areas, but represents the general characteristics of the entire region. The main causes of population decline include negative natural growth (particularly in Serbia and Bosnia and Herzegovina) and high out-migration rates. It is estimated that since the 2000s about 4.9 million people (nearly 25 percent of the total population), have left the region (Matković, 2017). The large labor outflows relative to population size have continued, with Bosnia-Herzegovina and Albania as the major sending countries with respect to their populations, followed by Serbia. This trend is less evident in other countries in the region, which experienced higher out-migration in previous decades. However, reference countries, particularly Romania and Lithuania, also faced out-migration-related issues, yet some of them experienced population growth (Slovenia and Turkey).

The intensity and the scope of out-migration have altered the demographic structure and reproductive base of the rural communities, along with their livelihoods. As a result, the provision of certain facilities and services in rural areas is low and is hindered by high provision costs, while the rural economy suffers from poverty, lack of job opportunities, and degradation of natural resources (Lampietti *et al.*, 2009; Bélorgey *et al.*, 2012; Pejin-Stokić and Grečić, 2012; Bogdanov and Babović, 2016). Rural labor markets in all countries are characterized by high levels of unemployment, low rates of job creation, and a lack of alternative employment and income opportunities (Matković, 2006; Bogdanov and Cvejić, 2011; Cvejić *et al.*, 2010). Unemployment rates are significantly higher in the Western Balkan countries than in all of the

Table 34.6 Rural population, GDP per capita, unemployment rates, and migration rates

Country	Rural population (2016)[A]		GDP per capita, PPP, constant 2011 $ (2016)[B]	Unemployment rates, % (2016)[C]		Net migration rate, % (2010–2015)[D]
	%	In./km²		Rural	Urban	
Western Balkans						
Albania	41.6	44.8	11,356	–	–	−3.19
Bosnia-Herzegovina	52.5	37.4	11,338	29.0	25.7	−4.33
Kosovo	–	–	9458	35.2	24.8	+0.17
Montenegro	33.9	–	15,729	–	–	−0.48
North Macedonia	42.4	40.2	13,113	21.9	22.6	−0.43
Serbia	44.2	–	13,721	11.9	17.6	−1.37
Reference countries						
Bulgaria	25.7	17.6	17,793	10.2	4.8	−0.32
Lithuania	32.6	15.8	28,032	10.8	5.2	−4.71
Romania	46.1	41.5	21,782	6.5	5.5	−1.48
Slovenia	46.0	53.7	29,930	7.2	8.8	+0.83
Turkey	25.9	28.4	23,757	9.4	11.3	+2.25

Sources: (A) World Bank (2017c); Gollopeni (2015) for Kosovo; (B) World Bank (2017d); (C) ILO (2017); (D) UN (2017). Net migrations rate is the difference between immigrants and emigrants over a period, divided by the population.

reference countries, with Serbia representing the only case where unemployment rates, at least in rural areas, are comparable to those of the reference countries. No data are available for Montenegro and Albania.

Table 34.7 provides a proxy of the quality of life suggesting that the general perception in terms of general life satisfaction, living standard, and quality of public services in the Western Balkans region is lower than that of the reference countries.

Despite diverse situations, common challenges in the region are also observed in relation to infrastructure, telecommunications, and public services. Table 34.8 shows that the density of roads is generally lower than that of the reference countries. Such a poor level of infrastructure development represents an obstacle to transport and logistics and to the development of more integrated and modern food supply chains.

Data on mobile phone penetration reveal that mobile phone subscriptions in Montenegro and Serbia clearly exceed other countries in the region and most of the reference countries, which demonstrates a relatively good level of development, while Bosnia and Herzegovina and North Macedonia are lagging behind. Fixed telephone subscriptions are very low in Albania and at a similar level in other countries. In the case of Albania, this is probably related to historic reasons as the landline phone network was not developed under the communist regime.

While the use of internet seems to be similar in the Western Balkans and the reference countries, broadband subscriptions are clearly fewer. Even in Bulgaria and Romania, which are similar to the Western Balkan countries in many other respects, broadband use is more widespread. It is particularly low in Albania, if compared to the other Western Balkan countries.

Table 34.7 Quality of life according to citizen perceptions, measured on a scale from 0 to 10

Country	How satisfied are you with your life these days?	Satisfaction with current living standard	Average satisfaction with public services
Western Balkans			
Albania	4.9	5.2	5.5
Montenegro	6.3	6.0	5.8
North Macedonia	5.1	5.2	4.7
Serbia	6.3	5.7	5.6
Reference countries			
Bulgaria	7.3	5.6	5.1
Lithuania	6.5	6.4	5.9
Romania	6.5	6.7	5.6
Slovenia	6.9	6.4	6.0
Turkey	6.0	6.2	6.4

Source: Eurofound (2016).

Table 34.8 Rural road networks and communication networks, 2016

Country	Motorway length[A]	Other roads length[A]	Mobile cellular[B]	Fixed telephone[B]	Using internet[C]	Broadband subscription[C]
	Km per 1000 km²		Per 100 people			
Western Balkans						
Albania	–	137	115.1	8.5	66.3	9.1
Bosnia-Herzegovina	2.5	447	96.8	21.2	60.3	18.8
Kosovo	7.3	185	54.9	–	88.8	–
Montenegro	–	624	165.6	23.6	69.9	18.3
North Macedonia	10.1	554	98.5	17.4	72.2	18.3
Serbia	8.9	581	130.2	38.4	67.1	20.8
Reference countries						
Bulgaria	6.8	177	125.8	20.7	59.8	23.8
Lithuania	5.0	1331	144.6	18.3	74.4	29.5
Romania	3.2	371	115.8	20.8	59.5	22.5
Slovenia	38.4	1887	114.8	35.1	75.5	28.3
Turkey	3.3	39.7	94.4	13.9	58.3	13.2

Source: (A) EUROSTAT (2018); EEA (2015) for Bosnia-Herzegovina; (B) ITU (2017a, 2017b); Eurostat (2016) for Kosovo; (C) ITU (2017c, 2017d); ASK (2017) for Kosovo.

Filling the development gap in rural areas

From the beginning of the 2000s onwards, the national agricultural policies of Western Balkan countries had undergone a number of important transformative processes. Although agricultural policies of all countries (except for Albania) had a similar starting point rooted in the policy framework and concept of Yugoslavia, and shared common institutional infrastructure, the paths, scale, and pace of reforms have been different. The heterogeneity of the agriculture sector and different roles it has in the regional and wider international agri-food markets have caused countries to take divergent paths and different priorities according to their specific contextual needs. However, the common characteristic was that agricultural policies in all countries were largely driven by overall economic, political, and social challenges that region had faced.

Besides focusing just purely on economic aspects of the agricultural sector, which still predominates rural livelihoods in the Western Balkan countries, we have taken a broader look at the overall levels of development of societies in the countries of interest. We tried to compile and analyze the indicators which would lead us to understanding the sustainability of development and economic growth in the countries concerned, as well as levels of inequality and well-being of all inhabitants. We made comparisons with a group of selected countries, most of them EU member states, but also Turkey, in order to understand what would be the level of the development gap to be filled for the Western Balkan countries to catch up (when and where at all necessary) with the levels of their peer EU member states.

This work has shown that Western Balkan countries have strong potential in their agriculture sectors, but generally still face convergence challenges also in light of the relation with the reference countries. Although, Western Balkan countries have a larger contribution of the agriculture sector to GDP, sector productivity and its growth are far from those of many of the EU member states, yet not too far from Romania and Bulgaria. This situation is the result of decades of under-investment, weak institutions, and slow pace of reforms. However, some countries (or their regions) and sub-sectors are exceptions to this general trend. For example, in Serbia, there is a dual agriculture sector comprising both modern big farms and traditional small family farms, where intensity of farming ranges from high (Vojvodina), through moderate (Šumadija and West Serbia), to very extensive farming (South Serbia). Overall, in the regional context Serbia stands out as having a comparative advantage due to fertile agricultural soil in part of its territory, whereas other countries are competitive in few sub-sectors/products, mainly on regional markets. Yet, the potential for the agriculture sector to develop further is significant and it relies on natural resource endowments, including soil quality and a favorable climate, as well as proximity to the EU market.

With regard to the EU accession some important gaps still remain to be overcome. This includes developing an effective and EU-compliant food safety system to ensure competitiveness in international markets and the protection of public health, improving performances of value chains, upgrading infrastructure and logistic services, boosting the rural economy through income diversification and value added, and improving the rural environment and the countryside (Bogdanov *et al.*, 2017).

In spite of frequent shifts in policy directions and implementation mechanisms, in recent years there is visible progress towards a more comprehensive and integrated policy framework. The most powerful impetus to accelerate the institutional and policy reforms is the progress in accession to the EU. Within that process, new mid- and long-term strategic documents governing agriculture and rural development were adopted and policy objectives, priorities, and instruments set out. The EU principles of rural policy and its operational framework (e.g. strategy-setting, participation, networks, and partnerships), as well as rules governing the support for rural development (e.g. co-financing, compliance with the minimum standards provided, and preparing business plans) are driving forward structural reforms in the sector. The experience of Central and Eastern European countries with rural development policy shows that rural issues were entered in the later stages of transition, which was closely tied to the availability of European funds for pre-accession assistance (Bogdanov *et al.*, 2017).

Strategic documents of all countries recognize the relevance of agricultural restructuring and rural development policy, where policy objectives and measures are shaped according to the principles and strategic directions compatible with the EU programming guidelines. Accordingly, the institutional capacity building and increase of budgetary allocations for second pillar measures are envisaged. In terms of policy objectives and priorities, in all countries emphasis is given to: (a) improving farm viability and competitiveness of the agri-food sector; (b) sustainable management of natural resources and mitigation of the effects of climate change, and (c) improving the quality of life of rural people and balanced development of rural areas. Besides, each country set out its own priorities to address specific needs, such as: income stabilization of farmers (Bosnia and Herzegovina, Kosovo, and Serbia), strengthening the food chain (North Macedonia, Kosovo, and Serbia), investment in human capital, transfer of knowledge and innovation (Albania, FYR Macedonia, and Kosovo), strengthening the social structure of rural areas (Serbia, Kosovo), etc.

National support to agriculture and rural development

State support to agriculture plays an important role in its development and is fundamental for boosting growth and meeting development objectives. Even though all countries in the region have developed multi-annual strategic programs and action plans for agriculture and rural development, which clearly state their commitment to adopt the goals and priorities of the Common Agricultural Policy, the data on public expenditures reveals that, after several years, these priorities are not fully reflected in funding policy support measures (Volk *et al.*, 2019).

In recent years, public expenditure on agriculture and rural development has risen in all Western Balkan countries reflecting the priority that governments are giving to the agriculture sector for economic development and progress to EU integration. Yet, the budgetary support in some countries (Albania, Kosovo, and Serbia) still indicates periodic ups and down.

Moreover, some direct producer support measures that are not in accordance with EU principles are still implemented. The funding of rural development in a few countries/territories is decreasing, while some countries are still experimenting with various approaches in terms of measures, beneficiaries, and amounts of support (Volk *et al.*, 2019). In comparison with the EU average, the budgetary expenditure in the Western Balkans is relatively low and has a limited potential to address development issues. The data for 2017 shows that support per hectare of UAA amounted from about 68.7 euro per hectare in Serbia to 188.6 euro per hectare in North Macedonia, representing only 15–42 percent of the EU-28 average (Figure 34.2).

More important than the level of support is the composition of budgetary expenditures. In general, the subsidies for market and direct support measures can help market development, introduction of new technologies, and reduce production risks. Yet, once their objectives have been achieved, they are likely to create new distortions and increase profit margins at the expense of broader agricultural sectors growth, while burdening the public purse. On the other side, rural development measures are intended to raise agricultural productivity and to promote structural change.

In the Western Balkans, market and direct producer support measures still prevail, especially in Serbia, Bosnia and Herzegovina, and North Macedonia. Yet, area and headage payments prevail over decoupled payments, which are the dominant support in the EU.

The budgetary funds for rural development measures are low and unstable, while the composition of funding by main groups of measures is incompatible with the EU (Figure 34.3). The level of budgetary funds for structural and rural development support varies from below 2.7 euro per hectare in Bosnia and Herzegovina, to 51 euro per hectare in Montenegro (135.4 euro per hectare in the EU-28). Low funding of second pillar measures does not allow key structural

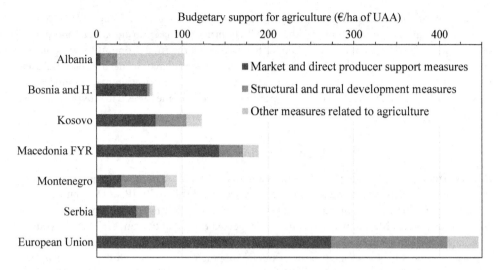

Figure 34.2 Budgetary support for agriculture, per hectare of UAA, in Western Balkan countries/territories and in the EU (€/ha), 2017

Source: Volk *et al.* (2019).

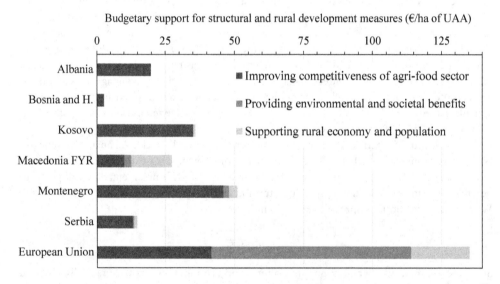

Figure 34.3 Budgetary support for structural and rural development measures

Source: Volk *et al.* (2019).

problems of agriculture and rural areas (e.g. technological developments, activation of land market, and reaching sustainability of farms in marginalized areas) to be addressed.

When it comes to the composition of rural development support, on-farm investment support for improving the competitiveness of agriculture dominates (except in North Macedonia), contrary to the EU where the expenditures for this group of measures represents less than a third of funds dedicated to the second pillar (Figure 34.3).

Funding of measures intended for improving the environment and the countryside in Western Balkan territories is minor, although all countries face land abandonment and consequent negative environmental changes. Funds for supporting the rural economy and population are also rather weak, except in North Macedonia. All countries have financed some infrastructure projects in rural areas, as well as investments for on-farm diversification of economic activities in the field of rural tourism. Yet, the support for this group of measures is too low considering the need to prevent stagnation of rural areas and further exodus.

EU pre-accession assistance

Besides national funds, EU pre-accession assistance provides important means to facilitate reforms and development in the agri-food sector. During 2014–2020, IPARD (rural development programs under the Instrument for Pre-Accession Assistance) allocations to Albania, Montenegro, North Macedonia, and Serbia are expected to add up to around 350 million euros. This amount when complemented by 25 percent share of national public funds (which is compulsory), increases to 466 million euros of public support to the agri-food sector, which then needs to be matched by private beneficiaries. Therefore, the total amount of IPARD-related investment in the agri-food sector in the Western Balkans is expected to be slightly below 1 billion euros. These investments, to a large extent, will aim at increasing the competitiveness of the sector and compliance with national and EU standards.

Moreover, IPARD represents not only financial means to support investments in the private sector. It has the overall catalytic effect of large-scale policy, institutional and administrative reforms in the public sector, and gradually changes ways of working in the private sector. While setting up management and control systems for handling assistance, the IPARD approach pursues public administration reform in agricultural administrations. IPARD implementation requires presence not only of direct management structures, such as paying agencies and managing authorities, but also of all other public bodies, without which good functioning of the agricultural sector would not be possible, such as: veterinary agencies, food safety authorities, environmental bodies, extension services.

By 2019, four Western Balkan countries had implemented IPARD: Albania, Montenegro, North Macedonia, and Serbia. While North Macedonia already has experience with IPARD, in the other countries first contracts were signed only in 2019. If implementation will prove to be effective, efficiency of the agri-food sector and overall quality of life in rural areas in the Western Balkans should improve over the coming years.

Conclusions

Since the 1990s, a number of important political and economic events have radically changed the overall situation in the Western Balkans. In addition to the common problems encountered by all transition countries in Southeast Europe, the transition period in the Western Balkans was marked also by wars and ethnic conflicts, deep economic recession, and the break-up of the Yugoslav monetary and economic union, and the imposition of trade barriers by the newly created states. Political instability has slowed down the structural reforms, which subsequently resulted in developmental delay.

The agriculture sector remains a backbone of national economies in the Western Balkans, with a high contribution to the countries' GDPs, and employment and external trade (particularly import). Though the region has diverse and rich land resources and a favorable climate for a vibrant agri-food sector, many obstacles for its growth remain.

Besides positive developments in some sub-sectors, the overall agriculture of Western Balkan countries is characterized by relatively lower labor productivity compared to that of neighboring countries and those countries that joined the EU during the 2000s. The rural economies of all countries in the region suffer from depopulation, out-migration, and lack of jobs. The negative side effects of shrinking rural populations are multidimensional and complex. These include changes in the rural environment, land use and land cover, but also negative impacts on rural livelihood and the economic and social fabric of rural areas. Weak infrastructure and logistics also prevent more effective productivity growth and reduce the capacities for small farmers to increase their income.

Reform of agricultural policy and institutional structures related to the EU accession are at the top of the agenda of the national ministries. Yet, Western Balkan countries still have, to different degrees, substantial work ahead in aligning legislation and meeting the established criteria. Administrative structures and resources for the implementation of rural development measures under IPARD are advancing well.

The agricultural sectors and rural areas of Western Balkan countries need a boost and a new push to move beyond subsistence farming. Achieving sustainable growth of the agriculture sector and rural economies largely depends on some fundamental obstacles being overcome. These include: reducing farm fragmentation, increasing labor productivity by income diversification, adapting to climate change, and capitalizing comparative advantages by investing in value added and food quality and safety.

Yet, diversification of rural economies in the Western Balkan countries depends on many interrelated factors that simultaneously impact overall regional development. In general, at the macro level systematic efforts should be undertaken to create innovative, sound, and coherent macro-economic policies, which will provide the solid base to promote growth, encourage private sector investors and employment, increase productivity, and enable human capital development. On the other side, at the local level, there is a need to create a business environment conducive to entrepreneurship, domestic investment, and job creation. The quality of infrastructure, quality of rural labor, and access to regional markets are crucial production factors in satisfying rural development needs. Meeting these require a more holistic and integrated approach, which goes beyond a simple increase of budgetary funding for agriculture and investment in rural development.

Therefore, raising the level of political awareness and commitment to rural revitalization can help ensure more effective policies and their implementation in the Western Balkans. To scale up rural economy growth and to achieve self-sustaining development, policy focus should be placed upon a more integrated territorial approach in policy-making. The ability of institutions and policy-makers to respond to the evolving rural development paradigm, addressing widening inequalities between rural and urban areas, environmental and climate change interactions, and contributing to multi-sectoral coordination and consultation mechanisms is critical to further the sustainable development of rural areas in the region.

Note

1 This manuscript represents solely the views of its authors and cannot in any circumstances be regarded as the official position of the European Commission.
2 The designation of Kosovo is without prejudice to positions on status and is in line with UNSCR 1244/1999 and the ICJ Opinion on the Kosovo declaration of independence.

References

ASK, Agjencia e Statistikave të Kosovës, 2017. Askdata platform. http://askdata.rks-gov.net/PXWeb/pxweb/en/askdata/askdata__Agriculture%20census%202014/?rxid=6c75a9aa-627c-48c6-ae74-9e1b95a9c47d.

Bélorgey, N., Garbe-Emden, B., Horstmann, S., Kuhn, A., Vogel, D., Stubbs, P., 2012. *Social impact of emigration and rural–urban migration in Central and Eastern Europe*. European Union, Cologne.

Bogdanov, N., Babović, M., 2016. *The impact of emigration on structural changes in Serbian agriculture*. IAMO Forum 2016, Rural Labor in Transition: Structural Change, Migration and Governance, June 22–24, 2016, Halle (Saale), Germany.

Bogdanov, N., Cvejić, S., 2011. *Poverty and social exclusion in rural Serbia: Position of family farms*. Ekonomika poljoprivrede 58, Belgrade.

Bogdanov, N., Rodic, V., Vittuari, M., 2017. *Structural change and transition in the agricultural sector: Experience of Serbia*. Communist and Post-Communist Studies 50, 319–330.

Cvejić, S., Babović, M., Petrović, M., Bogdanov, N., Vuković, O., 2010. *Socijalna isključenost u ruralnim oblastima Srbije*. UNDP, Beograd.

Eurofound, 2016. *European quality of life survey*. www.eurofound.europa.eu/data/european-quality-of-life-survey.

European Commission, 2018. *A credible enlargement perspective for and enhanced EU engagement with the Western Balkans*. Strasbourg, June 2. https://ec.europa.eu/commission/sites/beta-political/files/communication-credible-enlargement-perspective-western-balkans_en.pdf.

European Environment Agency, 2015. *Country profile: Drivers and impacts (Bosnia and Herzegovina)*. www.eea.europa.eu/soer/countries/ba/country-introduction-bosnia-and-herzegovina-2.

Eurostat, 2013. *Farm structure survey 2013 - main results*. https://ec.europa.eu/eurostat/statistics-explained/index.php?title=Farm_structure_survey_2013_-_main_results&oldid=271613.

Eurostat, 2016. *Enlargement countries: Information and communication technology statistics*. https://ec.europa.eu/eurostat/statistics-explained/index.php/Enlargement_countries_-_information_and_communication_technology_statistics#Mobile_phone_subscriptions.

Eurostat, 2018. *Database*. https://ec.europa.eu/eurostat/data/database.

FAOSTAT, 2018. *Data, crops*. www.fao.org/faostat/en/#data/QC.

Instat, 2012. *Agriculture census*. www.instat.gov.al/en/themes/censuses/agriculture-census/#tab2.

International Labour Organization (ILO), 2017. *Unemployment and labor underutilization*. www.ilo.org/ilostat/faces/ilostat-home/home?_adf.ctrl-state=jyp979o_4&_afrLoop=22164493141878#!.

International Telecommunication Union (ITU), 2017a. *Mobile-cellular subscriptions*. www.itu.int/en/ITU-D/Statistics/Documents/statistics/2018/Mobile_cellular_2000-2017_Dec2018.xls.

International Telecommunication Union (ITU), 2017b, *Fixed-telephone subscriptions*. www.itu.int/en/ITU-D/Statistics/Documents/statistics/2018/Fixed_tel_2000-2017_Dec2018.xls.

International Telecommunication Union (ITU), 2017c. *Percentage of individuals using the internet*. www.itu.int/en/ITU-D/Statistics/Documents/statistics/2018/Individuals_Internet_2000-2017_Dec2018.xls.

International Telecommunication Union (ITU), 2017d. *Fixed-broadband subscriptions*. www.itu.int/en/ITU-D/Statistics/Documents/statistics/2018/Fixed_broadband_2000-2017_Dec2018.xls.

Kotevska, A., Bogdanov, N., Nikolic, A., Dimitrieski, D., Stojcheska, A.M., Tuna, E., Milic, T., Simonovska, A., Papic, R., Petrovic, L., Uzunovic, M., Becirovic, E., Andjelkovic, B., Gjoshevski, D., Georgiev, N., 2015. *The impact of socio-economic structure of rural population on success of rural development policy: Macedonia, Serbia and Bosnia and Herzegovina*. Association of Agricultural Economists of Republic of Macedonia, Skopje. www.publicpolicy.rs/documents/49b4bd527097111e95af76861fe17965c7264610.pdf.

Lampietti, J.A., Lugg, D.G., Van der Celen, P., Branczick, A., 2009. *The changing face of rural space: Agriculture and rural development in the Western Balkans*. World Bank, Washington, DC.

Matković, G., 2006. *Overview of poverty and social exclusion in the Western Balkans*. Stanovništvo 44(1), 7–46.

Matković, G., 2017. *The welfare state in Western Balkan countries: Challenges and options*. Center for Social Policy, Beograd, Serbia. http://futureofthewelfarestate.org/wp-content/uploads/2018/04/The_Welfare_State_in_Western_Balkan_Countries_Position_Paper.pdf.

OECD, 2006. *The new rural paradigm: Policies and governance*. OECD, Paris. www.oecd.org/cfe/regional-policy/thenewruralparadigmpoliciesandgovernance.htm.

OECD, 2016a. *Rural 3.0: A framework for rural development*. Policy Note. OECD, Paris. www.oecd.org/cfe/regional-policy/Rural-3.0-Policy-Note.pdf.

OECD, 2016b. *Innovation, agricultural productivity and sustainability in Turkey.* OECD Food and Agricultural Reviews, Paris. www.oecd.org/innovation/innovation-agricultural-productivity-and-sustainability-in-turkey-9789264261198-en.htm.

Pejin-Stokić, Lj., Grečić, V., 2012. *Social impact of emigration and rural–urban migration in Central and Eastern Europe.* Final Country Report, Serbia. VT/2010/001. European Commission.

Standing, G., 2017. *Universal basic income is becoming an urgent necessity.* The Guardian, January 12. www.theguardian.com/commentisfree/2017/jan/12/universal-basic-income-finland-uk.

Stiglitz, J.E., 2015. *The origins of inequality, and policies to contain it.* National Taxation Journal 68(2), 425–448. http://dx.doi.org/10.17310/ntj.2015.2.09.

United Nations (UN), Population Division, 2017, *Net number of migrants, both sexes combined (thousands).* https://population.un.org/wpp/DataQuery/.

Volk, T., Erjavec, E., Ciaian, P., Gomez y Paloma, S., 2016. *Analysis of the agricultural and rural development policies of the Western Balkan countries.* JRC Technical Reports, EUR 27898 EN. http://seerural.org/wp-content/uploads/2016/08/JRC-Technical-Report-2016_Analysis-of-the-agricultural-and-rural-development-policies-of-the-Western-Balkan-countries.pdf.

Volk, T., Rednak, M., Erjavec, E., Rac, I., Zhllima, E., Gjeci, G., Bajramović, S., Vaško, Ž., Kerolli-Mustafa, M., Gjokaj, E., Hoxha, B., Dimitrievski, D., Kotevska, A., Stamenkovska, I.J., Konjevic, D., Spahic, M., Bogdanov, N., Stevović, M. (authors), Ilic, B., Pavloska-Gjorgjieska, D., Ciaian, P. (Eds.), 2019. *Agricultural policy developments and EU approximation process in the Western Balkan countries.* EUR 29475 EN. JRC Technical Reports No. JRC114163. Publications Office of the European Union, Luxembourg. DOI: 10.2760/583399.

World Bank, 2017a. *Data. Agriculture, forestry, and fishing, value added (% of GDP).* https://data.worldbank.org/indicator/NV.AGR.TOTL.ZS.

World Bank, 2017b. *Data. Employment in agriculture (% of total employment) (modeled ILO estimate).* https://data.worldbank.org/indicator/SL.AGR.EMPL.ZS.

World Bank, 2017c. *Data. Rural population (% of total population).* https://data.worldbank.org/indicator/SP.RUR.TOTL.ZS.

World Bank, 2017d. *GDP per capita, PPP (current international $).* https://data.worldbank.org/indicator/ny.gdp.pcap.pp.cd.

World Integrated Trade Solutions (WITS), 2017. *Trade statistics.*

PART VI

Comparative rural policy case studies

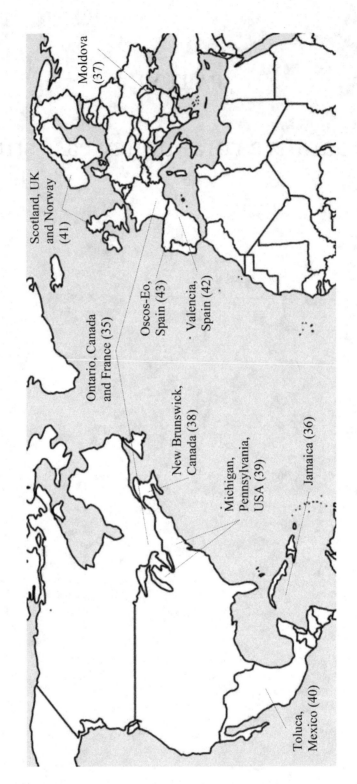

Moldova (37)

Scotland, UK and Norway (41)

Oscos-Eo, Spain (43)

Valencia, Spain (42)

Ontario, Canada and France (35)

New Brunswick, Canada (38)

Michigan, Pennsylvania, USA (39)

Jamaica (36)

Toluca, Mexico (40)

Location of case studies of Part VI

35

PERI-URBAN AGRICULTURAL POLICIES IN CANADA AND FRANCE

*Mikaël Akimowicz, Harry Cummings, Charilaos Képhaliacos,
and Karen Landman*

Introduction

Ontario's Greenbelt, a top-down zoning program, and Toulouse's Scheme for Territorial Consistency (InterSCoT), a bottom-up local planning project, both aim to maintain dynamic peri-urban farming sectors in Ontario and France, respectively. This chapter offers a critical analysis of their impacts, suggesting that the preservation of farmland is not enough to maintain a sustainable peri-urban farming sector. Instead, spaces where farmers can share perceived barriers to their farming projects are essential to coordinate actions among the sector.

Policy context

The spatial expansion of cities rapidly consumes near-urban landscapes and puts pressure on nearby natural and agricultural land (European Environment Agency, 2006; Beesley, 2010). To preserve agricultural, natural, and recreational areas proximate to sprawling cities, different types of policies have been implemented. Among the stated objectives of such policies, maintaining a dynamic agricultural sector has become a common concern. However, the proximity of urban centers and markets increases farmers' business uncertainties while also providing them with new opportunities to diversify their incomes (Vandermeulen *et al.*, 2006; Darly and Torre, 2013; Berdegué *et al.*, 2015). In this context, farmers can adapt their farming systems through new projects and investments. The literature shows that near-urban farmers' strategies usually lead to diversifying farm income sources or exiting the farming sector (Inwood and Sharp, 2012; Clark and Munroe, 2013; Singh *et al.*, 2016). In general, on-farm diversification consists of diversifying agricultural production, processing products, or developing on-farm services, whereas off-farm diversification involves finding off-farm employment or developing off-farm services.

This case study investigates the impact of Ontario's Greenbelt in Canada and Toulouse's Scheme for Territorial Consistency (InterSCoT) in France, two policies that aim to regulate urban sprawl and maintain a dynamic near-urban agricultural sector. Both policies impact an area of approximately 800,000 ha. Whereas Ontario's Greenbelt consists of a top-down zoning program, Toulouse InterSCoT is a bottom-up local planning project. After a critical analysis of the processes that have resulted in the implementation of Ontario's Greenbelt and Toulouse InterSCoT, the respective impacts on farm investment are analyzed with a focus on farmers' futurity – i.e. farmers' confidence and engagement for the future (Commons, 1934). The results of this research, based on in-depth interviews with farmers, suggest that the preservation of farmland is not enough to maintain a sustainable peri-urban farming sector. Rather, spaces where farmers can share perceived barriers to their farming projects and needs are essential to improve the coordination of territorial stakeholders.

Policy design

Toronto, Canada and Toulouse, France are two dynamic metropoles characterized by rocketing demographic growth (Ontario Ministry of Municipal Affairs, 2016; Institut National de la Statistique et des Etudes Economiques, 2016). Due to fertile soils, a dynamic agricultural sector had previously developed on these lands. In both cases, the agricultural sector was connected with nearby urban markets. In recent years, population growth in these regions has combined with preferences for land-consuming detached housing and access to automotive-based transportation, resulting in an increasing consumption of land for these sprawling cities. Consequently, farmland surrounding the two metropoles has rapidly been developed into residential areas (Ontario Ministry of Municipal Affairs, 2016; Institut National de la Statistique et des Etudes Economiques, 2016). Despite less than 1 percent estimated farmland loss (see Table 35.1), this loss usually affects higher quality soils and land fragmentation often results in the abandonment of surrounding farmland.

To preserve dynamic agricultural activity at the periphery of these urban areas, decision-makers have implemented two different policies which show clear differences in terms of legislative content (Table 35.2). In Canada, Ontario's Greenbelt Plan is a top-down approach implemented by the provincial government. Promulgated in 2005, the policy took approximately a year to design and builds on zoning which encompasses existing conservation plans – the Niagara Escarpment Plan and the Oak Ridges Moraine Conservation Plan – as well as the Provincial Policy Statement (Ontario Ministry of Municipal Affairs and Housing, 2005). The Greenbelt Plan strengthens existing legislation regarding farmland protection which, in Ontario, is implemented at the municipal level; according to this legislation, municipal plans *shall conform* with both the Provincial Policy Statement and the Greenbelt Plan. In addition, a Greenbelt Council is appointed by the Minister of Municipal Affairs to (i) provide advice on the administration of the Greenbelt and (ii) guide the provincial government on the implementation of the Greenbelt Plan.

In France, Toulouse InterSCoT is a bottom-up approach that was initiated by the nominated representative of the national state, the *Préfet*, who launched a collective reflection with the local

Table 35.1 Lost farmland in Ontario's Greenbelt and Toulouse InterSCoT

Geography	Loss of farmland	Period	Loss per year	Lost farmland/ Total area (%)	Note
Ontario's Greenbelt	30,764 ha	2006/11	3153 ha/year	0.8	Non-utilized farmland between two censuses
Toulouse InterSCoT	2,400 ha	2010/13	800 ha/year	0.2	Developed farmland

Table 35.2 Characteristics underlying Ontario's Greenbelt and Toulouse InterSCoT

Policy	Approach	Initiator	Policy design	Tool	Governance
Ontario's Greenbelt	Top-down	Ontario Provincial Government	1 year	Zoning	Greenbelt Council
Toulouse InterSCoT	Bottom-up	State representative	9 years	Regional planning	Association for Public Interest (GIP)

elected representatives in 2001. In 2010, this reflection resulted in the definition of a strategy organized on four axes – control, polarize, connect, and pilot – and in four sub-areas (SCoTs), where these axes can be adapted according to local specificities. In the end, more than 400 municipalities have pooled resources to strategically construct the territory delimited by the group of municipalities. The verb *to construct* is used on purpose to highlight the negotiations that were involved in defining the territorial project. The Groupement d'Intérêt Public (GIP, Public Interest Group) governance body is supported by the Agence d'Urbanisme et d'Aménagement Toulouse aire métropolitaine (AUAT, or the Agency for the Planning and Development of Toulouse Metropolitan Area), a planning agency in charge of coordinating Toulouse InterSCoT policy. AUAT acts as an interface to collectively reflect, work, and elaborate projects. Their goals are to (i) strengthen the consistency of the policies implemented at the SCoT level and (ii) support sustainable cooperation in the territory between the SCoTs, municipalities, and other territorial actors.

Policy evaluation

This comparative assessment is based on the analysis of 40 in-depth interviews with Canadian (20) and French (20) farmers. During the interviews, farmers' mental maps of investment decision-making were collected. These mental maps consisted of a graphic representation of the factors affecting their investment decision-making and the responses to a questionnaire designed to collect technical information on farm operations and households (see Figure 35.1) (Akimowicz et al., 2016; Akimowicz and Képhaliacos, 2018).

The first striking difference between the two case studies concerns the stringency of land protection. In Ontario's Greenbelt, farmland is strongly protected at the provincial level; it can be developed in a limited number of cases only, which includes farmers' houses and farm buildings. On the other hand, in Toulouse InterSCoT, farmland protection is planned at the (inter-) municipal level, which means it can be revised as frequently as the (inter-)municipal decision-makers decide. Therefore, land protection is more stringent in the Greenbelt than in the Inter-SCoT. For farmers, these relative stringencies result in productive environments, which seem *a priori* more favorable in the Greenbelt than in the InterSCoT since land access uncertainties are lower in the Greenbelt. In other words, the certainty that agricultural land will not be developed serves as a guarantee that investments will not generate sunk costs. From a theoretical point of view, farmers thus have an incentive to invest in the Greenbelt.

In both cases, guidelines ruling land transfers – the Greenbelt Plan and Toulouse InterSCoT strategic vision – are interpreted and implemented at the municipal level. In Ontario's Greenbelt, farmers stated that multilayered legislation and a lack of consistency in the interpretation of legislation by municipalities can create inequalities among farmers. These issues regarding

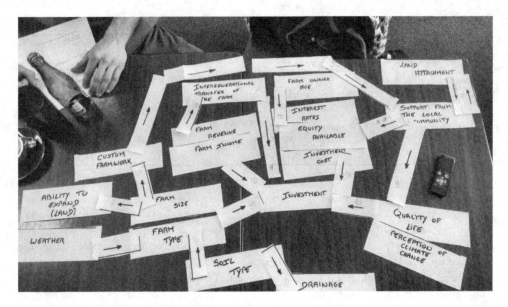

Figure 35.1 Mental map of a farmer operating in Ontario's Greenbelt

legislation can also complicate farmers' decision-making when one piece of farmland crosses municipal boundaries. Due to time shortages to align investment projects with each municipality's legislation, this situation can prevent farmers from investing. On the contrary, the collaboration spaces that result from the creation of the Toulouse InterSCoT governance body and the existence of specialized organizations seem to provide decision-makers with opportunities to improve the consistency of planning decisions. Examples of these specialized organizations include the Agricultural Chamber – a consular farm organization – and SAFER – a private organization in charge of regulating the farmland market. Indeed, these organizations have developed territorial and sectoral expertise on agricultural matters which can be mobilized by decision-makers. The resource pooling at the InterSCoT level and the coordination of potential actors could therefore improve agriculturally oriented policies.

As outlined above, policy-makers need to regulate local farmland markets to implement agricultural policies in peri-urban areas. In this research, the characteristics of the governance bodies – i.e. top-down versus bottom-up – seem to result in sharp differences in actions to regulate respective farmland markets. Prior to the implementation of the Greenbelt Plan, Ontario's farmland market was regulated through thresholds for lot severances that are still in operation. Nowadays, a minimum farm lot size of 100 acres is still commonly implemented in the municipalities within the Greenbelt. Farmers explained that these thresholds severely constrain their land investment capacity due to high land prices. Farmers wishing to start fruit and vegetable farm operations, which only need a few acres, were especially critical of the minimum lot size policy. In Toulouse InterSCoT, SAFER regulates the farmland market in a more ad hoc manner. First, an agricultural plan, designed at the department level (which is a larger administrative area than the InterSCoT) sets minimum farm economic sizes. Then, each time a transaction on agricultural land takes place, SAFER receives a notification from the notary in charge of the transaction. If the transaction does not comply with the agricultural plan, SAFER can pre-empt the transaction and acquire the land; SAFER must then redistribute the land within five years to farmers who follow the priorities defined in the agricultural plan. The land can sometimes be used for non-agricultural projects. During the interviews, critics emerged. Farmers perceive that some types of farming projects are prioritized by SAFER despite the departmental plan. In their opinion, alternative farm projects are rejected, which could be interpreted as a consequence of the tools used by SAFER to assess farm economic viability. In addition, non-agricultural land reallocations were highly criticized by farmers, who do not understand the decision-making criteria behind these allocations. This misunderstanding could be explained by SAFER's private status, in which the organization funds its activity by charging fees on land transactions.

More generally, due to differences in the governance bodies of Ontario's Greenbelt and Toulouse InterSCoT, the respective agricultural value chains are impacted differently. In the Greenbelt, upstream and downstream value chain actors have gradually left the area in anticipation of the decline of agricultural activity. Indeed, the dismantling of the agricultural value chain is a major constraint for farmers. On the one hand, they face extra costs since it is more difficult to access services such as veterinarians, abattoirs, and information. On the other hand, new farmers with a project they would like to pursue are reluctant to locate their activity in a production environment where partner actors are missing. In the InterSCoT, the situation is mixed. Whereas fruit and vegetable farming had slowly disappeared in northwest InterSCoT and cash-crop farming had persisted in southeast InterSCoT, urban pressure seems to have inversed this trend with an increasing demand to start fruit and vegetable farm operations, and a reorganization of the cash-crop industry characterized by an increasing number of custom farm-work enterprises (i.e. farmers who do not farm enough land to justify their machinery and decide to rent out their labor, equipment, and knowledge).

Conclusions

In this chapter, the impacts of Ontario's Greenbelt and Toulouse InterSCoT, two policies designed to preserve a dynamic agricultural sector in proximity to sprawling metropoles, were investigated. The results suggest that, despite lower land access uncertainty in Ontario's Greenbelt – which was expected to support farm investment more effectively, the lack of political representation of agricultural interests and the progressive dismantling of the agricultural value chain have inhibited the viability of the agricultural sector. In addition, Ontario's Greenbelt farmers' mistrust of the political process contributes to opposition, which is also highlighted in Toulouse InterSCoT between urban decision-makers and traditional rural actors who have developed a vision of the agricultural sector strengthened by years of political dominance in rural areas. In peri-urban areas, this rural vision is confronted by other perspectives, in particular the urban-linkages vision of non-traditional agricultural actors who do not share the same beliefs and norms of the more traditional stakeholders. It is thus not surprising that young farmers are more attracted by the new opportunities offered in the urban-influenced Ontario Greenbelt.

This lack of coordination is highlighted by the political misrepresentations of farmers in both governance bodies. The misrepresentation of farmers' interests prevents governance bodies from clearly identifying farmers' needs and implementing actions that could improve the viability of the agricultural sector. However, decision-makers seem to have recognized this lack of coordination. During the ten-year review of the Greenbelt Plan, a consultation process based on the organization of 29 open houses throughout the Greenbelt and the analysis of input from more than 42,000 individuals has resulted in a better understanding of stakeholders' points of view. In Toulouse InterSCoT, traditional agricultural institutions such as the Agricultural Chamber, SAFER, and farmers' unions are to be progressively involved in policy planning by the urban bodies, such as SCoT Toulouse Métropole and AUAT. This increasing collaboration seems to be a first step towards a better coordination of local stakeholders.

References

Akimowicz, M., Képhaliacos, C., 2018. *Coordonner la construction territoriale par une vision du futur. Les dynamiques d'investissement agricole dans l'InterSCoT toulousain.* Economie Rurale 365, 27–47.

Akimowicz, M., Cummings, H., Landman, K., 2016. *Green lights in the Greenbelt? A qualitative analysis of farm investment decision-making in peri-urban southern Ontario.* Land Use Policy 55, 24–36.

Beesley, K.B., 2010. *The rural–urban fringe in Canada: Conflict and controversy.* Brandon University, Brandon, MB.

Berdegué, J.A., Carriazo, F., Jara, B., Modrego, F., Soloaga, I., 2015. *Cities, territories, and inclusive growth: Unraveling urban–rural linkages in Chile, Colombia, and Mexico.* World Development 73, 56–71.

Clark, J.K., Munroe, D.K., 2013. *The relational geography of peri-urban farmer adaptation.* Journal of Rural Community Development 8(3), 15–28.

Commons, J.R., 1934. *Institutional economics: Its place in political economy.* University of Wisconsin Press, Madison, WI.

Darly, S., Torre, A., 2013. *Conflicts over farmland uses and the dynamics of "agri-urban" localities in the Greater Paris Region: An empirical analysis based on daily regional press and field interviews.* Land Use Policy 33, 90–99.

European Environment Agency, 2006. *Urban sprawl in Europe: The ignored challenge.* European Environment Agency, Luxembourg.

Institut National de la Statistique et des Etudes Economiques, 2009 *Toulouse, moteur de la forte poussée démographique en Midi-Pyrénées.* www.insee.fr/fr/statistiques/1293293 (accessed 5.6.17).

Institut National de la Statistique et des Etudes Economiques, 2016. *Une consommation foncière deux fois plus rapide que l'évolution démographique.* www.insee.fr/fr/statistiques/2501732 (accessed 5.6.17).

InterSCoT, 2010. *Vision stratégique de l'InterSCoT de l'aire urbaine de Toulouse.* www.apur.org/sites/default/files/documents/TOULOUSE_InterSCoT_VisionStrategique.pdf (accessed 5.6.17).

Inwood, S.M., Sharp, J.S., 2012. *Farm persistence and adaptation at the rural–urban interface: Succession and farm adjustment.* Journal of Rural Studies 28(1), 107–117.

Ontario Ministry of Municipal Affairs, 2016. *Proposed growth plan for the Greater Golden Horseshoe.* Queen's Printer for Ontario.

Ontario Ministry of Municipal Affairs and Housing, 2005. *The Greenbelt Act.* Queen's Printer for Ontario.

Singh, C., Dorward, P., Osbahr, H., 2016. *Developing a holistic approach to the analysis of farmer decision-making: Implications for adaptation policy and practice in developing countries.* Land Use Policy 59, 329–343.

Vandermeulen, V., Verspecht, A., Van Huylenbroeck, G., Meert, H., Boulanger, A., Van Hecke, E. 2006. *The importance of the institutional environment on multifunctional farming systems in the peri-urban area of Brussels.* Land Use Policy 23(4) 486–501.

36

A NON-PROFIT AS A POLICY ACTOR?

A case study of the Breds Treasure Beach Foundation in Jamaica

Matthew Pezold

Introduction

The Caribbean is a developing region of the world that has struggled to overcome challenges caused by corrupt governmental programs and agencies. Investors, economic developers, and developmental agencies, such as the World Bank, have expended much effort and many resources in the Caribbean but with limited success (Blumberg, 2010; Bowen, 2009; Henry and Miller, 2009; McConney *et al.*, 2003; Wint, 2003). Economic policy efforts, found largely within the tourism, manufacturing, and mining industries, have led to a general economic expansion across the region. However, many rural Jamaicans are excluded from these economic gains while facing additional economic pressures due to the environmental shocks caused by hurricanes, droughts, and depleting fishing stocks. Poverty and crime are commonplace, and there is a strong distrust of government. This distrust is widely attributed to many misplaced efforts and failed attempts to address poverty, crime, and corruption by governing bodies (Bowen, 2009; McConney *et al.*, 2003; Wint, 2003). More recently, fiscal austerity measures imposed by the International Monetary Fund have only made it more challenging to implement and fund rural policy programs (IMF, 2015). Consequently, much of the region has low expectations of elected officials, and a strong dose of skepticism is directed towards new policy solutions. Direct observations and research by the author are congruent with these regional studies (Pezold and Artz, 2010).

The author has direct experience working and researching in rural Jamaica. In 2010, he conducted qualitative research investigating the role of social capital in household wealth creation. The comparative case study of fishers and farmers was located in Treasure Beach because it is uniquely open to outsiders and has high stocks of social capital (Pezold and Artz, 2010; White, 2015). In investigating social capital, Pezold and Artz (2010) found that non-traditional leadership engaged in innovative policy creation. The community leadership of Treasure Beach circumvented ineffective officials by adopting social enterprise practices that allow community problems to be addressed through effective policy creation and implementation.

Treasure Beach

Treasure Beach is a small coastal fishing, farming, and tourism community of approximately 3000 people, located on the southwestern coast of Jamaica (2011 Census). The community stretches 6 miles along the coast and about 4 miles inland, and it is located in the parish of Saint Elizabeth. Treasure Beach is a quiet and remote destination for vacationers and is reached via winding, two-lane roads that connect it to international airports that are 100–140 km (2.5 hours) away.

Treasure Beach includes four fishing beaches and a number of small villages. The environment is semi-arid desert with a mixture of rolling fertile foothills and rocky outcroppings (Semenovyvh, 2014). The red fertile volcanic soils of Saint Elizabeth and Treasure Beach are considered the heart of Jamaica's breadbasket. Here, fishers and farmers catch or raise the products that they sell to "higglers" (vendors) or to the local hotels.

Alongside farming and fishing, ecotourism and boutique hotels have gradually developed as an informal policy that supports the local fisher and farmer households (Semenovyvh, 2014). The livelihoods of fishing and farming households in Treasure Beach are closely tied to the environment and there are many factors that can disrupt a farm, fishery, or the local tourism industry – such as hurricanes, earthquakes, floods, droughts, overfishing, and pollution (Pezold and Artz, 2010). Safety nets such as employment, health, life, property, or crop insurance are rare, which would help reduce household economic vulnerabilities (St. Elizabeth Municipal Corporation, 2017). Due to environmental factors, many rural households in the community face an insecure stream of income, which makes it difficult to accumulate household wealth, or to invest in one's children, business, or community.

Community governance

Corruption and crime are common in Jamaica (St. Elizabeth Municipal Corporation, 2017; Wint, 2003). Solid concrete walls protect Jamaica's houses, businesses, and resorts, while metal grills guard the doorways and windows. Conspicuously, these physical barricades are absent in the rural community of Treasure Beach (Semenovyvh, 2014; White, 2015). Despite the lack of barricades, there is a strong mistrust of government officials in this small community. Despite this mistrust, Treasure Beach has found a way to promote development though indirect involvement of the local, regional, and national governments, as well as through international organizations. In this rural community, non-profits, cooperatives, and community organizations work together to create policies and services that improve the well-being of the community (Pezold and Artz, 2010; Price, 2014; Semenovyvh, 2014). One non-profit, which will be highlighted in this chapter, is the Breds Treasure Beach Foundation (Breds, 2017).

A leading policy-maker for the community, Breds is a non-profit organization established in 1998 to promote education, sports, cultural heritage, and emergency health care in Treasure Beach. The term "Breds", short for Brethren, is a familiar and friendly way of hailing a person from the local fishing community (Breds, 2017). It represents a closeness of kinship and a duty to support the well-being of one another. In response to ineffective governance and a palpable cynicism of government agencies, Breds has arisen as an innovative, responsive, and effective hub of policy creation. Breds operates as an independent body comprising community stakeholders that are embedded in the rural community. These stakeholders and board members include entrepreneurs, educators, and community members. One entrepreneur in particular is a local official that brings a high level of human, social, and political capital to the table, which he leverages for the good of the community (Pezold and Artz, 2010; Semenovyvh, 2014).

As an organizational model, Breds resembles a social enterprise. Social enterprises are formed to either generate financial resources or provide services that are used for the good of the community (Chell *et al.*, 2010; Sepulveda, 2015). Breds provides health and educational services and it works to foster economic opportunity by applying business solutions to the challenges that the community faces. Business-based solutions are common in Breds because many of its board members are successful entrepreneurs, and they come to the table with a degree of creativity and a willingness to take risks. Major policy accomplishments include: (1) purchasing and running an emergency ambulance service, (2) building a multisport sports tourism park to generate tourism income while simultaneously providing recreational and educational opportunities for the youth, (3) building new classrooms and providing new technology, and (4) managing a fish sanctuary, in order to allow depleted fish stocks to recover (Breds, 2017).

Policy creation

Breds does not self-identify as a policy-maker, but it is a community organization seeking to solve policy problems. It was widely known within the community that the livelihood prospects for the community's youth were in decline, and that declining fish stocks and increasing food imports were making fishing and farming economically unviable (Breds, 2017; Pezold and Artz, 2010; Semenovyvh, 2014). Concern for the future of the community-led local business leaders and educators to come together and to form Breds. Leadership then began to explore how resources and policies could help strengthen the community. Breds' main policy objective is the building of a more vibrant community. To do this, they would protect the environment and the local culture, support the local economy and existing livelihoods, and they would invest in the youth (Breds, 2017). Breds' policy objectives include three overlapping policy areas: (1) health, (2) education, and (3) the economy. To promote these objectives Breds uses enterprise and innovation both to create new policy and to promote economic and environmental sustainability.

Health policy creation

Breds sought to support public health by addressing the lack of local health care in the community. The non-profit saw the lack of emergency care as an acute need, so it leveraged political and social networks and wrote grants to obtain an ambulance (Breds, 2017). Today, they have a voluntary ambulance service that supports the health of the community as well as the tourists. Having achieved early success in creating a health policy, they looked to address the high occurrence of drownings in the community. Breds found that the majority of children and adults in the community were unable to swim, and they found a partner to provide swimming instruction (Breds, 2017). Starting in 2016, they collaborated with the non-profit Likkle Swimmers (Likkle Swimmers, 2016) to raise funds to staff a summer youth swimming program. Today hundreds of children in the community are avid swimmers. This policy directly addressed the immediate concerns of health and safety, while also supporting long-term economic development, because it expanded the skillset of youth making it possible to safely consider fishing, or other water-based tourism enterprises.

Education policy development

The schools surrounding Treasure Beach were considered adequate but overcrowding and lack of student engagement was seen as an ongoing issue. Breds identified several ways to address these issues. One policy initiative involved collaborating with another non-profit, Food for the Poor, to build additional classrooms for the early childhood program (Breds, 2013). This policy leveraged their social capital to connect local schools with Food for the Poor, which built hundreds of early childhood classrooms across Jamaica (Breds, 2013). A second policy initiative was with EduSport. EduSport is a UNICEF program that uses sports as a vehicle to increase learning in children (Brown *et al.*, 2016). Together, EduSport and Breds worked to supplement and enrich the local physical education program and to promote general classroom engagement.

Breds developed a policy initiative that utilizes the Breds Treasure Beach Sports Park and Academy (see further discussion below) while promoting instructional collaboration with the local teachers and UNICEF Jamaica. Together they developed a new curriculum with EduSport, which uses sports to teach mathematics and science, along with physical education programming (Breds, 2012). Program reviews indicated increased school attendance, increased self-esteem, and increased performance for its participants (Breds, 2012). Numerous other educational needs exist, and Breds continues to develop new policies, partnerships, and fundraising efforts. Such efforts have included support in the hiring of additional school teachers, to increase access to technology and the internet, to fund academic scholarships, and to secure access to additional school supplies (Breds, 2013).

Economic policy development

As a foundation, Breds leverages its enterprising and managerial skills to promote youth development. Two major policy initiatives have been completed, and their crowning jewel is the Breds Treasure Beach Sports Park and Academy. This initiative is the product of a strongly held belief that Jamaicans have a great athletic legacy (established by decorated athletes such as Usain Bolt, Shelly-Ann Fraser-Pryce, Lennox Lewis), and that the overall potential of local youth was underdeveloped (Breds, 2012; Issuu, 2013). This strong belief led Breds to create a development policy that culminated in the construction of the sports parks and learning academy (Breds, 2012). Projected policy goals for the sports park include the development of leadership skills via sports, the development of the athletic potential of the youth, and the creation of sports tourism (Canadian Urban Institute, 2013; Ministry of Tourism, 2017; Issuu, 2013). To complete this policy initiative, Breds raised funds from governmental agencies and from international grants.

As a developmental policy, the sports park was designed to attract athletes from across Jamaica and the world. This would in turn increase competition levels and create new training opportunities, thereby elevating the athletic skills of the rural youth. In addition, sporting events would bring new revenue into the community, benefiting local businesses and their employees (Canadian Urban Institute, 2013; Ministry of Tourism, 2017; Issuu, 2013).

In the spring of 2010, the author was conducting research in Treasure Beach, which serendipitously occurred during the initial planning of the sports park and academy. A few years later, the multistage project was completed and the sports park and academy continues to refine and improve its facilities. The park regularly hosts sporting events and sports camps for the youth, and even brings in international celebrities such as Venus and Serena Williams and Lennox Lewis (Do Good Jamaica, 2017). The program continues to thrive and evolve, and it appears to be strengthening the community and creating more economic opportunity.

A second economic policy addresses environmental concerns. As Breds is regarded as a successful and trusted organization in the community, the Jamaican government created a new regulatory policy that placed Breds as the regulatory body over the newly established Galleon Fish Sanctuary (Breds, 2017). Since 2011, the Breds foundation has managed and enforced the fishing ban policy within the sanctuary. Today, the fish sanctuary serves as an educational zone to teach individuals about marine diversity and recovery, and is a destination for marine tourism. The sanctuary also addresses economic policy because it supports the restoration of the fish population, which benefits local artisanal fishers and the tourism industry. Ongoing studies in the fields of marine biology and geography confirm that the fish are increasing in size and number, and that portions of the shoreline are stabilizing (Caribbean Climate, 2014; Figueroa, 2014; Geier, 2017).

Breds has proven to be successful in constructing policies and following through in implementing policy initiatives. The non-profit has taken its social and enterprising vision and applied it in many ways, whether purchasing an ambulance for the community, developing new educational curriculum, or building a successful sports park and academy. These examples illustrate an informal policy cycle, and how Breds works to identify community problems (health, education, economy), much as a business might seek to serve an underserved market. To respond to the needs of the community, it develops a policy, searches for collaborators and financial resources, and implements its policy. Breds later evaluates this policy and builds upon it, while seeking to address related issues.

Observations and recommendations

Breds offers a compelling example of how innovative non-profits can use social enterprise and innovation to serve as a policy creation hub. Breds plays a central role in Treasure Beach by creating policy and overcoming mistrust by grassroots collaboration, grant writing, and by seeking governmental and nongovernmental support. Non-profits such as Breds have the capacity to harness social, political, human, and financial capital and to direct these resources towards creating effective and meaningful policy that addresses the health, educational, and economic concerns of its rural community.

Pragmatism aside, questions remain regarding the sustainability, transparency, and inclusiveness of current and new policies. Additionally, one might question the appropriateness of a non-profit serving as a policy creator. Other questions include: Is a rigorous evaluation process always used, before new policy is adopted or discontinued? Is there succession planning for the next generation of leadership? What happens if the current leadership resigns? Who would fill the leadership vacuum? Is Breds' policy creation process sustainable in the long-term and, are the policies financially sustainable? Do the business interests of the leadership represent a conflict of interest when policy is created and implemented? Is the organization truly representative and responsive to the needs of the entire community? Are the interests of the farmers, fishers, and community members consistently considered when creating and implementing new policy? Are their opinions welcomed and taken into account? Are third-party evaluators welcomed to perform routine audits? Despite the concerns raised, Breds serves as a unique illustration of how a rural community has found a way to create policy that addresses real needs in its fishing and farming community.

Breds demonstrates how trusted and embedded leadership can gather the resources and talents found in the local community and link them to external resources in order to create policy and a vision for a more resilient and prosperous community. Breds demonstrates that unofficial policy creators can use social capital to overcome trust and corruption, in order to create responsive policy. Other rural policy creators can take inspiration from Breds' model of policy creation. A lack of institutional trust or resources need not stop the creation of rural policy, if creative, trusted, and well-connected leaders from the local community band together as a socially oriented non-profit. Responsive rural policy must be creatively evolving while being careful not to forget those who are most vulnerable in the community: the small farmers, artisanal fishers, women, and their families. Admiringly, Breds worked to address problems concerning health, education, and the economy while using its entrepreneurial expertise and its social capital in the creation of innovative polices. Throughout the process, Breds sought to implement policy with an understanding of the vulnerabilities and needs of the farmers and fishers, which was evident when they began to police the Galleon Fish Sanctuary. Breds, perhaps an unlikely policy creator, points towards an enterprising form of policy creation, which might prove viable for other rural areas that are looking for ways to make their communities healthier, more vibrant, and more sustainable.

References

Blumberg, A., This American Life, 2010. *If you were stranded on a desert island and could only bring one economic plan ...*. www.thisAmericanlife.org/radio-archives/episode/410/social-contract?act=2.

Bowen, G., 2009. *Social capital, social funds and poor communities: An exploratory analysis.* Social Policy and Administration 43(3), 245–269.

Breds, 2012. *Breds – Treasure Beach Foundation.* www.youtube.com/watch?v=IsVyVzpKqvQ.

Breds, 2013. *Breds – Treasure Beach Foundation.* www.facebook.com/BredsTreasureBeachFoundation/.

Breds, 2017. *Breds – Treasure Beach Foundation.* www.breds.org/.

Brown, A., Tortello, R., Sheil, R., 2016. *EduSport: Using games to improve the Jamaican educational experience – UNICEF Jamaica.* UNICEF Jamaica. https://blogs.unicef.org/jamaica/edusport-games-improve-jamaican-education/.

Canadian Urban Institute, 2013. *The Greater Treasure Beach Sport Tourism Strategy.* https://canadianurban institute.files.wordpress.com/2013/06/gtb_st_strategy-final_jan2013.pdf.

Caribbean Climate, 2014. *Galleon Fish Sanctuary video wins at Cinefish Conference.* https://caribbeanclimate-blog.com/2014/12/01/galleon-fish-sanctuary-video-wins-at-cinefish-conference/.

Chell, E., Nicolopoulou, K., Karatas-Özkan, M., 2010. *Social entrepreneurship and enterprise: International and innovation perspectives.* Entrepreneurship and Regional Development 22, 485–493.

Do Good Jamaica – Blog, 2017. *Building a strong foundation: The Breds Treasure Beach Sports Park and Academy.* http://dogoodjamaica.org/blog/2017/08/03/building-a-strong-foundation-the-breds-treasure-beach-sports-park-academy/.

Figueroa, E., 2014. *Sanctuary.* www.youtube.com/watch?v=iQ77ehlSrlo.

Geier, K., 2017. Beach form, change, and mangrove interactions along Galleon Fish Sanctuary, south coast Jamaica (MSU Graduate Theses). https://bearworks.missouristate.edu/theses/3197.

Henry, P., Miller, C., 2009. *Institutions versus policies: A tale of two islands.* American Economic Review 99(2), 261–267.

IMF – International Monetary Fund, 2015. *Jamaica.* IMF Country Report No. 15/343. www.imf.org/external/pubs/ft/scr/2015/cr15343.pdf.

Issuu, 2013. *The Greater Treasure Beach Sports Tourism Strategy.* https://issuu.com/mymind101/docs/gtrtreasurebeach_sts_full_version_.

Likkle Swimmers.com, 2016. *Likkle Swimmers.* www.likkleswimmers.com/.

McConney, P., Baldeo, R., Robin, M., 2003. *Guidelines for coastal resource co-management in the Caribbean: Communicating the concepts and conditions that favor success.* Caribbean Conservation Association (CCA).

Ministry of Tourism, 2017. *New "JAMAICA Sport" entity launched to develop sports tourism locally.* www.mot.gov.jm/news-releases/new-%E2%80%98jamaica-sport%E2%80%99-entity-launched-develop-sports-tourism-locally.

Pezold, M., Artz, G., 2010. *The role of bridging and linking social capital in household wealth: A case study of two livelihoods in Treasure Beach, Jamaica.* University of Missouri–Columbia, Columbia, MO. http://hdl.handle.net/10355/10569.

Price, Z., 2014. *Jamaica "home of community tourism": An analysis of authenticity and women's everyday geographies.* York University, Toronto, Ont. http://hdl.handle.net/10315/28183.

Semenovyvh, O., 2014. *Small and medium-size enterprise leadership in sustainable development: A case study of the tourism industry in Jamaica* (Master's Thesis). University of Waterloo, Waterloo, Ont.

Sepulveda, L., 2015. *Social enterprise: A new phenomenon in the field of economic and social welfare?* Social Policy and Administration 49, 842–861.

St. Elizabeth Municipal Corporation, 2017. *St. Elizabeth Local Sustainable Development Plan: 2030 and Beyond.* http://stelizabethmc.gov.jm/sites/default/files/resources/selsdp.pdf.

White, T., 2015. *Stepping out from the Crowd: (Re)branding Jamaica's tourism product through sports and culture* (Master's Thesis). http://thekeep.eiu.edu/theses/2367.

Wint, E., 2003. *Social capital: Red herring or right on? The Jamaican perspective.* Development in Practice 13, 409–413.

37

POST-SOVIET RURAL AREAS TOWARDS EUROPEAN INTEGRATION

The difficult transition of Moldova

Simone Piras

The Republic of Moldova is a rural post-Soviet country located on the border of the European Union. After having been an important provider of agri-food products to the rest of the USSR, later Community of Independent States (CIS), it decided to pursue integration into the European economic space. In 2014, Moldova and the EU signed an Association Agreement that includes a Deep and Comprehensive Free Trade Agreement. This represents both an opportunity and a risk for Moldovan rural areas, where the majority of the population lives and where agriculture is still the main economic activity. To access the EU market, Moldovan agri-food products must comply with more advanced safety regulations. Compliance implies a process of modernization of small family farms created after land privatization. International and domestic development agencies are assisting Moldova in introducing reforms to foster agricultural productivity and reduce rural poverty. This chapter provides an overview of Moldovan rural areas in the framework of this process and assesses the outcome to date.

Introduction

The Republic of Moldova is a landlocked post-Soviet country situated at the southeastern border of the European Union (EU). It lacks both mineral resources and significant industry and lies far from important trade routes. Nevertheless, its fertile black soil and relatively mild climate has favored the development of agriculture. Thus, arable land and permanent crops make up 64 percent of its territory of 33,846 square kilometers – one of the largest shares in the world (WB, 2017). Furthermore, 66 percent of the country's population of 3.5 million live in rural areas – the highest percentage in Europe (NBS, 2017).

Until 1991, Moldova was a federal Republic of the Soviet Union and its rural areas evolved according to the rules of a planned economy. After the collapse of the USSR, rural development policies had to adapt to the new free-market conditions. However, the main purchaser of the country's agri-food products and provider of financial resources had disappeared. Since the fall of the USSR, investments have been lagging and today's rural areas lack infrastructure and non-farm employment opportunities. Export markets have become dominated by large corporate farms, while most rural households have focused on subsistence agriculture, resulting in huge out-migration and high poverty rates. In response to these challenges, since the mid-1990s the government has adopted a strategy of pursuing closer ties with the EU in the framework of the European Neighbourhood Policy in order to trigger economic development. This approach is expected to provide a secure market for Moldovan agri-food products, better work opportunities for Moldovan migrants, and financial assistance to modernize the agricultural sector and improve living conditions in rural areas. These efforts intensified after 2009, when a pro-EU political coalition won a parliamentary majority. Although pro-EU forces have been in power since then, the process of coming closer to the EU has not been able to reverse the outflow of population.

Development of Moldovan rural areas from the USSR to EU integration

Most studies on the Republic of Moldova, including this chapter, focus on Bessarabia, the western region of the country. Transnistria (the industrialized territory east of the Dniester River) seceded from the country in 1990, and although it has not achieved international recognition, it is not controlled by the national government. Bessarabia accounts for 30,355 square kilometers and has three million residents (NBS, 2017).

Until 1991, Moldova was a net supplier of agri-food products (primarily wine, spirits, fruits, and vegetables) to the rest of the Soviet Union, receiving energy and industrial products in exchange. Its agri-industrial complex was dominated by huge collective and state farms which, apart from engaging in agricultural production, were also responsible for providing services and managing rural infrastructure. The only private agriculture consisted of small subsistence plots allocated to households, which comprised 7 percent of total farmland. In this system, full employment and social services in rural areas were maintained by means of generous financial transfers from the center of the Union, despite the low productivity and lack of innovation. This support favored population growth, which has led to Moldova currently having the highest population density among European post-communist countries despite lacking large urban areas.

The dismantling of collective and state farms started in 1998. The privatization of their assets was implemented through the distribution of equivalent shares of value (Lerman, 2009), including "small shares" (former household plots) and "big shares" (quotas of the land farmed collectively) (Möllers *et al.*, 2016). In the new system, private initiative had to become the driver of economic growth and resources had to be allocated according to free-market rules. Reformers expected mid-sized commercial family farms to emerge through land market transactions, which were assumed to trigger rural development. Instead, most land recipients have engaged in subsistence agriculture on their "small shares", while leasing their "big shares" to the large corporate farms that succeeded their Soviet counterparts (Lerman and Sutton, 2008; Lerman *et al.*, 2008; Small, 2007). The land market developed slowly in Moldova; before 2008, less than 2 percent of land changed owners, with the average transaction involving only 0.1 hectares (Cimpoie , 2010). Farm growth and consolidation programs failed due to smallholders' lack of confidence and limited participation (Cimpoieş, 2010). Furthermore, no alternative organization was created to provide social services and manage rural infrastructure – including irrigation facilities, which fell into disrepair (Gorton and White, 2003).

In 1998, Moldova was severely hit by the Russian financial crisis, which led to the beginning of mass migration. The majority of Moldovans migrated to Russia and Italy. Estimates of the number of international migrants vary: for 2014, state border authorities gave a figure of 762,000 (IOM, 2016). Out of 342,000 temporary migrants, 72 percent came from rural areas, and the largest age group (35 percent) was represented by 25 to 34-year-olds (IOM, 2016). This represents a mass exodus of the labor force. In turn, migration resulted in a sizeable inflow of remittances, which peaked at 35 percent of GDP in 2006 and declined to 22 percent by 2016 (WB, 2017). Particularly in rural areas, remittances have accounted for double the share of family income compared to cities (23 percent vs. 12 percent in 2016) (NBS, 2017).

In 2011, there were 850,000 active family farms in Moldova (NBS, 2011) – one for every 4.2 inhabitants, signifying the highest incidence among European and Central Asian countries (author's elaboration on data from the Food and Agriculture Organization of the United Nations, 2014). These farms were small (71 percent were smaller than 1 hectare, 99.7 percent below 10 hectares); operated with rather old machinery or none (one tractor for every 54 farms, of which 83 percent are older than ten years); lacked irrigation facilities; and relied almost exclusively on family labor (NBS, 2011). As a result, a large majority (86 percent) of family farms produced only for their own consumption, while less than 9 percent sold more than half of their output (NBS, 2011). Despite their small size and subsistence focus, family farms used 43 percent of the total agricultural land (NBS, 2011) – a much larger share than in Russia or Ukraine, where in 2008 corporate farms used around 80 percent of the land (Lerman and Sutton, 2008).

Apart from family farms, there were around 3500 farms with juridical status (mostly corporations) with an average size of 369 hectares. These commercial farms represent the country's main exporters. They produce primarily low value-added crops (e.g. cereals, oilseeds, sugar beet), because of "the relatively low production cost, availability of agricultural machinery allowing the rapid cultivation of large areas, relatively simple and cheap post-harvest facilities, as well as assured markets for these commodities" (Moroz et al., 2015, p. 12). Apart from a few tractor drivers who are permanently employed, they hire mostly seasonal workers (Personal communications, June 2015). Furthermore, the growing mechanization of agriculture has reduced labor demand – from 125 jobs per farm in 2004 to 47 in 2012 (Moroz et al., 2015, p. 25). Hence, these farms do not represent a viable employment opportunity for rural households.

After land privatization, the total national output of corporate farms remained always below its 1995 value (in real terms) until 2014. In contrast, the output of family farms has increased constantly: since 2004, it has accounted for over 1.5 times its 1995 value, and in 2014 it was even twice that value. The only exceptions were in 2007 and 2012, when Moldovan agriculture suffered due to heavy droughts. Since 1999, family farms have accounted for around 70 percent of national agricultural output, although they declined to 60 percent after 2010. Considering that they farm less land, family farms are more efficient and productive than corporate farms (Lerman and Sutton, 2008). Despite their efficiency, the weakness of the institutions that should ensure fair competition and the tight constraint of credit prevent them from modernizing and becoming viable rural businesses. Corruption is by far the most problematic barrier to doing business, followed by political and governmental instability, access to finance, and inefficient bureaucracy (Schwab, 2017). The credit shortage is due to three main reasons: (1) smallholders lack collateral besides their land, while banks tend to make excessive requests (or to undervalue their assets); (2) supply is limited almost exclusively to short-term loans; and (3) there is a lack of instruments to facilitate access to credit, like guarantee funds (Moroz et al., 2015).

In 2016, agriculture accounted for 12 percent of the Moldovan GDP and employed 34 percent of the labor force; in rural areas, the latter was 58 percent (NBS, 2017). Considering that most land recipients do not register their farms and that many pensioners cultivate their land to supplement their low income, real agricultural employment is probably much higher. The prevalence of informal agricultural labor can also explain the low share of active population in rural areas, which was 41 percent in 2016 (NBS, 2017). In turn, in 2016 49 percent of off-farm salaried workers were based in the capital city, although it holds only 23 percent of the population (NBS, 2017).

The dynamics described above have resulted in high poverty rates in rural areas of Moldova. Poverty has been decreasing in the last decade (from 30% in 2006, to 13% in 2013, to 10% in 2015), but this trend has been less prevalent in rural areas (from 34% in 2006 to 19% in 2013). Thus, the gap between urban and rural areas has widened. Furthermore, the poverty decline has been mostly due to the inflow of remittances. In 2009, when the international financial crisis caused many migrants to return home (Piras, 2012, p. 149), rural poverty peaked at 36 percent (WB, 2017).

EU integration and agricultural and rural development policy

Since the second half of the 1990s, Moldova has been particularly eager to negotiate its economic integration into the EU economic space. Simultaneously, in 2004 the EU launched the European Neighbourhood Policy (ENP) with a view to ensuring stability and prosperity within its eastern and southern neighbors. In the framework of the ENP, the Prague Summit of 2009 established the Eastern Partnership, which involves six countries including Moldova.

The process of EU integration has mainly taken the form of trade liberalization. From 1999 to 2006, Moldova benefited from the so-called System of Generalised Preferences, which was then replaced by a potentiated version. The latter granted duty-free status to almost all goods produced in Moldova, with the notable exceptions of wines, spirits, sugar, meat, meat preparations, fruit, and vegetables, although these products represent the core of the country's exports. In 2008, the EU approved the so-called Autonomous Commercial Preferences, an asymmetric trade regime that granted duty exemptions for all goods produced in Moldova excluding, again, almost all agri-food products. A relevant share of the Moldovan non-agricultural exports to the EU is made up of clothing and accessories, furniture, and electric appliances and parts (NBS, 2017). These trade patterns suggest that this EU trade policy favored the relocation of related industries to Moldova in order to take advantage of low labor costs. In 2011, the tariff-rate quotas for wine, barley, wheat, and maize were raised. Finally, in June 2014, Moldova and the EU signed an Association Agreement, which also includes a Deep and Comprehensive Free Trade Agreement (DCFTA) and whose provisions have been in full effect since July 2016.

Most chapters of the DCFTA had already been negotiated in 2012, but agri-food products remained a divisive issue since Moldova wanted to achieve complete access to the EU market. However, access is contingent on compliance with the *acquis communautaire* in the fields of standards, quality infrastructure, sanitary, and phyto-sanitary safety. For this reason, the DCFTA foresees financial and legal assistance in related reforms. For example, a country-specific agreement signed in March 2015 in the framework of the European Neighbourhood Program for Agriculture and Rural Development allocated 64 million euros for modernizing the agri-food sector.

Following the government's policy of EU integration, agricultural and rural development policies were also tied to this broader goal (FAO, 2012). The National Development Strategy *Moldova 2020*, approved in 2012 by the government, highlights the need to transition the labor force from the low-productivity farming sector towards industrial and service sectors. As for rural development, this document focuses mainly on the building of a modern road infrastructure, which has already received substantial financial support by foreign donors. Within the framework of *Moldova 2020*, the Ministry of Agriculture and Food Industry adopted the *National Strategy on Agriculture and Rural Development (2014–2020)*, whose stated objectives are to increase the competitiveness of the agri-food sector in both domestic and EU markets by means of modernization and market integration, ensure the sustainable management of natural resources in agriculture, and improve living standards in rural areas. The government's strategic priorities include the promotion of food safety standards, the restructuring of the wine sector (for which Moldova is well known), the development of modern market infrastructure, and the reorganization of the farm subsidy scheme. Farm subsidies are managed by the Agency for Interventions and Payments in Agriculture, established in 2010 with the support of USAID and the World Bank. Although until now, the provision of subsidies has been "first come, first served", a transition to pre-investment selection based on a business plan should take place to foster efficiency (Personal communication, June 2015).

Apart from the EU, which is a major donor, many other international and domestic development agencies are active in the country: the FAO, the World Bank, USAID, and IFAD, among others. These organizations work side by side with the national government and the EU to help implement the *Strategy on Agriculture and Rural Development*. The FAO, for example, which has rural smallholders as its main target, focuses on migration-related issues like employment opportunities and the investment of remittances in agriculture (FAO, 2016).

Moldova has been a member of the Community of Independent States (CIS) since 1994. CIS countries, primarily Russia, have provided a secure market for agri-food products. Indeed, "Moldova" is a renowned brand there, especially for wines, spirits, and fresh products (FAO, 2012). However, the search for EU integration resulted in dramatic changes in Moldova's trade relations. The share of agri-food exports directed eastward decreased from 77 percent in 2001 to 26 percent in 2015, while the share directed towards the EU grew from 18 percent to 53 percent. A major downturn in relations with Russia dates to 2006, when Moscow banned Moldovan wines. Moldova went from the number one supplier of the Russian market to the 23rd. This ban lasted until 2011, but was then renewed in 2013. In 2014, Russia imposed trade bans and import duties on Moldovan meat and fruits, causing a drop in agricultural prices and a loss of rural profits and jobs. Surplus products could not be exported to the EU due to trade restrictions and because European consumers are not used to Moldovan products such as the varieties of apples grown in the country (Personal communication, June 2015). Furthermore, transport costs are too high for alternative markets to represent a viable option in the short-term (Personal communication, June 2015). Even the FAO recognizes the need to elaborate a strategy to mitigate the heavy social costs of the loss of the Russian market, at least as long as Moldovan products cannot access the EU market (Personal communications, January 2015). Due to these quarrels, agri-food exports have increased less than total exports, and their incidence has declined from 73 percent in 1997 to 46 percent in 2016. This sharp decline has negatively affected the overall economic performance of the country in 2006 and 2014, when Russia imposed the trade bans.

Conclusions and recommendations

To date, the process of Moldovan integration into the EU economic space has not successfully activated a virtuous cycle of sustainable rural development to overcome the imbalances generated by the country's transition from planned to market economy. Poverty has decreased, but the gap between urban and rural areas has widened and out-migration has not slowed down, resulting in population decline and aging. Rather than by agricultural development, poverty alleviation has been driven by remittances, as recognized also in the National Development Strategy *Moldova 2020*. Off-farm employment opportunities are still lacking, and only a limited number of remittance recipients invest in agriculture (Piras *et al.*, 2017).

These poor results are due to a number of unresolved contradictions in the development strategy of Moldova. These contradictions range from the rifts between EU integration and maintaining relations with Russia, to the need to promote both agricultural productivity and job creation, and conflicts between export-oriented corporations and family farms. This chapter offers several conclusions to explain the implications of these contradictions. First, given that Moldova cannot integrate into the EU economic space while maintaining access to the Russian market, policy-makers should have avoided a confrontational attitude with Moscow to grant a smoother phasing out. Instead, the deterioration of ties with Russia was not offset by new-found access to the EU market (not considering that Moldovan products are more competitive in Russia). Second, the achievement of visa liberalization with the EU in April 2014 and result-ing access to more competitive salaries fostered out-migration, but did not improve agricultural productivity since remittances are mostly spent on consumer goods. Third, while family farms can receive financial support for farm modernization, business opportunities are limited by underdeveloped internal markets, the monopolization of export markets by large corporate farms, and strong competition with imported goods on the modern retail market of the capital. Fourth, due to their greater human and financial resources, corporate farms are the main bene-ficiaries of farm modernization measures, which result in further mechanization and ultimately lead to the loss of rural jobs. Corporate farms tend also to monopolize the land rental market, limiting growth opportunities for family farms to marginal and less productive land (Personal communications, April–June 2015). Finally, the disappearance of traditional peasant farms, which is likely to be aggravated by productivity-driven policies, is causing the break of the thick social ties built around farm activities in rural areas. Nevertheless, the social function of these institutions is barely recognized by the government (Personal communications, April–June 2015).

In order to activate a virtuous cycle of sustainable rural development, Moldovan policy-makers should work towards solving the above-mentioned contradictions. First, as long as agri-food products cannot access the EU market, starting a dialogue with Russia aimed at rekindling economic ties would help mitigate the negative effects of trade redirection. The election of a pro-Russian president of Moldova in 2016 suggests that the population longs for a more balanced foreign policy and also indicates that keeping a confrontational attitude towards Moscow could cause the whole project of European integration to fall through.

Second, to achieve a fairer distribution of agricultural incomes, policy-makers could intro-duce norms that favor the access of middle-sized family farms to land and foreign support as opposed to large corporations. This kind of policy could also favor the investment of remit-tances in agriculture, since smallholders tend to prefer small intensification projects rather than farm growth as a development strategy (Piras *et al.*, 2017). To overcome the problems related to fragmentation, such as the management of mechanization services or the submission of funding applications, producer associations must be incentivized (Personal communication, June 2015). This represents a challenge due to the bias against cooperatives inherited from Soviet times.

Third, policy-makers should ensure that the profits derived from agri-food exports are re-invested (or redistributed) locally. This reinvestment could favor the diversification of the rural labor market and allow the replacement of foreign aid with internal resources, ultimately ensur-ing the sustainability of rural development.

Finally, policy-makers should consider that a loss of rural population is unavoidable in free-market conditions, as the inflow of resources that allowed population growth in Soviet times was not the result of efficient market allocation. Hence, they should set a realistic target in terms of rural population size and design policy incentives accordingly, favoring priorities such as facilitating labor reallocation across sectors. However, in order for these incentives to be effective, the strengthening of rule of law and an effective judiciary system must be prioritized in accordance with the Association Agreement.

References

Cimpoieș, D., 2010. *The economics of land fragmentation in the individual farm sector of Moldova.* Știința Agricolă 2, 101–108.

FAO – Food and Agriculture Organization of the United Nations, 2012. *Assessment of agriculture and rural development sectors in the Eastern Partnership countries: The Republic of Moldova.* FAO regional office for Europe and Central Asia, Budapest. www.fao.org/docrep/field/009/aq675e/aq675e.pdf.

FAO – Food and Agriculture Organization of the United Nations, 2014. *The state of food and agriculture 2014: Innovation in family farming.* FAO, Rome. www.fao.org/3/a-i4040e.pdf.

FAO – Food and Agriculture Organization of the United Nations, 2016. *Country programming framework for the Republic of Moldova (2016 to 2019).* FAO, Rome. www.fao.org/3/a-br870e.pdf.

Gorton, M., White, J., 2003. *The politics of agrarian collapse: Decollectivisation in Moldova.* Eastern European Politics and Society 17(2), 305–331.

IOM – International Organization for Migration, 2016. *Extended migration profile of the Republic of Moldova 2009–2014: Analytical report.* International Organization for Migration, Mission to Moldova, Chișinău. www.iom.md/sites/default/files/publications/docs/EMP%202009-2014%20ENG.pdf.

Lerman, Z., 2009. *Land reform, farm structure, and agricultural performance in CIS countries.* China Economic Review 20(2), 316–326.

Lerman, Z., Sutton, W.R., 2008. *Productivity and efficiency of small and large farms in transition: Evidence from Moldova.* Post-Soviet Affairs 24(2), 97–120.

Lerman, Z., Serova, E., Zvyagintsev, D., 2008. *Diversification of rural incomes and non-farm rural employment: Survey evidence from Russia.* Journal of Peasant Studies 35(1), 60–79.

Möllers, J., Herzfeld, T., Piras, S., Wolz, A., 2016. *Structural transformation of Moldovan smallholder agriculture: Implications for poverty reduction and shared prosperity.* World Bank Group, Washington, DC. www-wds. worldbank.org/external/default/WDSContentServer/WDSP/IB/2016/06/23/090224b0843f61cc/1 _0/Rendered/PDF/Structural0tra0nd0shared0prosperity.pdf.

Moroz, V., Stratan, A., Ignat, A., Lucasenco, E., 2015. *Country report: Republic of Moldova.* National Institute for Economic Research, Chișinău. www.agricistrade.eu/wp-content/uploads/2015/05/Agricis-trade_Moldova.pdf.

NBS – National Bureau of Statistics of the Republic of Moldova, 2011. *General agricultural census 2011. National results, 1 Volume.* National Bureau of Statistics of the Republic of Moldova, Chișinău. www. statistica.md/public/files/publicatii_electronice/Recensamint_agricol/RGA_2011_date_definitive. pdf.

NBS – National Bureau of Statistics of the Republic of Moldova, 2017. *Statistical databank "Statbank".* www.statistica.md/pageview.php?l=en&idc=407.

Piras, S., 2012. *La Moldova post-sovietica.* Aracne, Rome.

Piras, S., Vittuari, M., Möllers, J., Herzfeld, T., 2017. *Remittance inflow and smallholder farming practices: The case of Moldova.* Land Use Policy. DOI: 10.1016/j.landusepol.2017.10.050.

Schwab, K., 2017. *The global competitiveness report 2017–2018.* World Economic Forum, Geneva. www3. weforum.org/docs/GCR2017-2018/05FullReport/TheGlobalCompetitivenessReport2017% E2%80%932018.pdf.

Small, L.A., 2007. *East meets West: Utilising Western literature to conceptualise post-Soviet agrarian change.* Journal of Peasant Studies 34(1), 29–50.

WB – World Bank, 2017. *World Bank open data.* http://data.worldbank.org/.

38

"WHY LOCAL GOVERNMENTS?"

An ongoing debate in rural New Brunswick, Canada

Michelle Landry

New Brunswick, a small east coast province, is one of the most rural provinces in Canada. According to the 2011 census and using Statistic Canada's "rural area" definition,[1] New Brunswick is the second most rural province after Prince Edward Island with 48 percent of its population living in rural areas (Statistics Canada, 2011). The total population is 747,101 inhabitants (Statistics Canada, 2016). There are only two census metropolitan areas:[2] Greater Moncton and Saint John with a population of respectively 144,810 and 126,202. Moreover, 30 percent of the population reside in unincorporated areas called Local Service Districts (LSDs)[3] and, as such, do not have a local government.

Since the 1970s, the territorial organization of local governments in the province has been recognized as problematic (Finn, 2008). Nevertheless, only since 2005 has this situation been directly addressed by a provincial government, though with a timid and voluntary approach (Landry, 2007; Finn, 2008). LSDs can now amalgamate with others or with a municipality to form a "Rural Community", a municipal status with more flexibility in service provision. Nonetheless, more than ten years later, only eight Rural Communities have been formed, reducing the proportion of LSD population by only 6 percent (Statistics Canada, 2001, 2016).

This case study will first explain the historical reasons of the situation and the principal problems it causes. The low enthusiasm for municipalization in the province will then be discussed by submitting a few hypotheses drawing from an ongoing research project.

From county abolition to Rural Community status

Having such a large proportion of inhabitants living in unincorporated areas and depending directly on the provincial government for service provision is quite unusual in Canada. This situation goes back to an important reform that took place in the 1960s in New Brunswick. From 1877 to 1967, a two-tier system was in place with municipalities and counties managing education, health, social services, and some aspects of the justice system. In areas with no municipal government, the county was the only local government. Wanting to address rural–urban disparities and to better take advantage of federal regional development programs, the liberal provincial government of Louis J. Robichaud (1960–1970) put in place the Royal Commission on Finance and Municipal Taxation in 1962, chaired by Edward Byrne. The recommendations of the Byrne report resulted in the Equal Opportunity Program, one of the most ambitious local administrative reforms in Canada, affecting approximately 125 provincial laws in New Brunswick (Young, 2001; Cyr, 2001). County councils were abolished and the most important services to people – health, education, social services, and justice – were centralized at the provincial government level. Centralization was viewed as the most effective means to reduce regional inequalities, thus providing equivalent services in all parts of the province. When county councils were abolished, the areas outside municipalities were divided in administrative divisions for service provision called Local Service Districts (LSDs). Villages were also given the same powers as other municipalities, which resulted in the creation of approximately 90 villages (Cyr, 2001). According to Martin (2007), public servants were confident that the rural population, thus the LSD population, would diminish referring to modernization and urbanization theories of the time. Nevertheless, the LSD population continued to grow and was still growing in the first decade of the new century (Bourgeois and Strain, 2009).

As early as 1975, problems with the territorial organization started to be acknowledged by the Hatfield provincial Conservative government (1970–1987), which ordered a report (1976) but did not apply its recommendations (Finn, 2008). The McKenna provincial Liberal government (1987–1997) did execute some town amalgamations but did not address the larger problems associated with the unincorporated communities (Bourgeois, 2005). Camille Thériault, Liberal premier from May 1998 to June 1999, formed a Municipality Act Review Panel which presented its recommendation to Bernard Lord's Conservative government elected in June 1999. A regulation was finally adopted in 2005 to encourage municipalization, in other words the incorporation of LSDs under a new status called "Rural Communities". It is a voluntary approach permitting the creation of "Rural Communities" by amalgamating several LSDs or LSDs with a village or different villages if the new entity would have a population of at least 3000 or a \$200 million tax base (Department of Environment and Local Government, 2017).[4]

Local governments in New Brunswick

As of January 2018, there are 103 municipalities (8 cities, 1 regional municipality, 26 towns, 60 villages and 8 Rural Communities) and 236 Local Service Districts (LSDs) in New Brunswick (Department of Environment and Local Government, 2014).[5] In terms of surface area, there is a very small proportion of the territory that is incorporated. The LSD population is also relatively spread out (Figure 38.1).

An LSD is not a municipality, it is an administrative division for the provincial Department of Environment and Local Government, who is responsible for providing the services in these areas (e.g. road maintenance, snow removal, and street lighting). It does not have a council or any staff. Its inhabitants can only elect in a community assembly an advisory committee and a representative.

Land planning and waste management in LSDs as well as municipalities are managed by one of the 12 Regional Service Commissions. All mayors sit at the board of its Regional Service Commission, but only a certain number of LSD representatives are represented. As stated by the province:

> Each Regional Service Commission Board will be accountable to their member Municipal and Rural Community councils. Those councils are in turn, accountable to their taxpayers. For Local Service Districts, the Commission will be accountable to the Province which, as administrator of services in LSDs, is accountable to LSD taxpayers.
>
> *(GNB, 2018)*

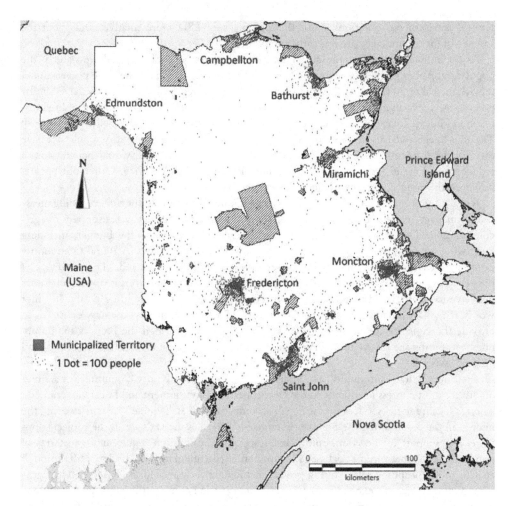

Figure 38.1 Population density in municipalized and unincorporated territory in New Brunswick

Source: Statistics Canada, 2016 Census of Population. Mapping produced by Josée Guignard Noël, CIRLM, 2018.

The local governance territorial organization is costly for the province because LSD tax rates are kept low. Property tax rates in LSDs have not been increased since 1984 and the tax income does not cover the cost of the services provided. Bourgeois and Strain (2009) estimated the difference to be 39.6 million dollars. In other words, the provincial government subsidizes the services in LSDs which is not the case for municipalities, even very small ones. It is also a burden for adjacent municipalities since the LSD population use facilities in nearby municipalities. Increasing fees for outside individuals and families who use the facilities, however, has a dissuasive effect, therefore reducing users. In an urban planning perspective, the fact that these areas have lower tax rates than the municipalities can also foster urban sprawl. From a development point of view, the territorial organization is also ineffective because these communities are not organized to leverage their community development. For example, LSDs do not have direct access to the Federal Gas Tax Fund which provides funding for infrastructure in Canadian municipalities. Because LSDs do not have a municipal council or staff to work on developing services and projects, questions about the legitimacy of LSD representatives and about the absence of local democracy are regularly raised.

As for municipalities the only difference between the city, town, and village status is the population. Although they have different financial capacities, they have the same powers under the Municipality Act. Rural Communities and the one regional municipality have similar powers, but they can negotiate to leave certain service provision to the Department of Environment and Local Government. The regional municipality status was created when the town of Tracadie-Sheila and 18 surrounding LSDs amalgamated so that the new entity would not have to carry the burden of maintaining the roads in the former LSDs and would benefit from a reduced cost for the Royal Canadian Mounted Police (RCMP) service. Other powers are, however, the same as city, towns, and villages.

Rural Communities, unlike LSDs, can elect a council, they can adopt rural planning measures to manage residential and commercial development or to protect water supplies or agricultural land. The council of a Rural Community has power over the budget, including borrowing power, property tax rates, and the power to adopt bylaws. A Rural Community can also have an office and hire staff to better address its population's needs. The advantage of the "Rural Community" status is that it can progressively gain the powers it wants and it does not have to assume road maintenance in the former LSDs which would be costly. In other words, if a village amalgamates with LSDs to form a Rural Community, the new entity has to provide the same services on the former village's territory, although the Rural Community does not, for instance, have to maintain the provincial roads in the former LSDs if the council does not wish to.

To form a Rural Community, a municipal council, an LSD advisory committee, or a group of citizens must express its interest to the Department of Environment and Local Government. Then, a local regional services manager will accompany local stakeholders to start assessing the interest in the community, the population targeted, as well as the tax base. If the project seems to receive support in the communities and respects the minimum requirements in terms of population (3000 persons) or tax base ($200 million), department agents, "undertake a thorough analysis of the proposed restructuring project including a review of local services, budget projections of revenues and expenditures (money coming in and going out), tax rates and how they differ across areas given service delivery differences, geographic boundaries, etc." (Department of Environment and Local Government, 2017). Public consultations are then formally organized and the decision on the project is determined by a plebiscite[6] in the concerned LSDs and the adoption of resolutions in the concerned municipal councils.

Municipalization here and there

Regardless of the problems and challenges related to unincorporated communities, very few community restructuring projects have been initiated and few have succeeded since the adoption of the Rural Community Incorporation and Restructuring Regulation under the Municipality Act in 2005. Since 2005, only 25 projects were formally submitted to a municipalization process and have reached an outcome (Table 38.1). Some of these projects are second versions of a failed one. Of these, 16 were to form or to amalgamate to form a Rural Community and one to amalgamate as a regional municipality; seven were about annexing LSDs to an existing municipality, one of which was with an existing Rural Community; and one was regarding the incorporation of a LSD to become a village.

In total, one regional municipality and eight Rural Communities were created and the non-municipalized population only decreased by 6 percent (Table 38.2).

Table 38.1 Formal process to municipalize LSDs 2005–2018

Descriptor	Failed	Succeeded	Total
Process to form a rural community	8	8	16
Plebiscite to form a regional municipality	0	1	1
Annexation to a municipality (including to an existing rural community)	3	4	7
LSD incorporation to village	1	0	1
Total	12	13	25

Table 38.2 Proportion of the population by type of communities, 2006, 2016

Type of community	2006 (%)	2016 (%)	Variation (%)
Local Service District	36	30	−6
Municipality	63	69	+6
First Nation Reservation	1	1	0
Total	100	100	–

Source: Census 2006 and 2016 in Geosuite 2016.

Thus, as of June 2018, only eight Rural Communities and one regional municipality have been formed since the adoption of the 2005 regulation. Two of the successful creations of a Rural Community occurred after a second referendum, one after a favorable outcome without the consent of a village (classified as failed), and one after a negative outcome of a broader project. As shown in Table 38.1, some LSDs also accepted to merge with an existing municipality. As mentioned before, 30 percent of the province's population still resides in unincorporated LSDs, showing very slow progress towards full municipalization.

Research is currently performed on why there is so little appetite for municipalization. This issue seems more complex than one would think. This study aims to better understand the perceived roles of municipalities and what motivates people to mobilize for or against the incorporation of their community. In other words, why would someone want its community to become a municipality and why would one oppose it? What advantages and disadvantages do people see in being part of a municipality? These are questions that are not even raised in other parts of the country since it is very normal that most of the population live in some kind of municipality. At this point in the research, it is possible to offer a few hypotheses linked to taxation, the perceived development benefits, and the decision-making process.

One of the principal arguments put forward against municipalization is the fear of seeing a property tax increase. Even though in the case of the creation of a Rural Community the tax increases were demonstrated to be minimal, the idea of a possible increase seems to have a large impact on the outcome. A property tax increase is generally unpopular as it is perceived to be arbitrary (Sheffrin, 2013). This type of opposition could also be stimulated by the fact that many rural New Brunswick inhabitants live in relative poverty (Bums et al., 2007; GNB, 2013).

This opposition might also be correlated with the fact that these areas have very limited community infrastructure and services and it seems people think that the development will keep being centralized in the largest municipalities of the region, one way or the other. In other words, the benefits of amalgamation and incorporation for rural residents are not clear. Preliminary observations indicate that the inhabitants of unincorporated areas do not believe amalgamation will change anything in their situation, in other words that amalgamation is very unlikely to contribute to the overall development of their community. In fact, it is important to ask to what extent people see municipalities as development agents. With this mind set and joined with the fear of tax increases, the status quo seems to be the safest option.

The third factor that needs to be investigated is the process. The burden of convincing reluctant people to accept an amalgamation project resides mostly on the shoulders of citizens. The issues regarding the financial aspects of these projects are very complex and very hard to communicate. It seems even harder to communicate clear information effectively when it mostly comes from unofficial sources. Moreover, the fact that most of these projects discuss municipalization and amalgamation issues at the same time reduces the chances of success. The results show that residents are not necessarily against municipalization, it is often more opposition to the amalgamation combined with something in the process that triggers opposition to the project at stake. Overall, it is necessary to better understand the dynamic in the Department of Environment and Local Government. Are there enough resources dedicated to support community incorporation initiatives? What is the impact of the political implications in the department? How could the process be ameliorated?

Conclusions

Having one-third of the population of the province living in non-municipalized territory is quite unusual, costly, and ineffective in terms of stimulating local development. It also poses challenges in terms of the legitimacy of local representatives on the Regional Service Commission and on the broader issue of local democracy. Since 2005, local services districts can amalgamate between themselves or with a village to form a flexible form of municipality called a "Rural Community". This voluntary approach does not seem to lead to a solution, as many communities reject municipalization by local referendum. There is thus a glaring need for a better understanding of the deeper issues related to this low appetite for municipalization.

Notes

1 Population outside population centers, which are defined as "having a population of at least 1000 and a density of 400 or more people per square kilometre" (Statistics Canada, 2017a).
2 "A census metropolitan area must have a total population of at least 100,000 of which 50,000 or more live in the urban core" (Statistics Canada, 2017b).
3 Calculations based on the 2016 Census data in Geosuite 2016, Statistics Canada.
4 At first, the threshold was 2000 inhabitants and a fiscal plate of 100 million dollars.
5 Numbers adjusted according to recent local referendums.
6 At first, the process did not include a local plebiscite. If there was not 20 percent of the population of an LSD that expressed its opposition to the minister, the incorporation process would go forward.

References

Bourgeois, D., 2005. *Municipal reforms in New Brunswick: To decentralize or not to decentralize?*, in: Lesage, E., Garcea, J. (Eds.), *Municipal reforms in Canada: Municipal governance for the 21st century*. Oxford University Press, Don Mills, Ont., pp. 242–268.
Bourgeois, D., Strain, F., 2009. *New Brunswick*, in: Sancton, A., Young, R.A. (Eds.), *Foundations of governance: Municipal government in Canada's provinces*. University of Toronto Press, Toronto, Ont., pp. 186–222.
Bums, A., Bruce D., Marlin A., 2007. *Rural poverty discussion paper*. Presented to Rural Secretary, Government of Canada, Ottawa, Ont.

Cyr, G., 2001. *La réforme municipale de 1967 au Nouveau-Brunswick*, in: *L'ère Louis J. Robichaud 1960–1970: actes du colloque.* Institut canadien de recherche sur le développement régional, Moncton, NB, pp. 143–167.

Department of Environment and Local Government, 2014. *Communities in each of the 12 Regional Service Commissions (RSC)/Les communautés dans chacune des 12 Commissions de services régionaux (CSR).* Government of New Brunswick. www2.gnb.ca/content/dam/gnb/Departments/lg-gl/pdf/Plan/Communities Communautes.pdf.

Department of Environment and Local Government, 2017. *The community restructuring process.* Government of New Brunswick. www2.gnb.ca/content/gnb/en/departments/elg/local_government/content/community_restructuring/process.html.

Finn, J.-G., 2008. *Building stronger local governments and regions: An action plan for the future of local governance in New Brunswick.* Report of the Commissioner on the Future of Local Governance.

GNB – Government of New Brunswick, 2013. *Profile of New Brunswick labour force.* www2.gnb.ca/content/dam/gnb/Departments/petl-epft/PDF/Emp/Profile-NB-LabourForce.pdf.

GNB – Government of New Brunswick, 2018. *Structure of the new Regional Service Commissions.* www2.gnb.ca/content/gnb/en/departments/elg/local_government/content/promos/action_plan_local_governance/structure.html.

Landry, M., 2007. *Le nouveau projet de "Communautés rurales" au Nouveau-Brunswick: Une occasion d'acquisition de pouvoirs et d'autonomie pour les Acadiens?* Francophonies d'Amérique 23–24, 15–29.

Martin, G.R., 2007. *Municipal reform in New Brunswick: Minor tinkering in light of major problems.* Journal of Canadian Studies 41(1), 75–99.

Sheffrin, S.M., 2013. *Tax fairness and folk justice.* Cambridge University Press, New York.

Statistics Canada, 2001. *Census of population.*

Statistics Canada, 2006. *Census of population.*

Statistics Canada, 2011. *Population, urban and rural, by province and territory.* www.statcan.gc.ca/tables-tableaux/sum-som/l01/cst01/demo62a-eng.htm.

Statistics Canada, 2016. *Census of population.*

Statistics Canada, 2017a. *Population centre (POPCTR): Detailed definition.* www.statcan.gc.ca/pub/92-195-x/2011001/geo/pop/def-eng.htm.

Statistics Canada, 2017b. *Census metropolitan area (CMA) and Census agglomeration (CA).* www12.statcan.gc.ca/census-recensement/2011/ref/dict/geo009-eng.cfm.

Young, R., 2001. *Le programme chances égales pour tous: une vue d'ensemble*, in: *L'ère Louis J. Robichaud 1960–1970: actes du colloque.* Institut canadien de recherche sur le développement régional, Moncton, NB, pp. 23–37.

39

A COMPARATIVE CASE STUDY OF THE MAIN STREET PROGRAM IN THE UNITED STATES

Glenn Sterner

Rural development policy in the United States often sees tensions between the three levels of government: federal, state, and local (Sterner *et al.*, 2015). Particularly in rural American communities, there is a local sensitivity to external policy development and programmatic implementation, specifically those seen as instituted by the state and especially federal levels (Swanson, 2001). These tensions, among other factors, can affect the outcomes of local implementation of these programs (Durlak and DuPre, 2008). To examine how federal program development and implementation may create tensions at the state and local levels, this chapter highlights a comparative case study of the Main Street Program. This federally designed program, implemented through the National Trust for Historic Preservation, emphasizes community revitalization while encouraging historic preservation of America's downtown main streets. Utilizing qualitative key informant interviews and archival data analysis of participants in four rural localities across two states, the objectives of this chapter are to: (1) examine the impact of state-level policies on local implementation of federal-level programs, comparing two states in their implementation of the Main Street Program; and (2) extrapolate the tensions and positive aspects of implementing a federal program in four rural communities.

The chapter begins with a contextualization of the Main Street Program, followed by the methods for data collection and construction of the comparative case study. The chapter then describes the implementation of the Main Street Program across two cases, Pennsylvania and Michigan. The chapter presents several key findings from the local perspectives associated with programmatic implementation including: the importance of state capacity development in program implementation, the impacts of state tax structures and policies on local development, and the need for feedback loops for state and local individuals to federal agencies. The chapter concludes with recommendations for policy-makers at the federal level.

The Main Street Program

The Main Street Program is a national community development initiative in the United States that promotes revitalization of communities while encouraging preservation of local assets (Main Street America, 2017). States establish a charter with the National Main Street Center, now an independent subsidiary of the National Trust for Historic Preservation. Upon successful creation of a charter, states are able to certify communities that meet the requirements for the Main

Street Program. Each community must apply to be part of the Main Street Program, and each state must determine mechanisms to fund local initiatives.

The program is popular in both rural and urban areas, with over 1600 affiliated neighborhoods and communities (Main Street America, 2017). A community must designate a Main Street district, a downtown area that is the focal point for development initiatives. While the Main Street district may serve as the hub for activity of the initiatives, the goal of the program is to assist and aid in revitalization that would benefit the entire community. Recognized as a robust economic revitalization opportunity, nationally this program has generated $70.25 billion in community investments in physical improvements, rehabilitated 268,053 buildings, increased local growth by 584,422 jobs, and increased businesses by 132,092 (Main Street America, 2017).

Methods

This comparative case study draws heavily from Sterner (2015) and is based on qualitative research methods (Yin, 2009), approved by the Human Subjects Institutional Review Board (IRB) of the Pennsylvania State University. Michigan and Pennsylvania were chosen as comparative states due to similar historical contexts of agriculture, extraction, and manufacturing, and their large rural population. Four rural municipalities that participate in the Main Street Program were selected, two in the state of Michigan and two in the state of Pennsylvania. Individuals were interviewed from each of these four locations to provide feedback on the state's implementation of the Main Street Program.

The case studies were compiled from archival data and key informant interviews with individuals at the state and local levels. Archival data included publicly available information through state and local websites, but also used information provided by state and local offices documenting their application and reporting mechanisms to Main Street offices. Key informants were identified through a snowball sampling methodology (Creswell and Poth, 2017). The points of contact from the Main Street offices in the four localities and two state offices served as the initial key informants, and additional key informants were identified through those individuals' recommendations and examination of archival records of the locality's involvement in the implementation of the Main Street Program. In total, 31 individuals were interviewed, 19 in Michigan and 12 in Pennsylvania. All were involved in local and state implementation of the Main Street Program. State-level information was compiled into two separate narratives presented below to highlight the differences in policy and programmatic implementation. Themes from the analyses of interviews with regards to state implementation are presented after the state-level narratives.

State-level implementation

This section explores the implementation of the Main Street Program in two states: Michigan and Pennsylvania. Through the examination of these cases, it is possible to see the difference in their approaches. These practices influenced the feedback provided by the local individuals involved in the implementation of the Main Street Program in their rural community.

Michigan main streets approach

The Main Street Program in Michigan is administered through the Michigan Main Street Center (referred to hereafter as the Center), administratively located in the Michigan State Housing Development Authority (MSHDA). MSHDA relies very little on general fund money from the state due to its revenue-generating programs. No general fund money is utilized to institute the Center; its funding comes entirely from MSDHA revenue. The Main Street Program is highly successful in Michigan, attributed with over $297 million in community investments, 556,091 volunteer hours, 1047 new businesses created, and 1060 building façade improvements since its implementation in 2003 (Michigan Economic Development Corporation, 2018).

Michigan communities may progress through three levels of membership in the Main Street Program. Communities must initially apply for Associate Level membership through the Center. At this level, communities are not yet certified as "Main Street communities", but gain access to Center training programs.

The second level, Select Member, requires an extensive community application that demonstrates its capacity to be successful as a Main Street designated community at the state and national levels. During five years as a Select Member communities are eligible for more advanced trainings, application-based services, and grants. Select Member communities must maintain certain standards and requirements through all five years, reporting evidence to the Center, or they will be entered into a remediation process, with dedicated assistance from Center staff.

At the end of five years at the Select Level, a community may elect to apply for Master Level status to maintain its Main Street affiliation. The reporting obligation for Master Level communities is not as strict. They must still maintain the standards of the Main Street Program, however, and will be required to go into a remediation program if they do not. Additionally, Master Level communities serve as mentors to Associate Level communities. Master Level communities have the choice to renew their affiliation every two years indefinitely.

Community participation in the Michigan Main Street Program does not come with funding; the local community must provide all funding for its program. At the Select Level, communities are required to hire a Main Street Manager to coordinate the efforts of their Main Street Program.

Local Main Street districts are typically located within a community's Downtown Development Authority (DDA) district, the economic center of a municipality, and the DDA becomes the administrative home for the local Main Street Program. In Michigan, a DDA is run by a group of individuals, typically appointed by the city council, at least half of whom are required by state law to own a business in the DDA district. DDAs receive tax dollars from the businesses in the DDA district. These funds then typically help to support the salary of the Main Street Manager and Main Street initiatives. The Main Street Program may also supplement this funding with additional revenue-generating efforts such as charging fees for events or donations from businesses.

If a community does not have an existing DDA or other local mechanism to coordinate a Main Streets Program, the community must form a 501c3, non-profit organization and raise money to fund Main Street initiatives and the hiring of a manager. Of the 19 Main Street designated communities in Michigan, only two are non-profits of this type.

Pennsylvania main streets approach

In Pennsylvania, the Main Street Program is instituted through the Department of Community and Economic Development (DCED) and is called the Keystone Main Street Program. Communities apply to be part of the Keystone Main Street Program and must meet the requirements set by the state and national Main Street Program. If successful in their application, they receive Main Street designation for five years after which the community may reapply for the distinction. The state provides no funding to Main Street communities, but they are given priority

access to application-based state grant programs. Similar to Michigan, this initiative has positively affected Pennsylvania communities from 1987 to 2016 through the investment of $1.3
billion, 919,000 volunteer hours, the founding of over 6800 new businesses, and the creation of
over 20,500 new jobs (Fontana, 2017).

Once a community is designated a Main Street community, it is also provided free technical
and educational assistance. The DCED contracts with the Pennsylvania Downtown Center
(PDC), a non-profit organization, to provide local assistance with application creation and local
program support. This organization also oversees the application process to the DCED, certify-
ing communities who apply for Keystone Main Street Community status. The PDC serves as
the regulatory body for the Main Street organization in Pennsylvania. Of the 47 states that have
Main Street Programs, only eight are affiliated with or have contracts with non-profit organizations like the PDC.

Communities that do not elect to apply to the Keystone Main Street Program may apply
directly to the PDC to be designated a Main Street community. This distinction does not permit
them any priority access to funding and requires that they pay for certain technical services that
Keystone Main Street communities receive free. Pennsylvania communities may therefore be
classified into two categories: Keystone Community Main Street Communities and Main Street
Communities.

Creating a Main Street Program at the local level in Pennsylvania requires the creation of a
non-profit organization that will institute the program. Although a municipal government
applies to be considered a Main Street community, a separate authority associated with the
municipal government or an independent non-profit organization administers the program.
Municipal governments may support the funding of the authority or non-profit organization,
but there is no requirement to do so.

There are two main options for providing funding for the salary of the Main Street Manager
and for program initiatives. The first is through the use of Business Improvement Districts (BIDs),
where businesses and other organizations in the BID pay a fee to the administering authority or
non-profit organization. If a BID is already in place, it can encompass a Main Street district, or a
BID may be created when a Main Street district is designated. The second typical option is to
create a non-profit organization and use fundraising as a fiscal strategy. This requires incorporation
at the state and federal levels, as well as applying for 501c3 status through the IRS.

Local perspectives on the state implementation of the Main Street Program

After examining each state's approach to the Main Street Program, the key differences in implementation across Michigan and Pennsylvania are in the local support mechanisms at the state
level and local restrictions for revenue generation. These two themes were evident in the results
from the interviews of local individuals involved in implementing the Main Street Program in
rural communities.

With regard to state support for local initiatives, results indicated strong appreciation for the
guidance and support for moving through the three levels of a Main Street community. Residents had generally favorable appreciation for the structure provided in Michigan. However,
some noted fatigue resulting from the large number of forms involved in the reporting process.
In Pennsylvania, the structure of state-level implementation created confusion at the local level,
and the lagging state-level support was viewed unfavorably by local individuals implementing a
Main Street Program.

The local tax structures in each state affected local implementation. By providing an easier
way to gain revenue through tax generation in Michigan, local residents could focus more on

community organizing and development rather than revenue generation. In Pennsylvania assessing a fee to local businesses created animosity with the business community, creating the semblance of another tax business owners were required to pay. Additionally, community members in Pennsylvania expressed burnout due to the need to create both a Main Street structure and a non-profit organization simultaneously.

Interviews with state staff revealed a need for feedback mechanisms linking state actors to the national program. The coordinators of the programs across states noted they would appreciate direct lines of communication to the national organization for changes to reporting, programmatic structures, and policy alteration. Local residents found more frustration in lack of feedback mechanisms with the state level in both states, rather than a need for direct communication to the national offices. However, these local individuals noted a direct feedback to national offices would ensure that difficulties encountered with their state organizing offices' practices could be communicated more efficiently to impact oversight policies.

Recommendations for national-level program development

When developing national programs and policies for implementation at the local level, it is essential to take into consideration state and local rural policy effects. In the designing of these initiatives, federal organizations and agencies should consider the following recommendations drawn from this case study:

1   *Develop capacity at the state level for local support.* If the program is to be administered through state agencies, it is essential that the appropriate individuals and organizations have the proper structure, training, guidance, and capacity to work with local individuals for effective implementation. While flexibility is necessary when addressing the needs across states, guidelines should be developed to ensure states are prepared to enhance local assets for implementation, especially in rural areas where resources are at time lagging compared to urban areas.
2   *Consider local restrictions on revenue generation.* State-level policies can greatly affect how a program is administered at the local level, as evidenced in this case study. This can include policies with regard to tax generation, tax utilization, and administrative restrictions.
3   *Ensure direct local feedback loops.* State-level individuals may filter feedback specifically from local individuals. By providing a mechanism that allows for local individuals who implement programs and policies directly to the national level, it allows for greater clarity in the tensions and positive aspects for alterations. Additionally, providing more effective state-level feedback and communication with national offices can assist in positively impacting state implementation. Finally, this may provide a greater sense of trust among rural communities that tend to have a greater distrust of external agency policy and programmatic development and implementation.

Following these recommendations can help those developing national programs and policies to alleviate state and local policy issues presented when implementing a national program at the local level, especially within rural communities. It is uncertain whether the tensions presented here are unique to rural communities. Rather, additional research should provide opportunities to examine differentiation in local implementation needs between rural and urban communities to enhance the efficacy of federal policy and program implementation.

References

Creswell, J., Poth, C., 2017. *Qualitative inquiry and research design: Choosing among five approaches*, 4th edition. Sage, Thousand Oaks, CA.

Durlak, J., DuPre, E., 2008. *Implementation matters: A review of research on the influence of implementation on program outcomes and the factors affecting implementation.* American Journal of Community Psychology 41, 327–350.

Fontana, B., 2017. *Looking back – and thinking ahead.* Center Piece, Summer, 2–3. https://padowntown.org//assets/Summer_2017_CenterPiece.pdf.

Main Street America, 2017. *Main Street programs.* www.mainstreet.org/mainstreetprograms.

Michigan Economic Development Corporation, 2018. *Michigan Main Street.* www.miplace.org/communities/mms/.

Sterner, G., 2015. *An examination of community organizing processes to assess the potential for increasing innovation in practice* (PhD Thesis). Pennsylvania State University. https://etda.libraries.psu.edu/files/final_submissions/10273.

Sterner, G., Alter, T., Watson, J., Kleinman, P., Bryant, R., 2015. *Community implementation dynamics: Nutrient management in the New York City and Chesapeake Bay watersheds.* International Journal of Rural Law and Policy, Special Edition 1: Soil Governance. http://epress.lib.uts.edu.au/journals/index.php/ijrlp/article/view/4366.

Swanson, L., 2001. *Rural policy and direct local participation: Democracy, inclusiveness, collective agency, and locality-based policy.* Rural Sociology 66(1), 1–21.

Yin, R.K., 2009. *Case study research: Design and methods*, 4th edition. Sage, Thousand Oaks, CA.

40

COMMUNITY-MANAGED FORESTRY IN PALO SECO, MEXICO

Andrew Peach and John Devlin

Introduction

This chapter presents an example of a successfully managed community forestry enterprise in Mexico called Palo Seco. The paper provides a brief overview of the history of forestry in Mexico and then discusses forest management and community benefits in Palo Seco. Mexican forestry policy requires logging permits and the approval of these permits is based on Palo Seco's demonstrated commitment to conservation and forest health, which means they must prioritize spending to maintain and improve the forest. But at the same time Palo Seco has been able to fulfill a strong social mission through infrastructural building projects that have improved the community in terms of housing, education, health, and social spaces. The research demonstrates that forest management policy based on community management can both protect the resource base and generate important social benefits.

The chapter is based on 16 semi-structured interviews conducted in Palo Seco over several weeks through February 2015. Interviewees were of different ages and genders, and interviews lasting between 35 and 90 minutes were conducted both in homes and in the forest during work breaks. Several days were also spent in the forest observing the harvesting of timber, accompanying a group of forestry workers to a training session in the municipal capital Coatepec Harinas, and general observation in the community. Several documents were reviewed outlining the details of the community forest management plan and harvest allocation (*aprovechamiento*) as well as the community's codified laws and customs (*reglamentos internos*). All fieldwork was conducted with the support of both the local administration and faculty members at the Universidad Autónoma del Estado de México (UAEM) and the Instituto de Ciencias Agropecuarias y Rurales (ICAR).

History of forestry in Mexico

The history of forestry in Mexico falls into two main periods (see also Chapter 26 for more details). Following the Mexican Revolution and throughout the twentieth century forest management fell under central state control. The revolution implemented an extensive land reform with an estimated 55 percent of Mexico's land redistributed to agrarian communities (Fox and Gordillo, 1989). The 1917 constitution also defined two new organizational structures: *ejidos* and *comunidades*. *Ejidos* were communal land grants given to landless farmers. *Comunidades* were similar, although they were granted to farmers that could demonstrate that they had been dispossessed of their traditional landholdings under the previous regime (Klooster, 2003). President Lazaro Cárdenas, in office from 1934 to 1940, distributed some 18 million hectares of land, affecting over 800,000 people, raising the share of agricultural land in farmer ownership to 47 percent (Klooster, 2003; Knight, 1994).

However, at the same time conservationists were focusing on Mexico's forests which were important to protect the country from droughts, floods, and damaging winds (Boyer, 2007). The conservationists saw farmers using primitive, unscientific methods as a deforestation threat and believed that state control was necessary to protect the forests. They called on government to teach rural communities how to harvest forests in a scientifically and centrally approved manner while tightly regulating the industry. The Forestry Law of 1926 established tight controls over everything from the cutting of trees to the transportation of the lumber and required forestry *ejidos* to form cooperatives, using a rigid administrative structure meant to maximize top-down control (Boyer, 2007).

Although this forestry law was removed in 1940, it left a lasting legacy. First, the basic structure of the institutional organization of *ejido* administration and collective decision-making was put into place, providing, in principle, a national framework of self-organization and self-government at the local level (Bray, 2013). Second, the rhetoric of mistrusting farmers and rural communities due to their perceived backwardness and shortsighted behavior continued to influence the way that other administrations shaped forestry policy (Boyer, 2007). A new forestry code in 1940 encouraged the creation of Industrial Forest Production Units (UIEFs), semi-public corporations meant to manage rationally the extraction of timber on an industrial scale (Boyer, 2005). *Ejidos* were given a stumpage fee for the amount of wood removed from their property. This continued until 1956 when forest engineers raised the alarm about the rate of deforestation in the country, claiming that at least 38 percent of the nation's forests were so damaged that any further harvesting would render them extinct (Klooster, 2003). This led to massive logging bans throughout much of the country.

Many communities responded to the bans by clearing forests for agricultural land or by logging illegally. These problems were exacerbated by the 1960 Forestry Law that increased the power of parastatal concessionaires while also expanding the complex system of rules and regulations. Foresters were required to seek permits and documentation for every tree felled (Klooster, 2000).

The second wave of forestry policy began in the 1970s as some in the Ministry of Agriculture argued that farmers were only destructive because government policy continually alienated them (Klooster, 2003). Farmers, they argued, would be the most effective stewards of their forests if they perceived the forest as a permanent source of resources and benefits. In 1973 many forestry bans were repealed, and a new office was created whose objective was to increase the number of *ejidos* that owned and managed their own forest businesses. This was expanded in 1976 with the creation of the Programa Nacional de Desarrollo Forestal (National Program for Forestry Development), which sought to address possibilities of linking production *and* conservation (Klooster, 2003). As parastatal concessions ended and *ejidos* began managing their own forests their income increased by as much as 300 percent (Klooster, 2000). The Forestry Law of 1986 officially ended the era of concessions (Klooster, 2003). This period saw Mexico's forest policy transition from top-down control that marginalized *campesinos*, to a grassroots approach that focused on community management seeking both conservation *and* production.

The end of centralized support also saw the last of the parastatals dismantled and the end to UIEFs. Legal changes in 1992 shifted responsibility of management onto local producers and allowed *campesinos* to utilize customary access rules and codify them in *reglamentos internos* (Bray, 2013). In 1997 a new forest development program Programa para el Desarrollo Forestal (PRO-DEFOR) was established and in 2001 the Comisión Nacional Forestal (CONAFOR) was created. PRODEFOR acts as the national regulatory body of CONAFOR and is responsible for approving and monitoring the operational plan that every community must have in order to operate a legal forestry operation (SEMARNAT, 2012). Apart from the approval and monitoring of the operational plan to ensure compliance with forestry conservation efforts the state now maintains a largely hands-off approach to community forestry in Mexico. Regulations still exist and are strictly enforced in order to prevent deforestation, but communities are now able to design and plan their own models that ensure maximum local control of forest resources. The right to extract timber is regulated but communities have full right to the value of the timber that is extracted (Bray, 2013).

Palo Seco

Palo Seco is a small *ejido* that operates within the community of Portrero Redondo, a small rural hamlet of between 500 and 700 people. Portrero Redondo is located in the Parque Nacional Nevado de Toluca (PNNT), about 100 kilometers outside of Toluca and 20 kilometers from the municipal center Coatepec Harinas. The Parque was created in 1936. It officially covers an area of 51,000 hectares (Candeau Dufat and Franco Maas, 2007). Forestry is the main economic activity of the majority of the 50-plus *ejidos* in the park, but they also engage in agriculture, producing potatoes, oats, pulses, and corn (Valencia *et al.*, 2013). Poverty characterizes the communities of the Parque and migration to urban centers or the United States is a common strategy for working-age adults (Valencia *et al.*, 2013).

All of the households in Portrero Redondo are located along the main road that can be traversed in under 15 minutes on foot. There are also two churches near the center of the hamlet, one Catholic and one Evangelical, and a medical clinic that is open every Thursday and services several neighboring communities as well. Removed from the main hamlet by 100 meters of forest is another cluster of buildings around a soccer field. These buildings consist of an auditorium, a primary and secondary school servicing students up to the age of 14, public washrooms, and a small trout farm on the river. Scattered throughout the households in the hamlet are several small convenience stores in the front rooms of houses, selling toiletries, some food products, and cards for recharging cellphone minutes. Almost every household has plumbing and electricity.

Forestry is the main economic activity and almost all working-age men work in the forest. At 1900 m above sea level, Portrero Redondo is one of the highest communities in the Parque and agriculture is limited to corn and some livestock in the form mainly of sheep and turkeys. During the rainy season (mid-May–August) the community forages mushrooms from the forest, which they sell at the local market in Coatepec Harinas and as far away as Mexico City. Some community members travel to other communities for work, but due to Portrero Redondo's isolation this is not common. Households also receive financial support from the federal government in the form of the *Prospera* (previously *Oportunidades*) which provides cash payments to households below a certain poverty threshold on a bimonthly basis in exchange for school attendance and health clinic visits (SEDESOL, 2014).

The *ejido* Palo Seco is a distinct organization located within the community of Portrero Redondo. Only 74 individuals – 68 men and 6 women – are members of the *ejido*. The *ejido* was created in 1940, and given ownership of 470 hectares of forest, with another 800 hectares added in 1941. With 74 *ejiditarios* Palo Seco is a small *ejido*. For comparison, the neighboring *ejido* Telar has close to 150 *ejiditarios* and the municipality's largest *ejido* Coatepec has over 1500. Being an *ejiditario* entails certain rights and responsibilities. Rights include an ownership stake in the forest and other *ejido* resources. These are realized in both dividend payments from economic activities and in the right to vote and take part in decision-making. They also include access to the forest for non-economic activities such as firewood collection. Responsibilities include attendance at monthly assemblies; adherence to and enforcement of all locally defined rules and regulations; and participation in all *faenas* (chores). These chores include reforestation, keeping the forest floor clean, patrolling the forest for fires and illegal logging, cutting and cleaning pathways through the forest to help prevent forest fires. These are done on a regular basis. They tend to consume about one full day a week. The costs of membership are quite high at one working day out of seven. These are days that cannot be used in the field working on subsistence agriculture, or in town searching for other work, or simply relaxing at home.

Palo Seco has an elected leadership of three members: the *comisariado*, a cross between a mayor and a company president, and two advisors that handle finances and other administration. They operate under three-year terms, which can be renewed, and are elected by a majority vote of all 74 *ejiditarios*. Decisions regarding the *ejido* and the forestry operation are made at monthly assemblies on the last Sunday of every month, which are coordinated by the *comisariado* and his two secretaries.

Although forestry has always been the primary economic activity of the *ejido* it was not granted a *manejo forestal* (forest license) until 1996. Previous to this all logging and sale of lumber was illegal. During the 1990s the *comisariado* became convinced that by legitimizing their actions through obtaining a *manejo forestal* the *ejido* could create a far more stable economic environment that would ensure steady work to *ejiditarios* and create more benefits for the community at large. After convincing the majority of *ejiditarios* to follow this plan the *ejido* hired a forestry engineer who undertook a study of the forest's overall health, a study which is required before a *manejo* can be approved by Probosque, the agency of the state of Mexico for forest protection.

A *manejo* details how, over a ten-year period, the *ejido* will protect the health of the forest and foster its growth and details the quantity of lumber that can be extracted (the harvest allocation or *aprovechamiento*) and dictates the manner in which this must happen. The *aprovechamiento* depends on the health of the forest, with the volume relating to a percentage of total new growth. The *aprovechamiento* is granted only if certain aspects of the conservation mandate are upheld. The *ejido* is responsible for the *manejo* and if they do not adequately protect, restore, and conserve their forests they will lose the privilege of harvesting trees.

The strategy proposed by the engineer, which is still used today, called for careful selection of the oldest trees; trees that were sick, or had stopped producing seeds; allowing the robust healthy trees to grow and propagate. The forest is divided into 12 sections, one of which is harvested each year while the other 11 are left dormant for natural reforestation. At the beginning of each season the engineer marks with spray paint the oldest and sickest trees that can be extracted. Any trees cut down without the marking would be noted by state inspectors and could jeopardize the *ejido*'s *aprovechamiento*. In 19 years Palo Seco has not faced any sanctions.

The 11 sections that are left dormant are subject to another program titled "Payment for Hydrological Environmental Services". This program provides 1000 pesos for every protected hectare. This payment is received annually and added to the funds raised through the sale of lumber, providing an economic incentive to the *ejiditarios* to protect their entire forest and ensuring that all 12 sections are economically productive every year.

Community benefits

Community members on Portrero Redondo are expected to uphold the rules created by the *ejido* regarding forest usage and management. In return for compliance they receive benefits from the forest and the forestry program. These include access to relatively unlimited firewood for household consumption (a very important benefit because it is the main fuel used by households to both cook their food and heat their buildings). During the rainy season another benefit is the collection of wild mushrooms for both household consumption and commercial purposes. In addition, the community benefits from a wide variety of building projects. Funds are designated by the *ejido* each year for construction of safer and more stable homes. Up to 2015 there had been 46 houses built or rebuilt. Other projects have included a potable water network that delivers drinkable water to every home in the community and an electricity grid that also reaches nearly every home. The projects are funded by a percentage of the money raised by the *ejido* through the sale of wood and the payment received for environmental services.

The benefits provided through the forestry program outweigh the costs. Before the forestry program was established the community suffered from a shortfall of employment and the most common solution was migration. Now many working-age individuals have returned to Portrero Redondo due to the benefit of employment offered by the forestry program. Furthermore, the younger generation of community members is now less tempted by opportunities abroad as they see gainful employment in the forest.

The cost for non-*ejido* community members is the large number of rules and regulations that they must follow with respect to the use of the forest. This perceived "loss of rights" is considered the cost that each community member must pay. Interviewees spoke almost unanimously about the positive changes that had occurred in the community between the time they obtained their first *manejo forestal* and the present. It is apparent that for the vast majority of community members the benefits of the forestry program certainly outweighed the costs.

Some community members did speak of isolated instances in which they were unhappy with certain decisions that were made by the *ejido*. They commented on the amount of money the *ejido* spends entertaining guests and on the purchase of a truck used primarily by the *comisariado* while on *ejido* business. But these are isolated instances in which community members have been disappointed with the *ejido*'s decisions.

Conclusions

The success of the forestry program is demonstrated by the fact that Palo Seco is held up in Mexico as an example of exemplary environmental management. In 2010 the state government gave Palo Seco an award recognizing its successful forest management. Palo Seco has protected and conserved its resource base, has generated community benefits, and has maintained substantial community support. The attitude among *ejiditarios* in Palo Seco is one of optimism and pride at what they have accomplished. Ranked as the top *ejido* in the state of Mexico and in the top ten in the country this attitude is certainly not unfounded. When asked why they had done so well while other *ejidos* around them struggled to attain similar results, both in terms of the forest's health and in building social works for the community, the most common response was their unity. They are united by their common history, by strong leadership, by virtue of being a small *ejido* and community, and by their desire to improve the community and invest in the future.

The *ejido* is a peculiarly Mexican institution, and this might limit its generalizability outside the Mexican context. Also, Palo Seco is a single case of an *ejido* that has been upheld as an example among *ejidos* and may not be representative of the average *ejido* experience. Further research within Mexico and internationally, could examine different common property regimes to determine whether other institutional arrangements and policy environments supporting community ownership and management such as cooperatives or social enterprises have been able to achieve a similar balancing of costs and benefits where business, environment, and community are all successfully managed.

Acknowledgments

Thanks to the Universidad Autónoma del Estado de México (UAEM) and in particular Dr. Lidia Carvajal from the Economics Department for her assistance in helping us in Toluca. Thanks also to the Instituto de Ciencias Agropecuarias y Rurales (ICAR) and in particular the director Dr. Gabino Bernal, and also Dr. William Gómez, and Mr. Noe Agruirre, MSc. for their expert guidance in regional rural issues and for introducing and familiarizing us to the Nevado del Toluca and the leaders of Palo Seco. Thanks especially to all of the people of Palo Seco and Portero Redondo for allowing us to spend time in their community. Andrew Peach would especially like to thank Hugo Marin for organizing a place to stay and for shuttling him to and from the site, and to David and Jobita Marin for taking him in and providing him with food and hospitality for the duration of his stay.

References

Boyer, C., 2005. *Contested terrain: Forestry regimes and community responses in northeastern Michoacán, 1940–2000*, in: Bray, D.B., Merino Pérez, L., Barry, D. (Eds.), *The community forests of Mexico: Managing for sustainable landscapes.* University of Texas Press, Austin, TX, pp. 27–48.

Boyer, C.R., 2007. *Revolución y paternalismo ecológico: Miguel Ángel de Quevedo y la política forestal en México, 1926–1940.* Historia Mexicana 57(1), 91–138.

Bray, D.B., 2013. *When the state supplies the common: Origins, changes, and design of Mexico's common property regime.* Journal of Latin American Geography 12(1), 33–55.

Candeau Dufat, R., Franco Maas, S., 2007. *Dinámica y condiciones de vida de la población del Parque Nacional Nevado de Toluca (PNNT) en la generación de presión a los ecosistemas circundantes y de impactos ambientales a través de un sistema de información geográfica.* Investigaciones Geográficas (62), 44–68.

Fox, J., Gordillo, G., 1989. *Between state and market: The Campesinos' quest for autonomy in rural Mexico*, in: Cornelius, W., Gentleman, J., Smith, P. (Eds.), *Mexico's alternative political futures.* Center for US–Mexican Studies, La Jolla, CA, pp. 131–172.

Klooster, D., 2000. *Institutional choice, community, and struggle: A case study of forest co-management in Mexico.* World Development 28(1), 1–20.

Klooster, D., 2003. *Campesinos and Mexican forest policy during the twentieth century.* Latin American Research Review 38(2), 94–126.

Knight, A., 1994. *Cardenismo: Juggernaut or jalopy?* Journal of Latin American Studies 26(1), 73–107.

SEDESOL – Secretaría de Desarrollo Social, 2014. *Prospera: Programa de Inclusión Social.* www.prospera. gob.mx/Portal/wb/Web/conoce_prosper.

SEMARNAT – Secretaría de Medio Ambiente y Recursos Naturales, 2012. *Consulta Temática: Programa de Desarrollo Forestal (PRODEFOR).* http://dgeiawf.semarnat.gob.mx:8080/ibi_apps/WFServlet? IBIF_ex=D3_R_RFORESTA11_01&IBIC_user=dgeia_mce&IBIC_pass=dgeia_mce.

Valencia, B.V., García, M.O., Ramirez de la O, I.L., Bernal, G.N., Maas, S.F., 2013. *Análisis social sobre los habitantes de la comunidad de La Peñuela, Parque Nacional Nevado de Toluca, México: Valores y comportamiento entorno al turismo.* Estudios y Perspectivas en Turismo 22, 425–449.

41

LAND OWNERSHIP AND LAND MANAGEMENT POLICIES IN NORWAY AND SCOTLAND

Annie McKee, Heidi Vinge, Hilde Bjørkhaug, and Reidar Almås

Policy-makers and the general public argue that the pattern of landownership in Scotland is inequitable and inefficient, since the land (and its associated outputs) is concentrated in only a few, private hands. Critics argue that the scale of private landownership in Scotland maintains historical inequalities and injustices, and that alternative forms of land occupancy and smaller landholdings could lead to more productive land use and associated socio-economic benefits. With its rural political history of decentralization and multifunctional agriculture, Norway provides a fascinating and highly relevant comparison to the history of Scottish landownership and land use policy, due in part to the similar population size, yet significant difference in the proportion of the population with a stake in landownership and management. The so-called "Norwegian model" (i.e. the pattern of land tenure, in tandem with rural and agricultural policies) is heralded as the goal for equitable landownership and sustainable land management that is aspired to by Scottish policy-makers. This comparative case study discusses the Norwegian and Scottish models of landownership and management in an historical perspective, to draw recommendations for the ongoing land reform in Scotland, including the implementation of measures within the Land Reform (Scotland) Act 2016. Reflections on the consequences of change to the Norwegian model are considered in the conclusion.

Introduction: the policy problem in Scotland and its causes

The system of landownership in Scotland is dominated by large-scale private "estates", with significant power held by the private owner with regard to land use decision-making (McKee *et al.*, 2013). It is reported that 83 percent of rural land is under private ownership, and that 50 percent of this private rural land is held by only 438 owners (Wightman, 2010). The Scottish agricultural census of 2016 indicated an average holding size of 109 hectares (Scottish Government, 2016a). This average is misleading, however, as explained: "the distribution of agricultural area between holdings in Scotland is highly skewed, with a relatively small number of very large holdings accounting for a high proportion of the area" (see Scottish Government, 2016b). This case study explores the question of whether an alternative model of land governance and institutions, namely that found in Norway, can provide insights for the pattern of landownership in Scotland.

The process of displacement and eviction of a large proportion of the Scottish rural population of the Highlands and Islands between 1760 and 1860, the so-called "Highland Clearances", illustrate the exploitative power once in the hands of private landowners. This era in Scottish history demonstrates a number of the key themes that have shaped negative sentiment towards private landownership and the predominance of "land" as a major Scottish political issue (cf. Hunter, 2006; Sellar, 2006). Since this event in history, rural power imbalances have persisted due to feudalism (brought to a belated end by the Abolition of Feudal Tenure (Scotland) 2000), absentee landlordism, and rural community disempowerment.

It is argued that the scale and concentration of private landownership in Scotland maintains historical inequalities and injustices, and that alternative models of land occupancy and a greater diversity of landowner type could lead to more productive land use and associated socio-economic benefits (see review by Thomson *et al.*, 2016). Due to the power held by private landowners in Scotland there has been a push for land reform from members of the general public, lobbying organizations, and the current Scottish National Party (SNP) government.

Contemporary land reform in Scotland aims to redress these historical inequalities and injustices and ensure that land ownership and management is in the public (and private) interest. The stated objective of the recent land reform process by the Scottish government is that "Scotland's land must be an asset that benefits the many, not the few" (Scottish Government, 2014), and that rights to land must promote fairness and social justice.

This case study aims to provide recommendations for Scottish land reform policy through examining the pattern of land tenure, in conjunction with rural and agricultural policies, in Norway. It may be argued that much of what the Scottish government aspires to achieve through land reform processes – in terms of greater equality and transparency in landownership, as well as sustainable and empowered rural communities – already exists in the so-called "Norwegian model" of social democracy in land governance (cf. Bryden *et al.*, 2015).

Policy variables: the "Norwegian model"

Rural Norway is characterized by a pattern of small farms and multifunctional agriculture, with most farms incorporating both privately owned and privately managed "in fields" ("*innmark*") and communally-managed "out fields" ("*utmark*", which may be uncultivable or too upland for crops). The so-called "Norwegian model" of agriculture (i.e. the pattern of land tenure, in conjunction with rural and agricultural policies) is often revered internationally, given the small scale of farms in Norway: only 3 percent of the land is suitable for arable cropping, with an average farm size of 23.9 hectares in 2016 (Statistics Norway, 2017a). Agriculture in Norway is supported by a national production subsidy system (differentially allocated according to geography, commodity, and farm size), production and sales cooperatives (who participate in legally guaranteed market regulations), and a regulated land market (Almås, 2004). Norwegian farm structure plays a key role in maintaining communities in remote rural areas: 18.5 percent of the Norwegian population in 2017 live in a rural area, with a decline of 0.8 percent since 2016 (Statistics Norway, 2017b).

It is clear that the system of privately owned, large-scale estates that continues to constitute the majority of Scottish landownership (including agricultural areas and uplands) contrasts with the small-scale, partnership model of land governance demonstrated in Norway (cf. Bryden *et al.*, 2015). Critical disjunctures of history occur with the legal abolition of the aristocracy in Norway in 1821 and with the "absolute right to buy" granted to the "*Husmenn*" (tenant farmers, similar to Scottish crofters in scale) in the 1928 Norwegian Land Act ("*Jordloven*") (Bryden *et al.*, 2015). Subsequently, the Husmann class was replaced by small, owner-occupier farmers (Almås, 2004) leading to relative farm scale equality.

Comparing this situation to Scotland requires further understanding of the measures in the Land Reform (Scotland) Acts 2003 and 2016, and the key land laws in Norway.

Actions and strategies

The first Land Reform (Scotland) Act, passed in 2003, was one of the primary political object-ives of the new Scottish parliament post devolution, and considered by many a pioneering and controversial land law reform for Scotland. The first section grants rights of responsible access to the Scottish countryside, the second provides rural communities a right of pre-emption in the purchase of land entering the market, and the third permits crofting communities the right to compulsory purchase of land (i.e. the landowner is legally required to sell the land to the crofting community) (Sellar, 2006; Munton, 2009; Warren, 2009). Many academics and policy com-mentators have described and evaluated the different sections of this ground-breaking legislation (see for example: Warren and McKee, 2011; Lovett, 2011; Hoffman, 2013).

Since 2014, the SNP government has undertaken to extend legislative powers to enhance land reform processes. The Community Empowerment (Scotland) Act 2015 extends the com-munity "right-to-buy" to urban communities and allows community bodies to purchase land deemed "abandoned, neglected or causing harm to the environmental wellbeing of the com-munity" (Scottish Government, 2017). Subsequently, the Land Reform (Scotland) Act 2016 has introduced powers of compulsory land sale (i.e. landowner would be legally required to put the land up for sale) to such bodies, if transfer of ownership is assessed as furthering the achievement of sustainable development in relation to land, and where maintaining the status quo is con-sidered to be "harmful" to the local community and public interest. The power of private land-owners is further challenged in this latest legislation through increasing rights granted to tenant farmers and requirements for community engagement in land management decision-making, among other measures (Scottish Government, 2016c).

In comparison, landownership and farming in Norway are regulated by three key laws, trans-lated as the Allodial Act, the Concession Act, and the Land Act, most recently adopted in 1995 (Pollock, 2015). First, the "Odel law" (*Odelsrett*), has been in place since the middle ages in Norway, and historically permits the oldest male child to inherit the farm. This historic principle now constitutes the Allodial Act, which granted female children equal rights to male children in 1975. Today it remains that close family members in direct descending line of the landowner have pre-emptive rights of farm purchase. This distinctive legislative instrument maintains land in family ownership and avoids the fragmentation of properties in generational shifts (Almås, 2004; Forbord et al., 2014), thus mirroring Scottish succession law and the impact of primogeni-ture (cf. Harvie-Clark, 2015). The fundamental principle of the *odel* maintains strong connec-tions to rural areas by much of the population.

In Norway, the owners of farmland must be resident on their landholding (which is not required in Scotland, unless under crofting tenure; Crofting Commission, 2017), and they must undertake "active" farming on the land, which limits farm expansion through land purchase. The Concession Act regulates land purchases by legal persons and gives preference to buyers who state their occupation as farming (Forbord et al., 2014). Finally, the Land Act ("*Jordloven*") aims to ensure that all land resources are best used for society and farmers, through promoting rural settlement, employment, and agricultural development (Vinge, 2015). This key legislation confirms that it is the landowners' responsibility that land is "actively farmed" and that land is maintained in good condition. Farmland rental arises as an option for landowners who do not wish to be active farmers. The Land Act controls land renting and requires written ten-year contracts between landowner and tenant, which are submitted to the municipality (Landbruks-direktoratet, 2017).

Policy solutions? The applicability of the Norwegian model in Scotland

The "Norwegian model" can represent a system of equitable landownership and sustainable land management to which Scottish policy-makers and land reform campaigners aspire (Bryden *et al.*, 2015). In Scotland, the variables that have been the focus of change efforts include land-ownership scale, diversity of landownership types, the public interest in land, and sustainable development. In particular, community involvement in the management and ownership of land is a key feature of the policy landscape, with the current Scottish government seeking to enable "1 million acres" (i.e. 404,686 hectares) of land to be in community ownership by the year 2020 (Scottish Government, 2015). As at June 2017, there was 562,230 acres (i.e. 227,526 hectares) in community ownership (Scottish Government, 2017). Community landownership in both rural and urban Scotland is supported by the land reform legislation (previously outlined), as well as funding support from the Scottish Land Fund, among others, for property purchases. The Scottish Land Commission, a centralized, non-departmental government body, is tasked to oversee the land reform process in Scotland and fulfill the Scottish government's vision "where the ownership, management and use of land and buildings contributes to the collective benefit of everybody" (Scottish Land Commission, 2017).

In Norway, the question of land reform does not appear to feature in public or political discourse, although there is some consideration of the need for land consolidation due to the distances between rental units managed by "solo farmers" (and resulting environmental impacts, in terms of transport fuel emissions and the abandonment of marginal land). While promoting community landownership is not the intention of Norwegian rural policies, there exists a much greater proportion of the population with access to land, due to the scale of landholdings and extent of close farming connections within family histories. A further critical difference exists in the fact that municipalities in Norway are important landowners; therefore, rural communities are able to directly influence and access land use decision-making at the local scale.

The Norwegian model may be proposed as a suggested policy solution for Scotland. However, in order to achieve this aspiration, several potential changes in Scotland would allow greater alignment with the institutions and governance of land in Norway. These changes may include greater influence of local communities and local authorities in the allocation of land for rent, replicating the role of the municipality in Norway, and seeking to overcome barriers to new agricultural tenancies in Scotland (cf. Scottish Government, 2016c). Scottish policy-makers could review guidance regarding succession and inheritance to promote equality of landowner-ship between claimants on inheritance. Shortall *et al.* (2017) recommend that the cultural practice of passing on large landholdings intact to one son needs to be challenged in Scotland, and that opening up discourses about farm succession and offering access to formal advice could help to enable women to be treated equally on inheritance, as has become a social norm in Norway. Furthermore, it is important that the Scottish policy-makers seek to maintain social networks between members of the local farming community, and between the farming and non-farming rural community, as exists in Norway through strong rural connections and recreational activities (e.g. hunting and skiing clubs).

Evaluation of policy and conclusions

It is too soon for the most recent land reform legislation in Scotland to be evaluated (i.e. the Land Reform (Scotland) Act 2016), as the various measures contained in the Act are only now (at the time of writing) starting to be implemented. Time will tell whether the Act leads to effective change and fulfillment of the Scottish government's land reform intentions. Nonetheless, the case study presented illustrates the value of international comparison to gain insights and experiences from alternative perspectives and institutional settings. The following recommendations for the Scottish policy goal of land reform may therefore be derived, with relevance to land governance internationally:

1   An ongoing review of policy measures to ensure a balance of private and public rights and interests in land.

2   A dialogue regarding the implementation and evaluation of land reform measures, in order to overcome barriers to local community involvement in decisions relating to land (see McKee, 2015; McKee and Roberts, 2016).

3   Support for underpinning networks and developing social capital between rural actors (i.e. owners and managers of land, and those who live and work in rural areas).

4   Support mechanisms that create opportunities for equality in land access (e.g. beyond succession and inheritance), to avoid competition between land owners and countering trends of farm "cannibalism", through building cooperation and new business models.

To conclude, this case study also provides a comparative insight into Norwegian land policies, to highlight the consequences of potential future changes to the "Norwegian model". Similar to Scotland, Norway is not exempt from the pressure of neoliberalism, not least with regard to agricultural policies (Almås and Campbell, 2012), and dramatic increases in areas of rented farmland have been attributed to a shift in Norwegian agricultural and rural policy, towards supporting larger scale and more efficient agricultural production units (Dramstad and Sang, 2010; Forbord *et al.*, 2014). A debate is emerging regarding policy changes intended to increase competitiveness in global production markets (Bryden, 2016). Such legislative reform in Norway would have consequences for land prices, increasing the rate of land sales and land speculation, as well as influencing traditional rural community structures. In this regard, it is opportune for Norwegian policy-makers to consider and reflect on alternative land systems which are governed more directly by market forces, such as in Scotland (cf. Bryden *et al.*, 2015; Bryden, 2016).

Acknowledgments

Annie McKee acknowledges the receipt of a fellowship from the OECD Co-operative Research Programme: Biological Resource Management for Sustainable Agricultural Systems in 2016, and staff time supported by the Rural and Environment Science and Analytical Services Division of the Scottish government through the Strategic Research Programme, 2011–2016 and 2016–2021.

References

Almås, R., 2004. *From state driven modernisation to green liberalism 1920–2000*, in: Almås, R. (Ed.), *Norwegian agricultural history*. Tapir Academic Publishers, Trondheim, pp. 296–357.

Almås, R., Campbell, H., 2012. *Rethinking agricultural policy regimes: Food security, climate change and the future resilience of global agriculture*. Research in Rural Sociology and Development, Volume 18. Emerald Insight, Bingley.

Bryden, J., 2016. *Land reform proposals in Norway and Scotland – BBC debate*. https://johnmbryden.wordpress.com/2016/02/12/land-reform-proposals-in-norway-and-scotland-bbc-debate/.

Bryden, J., Riddoch, L., Brox, O., 2015. *Conclusions*, in: Bryden, J., Brox, O., Riddoch, L. (Eds.), *Northern neighbours: Scotland and Norway since 1800*. Edinburgh University Press, Edinburgh, pp. 282–286.

Crofting Commission, 2017. *Crofters duties and statutory conditions.* www.crofting.scotland.gov.uk/faq.

Dramstad, W.E., Sang, N., 2010. *Tenancy in Norwegian agriculture.* Land Use Policy 27, 946–956. DOI: 10.1016/j.landusepol.2009.12.008.

Forbord, M., Bjørkhaug, H., Burton, R.J.F., 2014. *Drivers of change in Norwegian agricultural land control and the emergence of rental farming.* Journal of Rural Studies 33, 9–19.

Harvie-Clark, S., 2015. *Succession (Scotland) Bill.* SPICe Briefing 15/48. August 26, 2015.

Hoffman, M., 2013. *Why community ownership? Understanding land reform in Scotland.* Land Use Policy 31, 289–297. DOI: 10.1016/j.landusepol.2012.07.013.

Hunter, J., 2006. *Fonn's duthchas: Land and legacy.* NMS Enterprises, Edinburgh.

Landbruksdirektoratet, 2017. *Driveplikt og jordleie.* www.landbruksdirektoratet.no/no/eiendom-og-skog/eiendom/driveplikt/driveplikt-og-jordleie#utleie-av-jord.

Lovett, J.A., 2011. *Progressive property in action: The Land Reform (Scotland) Act 2003.* Nebraska Law Review 89(4), 739–818. http://digitalcommons.unl.edu/nlr/vol. 89/iss4/5.

McKee, A.J., 2015. *Legitimising the laird? Communicative action and the role of private landowner and community engagement in rural sustainability.* Journal of Rural Studies 41, 23–36.

McKee, A., Roberts, D., 2016. *Good practice in overcoming barriers to community land-based activities.* Report for the Scottish Government, June 2016. www.gov.scot/Publications/2016/07/7298.

McKee, A., Warren, C., Glass, J., Wagstaff, P., 2013. *The Scottish private estate,* in: Glass, J., Price, M.F., Warren, C., Scott, A. (Eds.), *Lairds, land and sustainability: Scottish perspectives on upland management.* Edinburgh University Press, Edinburgh, pp. 63–85.

Munton, R., 2009. *Rural land ownership in the United Kingdom: Changing patterns and future possibilities for land use.* Land Use Policy 26(1), S54–S61.

Pollock, S., 2015. *International perspectives on land reform.* SPICe Briefing, July 10. The Scottish Parliament, Edinburgh.

Scottish Government, 2014. *A consultation on the future of land reform in Scotland.* The Scottish Government, Edinburgh.

Scottish Government, 2015. *1 million acres short life working group.* www.gov.scot/Topics/Environment/land-reform/MillionAcres.

Scottish Government, 2016a. *Results from the June 2016 Scottish Agricultural Census.* October 25. A National Statistics publication for Scotland.

Scottish Government, 2016b. *Structure of the agricultural farms in Scotland.* www.gov.scot/Topics/Statistics/Browse/Agriculture-Fisheries/agritopics/farmstruc.

Scottish Government, 2016c. *Land Reform (Scotland) Act 2016.* www.webarchive.org.uk/wayback/archive/20180129140056/http://www.gov.scot/Topics/Environment/land-reform/LandReformBill.

Scottish Government, 2017. *The Community Empowerment (Scotland) Act 2015: A summary.* February. www.gov.scot/Topics/People/engage/CommEmpowerBill/CEAMainSummary.

Scottish Land Commission, 2017. *Driving land reform.* http://landcommission.gov.scot/.

Sellar, D.W.H., 2006. *The great land debate and the Land Reform (Scotland) Act 2003.* Norsk Geografisk Tidsskrift – Norwegian Journal of Geography 60(1), 100–109.

Shortall, S., Sutherland, L.-A., McKee, A., Hopkins, J., 2017. *Women in farming and the agriculture sector.* Report for the Environment and Forestry Directorate, Rural and Environment Science and Analytical Services (RESAS) Division, Scottish Government, June 9. www.gov.scot/Publications/2017/06/2742.

Statistics Norway, 2017a. *Population and land area in urban settlements.* www.ssb.no/en/befolkning/statistikker/beftett/aar (accessed 1.30.18; last updated 12.19.17).

Statistics Norway, 2017b. *Structure of agriculture, 2016, preliminary figures.* www.ssb.no/en/jord-skog-jakt-og-fiskeri/statistikker/stjord.

Thomson, S., Moxey, A., Wightman, A., McKee, A., Miller, D., Brodie, E., Glass, J., Hopkins, J., Mathews, K., Thomson, K., McMorran, R., Bryce, R., 2016. *The impact of diversity of ownership scale on social, economic and environmental outcomes: Exploration and case studies.* Report for the Scottish Government, March. www.gov.scot/Publications/2016/07/1094.

Vinge, H., 2015. *Food security, food sovereignty, and the nation-state: Historicizing Norwegian farmland policy,* in: Trauger, A. (Ed.), *Food sovereignty in international context: Discourse, politics and practice in place.* Routledge, New York, pp. 87–105.

Warren, C.R., 2009. *Managing Scotland's environment,* 2nd edition. Edinburgh University Press, Edinburgh.

Warren, C.R., McKee, A. 2011. *The Scottish revolution? Evaluating the impacts of post-devolution land reform.* Scottish Geographical Journal 127(1), 17–39.

Wightman, A., 2010. *The poor had no lawyers.* Birlinn Limited, Edinburgh.

42

LOCAL POLICIES ADDRESSING POVERTY AND SOCIAL EXCLUSION IN RURAL SPAIN DURING THE RECESSION

Diana E. Valero

Introduction: local policies in rural Valencia

This chapter explores the policies addressing social exclusion and poverty implemented by municipalities in rural areas of Spain during the recession between 2008 and 2014. The case study included here reports on results from qualitative research with rural mayors. While poverty and social exclusion rates rose during the recession, in recent years local authorities have continued to face a reduction of their already scarce capabilities for action in a context of austerity policies, local reforms, and budgetary cuts.

The rural areas studied are in the Valencia region of the east Iberian Peninsula. These areas are within the interior of Valencia and Castellon provinces and the mountainous part of Alicante.[1] While most territory in the region is considered to be intermediate-rural or peri-urban areas with more or less dynamic economies, these areas face traditional rural demographic challenges (low population, low population density, high aging levels, and depopulation) and economic challenges such as high dependency on the primary sector (Esparcia and Noguera, 2001). From a policy perspective, the rurality of these areas is highlighted by the EU-defined indicator of urbanization (Eurostat, 2012), the list of Areas Facing Natural Constraints (European Commission, 2009), and the 2006 configuration of Local Actions Groups (LAG) (Esparcia and Escribano, 2015). However, the rurality of the region is masked in these general classifications due to its asymmetric population distribution. The Eurostat rurality indicator classifies Valencia and Alicante provinces as predominantly urban, with Castellon as an intermediate area (Eurostat, 2013). However, a closer look at the population distribution indicates that more than 70 percent of the municipalities in the Valencia region have fewer than 5000 inhabitants – which is the threshold used in Spain to characterize small rural municipalities (Law 45/2007). Of these, 40 percent have fewer than 1000 inhabitants.

Local councils are usually the only governmental authority with a presence in rural areas. These bodies follow the provisions made by national and regional norms. During the recession, Valencia councils were governed mainly by regional branches of the two big national political parties: PPCV (Popular Party – Conservative-Liberal Party, center-right) and PSPV-PSOE (Socialist Party, center-left). Less than 8 percent of mayors came from other parties. Among other issues, local councils address aspects of social welfare with particular attention to poverty and social exclusion.

Finally, regarding the actions of local governments in rural areas, it must be noted that the real capacity of small councils is limited by their material resources – human and economic resources in particular – whose provision usually depends on their population. Thus, with fewer inhabitants and reduced markets, rural councils have fewer resources to implement policies, a situation that is aggravated in rural areas where municipalities are small in demographic terms. In addition, there are competency restrictions limiting the action of local councils depending on the population size of the municipality. For instance, municipalities with fewer than 5000 inhabitants are not required to provide the same public services as bigger municipalities and in some cases must do it under the coordination of the provincial councils.

The policy field: social exclusion in rural areas

Social exclusion refers to the complex generation of social problems beyond the traditional notion of poverty. Fighting social exclusion has become one of the main social policy objectives under EU direction. Different international studies (Bertolini *et al.*, 2009; Copus, 2014) have noted that the factors that cause unequal relations between rural areas in Europe are diverse. Neo-endogenous development approaches like the new rural paradigm (OECD, 2006) suggest that these differences are based on the distribution of internal resources (natural, economic, socio-demographic, organizational, and cultural-identity resources) and relational factors (social capital, social relations, network dynamics) (Shucksmith, 2012). The field of rural poverty research requires new investigation into the influence of local institutions on the risks of poverty and exclusion, in particular to explore the links between policy interventions and poverty in rural areas (Weber *et al.*, 2005).

From a holistic point of view, Reimer (2004) and Philip and Shucksmith (2003) described the risks of social exclusion in rural areas as failures in different social subsystems: private markets (labor markets, retailing, housing), public systems (access to services, paternalism and clientelism, participation), voluntary systems (associations) and family, and support networks. Thus, policy must address social development in rural areas in a comprehensive way to prevent and avoid social exclusion and should involve all the social subsystems where failures act as exclusion vectors. Public action should not be limited to targeting poverty and vulnerability assistance but must also include measures to empower both disadvantaged people and the community in general.

The economic recession that began in 2008 increased and accelerated circumstantial and structural social exclusion processes (Valero *et al.*, 2016). These include the rise of underemployment and unemployment, lower income and consumption levels (Petmesidou and Guillén, 2014), cutbacks in service delivery, and the overall rationalization of social aid (Guillén *et al.*, 2016). In rural areas, the crisis was particularly visible through the rise of unemployment rates and the loss of private and public services, which could act in some cases as push factors for out-migration, particularly among young people (Bock *et al.*, 2015; De Lima and Valero, 2014).

The research: a qualitative analysis of council actions

The actions of local governments to reduce social exclusion were studied qualitatively through fieldwork carried out during the spring of 2014 in the rural areas of the Valencia region. Thirty municipalities were selected according to their populations and the political orientation of their local councils, which were chosen to represent their geographic, demographic, and political

Table 42.1 Types of council actions against social exclusion

		Target group	
		Individual/group	Community
Aim of the action	Promotion	Selective promotion Actions aimed to empower or foster the development of particular individuals/groups	Community promotion Actions aimed to promote community development
	Care	Selective care Actions aimed to take care of the needs of particular individuals/groups	Community care Actions aimed to take care of an existing need affecting the community in general

diversity. Of the municipalities included in the study, 90 percent were rural areas where the EU LEADER program is applied to supported rural development projects, and almost half belong to rural areas targeted for revitalization according to the Spanish sustainable rural development policy. The remainder were located in intermediate-rural areas and peri-urban areas. Mayors of the selected municipalities were interviewed in depth about social exclusion in their area, the activities implemented by the respective councils, and the resources mobilized.

The actions reported were analyzed following a two-step process. First, the actions were classified according to the social subsystem in which they operate (provision of public services, public participation, market systems, associations, and civil society). Then, for each one of the social subsystems identified, the actions were classified in the four categories in Table 42.1 according to their scope. In general, literature on the subject agrees that promotion actions are more effective at coping with social exclusion than simple care actions and that the optimal scenario should include actions that promote community development (Brugué and Goma, 1998).

Second, a qualitative comparative analysis based on fuzzy sets (fsQCA) (Ragin, 2008) was performed to examine how the actions implemented to fight social exclusion related to the political affiliation of the councils. A profile of the actions of every council in public and non-public subsystems was developed to identify different strategy scenarios: a minimum scenario, in which councils limited their actions to selective care; an intermediate one, in which councils included actions on selective promotion and/or community care; and an optimal one, in which councils acted on community promotion. Each scenario was configured as an independent fuzzy set, and the political affiliation of the councils was explored through necessity and sufficiency tests on those different scenarios.

Findings

Actions of local councils

The findings of these interviews show that local authorities in Valencian rural areas employ a significant range of care actions to address explicit and urgent social needs (e.g. poverty) as well as promotion actions seeking to prevent social exclusion and promote social development (e.g. providing sources of employment).

From the point of view of the failures in different social subsystems (Reimer, 2004; Philip and Shucksmith, 2003), the type of actions implemented by the councils (care or promotion, selective or community) tends to vary depending on the social subsystem to which it is addressed.

Regarding *public services*, councils are limited by regulations and provisions of the central and regional (autonomous) governments. The provision of public services must follow community approaches in transportation, education, and health-care services. For the mayors, the most important field of public action relating to social exclusion was social services. In this field, there is a prevalence of concrete measures focused directly on addressing poverty and exclusion (e.g. provision of food, clothing, and household goods; financial aid for the payment of basic household supplies; birth benefits; community kitchen; specific care services for abused women or drug abusers; meal programs for the elderly) while wider and bolder social policies (e.g. gender equality plans) appeared only occasionally. *Public participation* policies included a variety of actions ranging from personal advice to local development forums, although their core was still developed with an approach of individual/group care focused on information activities.

Regarding *market systems*, the labor market was the most important system for the mayors interviewed. The councils focused on care or promotion of unemployed people (e.g. job search guidance and employment plans or vocational training) as well as community development measures aimed at creating jobs in the locality (local development projects). Actions concerning commercial and professional services, agricultural markets, and housing markets also have different orientations regarding the selective-community and the care-promotion axes. Regarding *voluntary systems and civil society*, actions also varied from supporting the activities of the civil associations through allocation of resources (selective care) to promoting their active role in the community (community promotion) by the co-production of socio-cultural services.

The areas of highest concern were social services and the labor market. All councils implemented actions in those fields (see Table 42.2). There were, however, no promotion actions in the field of transportation services, neither individual/group nor community care among socio-cultural and sports services; no individual/group promotion in the field of health services; and no community care in the labor market. The weak diffusion of other types of action should also be noted. For example, there was very little individual/group care in transportation and health-care services, community development for social services, and individual/group development in housing.

Table 42.2 Extension across local councils of the types actions implemented in the different social subsystems

Services	Selective care	Community care	Selective promotion	Community promotion	No council
Transportation services	★	★★	–	–	
Education services	★★	★★★★	★★	★★	★ < 5%
Healthcare services	★	★★★★	–	★★	
Social care services	★★★	★★★★★	★★	★	★★ 5%–33%
Culture, leisure, and sport services	–	–	★★	★★★	
Participation	★★	★★	★★★	★★★	★★★ 33%–66%
Labor market	★★★	–	★★★	★★★	
Retailing and professional services	★★	★★★	★★	★★	★★★★ 66%–95%
Agriculture	★★	★★	★★	★★	
Housing	★★★	★★	★	★★	★★★★★ > 95%
Associations	★★★	★★	★★★	★★	

Strategic orientation of local councils

All these actions together constitute a catalogue of measures implemented by rural councils seeking to fight social exclusion. Among the municipalities examined, there was no single archetype. Instead, each individual council pursued a unique combination of different actions. It was assumed that each council chose to carry out those measures that best fit their respective socio-community needs, available resources, and strategic orientation.

The second theme of analysis explored the political dimension of the councils. The hypothesis was that each council would plan its actions according to its values and program guides (aspects related to political parties and ideology), and in accordance with other resources that may be mobilized depending on the council's political party (e.g. information and economic resources). The results from the fsQCA analysis supported that hypothesis. On the one hand, councils that tended to limit their actions to care-oriented measures in the public spheres (provision of public services and participation) were often mayors from the conservative Partido Popular (PP) who had held that position for a long time. On the other hand, strategies that combined care actions with development actions were pursued by center-left PSOE mayors who were relatively new to the position (having served one or two terms). These results reaffirm the idea that, despite the significant limitations shared by all rural councils as institutions, they have some degree of ability to design and implement their own local social policy based on local political values and orientations.

Conclusions: governance challenges and possibilities for local policies in rural areas

The findings offered by this chapter show that local authorities in rural areas put into play a significant range of actions addressing explicit and urgent social needs while also seeking to limit the development of social exclusion processes through welfare services, adjustments of private markets, and increased civil society engagement. Thus, rural councils pursue distinctive social development strategies. From a policy perspective, the use of population thresholds to distribute resources and allocate powers to municipalities hinders the policies that rural councils may implement to address problems of social exclusion. In countries where a low population is a core feature of rural areas, as in Spain, these areas also face a higher level of social vulnerability as a consequence of the dynamics triggered by a weak demography: fragile economies, outmigration, and low employment opportunities. Population thresholds result in local councils with small populations having fewer material resources and limited powers. These constraints translate into a more limited capacity of action, feeding back into the communities' vulnerabilities and exclusion risks.

Despite the limitations, rural councils still have a clear say in deciding what to do in their villages. Their choices of action are shaped by resource availability and politics. The political composition of a given council is closely related to the type of measures that are implemented. From a governance point of view, it would be interesting to study similar issues in countries that have undertaken processes of municipal amalgamation such as Finland, Canada, or Greece. Amalgamation may mean changes in the political configuration of the community and local government. The challenges facing effective social policies in rural areas depend not only on the provision of services, but also on the general configuration of the governance system that distributes power and resources among the different government levels.

Note

1 The Valencia region (Valencia Autonomous Community) is one of the 17 Autonomous Communities in Spain, and it comprises three provinces: Castellon, Valencia, and Alicante. The chapter is dedicated to exploring local policies in rural areas in the Valencia region, and when referring to the Valencia province, it will always be specified.

References

Bertolini, P., Montanari, M., Peragine, V., 2009. *Poverty and social exclusion in rural areas.* Report to Directorate General for Employment, Social Affairs and Equal Opportunities, European Commission. http://ec.europa.eu/social/BlobServlet?docId=2087&langId=en.

Bock, B., Kovács, K., Shucksmith, M., 2015. *Changing social characteristics, patterns of inequality and exclusion*, in: Copus, A.P., De Lima, P. (Eds.), *Territorial cohesion in rural Europe.* Routledge, London, pp. 193–211.

Brugué, Q., Goma, R., 1998. *La dimensión local del bienestar social: el marco conceptual*, in: Brugué, Q., Goma, R. (Eds.), *Gobiernos locales y políticas públicas: bienestar social, promoción económica y territorio.* Ariel, Barcelona, pp. 39–56.

Copus, A.K. (Ed.), 2014. *TIPSE: The territorial dimension of poverty and social exclusion in Europe.* Final Report. EU – ESPON. www.espon.eu/main/Menu_Projects/Menu_AppliedResearch/tipse.html.

De Lima, P., Valero, D.E., 2014. *The territorial dimension of poverty and social exclusion in Europe. Case study report: Albacete, La Manchuela, Spain.* TIPSE – The Territorial Dimension of Poverty and Social Exclusion in Europe, EU – ESPON. www.espon.eu/main/Menu_Projects/Menu_AppliedResearch/tipse.html.

Esparcia, J., Escribano, J., 2015. *Programas europeos y el enfoque territorial*, in: Hermosilla, J., Iranzo, E. (Eds.), *Atlas de los recursos territoriales valencianos.* Universidad de Valencia, Valencia, pp. 268–276.

Esparcia, J., Noguera, J., 2001. *Los espacios rurales en transicion*, in: Romero, J., Morales, A., Salom, J., Vera, F. (Eds.), *La periferia emergente. La Comunitat Valenciana en la Europa de las regiones.* Ariel, Barcelona, pp. 343–371.

European Commission, 2009. *Less-favoured areas EU-27 (Version 2.4).* http://ec.europa.eu/agriculture/rurdev/lfa/images/map_en.jpg.

Eurostat, 2012. *Degree of urbanisation classification: 2011 revision.* http://ec.europa.eu/eurostat/statisticsexplained/index.php/Degree_of_urbanisation_classification_-_2011_revision.

Eurostat, 2013. *Updated urban–rural typology: Integration of NUTS 2010 and the latest population grid.* http://ec.europa.eu/eurostat/statistics-explained/index.php/Urban-rural_typology_update.

Guillén, A.M., González-Begega, S., Luque Balbona, D., 2016. *Austeridad y ajustes sociales en el sur de Europa. La fragmentación del modelo de bienestar mediterráneo.* Revista Española de Sociología 25(2), 261–272.

OECD, 2006. *The new rural paradigm: Policies and governance.* Organisation for Economic Co-operation and Development, Paris.

Petmesidou, M., Guillén, A.M., 2014. *Can the welfare state as we know it survive? A view from the crisis-ridden south European periphery.* South European Society and Politics 19(3), 295–307.

Philip, L.J., Shucksmith, M., 2003. *Conceptualizing social exclusion in rural Britain.* European Planning Studies 11(4), 461–480.

Ragin, C.C., 2008. *Redesigning social inquiry: Fuzzy sets and beyond.* University of Chicago Press, Chicago, IL.

Reimer, B., 2004. *Social exclusion in a comparative context.* Sociologia Ruralis 44(1), 76–94.

Shucksmith, M., 2012. *Class, power and inequality in rural areas: Beyond social exclusion?* Sociologia Ruralis 52(4), 377–397.

Valero, D.E., Escribano, J., Vercher, N., 2016. *Social policies addressing social exclusion in rural areas of Spain and Portugal: The main post-crisis transformational trends.* Sociologia e Politiche Sociali 19(3), 83–101.

Weber, B., Jensen, L., Miller, K., Mosley, J., Fisher, M., 2005. *A critical review of rural poverty literature: Is there truly a rural effect?* International Regional Science Review 28(4), 381–414.

43

INTEGRAL MOUNTAIN DEVELOPMENT IN SPAIN

An historical review

Pedro Fiz Rocha Correa

Introduction

Mountains are key territories that provide basic resources such as energy, water, and biodiversity, as well as a home for different human livelihoods that traditionally coexisted in equilibrium with the ecosystem. In recent decades, the larger part of Southern European mountain societies has been suffering from a process of aging and abandonment, which has caused environmental and social imbalances. Traditionally, mountain areas have been a locus for rural policy debate in Europe. They provide an ideal laboratory for the implementation of innovative rural policies due in part to the fact that, in many cases, mountain societies and economies can be more easily isolated from urban dynamics.

The European policy towards mountain territories has been mainly sectoral (Lacoma, 1993). In 1975, there was an initial attempt to enlarge the policy scope to include socio-economic aspects through the EEC Directive 268/75 on Mountain Farming. In some countries, including France and Spain, there were regulatory efforts to introduce integrated mountain programs in the 1980s (Amato, 1988). Among these were the 1982 Spanish Mountain Agricultural Law and the Oscos-Eo Integral Development Program (1985), a pilot program applied under the Spanish Law which sought integral development based on the promotion of active local participation and integrated multi-sourced funding with broad territorial scope. This program included a wide range of initiatives related to rural development, which set it apart as an exemplar in Spain for rural tourism, education, provision of basic services, land reallocation, and the implementation of LEADER initiatives (French acronym for "Liaison Entre Actions de Développement de l'Économie Rurale", meaning "Links between the rural economy and development actions").

Thirty years after its implementation (1985–1995), the impact of the program is still evident in Oscos-Eo, while some of the outputs are now more visible. However, the experience is little known despite the relevance of its results for a wide range of development areas (Orea and Díaz-Ambrona, 1993). Its integral scope may serve as a model for rural development policy in general, and in mountain territories in particular. In this chapter, the policy framework of the Oscos-Eo Integral Development Program is described, and its lessons identified.

Policy framework

The European policy

The Council Directive 75/268/EEC of 28 April 1975 on *mountain and hill farming and farming in certain less favored areas* proposed a shift from sectoral to socio-structural policies, from a solely productive logic towards a more social and environmental model. The Directive was also a first step towards the current rural development policy or the second pillar of the Common Agricultural Policy (Delgado Serrano, 2004). The Directive refers to depopulation, the fragility of mountain ecosystems, and the importance of protecting such areas, the added difficulties of these territories, the persistent deterioration of agricultural incomes, and the comparative disadvantages for farms in terms of production costs and natural limitations. In 1984, compensatory allowances for natural disadvantages, which were the main subsidy derived from the Directive, represented 55 percent of the European Agricultural Guidance and Guarantee Fund (Gómez Benito, 1987) – or 5 percent of the Common Agriculture Policy budget. This budgetary allocation reflects the importance given to the measure by the EU. In 1985, the Regulation (EEC) No. 797/85 was derived from, and completed, the 1975 Directive. This regulation stressed social and environmental concerns, as well as the link between the viability of farm holdings through diversification and the improvement of infrastructure. It thus reinforced the regional dimension of EEC socio-structural policy.

The Spanish Law for Mountain Agriculture (LAM)

The Spanish Constitution of 1978 specifies in article 130.2 that special treatment will be given to mountain areas. As a result, in 1982 Law 25/1982 (Ley de Agricultura de Montaña, LAM, or the Mountain Agriculture Law) was approved. Its main objectives were to:

- facilitate the social and economic development of mountain areas, especially in agricultural aspects;
- maintain an adequate population;
- attend to the conservation and restoration of the physical environment as human habitat.

The LAM, which is still in effect, is focused on the agricultural, livestock, and forestry sectors. However, its articles go beyond agrarianism and relate to environmental and other non-agricultural activities such as handicrafts in small industries, recreational activities, tourism, and services that are a necessary complement for agriculture (Oliván del Cacho, 1994).

Despite its name, the LAM is the first regulatory effort in Spain that approaches the problem of the mountain zones from an integral perspective and in line with the European legislation discussed above. The LAM was implemented via the elaboration and application of Integral Development Programs. The main objectives of LAM and the governance and management of the Integral Development Programs were pursued through the creation of a management agency (Rocha, 1988).

The Oscos-Eo Integral Development Program

Oscos-Eo district

In 1985, the regional government of Asturias (Spain), one of the most mountainous regions of Europe, introduced a program for Integral Rural Development in the District of Oscos-Eo under LAM. Oscos-Eo is in the western part of Asturias on the Cantabrian coast of Spain. The district covers a little more than 500 km^2 and, in 1985, had about 15,000 inhabitants living in over 350 villages organized in seven municipalities. Three of these are in the highest part of the district, two in the basin of the Eo river, and the other two by the sea at the mouth of the Eo. Some 5000 of the region's inhabitants lived in the higher part of the territory which was facing rapid depopulation, having suffered an emigration of 50 percent of total inhabitants in the previous 25 years (SADEI, 1984). This population was also aging, with 30 percent of the population older than 60 years and the average income at less than half of the regional mean. The economic activity of the region was mainly focused on dairy farming in the lower parts and meat/beef in the highlands, with agrarian employment over 85 percent (Rocha, 1988). This was supplemented with ironworking, weaving, and a small-scale timber industry.

The Integral Development Program (IDP)

As established by the LAM, the regional government of Asturias elaborated an Integral Development Program (hereafter the program). The program, named the "Programa de desarrollo integral de la zona Oscos-Eo", was approved by the regional government of Asturias in 1986 (EDEFI, 1986). The program was to be implemented with the participation of other public administrations and was bolstered by strong support from local actors, both public and private.

The program's design was based on a previous study that had collected baseline data on the area (SADEI, 1984). The report from that study describes the socio-economic and demographic situation and its evolution in the previous decades, together with an exhaustive inventory of resources and necessities in the territory. The document contained an in-depth survey of the inhabitants of Oscos-Eo about their attitude towards the future and opportunities for development. The residents highlighted their will to stay in the territory and the necessity to rectify the serious infrastructure shortages in the district, in which 200 out of 350 population centers lacked basic road and electricity services (SADEI, 1984).

The report served as the basis for the elaboration and planning of the program itself, which was developed by an external company and secured the support of technicians from national, regional, and local public authorities. The main objectives of the program were: (a) to develop an economic base for the inhabitants of the area and correct existing income imbalances in relation to other areas of Asturias, (b) to curb depopulation, (c) to generate continuous growth to assure stable social and economic development, (d) to conserve the environment while taking advantage of the territory's natural resources, (e) to ensure an adequate level of community social, educational, cultural, and sports services, and (f) to preserve the area's historical-artistic heritage and its cultural and traditional values (EDEFI, 1986).

The program sought to define a long-term development strategy with two phases of five years each (1986–1990 and 1991–1995), and with a pre-phase (1984–1985) as a period to construct basic infrastructure. The division of planning into two periods allowed for the correction and reorientation of actions and strategies at the end of the first phase to guide the second phase (Rocha, 1992b). The first phase targeted initiatives that could achieve maximum economic, social, and psychological effects to strengthen the confidence of the community, seeking to generate a development *momentum*. It was intended that activities carried out successfully in the short term would establish program credibility. The investments in the program reached 221 million euros in present-day terms (22,595 million 1995 pesetas), with 62 percent invested by the public administration and the remainder through private initiatives (EDEFI, 1995).

Governance and management structure: the Oscos-Eo agency

To develop the program, an agency was created with the function of coordinating and managing the different budgets, animating the activities of all administrations involved in the program, and establishing relationships with local inhabitants and associations by promoting their active participation (Rocha, 1992a).

The agency had a high degree of autonomy and was dependent on the Coordination Committee, which carried out the decision-making and comprised representatives of the regional, national, and local administrations, the manager of the agency, and a representative of the Oscos-Eo Mountain Associations, all on a parity basis. These open and individual membership associations were promoted and regulated under the umbrella of the LAM in mountain areas and granted participation in the Coordination Committees of the Integral Rural Development programs.

The staff of the agency was multidisciplinary in its composition, including agricultural technicians, economists, architects, urban planners, sociologists, archaeologists, and tourism technicians. The agency's activity stressed the mobilization of the population through assemblies, meetings, and field visits. For example, there were *explanatory meetings* with the residents to explain the program, as well as other meetings to discuss certain actions such as the reallocation of land. The involvement of the local population was emphasized at all levels of the process (Pérez Prieto, 1988). The agency's objective was to promote the extension, demonstration, and advocacy of agriculture and other sectors to empower the population through knowledge but, more importantly, through the promotion of a participatory culture.

Main actions

The program anticipated the implementation of 19 sub-programs during its two phases, with 59 percent of the total investments allocated for the first phase and 30 percent for the second phase. There was also an introductory phase in 1985 and 1986 with an investment of 2525 million pesetas mainly in basic infrastructure, constituting 11 percent of the total (EDEFI, 1995). The investments were of three types: infrastructure, community services, and economic promotion. Table 43.1 contains more details of these programs.

- *Infrastructure*: Out of the 19 sub-programs, more than half were assigned to infrastructure, with an overall expenditure of 24 percent of the total investment. This budget item included all basic networks: water, roads, electrification, radio, television, and sanitation, highlighting the investment in the sanitation of the Eo river mouth and road infrastructure.

Table 43.1 Investments in the Oscos-Eo Program (in millions of 1995 US dollars)

Sector	1985	1986	1987–1990	1991–1995	Total
Agriculture	3.60	3.60	65.70	33.50	106.30
Craft, trade, and small industry	–	–	7.00	6.20	13.20
Tourism	0.02	0.80	2.80	1.50	5.10
Community services	0.20	0.40	7.70	5.50	13.90
Infrastructure	6.30	5.50	23.00	9.40	44.20
TOTAL	10.20	10.30	106.20	56.00	182.70

Source: EDEFI (1995).

- *Community services*: This segment accounted for the 8 percent of investments, concentrated in education, health, social and cultural services, and restoration of traditional rural housing. Education was the key focus, with major efforts put towards the construction and amelioration of the educational centers network. Furthermore, Oscos-Eo pioneered the implementation and management of two educational programs in Spain: the *"escuela rural agrupada"* (grouped rural school), an educational model based on the mobility of teachers among other aspects, and *"preescolar en casa"* (pre-schooling at home), an action promoted by parent–teacher associations for the education of children under three years of age (Rocha, 1992b). Another successful plan was the creation of a network of cultural centers and libraries, in many cases located in public buildings of historical and cultural importance. Regarding health, the program articulated the health centers network around the Health District Centre of Vegadeo.

- *Economic promotion*: The development of the area's economic potential received 68 percent of total investments. The goal of this investment was to activate the local economy and increase employment, with a special focus on youth. The budget targeted three areas: agriculture; craft, trade, and small industries; and tourism. Agriculture accounted for 85 percent of this segment, highlighting the consolidation of small plots into larger production units affecting more than 20,000 ha (70 percent of the total Utilised Agricultural Area (UAA) and 75 percent of farm holdings in Oscos-Eo). This action established the basis for the regional plot consolidation model and introduced, for example, the presence of archaeologists in case of archaeological remnants. This consolidation facilitated farmers' adoption of improvement plans promoted by CAP (Council Regulation (EEC) No. 797/85 on improving the efficiency of agricultural structures). Of 1800 farm holdings, more than 1200 applied some kind of improvement scheme. Although the farm holdings from the Oscos-Eo lowlands specialized in dairy cattle and the highlands in beef cattle, there was a significant process of farm diversification. The process was accompanied by a considerable public diffusion effort, as well as advising and training of farmers supported by the Research and Experimental Centre of Villaviciosa. The plot consolidation plan included forestry management that allowed clearing of the most favored areas for agricultural uses and fostered the forestation of the rest. The clarification of forest land ownership and improved use meant a decrease in the number of forest fires, which have traditionally been a threat in Oscos-Eo.

The budget allocated to craft, trade, and small industry accounted for 7 percent of the total expenditure. This segment included entrepreneur initiatives in the traditional iron and loom industries, as well as in the agri-food, timber, and aquaculture sector. Rural tourism played a key role in the development of Oscos-Eo. Accounting for 3 percent of investments, the successes in this sector had a deep impact at the national level. In 1986, the program launched the Rural Tourism Centre of Taramundi, a pioneer initiative in Spain consisting in the construction of a four-star hotel and various apartments promoting a new model of rural tourism. The facilities were accompanied with the restoration of important ethnographic constructions in Oscos and the recuperation of traditional high-natural value tourist routes. The project was a result of the joint action led by DITASA, a public–private society formed by the regional government, the municipality, and various residents of Taramundi. The General Secretary for Tourism, the highest tourism authority at the national level, contributed with an important subvention to the initiative, supporting the involvement of the Consejo Superior de Investigaciones Cientificas (CSIC – Superior Council for Scientific Research) in the design of the project. From this pilot experience would result the key successes for the tourism planning of the district, supported financially by the Community Program LEADER I.

In 1990, the European Commission launched the LEADER Initiative – known as LEADER I – a pilot experience for the promotion and development of non-agrarian investments to foster the diversification of rural economies towards tourism, craft industry, and trade. The main feature of LEADER was the importance given to the participation and involvement of local actors: the general population, associations, and local government (Coimbra, 2006). LEADER I was continued by LEADER II in 1995, and LEADER + in 1999. Overall, the LEADER Initiative was the program with the greatest economic endowment per inhabitant out of all EU programs. Oscos-Eo participated in the LEADER Initiative from the beginning. The participation of the Community funds has become important since the 1990s, mainly embodied in the Common Action Plan (primarily through plot consolidation) and the LEADER I Program (by means of diversification of economic activities, especially rural tourism).

Results

The program was active for ten years (1985–1995), generating a deep impact on not only territorial policy, but also on the national and European scales. These impacts included the awarding of the Great Prize of the European Commission on Tourism and Environment in 1995. Table 43.2 describes the connections between LAM's objectives and the result of the program. This prize recognized Oscos-Eo as an example of public–private cooperation for development. In 2017, Oscos received the award Pueblo Ejemplar de Asturias (Exemplary Town of Asturias Award) granted by the foundation Princesa de Asturias and delivered by the King of Spain during a visit to the district. Other recognitions were the best rural hotel of Spain (2003) for the La Rectoral Hotel of Taramundi. In 2017, the Regional Health Ministry of Asturias ranked Oscos-Eo with the highest quality life index of all Asturian districts. The distinction came three decades after the beginning of the program, when Oscos-Eo was considered the most deprived district of the region in all indexes.

Table 43.2 Comparison between LAM objectives and program achievements

Main objectives – LAM	Achievements of Oscos-Eo Program
Facilitate the social and economic development of mountain areas, especially in agricultural aspects.	Agriculture ordinance plan for agriculture management and plot consolidation. Strong increase in the size and profitability of farm holdings (mainly cattle) and agriculture diversification with the introduction of new productions. At the social level, recognition as the Asturian District with the highest quality life in 2017 by the Regional Health Ministry.
Maintain an adequate population	Even though the District followed the general population regression of rural areas, its impact was less marked than in other areas and Oscos-Eo did not lose any population center over the last thirty years.
Attend to the conservation and restoration of the physical environment as human habitat	Restoration of the architectonic heritage including rural housing. Great prize of the European Commission on Tourism and Environment in 1995, UNESCO Biosphere Reserve from 2007

The Oscos-Eo Program ended abruptly in 1995 due to a political change. The new government dissolved the Coordination Committee and closed the agency against the will of the local administrations and the population. Afterwards the district municipalities applied to the LEADER II call, and later LEADER +, to maintain a minimum structure for the management of development in Oscos-Eo. This management promoted and achieved the inclusion of the district as a UNESCO Biosphere Reserve in 2007.

Integral rural development: best practices from Oscos-Eo

Oscos-Eo presents key aspects from which other regions could adapt and learn, many of which have already been successfully transferred. The program followed the principle of joint action, with the integration of different funds from diverse administrations and financial schemes in support of the same strategy. In Oscos-Eo, the multi-fund strategy was especially notable due to the involvement of the EEC, with national, regional, and local authorities. The program initiated a wide range of initiatives and showed the capacity to fulfill the requirements demanded by all administrative levels, especially those related to the EEC, which Spain joined in 1986.

The active participation of the local community was a key factor in the implementation of the program, including in the design and planning phase with the inclusion in the Coordination Committee of municipalities and Mountain Associations. The effort made to involve the local population encouraged their transformation into active agents for their own development, a key resilience factor that helped to maintain the expectations of the district for a successful future in a context of strong depopulation all over northern Spanish mountain areas, which has had lasting positive implications for the region.

Another characteristic of Oscos-Eo was its status as a pilot project which, together with the priority given by the LAM, served as a catalyst for the improvement of different policies under the principle that *pilot projects can overcome formal obstacles*. In this sense, many of the actions initiated by the program were consolidated at the regional level, including plot consolidation, education, and health services. In other cases, it was the business models that laid the foundations for what rural development was to become in Spain. The case of the rural tourism nucleus of Taramundi is still an exemplar of the sustainable tourism model in Spain, with accommodations continuously meeting rural occupancy and revenue levels much higher than the Spanish mean.

The configuration of a multidisciplinary working group in the agency facilitated an original approach to complex and different situations which propelled it into success. This characteristic, which was uncommon at that time in policy implementation, together with the pioneer focus of the program and its wide range of objectives, stimulated a number of innovative models and methodologies that have been replicated at the regional and even national levels.

The program met expected budgetary targets in quantitative terms, as well as the qualitative efficiency achieved by the fulfillment of the 19 sub-programs. The integral development model that it employed aims for efficient resource use; in Oscos-Eo, all locally initiated infrastructure such as roads and water were made using voluntary contributions from residents. This participation not only signified economic efficiency but also reflected the strong buy-in of the different levels of the community.

One of the aspects that allowed the program to succeed was the positive disposition of the Asturias government towards the development of rural areas. In the 1980s, the majority of Asturian inhabitants were concentrated in the central triangle area shaped by three industrial cities, with the rest of the region (10,000 km²) inhabited in dispersed population centers. During the 1980s, Asturias was the region most affected by industrial restructuring and had a marked deficit in rural infrastructure. In this context, Oscos-Eo was considered the most depressed district of the region. In 1986, the regional government invested 10 percent of the regional budget in Oscos-Eo, even though it counted for only 1.6 percent of the Asturian population. That year, the government's strategy revolved around the slogan "Asturias will take off when its wings get reinforced". In addition, there was a strong campaign vindicating the natural values of Asturias whose promotional slogan "*Asturias, paraíso natural*" (Asturias, natural paradise), is still central in the regional tourism promotion.

There is a consensus among associations and professionals related to rural development and improvement of mountain territories about the necessity for specific policies directed towards these social spaces. However, unlike in the 1980s and 1990s, there is now a lack of political will to tackle the challenges of mountain areas with a long-term strategy. The lack of political interest is especially relevant considering that the LAM is still in effect and the Spanish Constitution emphasizes the special treatment for mountain areas for rural development.

Since the 1980s, the concept of integral development has been fading. The term has almost disappeared from the public and academic debate. Key ingredients such as the active involvement of local inhabitants in decision-making or the necessity of decentralization to promote real development momentum are lost from view. The case of Oscos-Eo shows that an integral approach can succeed. Integral development must be implemented in other Spanish mountain areas if the dramatic abandonment of their population centers is to be reversed and the fall of the final Damocles sword is to be prevented.

References

Amato, A., 1988. *Una política para las zonas de montaña*. European Community, Brussels.

Coimbra, E., 2006. *Aplicación de programas de desarrollo leader en Oscos Eo: Su incidencia en el empleo*. Oscos Eo, November.

Delgado Serrano, M., 2004. *La política rural Europea en la encrucijada*. MAPA. www.mapa.gob.es/ministerio/pags/biblioteca/fondo/pdf/46954_all.pdf.

EDEFI – Española de desarrollo financiero, 1986. *Programa de desarrollo integral de la zona Oscos-Eo*. Consejería de Agricultura y Pesca, Principado de Asturias.

EDEFI – Española de desarrollo financiero, 1995. *Memoria del programa de desarrollo integral de la zona Oscos-Eo*. Consejería de Agricultura y Pesca, Principado de Asturias.

Gómez Benito, C., 1987. *La política socioestructural en zonas de agricultura de montaña en España y en la C.E.E.* Ministerio de Agricultura, Pesca y Alimentación, Secretaría General Técnica, Madrid.

Lacoma, J.Á.M., 1993. *La política de desarrollo de las zonas de montaña en el marco de la Comunidad Europea*. Inst. de Estudios Altoaragoneses, Diputación de Huesca.

Oliván del Cacho, J., 1994. *El régimen jurídico de las zonas de montaña*. Civitas, Madrid.

Orea, D.G., Díaz-Ambrona, H., 1993. *El plan Oscos-Eo: un ejemplo de desarrollo rural a estudiar*. Agricultura: Revista agropecuaria y ganadera (732), 550–553. www.mapa.gob.es/ministerio/pags/biblioteca/revistas/pdf_Agri/Agri_1993_732_550_553.pdf.

Pérez Prieto, V., 1988. *Plan Oscos-Eo: un programa de desenvolvemento integral nunha zona de montaña*. Entrevista a Pedro Rocha. Revista Irimia (290), 6–7. Rocha, P., 1992a. *Plan de desenvolvemento rural integral Oscos-Eo Asturias*. Dirección Xeral de Servicios Sociais, Santiago de Compostela.

Rocha, P., 1992b. *Programa de desarrollo Osco-Eco: Cinco anos de experiencia de desarrollo integral en una comarca de montana de Asturias*. Presentado en El Turismo Rural en el Desarrollo Local. Laredo (Espana). July 22–26, 1991.

SADEI – Sociedad Asturiana de estudios económicos e industriales. 1984. *Los Oscos y La Cuenca Del Eo: Situación y perspectivas 1980*. Consejería de Agricultura y Pesca del Principado de Asturias.

INDEX

Page numbers in **bold** denote tables, those in *italics* denote figures.

Printed in the United States
by Baker & Taylor Publisher Services